PART 9
EDITING AND PROOFREADING YOUR WORK

W9-AVJ-365

Why Do You Need This New Edition?

Six Great Reasons to Buy This New Edition of *The DK Handbook!*

This edition of *The DK Handbook* was created with input from hundreds of college students like you. We worked closely with real students using their handbook to solve real problems in their writing. They told us where they got stuck or frustrated and we listened. Student advisors gave us feedback about how to make a handbook that would be more useful and valuable for them.

1. Samples from a student research project illustrate the writing process from beginning to end, helping you to see how to focus and develop your ideas at each step in the process.

2. A new section on how to use your thesis statement to organize your paper helps you avoid the dreaded blank-page syndrome!

3. Do you have a hard time knowing what to say when you need to read and respond to a classmate's paper? A new section on peer response can help you give better feedback to your classmates.

4. Do you need strategies for how to revise a paper? A new section on revising your writing helps you use feedback, craft a revision plan, and improve your style.

5. Do you need help with proofreading? A new section on editing and proofreading shows you what to look for and how to catch and fix errors more effectively—before you turn in your final paper.

6. A new sample research paper in updated APA style shows you how to organize and format research papers for your projects in the social sciences.

PEARSO

The DK Handbook

Second Edition

ANNE FRANCES WYSOCKI
University of Wisconsin, Milwaukee

DENNIS A. LYNCH
University of Wisconsin, Milwaukee

Longman

Boston   Columbus   Indianapolis   New York   San Francisco   Upper Saddle River
Amsterdam   Cape Town   Dubai   London   Madrid   Milan   Munich   Paris   Montreal   Toronto
Delhi   Mexico City   São Paulo   Sydney   Hong Kong   Seoul   Singapore   Taipei   Tokyo

Text design, page layout,
and cover design:
Stuart Jackman

Pearson Longman
Executive Editor: Lynn M. Huddon
Senior Development Editor: Michael Greer
Senior Supplements Editor: Donna Campion
Senior Media Producer: Stefanie Liebman
Senior Marketing Manager: Susan E. Stoudt
Production Manager: Bob Ginsberg
Project Coordination: Elm Street Publishing Services
Cover Design Manager: Wendy Ann Fredericks
Cover Photos (*clockwise from top left*): Heidi Kristensen/iStockphoto; David
    Fischer/Digital Vision/Getty Images; Oleg Prikhodko/iStockphoto; Research
    in Motion Limited; and Kaoru Fujimoto/Taxi/Getty Images
Photo Researcher: Pearson Image Resource Center
Image Permission Coordinator: Nancy Seise
Senior Manufacturing Buyer: Alfred C. Dorsey
Printer and Binder: RR Donnelley & Sons Company/Crawfordsville
Cover Printer: Lehigh-Phoenix

For permission to use copyrighted material, grateful acknowledgment is made to the copyright holders on pp. 603–606, which are hereby made part of this copyright page.

Library of Congress Cataloging-in-Publication Data

Wysocki, Anne Frances, 1956-
   The DK Handbook / Anne Frances Wysocki; Dennis A. Lynch.--2nd ed.
      p. cm.
   Includes index.
   ISBN 978-0-205-73076-6
   1. English language--Rhetoric--Handbooks, manuals, etc. 2. Report writing--Handbooks, manuals, etc.
3. English language--Grammar--Handbooks, manuals, etc. I. Lynch, Dennis A., 1950-II. Title
   PE1408.W97 2011
   808'.042--dc22

                                                                    2009043479

12345678910—DOC—13 12 11 10

Longman
is an imprint of

www.pearsonhighered.com

ISBN-13: 978-0-205-73076-6
ISBN-10:   0-205-73076-0

PREFACE

We wrote this handbook because we wanted to create a resource that would be useful for students.

Because we found the process so valuable (and eye-opening) when we were developing the first edition, we once again commissioned a series of formal usability studies for this second edition, to test the handbook by putting it in the hands of students. We asked a group of students to use this handbook to carry out the kinds of tasks they routinely use a handbook for in their composition classes, such as evaluating sources for a research assignment, documenting sources, and reviewing and editing texts. These usability studies generated many hours of video footage that helped us to learn, by direct observation, how and why students sometimes got stuck at certain points in the tasks assigned them. We also conducted a series of four-week student diary studies to find out when and how students used their handbooks in the context of their composition courses. Nearly 200 students participated in this project, and their responses helped us focus on those parts of the handbook students used most often.

Teachers using the first edition, reviewers, and focus group participants also contributed many suggestions and ideas that shaped our work on this second edition. While our original vision and design principles carry over from the first edition, we have made substantial revisions to both the content and organization of the handbook. In all of these revisions, our goal has been to create a handbook that is useful to the growing community of teachers and students who use *The DK Handbook*.

On pages vi and vii, we highlight some of the notable new content and features in this edition.

WHAT'S NEW IN THIS EDITION?

1 New emphasis on composing and developing arguments: A new section in Part 4, *Using a thesis statement to organize an academic paper*, offers students step-by-step strategies for composing an argument. An extended student example shows how a thesis statement can be used to develop a structure for a paper.

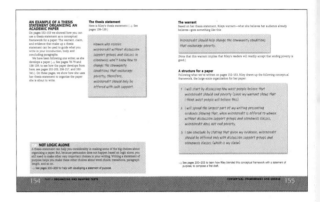

2 Expanded coverage of peer review and response: In response to suggestions from both teachers and students, a new section in Part 5 on *Responding to the writing of your peers* offers students concrete strategies for peer response and classroom workshops, including an annotated sample student response to another student's draft.

3 New coverage of the editing and proofreading process: Part 9 begins with an expanded section on editing and proofreading (pages 450-455) to help students understand what to look for in their own writing, and to give them practical strategies for finding and correcting common errors.

4 New complete annotated sample research paper in APA style: Our revised and updated APA coverage now includes a complete sample paper, to support teachers and students who want a model from the social sciences and to support writing in the disciplines and similar programs.

5 New focus on the revision process: Part 6, *Revising with style*, includes new sections on revising strategies, developing a revision plan (including a sample revision plan), and revising for different audiences. A new *Revision Checklist* on page 672 also provides a set of criteria students can use to assess their own revision goals.

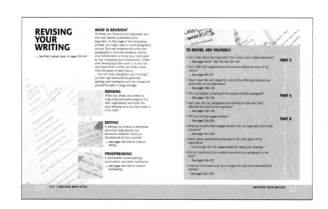

6 Redesigned documentation coverage: Based on user feedback, our sample citations are presented in a new layout, making it easier to locate each type of source and to support students who look for examples first. MLA and APA examples have been updated to incorporate recent changes in both styles.

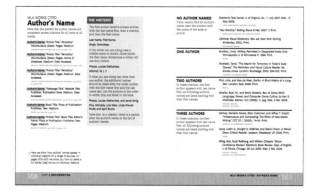

7 New pathways to support student readers: New menus on the inside back covers, *A Writer's Concerns* and *Questions about Research*, help students find what they need in language familiar to them. A student wondering "how much of my own opinion can I put in a paper?," for example, would be able to find answers to that question by using the *Writer's Concerns* menu, which would lead her to coverage of thesis, supporting evidence, and a discussion of the difference between fact and opinion.

8 New support for speakers of languages other than English: A new guide at the beginning of Part 7, combined with an expanded number of topical discussions highlighted in Part 9, helps English language learners find guidance and advice on a number of stylistic and structural challenges unique to written English.

WHY AND HOW WE WROTE THIS HANDBOOK

We wrote this handbook to be useful. We want to be useful to a community that matters to us, the community of writing learners and writing teachers.

We want those who use this book to use it with confidence and even delight so that they can then write with confidence and take delight and satisfaction in the shape and effectiveness of their words.

These are some of the core principles of the handbook's design.

1 Pages can be designed to support the conceptual work of learning.

Our handbook's **layered structure** helps learners move from the general to the specific. Each new topic begins with a two-page spread that is a **topic overview**; each overview helps students grasp quickly and visually the key steps of processes and concepts.

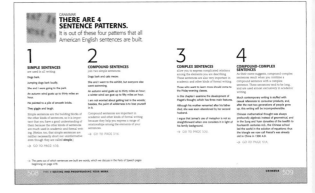

Students needing more information can turn to the detail pages following each overview. The **detail pages** expand on one step or concept at a time, helping learners **zoom in** on strategies or ideas.

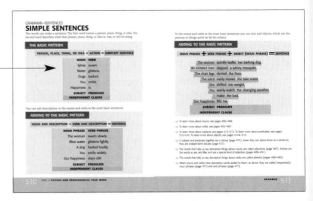

Application pages (again, made up of two-page spreads) present illustrated examples demonstrating how to apply processes.

2 Consistent and uncluttered layout helps learners find what they need.

Each topic fits on its two-page spread, making information and ideas readily graspable visually and so conceptually. The topic of every two-page spread appears dependably at its top left corner. Because finding and seeing information is made easy, students can focus on what they need to learn instead of on finding it

3 Students search for visual and verbal patterns that match the problems they wish to solve.

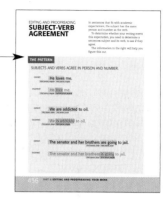

Pattern pages provide learners with straightforward visual explanations of compositional processes or grammatical structures. If students can see a pattern, they can hold it in their minds for later application.

4 Students look for examples first.

Our handbook's design puts examples front and center. We've included as many examples—of sentences, student writing, or source evaluation—as we could and we built explanations inductively from the examples. We want students to find easily what will help them solve their writing and editing concerns—and then we want them to remember the pattern of what they learn so they can apply it later.

5 The processes of research and documentation can be presented visually.

Many of our reviewers told us how frustrated students are by the details of documentation. So we worked to make visible the patterns of documentation, so that students won't feel as though each citation requires starting anew.

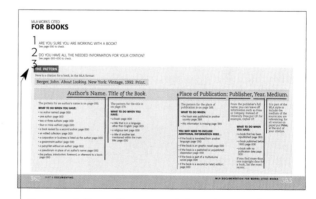

Documentation pattern pages help students see the underlying elements of a citation, reinforcing the basic process used to build a citation for any type of source.

SUPPLEMENTS

MyCompLab empowers student writers and facilitates writing instruction by uniquely integrating a composing space and assessment tools with market-leading instruction, multimedia tutorials, and exercises for writing, grammar and research.

MyCompLab is an eminently flexible application that instructors can use in ways that best complement their course and teaching style. They can recommend it to students for self-study, set up courses to track student progress, or leverage the power of administrative features to be more effective and save time. **Learn more at www.mycomplab.com.**

Interactive Pearson eText: An e-book version of *The DK Handbook* is also available in MyCompLab. This dynamic, online version of the text is integrated throughout MyCompLab to create an enriched, interactive learning experience for writing students. In addition, a series of **DK Handbook online learning modules** offer students guided instruction and in-depth practice on key topics including evaluating sources, revising, documentation, grammar, and punctuation. Look for links to these online modules in the eText and in the book wherever you see this icon:

Explore these topics online:

Choosing sources

www.mycomplab.com

The DK Handbook is also available as a **CourseSmart etextbook**. This is an exciting new choice for students, who can subscribe to the same content online and search the text, make notes online, print out reading assignments that incorporate lecture notes, and bookmark important passages for later review. For more information, or to subscribe to the CourseSmart etextbook, visit www.coursesmart.com.

A booklet of **Exercises** to accompany *The DK Handbook* provides assignments and activities that allow students to practice the writing and grammar lessons in the handbook. Instructors can assign the exercises according to their own teaching styles and their students' needs. The variety of short answer and open-ended questions also allows instructors to use the exercises as both an assessment and a diagnostic tool.

A separate **Answer Key** is available to instructors for this Exercises booklet.

An **Instructor's Resource Manual**, developed by Anne Wysocki, Dennis Lynch, and Kristi Prinz, offers guidance to new and experienced teachers for teaching composition with The DK Handbook and using its media resources.

VangoNotes. VangoNotes are study guides in MP3 format that enable students to download handbook information into their own players and then listen to it whenever they wish. The notes include "need to know" tips for each handbook chapter, practice tests, audio flash cards for learning key concepts and terms, and a rapid review for exams. For more information, visit www.VangoNotes.com.

ACKNOWLEDGMENTS

Lynn Huddon got us started on this project, kept her humor and patience, and contributed finer features. Michael Greer's intelligence, thoughtfulness, humor, and energy are present on every page, and his evenness and encouragement are also a reason this book is now in your hands. Joe Opiela gently kept us focused and determined. Stuart Jackman kept us colorful and delighted us with each new page. Megan Galvin-Fak and Susan Stoudt have creatively and energetically thought about how to get this book into people's hands and infectiously kept us excited. In working with our advisory board and focus groups, Laura Coaty kept us thinking about this work's real applications. Bob Ginsberg and Heather Johnson managed the production process with grace and style. And Tharon Howard carried out the smart and detailed user testing—with live students—that helped us understand how others really do use handbooks.

We thank (and will continue to thank for a long time) all the above for the extraordinary efforts they have made on behalf of this book—but nonetheless our most emphatic thanks go to our reviewers (listed to the right) and student diary study participants (listed on page xii), whose generosity with their time and care for student learning has contributed to and strengthened every bit of this book.

Craig Bartholomaus, Metropolitan Community College - Penn Valley; Joel R. Brouwer, Montcalm Community College; Shanti Bruce, Nova Southeastern University; Sue Buck, FCCJ Downtown Campus; Tami Christopher, University of Bridgeport; Joe Davis, North Iowa Area Community College; Rosemary B. Day, Central New Mexico Community College; Sarah DeBacher, University of New Orleans, Lakefront; Chitralekha Duttagupta, Utah Valley University; Carrie Finn, Wartburg College; David FitzSimmons, Ashland University; Hank Galmish, Green River Community College; Janet P. Gerstner, San Juan College; Baotong Gu, Georgia State University; Jane Hammons, University of California, Berkeley; Will Hochman, Southern Connecticut State University; Christine Laursen, Westwood College; Beverly Neiderman, Kent State University; Deborah Craig Nester, Northwest Florida State College; Gregory M. Neubauer, West Liberty State College; Steven L. Penn, Morehead State University; Kate Peterson, University of Minnesota; Paige Reynolds, College of the Holy Cross; Paul Michael Rogers, George Mason University; Vicki Schwab, Manatee Community College; David Sharpe, Ohio University; Julie Marie Strickland, Georgia Southern University; Charrolee Thompson, Massasoit Community College; Carrie Hall Tomberlin, Bellevue Community College; Anne Wilson Twite, Eastern New Mexico University, Ruidoso; Marilyn Weymouth Seguin, Kent State University; Mary M. Williams, Midland College; Justin Williamson, Pearl River Community College; Gary J. Wingenbach, Texas A&M University.

Students from seven campuses participated in our diary study and taught us much about how they used their handbooks. We are grateful to all of them, and to their teachers, who helped coordinate an extended survey process:

Susan Achziger, Community College of Aurora; Craig Bartholomaus, Metropolitan Community College - Penn Valley; Rosemary B. Day, Central New Mexico Community College; Uma Krishnan, Kent State University; Beverly Neiderman, Kent State University; Troy D. Nordman, Butler Community College; Josephine Walwema, Clemson University.

Throughout the development of the first edition, members of our editorial advisory board provided ideas, enthusiasm, and constructive criticism, and we want to thank them again here for all the work they did for us:

Kathryn Adams, Allan Hancock College; Diann Baecker, Virginia State University; Deborah Coxwell-Teague, Florida State University; Mark Crane, Utah Valley State College; David Elias, Eastern Kentucky University; Dan Ferguson, Amarillo College; Jacqueline Gray, St. Charles Community College; Ina Leean Hawkins, National Park Community College; Joel Henderson, Chattanooga State Technical Community College; Klint Hull, Lower Columbia College; John Hyman, American University; Ann Jagoe, North Central Texas College; Elizabeth Joseph, Eastfield College; Michael Knievel, University of Wyoming; Lydia Lynn Lewellen, Tacoma Community College; Sharon James McGee, Southern Illinois University, Edwardsville; James McWard, Johnson County Community College; Jeffrey Michels, Contra Costa College; Connie Mick, University of Notre Dame; Beverly Neiderman, Kent State University; Janet Kay Porter, Leeward Community College; Jane Rosecrans, J. Sargeant Reynolds Community College; Lisa Sandoval, Joliet Junior College; Joseph Scherer, Community College of Allegheny County, South Campus; Deidre Schoolcraft, Pikes Peak Community College; Bonnie Spears, Chaffey College; Kristine Swenson, University of Missouri, Rolla; Karen Taylor, Genesee Community College; Eula Thompson, Jefferson State Community College; Gina Thompson, East Mississippi Community College; Christopher Twiggs, Florida Community College at Jacksonville; Justin Williamson, Pearl River College; Geoffrey Woolf, Cincinnati State Technical and Community College.

PART 1
A PROCESS FOR COMPOSING

CONTENTS

available designs

??? the redesigned

WHAT IS COMPOSING?

Composing a paper, you arrange words into sentences into paragraphs, hoping that the arrangement will engage your readers. Composing a poster, you arrange words, photographs, and colors, so that viewers will want to look at the poster and heed its purposes. Composing a podcast, you arrange voices and other sounds so that others want to listen. In other words, composing—as we use it in this book—refers to written, visual, oral, and mixed-media texts that you create.

The New London Group—British and American teachers who research how we learn to communicate—argues that composing requires three steps:

1 No matter the medium—written, visual, oral, or a mix—we compose with elements and arrangements already familiar to others. These existing elements and arrangements are called *Available Designs* by the New London Group.

2 As we compose our texts out of available designs, we are *Designing*, trying out new shapes and combinations of what is available.

3 When we finish composing, we have made the *Redesigned*, something new out of past possibilities. The redesigned, in turn, becomes new available designs for our, or others', future composing.

This process shapes what we propose in this handbook. If you are to be an effective and satisfied composer, you need to learn the designs that are available to you—the conventions, grammars, and expectations—so you can make what audiences can understand but also so that you can design for your own purposes.

WHAT IS RHETORIC?

Rhetoric is a method for understanding how communication happens.

Rhetoric developed in the western Mediterranean area over 2,000 years ago as political systems became democratic and as legal institutions came into being. People saw that audiences were moved by some speeches and writings more than by others, and that some speeches and writings not only failed but achieved the exact opposite of what their composers had hoped.

Some people—*rhetoricians*—started systematically studying why some speeches and writing were more effective than others.

The result of the rhetoricians' studies was rhetoric.

AUDIENCE

Rhetoric begins with the understanding that writers (and composers of any text) address audiences. Audiences are not mindless and automatically under a composer's sway; instead, audiences come to texts with beliefs, values, and ideas. Using rhetoric, composers consider the relationships they can build with audiences so that audiences will want to listen and engage with the composer around the issue at hand.

CONTEXT

Where and when do composer and audience meet? Is it face to face or through an essay? Late Saturday night or early Monday? How will recent events influence an audience's attitude? Rhetoricians recognize that composers need to consider the contexts of communication because the contexts shape how audiences respond.

PURPOSE

The earliest rhetoricians realized that composers need to have purposes. This might seem so obvious as to be useless, but if composers cannot articulate their purposes in detail, then they cannot decide how to proceed in composing. (As when one young woman went to court to appeal a ticket for driving through a red light, it was only after her appeal was denied that she realized her purpose was not to tell the judge how the traffic light was hidden by a truck, but rather how she did not know there even was a traffic light where she should have stopped.)

STRATEGIES

Once composers have a sense of audience, purpose, and context, they can begin making all the particular decisions—big and small— that shape a composition. Composers need to consider how a choice of a particular word, just as much as a choice of what comes first in a text, are likely to affect an audience's attitude toward a purpose.

■ ■ ■

RHETORICAL SITUATIONS

The combination of audience, purpose, and context make up what rhetoricians (starting in the twentieth century) call *the rhetorical situation*. This term helps us keep in mind that communication is not a simple transfer of information but is rather an interaction of real, complicated people within the real, complex events of lives and cultures.

Even classrooms are rhetorical situations, where writing an essay involves people with different cultural and educational backgrounds: students and teachers. How do you use the audiences, purposes, and contexts of classrooms—and the strategies available to you—to learn to communicate as you hope?

■ ■ ■

THIS HANDBOOK

This book is about helping you discover as much as you can about your audiences, purposes, and contexts so that you can use the available strategies of writing (and also, to a lesser extent, of visual and oral communication) to construct the connections you want to build with your audiences.

WHAT IS RHETORIC?
AUDIENCE

WHO WILL BE READING, VIEWING, OR HEARING WHAT YOU COMPOSE? WHAT ASPECTS OF YOUR AUDIENCE MATTER TO WHAT YOU HOPE TO ACHIEVE?

That a text you are composing has to be shaped for other people is the central concern of rhetoric.

Perhaps the need to think about your audience when you compose seems obvious to you, but the understanding that we write and compose texts for others takes a while to develop.

Before college, most writing education focuses on grammar, research, and the logical structures of writing. Before college, most people move in fairly small circles of friends and family, and so their communications are informal and relaxed: Most often, people in high school know well the people to whom they are writing and speaking. After high school, when we go to college, start working to support ourselves, and start taking more active roles in our communities, we have to learn how to communicate with people we may not know so directly.

We need, in other words, to build upon what we learned about writing in high school: We need to start thinking about the people who read, view, or hear what we compose, and how those people are likely to respond to the many choices we make while composing.

AUDIENCES ARE NEVER FULL, REAL PEOPLE

Even when you are talking with your mother or best friend, you are addressing only some part of that person. Your mother is your mother, after all, and so you speak to her as *mother*; she may also be a boss, an employee, a sister, a daughter—but, when **you** talk with her, you are addressing only that part of her that is *mother*.

Likewise, when you write work memos, they go to your boss and co-workers insofar as they have the role of **boss** and **co-worker**; you do not address the sides of them that are *parent*, *churchgoer*, or *novel reader*.

In addition, people have rich emotional and intellectual lives and different cultural backgrounds. When you compose texts for others, you focus on a particular topic and hope your audience will pay attention to your concerns. What emotions play around your topic—and how can you compose to arouse or to dampen those emotions? What possible opinions and values might your audiences hold on your topic—and how can you compose to focus their attention on some particular aspect they might not have considered before or are likely to dismiss?

Audiences, in other words, are always a bit imaginary, in that you ask them to step into the roles and beliefs that the purposes and contexts of your composing require. You call audiences into being from where they really are.

→ Because the consideration of audience is so important, a whole part of this book is focused on shaping writing for audiences. See pages 193–218.

WHAT IS RHETORIC?
CONTEXT

WHERE ARE YOUR READERS AT THE MOMENT THEY ENGAGE WITH THE TEXT YOU ARE COMPOSING?

WHAT IS GOING ON AROUND THEM? HOW ARE THE PLACE AND TIME LIKELY TO AFFECT HOW THEY READ?

How can you take those circumstances into account while composing so that the text fits its context and reaches its readers?

LOCAL AND IMMEDIATE CONTEXTS

When you write an essay for a class, the teacher has to respond to your essay as well as to the essays of everyone else in your class, usually at night or on the weekend, at home. How is this likely to shape how your teacher reads?

When you write a memo at work, your boss or co-workers will receive the memo amid a pile of other paperwork, in the middle of distracting days. How is this likely to shape how they read?

When you design a flyer for a campus event, it goes up on walls or telephone poles alongside hundreds of others; it has to attract the attention of people who are hurrying by, ten feet away.

When you design a website for a non-profit organization, readers will probably read it alone, at their computers.

Each of these circumstances, describing the particulars of how audiences come to texts, can help you consider composing. What do you need to do to show a tired, weary-eyed teacher that you've done what an assignment asked? How can you compose a memo so that your busy boss and co-workers will understand exactly what you want? What photographs and words—and what sizes, and how many—can help you attract the eyes of a passing poster audience? What words, colors, and photographs can help you take advantage of the intimacy of a computer screen reader?

The more you can imagine the time and place in which someone will read your text, the more you can shape the text to fit when and where the text will be read.

LARGER CONTEXTS

What are the values and concerns of your time and place? What has happened recently—in your town or country or in the world—that might affect how someone responds to a text?

For example, after September 11, 2001, no one could write an editorial about travel or world events without taking September 11 into account. It was a long time before people felt it was appropriate to tell jokes and be humorous about politics or world events.

But also imagine that your town is struggling over whether to allow Wal-Mart to build a megastore or over how to find funding to keep the hospital open or the factory from shutting down. If you were to write a letter to the editor about school funding, for example, or about the need for a new stoplight on your corner, taking into account those larger community concerns shows readers that you understand the consequences of what you argue—and so readers are more likely to listen.

Composing texts while mindful of the larger contexts in which your readers move can help you figure out what tone of voice to use, the beliefs and values that shape how readers read, and the mood your readers are likely to be in. Considering all these details helps you understand how and why readers might respond. It helps you build bridges to readers, and thus helps you shape a text that readers are more likely to read, understand, and want to engage.

WHAT IS RHETORIC?
PURPOSE

WHAT DO YOU WANT TO HAPPEN AS A RESULT OF YOUR COMPOSING EFFORTS?

What do you hope your audience will think, feel, believe, or do after engaging with you through your text? What do you want to learn through engaging with your audiences?

PURPOSE IS NOT THE SAME AS THESIS

A thesis is the idea—usually with reasons—you hope readers will take away from a piece of argumentative writing. But when you compose such writing, you hope readers will do something with that idea: Do you hope they will write to their national or state political representatives, buy energy-saving light bulbs, or think a little differently about religion or women's lives?

Purposes take into account the emotions and possible actions of readers as well as their thoughts.

PURPOSES ARE NEVER SIMPLE

Here are some purposes for composing:

"I hope that my paper will encourage readers to feel angry enough about teacher salaries in this district that they will join the demonstration to be held at the state capitol next month."

"Because of my poster, I'd like my audience to look more carefully at how others treat pets, knowing there is a relation between pet abuse and child abuse."

"I want my readers to be happy that women's rights have advanced so much in the last century, and to understand why it's important to protect those rights. I want them to see the connection between what happened in the last century and the improved lives of their mothers, sisters, daughters, and themselves."

By thinking about purpose, you start thinking about what your writing and composing need to do, and you start thinking concretely about how to do it.

IMAGINING PURPOSE

As with audience, you need to imagine your purpose as closely as you can: If you picture for yourself exactly the response you hope the text you are composing brings about, you will be more likely to compose texts that appeal in concrete and engaging ways to audiences.

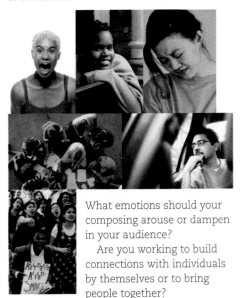

What emotions should your composing arouse or dampen in your audience?

Are you working to build connections with individuals by themselves or to bring people together?

Are you hoping people will take specific action, or quietly consider an issue in more depth?

→ Considerations of purpose weave throughout the rest of this book, but if you want specific help with purpose, see page 15, and pages 200–203.

WHAT IS RHETORIC?
STRATEGIES

WHAT ARE THE CHOICES YOU CAN MAKE AS YOU COMPOSE A TEXT?

What words, or tone of voice, or colors will you choose? What should come first? What examples will you use? Will you use photographs or charts? Which typefaces?

Every choice is a strategy affecting how your audience responds. Your choices depend on your purpose, context, and audience.

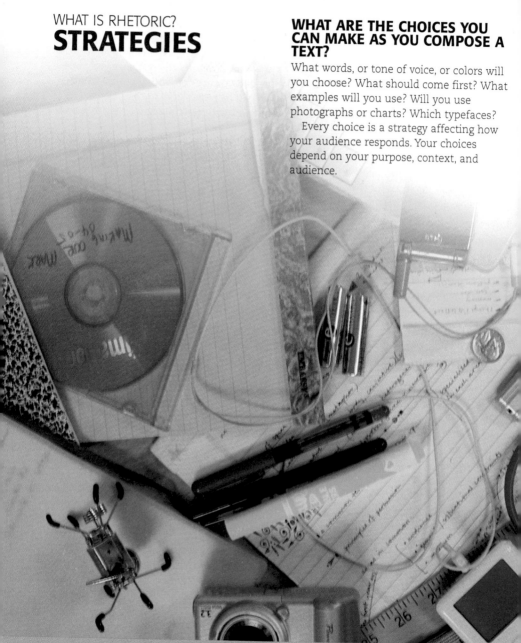

IN TERMS OF STRATEGIES,

becoming an effective composer of texts involves:

1 Your ability to identify the widest possible range of choices—of strategies—available to you in your rhetorical situation.

2 Your ability to shape choices to address your audience, given your purpose and context.

Regarding the first ability: When you first start considering a text you have to compose (or even when you are partly into composing it), if you list every choice you could make, you'll see how much room there is for you to experiment with possibilities; you're more likely therefore to achieve your purposes. (You'll also probably realize the impossibility of listing every possible strategy—but it's useful to try.)

Regarding the second ability: If you want your audience to write to their congressional representatives to support a bill funding more space exploration, don't begin with a discussion of where the money should come from: That starts your readers thinking about why space exploration might be too expensive. Start instead with a discussion of the wonders of space, and then describe the medical and industrial advances resulting from space exploration; your audience is more likely to approach your request with a positive point of view.

You can consider every possible strategy in light of how your readers are likely to respond, and how your choice will shape their attention and thus their receptiveness to your purpose.

THE STRATEGY OF ARRANGEMENT

In the example of space exploration, the strategy we discussed is arrangement. Arrangement is about what comes first in a composition, and what follows.

For some rhetorical situations, audiences expect certain arrangements. When you write a business letter, the letter starts with a date and a greeting, and then discusses the matter at hand, with (often) a final paragraph suggesting what the next actions should be. Scientific papers are usually arranged with an abstract first, then a description of experimental method, then a description of the results of the experiments, then a discussion of the results, and finally a list of other papers consulted during the research.

→ Because arrangement is such a crucial strategy in composing, a whole part of this book is devoted to it; see pages 141–192.

THE STRATEGY OF MEDIUM

Sometimes you enter a composing situation with all choices open to you, including that of the medium. If, for example, you have been asked to help a nonprofit organization improve its outreach to teenagers, would you recommend composing webpages or brochures, organizing a fair or school visits, or handing out printed T-shirts at the mall? Each of these media engages with the audience in different ways, and so can help you achieve your purpose in different—and differently effective—ways.

RHETORIC AND A PROCESS FOR COMPOSING

People who study writers and writing have learned that all effective writers have processes they follow to develop writing. These processes differ in their particulars from writer to writer, but generally—when it comes to composing a research paper—the processes contain the steps shown on the next page.

(Keep in mind that, although the process looks linear, writers often move back and forth through the steps, especially between revising and getting feedback, as they produce several drafts of the work.)

With each step, you become more certain about audience, context, purpose, and—eventually—strategies, until it is time to declare a project finished.

We include the chart on the right at the beginning of each part of this book to help you stay oriented in a project.

Understanding your project   At this step, you develop your first, tentative, ideas of your audience, context, and purpose.

Getting started   Mulling over different ways of understanding audience, context, and purpose helps you determine what and where you need to research.

Asking questions   How does your research help you understand how your audience, context, and purpose relate to each other—and vice versa?

Shaping your project for others   Here, you focus on audience, and how their understandings and expectations shape what and how you will compose.

Drafting a paper   Given your understanding of audience, context, and purpose, what strategies might help you compose most effectively?

Getting feedback   Once you have a draft, listen to how your audience reads and understands: What worked in your composition, and what didn't?

Revising   In response to feedback, how can you refine your strategies better to fit your audience, context, and purpose?

Polishing   Now you know exactly what your audience, context, purpose, and strategies are, and can polish them into a solid, shining, finished composition.

RHETORIC AND A PROCESS FOR
COMPOSING

UNDERSTANDING YOUR PROJECT OR ASSIGNMENT

To understand any new project or assignment—whether you are in school, at work, or anyplace else where you need to develop communication—you need to understand the rhetorical situation of the project or assignment:

❑ **Who is your audience?**

❑ **What is the context?**

❑ **What is the purpose?**

UNDERSTANDING A CLASS ASSIGNMENT

❑ **Who is your audience?**

In a writing class, you will often hear that the audience is your classmates— but probably your teacher will give you a grade on how well you address the concerns and beliefs of your classmates, so the teacher is also a very important part of your audience. (Sometimes teachers ask you to write for other audiences besides the class; you will have to ask how you are to learn about those audiences.)

❑ **What is the context?**

The classroom is the immediate context, of course—but so is your campus and its values and recent events. The values of the community around the school, current national and international events—how are these likely to shape how your audience will read? What has happened recently in their individual and shared lives that shapes how your audience thinks and feels, in general and on the topic you are considering?

What is the purpose?

Three levels of purpose shape class writing assignments:

- There are the teacher's purposes. You might be asked to demonstrate that you can produce polished prose; carry out research, integrate it into a paper, and document it; and develop and produce a persuasive argument. Look at each new assignment for explicit statements of what the teacher hopes you will learn; if they are not there, ask.

- You can have your own purposes for your own learning: If there are skills on which you need to focus (some particular aspect of grammar, or transitions, or writing complex paragraphs), how can you work them in?

- Your paper will have its particular purposes, such as *I want to persuade the people in class that replacing the light bulbs in their houses with compact fluorescent bulbs is a useful thing to do* or *I would like to persuade people to write to their representatives about health care.*

When you wish to understand what a teacher hopes you will achieve, look for the following terms in an assignment:

summarize: to describe as concisely as possible the main points of writing

define: to explain a term or concept

inform: to tell others about an issue, with supporting examples and data

analyze: to break a process or object into its conceptual parts while showing how the parts relate to make a whole

persuade: to present your opinions on a topic using evidence, so that others might come to agreement with you

COMPOSING TO LEARN

Once you have done some thinking about these questions, you will help yourself tremendously if you reflect on the assignment in writing, asking any questions that come up, as the person who wrote the following did:

> The assignment says that I am to write an argumentative research paper on a topic of my choice providing lots of evidence, with the class as my audience. I've written research papers before, but I don't know what "argumentative" means with a research paper, so I have to ask about that. But that sounds like the overall purpose for the teacher, to show that I know how to make research be an argument. (I'm also not sure what counts as evidence; I'll have to ask.)
>
> And I don't really know the people in class yet, but they seem to be just like everyone else I know on this campus, so I can ask my friends to help me think about this paper.
>
> The context? Well, it's this writing class—so I guess that means I also have to be careful about how I write. But last night Liv's mother talked about how she makes really small loans to women in other countries—so maybe that's something to write about.

UNDERSTANDING OTHER PROJECTS

Here are questions to help you start your initial thinking about new communication projects. Later parts of this book will help you continue to develop your understanding of your rhetorical situation, as your questions and concerns become more focused with further work.

☐ **Who is your audience?**

What particular people will read, see, or hear the communication I am building? What are my relationships with those people? What values and beliefs do they hold concerning the topic of the communication? Why should this communication matter to them? What will be most important to them in this communication? Is there an immediate audience and then a secondary audience (as, for example, when someone writes a report for a boss, who will then pass the report on to the next boss)?

➡ Part 5 of this book goes into detail about audiences; see pages 194–199.

☐ **What is the context?**

Where and when will my audience receive the communication from me? How does that context shape them to respond? Are there any recent events that might affect how they respond?

☐ **What is the purpose?**

Why am I doing this? What am I hoping to achieve? What should my audience think, feel, or do when they are finished reading? What relationships am I hoping to build with my audience?

➡ Part 5 of this book goes into detail about purposes; see pages 200–203.

PART 2
FINDING IDEAS

2 FINDING IDEAS

CONTENTS

WHERE ARE WE IN THE PROCESS FOR COMPOSING?

Understanding your project

Getting started
    Finding a topic
    Narrowing the topic
    Developing research questions
    Finding sources
    Keeping track of sources

Asking questions

Shaping your project for others

Drafting a paper

Getting feedback

Revising

Polishing

ARE YOU READY TO USE THE NEXT PAGES OF THIS BOOK?

NO…

Are you working at understanding your assignment? Are you still trying to figure out what an assignment asks of you?

If this is your situation, then, no, you are not ready for the next pages.

Until you have a pretty clear idea of your assignment, you will have trouble making a confident and on-target beginning.

→ For help with understanding an assignment, see pages 14–16.

YES.

Can you confidently state in your own words what you believe the assignment asks of you?

If this is your situation, we believe the next pages will help you develop a topic and begin researching it.

COMPOSING TO LEARN & COMPOSING TO COMMUNICATE

When are you writing for yourself, and when are you writing for others?

This is a distinction rarely taught in high school, but it is a distinction that confident, successful writers use all the time.

To understand this distinction, you have to understand that other people are not likely to understand your ideas when those ideas fall out of your head and onto paper. Many people just starting to take writing seriously believe there is something wrong with readers if the readers don't understand such a piece of writing ... but how could readers understand, if they do not live inside your head and know exactly the same things you know, the things you take for granted in putting one idea next to each other?

All composing starts as composing to learn. Effective and successful writers understand that sometimes they need to lose themselves in their own words in order to figure out what ideas matter to them.

They also recognize, however, that sometimes they need to look at their ideas from a little distance: This helps them make their ideas, and the connections between those ideas, explicit for readers.

If you can recognize when you are composing to learn and when you are composing to communicate, or if you can recognize that sometimes you need to back off from shaping your ideas for readers in order to figure out your own ideas, your composing process will be quicker and easier and will yield stronger results.

COMPOSING TO LEARN

If you are writing, sketching, or reading to figure out what *you* think, believe, or feel, then you are composing to learn. You have no one else in mind as you work: You are simply working things out for yourself. In this stage, you don't think about audiences.

Composing to learn can take place on scraps of paper, in journals, on white boards, on dinner napkins, in dreams.

COMPOSING TO LEARN SUPPORTS...

JOURNALS, DIARIES, AND MEMORIES

This is writing meant to be read only by you. Only you will fully understand it.

COMPOSING TO COMMUNICATE

When you alertly shape your ideas so that others can understand them, you are composing to communicate. You make overt connections between ideas. You consider how others might respond, and you shape all aspects of a text so that others can understand what you do.

Composing to communicate requires composing to learn. Until you have a pretty good idea of what matters to you, you can't know what it is you want others to hear or see.

PART 2 OF THIS BOOK IS ABOUT COMPOSING TO LEARN

At the earliest stage of composing, you need to let yourself wander through a wide range of perspectives on a topic. By letting yourself wander, you are more likely to come upon ideas that resonate for you and your audience. That is why Part 2 of this book is set up to help you identify and narrow a topic and then find a wide range of supporting sources.

A RESEARCH PROCESS

What moves writers from step to step of the composing process is research.

At each step of their composing process, successful writers articulate for themselves exactly what they know—and so they come to understand what they still need to learn and research.

Almost all writers—all composers in almost any medium—start by researching an idea or topic that interests them. By doing initial broad research into their area of interest, they learn what aspects of the topic might be of concern to their audiences.

Once writers have a narrowed topic, they can generate questions about the topic. These questions help writers learn what further research—now very focused research—they need to do.

Through this work, writers are moving toward a thesis statement. A thesis statement arranges, logically, the parts of an argument about the topic being researched.

Once they have a thesis statement, writers can then build a statement of purpose, which uses a thesis statement and a writer's knowledge about an audience to describe the various compositional strategies that will help the writer reach the audience.

With all that research behind them, writers are well prepared to draft an effective and strong composition.

TIP: THE RESEARCH PROCESS IS NOT LINEAR

The graphic to the right makes the research process look fast and streamlined. It isn't. You will probably repeat steps as you come across sources that lead your thinking in new directions or as you think more about your own position.

global warming politics the economy immigration electronic voting education video games the draft globalization music health war file sharing

GENERAL TOPIC

RESEARCH

how electronic voting can be manipulated in U.S. national elections

file sharing and the success of new bands

the effects of charter schools on local public schools

NARROWED TOPIC

RESEARCH

What is electronic voting? What makes electronic voting machines better (or worse) than other voting methods? Who oversees electronic voting machines? Who makes electronic voting machines? Who recommends electronic voting machines? Who owns electronic voting machines? Who says we shouldn't use electronic voting machines? How can someone tamper with electronic voting machines?

QUESTIONS TO GUIDE RESEARCH

RESEARCH

Voting machines developed and owned by private companies that tally the vote themselves are not accountable to the voting public; therefore, government-developed and -owned electronic voting machines that print receipts for voters have a higher degree of accountability.

THESIS STATEMENT

RESEARCH

Because I am writing to people in class, many of whom will not have ever voted, I need to explain about different kinds of voting machines—and how each one causes troubles in tracking and counting votes. I also need to show how electronic voting machines—given how they are now developed—seem more vulnerable to tampering and fraud than other existing kinds of voting, and why this should matter to all of us.

STATEMENT OF PURPOSE

RESEARCH

FINISHED WRITING

RESEARCH BROADLY, THEN DEEPLY

GENERAL TOPIC

RESEARCH

NARROWED TOPIC

RESEARCH

QUESTIONS TO GUIDE RESEARCH

RESEARCH

THESIS STATEMENT

RESEARCH

STATEMENT OF PURPOSE

RESEARCH

FINISHED WRITING

During the early stages of research, *general and popular sources* can help you research broadly to get a general sense of what matters to people. Online sources like Google and Wikipedia and popular magazines like *Time* and *Newsweek* can provide help with this broader, preliminary inquiry.

During the later stages of research, *academic journals and other specialized sources* can help you deepen your research and develop your thesis. In academic and other kinds of formal writing, audiences also expect you to provide multiple sources to support your main points.

→ See pages 38–43 for more on kinds of sources and the expectations audiences have about them.

A SKETCH OF ONE WRITER'S PROCESS

GENERAL TOPIC
file sharing

RESEARCH

NARROWED TOPIC
file sharing and the careers of new bands

RESEARCH

QUESTIONS TO GUIDE RESEARCH
Developing guiding questions can help you know what information you need and so what focused research to carry out. Doing this research helps you gain a better sense of what is at stake, for whom, and why—and so helps you understand how to shape your writing. Who shares files? How many files are shared in a year? What is file sharing? What are different ways to file-share? What kinds of files are shared? Are there competing interpretations of what counts as file sharing? Who assigns different interpretations? Who decides whether file sharing is good or bad? What criteria do they use? Some people think file sharing is always theft; are there conditions under which it is beneficial? Who benefits from file sharing? Who doesn't? Do the effects of file sharing differ when different kinds of files are shared? What aspects of file sharing ought to be protected? When should file sharing be prohibited?

RESEARCH

THESIS STATEMENT
A thesis statement is logic: It offers reasons for your position that will be persuasive to your intended audience. Musicians who make their music freely available online attract new audiences, and so sell more of their music than those who do not share their music online.

→ See pages 96–97 for more on thesis statements.

RESEARCH

STATEMENT OF PURPOSE
Writers use statements of purpose to shape a thesis statement for a particular audience. A statement of purpose helps a writer think through the details (such as tone of voice, arrangement, or kinds of examples) of how to present a thesis to an intended audience.

→ Because a statement of purpose is usually several paragraphs long, we cannot give an example here; see pages 200–203 for examples.

In this part of the book, we help you work on developing a narrow topic and questions to guide your research into that topic. Part 3 helps you develop a thesis statement. Part 4 helps you develop a statement of purpose.

GETTING STARTED WITH RESEARCH

ONE PERSON'S PROCESS

Here is how Jessica Rankin, a Senior Technical Writer for a large corporation, describes her research—including how she gets started—when she has to write manuals about a new software product:

I begin by researching and reading the feature specification documents that an engineer writes for the product. These contain descriptions of the feature and what types of things the feature should be used for. After reading through these documents, I usually have a general idea of what the feature is supposed to do, the main parts that would need to be clarified for a user, and where it has been integrated into the software. From there, I go to the software and start playing with the feature to see if it correlates to the feature specification that was written for it. At this point, I have identified odd behaviors and areas that are not intuitive to the general user. These become my starting points for what I document and discuss with the engineer. I act as his first usability tester and I can see the areas that I feel need further development in terms of documentation. Plus, the dialogue that is established between the two of us allows for greater flow of information when changes come up in the feature after development has gotten further along. I know this iterative process has come to a close when the feature no longer changes and I have no further questions about the feature. The real test comes when an outside peer who isn't familiar with the feature reviews my research and documentation. The outside peer is my gauge: Have I conveyed enough information to give the most basic user a good understanding of what they're using?

SETTING UP A SCHEDULE

Unless they are projects you start out of general interest, research projects almost always have due dates—so part of getting started with a research project is figuring out how to schedule your work to be done on time. Making a schedule is also a useful way to remind yourself of just how much work goes into a research paper that is worthy of your efforts and is a learning opportunity. Start with the due date, and work backward. Here is one student's schedule (you may have less time):

Research Paper

DUE DATE	12/15
date assigned	11/1

STEPS	DATE TO COMPLETE STEP
Analyze project (p. 14)	11/2
Find & narrow a topic (pp. 26–33)	11/6
Develop questions for guiding my research (pp. 34–37) and figure out the kinds of research I need to do (pp. 38–43)	11/7
[Will I need to do any interviews, surveys, or observations? (pp. 78–79)]	
[Do I need to do archival research? (pp. 76–77)]	
Carry out my research (pp. 60–79) and start keeping running list of sources (pp. 82–83)	11/14
Develop working thesis (pp. 102–103)	11/16
Do further research required by my thesis (pp. 104–113)	11/23
Evaluate sources, deciding what to include (pp. 130–143)	11/24
Develop statement of purpose (pp. 160–165)	11/25
Develop Works Cited list (pp. 328–350)	11/30
First draft due	12/1
Receive draft back with comments	12/8
If more research is necessary...	12/10
Revise first draft	12/13
Edit first draft	12/14
Get Dad to proofread it for me	12/14
FINAL DRAFT DUE	12/15

FINDING A TOPIC

WHAT A TOPIC IS

A topic is a general area of interest. It's often just a name or a word or two, or two ideas together:

- computer game violence
- children's education
- automobiles
- racism
- women's rights
- sports and advertising
- health and aging
- microloans
- viruses

A topic is a place to start, but it is too broad for a paper; you have to narrow it by doing research that helps you shape your topic for a particular audience in a particular context.

IF AN ASSIGNMENT GIVES A GENERAL TOPIC

You may be given broad guidelines within which to choose a topic. For example, in a history class you might be asked to *Write a short biography of a person who lived through World War I* or *Find two articles that take different positions on an event we've discussed and compare the two articles.* Start by identifying an area—a topic—within the parameters of the assignment, an area in which you want to do further research. If an idea does not immediately spring to mind, use the recommendations on the opposite page to help you choose.

IF YOUR ASSIGNMENT ASKS YOU TO CHOOSE A TOPIC

In writing classes, you are often asked to write a research paper on a topic you choose. Sometimes a topic comes immediately to mind; if not, try:

- **Asking yourself some questions.** What current issues matter to you—or are affecting a friend or someone in your family? What current events or issues do you not understand?

- **Talking to others.** Ask friends and family members what matters to them these days, and why.

- **Going online.** Some library and writing center websites provide lists of current topics that are rich with possibilities for research.

  Old Dominion University Libraries' Idea Generator <*http://www.lib.odu.edu/ libassist/idea/index.php*>

  University of Illinois at Urbana–Champaign Library's Topic Ideas <*http://www.library.uiuc.edu/ugl/ howdoi/topic.html#ideas*>

Once you have a list of possible topics, try these strategies to determine which you want to develop further:

- **Write a little bit on each possible topic.** Use these questions to help:

  Audience questions: Why might my audience care about this topic? What might they already know about it?

  Context questions: Does this topic seem rich enough to help me write a paper of the length asked by the assignment? Does it seem complex enough for the assignment? What is happening locally/nationally/ internationally around this topic?

  Purpose questions: How does this topic help me address the assignment's purposes? Will this topic expand my learning? How can I shape this topic into a purpose that will interest my audience?

  → See pages 2–9 to review the concepts of audience, purpose, and context.

- **Do a Google search on the topic.** Does it look like there's lots of interest in the topic? What are people's different positions on the topic? Do the webpages you visit suggest other, related topics, or other directions for research?

TIP: GET STARTED EARLY

Given the time constraints of school—and of producing a solid research paper—you usually need to decide quickly on a research topic. If you start working early enough, you'll have time to explore possibilities and find a topic that engages you.

Keep in mind, too, that a research paper takes shape in many stages, and you will (if you start early) have time to modify your topic and the research questions that grow out of it as you deepen your understanding of your topic. Leaving this work until the night before doesn't necessarily doom you to failure—just to fear, nerves, and the temptation to let someone else do the work for you.

NARROWING A TOPIC

A TOPIC HAS TO BE NARROWED DOWN BEFORE IT CAN HELP YOU SHAPE RESEARCH AND WRITING

Imagine you want to write about the 1960s, and you tell this to one of your slightly more obnoxious friends, who responds, "Groovy! Are you going to tell us about the Vietnam War and the draft and hippies and the free speech movement and the civil rights movement and the Black Panthers and Women's Rights and the deaths of Jimi Hendrix and Janis Joplin and then there's Woodstock and the Young Republicans…? And do you want to talk about the 1960s in Africa, Asia, and Europe?"

You probably already had some idea of where within that long list you wanted to focus, but **until you can make your focus clear and specific to others, simply being able to name your topic sets you up to be unfocused**. If you are unfocused, your writing will also be unfocused and you will find it hard to plan and organize your paper.

STARTING TO NARROW A TOPIC THROUGH INITIAL, BROAD RESEARCH

One way to find possibilities for narrowing a topic is to start researching the topic using general and popular research sources, as in this example where a Google search on the topic, talking with friends about the topic, and reading the paper and watching television give this writer a sense of how to focus the topic:

TOPIC:
microloans

GOOGLE SEARCH:
Microloans are small loans (usually under $100) made to people without credit, usually in developing countries; they support self-employment and are often made to women because then the whole family benefits; one example is the Grameen bank in Bangladesh, whose founder won the Nobel Peace Prize in 2005.

READING THE PAPER:
The New York Times has an editorial by Nicholas Kristof on how anyone in the U.S. can loan even a little bit of money to individuals in other countries, through websites like kiva.org.

TALKING TO OTHERS:
A friend's mother has made loans to women in other countries (through online organizations) so that the women can buy sewing machines and start businesses; all the loans she's made have been repaid.

TELEVISION SHOW:
Small Treasures: Microcredit and the Future of Poverty on PBS says that many microloans are to small businesses that make products out of what others have thrown away, like a woman who makes shopping bags out of discarded cement bags.

After such initial research, this writer could narrow the possibilities to these:

• Microloans and the role of women in developing countries

• Small business options for people living in poverty

• Ways of using your money to help others

• Alternative approaches to traditional economic development

HOW DO YOU KNOW WHEN YOU HAVE A NARROWED TOPIC?

A NARROWED TOPIC IS LINKED TO AN ISSUE OR CONTROVERSY THAT WILL BE OF INTEREST TO YOUR AUDIENCE

Using what you know about your audience, use your initial, broad research (as described on the previous page) to find possible areas that might be useful, surprising, or provocative to your audience.

For example, if you are writing about the 1960s for a class research paper, you probably already have some sense of how others in class think about what happened in the 1960s. If everyone else thinks of the 1960s in terms of free love and music, then imagine how you will catch their attention if you can narrow your topic to *How the conservative movement of the 1980s and 1990s in the United States is a response to the social movements of the 1960s.*

TIP: KEEP YOUR MIND OPEN

While doing initial informal research, cast a wide net and keep as open a mind as possible. The wider you look for information on a topic, the more likely you are to be surprised by what you find—and being surprised can help you be more interested and engaged and thus write more strongly.

Also, don't look only for sources that support your initial thoughts on a topic. Seek a range of positions so that you have the widest sense of how people are thinking. (In Part 3 of this book we help you evaluate the sources you find through your research so that you can decide what is most useful for your project.)

NARROWED TOPICS

Notice how narrowed topics usually relate a general topic to specific places, times, actions, or groups of people. A narrowed topic can focus on one aspect of a general topic (as in the examples below about the Internet or religion), and relate that aspect to a place, time, action, or group.

GENERAL TOPIC		NARROWED TOPIC
women in the workforce	→	the number of women in politics in the United States the last fifty years
advertising	→	advertising and democratic participation in the United States
water as a resource	→	water management in the Middle East
the Internet	→	how corporations shape Internet social networking sites
poetry	→	poetry written by people rooted in two cultures
racial profiling	→	racial profiling and law-enforcement policies
global warming	→	global warming education in elementary schools
sports	→	college sports training and men's body images
religion	→	the tax-exempt status of churches and their role in political races
technology	→	the development of the compass, gunpowder, and papermaking in China
the civil rights movement	→	organizational strategies of the civil rights movement

TIP: USE GOOGLE TO TEST YOUR TOPIC

There are two ways Google can tell you if your topic is narrow enough:

- If the first websites that Google suggests come from academic sources or respected organizations, your topic is narrow enough to be worth further research. (Pages 39 and 44–53 can help you determine if the sources are academic.)
- If Google responds with hundreds of millions of possible links, your topic is not yet focused enough.

OTHER STRATEGIES FOR NARROWING A TOPIC

BRAINSTORMING

Brainstorming is letting your brain run loose to jump from one idea to the next. Coming up with ideas that will engage an audience can sometimes happen when you think hard and with focus; other times you need simply to let your brain's associative abilities do what they will.

You can brainstorm alone or with others; with others, you have the advantage of playing off each other's ideas. In either case, work in the same way:

- Set aside five or ten minutes.

- For that five or ten minutes, say your topic out loud, and then say out loud—but also write down—every single thought that comes to mind in response.

- Do not stop to judge. If an idea seems too absurd to record, record it nonetheless: It might lead to something you can use. (And let yourself laugh: The energy of laughter is part of what makes brainstorming work.)

- If you hit a dead end, go back to an earlier term and see what other associations you have with it. (Try thinking of synonyms or opposites to spur your thinking—or come up with as absurd an association as you can.)

- At the end, read your ideas out loud to see if anything else comes up. If one or two ideas seem useful or potentially fruitful now, hold on to them. Otherwise, put the list aside and look at it the next day.

FREEWRITING

Freewriting is a little like brainstorming on paper. Give yourself five minutes, and just write on your topic. As with brainstorming, just record whatever ideas come up: Let one idea lead into the next without stopping.

Freewriting becomes easier the more you do it; it's a good way to help your mind run more easily, and it's a practice of many successful writers.

At the end of your time limit, read over what you have written to see if any ideas stand out for development. If not, put the writing aside and go back to it later.

CLUSTERING

Like brainstorming and freewriting, clustering is a strategy for making your ideas visible to yourself—but instead of writing, you draw. Clustering helps you see relations among ideas, which can help you see potential arrangements you can use later when you start writing your paper.

To cluster, write your topic in the center of a page. Around the topic, write down as many related ideas as you can. Turn to each of those related ideas, and see what other ideas relate to them. If one idea suggests a chain of related ideas, follow it.

Below is the cluster Shelly made in thinking about body image, which led her to think about how the media shape our sense of our bodies and how our body image affects our health; by doing this clustering, and thinking about how pro-ana sites work, she came up with this narrowed topic: *body images in the media produced for you by others, and body images in the media that you produce about yourself.*

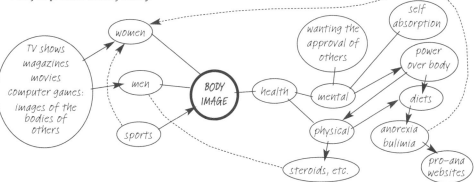

TIP: USE IDEA MAPPING TOOLS

There are free online applications that can help you cluster ideas (in information design and management, clustering is called **mapping**):
try FreeMind <http://freemind.sourceforge.net/wiki/index.php/Main_Page> or
CMapTools <http://cmap.ihmc.us/>.

QUESTIONS TO GUIDE RESEARCH

Once you have a narrowed topic, you can go online or to the library to start doing more focused research. But if you take time to carry out one more step—generating questions to help guide your research—you will have a better sense of what you need to find to write a solid paper, and where to look for that information.

On the next page, we show you one way to generate questions on your topic. Doing this can help you see

- areas of research you might not have considered otherwise.
- possible ways for shaping your purpose.
- questions your audience might have that you need to address.
- the specific research directions you need to take.

You may not need to address all the questions you develop, but you won't know for sure until you start using them to dig into sources with focus.

THE ORIGINS OF THESE QUESTIONS

Courtroom observations helped rhetoricians see that most questions fit into a set of categories. Rhetoricians called the categories **stases**, the plural of **stasis**, the Greek word for **place**. Stasis questions—like the ones to the right—help communicators determine what is at stake in any argument and the complexity of what is at stake.

KINDS OF QUESTIONS TO GUIDE RESEARCH

These categories can help you not only invent questions to ask but also determine which questions are likely to lead to rich research, as we show on the next pages.

QUESTIONS OF FACT

- What happened?
- Who was involved?
- Where did it happen?
- When did it happen?

QUESTIONS OF DEFINITION

- What is the thing or issue under discussion? What is it made of?
- What is the expected way (in the particular context) of using the thing, word, title, or expression?

QUESTIONS OF INTERPRETATION

- How do we understand and make sense of what happened?
- How are we to incorporate facts and definitions into a story that makes sense to us?

QUESTIONS OF CONSEQUENCE

- What caused what happened? What changes—to which persons, processes, or objects—led to the issue at hand?
- What are the effects of what happened? What changes might result from what happened?

QUESTIONS OF VALUE

- Is what is at stake good, useful, worthy of praise, or worthy of blame?
- What audiences will value the matter at hand? What do people say about the issue?
- Which of our (or our audience's) values are called upon as we make judgments about what happened?

QUESTIONS OF POLICY

- Given the circumstances, what should we do?
- Given the circumstances, what rules should we make or enforce?
- Given the circumstances, what laws should we write?

USING RESEARCH QUESTIONS TO DEVELOP A TOPIC

USING THE QUESTIONS

Use the research questions to generate as many other questions on your narrowed topic as you can, as the examples to the right suggest.

Doing this work will help you gain a sense of questions your audience might have, questions your research and composing will need to answer.

Generating questions will also help you see what research you need to do to gain authority on your topic.

Finally, generating questions will help you see whether your initial opinion on your topic is sufficiently informed. You will learn whether your opinions really are the ones you want to hold.

■ ■ ■

When you use the research questions to help you generate more questions, just let the questions come: Don't judge them, but let one question lead to another. The more questions you can generate, the more you will have a sense of what further research you need to do.

→ See pages 42–43 for using the questions to help you determine the kinds of research to do.

DEVELOPING SEARCH TERMS FOR ONLINE AND DATABASE SEARCHES

From your questions, pick out words and phrases directly related to your topic, and use them in search engines.

Here are terms coming from all the questions Kwan generated to the right:

stem cell, stem-cell research, viable stem-cell treatments, stem-cell treatments, stem-cell controversy, stem-cell controversies, stem-cell results, paralysis, stem-cell therapies, consequences of stem-cell research, results of stem-cell research, stem-cell policy, stem-cell research in Europe, stem-cell research in Asia

→ Page 67 shows how to combine several terms to do a very focused search.

TIP: TRY TO ANSWER ALL THE QUESTIONS YOU GENERATE

Even though (as you will see in coming pages) you will eventually further narrow your research to focus on one or two questions, using your research to find answers to all the questions you generate will help you:

1 Learn the broad information you will need to give your readers at the beginning of your writing so that they understand why the topic matters.

2 Develop the most thorough and complete answers in your writing.

USING THE RESEARCH QUESTIONS, EXAMPLE 1

Kwan chose the topic of stem-cell research for an argumentative research paper, and has narrowed his topic to the possibilities of stem-cell treatments for paralysis. Using the research questions, he brainstorms the following questions:

QUESTIONS OF FACT
What are researchers able to do now with stem cells to help paralysis? How far away do viable stem-cell treatments seem?

QUESTIONS OF DEFINITION
What are stem cells? What is stem-cell research? What is paralysis?

QUESTIONS OF INTERPRETATION
Do stem-cell treatments cure paralysis? Should paralysis always be treated?

QUESTIONS OF CONSEQUENCE
What happens to people who have stem-cell treatments for paralysis? How do stem-cell therapies work in treating paralysis?

QUESTIONS OF VALUE
Who thinks stem-cell research is worthwhile, and who doesn't? Why? What values are called upon as people make judgments about stem-cell research? What values aren't called upon? Are the bad results of stem-cell research offset by the good results?

QUESTIONS OF POLICY
What are the different policies we could have toward stem-cell research and paralysis? What are the policies of other countries on stem-cell research?

USING THE RESEARCH QUESTIONS, EXAMPLE 2

Eva has chosen the topic of road building, and has narrowed her topic to the effects of road building on rural communities. Using the research questions, she brainstorms the following questions:

QUESTIONS OF FACT
Who decides where & when roads are built? How expensive is a new road? What affects the cost of a new road? Who pays for roads in rural areas?

QUESTIONS OF DEFINITION
What counts as a new road? What, really, is a road?

QUESTIONS OF INTERPRETATION
What do new roads bring to a rural community? What do existing roads bring to a rural community?

QUESTIONS OF CONSEQUENCE
What happens when a new road is built in a rural community—or not? Who or what is affected when a new road is built, and how?

QUESTIONS OF VALUE
Are the consequences of new roads good—or bad—for a community? For whom or what are new roads good or bad (including nonhumans)? What values are at stake in making judgments about whether roads are good or bad? What values underlie the different laws that exist about road building?

QUESTIONS OF POLICY
What laws already exist about the development of roads? How have laws and policies changed over the years?

KINDS OF SOURCES, KINDS OF RESEARCH

You have a narrowed topic and a series of questions that can help you learn more about your topic, in a focused and organized manner.

Now you need to determine where to look to find answers to your questions. In these pages we cover

- **KINDS OF SOURCES** for research
- **KINDS OF RESEARCH**
- **USING YOUR GUIDING RESEARCH QUESTIONS** to determine what kinds of sources and kinds of research to carry out
- **WHERE TO FIND THE SOURCES** for the research that will help you answer your questions

UNDERSTANDING DIFFERENT KINDS OF SOURCES

Sources are the texts—written, filmed, videotaped, recorded, photographed—from which you learn about your topic. Sometimes sources provide evidence and examples to use in your writing or other composing.

PRIMARY AND SECONDARY SOURCES

To determine whether a source is primary or secondary, ask yourself if you are reading someone's original words or reading *about* the person. In a paper about Ida B. Wells, for example, speeches and books by Wells are primary sources; commentary about Wells by other writers is a secondary source.

Examples of primary sources:

- Novels, poems, autobiographies, speeches, letters, diaries, blogs, e-mails.
- Eyewitness accounts of events, including written, filmed, and photographed accounts.
- Field research (surveys, observations, and interviews) that *you* conduct.

Examples of secondary sources:

- Biographies.
- Encyclopedias.
- News articles about events.
- Reviews of novels, poems, autobiographies, speeches, letters, diaries, e-mails, blogs.

Knowing the distinction between primary and secondary sources helps you seek out both kinds, and cover all the bases in your research.

SCHOLARLY AND POPULAR SOURCES

This distinction depends on the authority and reliability of the information in the sources.

In scholarly sources:

- Authors have academic credentials: they have studied the topic in depth and know how to weigh and present different sides of the topic.
- The sources used by the writer are listed so readers can check that the sources have been used fairly.
- Topics are examined at length.
- Their purpose is to spread knowledge: These sources are usually found in libraries; they contain little or no advertising.

In popular sources:

- Authors are journalists or reporters, usually without academic study in the topic.
- The sources are not listed.
- Topics are addressed briefly.
- Their purpose is to be quickly informative or entertaining: You find these sources at newsstands and stores, and they contain advertising.

Starting research with a range of popular sources can help you quickly get an overview of available perspectives on a topic. But the expectation for an authoritative research paper is that most of its sources are academic.

KINDS OF RESEARCH

Most research projects require you to do different kinds of research, seeking sources in different places and seeking different kinds of sources. Here are general categories of the kinds of research you can carry out, in recommended order:

ONLINE RESEARCH

Not everything is online—nor does Google link to all that is online.

Unspecialized search engines—like Google and Yahoo!—are useful for the following, usually early in research:

- Developing a sense of popular opinion on topics.
- Finding popular sources on topics, in both popular magazines and in blogs.
- Finding person-on-the-street quotations.
- Finding links or references to academic sources.

Specialized search engines provide access to material to which popular search engines often don't have access.

→ See pages 66–67 for descriptions of some specialized search engines.

TIP: USE VISUAL AND AUDIO SOURCES

With any of the research sites we mention here you can do *visual research* and *aural research*. Almost all the kinds of research we mention access not only print sources but also photographs, videos, historic printed matter such as brochures and posters, and speeches. If any visual or aural sources can support your research, search for them online and ask librarians about them.

LIBRARY RESEARCH

There are two ways to use most libraries these days: in person and online.

We encourage you to get to know, in person, a reference librarian at your library: Being able to have a conversation with a librarian about a topic can help you open up new approaches you might not have considered of on your own. A reference librarian can help you with both in-library and online uses of the library's resources.

In-library resources include the obvious books, journals, and reference materials. But some libraries also house historical or art archives, as well as map and government repositories. If you do not know how to find these—or even what materials are available—see if your library gives tours or workshops; knowing what is in your library can help you find creative possibilities for research.

Online library resources can include catalogs of the library's holdings and databases of newspapers and journals from across disciplines. (Later we discuss how to use such databases.)

Finally, libraries usually give you access to interlibrary loans: If your library does not have a book or journal you need, they can order it for you from another library.

RESEARCH IN ARCHIVES AND SPECIAL LIBRARY COLLECTIONS

Physical archives include local history associations or museums that have collections of old manuscripts, furniture, clothing, or other items. Such archives are usually private or provide limited access in order to protect their collections; they have different access policies that you can learn by contacting the archive. To find archives that might be close to you, do an online search using *archive* or *museum* as a keyword along with the kind of information you are trying to find, look in the phone book under *museum*, or ask a librarian.

Virtual archives are online collections of digitized materials such as letters, posters, photographs, or speeches.

Many libraries also have special collections of paintings and prints, films and video, and sound recordings—often not digitized. If you are writing on a topic that has a historical dimension, or are just curious, such special collections can be fascinating.

→ For more information on finding and using both physical and virtual archives and special collections, see pages 70–71.

FIELD RESEARCH

Interviews, observations, and surveys are all forms of research. To carry them out, you have to go out *into the field*—which could be a suburban strip mall, urban nonprofit organization, classroom, or rural farm.

→ For more on carrying out interviews, observations, and surveys, see pages 72–73.

DETERMINING WHERE TO RESEARCH

WHAT SOURCES AND RESEARCH WILL HELP?

Almost all research writing starts by grounding its readers in definitions and facts on the topic, and then focuses on interpretation of the issue to show a problem (which could be a consequence of an event) or to argue for certain policies. Once you have focused questions, use this chart to choose kinds of sources and research.

	primary source	secndary source	academic sources	popular source	online research	library research	archival research	field research
QUESTIONS OF FACT								
encyclopedias, atlases, and other reference works		✓	✓	✓	✓	✓		
statistics	✓			✓	✓	✓		
government or organizational documents	✓				✓	✓	✓	
firsthand accounts (interviews, autobiographies)	✓				✓	✓	✓	✓
photographs of events	✓				✓	✓	✓	
trial transcripts	✓					✓	✓	
surveys and polls	✓				✓	✓		✓
QUESTIONS OF DEFINITION								
dictionaries (for general audiences as well as specialized)	✓	✓	✓	✓	✓	✓		
academic journal articles		✓			✓	✓		
QUESTIONS OF INTERPRETATION								
editorials and opinion pieces		✓		✓	✓	✓		
partisan news sources		✓			✓	✓		
people's stories	✓				✓		✓	✓
artwork (movies, novels, short stories, documentary photography)	✓				✓	✓	✓	
position statements		✓			✓	✓		
biographies	✓	✓	✓			✓	✓	
academic journal articles			✓			✓		

As you move forward with a research project and develop a thesis statement, you will know which of these categories of questions most guides your work. This will help you know where to focus your last research efforts as you gather the last evidence to support your work.

→ To develop a thesis statement, see pages 96–97.

	primary source	secndary source	academic sources	popular source	online research	library research	archival research	field research
QUESTIONS OF CONSEQUENCE								
statistics	✓	✓			✓	✓		
historical accounts	✓			✓	✓	✓	✓	
photographs of the aftermaths of events		✓		✓	✓	✓	✓	
academic journal articles					✓	✓		
the items listed under INTERPRETATION								
QUESTIONS OF VALUE								
organizational mission statements	✓				✓			✓
voting results	✓				✓	✓	✓	
surveys and polls	✓				✓	✓		✓
position statements	✓				✓	✓	✓	
academic journal articles			✓			✓		
the items listed under INTERPRETATION								
QUESTIONS OF POLICY								
government decisions	✓				✓	✓	✓	
organizational policy statements and decisions	✓				✓	✓	✓	✓
business records	✓				✓		✓	✓
trial decisions	✓				✓	✓	✓	
academic journal articles		✓				✓		

KINDS OF SOURCES,
KINDS OF RESEARCH

CHOOSING SOURCES THAT HELP YOUR RESEARCH AND SUPPORT YOUR ARGUMENTS

Compositions that audiences take seriously offer as much support as possible from a range of supporting sources. The kinds of sources appropriate for your argument depend on the argument you are making, the audience to whom you are making the argument, and your context.

Explore these topics online:

Choosing sources

www.mycomplab.com

CHARACTERISTICS THAT DISTINGUISH SOURCES

On the next pages, we describe different often-used sources so you can judge their appropriateness for your purposes. We use the following criteria:

- **AUDIENCE**

  If a source is aimed at a general audience, the information it offers will generally be broad but shallow.

  Sources for academic or other specialized audiences will usually be more developed and better supported.

- **WRITERS**

  When writers are paid by the company or organization for which they write, they might offer opinions and information that are in line only with the goals of the company or organization.

- **APPEARANCE**

  A professional appearance is a reflection of an overall ethic of care and attention to detail.

- **FORMAT**

  If information is presented alongside advertisements, it can mean that the advertiser has some say in what information is presented.

- **LANGUAGE**

  Sources using informal language are for general audiences; although they are easier to read, such sources are considered less authoritative than sources that use the language and vocabulary of specialized disciplines.

- **REVIEW**

  If a source's information is reviewed by people who are unpaid and have no connection with the publisher, readers will grant it more authority.

- **BIBLIOGRAPHY**

  Your readers will consider as most authoritative those sources that provide information that allows them to check the sources—such as a Works Cited list or other kind of bibliography.

- **WHEN TO USE**

  We make general suggestions for using sources in ways readers will trust—but keep in mind that you always need to consider your readers, your purposes, and your context in making choices about what kinds of sources to use and how to use them. If you have any questions about using a source, ask several people from your intended audience how they would respond to your use of the source.

OTHER KINDS OF SOURCES

Almost any composition can be a source: You can cite song lyrics to show how hip-hop artists interpret current events differently than mainstream media; you can use a computer game screenshot to discuss representations of women; you can interview a neighbor about the history of local development.

We cannot possibly list all the sources you might use because what you use is limited only by what will engage your audience, given your purpose. The characteristics we consider on these pages can help you decide whether and how to use sources we have not listed.

CHOOSING SOURCES—**PERIODICALS**

They are called *periodicals* because they are published periodically: daily, weekly, monthly, quarterly.

DAILY NEWSPAPERS

WHEN TO USE: When you write for a general audience, examples and supporting evidence from newspapers can be appropriate.

AUDIENCE: General public

WRITERS: Newspaper employees (*staff writers*) or freelance journalists who are paid; writers who work for news services; a writer's credentials often are not given.

FORMAT: Articles can have illustrations or photographs, and newspapers contain advertising.

LANGUAGE: Nontechnical, informal

REVIEW: Articles are assigned to writers and reviewed by editors working for the newspapers.

BIBLIOGRAPHY: References might be mentioned in the text, but there are usually few ways given for readers to check a writer's sources.

POPULAR JOURNALS

WHEN TO USE: When you write for a general audience, examples and supporting evidence from popular journals can be appropriate.

AUDIENCE: General public

WRITERS: Employees of the journal (*staff writers*) or freelance journalists who are paid; a writer's credentials often are not given.

FORMAT: Articles can have illustrations or photographs, and popular journals often contain advertising.

LANGUAGE: Nontechnical, informal

REVIEW: Articles are selected and reviewed by editors working for the journal.

BIBLIOGRAPHY: References might be mentioned in the text, but there are usually few ways given for readers to check a writer's sources.

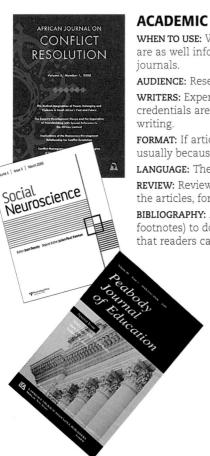

ACADEMIC JOURNALS

WHEN TO USE: When you want to show readers that your arguments are as well informed as possible, draw on the research in academic journals.

AUDIENCE: Researchers, scholars, specialists

WRITERS: Experts or specialists in a field or discipline, whose credentials are often provided and who are usually not paid for writing.

FORMAT: If articles contain illustrations, charts, tables, or maps, it is usually because they directly support the articles' arguments.

LANGUAGE: The specialized language of a field or discipline

REVIEW: Reviewers who are recognized experts in the field review the articles, for no pay.

BIBLIOGRAPHY: Articles end with a list of works cited (and/or contain footnotes) to document the research performed by the writer so that readers can check the sources.

CHOOSING SOURCES—**BOOKS**

NONFICTION BOOKS
Such books may have more than one author but be written with a single voice throughout.

WHEN TO USE: Because of the review process, such books tend to have authority for readers.

WRITERS: Publishing companies solicit writers or accept proposals and choose what to publish.

REVIEW: Publishers approve the writing and can arrange for fact-checking.

BIBLIOGRAPHY: References are usually mentioned.

REFERENCE BOOKS
These books provide factual information such as definitions or statistics.

WHEN TO USE: To provide definitions of words unknown to an audience or to support factual claims. Conventionally, use reference books sparingly in academic writing.

WRITERS: Authorities on a topic usually write entries in reference books.

REVIEW: Publishers approve the writing and check facts.

BIBLIOGRAPHY: References may be given.

EDITED COLLECTIONS
An edited collection is a series of essays written by multiple authors, bound into one book.

WHEN TO USE: Because of the review process, such books tend to have authority for readers.

WRITERS: Publishing companies solicit writers or accept proposals and choose what to publish.

REVIEW: Publishers approve the writing and can arrange for fact-checking.

BIBLIOGRAPHY: References are usually mentioned.

CORPORATE AUTHOR
Companies publish annual reports on their finances and accomplishments; they might publish books or pamphlets relevant to their products or services.

WHEN TO USE: The company's reputation on the topic about which you are writing will shape how readers respond to your use of such sources.

WRITERS: Written by a company employee or by a writer hired for the purpose

REVIEW: A company might set up a review.

BIBLIOGRAPHY: References might be mentioned.

GOVERNMENT AUTHOR
The U.S. government publishes a wide range of books, pamphlets, guides, and reports on health, agriculture, economics, statistics, education, and other issues.

WHEN TO USE: When your readers will accept the authority of the government on a topic

WRITERS: Writers can be government employees or people hired because of their expertise.

REVIEW: The writing can be reviewed by others in the same or other government agency.

BIBLIOGRAPHY: References may or may not be given.

CHOOSING SOURCES—**WEBPAGES**

Just as there are many kinds of books, there many kinds of webpages.

Because there are so many kinds of webpages, and because webpages can be published by anyone with design abilities and access to hardware and a server, it is often hard to judge webpages' potential to support your research. On these next pages, we provide strategies for recognizing kinds of webpages as well as considering what kind of webpage might be appropriate to support the arguments you are making.

As always, keep in mind that—as with any source—the appropriateness of a webpage for supporting your argument depends on the argument you are making, the audience to whom you are making the argument, and your context. The most important question you can ask yourself in considering whether to use a source is **"Will the audience to whom I am writing see the makers of this website as authoritative on the issues with which I am concerned?"** (Keep in mind, though, that sometimes you will use sources to show how the opinions and ideas of some writers are not well argued or well supported.)

→ For ideas on judging the relevance and credibility of websites, see pages 124–137.

PERSONAL WEBSITES AND BLOGS

These present the very personal opinions of individuals who may or may not have credentials to write on a particular topic.

AUDIENCE: General public or people interested in the particular topic addressed by the website or blog

WRITERS: Such websites can be produced by anyone with at least minimal technical understanding and access to a computer and the appropriate software.

APPEARANCE: Such websites can look amateurish or completely professional; they may or may not have ads. Look at the URL or on the page bottom to see if the website is sponsored by a company or organization.

LANGUAGE: Nontechnical, informal

REVIEW: No one reviews this information except the writer.

BIBLIOGRAPHY: Writings can be accompanied by source lists or links to supporting webpages.

WHEN TO USE: If the writer is an authority on the topic you are researching and your audience is likely to have heard of the person, you can use the writings to support claims you make—but you will probably also want to offer other support. If the writer is unknown to you, it is probably a good idea to use the person's opinions only as illustration of opinions people might hold on your topic.

GROUP BLOGS

People who care about similar issues work on a blog together; each contributes individual entries.

WHEN TO USE: If the writers are well respected in their fields or disciplines, citing their opinions can support your writing—but keep in mind that when you are writing an academic paper, citing a blog will not have as much authority as citing an article published in a journal.

AUDIENCE: Because group blogs are usually on a shared set of interests, the audience is people interested in those issues.

WRITERS: Because these writers want to be read, they are usually careful to choose each other on the quality of their knowledge and writing.

APPEARANCE: Group blogs tend to be carefully presented so that their appearance encourages others to take the blog seriously. Advertising on the blog can indicate that the blog is taken seriously enough that others want to advertise there, or it can mean the writers are trying to make money. Academic group blogs rarely have advertising.

LANGUAGE: The writing indicates the audience the blog wants to attract: Is it academic, or conversational, or…?

REVIEW: Because writers for these blogs want to be read and care about the reputation of the blog, they often discuss with each other the quality of the writing.

BIBLIOGRAPHY: Writings can be accompanied by source lists or links to supporting webpages.

CORPORATE WEBSITES AND BLOGS

These present information about and opinions of companies, which can be large or very, very small.

WHEN TO USE: Because such websites are usually promotional, the information you find on them will rarely be useful for supporting arguments, unless you are writing about the company itself or using the company's website as an example of how companies operate.

AUDIENCE: General public, consumers, people interested in the particular topic addressed by the website or blog

WRITERS: Employees of the company or freelancers

APPEARANCE: Such websites can look amateurish or professional, depending on the ethos the company wishes to present and the resources they allocate. Well-established companies will have their name in their URL. The company name and contact information should be somewhere on the main page.

LANGUAGE: The language reflects the company's purposes: friendly and informal to appeal to customers, or formal to show the company's solidity.

REVIEW: Corporate webpages might be reviewed by lawyers to protect the company from lawsuits; otherwise, content is approved only by the company.

BIBLIOGRAPHY: Writings can be accompanied by source lists or links to supporting webpages.

NONPROFIT WEBSITES

*According to the Internal Revenue Service, an organization is nonprofit if its income does not go to stockholders, directors, or anyone else connected with the organization; instead, its income supports only the work the organization does. A nonprofit's URL usually ends in **.org**.*

WHEN TO USE: Generally, the facts and statistics you find on the websites of nonprofit organizations are reliable—although remember that organizations want to present information that supports their purposes. It is always useful to find additional supporting information. (You can always use an organization's description of itself in your writing when you want readers to know about an organization.)

AUDIENCE: Anyone interested in the work done by the organization, perhaps to donate or to learn more about the organization.

WRITERS: The website might be composed by an employee of the organization or by someone hired to represent the organization.

APPEARANCE: Organizations try to present themselves as competent and dependable in order to gain support from those who see the site.

LANGUAGE: Generally, nontechnical, informal language for general audiences

REVIEW: The organization approves what is on the website.

BIBLIOGRAPHY: Writings can be accompanied by source lists or links to supporting webpages.

GOVERNMENT WEBSITES

*U.S. government website URLs usually end in **.gov**. State websites end with the two-letter abbreviation for the state followed by **.gov**.*

WHEN TO USE: Use government websites when you want to give statistics or the wording of policies. Because claims made about science or social research can be shaped for political ends, use such claims in your writing only if you can back them up with support from disinterested parties whom your readers will trust.

AUDIENCE: General public; specialists looking for information the government compiles

WRITERS: The website might be composed by a government employee or by someone hired as a freelancer.

APPEARANCE: The look of government websites will tell you whether the site has been designed for general-audience or specialist use.

LANGUAGE: The language of government websites can range from friendly and informal to highly technical, depending on the intended audience.

REVIEW: Governmental websites are supposed to adhere to accessibility, writing, and navigational policies established within agencies as well as across some agencies.

BIBLIOGRAPHY: Writings can be accompanied by source lists or links to supporting webpages.

ONLINE PERIODICALS

Distinguish among online periodicals just as you would among print periodicals, as on pages 46–47.

WHEN TO USE: Use each kind of periodical as you would use its print counterpart, as described on pages 46–47.

AUDIENCE: Depending on the periodical, the audience can be general or highly specialized, academic or popular.

WRITERS: If the periodical is an online version of a print periodical, then the writers for both versions are usually the same people. Online-only journals can have paid writers or volunteer writers.

APPEARANCE: Such websites can look amateurish or completely professional, depending on the organization behind them and their purpose.

LANGUAGE: The language will depend on the audience and purpose.

REVIEW: Online versions of print periodicals tend to have the same review policies as the print version. Academic periodicals will generally have some sort of review policy for articles; look on the website to find out. For other periodicals, the website might include such policies.

BIBLIOGRAPHY: Academic periodicals will provide sources and ways to find those sources; other periodicals may or may not provide sources.

DATABASES OF JOURNALS

Through your school library, you probably have access to these databases, which are like search engines into collections of periodicals: You enter terms for topics of interest to you, and the database returns to you listings of articles in which those terms appear. Databases are usually specialized. Each database provides access to a particular subject, such as medicine, law, literature and the arts, newspapers, or engineering.

WHEN TO USE: Any time you want to find a generally credible range of articles to help you think about your topic or to support your claims, use online databases of journals.

→ See pages 58–65 for more information on using databases.

AUTHORITY: Unless you are writing about databases, you are not going to be citing databases; you will instead be using them to find periodical articles that help you think about your writing or that support your points. Because of this, the authority of databases is not an issue to consider in your use of them.

ONLINE REFERENCE WORKS

These can be online versions of print reference works or reference works created only to be online.

WHEN TO USE: Generally, make only limited use of reference works: They are best used for giving a quick fact or an authoritative definition of a term. Readers of academic research papers expect you to use a range of sources, but they especially expect you to use specialized sources primarily.

AUTHORITY: The information and thus authority of these sites is the same as that of print reference sources.

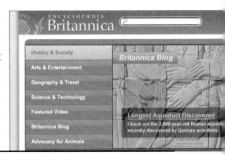

ONLINE REFERENCE WORKS—WIKIPEDIA

Wikipedia is a particular kind of online reference, developed by volunteers who write on topics of interest to them and who edit each other's entries. Teachers consider Wikipedia use to be controversial because the entries can be shaped by nonspecialists; because there are no easy ways to check the authority and accuracy of any particular entry; and because the ease of using Wikipedia sometimes encourages writers not to seek further support for their arguments.

WHEN TO USE: Wikipedia is useful in the early stages of research, when you are looking for quick and preliminary information to help you learn how others think about a topic—just as you can use Google or any general encyclopedia. In addition, your audience (including your teacher) will probably not object if you use Wikipedia as the source for the definition of a term in your writing.

When you are ready to research a topic in depth, Wikipedia can help you go deeper because many entries include good listings of further resources—but citing Wikipedia in a Works Cited listing shows readers that you have probably done only quick and dirty research.

FINDING SOURCES

SEARCHING

In shaping your narrowed topic into a statement of purpose, you've determined that a kind of source—a scholarly journal, an oral history, or census statistics—will help you. Finding this particular source means you have to understand how sources are organized (or "catalogued").

Prior to the Internet, libraries had card catalogs for their materials. For every book, journal, map, or governmental record kept in a library there was a small card that listed the object's title, author, date, and place of publication; a few keywords about the object's topic; and a general subject area into which the object's contents fit.

Now, instead of those cards, library objects are associated with online records in databases, which carry the information that used to be on the cards. The **library computer system** provides a webpage into which you type search terms; the database compares your search terms to all the terms listed in the database records and then shows you any matches.

Online search engines that give you access to sources outside of libraries look at webpages of all kinds and develop their own database records for those pages, based on what words are on the page or in its code. When you use a search engine, it compares your search terms to its database and shows you the matches.

Both processes are similar, and both require that you know how to generate search terms that will help you find useful sources.

BE SPECIFIC

Having a narrowed topic will help you find sources that specifically address your questions.

It is useless to enter one word into a search engine. Try two words and then three: **cars fuel** or **cars ethanol**—and then **cars alternate fuels**.

In library catalogs and databases, you can enter the key terms from your narrowed topic; you can also enter any synonyms for those terms.

In search engines like Google, you can enter the key terms from your narrowed topic—but you can also enter a question such as "Does ethanol provide better mileage than a hybrid car?" and receive the most focused information possible from the websites to which Google has access. Use the research questions you generated for such searches.

→ See page 67 to help you with this.

TRY ALTERNATE TERMS

If you cannot readily think up synonyms for the key terms of your narrowed topic, use a thesaurus, or ask someone else what other terms come to mind for your topic. The more terms you can use, the more likely you are to find helpful sources.

ASK FOR HELP

Teachers, librarians, and people in your class who seem to be good at searching are usually happy to help.

CHECK THE SEARCH ENGINE'S HELP TIPS

All search engines—the library's online catalog, a library database, or a general search engine—have a link to help or usage tips. Read this information so that you can take advantage of the particular features of a search engine.

USE A FAMILIAR SEARCH ENGINE TO FIND SOURCES YOU CAN THEN CHECK IN A MORE SPECIALIZED SEARCH ENGINE

Library joural databases can have confusing interfaces; many people, including faculty, use Google to find a source and then check to see if it's in their library. For example, you might find through Google an academic article exactly on your topic. You can then enter into your library's journal database the journal name, author, and date to have access to a full-text version of the journal. (Similarly, some researchers use Amazon.com to find books because they can usually read some of the book and check reviews. If the book looks useful, they will then see if their library has it. This is useful only for recently published books.)

PERSIST

The more creative you are with your terms and the longer you search during this stage, the more information you will find that pushes you to weigh differing opinions. This sort of thinking leads to writing others want to read.

LIBRARY RESEARCH

USING LIBRARY INDEXES

If you think information you need will be in a print source that was published before the rise of networked computers (or, roughly, before the early 1990s), then you are likely to be successful with the print indexes in your library for journal articles, newspapers, and books in several subject areas. A reference librarian can help you find the appropriate index.

TIP: GET TO KNOW A REFERENCE LIBRARIAN

Reference librarians know a tremendous amount about different kinds of sources and how to find them, in print and online. Whenever you have research questions, ask your librarian.

You can help your librarian help you if you have specific questions. "I need some statistics about how many manufacturing jobs have been lost in the U.S. in the past 10 years. What are the best places you can suggest for finding that information?" will help the librarian find you useful and specific information. "I want to learn something about job loss in the U.S." is less likely to do so.

USING LIBRARY CATALOGS

Most library catalogs have similar features to the one below. The features may show up in different places on-screen or in checkboxes instead of pop-up menus—but they will work in the same way. To prepare to use such a catalog, be sure you have a focused set of search terms, as we describe on page 55.

Pop-up menus

These pop-up menus allow you to choose how you want to search for a source. You can search using just a word or phrase or just the subject, or you can combine searches, looking for a periodical title and a word or phrase together.

Search selection

If your campus is part of a system of schools or has multiple libraries, this option allows you to search within just one of the available libraries.

Choose a language

If you are searching for a source in a specific language, this option allows you to choose from a range of available languages.

Choose your source

With this option you can choose to search specifically for a book, magazine, map, poster, or for any other type of source the library has.

Select the location of your search

This library has different archives and collections; the *location* option allows you to search within one specific location or across all of them.

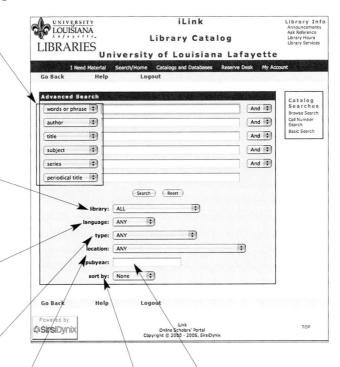

Sort the search results

This option allows you to see the search results sorted by year, author name, or title.

Select the time period of your search

If you are searching for sources from a specific year or range of years, enter that information here.

USING LIBRARY JOURNAL DATABASES

Most scholarly journals are now online—and not accessible through Google.

Different companies provide subscriptions for online access to scholarly journals; your college library subscribes to some. Different subscription services give access to databases in different disciplinary areas. For example, some services provide access only to engineering or to humanities databases.

These databases often provide only basic bibliographic information for a source—the article title, author's name(s), date and place of publication, and journal or periodical name—and an abstract giving a brief description. Once you find this information, you have to find out if your library has a subscription to the journal or periodical so that you can see the full article.

More frequently, however, these databases provide full-text versions of journal articles and periodicals you can read online.

STEPS IN USING DATABASES

1 Find the database search page on your library website.

2 Choose a database to search.

3 Use the database's search features to find references to relevant articles.

4 Choose the references that seem the most relevant.

5 Once you decide on the most relevant references, get hold of the articles.

TIP: DATABASE? Or GOOGLE?

The scholarly sources to which these databases can give you access are focused, detailed, and scholarly—and not accessible through Google (although they *might* be through Google Scholar).

The scholarly sources available on databases carry considerable authority for readers, but they also require effort on your part to find and to read. These sources will therefore be most useful to you when you have a solid, narrowed topic or statement of purpose to shape your searching. You can use Google first, to help you narrow your topic and find search terms—and then use databases for more scholarly results.

→ See Part 5 on statements of purpose.

WHAT IS A DATABASE?

When you have lots of data—journal articles, sports statistics, census numbers—it must be organized if it is to be searchable. In a computer database, journal articles can be organized by tags—records—such as the title, author, keywords, and so on; the database software can then use your search terms to find records that match.

1 FINDING THE DATABASE SEARCH PAGE ON YOUR LIBRARY WEBSITE

On the main page of your school library's webpage will be some sort of link to the databases. There may be an option labeled **Resources for research**, **Indexes and Databases**, or **E-Resources**.

Clicking such a link will take you to a screen where you can choose the database to search, as on page 60.

2 CHOOSING A DATABASE TO SEARCH, PART 1

First, it helps to know some of the popular databases that give you access to general information. The following databases, with short descriptions, can help you choose which might be useful to your research purposes:

ABI/INFORM
(information from 1971 to the present)
This database covers U.S. and international business and management topics, with information on 60,000 companies.

AH SEARCH
(information from 1984 to the present)
This is an index to more than 1,150 arts and humanities journals and over 7,000 science and social sciences journals.

ALTERNATIVE PRESS INDEX ARCHIVES
(information from 1969 to 1990)
This is the archives for the AH Search database, and includes book, film, and television reviews, obituaries, and bibliographic information as well as articles.

CSA ILLUMINA
This is a database of other databases, giving you access to more than 100 full-text and bibliographic databases in the arts and humanities, natural sciences, social sciences, and technology.

EXPANDED ACADEMIC ASAP (information from 1980 to the present)
This database covers subject areas in the humanities, technology, social sciences, and sciences, with full-text articles available. The database includes scholarly journals, news magazines, and newspapers.

FIRSTSEARCH
This database searches other databases, giving you access to educational, literary, medical, and religious topics; Latin American journals; government publications; conference proceedings; and the World Almanac.

JSTOR
JSTOR gives access to academic journals (dating back to 1665 in one case) in the arts and sciences; health, biology, and general science; and business. (Your library may not subscribe to all the areas JSTOR covers.)

LEXISNEXIS ACADEMIC
This provides full-text access to news, business, legal, and reference information.

PSYCFIRST
(information from 2002 to the present)
This database gives you access to citations and abstracts about worldwide research in psychology and related fields.

CHOOSING A DATABASE TO SEARCH, PART 2

Because there are hundreds of databases, your first step in working with the databases to which your library subscribes will probably involve a webpage that looks like the one below, which helps you choose among available databases. (The screen below comes from Michigan Technological University's Van Pelt Library website.)

Your college library's page for searching databases may not have all the features of the page shown below, but it will be similar.

Such a screen gives you many options for finding databases useful to you, as the callouts below indicate.

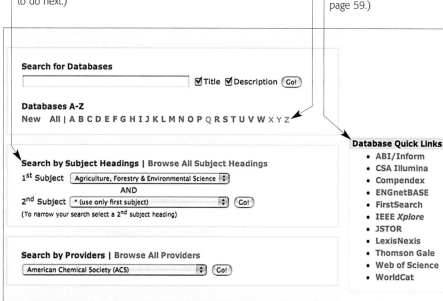

If you know the name of the database you want

Type its name in the *Search for Databases* box, or use the alphabetic search option to access it.

If you are new to using databases, or are searching in a new subject area, start here

These pop-up menus (which might be checkboxes on other webpages) give you access to lists of databases chosen because of their relevance to specific subject areas. Look at the list of subjects, and choose the one (or two) in which your topic best fits. (On the next pages, we show you what to do next.)

If you have some familiarity with popular databases

These are links to some of the most used databases. (Some of these are described on page 59.)

Search for Databases

☑ Title ☑ Description (Go!)

Databases A-Z

New   All | A B C D E F G H I J K L M N O P Q R S T U V W X Y Z

Search by Subject Headings | Browse All Subject Headings

1st Subject [Agriculture, Forestry & Environmental Science ▼]

AND

2nd Subject [* (use only first subject) ▼] (Go!)

(To narrow your search select a 2nd subject heading)

Search by Providers | Browse All Providers

[American Chemical Society (ACS) ▼] (Go!)

Database Quick Links

- ABI/Inform
- CSA Illumina
- Compendex
- ENGnetBASE
- FirstSearch
- IEEE *Xplore*
- JSTOR
- LexisNexis
- Thomson Gale
- Web of Science
- WorldCat

CHOOSING A DATABASE TO SEARCH, PART 3

If you are researching a geographic topic, for example, you may find that the **Database Quick Links** databases listed in the dialogue box to the left don't get you what you need; in such a case, choose **Geography** from the **Search by Subject Heading** option on the screen shown to the left.

Below is the result of such a choice. This is a list of the databases to which this library subscribes that will most likely help you find geographic information.

How do you choose which databases to search?

Read the descriptions of the databases' scope

Look for descriptions that seem most focused in your area of interest. Below, the descriptions of scope suggest that GEOBASE, ScienceDirect, and Web of Science might be the best places to start.

Which databases give you full-text access?

Full text means that you will see the article online and not just its bibliographic information. If articles do not have full-text access, use the bibliographic information to see if your library has the journal you need; you might need to order it through interlibrary loan.

	Full Text Available Show All	Access Restrictions
Academic OneFile Coverage: 1995 - Present	F	M
Scope: premier source for peer-reviewed, full-text articles from the world's leading journals and reference sources. With extensive coverage of the physical sciences, technology, medicine, social sciences, the arts, theology, literature and other subjects.		
Article1st Coverage: 1990 - Present		M
Scope: contains bibliographic citations for items listed on the table of contents pages of over 12,600 journals in all subject areas.		
GEOBASE Coverage: 1980 - Present		M
Scope: contains citations with abstracts covering worldwide literature in geography, geology, and ecology.		
Google Scholar Coverage: 1900 - Present	F	M
Scope: web search engine designed specifically to locate scholarly literature, including peer-reviewed papers, theses, books, preprints, abstracts and technical reports across broad areas of research. **Access Note:** click here for additional information about Google Scholar. Also if you are coming from off campus you will be asked for your ISO Login and Password. This will grant you full text access to those full text resources that the JRVP library has secured.		
ScienceDirect Coverage: 2003 - Present	F	M
Scope: extensive and unique full-text collection covers authoritative titles from the core scientific literature. ScienceDirect is designed as a basic electronic version of Elsevier Science print allowing you to access full-text articles published since 2003.		
Social Sciences Abstracts Coverage: 1983 - Present		M
Scope: covers periodicals in anthropology, economics, geography, law and criminology, political science, social work, sociology, and international relations.		
Web of Science Coverage: 1973 - Present		M
Scope: offers Web of Science access to ISI Citation Indexes (Science Citation Index Expanded, Social Sciences Citation Index and Arts and Humanities Citation Index), which contains multidisciplinary, high quality research information from the world's leading science, social science and art and humanities journals. **We now have unlimited access to WoS.**		

TIP: **THE EARLY STAGES OF RESEARCH**

Keep in mind that you need to search more than one database when you are in the early stages of research looking for broad background information.

3 USING A DATABASE

Once you have chosen a database to search, you will see on your screen the search tools particular to that database; every database company presents this information differently.

WHAT DATABASE SEARCH SCREENS USUALLY HAVE IN COMMON

Here is the initial search screen for the LexisNexis database.

Start by entering your search terms

With most database searches, you will probably start by entering your search terms into the text entry box and then clicking *Search*.

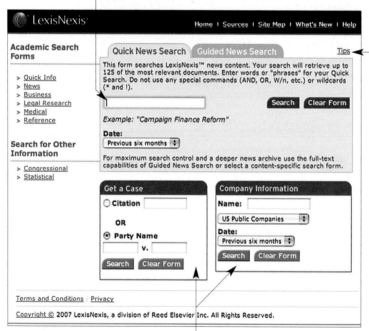

Using the database tips

As you become more comfortable with database searches, you can become more fluent by checking out how the database creators recommend you use their search features.

Explore the features of the database

Database search screens can be somewhat visually daunting, in part because they offer researchers so many possible ways to research. As you become more at ease with these sorts of searches, you will make your work and research richer if you take time to explore the features of the databases that most tie to your interests.

Searching databases that give you access to other databases

Sometimes, when you choose a database following the advice we've given in step 2, you will come to a screen like the one below; this screen shows that you have chosen a database that gives you access to still other databases. These other databases tend to be focused and specialized.

To use a screen like this, look over the databases that are listed just as you would in step 2. Choose those databases that look most relevant to your topic. When you click **Continue to Search**, you will come to a screen similar to the one shown at left, where you can enter your search terms.

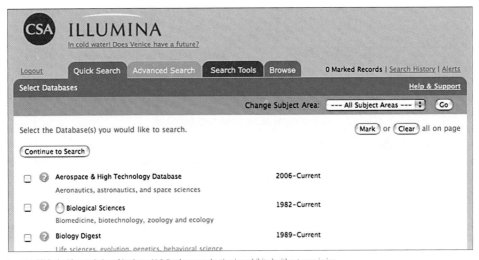

Image published with permission of ProQuest LLC. Further reproduction is prohibited without permission.

TIP: FINE-TUNING DATABASE SEARCHES

Just about every database search screen will give you a choice between a **Quick Search** and an **Advanced Search**. In **Quick Search**, you simply enter your search terms. In **Advanced Search**, you will have some set of options: You might be able to specify that the database search for articles only from within the last five years or from twenty years ago; you might be able to specify very specific subject areas for the search, or that you want only full-text searches or searches in a specific language.

Such fine-tuning can help reduce your search time if you know you need such specific information.

4 CHOOSING THE REFERENCES THAT SEEM MOST RELEVANT

After you have entered your search terms into a database search screen and clicked **Search**, you will see a screen like the one below (each database will look slightly different). This is the list of articles in the database that match your search terms.

Understanding the search results

This search was made by someone looking into recent cultural notions of beauty and the ways they affect how women think about themselves. This information shows that this researcher used the search terms *beauty* and *culture*, and was looking for articles published between 1995 and 2007. (Note that there were 4,017 matches—an indication that this search could be narrowed even more.)

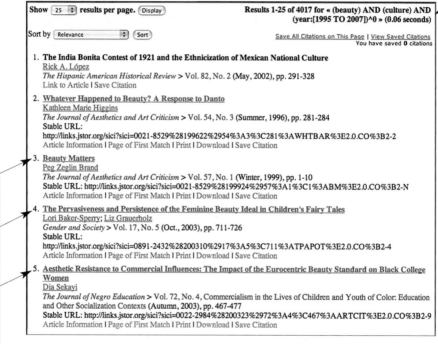

Three promising articles

Given this researcher's purposes, these three articles look promising. He won't know for sure until he looks at the full articles, but the titles of these three suggest that they will address his concerns. (Number 2 looks as though it was written specifically in response to another article, and so won't be useful.) Note that these are not the first articles in the list; note also that there are 4,012 more articles to consider. How would you narrow this search?

- The database listing to the left is from a full-text database; clicking any of the links will take you to the listed article, which you can then read.

- Sometimes, however, you will get a listing like the one below, which has no link to access a full-text version.

A listing with no link to a full-text version

In such cases, look for links like these, which allow you to see if your library carries the journal from which this article comes and, in case your library doesn't, to see other libraries that have the journal. (If your library does not carry the journal, you will need to use your library's interlibrary loan service; ask a librarian for help with this if you've never used this before.)

Availability:	Check the catalogs in your library.
	• Libraries worldwide that own item: 347
	• Search the catalog at J Robert Van Pelt
Author(s):	Charles, S
	Reprint Address: Charles, S; Univ Sherbrooke, Sherbrooke, PQ J1K 2R1, Canada
	Research Address: Univ Sherbrooke, Sherbrooke, PQ J1K 2R1, Canada
Title:	**The meaning of beauty. From its origins to modern culture**
Source:	*DIALOGUE-CANADIAN PHILOSOPHICAL REVIEW* 40, no. 2 (SPR 2001): 416-419
	Additional Info: CANADIAN PHILOSOPHICAL ASSOC: MORISSET HALL #375, UNIV OTTAWA, OTTAWA, ONTARIO K1N 6N5, CANADA
Standard No:	**ISSN:** 0012-2173
Language:	French
Reviewed Item:	**Author:** Ferry, L **Publication:** 1998 **Language:** French
References:	**Number:** 1
	SUBJECT(S)
Journal Subject:	PHILOSOPHY -- H UA
Cited Reference:	FURRY, L, 1998, SENS BEAU ORIGINES C
Article Type:	Book Review
Accession No:	000169393900022
Database:	AHSearch

TIPS: WORKING WITH DATABASES

- As with all research, database work takes time. You will need to try more than one database, performing variations on your basic search in each. Have patience, and look for the sources that expand your thinking on your topic.

- If you use an article from a database in your writing and are working with MLA formatting, see pages 358–359 for formatting the citation.

FINDING SOURCES
ONLINE RESEARCH

SEARCH ENGINES AND SEARCH DIRECTORIES

Search engines work because they access large databases of websites, which have been collected by automated programs called *spiders* or *robots*. The websites are indexed: The words and phrases they contain are compiled into lists that are structured for easy computer searching.

When you enter your search terms, the search engine compares your terms to its indexes, and returns to you a list of websites containing your terms.

Search directories are similar to search engines because each compiles databases of websites—but a directory lists or searches through only the sites that have been inspected for their relevance.

Because each search engine or directory has been designed to search the Web differently, and to index its terms differently, different search tools can return differing results for the same search terms—so you are more likely to find helpful information by using more than one search tool.

You are probably familiar with Google and Yahoo!, which are generalized search tools, but also check the tools on the next page, designed to aid academic searches.

RESOURCES FOR KEEPING TRACK OF YOUR ONLINE RESEARCH
—and for taking advantage of other people's searches

If you do lots of online searches and have not yet learned about diigo *<http://www.diigo.com/>* or delicious *<http://delicious.com/>*, check them out. Each site works a little differently, but each gives you ways to save and organize links that matter to you.

In addition, each site gives you ways to search other people's collections of website links on topics related to yours; by looking at how others have labeled—or *tagged*—their finds, you can also learn new terms to use for further searching.

SOME USEFUL SEARCH DIRECTORIES

INFOMINE: SCHOLARLY INTERNET RESOURCE COLLECTIONS
<http://infomine.ucr.edu>

Infomine is constructed by college and university librarians to be a library of resources specifically for college and university students and faculty. Infomine links you to databases, electronic books and journals, and other useful resources.

ACADEMIC INDEX
<http://www.academicindex.net>

A librarian developed this search tool, which searches through databases of information on topics of academic interest and quality, compiled or recommended by librarians, teachers, and researchers.

LIBRARIANS' INTERNET INDEX
<http://www.lii.org>

This publicly funded directory also sends out a free weekly newsletter of websites that are chosen and organized by librarians.

GOOGLE SCHOLAR
<http://scholar.google.com>

Google Scholar can point you to academic sources because it indexes many journals and papers, but often you won't have access to the full-text versions and will still need to find full-text through a library database (→ see pages 58–65).

TIPS: USING ONLINE SEARCH TOOLS

- *Use more than one search engine.* Because each search engine searches the Web differently than others, different engines give different results for the same search terms—so you are more likely to find helpful information by using different engines.

- Most search engines have both *a simple search*—where you enter a few search terms—and *an advanced search*, where you can specify date ranges, the kind of file you want (html, pdf, or doc), or that the search results be only webpages containing noncopyrighted information. When you have a narrowed topic or know you need information from 1995, for example, use these features. Explore these features in your favorite search engine so that—when you have a very focused search to carry out—you know what is possible.

- Many search engines will allow you to carry out a *boolean search*. George Boole, a nineteenth-century mathematician, developed ways for thinking logically about how terms interact. His system is used in computer searches, in which you can use the words AND, OR, NOT, and XOR (always in capital letters) to help narrow your search.

  If you are researching the Buddhist concept of Nirvana, you could enter these terms so as not to be deluged with returns about music: ***Nirvana AND Buddhism NOT Cobain***

  To search once with synonyms instead of doing two searches: ***women AND workplace OR office***

  Be sure to check the advanced search features of the search engine you are using for its particular approach to boolean searches.

ONLINE REFERENCES

There is a wide range of online reference materials on all subjects. Your library will probably have an online listing of all kinds of reference materials, longer than what we can include here. Here are links to some widely used sources:

BARTLEBY.COM

<http://www.bartleby.com/>

Bartleby.com gives you searchable access to dictionaries, quotations, thesauruses, usage and style references, and literature and poetry.

THE INTERNET MOVIE DATABASE

<http://us.imdb.com/>

If you are discussing a movie, this database provides you with information about the actors, directors, and writers and gives you links to reviews.

ONELOOK

<http://www.onelook.com/>

This website gives you access to over 900 dictionaries.

PERRY-CASTAÑEDA MAP COLLECTION

<http://www.lib.utexas.edu/maps/ map_sites/map_sites.html>

The library of the University of Texas at Austin has produced this long list of links to all kinds of maps.

STATISTICAL RESOURCES ON THE WEB

<http://www.lib.umich.edu/govdocs/ stats.html>

The library of the University of Michigan maintains this very valuable website of links to sites that track statistics about the environment, housing, the cost of living, and education, among many other topics.

WIKIPEDIA

<http://en.wikipedia.org/wiki/Main_Page>

Wikipedia is an online encyclopedia written and edited by users who wish to contribute their knowledge. This is a controversial website for teachers precisely because anyone can edit and contribute. Wikipedia is a good place to start research, when you are composing to learn: It can be a quite accurate source that gives you deeper openings into a topic. You should always check with your teacher to learn his or her position on this source. In general, however, know that using Wikipedia as a source in an academic paper will not give your paper the authority you probably want it to have—and using Wikipedia as your only source is a sure way to show readers that you have not done appropriate research.

ONLINE NEWSPAPERS

ONLINENEWSPAPERS.COM

<http://www.onlinenewspapers.com/>

This website, out of Australia, gives you access to hundreds of newspapers around the world (many in English).

ONLINE ARCHIVES

→ See page 71.

GOVERNMENT SOURCES

Every government agency has a website, so if you are looking for educational or agricultural information, for example, check the websites of the Department of Education or the Department of Agriculture. Keep in mind that some of the information is shaped by the political ends of the current administration.

THE U.S. CENSUS BUREAU
<http://www.census.gov/>

The Census Bureau compiles a wide range of statistics on the U.S. population and economic systems.

MEDLINE PLUS
<http://www.nlm.nih.gov/medlineplus/>

The U.S. National Library of Medicine and the National Institutes of Health provide this nonspecialist information on health and medical issues. The site also provides a medical dictionary and encyclopedia.

THOMAS
<http://thomas.loc.gov/>

This website helps you search for U.S. government legislative information such as what is happening in Congress and its bills and resolutions.

THE WORLD FACTBOOK
<https://www.cia.gov/library/publications/ the-world-factbook/index.html>

The U.S. Central Intelligence Agency regularly updates this website of information about every country in the world. You can learn about a country's population, geography, government, and so on.

PHOTOGRAPHIC AND OTHER VISUAL RESOURCES

Many museums have collections of photographs; many U.S. government agencies also have collections of photographs. For example, check the NASA Image Exchange *<http://nix.nasa.gov/>* or the National Oceanic and Atmospheric Administration's Photo Library *<http://www.photolib.noaa.gov/>*.

NYPL DIGITAL
<http://www.nypl.org/digital/>

The New York Public Library offers this resource of "520,000 images … including illuminated manuscripts, historical maps, vintage posters, rare prints, photographs, illustrated books, and printed ephemera."

PRINTS AND PHOTOGRAPHS ONLINE
<http://www.loc.gov/rr/print/catalog.html>

This website is part of the U.S. Library of Congress. Many of the visual materials available here—posters, photographs, maps, magazines—are copyright free, but you need to check.

WIKIPEDIA: PUBLIC DOMAIN IMAGE RESOURCES
<http://en.wikipedia.org/wiki/ Wikipedia:Public_domain_image_resources>

This webpage contains a long, categorized list of online photograph and other visual text resources.

→ To cite photographs and other visual texts in your writing, see pages 389–393 for MLA style and pages 436–437 for APA style.

ARCHIVAL AND SPECIAL LIBRARY COLLECTION SOURCES

SPECIAL LIBRARY COLLECTIONS

Duke University has special collections related to women's history and culture, to African and African American Documentation, and to the history of sales, advertising, and marketing. Haverford College has special collections of materials related to the Quakers. The University of Idaho and the University of Utah have special collections on the history of their states.

Check your library's website to see what special collections it holds.

PHYSICAL ARCHIVES

Archives store documents of historic interest such as letters, diaries, newspapers, sermons, and postcards. Archives can store the documents of a town or county, a church or synagogue, or a person or family; they can be about labor history or African American music.

Many small museums, historical organizations, and libraries have archives of local materials. Some archives collect materials related to the life of a political or literary figure who was from or lived in the area.

To find archives in your area, look in the phone book under **Historical Organizations** and **Museums**.

To learn about archives at your university, check the library website, which will list the library's collections.

Archival research can be captivating: Holding a pioneer woman's diary from the 1860s will give you an exciting sense of differences in lives then and now—and using the diary's words in your writing will give your writing life and authority.

VIRTUAL ARCHIVES

Many physical archives have digitized their materials and made them available online. (If you use a virtual archive, keep in mind that digitization is time-consuming and costly; an archive may have only a small portion of its collection online, so you may still want to try to visit the physical archive if possible.) Each archive will have its own system for searching its collection. Individual archives might also tell you how they would like to be cited if you use their materials in your work.

Some rich virtual archives are

THE INTERNET ARCHIVE

<http://www.archive.org/index.php>
This is an archive of video, music, sound, and texts.

THE LIBRARY OF CONGRESS'S AMERICAN MEMORY PROJECT

<http://memory.loc.gov/ammem/index.html>
This collection gives you access to "written and spoken words, sound recordings, still and moving images, prints, maps, and sheet music that document the American experience."

THE NATIONAL ARCHIVES OF THE UNITED STATES

<http://www.archives.gov/research/arc/education/>
The Archives have a tremendous collection of materials (primarily government related) about this country. You have to go to the archive to look at most materials, but some are available digitally. If you are carrying out research in genealogical, social, political, or economic areas, check out the archives that have been put in searchable databases:
<http://aad.archives.gov/aad/>

THE UNIVERSITY MUSEUMS AND COLLECTIONS

<http://publicus.culture.hu-berlin.de/umac/>
This is an international database giving access to 150 museums.

→ Page 369 shows a citation in MLA style for an online text and image archive; pages 383 and 390 show citations for a book and a chart from online archives.

→ Page 369 shows a citation in MLA style for an online text and image archive; pages 383 and 390 show citations for a book and a chart from online archives.

TIP: FINDING ARCHIVES OUTSIDE YOUR LOCAL AREA

Go online if historical materials will answer your research questions and there are no useful local archives.

Using your search terms, do at least three searches:

your topic + **archive**
your topic + **special collection**
your topic + **museum**

Try out variations on your topic, too, because you cannot know how websites describe themselves and are cataloged by a search engine.

For example, if you were researching organizational strategies used in the civil rights movement, you could do a Google search with the terms **civil rights movement** and **archive**. Among other useful links, this search turns up a link to the "Voices of Freedom" website at Virginia Commonwealth University, where you can listen to a recording of Dr. Joyce E. Glaise speaking about the church's role in organizing.

Keep in mind that such searches may not turn up materials you can access digitally, but may suggest books you can order through your library's interlibrary loan service.

FIELD RESEARCH SOURCES

Field research can be performed in more depth than we can describe here. Your teacher or a librarian can help you find further information.

→ See page 104 on evaluating field research.

TIP: GETTING PERMISSION FOR FIELD RESEARCH

Almost all colleges and universities have an Institutional Review Board (IRB), a committee that ensures the proper treatment of those who participate in research studies. Such boards were started to oversee medical and other kinds of technological research, but their responsibility has spread to cover research in the humanities and social sciences.

Every campus's Institutional Review Board will have different policies for field research carried out in writing classes. If you will use the results of your field research only in a classroom paper, it is possible you do not need IRB permission—but the only way to know is to ask your teacher. (If a teacher requires you to do field research, the teacher might have gotten approval for the whole class, or will help you through the process.)

If you think you might do field research on your own, ask your teacher what permissions you need.

INTERVIEWS

You can interview experts on the topic you are researching, people who have lived through an event central to your research, or those who have opinions about your topic.

Here is a sample e-mail for requesting an interview:

Dear Professor/Ms./Mr./Dr. [Name],
For my writing class, I am doing research into [your topic] and would like to interview you, informally, on this topic.

If you are willing, I would need only 30 minutes of your time. I would like to use a tape recorder during the interview.

If an interview is amenable to you, here are several times in the next two weeks when I could come to your office: [list times here].

Sincerely, [your name]

PREPARE FOR AN INTERVIEW

• What would you like to learn from this person? Write down questions that can draw that information out of the person. (You can use the guiding questions for research you developed.)

AT THE INTERVIEW

• Start by thanking the person.

• Explain your research.

• Ask your questions, and don't hesitate to ask other questions that come to you as you listen.

• End with a "Thank-you!" Ask if you can contact her or him for clarifications.

AFTERWARD

• Send a thank-you e-mail or note.

• Call or e-mail for clarifications.

OBSERVATIONS

If you are researching the effects of video games on social relations among men, you could observe a group of friends playing a game together and then observe a group playing softball, to see if there are differences in how the friends interact. If you are writing about cell phone use among teenagers and adults, you could go the mall and count the percentage of teenagers and the percentage of adults using cell phones.

PREPARE FOR AN OBSERVATION

- Consider where you can observe without others being very aware of you so that they don't change their behavior because of your presence.

- Determine what kinds of actions or behaviors you want to observe and record.

- Determine how you will record what you see. (If you are doing multiple observations, set the same time limit for each one.)

WHILE OBSERVING

- Start your records with the time and date of your observation.

AFTERWARD

- If you have not learned what you thought you would, have you learned something else? Do you need to change your overall purpose, or do you need to do another observation, one set up slightly differently?

- Think about how you will justify your observations to your readers; you will need to include this in your writing.

SURVEYS

Small, focused surveys (the kind you are probably prepared to carry out, instead of state or national surveys) help you learn others' opinions about events or policies.

Small surveys can take two forms (which you can mix):

YES-OR-NO QUESTION SURVEYS

For example: *Do you think there should be a traffic light at the intersection of Bridge and Montezuma Streets?*

- Solicit quick decision making with no room for gray areas.

- Allow for tabulation to make arguments; for example, *Ninety percent of the respondents favor a traffic light.*

- Tend to get more responses because they are quick and easy to take.

OPEN-ENDED QUESTION SURVEYS

For example: *What additional school programs do you think would better prepare elementary school students to use developing technologies?*

- Solicit more thoughtful responses.

- Require interpretation. Sometimes answers group together and sometimes you get a range of very different responses. You will need to present the answers you get with explanations of what you learned.

Before you give your survey, test your questions on a few people to be sure respondents understand the questions and can answer them easily.

Also, consider how many people you need to survey so that your readers will accept that your results are well supported.

WHAT IF YOU CAN'T FIND ANYTHING ON YOUR NARROWED TOPIC?

If you are not finding information on your narrowed topic, there are several possible reasons:

- You have a creative and original topic.
- Your topic might not yet be narrow enough.
- You haven't yet found the right search terms or combination of search terms.
- You haven't yet found the right places to search.
- You have not yet learned how to use search tools comfortably.
- You are not putting in enough time.

IF YOU HAVE A CREATIVE AND ORIGINAL TOPIC

You have a decision to make: find a new topic, or continue searching?

Making effective arguments around creative and original topics is challenging, and can teach you much. You still need to find supporting evidence for the points you want to make, so you have to get creative with finding sources that inform you about the positions of others; you also have to be creative and careful with weaving those sources together into supporting evidence for the position you ultimately take. The following suggestions for generating search terms can still help you.

IT'S POSSIBLE YOUR TOPIC IS NOT YET NARROW ENOUGH

If Google or another search engine returns millions of responses on your topic—none of which seems to address what matters to you—go back to pages 28–33 to work on further narrowing your topic.

IF YOU HAVEN'T YET FOUND THE RIGHT SEARCH TERMS

- Be open to what you find: Remember that, at this stage of producing a research paper, you are trying to gather as much information as you can on a topic. You might need to shift the focus of your topic as you learn what information is available.

- Develop lists of synonyms for your terms. For example, if you are searching the topic of childhood obesity and its relationship to food advertising using cartoon characters, you are going to want to search with different combinations of the following:

    childhood, youth, young
    obesity, overweight, weight
    food, junk, diet, cereal, candy
    advertising, commercials
    cartoons, animation

    To find other words for searching, look for terms people use in the articles and websites you do find; ask others—teachers, librarians, and anyone you know who is good with words or reads a lot—what terms come to mind when you describe your topic.

- Keep track of other terms that come up as you search. In any article or webpage that seems at all close to your concerns, note what terms the authors use to describe your topic, and use those for further searches.

- Try a different search tool. Because each search tool works differently, different search tools will give you different results.

KNOWING IF YOU HAVE FOUND THE RIGHT PLACES TO SEARCH

If you have tried only one search engine or database, you need to try others. If you have tried multiple databases without luck, talk to your teacher or a librarian: They can help you determine other databases that might be fruitful.

But perhaps you are searching online when you need to be interviewing others or looking in an archive. Again, talking to a teacher or librarian about your narrowed topic—and about what you are hoping to learn—can help you find out where to look.

IT'S POSSIBLE YOU ARE NOT USING SEARCH TOOLS COMFORTABLY ENOUGH

If every time you do your research you get frustrated or confused, it is definitely time to make an appointment with your teacher, a librarian, or someone from your campus's Writing (or Learning) Center. Be specific about the help you need: First, describe your narrowed topic and what you are hoping to learn, and then describe the research you have carried out so far. Finally, ask for someone to sit by you while you search, to guide you and give advice.

IT'S POSSIBLE YOU ARE NOT GIVING YOUR RESEARCH ENOUGH TIME

If you expect research to take fifteen minutes or even an hour one night, you are wrong. Effective research requires patience, spread out over hours and days: It takes time to find the information that will help you be smart.

KEEPING TRACK OF SOURCES: Starting a running source list

As you find sources that are useful to you or that contain phrases or sentences that will attract your readers' attention, keep track of both the sources and the quotations. You can do this on paper or online.

Keep all this information in order to produce writing that meets current academic expectations. In the academic world, writers acknowledge the sources from which they draw their ideas and they make it easy for readers to check their sources. There are standard forms for showing this information in a research paper.

→ For information on the forms for documenting sources, see Part 8.

WHEN YOU FIND A SOURCE YOU MIGHT USE...

Enter any source you might use into a running list—like the sample to the right—recording the information you need for that kind of source:

→ For a book or part of a book, see pages 312–317 for the information you will need.

→ For a newspaper, magazine, or journal article, see pages 318–321.

→ For an article you find in a database, see pages 326–327.

→ For a webpage or website, see pages 322–325.

IF YOU THINK YOU MIGHT QUOTE WORDS FROM ANY SOURCE...

In addition to the information for the source, record the exact words you might quote, along with the number of the pages on which the words appear (if there are page numbers).

HELPING YOURSELF AVOID PLAGIARISM

Because respecting the work of others and therefore acknowledging when you use their work is so important in academic writing, find strategies to keep track of when you copy the words of others. Whenever you copy words off a website into your notes or into a paper, color-code or otherwise mark those words.

→ See pages 290–295 to learn more about plagiarism.

EXAMPLE OF A RUNNING SOURCE LIST

March 22, 2010

"Africa Debt Cancellation -- FAQ." January 2007. American Friends Service Committee.
<http://www.afsc.org/africa-debt/learn-about-debt/debt-faq.htm>

"Debt: The Illegitimate Legacy of Continent's Dictators." January 25, 2007. Africa News.
LexisNexis. Van Pelt Lib., Houghton, MI
<http://library.lib.mtu.edu:2082/universe/document?_m=62be476dbc43903fc53cef9fb4
3832d5&wchp=dGLbVzW-zSkVA&_md5= a9cda7d0ad24dda40259c9e16d4ddad1>

Meredith, Martin. The Fate of Africa: A History of Fifty Years of Independence. New York:
PublicAffairs, 2006.

TIP: KEEP A PAPER TRAIL

If you have the slightest feeling that you might use a source—to paraphrase or quote—keep track of it. It is awful to finish a paper only to realize you have a quotation whose source you don't remember: Either you have to remove the quote or you have to find the source.

TIP: CITE VISUAL SOURCES

If you use visual material made by others—such as charts, graphs, posters, photographs, and so on—you need to document the source.

→ For citing visual materials, see pages 389–393 for MLA style and pages 436–437 for APA style.

TIP: ORGANIZE YOUR LINKS

If you don't already know about them, take a look at websites like <www.diigo.com> and <delicious.com> for tracking your online sources. These websites can also help you see the research other people have carried out on your topic.

STARTING A PAPER

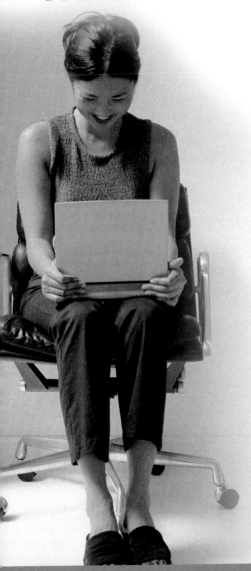

The night before she received an assignment to write a research paper, Riley was talking with a friend's mother and learned that, through an online organization, the mother makes small loans to women in other countries to help the women start or develop small businesses. The mother explained that this process of making small loans is called **microcredit** or **microloans** and is often set up to help women who might not otherwise have access to loans.

General topic

When she received her assignment, Riley decided to learn more about microcredit, and started her research.

Some of her initial research work is shown on page 29.

This initial research taught her that microcredit or microloans can also be called **microfinance**, and so she searched with this term as well as the two others. She learned how these small loans were started in Bangladesh in the 1980s and have since spread all over the world—and that such small loans are overwhelmingly made to women.

Narrowing the topic

Riley is curious about why microcredit focuses on women, so she decides to research **women and microcredit in developing countries**.

Questions for research

Based on what she had learned from her initial research, Riley brainstormed questions to guide her further research; the bold questions are those that matter most to her now:

QUESTIONS OF FACT
- How and where did microcredit get started?
- How large is a typical loan?
- How do the people who borrow the money pay it back?

QUESTIONS OF CONSEQUENCE
- Why is microcredit necessary?
- Who benefits from microcredit?
- What are negative results of microcredit?
- **How do microloans change women's lives?**

QUESTIONS OF VALUE
- Why are so many people praising microcredit now?
- Why are so many governments encouraging microcredit organizations in their countries?

QUESTIONS OF DEFINITION
- What is microcredit?
- How is it different from other kinds of loans?

QUESTIONS OF INTERPRETATION
- Why did microcredit get started?
- **Why are loans made mostly to women?**

QUESTIONS OF POLICY
- Who decides who will receive microcredit loans?
- What laws or other policies have been enacted to support microcredit?
- What kinds of organizations support microcredit?
- What organizations oppose it?

Choosing sources

From her initial work, Riley realized that her first Google searches were helping her answer questions of fact and definition but not other types of questions.

Because the questions that matter most to her are questions of interpretation and consequence, she used the charts on pages 42–43 to help her determine where to look.

1 She knew that stories of women who had received microloans would help her, but because she couldn't interview women in developing countries, she used Google to find microcredit organizations' websites, hoping they would have women's stories. She also looked for the organizations' mission statements, to see if they discussed why they focused on women.

2 Her library's online resources helped her search databases on current economic topics, as well as women's issues and newspaper editorials. (The ProQuest database suggested additional search terms: **women AND poverty AND microcredit OR microfinance**.)

3 The databases also helped her find organizational and governmental reports with statistics that might show how women's lives were changed because of small loans.

→ Riley didn't find any one source that answered all her questions, but she found many that helped her develop a thesis statement for her own argument—as you can see in Part 3, on pages 138–139.

HINTS & TIPS FOR FINDING IDEAS

HOW DO YOU KNOW IF YOU HAVE FOUND ENOUGH SOURCES?

In the earliest stages of research, you won't know, exactly, if you have all the sources that will help you develop an argument that will satisfy readers.

But you are researching broadly enough—finding enough sources—if you can answer most of the research questions you've generated.

HOW DO YOU KNOW IF YOU ARE KEEPING AN OPEN MIND?

You might think that you should have definitive answers to all your research questions. But—*especially for questions of consequence, interpretation, value, and policy*—if your research makes you hesitate over deciding between two or three possible responses, then you are keeping an open mind. If you can offer good reasons for several differing possibilities, then you are researching as you should.

Academic writing is rarely about offering final solutions to anything; there are few situations in life where the evidence obviously supports one final conclusion. Instead, you need to acknowledge the differing possibilities and offer the best evidence and arguments you can for the position you believe to be best.

HOW CAN YOU KEEP A TOPIC FRESH AND INTERESTING?

If you get bored with your topic, you won't enjoy the writing, your writing will reflect your emotion, and your readers will pick up on it.

Because there are different ways to get bored with a topic, there are different approaches for becoming unbored:

- Perhaps you've chosen a topic that isn't controversial or challenging enough to keep you engaged. Talk with a teacher or someone who knows about the topic to determine if you can make the topic more challenging or if you need a new topic.

- Sometimes topics become boring when you've done a lot of research and feel that you know all there is to know. If this happens, remember that not everyone knows what you do: If you talk to someone else and lay out why the topic should matter, you might see how writing about your topic can help others learn important information.

Explore these topics online:

Choosing sources

www.mycomplab.com

PART 3

ANALYZING
ARGUMENTS
& EVALUATING
SOURCES

CONTENTS

WHERE ARE WE IN THE PROCESS FOR COMPOSING?

Understanding your project

Getting started

Asking questions
   Critical thinking and questioning
   Evaluating sources
   Developing a thesis statement

Shaping your project for others

Drafting a paper

Getting feedback

Revising

Polishing

ARE YOU READY TO USE THE NEXT PAGES OF THIS BOOK?

NO…
Are you reading the assignment, wondering where to start?
Is your head full of possibilities of what you might research?
Are you staring at a database search screen wondering what search terms to enter?
If any of these is your situation, then, no, you are not ready for the next pages.

Until you understand your assignment, have a narrowed topic, and have read a range of sources on your topic, you won't be able to evaluate sources to know if they are relevant to your argument and credible to your audience and you won't be able to formulate the solid bones of an argument that is a thesis statement.

→ For help with understanding an assignment, see pages 14–16.

→ For help with narrowing a topic, see pages 28–33.

→ For help with researching a topic, see pages 34–53.

YES.
Do you have a narrowed topic and have you found a range of informative and useful sources on that topic?
If this is your situation, the next pages should help you with some of the critical thinking that goes into persuasive writing: developing a thesis statement and evaluating your sources for their relevance and credibility.

WHAT IS ANALYSIS?

Analysis is about breaking something into its pieces to learn how the pieces fit together into a whole.

To learn about and prevent diseases, doctors analyze bodies, looking at organs and bodily functions: They analyze the skeletal and muscular systems, the organs of digestion and sight, and the cellular processes of those different systems and organs. Once doctors understand how these different parts fit together, they can start questioning how a change in one part affects other parts, how (for example) a disease of the liver affects stomach functioning.

Similarly, social scientists analyze crises that are the result of human action (such as wars and economic depressions) and crises that result from a mixture of human and natural causes (deaths from heat waves or hurricanes). They try first to understand the political, social, economic, and techological structures of towns, cities, countries, and regions so that they can ask how actions and events affect those different structures. They hope in this way to learn what went wrong and how a similar crisis might be avoided in the future.

Similarly, communication specialists analyze the texts we give each other. Some specialize in analyzing political speeches, some in television advertising, some in film, some in literature, some in digital communication. These specialists bring different analytic tools to their work. In this book, we use the analytic tools of rhetoric.

In the upcoming pages, we follow the analytic scheme shown below, to help you move from analyzing to understand to analyzing to ask questions of a text.

ANALYSIS

By breaking a text down into its parts and identifying its main strategies, we can:

understand

If we can describe the parts of a text and how they fit together into a whole, then we can say we understand the text, and what its composer's purpose might have been in producing it.

ask questions

Once we understand a text, we can question it:

Does the text achieve the composer's purpose?

- Do the strategies used in the text fit with its purpose?
- Is the intended audience likely to be persuaded by the strategies used?

What do I think about that purpose and the strategies used to achieve it?

- Can I support the purpose?
- Are the strategies used valid?
- Do I accept those strategies, or think they are ethical?
- Do I think the text's composer respects the text's audience?

UNDERSTANDING AND ANALYZING TEXTS

In this book, we use the analytic tools of rhetoric to understand what the parts of a communication are and how those parts fit together to make a whole—and how the parts work to make a communicator's purposes clear to the intended audience in a particular context.

BEGINNING RHETORICAL ANALYSIS

Almost any rhetorical analysis begins with these two steps:

1 Determining the choices composers make in developing a text.

2 Considering how those choices help composers achieve their purposes with their particular audience in the context at hand.

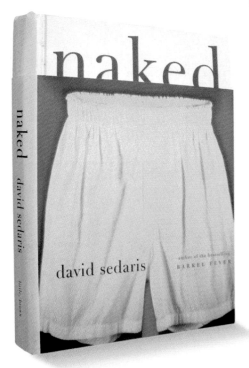

BEGINNING A RHETORICAL ANALYSIS OF A BOOK COVER

This example for starting a rhetorical analysis looks at the book cover to the left.

1 Determining the choices composers make in developing a text.

To do this, we list as many choices as we see, in any order:

- the book's title
- the book's size
- the typefaces used, and their size
- the placement of the elements, such as the title relative to the photograph
- any information about the book in addition to its title

- the book cover is different from what we usually see: The paper cover doesn't cover the whole, just part of it—so there must be something hidden under it
- the use of a photograph
- the colors used
- the overall feeling: humorous

2 Considering how those choices help composers achieve their purposes with their particular audience in the context at hand.

It's tempting to say that the cover's purpose (like any book cover) is to sell the book—and that is certainly part of the purpose. But if a cover helps persuade someone to buy the book, the cover must interest the buyer. If the buyer knows the author's writing, maybe the cover design doesn't matter; if, however, someone doesn't know the author, then the cover's purpose has to be about giving someone a strong, particular sense of what is inside **this** book. What do the strategies above suggest about *naked*?

The title and photograph are important choices because they are emphasized. The photograph is of boxer shorts, which for some reason in American culture are objects of silliness.

Their presence tells us this book is about fairly recent topics and not about people living long ago.

Naked is a word we apply to humans, not animals, and though it can imply serious things, the word can also imply awkwardness, like losing your clothes while swimming—or being caught in public in your underwear. Because the title is printed without a capital letter—which implies informality—and is combined with the photograph, we get the sense that this book is not about heavy topics. The cover also has only the one photograph, telling us that what is in the book is probably not complicated: This is, probably, not a book of detailed history. It is about people, possibly their awkward behaviors.

THERE ARE CATEGORIES FOR ANALYZING THE STRATEGIES USED IN COMPOSING...

as we discuss on the next pages. Also, analyzing a composition is easier when we compare it to another composition, as we do with this book cover on the next pages.

DEVELOPING A SENSE OF THE AUTHOR

WE MAKE ASSUMPTIONS ABOUT THE COMPOSERS OF TEXTS

Whenever you use a text, you develop a sense of the person who made it.

Listening to the radio, you probably develop—without thinking—a sense of any speaker's gender and age, and probably also a sense that the person is serious, funny, or well-informed. You could be wrong in all your assumptions—but that doesn't stop you from making such assumptions.

We make the same assumptions when we read and even when we look at photographs, posters, or video games: We develop, consciously or not, a sense of who made the text and whether the person is trustworthy, authoritative, knowledgeable, intelligent, and so on.

WE NEVER KNOW A REAL PERSON THROUGH THE ASSUMPTIONS WE MAKE

Text producers choose how they want to appear in their texts: Writers choose tone of voice, the evidence they use, and how they describe others. Because the evidence is limited—and sometimes carefully crafted—the sense we develop of composers is always limited and partial; we never get to know a **real** person through a text.

Composers can use any strategy available to them to shape how audiences understand who the composers are. In traditional rhetorical terminology, the sense that audiences develop about composers is called

ETHOS.

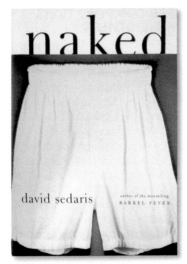

ETHOS IN BOOK COVERS

The context of book cover design says something about ethos. Rarely do writers design their own book covers; instead, a book's publisher chooses a designer. The designer works alone, or with an art director or photographer, but the work has to be approved by the publisher and (usually) by the author.

The ethos we associate with a cover is therefore not necessarily the ethos of the book—but the two should be close if the cover is to achieve its purpose of suggesting what the book is about. Notice that ethos can, therefore, be the result not of one person's decisions but of several people's.

The cover for *naked* looks professional, composed by someone who knows about using words, typefaces, and photographs together. Its humor suggests not only that the book will be funny but also that the person who made the cover has a sense of humor.

The cover for *The Little Friend* was composed by the same designer, and it too looks professional and has similar elements: one photograph, the title of the book, the author's name, and information about another of the author's books. Even though the strategies are similar, however, the second cover is a bit creepy: The extreme close-up on the face of a doll looking sideways suggests someone trying to see what's going on behind her, an undoll-like emotion.

Both covers show us someone who is able to suggest that objects have more life than we usually expect.

All these facets of this ethos—the professionalism, the humor, the attention to objects—suggest that these books are connected with makers who are clever and able to get readers to look below surfaces.

UNDERSTANDING AND
ANALYZING TEXTS

UNDERSTANDING APPEALS TO EMOTIONS

PEOPLE COMPOSE TEXTS TO MOVE OTHERS

Every text is composed for a purpose—and for that purpose to be achieved, the audience has to shift. The shifting can be as simple as the audience's attention being shifted from one object to another—but most often it is larger: a shift from passivity to engagement, from not knowing or caring about a topic to knowing and caring, from feeling hopeless to wanting to act.

In all of this, there is a shifting in the audience's emotion.

What emotions does an audience hold on a topic before they read, see, or hear a text—and what emotions does the composer hope the audience will hold afterward?

And—given the emotion a text's composer hopes an audience will feel after engaging with the text—what compositional strategies should the composer choose?

In rhetoric, a composer's use of strategies to shift an audience's emotions is called

PATHOS.

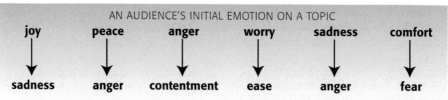

AN AUDIENCE'S INITIAL EMOTION ON A TOPIC

joy	peace	anger	worry	sadness	comfort
↓	↓	↓	↓	↓	↓
sadness	anger	contentment	ease	anger	fear

THE EMOTION YOU HOPE THEY WILL HOLD AFTER ENGAGING WITH YOUR TEXT

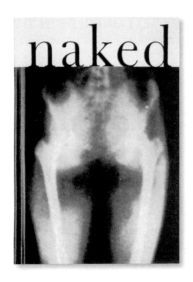

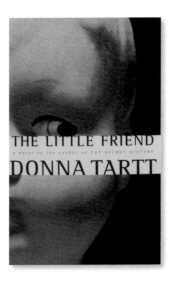

PATHOS IN BOOK COVERS

Earlier, we talked about how *naked*'s cover is about engaging with an audience's sense of humor: The title of the book and the photograph of boxer shorts are simple and funny. Perhaps we can say, then, that the cover's main pathos appeal is that of humor.

But there is another strategy we mentioned that we have not discussed: the part of the cover that comes off.

The boxer shorts are printed on a paper jacket that covers only part of the book. The jacket overlaps *naked*; the paper does not—as we expect with most book covers—cover the whole book; we are led to wonder what is under the cover, under the boxers.

In addition to its humor, the cover therefore also offers some interaction and provocation. It asks the audience to expect something under the cover ... and under the cover is an X-ray, a body more naked than we might have expected. Our emotions are called into play as we realize that we were

(perhaps) hoping to see something else but instead are given a very exposed naked body. We are teased by this cover—perhaps made to laugh, perhaps made to question why we were expecting to see something else.

The second book's title, *The Little Friend,* suggests childhood—but the photograph plays emotionally with the associations we probably have with childhood. A close-up photograph of a face engages us with the face's emotion. A close-up of a face turning its eyes toward shadows behind it suggests worry, concern, fear of something about to happen. When the face is a doll's, we have entered the realm of fairy tales and fantasy. The emotions encouraged by this cover are in your face, and unsettling.

UNDERSTANDING AND
ANALYZING TEXTS

UNDERSTANDING ARRANGEMENT
(including logic)

THE BREADTH OF LOGOS

Logos may make you think of logic, and that is appropriate: Both words developed from the same Ancient Greek word.

Logos, as a name for a strategy that looks at the arrangement of a text, includes logic. Logic is about how ideas are structured—arranged—to have a very specific kind of effect.

So when you hear the word **logos**, it is fine to think about all kinds of arrangements that are used to structure texts, including the particular set of arrangements we call **logic**.

EVERY TEXT UNFOLDS IN TIME

Even in posters and book covers, we see some elements first and some second because some elements are big or at the top. We have to look longer to see the arrangements of novels, essays, films, and video games. We may read a book's conclusion first, but in the table of contents we see that the composer put the chapters into a particular order. On a website we can look at individual pages in any order, but we see that the designers have designated one page as the home page—and we still have to look at each page starting at the top.

To move audiences, composers make choices about the order in which (they hope) audiences experience their work.

Choices about order can concern the

- **Large scale of a text.** What introduces someone to the text and what concludes it, or what does someone see first, then second, and so on?

- **Middle scale.** How are intermediate parts of a text given shape, such as sections or paragraphs in writing, the arrangements of one photograph in an advertisement that contains ten photographs, and so on?

- **Small scale.** In writing, the order of words in a sentence shapes how readers read; in sound recordings, background music or ambient sounds play behind main sounds, but still shape a listener's overall experience.

In rhetoric, a text's arrangements (including its logical arguments) are referred to as the strategy of

LOGOS.

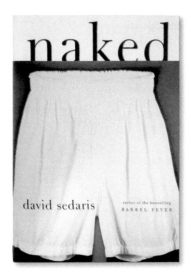

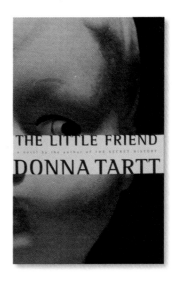

LOGOS IN A BOOK COVER

When readers first encounter *naked*, they probably notice the photograph first, because of its size, and then the title. The author's name is smaller than the title, and tied into the photograph.

When an author is well known, sometimes the person's name is larger than the title, but in this case we can see that the composers believed the suggestive title would probably attract more readers than the author's name—even though this author is now quite well known. Even smaller than the author's name, however, are two short lines of text that inform readers that this author has written another (best-selling) book; the cover's composers decided that this information is important enough to include, but not important enough to make bigger than any of the other elements. A final element of arrangement—of logos— is the strategy of having another photograph hidden under the first.

Whereas the arrangements of *naked* encourage eyes to move over the cover, putting together (and taking apart) the pieces, the arrangements of the cover of *The Little Friend* keep a viewer's eyes held close to the middle. The placement of the doll's eye right on top of the title—which is lined up closely with the author's name and information about another of the author's books—puts the points of visual interest of this cover close together. There is really nothing else to look at, so the arrangements support the pathos of this cover: We are aware of the darkness to the side, but we do not know what is there. This arrangement asks us to identify with the doll, to wonder what might be over there.

UNDERSTANDING AND ANALYZING TEXTS
A SAMPLE ANALYSIS ESSAY

As we wrote earlier, the first step of doing analysis is to analyze for understanding. Can you describe what you think the purpose of the text is, and for whom it was intended? Can you find evidence from the text— quotations, your observations about how ethos, pathos, and logos are used—that supports your understanding? If you can do that, then you understand a text.

Your understanding may differ from others' analysis of the same text, but as long as you can use as evidence the strategies you've noted, then you have built your own understanding. Listen to how others analyze, and notice how they use the evidence of the text.

On the opposite page is a written rhetorical analysis of one of the book covers we examined on the previous pages, as an example of how you can write such an analysis for understanding.

■ ■ ■

You'll notice that the writing uses some of the descriptions from the preceding pages; this is one way to develop an analysis: Write down your observations, and then use them to build a more formal analysis (such as one required by a class assignment).

The introduction

The introduction of the essay tells readers something of what the essay is arguing— but only enough to give readers direction and (the writer hopes) curiosity.

The subject of the essay

The writer of this short essay is careful to explain to readers what the explicit subject of the essay is.

Building to analysis

In order to get to an analysis of the book cover, this writer first lists pertinent strategies used by the cover's composer; after such a listing, the writer can analyze those strategies.

The conclusion

In the conclusion to the essay, the writer argues for the main strategy used by the composer of the text being analyzed, and (in the last sentences) shows how that strategy connects to the purpose of the text.

I would have thought a book cover made of a single photograph and a few words would give a reader only a bare, literal sense of the book, telling a reader, for example, that "this book is about boxer shorts." The book cover I analyze—designed by Chip Kidd for the book *naked* by David Sedaris —contains such limited elements, and yet it engages potential readers in puzzling out odd emotional relationships and so gets them engaged with the book even before they turn to page 1.

The cover of *naked* is composed, at first glance, of a simple photograph of bright white boxer shorts on a shaded blue background. The word "naked"—all in lower-case letters in a straightforward serifed typeface—is at the top, on a white background, partially covered by the photograph. The author's name is in the same typeface on top of the boxer shorts, along with a few words about another book he's published. This combination of elements is informal, straightforward, and balanced, with everything symmetric and centered. Based on such a description, this cover suggests a book that could be mundane and perhaps even boring. But boxer shorts are rarely on book covers, especially so large in proportion to everything else; to put them together with "naked" presented so informally encourages a reader to wonder where the shorts-wearing person is: Is that person running around naked somewhere?

But there is more to the cover. Kidd has readers wondering about who is wearing those shorts, but his design also suggests we might be able to find out. The boxers are printed on a paper jacket covering three-quarters of the book. The jacket partially overlaps "naked"; the overlapping, combined with how the paper does not—unlike most book covers—cover the whole book, leads readers to wonder what is under the cover, under the boxers.

In addition to its humor, the cover therefore also offers some interaction and provocation. It asks the audience to expect something under the cover … but what is under the cover is probably unexpected.

Under the cover is an X-ray of a lower torso, a body more naked than we might have expected. Readers are teased by this cover—perhaps made to laugh and perhaps made to question why they expected to see something else.

Most book covers show people or objects that give readers a literal sense of what is in the book: A book cover with a dog on a leash is about dog training; a book with a palm tree is about the South Pacific. Kidd has instead used the rhetorical strategy of pathos as his primary strategy: While the arrangement of elements (including the order of seeing the boxer shorts before seeing the bony torso) encourages readers to see the informal relationship between the elements, it is the humor and surprising interaction and discovery that give readers a sense of this book. A reader who looked at this cover and in response thought that this book was a funny but edgy intimate look at a man's life would not be far off. It is possible readers would buy this book—the general purpose of the cover—because they have gotten involved emotionally with that man's life only by picking up the book to look closer.

ANALYZING ARGUMENTS

Once you understand a text, you can make judgments about it.

- Do you agree with the arguments the text is making?

- Is there enough evidence to persuade you to agree? Does the evidence offered truly support the arguments being made?

- What are consequences of the arguments being made?

Experienced researchers and scholars do not respond only to isolated chunks of a text but instead try to be fair to the whole text, to how its various strategies build to a whole.

On the next pages we show steps for taking apart arguments to see whether enough evidence is offered (and thus also discuss kinds of evidence and how to judge different kinds). We suggest questions you can ask of texts to support your analysis of them.

JUDGING EVIDENCE, JUDGING SOURCES

In the next few pages on analysis, we help you judge the evidence offered in a text: Such judgments help you decide whether you accept the evidence and thus the arguments built on the evidence. Later in Part 3, we offer strategies for judging the relevance and credibility of sources you are considering using in your writing.

Judging the evidence of a text for yourself will help you decide later if your readers will see the text as a credible source that supports the arguments you are building.

This editorial was published in the *San Francisco Chronicle* in March 2007:

Food ad blitz

IT CAN'T be healthy for a 9-year-old—or any child—to be bombarded with an average of 21 food ads on television each day.

That's especially the case when most of the products being peddled don't come close to meeting the ordinary definition of the word "food."

According to the most exhaustive study yet done on advertising to children by the Kaiser Family Foundation in Menlo Park, one-third of all "food" ads are for candy and snacks. Just under a third are for cereals (almost all of them loaded with sweeteners). Ten percent are for fast foods.

Of the 8,854 ads reviewed, none was for fruits or vegetables.

All those commercials add up. So-called "tweens"—kids between the ages of 8 and 12—see some 7,600 food ads each year. On average, teenagers see slightly fewer—6,000 a year, or 17 a day, while 2-to-7-year-olds see 4,400, or 12 ads a day.

To view these ads as an inevitable, and even normal, part of childhood in America is not acceptable. As an authoritative report last year by the Institute of Medicine concluded, food ads have a direct impact on children's health. "Television advertising influences the food preferences, purchase requests and diets, at least of children under 12, and is associated with the increased rates of obesity among children and youth," the report found.

What's more, food ads swamp public-service advertising that promote fitness and nutrition. Children between ages 2 and 12 see a pitiful 164 such messages each year, or one every two or three days. Teenagers see one such PSA, on average, once a week.

Marketers of food products can, and must, do better. Last year, 10 of the top 10 food companies formed the "Children's Food and Beverage Advertising Initiative," and promised to devote at least half of their ads to healthier food messages that encourage fitness and nutrition.

This must be a serious effort on the part of the food industry—and must embrace more than just the major food companies. Given the high stakes—the health of future generations of Americans—it would not be premature for Congress to begin to exercise more oversight over the glut of food advertising intruding into the lives of children.

On the next pages, we offer strategies for questioning the arguments offered in this editorial. The strategies will help you:

- **Make judgments about sources you are considering using in support of your own composing.** If you question a source and find its arguments to be poorly made, you do not want to base your arguments on that source.

- **Make judgments about the validity and strengths of your own composing.** You can use the strategies we offer to be sure your arguments are well supported and are therefore more likely to be taken seriously by others.

ANALYZING ARGUMENTS
THESIS STATEMENTS

A THESIS STATEMENT CAN HELP YOU ANALYZE THE WRITING OF OTHERS

People who study how arguments work have studied the logic of thesis statements. They have learned that analyzing arguments to pull out their thesis statements—as we have done to the right for "Food Ad Blitz"—can help us better decide about being persuaded.

The ideas here about thesis statements come from the work of mid-twentieth-century philosopher Stephen Toulmin. Through his studies into the structure of argument, Toulmin developed an understanding of an argument's **evidence, claims,** and **warrants**.

When you read an argument written by someone else, you can decompose the writing: You can analyze the writing to pull out a thesis statement, along with its claims, warrants, and evidence—as we do on the opposite page.

Once you see the evidence, claim, and warrant pulled out so explicitly, how persuaded by "Food Ad Blitz" are you? Why?

A THESIS STATEMENT CAN HELP YOU ORGANIZE YOUR WRITING

Thesis statements structured like the one shown to the right help writers make decisions about how to turn a thesis statement into a full paper: They help writers make decisions about how to organize their writing, what evidence is strongest, and where to focus their energies in writing.

→ See pages 152–155.

GIVEN THE EVIDENCE OFFERED BY "FOOD AD BLITZ" (P. 95) AND THE WARRANT THE ARTICLE ASKS YOU TO ACCEPT, ARE YOU PERSUADED BY THE ARTICLE?

Here is the article's thesis statement, followed by an analysis:

> Food advertising on TV is affecting the future health of young people; *therefore*, Congress should have oversight of food advertising.

A THESIS STATEMENT IS COMPOSED OF THREE PARTS:

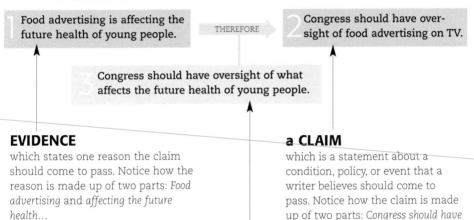

1 Food advertising is affecting the future health of young people.

THEREFORE

2 Congress should have oversight of food advertising on TV.

3 Congress should have oversight of what affects the future health of young people.

EVIDENCE

which states one reason the claim should come to pass. Notice how the reason is made up of two parts: *Food advertising* and *affecting the future health...*

In a thesis statement, evidence will be offered in a general form, but in a piece of writing—as in the "Food Ad Blitz" article—specific evidence will be offered: *A study by the Kaiser Family Foundation in Menlo Park reviewed 8,854 ads; none was for fruits or vegetables and the majority were for foods heavy in sugars. Another report, by the Institute of Medicine, says that food ads affect children's eating habits and thus their health, and are "associated with the increased rates of obesity among children and youth." Children see almost no ads that encourage healthy eating practices.*

a CLAIM

which is a statement about a condition, policy, or event that a writer believes should come to pass. Notice how the claim is made up of two parts: *Congress should have oversight ...* and *food advertising.*

a WARRANT

is an idea or value that links the evidence to the claim. A writer believes the audience is likely to accept the warrant without much argument— and so, while the warrant is not stated explicitly in a thesis statement but is implied, the strength of the thesis statement depends on whether the audience does indeed accept the warrant. Notice how the evidence and claim each repeat a similar phrase (*food advertising*); the warrant links the evidence and claim logically—by linking the parts that aren't repeated: *Congress* and *the future health of young people.*

WHAT COUNTS AS EVIDENCE

Evidence is what you offer audiences to persuade them that your position on a topic is worth considering.

There are many kinds of evidence composers can use to support their warrants; on these pages we consider:

1 EXPERT TESTIMONY
2 PERSONAL EXPERIENCE
3 ANALOGIES
4 FACTS (AND STATISTICS)
5 FIELD RESEARCH
6 SHARED VALUES
7 EXAMPLES

EXPERT TESTIMONY

An expert has special and thorough knowledge on a particular topic because of education, profession, study, or experience. Experts can be individuals or groups. Because of their knowledge, we believe we can rely on experts' judgments in the areas in which they know more than the average person.

Text composers can use the words of experts—their testimony—as authoritative backing on the topics about which the expert is knowledgeable.

In the editorial on page 95, for example, the Kaiser Family Foundation and the Institute of Medicine are both cited as experts; excerpts from reports they have published are offered as evidence in support of the editorial's arguments.

EVALUATING EXPERT TESTIMONY

If you are wondering whether to accept expert testimony:

- Do an online search on the person or organization. Does the person have credentials—education and experience—for offering the evidence? Does the organization specialize in the topic? Does the person or organization have an affiliation indicating potential bias?

- Ask others what they know about the person or organization.

When you compose your own texts:

- Ask people from your audience if they know and trust the experts you are citing.

- If your audience might not know an expert you are citing, include descriptions of the expert, saying why the expert has authority for you.

PERSONAL EXPERIENCE

Personal experience is what we know through living. Each of us has experienced families, schools, jobs, and romance; we've paid taxes, driven cars, eaten, shopped, and seen our communities change. Every experience—and especially repeated experiences—shapes our sense of how the world works.

Personal experience is limited evidence precisely because it is personal. Without considerable research, you cannot know how many other people share your experiences; you cannot know if they draw the same knowledge from their experiences as you do.

Because personal experience is limited, it ought to play only a small part in formal writing. It can serve as a single example in support of a point. An introductory anecdote about your experiences working in a fast-food restaurant can draw readers emotionally into an argument about the moral satisfactions of low-paying jobs, but you would need much more evidence to show that others found the same moral satisfaction.

The same holds true for using others' experiences as evidence. A friend who has been to Burundi on a missionary trip might have interesting observations about how donations are spent in that country, but those observations have little place in your writing unless your friend is also an expert on the economics of donations or unless the observations are backed up by other evidence.

Personal experience can become facts or statistics when it is joined with and examined alongside the experiences of others through field research.

EVALUATING PERSONAL EXPERIENCE

When you see others using personal experience as examples in their writing, whether the experiences are their own or belong to others, ask these questions:

- Is the experience used as logical evidence in support of the composer's ability to discuss this topic (ethos), or as an emotional appeal (pathos)?

- If the experience is used as logical evidence, does the writer acknowledge that the experience is necessarily limited? Is other evidence also given as support?

- If the experience is used to show that the composer has relevant experience for taking on the topic at hand, is the experience sufficient? Does the experience indicate that the composer has any bias on the topic?

- If the experience is used as an emotional appeal, does the emotion draw the audience away from what is at issue or does it help show why the issue might be worth the audience's attention?

When you compose your own texts, keep in mind the following:

- Be wary of generalizing from your own experiences. Always try to find out if your audience has shared the same experiences—and, if they have, ask if they have drawn similar conclusions to you.

- When you use the experiences, observations, anecdotes, or opinions of others, use them only to illustrate examples and to offer other evidence of the kinds we describe on these pages.

ANALOGIES

Analogies are quasi-logical structures: When you use an analogy, you compare—usually at length—two objects, events, or processes so that the more familiar can explain the less familiar. For example, a long description of how the brain is like a computer would be an analogy in which the composer relies upon the audience's knowledge of computers to explain how the brain works.

Similarly, to call the Internet the *Information Superhighway* is to use an analogy: One is to understand the abstract Internet networked system as being like a highway. Most people in the United States have experienced highways, and so can think of the Internet as a series of roads and interchanges with information traveling between locations in packets just like cars.

But analogies work more than descriptively. They carry assumptions from the more familiar object to the less familiar. For example, the *Information Superhighway* analogy carries the assumption that the Internet should be a public resource as highways are, and that the Internet should be regulated, supported, and repaired with public funds just as highways are.

Analogies can be used in small focused ways, or can shape the argument of a whole book: The writer Malcolm Gladwell, for example, one of whose short essays we examine later, has used a whole book to consider how *ideas can be contagious exactly as a virus is.*

The following analogy is a blog entry; the writer describes a day in which he and others from his company discussed leadership and teamwork:

I mentioned something I recently read on migratory birds in flight. This study found that a flock of birds in a V-formation can fly at least 70% farther than a bird on its own. Birds at the back of the V work much less because they can take advantage of the draft created by the birds at front. When a bird at the front tires, it drops out of the lead and goes to the back to rest. The V-formation also improves visual contact and communication.

I like to tell this story to show how natural teamwork should be. This story also highlights the importance of individual excellence and leadership. Every bird in the V-formation at some point assumes the leadership role at the front. Similarly, each member of my leadership team has a key responsibility to drive the priorities and vision for their area in the company, while at the same time being able to understand how that fits into the overall vision of our company.

The comments appearing after the blog entry develop the shortcomings of the analogy: If you carry out the analogy, as one person commented, it would be appropriate for the company's *top managers to drop out of the lead positions and for some others either to die or recover;* another points out that the V-formation is *a pattern learned over the millions of years of evolution* and so not easy for humans to learn or apply.

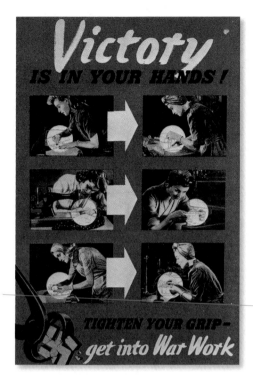

Visual analogies also exist. The example above comes from early in World War II, when—with so many men in battle—industries encouraged women to work in factories producing weaponry and machinery needed for the war effort. The poster above uses analogies between the work to which women were already accustomed—sewing and cooking—and industrial production. The visual analogies between the two kinds of work are offered as evidence that, if women can do the familiar work, they can also do the unfamiliar work.

EVALUATING ANALOGIES

In reading and developing analogies, consider:

- Analogies are an odd sort of evidence because they prove nothing. They do not guarantee that situations will play out as an analogy suggests.

  Instead, composers use analogies to shape an audience's attitudes. A compelling analogy can persuade audiences to consider an object or process in a positive light, which is a large part of any successful argument. A compelling analogy is therefore both a pathos appeal and a form of logos.

- When it is compelling, an analogy can so focus your perceptions that you cannot think outside the analogy. When you see an analogy being used as evidence in an argument, or want to use one yourself, try carrying out the implications of the analogy, as those commenting on the bird–human leadership example did.

  You can also explore how an analogy shapes thinking by coming up with alternative analogies. For example, consider how the *Internet as a Superhighway* analogy asks us to think of the Internet as roads and exchanges and implies that the Internet should be built and supported with public funds. To consider an alternative analogy, ask what implications accompany thinking of the Internet as a marketplace or huge library.

FACTS

A fact is a statement about an event or condition that exists or has happened. Facts are true or false, with no gray areas.

Facts are verifiable: They can be checked. If someone claims that it is a fact that cold climate turtles hibernate, we ought to be able to go see such hibernating turtles for ourselves.

Facts can be presented in words and through numbers, firsthand experience, illustrations, charts, and graphs.

Facts can be presented in diagrams, as in this explanation of swimmer's itch:

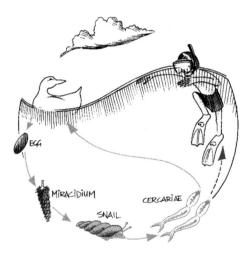

This diagram brings together small facts about a parasitic flatworm's life cycle in order to build a larger fact about how swimmers get infected with the worm.

Facts can be about historical events—

In the late 18th century, Haiti's nearly half million slaves revolted under Toussaint L'Ouverture. In 1804, after a prolonged struggle, Haiti became the first black republic to declare its independence.

—more recent events—

He graduated from Aurora College in 2011.

—or natural objects and events:

Jupiter is the largest planet.

The maximum age of a snapping turtle recorded in nature is 24 years.

STATISTICS—A KIND OF FACT

Statistics result from manipulations of sets of numbers.

Statistics can be presented in tables—

Table 1: DOCTORATE AWARDS by selected characteristics of recipients, 1995 and 2004	1995	2004
All doctorates	41,750	42,155
Male	61%	55%
Female	39%	45%

Source: National Science Foundation/Divisions of Science Resources Statistics, Survey of Earned Doctorates, 2004.

—be written—

In 2002, more than one-third (38 percent) of child maltreatment fatalities were associated with neglect alone. Physical abuse alone was cited in more than one-quarter (30 percent) of reported fatalities. Another 29 percent of fatalities were the result of multiple maltreatment types.

—or presented in charts or graphs:

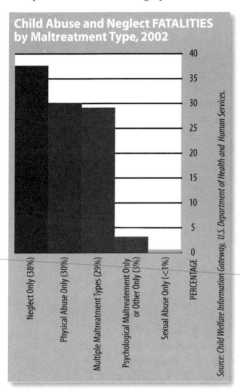

Child Abuse and Neglect FATALITIES by Maltreatment Type, 2002

40
35
30
25
20
15
10
5
0

PERCENTAGE

Neglect Only (38%)
Physical Abuse Only (30%)
Multiple Maltreatment Types (29%)
Psychological Maltreatment Only or Other Only (3%)
Sexual Abuse Only (<1%)

Source: Child Welfare Information Gateway, U.S. Department of Health and Human Services.

Charts, graphs, and tables allow viewers to make comparisons.

EVALUATING FACTS & STATISTICS

To evaluate these, ask the following:

- Are sources given for the facts and statistics? If so, are they authoritative? If not, do you trust the author enough to accept the facts?

- Do the facts and statistics support the conclusions that are based on them?

- Can you find other facts that contradict those you are questioning?

When you are using facts and statistics in your own compositions, consider:

- Will your audience accept the authority of the sources from which you've drawn the facts or statistics?

- Have you made clear how the facts support the points you are making?

- If you are working with a source that offers a wide range of facts or statistics— census data, for example—are you using the facts responsibly, using them fully, and not choosing only those that support your points?

TIP: USE FACTS, NOT OPINIONS

Zbigniew Boniek is the greatest male soccer player of all time.

The sentence above is an opinion: People can argue about who is the greatest soccer (or baseball or football) player of all time.

In 2006, Sharma Wing of Daniel Webster College scored the most points per game in Division III soccer.

The sentence above gives a fact: It can be verified by checking data collected about college soccer in 2006.

FIELD RESEARCH

If researchers are fair and open-minded, honestly researching what others think, their interviews, observations, and surveys create facts. When researchers compile information, they can demonstrate what a group of people think or believe in a particular place and time. For example, they can provide statistics about how many people desire a particular policy or, through interviewing older people in an area, show what Sunday activities were popular in 1950.

You can use the following questions both to evaluate field research carried out by others and to help you shape field research you might perform.

EVALUATING INTERVIEWS

- Did the interviewer ask open-ended questions, allowing those being interviewed to provide their opinions and beliefs?

- Did the interviewer present the interview fairly, showing where the words of the person interviewed were cut or edited?

- What sort of relationship does the interviewer appear to have had with those being interviewed? Does the interviewer seem hostile, or overly friendly?

EVALUATING OBSERVATIONS

- Does the researcher describe the methods and goals of the observation, and how those methods and goals may have shaped the research?

- Does the researcher appear to have approached the observation seeking particular results—or been open to whatever happened?

- Does the researcher appear to have observed well, or with too much focus?

- Are the researcher's results only positive, in support of the researcher's goals, or does the researcher note any observations that went against expectations?

EVALUATING SURVEYS

- Did the survey ask open-ended questions, allowing the person or people being interviewed to provide their opinions and beliefs?

- Was the number of people surveyed sufficient for providing support for any assertions a researcher is making based on the research? (To learn how many people need to be surveyed depending on what a researcher is trying to find out, see the article "Sample Size: How Many Survey Participants Do I Need?" <http://www.sciencebuddies.org/science-fair-projects/project_ideas/Soc_participants.shtml>.)

- Did the researcher seek information from an appropriately wide group of people, or only from those likely to give responses the researcher wanted?

SHARED VALUES

The editorial on page 95 relies on the warrant that *Congress should have oversight of what affects the future health of young people* (as shown on page 97). This warrant presumes the article's readers are concerned about young people's health. The editorial's writer does not argue for this value or offer evidence for it; the writer instead assumes that readers readily accept that value.

Composing an argument that does not rely on readers' values in this way is impossible. Even simple arguments such as *Don't do that—you'll get hurt!* work only if the person at whom they are directed believes that getting hurt is bad. The person making the statement doesn't have to explain this.

Longer and more complex arguments about going to war or about health care, for example, will appeal to shared values about patriotism, nationalism, the right of people to a doctor's care, or the right not to suffer.

Because the composers of texts rely on such shared values to encourage readers to accept their arguments, these values work to support arguments just as other kinds of evidence do.

EVALUATING SHARED VALUES

When you are questioning shared values or using them in your own work, keep in mind:

- Using shared values to support arguments depends on what the audience believes—so you must look at the values you assume as you argue and ask if audiences truly do believe the assumptions. Under what conditions does an audience accept them?

- People can hold contradictory values or accept some values only under certain conditions, as when some are against violence except in response to aggression. When you consider the values underlying an argument, ask if the assumptions hold in all cases or only in some.

- When you compose your own texts, be aware of the values you assume you and your readers share. If you do not make those values explicit to yourself, you will not be able to use them alertly in your writing—and so you may be surprised when your audience responds negatively.

EXAMPLES

Examples can make general or abstract arguments specific and concrete for audiences. Detailed examples can help audiences visualize what might otherwise be only conceptual.

Examples can be in a sentence—

Classes at our college emphasize personal attention, especially in the first year, when all classes are limited to fifteen students.

—or a paragraph:

What always amazed me about my father was how multifaceted he was. He was an intellectually curious physician living in a small town who had traveled the world, read at least a book a week up until he died, could continually kick my ass in Scrabble even though he didn't learn English until he was 23, and knew practically everything there was to know about classical music, Spanish wines, and French cinema. All I wanted to be when I grew up was as smart as my dad.

In each example above, a general statement comes first—Classes at our college emphasize personal attention and What always amazed me about my father was how multifaceted he was—followed by examples to show concretely what the terms **personal attention** and **multifaceted** mean to the writers.

Like analogies, examples do not prove anything. Rather, they help audiences better understand a point or concept, and so can enhance an audience's engagement with your work. Like analogies, they are logos and pathos appeals.

USING VISUAL EXAMPLES

Notice how the following selection uses both written and visual examples:

By immersing players in political or economic structures, the makers of *serious games* hope to encourage critical thinking and even activism. For example, in *Bacteria Salad* from Persuasive Games, players learn about agribusiness because they have to (in the words of the Persuasive Games website) "Harvest mass amounts of cheap produce and sell it for as much profit as possible. But watch out for floods and animal waste, or your greens might turn, uh—brown—and your customers will get E. Coli." As you can tell from the description, the game is humorous and, as the screenshot below shows, has lighthearted graphics, all to seduce players to engage critically with serious issues. I wonder, however, if the playfulness encourages or distracts from that purpose.

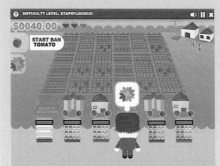

Screenshot of *Bacteria Salad* from Persuasive Games website.

EVALUATING EXAMPLES

Whether you are analyzing others' examples or considering how to use them in your own work, consider:

- Do the examples make clear the general or abstract point they are meant to explain? Do they distract from the point, or will audiences easily understand why the examples are there?

- How do the examples support the general or abstract points being made? Are the examples too specific, causing the general points to get lost?

- If more than one example is used to clarify a general or abstract point, are all the examples appropriate? Are the examples ordered to move from least complex to most, or from most known to least known?

In addition, for **visual examples**, consider the following:

- Are the examples used only to support and explain general points, or do they distract from the purpose?

- Are the examples labeled, both to give proper attribution and to help readers understand their relationship to the words?

TIP: CHOOSING KINDS OF EVIDENCE FOR YOUR COMPOSITIONS

On pages 34–37 in Part 2 we encouraged you to develop questions to guide research; on pages 42–43, we showed how those questions guide choosing research sources. Also use those questions to choose useful kinds of evidence. Decide which questions most guide your research; use the information below to help you develop evidence or find it in sources. Also use what we've written in Part 3 to evaluate your evidence.

QUESTIONS OF FACT: Facts!

QUESTIONS OF DEFINITION: Expert testimony (from a person or authoritative text) can help.

QUESTIONS OF INTERPRETATION: Expert testimony, analogies, personal experience, and field research can help persuade audiences to consider the interpretation you offer.

QUESTIONS OF CONSEQUENCE: Expert testimony, analogies, facts about what has already happened, and field research can be persuasive about what might result from a proposed action.

QUESTIONS OF VALUE: Expert testimony, personal experience joined with field research, and facts about people's behaviors help identify values.

QUESTIONS OF POLICY: Use expert testimony and facts.

TIP: SHARED VALUES

Shared values underlie every argument you make, so we have not mentioned them on the right. Nonetheless, because they underlie all arguments, working to identify them is central to analysis.

FURTHER QUESTIONS TO GUIDE CRITICAL READING

In the previous pages, we have been focusing on paying critical attention to logical elements of texts. Here, we offer you questions to help you consider an even broader range of choices composers make in their texts.

Once you have done preliminary analysis to be sure you understand a text, ask these questions to help you decide if you want to be persuaded by a text:

QUESTIONS ABOUT AUDIENCE

- Whom is the composer including in the audience? Who is excluded from the audience—and why?

- To what is the composer drawing the audience's attention? What might the composer be able to overlook by focusing the audience's attention in this way?

- What does the composer assume the audience knows or believes?

QUESTIONS ABOUT PURPOSE

- Why does this purpose matter at this time and in this place?

- Are there secondary purposes as well as a main purpose?

- Is the purpose clearly stated or easy to determine? If not, why might the composer have decided not to make the purpose obvious?

TIP: USING STYLE TO SUPPORT ANALYSIS

When you are analyzing writing, use Part 6 of this book, on style, to help you identify a writer's choices. Part 6 will help you name the strategies a writer uses for emphasizing parts of an essay and thus will help you figure out what is emphasized (logos) as well as how to describe the writer's ethos and pathos strategies. Such identifications help you see a writer's purposes more easily.

QUESTIONS ABOUT CONTEXT

- Where does the audience encounter the text? How might this shape their responses?

- When is an audience likely to encounter the text? How might this shape their responses?

- What events at the time of the text's production are likely to shape an audience's expectations about the topic?

QUESTIONS ABOUT ETHOS

- Does the composer have the appropriate background or experience for pursuing this purpose?

- Does the composer seem open to multiple perspectives? Is the composer treating those perspectives fairly?

- What cultural backgrounds and expectations shape the composer's positions?

- Is the composer using a tone of voice appropriate to the purpose?

- What role does the composer take toward the audience? Is the composer acting as a teacher, a lecturer, a parent, a peer, a friend? Is this role appropriate for the purpose?

- Is the composer respectful of the audience, treating them as intelligent, thoughtful people?

QUESTIONS ABOUT PATHOS

- What emotion is the intended audience likely to have about the issue? How does the text acknowledge that emotion, and try to shift it?

- Do the emotional appeals seem reasonable to you—or overblown?

- Are the emotional appeals appropriate to the issue?

QUESTIONS ABOUT LOGOS

- What claims, reasons, and warrants are explicit or implied in the text? (→ See pages 96–97.)

- What kinds of evidence does the composer use? (→ See pages 98–107.) Is that evidence relevant, credible, and sufficient? (→ See pages 124–137.) Do you know of or can you find evidence that points to different conclusions?

- Are the sources cited so that the audience can check them? If so, are the sources relevant and credible? (→ See pages 124–137.)

- Why might a composer start with particular examples or evidence? To what will these draw the audience's attention? (And from what will these examples distract attention?)

- How does the composition end? How will the end affect how the audience looks back on the rest of the composition?

TIP: GIVING EVIDENCE

If you are using these questions to do the preliminary analysis for writing a paper, include with your responses any evidence in the text that supports your responses. For example, when taking notes about ethos, you might write: *It feels as though the author is yelling at readers: All the sentences are short, emphatic, addressed to "you!" written as though readers know nothing about the topic….*

ANALYZING ARGUMENTS
CRITICAL
READING

To the right is a short argumentative essay about zero-tolerance policies in schools.

Read it through once, trying to ignore the questions we've put next to it. Come to your own understanding of the purpose, audience, and context for this text.

Then use the questions we've put here, which draw on the analytic approaches we've described in the last pages, to help you further develop your critical reading.

The beginning: Pathos and an example as evidence

The first sentences give an example and encourage readers to sympathize with the student before knowing anything else about him. Why might Gladwell start with an introduction dependent on pathos?

Naming

Why might Gladwell tell us the name of the tutor but not the student?

Evidence: A second example

What attitude does Gladwell want readers to have toward Bomar? Toward students now? How has Gladwell prepared his readers to have those attitudes?

TIP: ANNOTATING WHAT YOU READ

The comments we've added to this article suggest how you can mark up readings on your own, to keep track of your own questions and comments. By making such annotations, you'll see patterns in what you read, patterns that can help you determine purpose and other strategies. By making such annotations, you'll also see patterns in your responses—which will help you develop a focused analysis.

Pathos: How readers are addressed

Why do you think Gladwell addresses readers directly here? How might a reader respond to these questions?

No Mercy

Malcolm Gladwell

In 1925, a young American physicist was doing graduate work at Cambridge University, in England. He was depressed. He was fighting with his mother and had just broken up with his girlfriend. His strength was in theoretical physics, but he was being forced to sit in a laboratory making thin films of beryllium. In the fall of that year, he dosed an apple with noxious chemicals from the lab and put it on the desk of his tutor, Patrick Blackett. Blackett, luckily, didn't eat the apple. But school officials found out what had happened, and arrived at a punishment: the student was to be put on probation and ordered to go to London for regular sessions with a psychiatrist.

Probation? These days, we routinely suspend or expel high-school students for doing infinitely less harmful things, like fighting or drinking or taking drugs—that is, for doing the kinds of things that teenagers do. This past summer, Rhett Bomar, the starting quarterback for the University of Oklahoma Sooners, was cut from the team when he was found to have been "overpaid" (receiving wages for more hours than he worked, with the apparent complicity of his boss) at his car dealership. Even in Oklahoma, people seemed to think that kicking someone off a football team for having cut a few corners on his job made perfect sense. This is the age of zero tolerance. Rules are rules. Students have to be held accountable for their actions. Institutions must signal their expectations firmly and unambiguously: every school principal and every college president, these days, reads from exactly the same script. What, then, of a student who gives his teacher a poisoned apple? Surely he ought to be expelled from school and sent before a judge.

Suppose you cared about the student, though, and had some idea of his situation and his potential. Would you feel the same way? You might. Trying to poison your tutor is no small infraction. Then again, you might decide, as the dons at Cambridge clearly did, that what had happened called for a measure of leniency. They knew that the student had never done anything like this before, and that he wasn't well. And they knew that to file charges would almost

Evidence: Examples

How do we know anyone is *incorrigible* or a ***decent kid***? Gladwell seems to believe that these are obvious characteristics of people, but who gets to make these decisions, and based on what evidence?

Evidence: Research

How might readers respond to this move from the made-up stories of Jimmy and Bobby to the Tennessee study? Is there enough evidence given in this essay for us to check on the Tennessee study ourselves, to see if we agree with how it was conducted or with Gladwell's characterization of it?

Pathos: How readers are addressed

Gladwell now refers to himself and the audience together as *we*. By assuming we are all in agreement with what he writes, what might he be trying to achieve?

Evidence: Examples

Because of the temporal context surrounding the publication of this essay, Gladwell assumes that his readers know that he is referring in this parenthetical remark to events in Iraq and at Guantanamo; he is also assuming that his readers share his interpretation of the events. Why would he insert such a serious example in parentheses here, when all his preceding examples have involved students?

Evidence: Analogy

Gladwell takes someone else's analogy and turns it around. This analogy involves an event that many take extremely seriously and would not want to see used in a lighthearted way. Do you think Gladwell's overall purpose so far justifies his use of this analogy? What sort of reader, holding what sort of beliefs, would be likely to accept this analogy and find it appropriate? (And why might Gladwell use such a serious analogy here?)

certainly ruin his career. Cambridge wasn't sure that the benefits of enforcing the law, in this case, were greater than the benefits of allowing the offender an unimpeded future.

Schools, historically, have been home to this kind of discretionary justice. You let the principal or the teacher decide what to do about cheating because you know that every case of cheating is different—and, more to the point, that every cheater is different. Jimmy is incorrigible, and needs the shock of expulsion. But Bobby just needs a talking to, because he's a decent kid, and Mary and Jane cheated because the teacher foolishly stepped out of the classroom in the middle of the test and the temptation was just too much. A Tennessee study found that after zero-tolerance programs were adopted by the state's public schools, the frequency of targeted offences soared: the firm and unambiguous punishments weren't deterring bad behavior at all. Is that really a surprise? If you're a teenager, the announcement that an act will be sternly punished doesn't always sink in, and it isn't always obvious when you're doing the thing you aren't supposed to be doing. Why? Because you're a teenager.

Somewhere along the way—perhaps in response to Columbine—we forgot the value of discretion in disciplining the young. "Ultimately, they have to make the right decisions," the Oklahoma football coach, Bob Stoops, said of his players, after jettisoning his quarterback. "When they do not, the consequences are serious." Open and shut: he sounded as if he were talking about a senior executive of Enron, rather than a college sophomore whose primary obligation to Oklahoma was to throw a football in the direction of young men in helmets. You might think that the University of Oklahoma was so touchy about its quarterback being "overpaid" it ought to have kept closer track of his work habits with an on-campus job. But making a fetish of personal accountability conveniently removes the need for institutional accountability. (We court-marshall the grunts who abuse prisoners, not the commanding officers who let the abuse happen.) To acknowledge that the causes of our actions are complex and muddy seems permissive, and permissiveness is the hallmark of an ideology now firmly in disgrace. That conservative patron saint Whittaker Chambers once defined liberalism as Christ without the Crucifixion. But

The end

Why might Gladwell have waited until the end of his essay to mention the name of the student whose actions he described back at the very beginning of the essay? (In case you didn't know, Robert Oppenheimer was one of the people responsible for the atom bomb.)

Context and ethos

What does this essay's being published in the *New Yorker* tell you about Malcolm Gladwell and how others think of his writing? If you know nothing about this magazine, what might that tell you about how Gladwell was viewing his audience while he was writing?

punishment without the possibility of redemption is even worse: it is the Crucifixion without Christ.

As for the student whose career Cambridge saved? He left at the end of the academic year and went to study at the University of Göttingen, where he made important contributions to quantum theory. Later, after a brilliant academic career, he was entrusted with leading one of the most critical and morally charged projects in the history of science. His name was Robert Oppenheimer.

New Yorker, September 4, 2006, pp. 37–38.

Below is one possible way of analyzing Gladwell's evidence, claim, and warrant in the above essay. By separating these elements, you can have a better sense of whether you agree with these elements, whether you think they really do fit together logically, and whether you think the evidence works.

EVIDENCE: *Zero-tolerance* policies potentially prevent good people from developing to their full productive potential.

THEREFORE

CLAIM: We should apply discretion rather than zero-tolerance policies when responding to the bad behavior of youth.

WARRANT: Discretion in response to the bad behavior of youth will help good people develop to their full productive potential.

DETAILED EVIDENCE: *Facts:* The people who apply zero tolerance apply the policy outside their rightful realm, as the University of Oklahoma case shows. *Shared values:* Zero tolerance does not take into account the differences in people, as the Bobby and Jimmy examples show. Zero tolerance does not take into account the moral development of youth. Zero tolerance removes the need for institutional responsibility. *Appealing to readers' experiences:* Readers are likely to agree, based on their own experiences, that Robert Oppenheimer would perhaps not have gone on to do his important work if *zero tolerance* had been in use in 1925.

ANALYZING ARGUMENTS

A SAMPLE RHETORICAL ANALYSIS

On the opposite page, we show a written rhetorical analysis—a critical analysis—of Malcolm Gladwell's article "No Mercy," which we examined on the previous pages. You should be able to see how this essay grows out of the work of responding to the questions asked of the essay in the previous pages—as well as how this essay cuts to the heart of Gladwell's argument by questioning his warrant.

This rhetorical analysis is one example of how you can write such an analysis.

The beginning: Ethos

This writer gives a quick summary of the Gladwell article, to show that she has done the work of understanding the article. This builds her ethos positively, so her questioning of the article will thus be more persuasive to her readers.

The beginning

Now this writer helps her readers have a sense of what is to come by summarizing—quickly—her main concern about the Gladwell article; she will give evidence for this concern in the paragraphs to follow.

Analyzing ethos

The writer analyzes Gladwell's ethos: He is "confident … but not bullying" and wants to inspire others to think critically.

Logos: Evidence

Here the writer uses direct quotations from the Gladwell article to show that she has read carefully and is responding to specific Gladwell arguments.

→ See pages 300–305 for help with including direct quotations in your writing.

Ethos and pathos: The writer asks questions

After showing her readers the specific parts of Gladwell's writing that concern her, this writer can then raise the questions that motivate her concern.

How would her ethos be different if she had instead phrased these questions as statements? How does asking these questions engage readers (a pathos strategy)?

Ethos: Adding authority by using other sources

After some online searching, this writer found a published report that helps demonstrate that her worry is concrete and real. This source ought to have authority with readers because it is published by a government source—and also because the writer describes the detailed research on which the report is based.

No Justice, No Mercy?
Responding to Malcolm Gladwell

In his essay "No Mercy," published in the September 4, 2006, issue of the *New Yorker*, Malcolm Gladwell argues implicitly that current "zero-tolerance" policies hurt people more than we realize. For example, Gladwell tells about the brilliant physicist Robert Oppenheimer, who under today's policies probably would have been expelled from college and denied his important career because of dangerous actions he took as a graduate student. With this example Gladwell suggests that current students who are expelled for lesser offenses are losing future careers in which they might contribute to society. While there is much in Gladwell's argument with which I agree, his examples raise for me the question of who is to judge others, and how.

I appreciate the tone of Gladwell's writing. He is a confident writer, but not bullying. There is nothing in his writing to suggest that he thinks anyone who disagrees is somehow stupid or unthoughtful. Instead, Gladwell's writing seems more of a provocation, asking us to think on these matters because they have consequences. I appreciate being drawn into this issue by the range of examples and ideas Gladwell brings into his writing—but those examples lead me to my concerns.

As a possibility for how we might treat the poorly considered actions of the young, Gladwell uses the notion of "discretion," which he describes as being based in an awareness that "every cheater is different" (119). Therefore, Gladwell argues, we need to approach each case with an awareness of who has done the action, and why, in order to decide consequences: "Jimmy is incorrigible, and needs the shock of expulsion," Gladwell writes, but "Bobby just needs a talking to, because he's a decent kid" (119). But how does anyone know these things? What would someone have to do to get to know Jimmy or Bobby well enough to make these decisions with any certainty? And what sort of person would we want to make such decisions that have so much effect on the lives of others? To live together using the discretion that Gladwell asks us to have, we would need to find people who have the time and sensitivity to look carefully into the lives of others, and who have considerable training in understanding the patterns of someone's life so as to make valid decisions.

Meanwhile, however, many examples exist of discretion that is biased. For one, the United States Department of Justice's Office of Juvenile Justice and Delinquency Prevention published a report in 1995 in which the Office analyzed the available literature

Ethos: Adding authority by quoting the words of others

This writer could have summarized the findings of the report she is citing, but by quoting from it she is able to let the report speak for itself, which tends to be more persuasive to readers.

Concluding

After having given her own evidence in the preceding paragraphs, the writer now summarizes her position so that her readers can leave her writing with a clear idea of her argument. (→ See pages 232–233 on writing conclusions.)

Notice, too, how she shapes her words here: She neither dismisses Gladwell nor insists that she knows it all. How does this shape her ethos? What sort of emotional room does this leave for readers to respond?

Citing sources

→ See Part 8 (pages 289–448) for help with citing sources.

THIS WRITER'S USE OF LOGOS...

To the right is one possible analysis of this writer's use of evidence, a claim, and a warrant. If you think that this writer has written a persuasive short essay, consider the following:

1 In what order are the evidence, claim, and warrant presented in the writing? Why might they be presented in that order?

2 Notice that many other strategies weave into the writing, in support of both the logic of the claim, reason, and evidence, but also to persuade readers to have a sympathetic lean toward the writer's position: Logos matters tremendously, but it cannot stand alone.

on the treatment of minority youth in the juvenile justice system; after analyzing 250 published articles, with 47 being particularly relevant, the report argues that "processing decisions in many State and local juvenile justice systems are not racially neutral" (7).

Whether or not the juvenile justice system is the same now as it was in 1995, what the report shows is that racial bias can enter the system—even from people who are supposed to be professionals in deciding whether a young person committed an offense and how it should be treated. Other kinds of bias—based on class or gender, for example—also seem possible. If we do want discretion as the basis for responding to youth behavior, as Gladwell argues, how do we keep it fair?

I may sound as though I disagree with Gladwell. I do not. I think zero-tolerance policies in high schools harm the futures of people who are still too young to make certain decisions. But until an argument addresses how discretion can be applied knowledgeably and justly, without bias, I will sit uneasily with my beliefs.

Works Cited

Gladwell, Malcolm. "No Mercy." *New Yorker* 4 Sept. 2006: 37–38. Print.

United States. Dept. of Justice. Office of Juvenile Justice and Delinquency Prevention. "Minorities and the Juvenile Justice System: Research Summary." Washington: GPO, 1995. Print.

EVIDENCE: Discretion is often neither fair nor offered equally.

THEREFORE

CLAIM: Discretion is not enough for making decisions about the lives of young people.

WARRANT: Young people deserve fair and equal treatment.

DETAILED EVIDENCE: Facts: The writer also uses the expert testimony of the U.S. Department of Justice's Office of Juvenile Justice and Delinquency Prevention, and facts supported by that testimony. **Appealing to readers' experiences:** This writer appeals to the reader's own experiences by asking questions about how we make decisions.

ANALYZING ARGUMENTS
QUESTIONS TO GUIDE CRITICAL LOOKING

In the previous pages, we have been focusing primarily on alphabetic texts—but questioning photographs, graphic novels, advertisements, films and videos, and similar texts is equally important.

In our earlier discussions of how to understand what some book covers are doing rhetorically (→ see pages 84–93), we analyzed the covers in terms of the rhetorical choices made by their designers. You can analyze any visual text that way—and then can ask **the same questions on pages 108–109** to help you consider whether you think the text has been designed ethically.

Because visual texts often function differently in society than print texts, you can also ask questions like the following.

QUESTIONS ABOUT AUDIENCE

• Who can see this text? How does the placement of the text (in a museum, on the Internet, in a magazine) shape who can see it? Who won't be able to see it?

• What knowledge is required for an audience to understand the text? Does a viewer have to know something about the history of art, about consumer culture, or about celebrities?

→ The analysis of the book cover on pages 92–93 is one example of critical looking; another example is on pages 122–123.

QUESTIONS ABOUT PURPOSE

- Is the primary purpose of the piece to encourage people to buy or to enjoy? Keep in mind that in either case, you need to say more: If the purpose were simply to sell or to delight for all advertisements or cartoons (for example), then there would be no variety among these texts because they could all achieve their purposes in the same way. If the primary purpose is to encourage people to buy, then there will be secondary purposes such as making people feel they lack something, or that they too can have endless fun, or....

- Why might the text's composers have used a visual text instead of an alphabetic text to achieve their purposes?

QUESTIONS ABOUT CONTEXT

- Are you seeing the text in the context for which it was designed? Where was it designed to be seen?

- How would the text be different if you saw it someplace else? If you are analyzing a painting in a museum, how would it be different in your bedroom? If you are analyzing a comic book, how would the pages be different if you saw them in a formal newspaper like the *New York Times*?

- How would seeing this text change if the number of people around you changed?

QUESTIONS ABOUT ETHOS

- Was this text made by one person or by many? Is it attributed to an organization?

- What knowledge and abilities did the maker(s) of this text need in order to design or produce the text?

QUESTIONS ABOUT PATHOS

- Would you describe this text as simple or complex? Is it cheery or morbid? Active or calm? What features of the text encourage these responses?

- Does this text use pathos as its primary appeal to your attention?

- Where does this piece require you to stand or sit to see it well? Do you need to be close or far away?

- Do you feel that this piece is inviting you to come closer or do you feel as though it is yelling at you to move away? Why?

- How would this piece be different if the colors were different?

QUESTIONS ABOUT LOGOS

- What is made visible in this text? On what people, objects, or processes does this text ask you to focus your eyes?

- What arguments are made by the text?

- What are the parts of this text? Name every element you can visually differentiate.

- What elements of this text do you see first? Which second, which third? Why?

A SAMPLE ANALYSIS OF A VISUAL TEXT

The poster to the right was produced by the Mayor's Office of the City of New York as part of a campaign against domestic violence.

Pathos

This text is simple, composed of one photograph of a woman and a few lines of type. If we were looking at the original poster, the woman would seem almost life-size; as viewers, we are situated as though we were standing close to her, right behind her, as though we could touch her. What emotional relationship might this physical closeness encourage viewers to have with the woman and so the poster?

Pathos

The woman's body is bruised, and she is wearing a hospital gown. How might a viewer's attitude toward the woman and so toward the poster be different if she were wearing a low-cut dress instead?

Logos: Evidence

The poster gives one fact. What evidence is offered in its support? Whose authority is offered in support? Do we know if the fact refers just to high school students in New York City or to those in the entire United States? (Does that matter?) Why might the makers of this poster have chosen to present this fact written on this woman's bruised back instead of on a poster containing only words?

Audience

Who would be interested in this fact about high school students? Notice that the poster's composers have chosen to call attention to "high school students" and not "high school girls." Why might they have made this word choice?

Context

If the audience includes people in high school, then it is likely that the people running the campaign decided to make a poster because schools have many places where posters are easily seen. In addition, the particular visibility of posters says something about why the poster uses pathos as its major strategy: A poster has to catch the eye—quickly—of someone walking by.

Logos: Argument

This poster is encouraging viewers to make phone calls to stop abuse. Does it offer reasons to encourage this action? If so, what are they?

Logos: Arrangement

Why might these words be at the bottom of the poster rather than at the top?

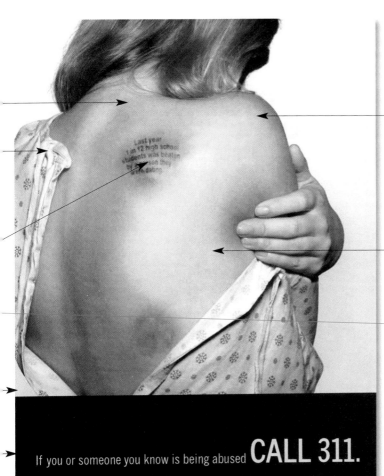

Pathos

Why do you think we are shown the woman from the back? What emotional connections does this ask the audience to make with the poster?

Pathos

Why do you think the woman is white? What does this suggest about how the poster's makers conceived of their audience?

If you or someone you know is being abused **CALL 311.**

In emergencies call 911.

Michael R. Bloomberg, Mayor   Yolanda B. Jimenez, Commissioner, Mayor's Office to Combat Domestic Violence

Logos: Evidence?

Does the support of the mayor of New York City for this poster serve as expert evidence?

EVALUATING SOURCES
with audience and purpose in mind

The previous pages have asked you to consider your sources carefully to see if you want to be persuaded by them.

Now you can also ask if your sources are appropriate to your composing purposes, given your current understanding of your audience and your purposes.

ARE YOU READY TO APPLY THE INFORMATION IN THE NEXT PAGES?

IF THIS IS YOUR SITUATION, THE ANSWER IS **NO**.

Midnight: Your eyes hurt, and the number of items returned from your database search is 5,652.

Go pack to pages 55 or 66-67 to learn more about how to narrow down your search terms so that you get fewer but more focused results.

IF THIS IS YOUR SITUATION, THE ANSWER IS **YES**.

You've got a solid research question (although you know you might need to tweak it once you start writing) and you've got a pretty good initial sense of the audience of readers you want to address in your writing. (If you are unsure about your research question, check pages 34–37. If you want to think about your audience a bit more, check pages 194–199.)

If you apply what we present in the next few pages, you will have a list of sources about which you know two important things, as we describe in the next paragraphs.

- ☐ ONE **relevance**
- ☐ TWO **credibility**

WHAT WILL THIS SECTION HELP YOU ACHIEVE WITH YOUR RESEARCH?

1 **Your sources will be relevant to your audience and purpose.** The sources will supply appropriate support for what you are arguing and will likely be accepted by your audience.

2 **Your sources will be credible to your audience.** Your audience ought to trust the sources, and thus will be more likely to trust any arguments you build based on those sources.

Because you need to know that your sources are both relevant and credible, the process of evaluating sources has two steps—one for evaluating relevance and the other for evaluating credibility.

JUDGING EVIDENCE, JUDGING SOURCES

On pages 98–107, we offered you strategies for judging the evidence offered in others' arguments. Your judgments about those arguments can help you decide if those arguments will be accepted by your readers if you were to use them as evidence in your own writing.

TIP: APPLYING THE CRITERIA IN ORDER

While the criteria of relevance and credibility are equally important, use the steps in order. Determining credibility often takes more effort than determining relevance, so you can save yourself some time by checking relevance first.

EVALUATING SOURCES
FOR RELEVANCE

ONE
relevance

☐ TWO
credibility

IF A SOURCE MEETS MOST OF THE CRITERIA TO THE RIGHT, HOLD ON TO IT.

When you are evaluating the relevance of a source, you are evaluating how likely most readers will believe that what is presented in the source is appropriate to your arguments.

Finding sources that meet all the criteria doesn't guarantee that they'll end up in your Works Cited list at the end of your paper—but sources that meet all the criteria are much more likely to help you write a solid, strong, and persuasive argument.

ask this:
IS THE KIND OF SOURCE
RELEVANT TO YOUR AUDIENCE?

☐ **Given your research question/ purposes, what kinds of sources are likely to be most appealing and persuasive to your particular audience?**

When you are writing an academic research paper, your audience is academic readers, who tend to respect books published by academic presses, academic journal articles, and specialized encyclopedias.

Academic audiences also respect the use of primary sources. (→ See page 39 on primary sources.)

Depending on your purposes, however, you might need to supplement such sources. For example, if you are writing about the role of women in space exploration, you might want to begin your essay with one woman's personal story about how she got into the U.S. space program; in such a case, you could look in popular periodicals or blogs for such stories—and those sources would be appropriate for your purposes.

DK Online Han...

online
DK Hand

Explore these topics online:

Evaluating sources

www.mycomplab.com

then this:
IS A PARTICULAR SOURCE
RELEVANT TO YOUR ARGUMENT?

☐ **Is the source on topic?**

This might seem too obvious a question to ask, but it isn't. You can save yourself a lot of time if, with each possible source, you ask yourself whether the source really does provide information that is focused on your topic.

☐ **Does the source have a publication date appropriate to your research?**

If you are writing about the current state of a rapidly changing topic—such as AIDS research—you need sources dated close to the moment you are writing; if you are writing about a past event or about past situations that have led to a current event, then you need sources from those time periods as well as from people in the present.

☐ **Does the source bring in perspectives other than those of the sources you've already collected?**

You do not want to collect sources that all take the same position, for two reasons. First, if all you can find are sources that take the same perspective on your topic, then your topic is probably not controversial or interesting enough to be the subject of a paper. Second, your audience is not likely to be persuaded by writing that does not consider multiple perspectives on a topic.

☐ **Does the source provide something interesting?**

Your audience wants to be intellectually engaged with your writing. As you consider a new source, ask yourself if it contains ideas or information that are interesting—funny, provocative, puzzling—and that support your points. Quoting or citing such ideas or information in your writing helps you write a more engaging paper.

☐ **Does the source bring in data or other information different from the sources you have already collected?**

This criterion is similar to the one preceding, but it asks you to consider how much data or other information is useful for you to collect in order to construct a persuasive position in your writing.

☐ **Does the source suggest other possible directions your research could take?**

We do want you to stay on track in your research as much as you want to stay on track, given that you have a deadline—but we also want you to stay open to the possibilities of reshaping or retouching your research question and purpose as you discover potentially new and exciting approaches.

EVALUATING SOURCES
FOR RELEVANCE: SAMPLE SOURCES

ONE **relevance**

TWO **credibility**

To the right are examples showing how to judge the relevance of a source based on your research question and audience.

Pedro's research question is

"What social actions ought the U.S. government take in the face of pandemics?"

He is writing for his classmates and teacher.

Aaliyah's research question is

"On the Internet, how do ideas spread like viruses?"

She is doing research for a marketing company whose directors are considering new online approaches.

Penenberg, Adam L. "Technorati: A New Public Utility." *WIRED News* 14 July 2005. Web. 5 Apr. 2006.

Fineberg, Harvey V. Interview. "Swine Flu of 1976: Lessons from the Past." *Bulletin of the World Health Organization* 87 (2009): 414–15. Print.

This source is **NOT RELEVANT**, given Pedro's purpose. Because *Wired News* is generally considered both reputable and hip, and because the story is fairly recent, this news story could help Pedro make his writing more interesting to his audience. The only connection this story has with Pedro's question, however, is through the analogy between the spread of ideas and the spread of diseases, which will not help Pedro think about how governments ought to counter viral pandemics.

This source is **RELEVANT**, given Pedro's purpose. Because the person being interviewed in this journal article discusses the interactions between scientists and public policy makers in relation to flu pandemics, this article can help Pedro understand the different pressures governments face in pandemics. The article is important for Pedro's research and is also recently published.

This source is **RELEVANT**, given Aaliyah's purpose. This online news story gives a specific example of how a particular idea spread on the Internet, and compares the spread of the idea to a virus. The story also defines terms that might be useful to Aaliyah because she will have to define terms for her audience.

This source is **RELEVANT** for Aaliyah. Because there is information in this interview about how viruses spread, Aaliyah can use this source to test and develop examples of how viruses and ideas do or do not spread in similar ways. The seriousness of this source—and its timeliness—will also appeal to her audience.

EVALUATING SOURCES
FOR CREDIBILITY: PRINT

ONE relevance

TWO credibility

IF A SOURCE MEETS MOST OF THE CRITERIA TO THE RIGHT, HOLD ON TO IT.

When you evaluate the credibility of a source, you are evaluating whether most of your readers will accept the facts and arguments you present.

Finding sources that meet all the criteria doesn't guarantee that they'll end up in your Works Cited list at the end of your paper—but sources that meet all the criteria are much more likely to help you write a well-supported and persuasive argument.

A NOTE

Some people are nostalgic for pre-Internet days because the institutions of print publication seem to make evaluating a source's credibility easy. The costs and complexities of print publication and distribution are behind that perception.

The printing of books, magazines, and newspapers is expensive. Those who provide the money want return on their investments, so they want readers to trust what is published. Print publishing therefore developed systems of editors and fact-checkers: Often when you buy a print text its credibility has been checked in different ways. (Libraries contribute to this system, too, because librarians often buy only books recommended to them by trusted sources.)

But, as you know, not all print texts are credible (think supermarket tabloids). Some publishers have political motivations, for example. You cannot therefore count on something you find in print to be absolutely reliable—and you also have to consider what criteria your audience will use for judging credibility.

Explore these topics online:

Evaluating sources

www.mycomplab.com

TIP: HAVE ANY QUESTIONS?
If you have any questions as you apply these criteria to a source, a librarian is a good person to ask.

DETERMINING THE CREDIBILITY OF A PRINT SOURCE

❑ **Who published the source?**

Look at page 39, on Understanding Different Kinds of Sources, to read about the motivations behind different kinds of publishers. A publisher's motivations can help you decide the level of credibility the source will have for your audience.

❑ **Does the author have sufficient qualifications for writing on the topic?**

Most print publications will tell you something about the author so that you can judge; you can also search online to learn about the author.

If you cannot find an author or sponsoring agency, is that because no one wants to take responsibility?

❑ **What evidence is presented?**

Is the evidence of a kind that fits the claims? What kind of evidence would be stronger?

❑ **Does the evidence seem accurate?**

❑ **Do the author's claims seem adequately supported by the offered evidence?**

❑ **Does the source try to cover all the relevant facts and opinions?**

If you are at the beginning of your research, this might be hard to answer, but as you dig deeper into your topic, you'll have a sense of the range of perspectives one can take on your topic, and you'll be able to judge how widely a source engages with the issues at stake.

❑ **What is the genre of the source?**

Is the source an advertisement (or does it contain advertisements)? Advertisers sometimes try to influence what is published near their advertisements to keep their appeal strong.

But it also matters if the source is an opinion piece, a thought-experiment or essay, or a piece of scholarship: Writers and readers have different expectations for different genres regarding how much (unsupported) opinion is appropriate.

❑ **Does the source make its position, perspective, and biases clear?**

When writers do not make their own biases clear, they often do not want readers to think about how those biases affect the writers' arguments.

❑ **Does the source make a point of seeking out different perspectives?**

If so, this is an indication that a writer is trying to understand a topic fully and not just giving a narrow view.

❑ **Does the writing seek to sound reasonable and thoughtful?**

Inflammatory language in a piece of writing is a sign that the writer is trying to move you solely through your emotional responses without engaging your thoughtfulness.

FOR CREDIBILITY: PRINT SAMPLE SOURCES

ONE **relevance**

TWO **credibility**

To the right are examples of how to judge the credibility of a print source based on your research question and audience.

Pedro's research question is

"What social actions ought the U.S. government take in the face of pandemics?"

He is writing for his classmates and teacher.

Aaliyah's research question is

"On the Internet, how do ideas spread like viruses?"

She is doing research for a marketing company whose directors are considering new online approaches.

Gorman, Christine. "How Scared Should We Be?" *Time* 17 Oct. 2005: 30–34. Print.

Fineberg, Harvey V. Interview. "Swine Flu of 1976: Lessons from the Past." *Bulletin of the World Health Organization* 87 (2009): 414–15. Print.

This source is **NOT CREDIBLE** for Pedro's audience and purpose. *Time* is well known but is not a science or policy journal; the author is not a scientist or lawmaker. Though the author quotes credible agencies, she does not give citations for us to check. The article's evidence is patchy because the questions are complex but the space for answering them is small. The language is almost inflammatory, to catch attention, not thoughts. Although this article is relevant to Pedro's question, Pedro and his readers should be skeptical about this article's depth. Pedro could perhaps use anecdotes from this article, but ought not make this a main source.

This source is **CREDIBLE** for Pedro's audience and purpose. Pedro's readers will respect the standards of this journal published by an international organization: The journal gives the scientific credentials of the person being interviewed and the decision to publish the article was made by other scientists (which ensures accuracy of evidence). The writing is exact, key words are defined, and inflammatory language is carefully avoided.

This source could be **CREDIBLE** for Aaliyah's audience and purpose, depending on how Aaliyah uses it. For all the reasons listed above, Aaliyah and her audience ought to be skeptical of this article. Given Aaliyah's purposes, however, the article covers enough different perspectives to be useful for developing the analogy between epidemics and Internet viruses—as long as Aaliyah notes her skepticism about the source.

This source is **CREDIBLE** for Aaliyah's audience and purpose. For all the reasons mentioned above, this source will carry weight with Aaliyah's audience, even if Aaliyah uses this source only to provide examples supporting her descriptions of viruses and how they spread.

EVALUATING SOURCES
FOR CREDIBILITY: ONLINE

ONE
relevance

TWO
credibility

DETERMINING THE CREDIBILITY OF AN ONLINE SOURCE

Use the criteria for evaluating print sources, with the following additions:

❏ **Who published the source?**

The domain name in the URL can indicate something about a publisher's credibility. (Example domain names are microsoft.com, whitehouse.gov, or lacorps.org.)

Look at the last letters in the domain name:

.gov A website created by an office of the U.S. federal government

.com A website created for a company that is seeking to publicize itself or sell products

.org A nonprofit organization—but anyone can register for the .org domain

.edu Colleges and universities

.mil U.S. military websites

.me.us A website for one of the fifty U.S. states: The first two letters are the abbreviation of the state name

.de A website created in a country other than the U.S.—but websites created outside this country can also use .com, .net, and .org

.net The most generic ending; Internet Service Providers (ISPs) as well as individuals can have websites whose URLs end in .net

What sorts of websites will your audience think are most appropriate and credible, given your purpose?

DK Online Handbook
online
DK Hand

Explore these topics online:

Evaluating sources

www.mycomplab.com

- **Does the author have qualifications for writing on the topic?**

  With some websites you won't be able to answer this because you won't be able to determine who the author is, either because no name is given or a pseudonym is used.

  If you cannot find the name of an author or sponsoring agency, perhaps no one wants to take responsibility or someone is worried about the consequences of publishing the information. If you are writing on a controversial topic, you could use information from such a site to describe the controversy and support the fact that there is a controversy—but you couldn't use the site to offer factual support for anything else.

- **What evidence is offered?**

  In the most credible print sources, authors list the sources of their evidence; the same holds true for websites. If you cannot find the source of the evidence used, the site is not as credible as a site that does list sources.

- **Does the source make its position, perspective, and biases clear?**

  Approach websites just as you approach print pages with this question, except that with websites you can also check where links on the site take you. A website may give the appearance of holding a middle line on a position, but if the websites to which it links support only one position, then question the credibility of the original site.

- **What is the genre of the source?**

  Some online genres, such as newspapers and magazines, mimic print genres; approach them with the same questions as you would their print equivalents.

  But webpages can easily be made to look like any genre. For example, some websites look like the informational material you pick up in a doctor's office. Just as when you receive such material in a doctor's office, however, you need to look carefully: Is the website actually advertising a company's treatments or products?

  Also keep in mind that blogs are a tricky genre to use as sources. There are many well-respected blogs published by experts; if you want to cite such a blog, you will need to give evidence why that particular blog is respected by other experts. On the other hand, if you are citing words from a blog solely to show a range of opinions on a topic, the blog's credibility will not be an issue.

ALSO:

- **How well designed is the website or webpage?**

  A site that looks professionally designed, is straightforward to navigate, and loads quickly suggests that its creators put time and resources into all the other aspects of the site; these characteristics could also indicate that the site was published by an organization rather than an individual. Do any of these factors matter for your purpose and audience?

EVALUATING SOURCES
FOR CREDIBILITY:
ONLINE SAMPLE SOURCES

To the right are examples of how to judge the credibility of an online source based on your research question and audience.

Pedro's research question is
"What social actions ought the U.S. government take in the face of pandemics?"
He is writing for his classmates and teacher.

Aaliyah's research question is
"On the Internet, how do ideas spread like viruses?"
She is doing research for a marketing company whose directors are considering new online approaches.

United States. Dept. of Health and Human Services. *HHS Pandemic Influenza Plan.* 8 Nov. 2005. Web. 4 Apr. 2006.

Wikipedia contributors. "Virus." *Wikipedia, The Free Encyclopedia.* Web. 7 Apr. 2006.

This source is **CREDIBLE** for Pedro's audience. It has been published under the authority of the government, which has been charged by its citizenry to provide accurate information on matters of such importance. This source has numerous links to issues Pedro will find useful, each of which includes a long list of sources from which the evidence has been drawn, and which each person can access and check. The perspective of this website is clear: It tries to be open to all the questions people like Pedro are asking and to provide information from all the relevant agencies, institutes, and scientific journals.

This source is (probably) **NOT CREDIBLE** for Pedro's audience. Although researchers have shown Wikipedia to be as dependable as *The Encyclopedia Britannica* and that Wikipedia is usually as up-to-date as possible, many audiences do not know this or understand how articles are composed in this online source. If Pedro feels compelled to use this source, he should find out his teacher's view—but even if his teacher approves, Pedro's writing will be more persuasive with backup from multiple sources. (He can use Wikipedia as a link to other sources, taking advantage of the Resources listed at the bottom of the Wikipedia page.)

This source is **CREDIBLE** for Aaliyah's audience because they believe government agencies are public and subject to oversight and that the advice provided is based on the best, most up-to-date evidence available. Because government websites can nonetheless be subject to partisan influence, Aaliyah—like Pedro—will still need to supplement this source with other sources in order to show broad agreement among a range of credible sources.

This source is (probably) **CREDIBLE** for Aaliyah's audience. Aaliyah's purposes are different from Pedro's: She will use the information on the Wikipedia site for defining terms rather than supporting her major arguments, and her overall purpose is speculative, so her audience will read her writing with a different expectation of credibility than will Pedro's audience. If, when she cites it, Aaliyah makes clear how information is compiled in Wikipedia, her audience is likely to accept it as credible.

USING ANALYSIS TO DEVELOP A THESIS STATEMENT

Riley has done initial online and library research into how microcredit changes women's lives in developing countries, as the notes on page 29 describe.

USING ANALYSIS TO DEVELOP A TOPIC

Because Riley asked the research questions she did (page 79), she was able to read her sources analytically, looking for specific information and judging the credibility of the sources she found. As she read, she looked for why women are the focus of microcredit and how microcredit changes women's lives.

While reading with those questions in mind, Riley noticed that most of the sources she read spoke glowingly about microcredit—but a few pointed out problems. Riley started looking for more sources to support or refute those claims about problems with microcredit.

By changing her search terms (**microcredit AND problems OR shortcomings**), Riley was able to find more sources that questioned some of the benefits of microcredit.

By reading analytically, she recognized that they tended to come from feminist perspectives—and so she is aware that various audiences will respond to those sources differently.

Because of this continued research, however, Riley believes that pointing out such problems is justified.

FIRST THESIS STATEMENT

A thesis statement has this basic form, as described on pages 96–97:

CLAIM + EVIDENCE

Based on her research, Riley writes:

> Microcredit keeps women in poverty and makes them vulnerable to familial violence; therefore, microcredit is not always good for women.

EVALUATING THE FIRST THESIS STATEMENT

Effective and engaging papers are most likely to develop from thesis statements that

1 Have a concrete and focused claim.

2 Have a debatable claim.

3 Give evidence supported by authoritative and relevant sources.

Using the three points above to think about what Riley has written, here's an evaluation of Riley's first try:

1 The claim that *microcredit is not always good for women* is vague and broad. What do **good** or **not always** mean here? Is Riley talking about all women everywhere?

2 Because so many sources wrote only positively about microcredit, Riley's claim is certainly debatable.

3 If Riley has found several authoritative and relevant sources providing evidence in support of her claim, then her claim will be supported—although it still is vague.

SECOND THESIS STATEMENT

After evaluating her first try, Riley writes:

> Women who receive microcredit without discussion support groups and classes in economics won't know how to change the community conditions that encourage poverty; therefore, microcredit should only be offered with such support.

EVALUATING THE SECOND THESIS STATEMENT

1 In her paper, Riley will have to explain more clearly what she means by *discussion support groups and classes in economics*, but this claim is concrete because it makes specific recommendations; it also focuses on a few recommendations rather than many.

2 For the same reasons as before, Riley's claim is debatable.

3 Riley's now knows more concretely the kinds of detailed evidence she needs. She will need to write about conditions that encourage poverty in communities and give evidence that microcredit programs that don't do what she recommends do not result in community change.

Explore these topics online:

Thesis statements

www.mycomplab.com

WHAT'S NEXT?

→ To see how Riley uses her thesis statement to organize for her first draft, see pages 154–155.

→ To see how the draft that Riley develops out of this thesis statement, see pages 204–213.

HINTS & TIPS FOR EVALUATING SOURCES

IF YOU ARE UNSURE ABOUT THE RELEVANCE OR CREDIBILITY OF A SOURCE…

Ask someone who might be more familiar with the source, such as your teacher, a librarian, or someone who has researched your topic before.

Knowledge about relevance and credibility of sources increases over time. Those who write repeatedly on similar research topics learn who respected writers and researchers are, and learn (in addition to what we've listed here) lots of subtle signs for what makes a source relevant and credible.

REMEMBER THAT FINDING A SUFFICIENT NUMBER OF SOURCES IS ONLY PART OF WRITING A PERSUASIVE PAPER

Have you ever started to read a letter to the editor or a blog that you had to put aside because the tone of voice was rude or obnoxious? The letter or blog might have had perfectly fine evidence in support of its arguments, but other choices the writer made in constructing the whole argument might have undone the worthiness of the research.

The same can happen to you in writing a research paper. Look on pages 200–203 for help with making choices about the other aspects of a research paper.

HOW DO YOU KNOW YOU HAVE COLLECTED ENOUGH SOURCES?

❑ **Do your sources approach your question from a range of directions?** Readers see it as a sign of careful and thoughtful research when writers consider a range of positions on a topic; you should not consider your research done until you have collected—and can reference—a range of positions.

❑ **Do you have the right range of kinds of sources?** With academic research papers, audiences usually expect sources that are academic. If your writing is for a nonacademic audience, using many kinds of sources can demonstrate that you have done broad and careful research.

❑ **Do you have enough sources to support every step of the argument you are making?**

❑ **Do you have enough sources to help you develop solid and well-supported responses to your research questions?**

❑ **Before you can finally decide if you have enough sources,** however, you need to know if you have the sources that will fully answer your audience's questions on this topic. Look to Part 5—where you turn your thesis statement into a statement of purpose—to help you decide if you really do have all the sources you need for your particular audience.

PART 4
ORGANIZING AND SHAPING TEXTS

CONTENTS

WHERE ARE WE IN THE PROCESS FOR COMPOSING?

Understanding your project

Getting started

Asking questions

Shaping your project for others
Choosing a genre
Choosing an overall organization
Arranging paragraphs

Drafting a paper

Getting feedback

Revising

Polishing

ARE YOU READY TO USE THE NEXT PAGES OF THIS BOOK?

NO...

Are you experimenting with the different parts of your thesis statement? Are you working at formulating a one or two sentence statement of your argument?

If this is your situation, then, no, you are not ready for the next pages.

Until you have a pretty clear idea of your thesis statement or main argument, you do not have the information you need to identify and so be able to organize the parts of your writing.

→ For help with a thesis statement, see pages 96–97 and 138–139.

YES.

Do you have a thesis statement that seems pretty solid to you? If someone asked you what you hope your writing will persuade others to consider, could you say this in a sentence or two?

If this is your situation, you have done the preliminary work of writing your own persuasive research paper. We believe that the information in the following pages will help you organize your composition logically and persuasively.

WHAT IS ORGANIZATION?

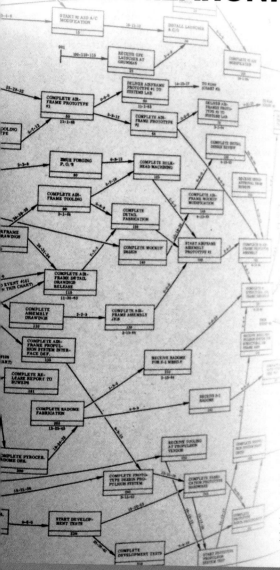

BUILDING A TEXT IS LIKE BUILDING A BUILDING

You make choices to shape your audience's experience similarly to how people experience buildings.

Think of when you first visited a new acquaintance. You went to the person's apartment or house, and from the street you got a sense of the building's age. Seeing the overall style of the building—Victorian, modern, suburban ranch, or fifties apartment block—you sensed what you would see inside. Once inside, you got a sense of the organization of the rooms—of the layout and floorplan—which indicated how you could move through the rooms. Then there were the individual rooms with their furnishings, which told you about how comfortable it was to live in this place and what people did there. There was also the color of the walls, and what was on the walls, and what was on the shelves....

As you moved from the outside to the inside, you moved from seeing large structures to seeing smaller ones, from big shapes to small objects.

MOVING THROUGH A TEXT IS LIKE MOVING THROUGH A BUILDING

First, you see the whole, which sets up expectations about the smaller parts. As you read, listen, or look, you see the floorplan—the overall structure; and then you notice the parts of the floorplan—the paragraphs or major divisions. Finally, you notice the details, such as tone of voice, sentence length, word choice, and so on.

In this part of the book, we focus on the major elements, the overall structure and paragraphs.

BUILDING

POSTER

AN ACADEMIC PAPER

FLOORPLAN

CONCEPTUAL
FRAMEWORK

CONCEPTUAL
FRAMEWORK

PART 4

ROOMS

MAJOR ELEMENTS

PARAGRAPHS

FURNISHINGS

DETAILED
ELEMENTS

SENTENCES
& WORDS

PART 6

ORGANIZATION IS ABOUT HOW YOU WORK AT EACH OF THESE LEVELS

At each level, you have many choices about how to place the relevant elements in relation
to each other in order to achieve your purpose, for your audience, given your context.

CONCEPTUAL FRAMEWORKS AND GENRES

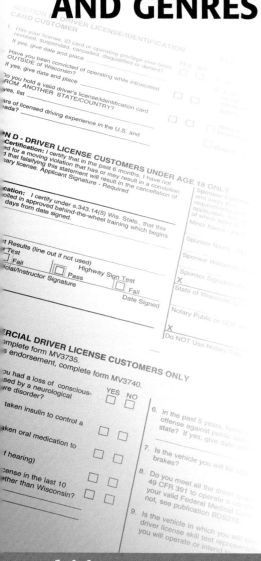

Imagine you are a clerk in a driver's license office, and there is no application form. Instead, each time someone needs a license, you say, "Please put the necessary information on a piece of paper." How many different sizes and shapes of paper would you receive, with how many different arrangements of information—and what would different people consider to be "the necessary information"? How messy would it be to try to work with all those different pieces of paper?

Think then of how a driver's license application form saves time and energy for both applicants and clerks.

When conceptual frameworks for organizing texts get used repeatedly—as with application forms for a driver's license—then they become "genres."

Genres save us time and effort because they help both composers and audiences know what to do and what to expect. There are movie genres (Westerns, comedy romances, horror movies), videogames (first person shooters, quests), fiction genres (fantasy, science fiction, romance). There are genres for writing as well: We list three of them to the right, and we trace out their major features in the pages that follow.

When you encounter a new rhetorical situation, you need to ask what genres your audience might expect, and how tightly you need to stay within the confines of the genre if you are to achieve your purposes.

→ In the following pages we focus on the larger features—the overall shapes and paragraph-level organizations—of the three genres to the right; to learn more about the styles of these genres— their sentence-level features—see pages 228–229.

	ACADEMIC GENRES	**WORKPLACE GENRES**	**POPULAR GENRES**
TEXTS	Academic papers, reports, articles in scholarly journals	Memos, proposals, resumes, project plans, progress reports, white papers, executive summaries	Magazines, newspapers, social networking websites, letters to the editor, letters of complaint, comics
AUDIENCES & PURPOSES	Academic genres help specialists build and share knowledge that is widely useful across the humanities, social sciences, sciences, engineering, and medicine.	Worksplace genres help people get work done quickly and efficiently—and so such genres address both how people work together as well as the products, services, and processes they use and produce.	Popular genres can be produced by anyone for broad general audiences: they can entertain, inform, or sell.
AUDIENCE EXPECTATIONS	Academic audiences expect academic texts to be: • serious • direct • explicit • objective and unbiased • supported with evidence • respectful of previous knowledge • cautious in their claims, only making claims that can be supported by evidence	Workplace audiences generally expect workplace texts to be: • short • focused • to-the-point • easy-to-read • full of immediately useful information supported by some degree of research	Popular audiences expect popular texts generally to be: • interestingly if not entertainingly composed • easy-to-read without a reader needing specialized knowledge to understand

CONCEPTUAL FRAMEWORKS AND GENRES
ACADEMIC GENRES

THE VALUES OF ACADEMIC GENRES

As you will see in the following pages, different disciplines have different expectations about how writing within the discipline is organized, but all academic disciplines share these general expectations:

ACADEMIC WRITING IS ABOUT BUILDING KNOWLEDGE.

Academic audiences expect that you approach writing seriously because through writing you add to our understandings of the world and each other. This means that you have to take existing arguments seriously, research and gather evidence methodically and honestly, and make only the arguments that you can support with evidence.

ACADEMIC WRITING USES LOGICAL DEVELOPMENT OF IDEAS AND TRIES TO BE OBJECTIVE AND UNBIASED.

Logic is about ideas that relate to each other because of their structure or form—as thesis statements do, and as papers that are organized around thesis statements do.

→ See pages 96–97 for an introduction to thesis statements.

→ See pages 152–155 on using a thesis statement to organize a paper.

The point of view of academic writing is rarely personal, rarely focused on the writer. Instead, the emphasis is on the argument being made and on ideas that benefit as many people as possible.

ACADEMIC WRITING LOOKS SERIOUS.

→ See pages 260–261, 330–341, and 396–409 for help with academic formatting.

ACADEMIC WRITING GETS TO AND STAYS ON THE POINT.

An introduction moves quickly to stating what the paper is about. The writer ought to be able to explain how each and every sentence helps move a reader to the conclusion. There shouldn't be digressions or stories.

→ See pages 234–235 on writing introductions to academic papers.

→ See pages 244-245 and 252-259 on being explicit in your writing.

ACADEMIC WRITING IS EXPLICIT.

Academic writers say directly what their writing is about. In fiction and creative nonfiction, writers often use figurative language to pull readers in and suggest an overall point without ever stating the point; academic writing doesn't do this.

Academic writers also give full definitions of the terms of their arguments because they understand that many readers have differing understandings of terms.

→ See pages 244-245 and 252-259 for more on the characteristics of explicit writing.

ACADEMIC WRITING ALWAYS HAS AN ELEMENT OF DOUBT.

Academic writers accept that there are very few thoughts and ideas that apply to everyone, everywhere, at all times. Instead, academic writers consider a range of reasons and opinions.

To this end, academic writers often use phrases like *These facts suggest ...* or *Given the available evidence, it would seem that ....*

ACADEMIC WRITING IS NOT CONVERSATIONAL.

Academic writers strive for a thoughtful tone of voice, and rarely tell jokes or use emotional language or colloquialisms (such as *no-brainer* or *oh, snap!*). In some disciplines, writers will use **I** and will use their own experiences as evidence or examples; reading examples of writing in a discipline will help you learn the particulars of the discipline. (For help with writing assignments in classes in disciplines that are new to you, ask your teacher.)

→ See page 464 for more on creating a serious tone.

Academic writing usually uses longer words and sentences, more vocabulary, and more complex grammar than spoken language. Some of the more complex grammatical forms that academic writing uses are:

→ dependent clauses, described on page 469.

→ complex, compound, and complex-compound sentences, described on pages 517–525.

ACADEMIC WRITERS ARE RESPONSIBLE FOR THEIR ARGUMENTS AND TO OTHER WRITERS.

Academic writers can't just say anything; instead, they must take responsiblity for any claims they make by giving supporting evidence and by helping readers check that evidence. In addition, they are responsible for showing when the evidence they offer comes from the work or words of others: Academic writers give careful and full acknowledgment of any use of the ideas of others.

→ Part 8 of this book is all about using the words and work of others; see pages 289–448.

WRITING IN THE HUMANITIES

Writing in the humanities can be creative, theoretic, or analytic. We focus on analytic writing, for you will be asked to produce such writing in literature, film, rhetoric, modern languages, art, philosophy, history, and gender studies classes.

When you write analytically, you focus on a text like a short story or film or on a topic as we described in Part 2. Whether you analyze a text or a topic, you analyze to understand **how** and **why** values and decisions come to be and their effects.

ANALYZING TEXTS

When you analyze a text, you can focus on one text, describing its parts and arguing how the parts create an overall effect. You might show how a poem's line lengths and soft vowel sounds evoke a reader's reflections.

You can also analyze a text by comparing it with other texts or by explaining how it (and perhaps other similar texts) embodies cultural values, events, and structures. You might compare contemporary graphic novels and short stories, to show how both use quick, pictorial description and argue that this echoes the timing of fast food or video edits.

ANALYZING TOPICS

When you analyze a topic, you do the work we described in Parts 2 and 3 of this book. You look to texts—books, journals, films, interviews—to help you learn about the topic and, using what you have learned from those other texts as evidence, you develop an argument focused on some aspect of the values, ideas, or effects of the topic.

ORGANIZING ANALYTIC PAPERS

1 A TITLE. Examples: "Counterfeit Motion: The Animated Films of Eadweard Muybridge" or "'To Protect and Serve': African American Female Literacies"

2 AN INTRODUCTION. In humanities papers, an introduction can begin with a relevant quotation or example to pique interest, but the introduction's purpose is to draw readers' attention to the question or problem being discussed and to make clear why it should matter to them.

THESIS: The main argument is usually explicitly stated in the introduction and is probably also repeated in the conclusion. Writers rarely leave readers to infer the argument. Subsequent ideas and information are related to the thesis; nothing is put into the text that doesn't support or further the thesis.

3 BODY. This contains the writer's analysis of the text or topic. Evidence supports the analysis: In the analysis of a text, the evidence is drawn from the text itself, through quotation; in the analysis of topics, evidence comes from a range of sources.

→ See pages 98–107 on the kinds of evidence used in humanities writing.

ARRANGEMENT OF IDEAS: Writers state the main argument in the beginning of the paper and then provide evidence for it; they do not lead the reader to the main argument.

→ Pages 96–97 and 152-155 explain some aspects of the logic used in academic writing.

Each paragraph usually picks up on and develops a point from the preceding paragraph, moving readers forward with little unnecessary repetition.

Writers consolidate or group issues that are related to make their writing less repetitive. They also signal the progression of their ideas using headings, transition sentences, and connecting words.

→ Pages 174-175 and 236-237 discuss transition sentences and connecting words.

EVIDENCE IN SUPPORT OF THE ARGUMENT. Evidence is given to support the main argument. Different disciplines will value different types of support and will use it in specific ways; but, in general, academic writers tend to avoid using only stories or examples to support a thesis.

→ See pages 98–107 for the types of evidence used in academic and technical writing.

→ See pages 150–151 to see the kinds of evidence valued in different disciplines.

The body of the writing is composed almost exclusively of evidence. Statistics, examples, and facts support any generalizations used in the argument.

4 A CONCLUSION. The conclusion summarizes the paper's argument while offering no new information.

5 WORKS CITED LIST. At the end of the paper, list any works by other writers that are cited in the paper. (→ See pages 352–394 to learn MLA style, most often used in the humanities.)

In addition, if the writer's purpose and the context of the writing make it appropriate, writing in the humanities can be expressive: Writers can use **I**, draw on their own personal experiences or those of others, and use narratives as evidence. Check with your teacher if you are considering doing any of this for a class assignment.

WRITING IN THE SCIENCES

Research reports by scientists and engineers usually follow a specific arrangement of parts and a specific style of writing. The arrangement directs readers' attention to how an experiment was performed; readers can then judge the results and perhaps replicate the experiment.

The arrangement that scientists and engineers have developed to support communications about experiments asks that any report have, in order:

1 **A title,** which describes the experiment. One example: *The Physiological Effects of Pallidal Deep Brain Stimulation in Dystonia.*

2 **An abstract,** which is a short and concise overview of the paper; abstracts allow readers to see quickly if a paper is relevant to their work.

3 **An introduction.** This states why the research was done, what was being tested, and the predicted results—the hypothesis. There might also be a review of earlier relevant research here.

4 **Methods.** Researchers describe the procedures they undertook to perform their experiments, including the materials and equipment used.

5 **Results.** Researchers describe what they learned from the experiment.

6 **Discussion.** Here, the researchers discuss their understanding of the results. Did the results support the hypothesis? Why—or why not?

7 **A conclusion.** In this section, the researchers describe possible implications of their experiment as well as possible further research.

8 **References list.** Any works by other researchers that are cited in the report—or any reports written at an earlier time by the authors—are listed at the end of the paper. (→ See pages 439–443 to learn CSE style, which is most often used in the sciences.)

In a scientific report, all the above sections are separated and are labeled by the names listed above.

In addition, scientific writing usually has the following features:

- Because experiments are supposed to be repeatable anywhere by anyone, the experiment is emphasized, not the experimenter—and so scientific writers rarely use the first person *I* or **we** in writing; instead, they often use passive voice.

  → See pages 238-239 and 465.

- Because scientific and engineering evidence is often quantifiable, writers use charts, graphs, and tables as evidence. Photographs of objects used in experiments are also used as evidence.

- Because science and engineering research is most often carried out in labs where many people work, or across labs, research reports often have multiple authors.

TIP: CLASS ASSIGNMENTS

If you are asked to write a report in a science or social sciences class, your teacher will probably expect you to include at least several of the parts described on these pages. If the organization or features are not described in the assignment, ask.

WRITING IN THE SOCIAL SCIENCES

As the term **social sciences** suggests, the disciplines that come under this name apply scientific methods to studying people as social groups and as individuals within social groups. The social sciences include anthropology, economics, education, geography, linguistics, political science, psychology, sociology, and speech communication. (At some schools, history and gender studies might be listed as social sciences, if those areas use primarily scientific approaches to support their research.)

In writing papers for the social sciences, the arrangements that have developed over time follow the overall pattern of science writing as on the opposite page, but within the steps are some differences:

1 **A title,** which describes the study being reported in the paper. One example: *What Determines Cartel Success?*

2 **An abstract** of 100–200 words that summarize the purpose of the study, its methods, and its results.

3 **An introduction.** This defines the problem that was studied, reviews previous writing on the problem, notes the gaps in the previous writing that the current study will address, and gives an overview of the methods used. Writers also tell readers why the research being described matters.

4 **Methods.** Evidence used in the social sciences is usually observational, because social scientists are making and testing claims about human behavior. The sorts of methods for gathering this evidence are surveys and questionnaires, observations, interviews, and fieldwork. (➔ See page 104.) In the methods section of the paper, the writer describes which of these methods was used, and the details of how the method was carried out (how many people were interviewed or surveyed, for example, and what questions were asked).

5 **Results,** a description of what can be learned from the research.

6 **Discussion.** The researchers argue how the results of the study do (or do not) help with the problem described in the introduction.

7 **A conclusion,** which summarizes the problem, the research carried out, and what was learned.

8 **References list.** Any works by other researchers that are cited in the writing are listed at the end of the paper.

If the social sciences paper is longer than about five pages, the above sections are labeled by the names listed.

Because the social sciences seek as much objectivity as possible, further features of social science writing echo what we have described for science writing:

• Use of passive voice.

• Use of charts, graphs, tables, and photographs as evidence.

• Multiple authors.

APA STYLE

The American Psychological Society (APA) has established the publishing and citation conventions most used in the social sciences.

➔ See pages 396-438 to see a sample paper in APA style and to learn APA citation conventions.

USING A THESIS STATEMENT TO ORGANIZE AN ACADEMIC PAPER

You know that a paper needs an introduction, a body, and a conclusion, but what goes into those sections—and why?

If a reader cannot figure out why one paragraph or section follows another in a piece of writing, the reader will be confused—and the writing will lose its force.

But **the reader** won't be able to figure out why one paragraph or section follows another if **the writer** hasn't figured it out. Writers must be able to say why each paragraph is where it is in a composition, why one paragraph comes before or follows another. To do this, writers need a conceptual framework.

A conceptual framework (which we introduced on page 144) is like a skeleton: It is a bare-bones idea about organization, a sense of what generally needs to come first, second, and third in a piece of writing.

Having a thesis statement for a piece of writing helps writers develop a conceptual framework. A thesis statement can show the major steps a writer needs to take and in what order; a statement of purpose helps the writer begin to flesh out those steps.

→ On pages 154–155, see how one writer uses a thesis statement to develop an organization for her paper.

DK Online Manual

online

DK Hand

Explore these topics online:

Thesis statements

www.mycomplab.com

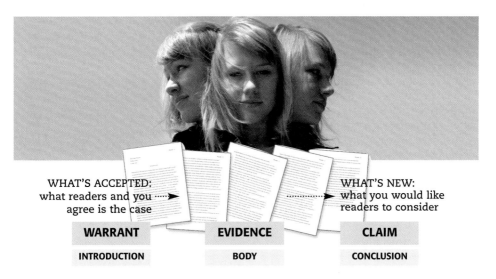

WHAT'S ACCEPTED: what readers and you agree is the case ·····➤ ············➤ WHAT'S NEW: what you would like readers to consider

| WARRANT | EVIDENCE | CLAIM |
| INTRODUCTION | BODY | CONCLUSION |

THESIS STATEMENTS, PERSUASION, AND ORGANIZING A PAPER

Those who developed the rhetorical method in ancient Greece noted that speeches were more likely to be persuasive when speakers started by discussing something about which they and the audience agreed: When speakers start by being in agreement with their audiences, audiences feel more generous toward the speakers and so are more likely to listen generously.

Because persuasive (or argumentative) research writing is about moving audiences to consider a different position than they may otherwise have held, those observations about persuasion led to the pattern diagrammed above for organizing persuasive compositions:

1 INTRODUCTION: Use your warrant
Start by dicussing something around which you and your audience hold the same values or opinions.

2 BODY: Give your best evidence
Offer your evidence for a new perspective on what you hold in common with the audience.

3 CONCLUSION: Make your claim explicit
Make your claim: Tie together for your audience how what they already accepted (the warrant), when seen through the lens of your evidence, points to the conclusion of your claim. (Note that your conclusion is the concluding part of your paper; this could be the last paragraph, but in a five-page paper is more likely the last two or three paragraphs; in a seven-page paper, this could be the whole last page.)

AN EXAMPLE OF A THESIS STATEMENT ORGANIZING AN ACADEMIC PAPER

On pages 152–153 we showed how you can use a thesis statement as a conceptual framework for a paper: The warrant, claim, and evidence that make up a thesis statement can be used to guide what you write in your introduction, body, and concluding paragraphs.

We have been following one writer, as she develops a paper (→ See pages 78-79 and 138-139; to see how the paper develops from here, see pages 202-203, 206-217, and 330-341.). On these pages, we show how she uses her thesis statement to organize the paper she is about to write.

The thesis statement

Here is Riley's thesis statement (→ See pages 138–139.)

Women who receive microcredit without discussion support groups and classes in economics won't know how to change the community conditions that encourage poverty; therefore, microcredit should only be offered with such support.

TIP: NOT LOGIC ALONE

A thesis statement can help you considerably in making some of the big choices about organizing a paper. But, because persuasion does not happen based on logic alone, you still need to make other very important choices in your writing. Writing a statement of purpose helps you make these other choices about word choice, transitions, paragraph length, and so on.

→ See pages 200–203 for help with developing a statement of purpose.

The warrant

Based on her thesis statement, Riley's warrant—what she believes her audience already believes—goes something like this:

> Microcredit should help change the community conditions that encourage poverty.

(Note that this warrant implies that Riley's readers will readily accept that ending poverty is good.)

A structure for a paper

Following what we've written on pages 152–153, Riley draws up the following conceptual framework, the large-scale organization for her paper:

1 I will start by discussing how most people believe that microcredit should end poverty (since my warrant shows that I think most people will believe this).

2 I will spend the largest part of my writing presenting evidence showing that, when microcredit is offered to women without discussion support groups and economics classes, microcredit does not end poverty.

3 I can conclude by stating that given my evidence, microcredit should be offered only with discussion support groups and economics classes (which is my claim).

→ See pages 200–203 to learn how Riley blended this conceptual framework with a statement of purpose, to compose a first draft.

CONCEPTUAL FRAMEWORKS AND GENRES

WORKPLACE GENRES

THE VALUES OF WORKPLACE GENRES

When you write for workplace audiences, keep the following five considerations in mind:

THE PLACES IN WHICH WE WORK DEVELOP THEIR OWN CULTURES.

Communities develop shared habits and expectations, and workplaces are no exception. Learning to write well professionally means learning the habits and expectations of a workplace: Is the workplace formal or informal, particularly focused on getting things done quickly or on group discussions aimed at consensus?

WRITING IN WORKPLACES NEEDS TO FIT THE CULTURE OF THE WORKPLACE.

All our earlier advice about audiences applies to workplace writing, but writing in workplaces is tied to how people in the organization solve problems, attend meetings, organize projects, manage tasks, evaluate documents and performance, use computer technologies, give presentations, run training sessions, and so on.

Connected to these activities is a range of specialized forms of communication with which you need to become familiar; each has general characteristics that you can recognize across various places of work and that also become adapted to specific workplaces. For example, workplace audiences all know the general form of a memo, but they also know the specific ways memos are written—and read—in their particular workplace.

BECAUSE WORKPLACES ARE ABOUT GETTING WORK DONE, PEOPLE AT WORK EXPECT WRITING TO HAVE A SINGLE PURPOSE AND BE EFFICIENT AND TO THE POINT.

For the sake of efficiency, workplace writers most often produce texts focused on to achieve a single, particular purpose—and so the purpose is usually stated directly and clearly, usually in the beginning of the text. Workplace texts are usually short, with a formal but courteous tone.

This doesn't mean the writing is mechanical—it still needs to address its human audiences—but it needs to be very focused.

→ See pages 244–245 for suggestions on how to shape writing that is focused, quick, and to the point.

OFTEN IN WORKPLACES YOU WILL BE WRITING FOR TWO (OR MORE) AUDIENCES.

In workplaces, where you may be writing a brochure or an instruction set to be read by potential consumers, it can be useful to keep in mind that you often have two audiences, a foreground audience and a background audience. The foreground readers are the customers or clients; the background audience is those in the business or organization who will be looking at what you produce and making comments or suggestions along the way.

LARGER WORKPLACES CAN HAVE STYLE GUIDES YOU NEED TO FOLLOW WHEN YOU ARE WRITING FOR CLIENTS OR CUSTOMERS.

Companies have such style guides to be sure all the documents they produce are consistent and represent the company professionally. Style guides can include guidelines for using the company's logo, specific phrases to use in writing (for example, a hardware company could specify that writers tell customers to *click a button* rather than to *click on a button*), and formats for different kinds of documents. If you are not given a style guide, ask if one exists.

TIP: GENRES FOR INTERNATIONAL WORKPLACES

The conventions of workplace genres are very much related to national culture. If you land a job with a company that has international offices, you may receive training in the forms of communication the company expects; if not, ask co-workers about the expected ways communication happens in the company.

If your company is in the United States but you must communicate with people in other countries, ask if the company will pay for you to take a workshop in cross-cultural communications or will hire a consultant who knows about communication expectations in the other countries.

MEMOS

Workplace memos can be delivered on paper or by e-mail. Used for brief communications—usually one page only—memos make announcements, ask questions, set up meetings, make requests, or confirm agreements.

Readers have come to expect memos to have the following parts:

- A heading
- An introduction
- A body
- A closing

A heading

At the top, memos have, on separate lines:
- the date
- the recipient's name (and title if appropriate)
- your name (and title if appropriate); sometimes writers initial their names
- a subject line

An introduction

Describe—quickly—your main purpose in writing the memo.

A body

Give the background information that supports or explains your purpose. If this information breaks into two or more parts, as in this example, consider using bold headings to make these parts easier to see.

A closing

Provide a one- or two-sentence summary, with contact information (if necessary). (Unlike letters, memos do not end with a signature.)

---

4 October 2006

To: STC Arts Project Teams
From: Jason Dryja
Re: New Print Project Protocol

stcarts enterprise

{design}
<writing>
[media]

I want to take this opportunity to congratulate you on three consecutive successful projects. You and your project team members have met all deadlines and I think we have impressed our clients.

We learned a good lesson along the way—that we need to develop additional project protocols: an in-house preflight checklist and a print check.

Preflight Checklist
When we are preparing to deliver a client's project files for printing, we need to ensure that we have labeled and included all necessary files and documentation for the printer. Each project will have its own preflight checklist depending on the printer that the client is using and the nature of the project. Every print project, however, will have basic checklist items:

- RGB conversion to CMYK
- Page layout files converted to EPS
- Trims
- Bleeds
- Linked art files
- Paper mock-up for printer review

Print Check
When using a local printer, we should either accompany the client or deliver preliminary files ourselves to ensure that the printer has all the necessary information and files that she needs to complete the print job successfully.

These new print-project protocols will become part of our new-member orientation materials, but I would like to implement them immediately, including current projects. If you have any comments, questions, or concerns about how we might implement these protocols, please feel free to contact me.

| 112 Walker. MTU. 1400 Townsend. Houghton MI. | 906.487.1197 |
| www.stcarts.org. | info@stcarts.org |

Dear Ms. Fisher:

I wanted to double-check that you are set for our class to visit the Keweenaw National Historic Park Library on Thursday, the 5th. We're planning on arriving around 4, and staying for about an hour; there will be 17 of us.

Thanks again for encouraging this visit: the people in class look forward to it.

Sincerely,
Anne Frances Wysocki
Michigan Technological University

E-MAIL (ONLINE MEMOS)

When you write e-mails within workplace settings, or to people in workplaces, follow the same considerations as for memos, but also keep the following in mind to develop professional messages:

- **Have a neutral-sounding e-mail address.** squirrlygrrrl@hotmail.com is fine for friends—but for formal communications, consider getting an e-mail account that uses your initials and last name. If your company or school gives you an e-mail address, use that for communicating with professors, staff, employers, and colleagues.

- **Write a subject that is descriptive but short and in a professional tone.** "Wanna meet?" is descriptive and short—but sounds like it's party time. For formal situations, "Budget meeting Tuesday 3pm?" is more appropriate.

- **Start with a salutation.** Until you have a relaxed relationship with others, the expected way for showing respect is to start a message with a formal salutation such as "Dear Professor:" or "Dear Dr. Murthy:" or "Dear Mo Folk:" (if you do not know someone's gender or title, write out the person's first and last names). Notice also that, in workplaces, the expected

punctuation following the salutation is a colon. When others end messages to you with their first names, then you can write to them using their first names. Otherwise, in any follow-up messages, address others the way they signed their e-mails.

- **State your purpose following the salutation.** Put two returns after the salutation, and then state your purpose.

- **Write the e-mail in short paragraphs separated by two returns.** Readers can rarely see whole messages at once, and e-mail software is rarely designed to support easy reading. Others can read more easily if they can see your paragraphs—so arrange your paragraphs to be short and easy to discern visually.

- **Avoid smiley faces.** They are appropriate only in informal e-mail.

- **Sign your message.** Even though your name is in the header, it is still considered polite to type your full name at the message end—until you know the person to whom you are writing well.

- **Keep in mind how easy it is for others to forward your messages.** If you do not want to risk the world knowing something, do not put it in an e-mail.

RESUMÉS

Resumés summarize the experiences and education that make you appropriate for a new job. Because a resumé (and cover letter; → see pages 162–163) is often how a potential employer first encounters an employee, it deserves time and attention. And because employers often receive hundreds of resumés, they look at them quickly. Therefore, a resumé needs to be:

- short, to the point, and easy to read.
- focused on the position for which it is being sent.
- accurate.

THE FORMAT OF A RESUMÉ

Name

Center your name at the top. Do not use nicknames. Bold your name, and put it in a slightly larger size (14 or 16 points).

Contact information

Be sure your address will be current for several months; if you are still in school or planning to move, put a permanent address. Most companies will contact you by phone or e-mail, so include both. Be sure whoever answers your phone knows to answer professionally; have a professional answering machine or voice mail message. Your e-mail address should be your name or initials; hotdude@hotmail.com does not suggest a reliable, focused employee. If it is appropriate to the position, include a Web or blog address—as long as your Home page or blog is professional in both presentation and content.

Shawnelle Ponder
sponder@mtu.edu

Address until 5/15/09
29401 Woodmar Drive Apt. Q
Huffton, Michigan 49938
(096) 270-8187

Permanent Address
4577 Pertin Drive
Detroit, MI 48221
(313) 688-1239

OBJECTIVE
To acquire an internship designing and developing educational materials in biological sciences/health

EDUCATION
Michigan Technological University, Houghton, Michigan
Bachelor of Science in Scientific and Technical Communication
Expected graduation date: April, 2012
Cumulative G.P.A. 3.75/4.00

EMPLOYMENT
Design Assistsant, MTU First-Year Programs, Houghton, MI (Summers 2009, 2010)
- Developed overall theme for and designed print materials (1- and 4-color) for Student Orientation
- Managed scheduling and production of print materials
- Oversaw development of related online materials
Communications Assistant, MTU Plant Biotechnology Research Center, Houghton, MI (2009-present)
- Performed educational outreach for the Center
- Designed, developed, and maintained educational component of Research Center website based on my research; Website visits increased by 125%

OTHER RELEVANT EXPERIENCE
Writing Coach, MTU Writing Center, Houghton, MI (Fall 2010-Present)
- Met with individual students to help develop their writing
- Participated in on-going research projects and presentations on student wrriting

RELEVANT COURSEWORK
Technical Writing, Technical Editing, Information Design, Interactivity Design, Usability, Graphic Design
Biology, Chemistry, Anatomy, Journalism, Creative Writing

COMPUTER SKILLS
Operating Systems: Windows, Macintosh, Linux
Language: C++, Java, HTML, CSS
Software: InDesign, Photoshop, Flash, Dreamweaver, Acrobat Professional, Microsoft Professional Suite

HONORS
Dean's List (2006, 2007, 2008)
Susan Lewis Anthony Memorial Award (2007)
University Student Award (2006)

EXTRACURRICULAR ACTIVITIES
Scientific and Technical Communication,student association, president (2010-2011)
Black Student Assocaition (BSA) (2009-present)
BSA Big Brother/Big Sister Mentoring Program (2009-present)
ExSEL Peer Mentoring Program (2009-Present)

REFERENCES
Available upon request

Objective

Fit this on one line only. If you are responding to an ad, use the job title as part of the objective.

Education

Don't include high school unless there is something about your high school education that is relevant to the position.

Employment

Put your most recent employment first. Start an entry with your title, followed by the place of employment and the length of time you held the position.

List your main accomplishments and responsibilities underneath the job title. Use action verbs in the past tense for past positions; use present tense for ongoing positions. If you have an accomplishment an employer will value, include it (such as *Website visits increased by 125%* under *Employment*).

Other relevant experience

List here—in the same format as for employment—experiences for which you received no pay but from which you gained abilities relevant to the position for which you are applying. You can include hobbies—if they are relevant.

Relevant coursework

List only those classes that are directly applicable for the position.

Computer skills

List these if the position requires computer skills.

Honors

List any awards, in the order in which you received them.

Extracurricular activities

If you belong to any clubs or societies relevant to the position, list them.

References

It is fine to say these are *Available upon request*—but do check with your references that they don't mind being contacted.

COMPOSING A RESUMÉ

- For entry-level positions, a resumé should be one page so that employers can scan it quickly.

- Use white or cream paper. Use good-quality paper, but don't use papers such as parchment or vellum unless they are appropriate for the position (graphic designer, for example).

- Use black ink.

- Use a typeface such as Times or Helvetica. (Times takes up less space and so fits more information on a page.)

- Use 11- or 12-point type.

- Use headings, bullets, and indents so that readers can see the parts quickly.

  → See page 261 on using headings.

- Look at your first draft; for each line in the body of the resumé, ask yourself, *Does this help an employer see my suitability for this position?* If the answer is no, remove or replace the information.

- If possible, get feedback from someone who works in or supervises the sort of position for which you are applying: Does this person find your resumé readable, appropriately formatted, and strong?

- Always have someone else proofread it for you. Because employers receive so many resumés, they are looking for reasons to exclude; don't give them such a simple one as a typo.

- Do not lie or pad your experiences.

COVER LETTERS

Unless a job advertisement requests only a resumé, always send a cover letter with your resumé. A resumé lists your accomplishments; in a cover letter you address an employer directly, to describe why you are a fit for the job.

GENERAL FEATURES

- Because employers receive many job letters and are always pressed for time, keep a cover letter to one page.

- Research the company by reading their website carefully or talking with people who work there; you need this knowledge for an effective letter.

- Put the cover letter on the same kind of paper as your resumé, and send originals, not copies.

- When you send a cover letter and resumé, put the cover letter on top. You can fold the two together to go into a regular-size envelope, or you can send them in a large envelope so that they remain uncreased.

- Make it perfect. Many employers will use even one typo as a reason for discarding a letter and resumé.

SPECIFIC FEATURES

Date

Name and address of recipient

A job listing should give you a name and address. If you are writing to inquire if a company has any job openings, you'll have to do some research: Call the company and ask a receptionist for the name of the person who does the hiring in the department where you would work; you can also often find this information online.

Salutation

Use *Dear* and the title of the person being addressed; if there is no title, use *Ms.* or *Mr.* Be sure to spell the name accurately.

Introduction

There are two kinds of cover letters:

- Those written in response to job advertisements.

- Those expressing interest in a company when you don't know if there is an opening.

Each kind of cover letter requires a different introduction.

For the first kind, include the name of the job—exactly as it is listed in the job ad—and any job number.

For the second kind, explain why you are writing to the particular company and how you learned about them, and describe the position you desire. If someone has recommended you to the company, say so.

March 1, 2008

Dr. Louisa Bramant
Community Education Director
Toivola Health Services
500 Campus Drive
Toivola, MI 49956

Dear Dr. Bramant:

A professor at my college whom you know, Dr. Richard Otherly, came to me to suggest that I write to you. He heard that I am looking for an internship in health education and said he thought I would be a perfect fit for your organization because of my knowledge and background. He did not know if you have any internship openings starting in early June (which is when I will be available for three to six months), but I am writing in hopes that you will keep me in mind should you have any openings.

From looking at your website, I see that your hospital provides a wide range of materials for helping people learn healthy habits or manage ongoing health issues. If you look at my resumé, which I've attached, you'll see that I have experience in both the technical and the scientific aspects of designing online educational materials for general audiences. In my position working at the Plant Biotechnology Research Center, my background education in biology and chemistry helped me communicate with the scientists whose work I translated into educational materials, and my technical knowledge and education in technical communication allowed me to suggest strategies for developing creative and effective learning materials. (When I redesigned the Center's educational website, visits to the website increased by 125%.) I know how to make interactive animations that help people see and so understand how plants uptake water, and I can imagine how useful an interactive animation about how insulin works (for example) would be on your diabetes education webpages. I also have experience developing print materials, should that be of use to you.

What my resumé doesn't show is that I am a solid and cheerful team player who gets things done on time. All my previous employers have commented on my responsibility and energy. I would be excited to be part of the good educational efforts your hospital is making, and hope that my qualifications appeal to you.

I would appreciate the opportunity to discuss an intership with you. I will contact you within the next ten days to see if you might have an opening and to see if you need any other information from me such as an application form, recommendations, or transcripts. Thank you for your time and consideration.

Sincerely,

Shawnelle Ponder

Shawnelle Ponder
29401 Woodmar Drive Apt. Q
Huffton, Michigan 49938
(096) 270-8187
sponder@mtu.udu

Body

Use your research in the company to show how your abilities fit the company's goals and values. Don't just repeat what's listed in your resumé but flesh it out: Give concrete examples, describe achievements, and help the potential employer see how you are suitable; be positive and enthusiastic.

Sum up

Let the person know that you will be contacting the company to request an interview.

Close

Use *Sincerely* or *Cordially*.

Signature and contact information

Leave four lines after the closing for your signature, and sign in blue or black ink. Type your name and full contact information, including your phone number and e-mail address.

CONCEPTUAL FRAMEWORKS AND GENRES
POPULAR GENRES

Popular genres does not mean genres everyone likes; instead, popular genres are those that can be produced **by** almost anyone or that are produced **for** broad general audiences—or both.

We give examples of four quite different popular genres here. As you look at the four, consider how the writers try to achieve their purposes by meeting audience expectations: How do they organize the parts of their texts to engage readers and make happen what they desire?

TIP: GOING ONLINE

The first three of the genres we present here can be produced in print or online. Here are some differences for composers to consider when using one or the other medium:

- Paragraphs and sentences are usually shorter online than in print. Generally, readers gain a stronger sense of a text's organization when they can see the text's divisions; because screen sizes are usually smaller than paper, you can help readers see a text's organization online by using smaller paragraphs.

- For the same reasons, separating paragraphs online by two returns rather than with an indent helps readers read more easily.

- Because it requires more time and effort, a letter printed on paper and sent through the mail—rather than an e-mail—will almost always show that the writer is more serious. Such letters often therefore seem more authoritative and worthy of respect.

In the last five and a half weeks, five schools in the United States and Canada have suffered the invasion of gunmen: Aug. 24, Essex, Vt.; Sept. 13, Montreal; Sept. 27, Bailey, Colo.; Sept. 29, Cazenovia, Wis. And now, Oct. 2, Nickel Mines, Pa.

In four of these five incidents, the gunman targeted girls and women.

At what point do a country and its news media note this lethally combustible cocktail of gender and guns?

Men and boys with guns are stalking and hunting women and girls in schools repeatedly. Until we see "the gun problem" as equally a problem of violence against women, nothing will change, and I fear that the mourning and shock will continue.

Daniel Moshenberg
Washington, Oct. 3, 2006
The writer is director of the Women's Studies Program at George Washington University.

LETTERS TO THE EDITOR

After any event—horrible events like the shootings referenced in the letter above but also happier events like fund-raising picnics for local fire departments—people want to be able to share their opinions with others. They want to join in the considerations about how we should think about what happened and how we should respond.

Letters to the editor are one existing genre of writing that allows this to happen. People who send letters to the editor reach the readers of the periodical to which the letters were sent, and so extend the reach of their ideas. These letters may seem small, but if they spark responses in readers, then their ideas start to ripple out and affect others.

Whether letters to the editor are published in print or online, audiences have similar expectations about them.

Letters to the editor are

- Short and to the point.
- Focused on one topic.
- About an issue of interest to the periodical's readers. In magazines, letters to the editor are always in response to earlier published articles; in local newspapers, they can be about current or local events.
- Begun with a statement of the issue before going on to the writer's position.
- Documents in which ethos is crucial. Unlike the example letter above, rarely in a letter to the editor are a writer's credentials given. Writers have to demonstrate why they should be heard, through giving their own credentials but also through choosing a fitting tone of voice, staying focused, and using examples and evidence.

LETTERS OF COMPLAINT

When they reach high frustration with a product or service, many people find that the following approaches bring results:

- Finding the name of the highest-level person responsible for the product or service, and writing directly to that person. (Sometimes you can find the name online; you can also call a customer service number and ask.)

- Keeping the letter short so that a busy person can read it quickly.

- Keeping it friendly and unemotional: The point is to get results with the help of someone who is on your side.

- Listing the facts: Describe the problem concisely but concretely and include any relevant dates, serial numbers, or order numbers.

- Describing a concrete—and fair—action the company can take: Make it easy for the recipient to know what to do.

- Stating a reasonable time—four to eight weeks—for hearing back.

- Including your full contact information.

Daryl Flack
Director, Customer Service
ME Consumer Appliances
7645 Industrial Way
Houston, TX 77013

February 27, 2008

Dear Mr. Flack:

On January 20, 2007, I paid $709 for an ME SpaceFit Microwave (model HEM1146) at Shrumm's Appliance Center in DeQueen, Arkansas. I have enclosed a copy of my receipt.

In the last month the paint on the inside top of the microwave started blistering, peeling, and falling into the food being microwaved.

I called the customer service numbers listed in the manual and was told that because the microwave is now out of warranty ME will only give me $75 toward the purchase of a new microwave—or will charge me $60 for a technician to come look at the problem.

I've used ME products for many years and have always praised them to others and am surprised that such an expensive product should become unusable after only 13 months. I hope you will do what you can to fix this.

To resolve this problem, I would appreciate it if you would replace this microwave at no cost to me.

I look forward to your reply and a resolution to my problem, and will wait until April 21 before seeking help from a consumer protection agency or the Better Business Bureau. Please contact me at the address or phone number below.

Sincerely,

Diana Franks

Diana Franks
357 Wasa Rd.
DeQueen, AR 71832
555-555-1234

MAGAZINE ARTICLES

Mass-market magazines focus on an area of reader interest: recent news events, knitting, NASCAR, kittens, do-it-yourself projects, or hip-hop music. The article to the right illustrates many of the considerations to which magazine article writers attend:

- Articles inform about one topic.

- Articles have succinct and often catchy titles.

- The opening is often catchy, to draw in readers.

- In spite of a magazine's focus, writers cannot assume a specialized audience and so do not use specialized vocabulary; magazine publishers want to attract a wide audience.

    For example, the article to the right comes from *Onearth* magazine, a publication of the Natural Resources Defense Council. The writer assumes that the magazine's audience—who read the magazine because of their interest in environmental issues—think global warming is a problem and know that carbon dioxide is a major contributor to global warming. Beyond that, however, the writer makes no assumptions about reader knowledge.

- Instead of specialized vocabulary, writers use common terms: **ruminant bad breath** instead of **ruminant halitosis**.

- The language is less formal than academic writing, can be humorous, and can address audiences directly, as in the first two sentences of the example to the right.

- Paragraphs and sentences are shorter than in academic writing.

- Articles are frequently accompanied by photographs and pull-quotes to entice readers. (A pull-quote is a one- or two-sentence extract from the article; the extract can either summarize the article or be a compelling introduction.)

A Nasty Gas Attack

LET'S DISPOSE OF ONE misconception right away. Cows expel methane from the mouth, not from, ahem, the other end. The average dairy cow belches or exhales between 30 and 130 gallons of methane each day as its forestomachs break down a diet of grasses heavy in tough cellulose fibers. With some 1.3 billion cows worldwide, ruminant bad breath acounts for 80 million tons of methane each year—a gas that is 20 times more efffective at trapping heat in the atmosphere than carbon dioxide.

Those alarming numbers have prompted scientists to look for alternative bovine diets that might reduce these levels of methane. Researchers at the University of Wales claim that feed containing garlic could reduce methane by as much as 50 percent. They also suggest that cultivating grasses with high sugar levels, such as white clover and birdsfoot trefoil, would reduce methane production by improving cows' digestive processes.

Would a change of diet have a negative effect on the quality of the meat? On the contrary: Improving the efficiency of the cows' digestion would mean that the energy lost with each burp would be redirected toward the creation of protein, amino acids, and fat—all the signatures of a good steak.

—BEN CARMICHAEL

BLOGS AND OTHER SOCIAL NETWORKING WEBSITES

A blog is not a blog unless it is written in reverse chronological order with places for reader response. Users need technological know-how to change the provided content categories of a MySpace or Facebook profile page. Beyond those constraints of arrangement that are built into the software underpinning these sites, however, blogs and other social networking sites give composers lots of wiggle room in word, color, and illustration choices.

The most important choice a composer of a social networking site profile has to make, however, ties to the overall purpose of these sites: Social networking sites exist to connect people to each other. Because connecting with people almost always involves getting personal, the largest decision composers of such sites have to make is just how much to reveal about themselves, given the long and very very public life of information on the Web.

ARRANGING TO CONNECT

Strategies for composing a blog or profile page that brings lots of responses include:

- being an authority on the topic about which you write.

- providing useful and well-researched information on a topic of interest to others.

- writing entertainingly.

- divulging interesting or provocative personal information.

- being famous.

- writing to ask questions of your readers so that they will want to respond.

- engaging with readers in comments.

- adding comments to others' pages.

STEVENBERLINJOHNSON.COM

THE DEPARTMENT OF BLOGIOLOGY STRIKES AGAIN

We couldn't help ourselves -- it was so fun calculating America's bloggiest neighborhoods, we had to go on and do the math on America's bloggiest cities, which led to my very first role in creating a USA Today infographic.

My colleague John Geraci does an excellent job explaining the results on the outside.in blog.

Email this • Save to del.icio.us (1 save) • Digg This! • outside.in: geotag this post

August 21, 2007 in Outside.in | Permalink | Comments (0) | TrackBack (0)

LIVE SBJ

I'm doing a little long overdue maintenance on the blog and the first change you'll see in the sidebar here: a list of all my upcoming public appearances.

THE BASICS

I'm a father of three boys, husband of one wife, and author of five books. In early 2007 I went and foolishly got myself a day job running the hyperlocal community site, outside.in that I co-founded the year before. We

You do not, obviously, need to have all those strategies working for you, but some combination will help you gain many readers or friends.

PERSONAL ARRANGEMENTS

Once information is posted online, it is stored on a server and can be copied and pasted elsewhere—so even if you have second thoughts about what you've posted and try to erase it, it will still be out there. Do you want what you post today to be available to people you don't know? Do you want what you post today to be available to people five or ten years in the future?

PROFESSIONAL ARRANGEMENTS

One of the pages shown below belongs to a writer seeking a professional presentation to attract book buyers; the other is designed to be understood by those who know its maker.

For a professional-looking site, audiences generally expect:

- A muted color scheme.
  → See pages 262–263.

- Lots of white space.
  → See pages 186–187.

- Writing that carefully reaches out to readers.
  → See Part 6 of this book for help styling your writing to engage readers.

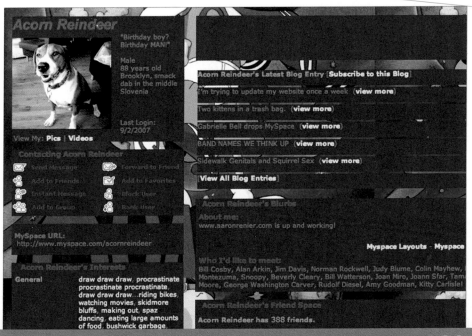

SHAPING PARAGRAPHS FOR AUDIENCE AND PURPOSE

In the preceding pages we've discussed the larger-scale organizational structures of different kinds of texts, and how and why to use them.

Now we discuss the next level of written organization, paragraphs.

PARAGRAPHS

Writing is not simply about conveying ideas to someone else. It also involves conveying the structure and relations of the ideas that have led writers to hold the beliefs, opinions, and values they do.

Paragraphs break reading—conceptually and visually—into units a reader can easily see. Because readers can see them, paragraphs help readers remember and so think about the structure and relations of the ideas in a text.

Readers' expectations about paragraphs have developed over several centuries. What we present on the next pages are current expectations about paragraphs in formal writing.

PURPOSES OF PARAGRAPHS

There are three main categories of paragraphs:

1 Introductory paragraphs, which orient readers to the general concerns of a paper.

2 Body paragraphs, where the main arguments of the writing are developed.

3 Concluding paragraphs, which summarize the paper's argument and add nothing new to the argument.

In the next pages, we focus on the body paragraphs. Such paragraphs can function to

- describe.
- define.
- narrate.
- give examples.
- compare.
- classify.
- use analogies.
- divide.

Paragraphs can also mix these functions.

In the coming pages, we give examples of and discuss some of these paragraph functions. Once you understand how paragraphs perform functions like these, you can shape paragraphs to function as you need for your own purposes.

→ Pages 232–235 address introductory and concluding paragraphs.

QUALITIES THAT READERS EXPECT IN PARAGRAPHS

UNITY

In the twenty-first century, readers expect a paragraph to contain sentences focused around only one idea or point.

COHERENCE

Readers expect the sentences of a paragraph to grow out of each other.

DEVELOPMENT

Readers expect paragraphs not to repeat the same idea over and over, but instead to add to their understanding of the idea being discussed, as it relates to the writing of which the paragraph is a part.

■ ■ ■

In the next pages we go over these qualities in order.

SHAPING PARAGRAPHS FOR AUDIENCE AND PURPOSE

UNIFIED AND COHERENT PARAGRAPHS

Whether you write for an academic journal or a music blog, readers these days expect paragraphs to be unified and coherent.

To be unified, each sentence of a paragraph is on the same topic.

To be coherent, each sentence of a paragraph will seem to a reader to follow directly from the sentence that preceded it. Writers use strategies like the following to achieve coherence:

- Repeating crucial words and phrases.

- Repeating crucial concepts by using synonyms for the concepts.

- Using pronouns to show that successive sentences refer to the same topic.

- Using parallel structures (➔ see pages 248–249).

- Using words that show relations and connections among sentences (➔ see pages 174–175).

- Having a consistent point of view.

- Using the same tense throughout.

When a paragraph is coherent, a reader should be able to draw connections between various parts of the paragraph, as the examples to the right show.

UNIFIED BUT INCOHERENT

It is possible to have paragraphs that are unified but not coherent:

Dolphins are highly intelligent mammals that live in the oceans. They are closely related to whales. Some people think they are gentle and cute. Dolphins are predators who can act violently. Dolphins can hear better than people. Some people think dolphins are a symbol of freedom and joy. The Dolphins are a football team in Miami.

The paragraph is unified because each sentence is on the topic of **dolphins**. The paragraph is incoherent because nothing else connects one sentence to the next. Instead, the paragraph offers random facts about dolphins—and Dolphins.

Another of the scorpion's exceptional features is the ability to glow under ultraviolet light, like a psychedelic poster.

The exoskeleton of the scorpion is made of a tough layer of tissue that feels like fingernail but is composed of another type of cuticle protein, chitin. This coat reflects the ultraviolet rays from moonlight and other light sources so brightly that even a black scorpion will be a fluorescent shade of green or pink. Fossilized scorpions from 300 million years ago still gleam brilliantly under ultraviolet light. The glow may have evolved to attract insects, which are drawn to ultraviolet light, or it may be an incidental byproduct of the chitin's chemical nature.

Whatever the reason, the unmistakable shine, visible from twenty feet away, makes it easy to spot scorpions at

UNITY

Every sentence in this paragraph is about the hard outer covering that is a scorpion's skeleton and, even more specifically, on how that covering responds to ultraviolet light.

COHERENCE

The writer keeps a scientfically descriptive tone in each sentence, and each sentence is in the present tense. Notice how the writer repeats one word, **chitin**, but uses synonyms to refer several times to the exoskeleton and its shiny nature.

■ ■ ■

...ground were the result of deep and personal individual reactions to a new environment.

The knottiest mystery of survival is how one unequipped, ill-prepared seventeen-year-old girl gets out alive and a dozen adults in similar circumstances, better equipped, do not. But the deeper I've gone into the study of survival, the more sense such outcomes make. Making fire, building shelter, finding food, signaling, navigation—none of that mattered to Juliane's survival. Although we cannot know what the others who survived the fall were thinking and deciding, it's possible that they knew they were supposed to stay put and await rescue. They were rule followers, and it killed them.

In the World Trade Center disaster, many people who were used to following the rules died because

UNITY

In this paragraph, the first sentence describes a **mystery**— and then every following sentence works to explain that mystery.

COHERENCE

In this paragraph, the writer has chosen a straightforward, emphatic tone throughout. The writer repeats **survival** often because that it is the paragraph's unifying idea. The writer refers to a young woman in two different ways. After a first reference to those who did not survive the airplane crash that the young woman did, the writer uses pronouns to refer to them.

LINKING WORDS THAT BUILD COHERENCE IN PARAGRAPHS

If you use words from the following list in a paragraph's sentences, you will help your readers understand why the sentences belong together. When you use the words below, you can repeat them to build parallel structures (➔ see pages 248–249) that also show how the sentences belong together. If you do use such repetition, read your paragraph aloud to be sure you have not built a boring, singsong rhythm (unless a boring, singsong rhythm supports your purpose).

To show that information in one sentence adds to information in a preceding sentence: *additionally, also, and, besides, equally important, furthermore, in addition, moreover, too*

To emphasize the information in a sentence: *indeed, in fact, of course*

To help readers understand that you are building a sequence of events or a description of a process: *again, also, and, and then, besides, finally, first...second...third, furthermore, last, moreover, next, still, too*

To build sentences to describe events that take place over time: *after a few days, after a while, afterward, as long as, as soon as, at that time, at the same time, before, during, earlier, eventually, finally, immediately, in the future, in the meantime, in the past, lately, later, meanwhile, next, now, simultaneously, since, soon, then, thereafter, today, until, when*

To help readers compare information in one sentence with that in another: *also, in the same manner, in the same way, likewise, once more, similarly*

To help readers see any important differences between your sentences: *although, but, despite, even though, however, in contrast, in spite of, instead, nevertheless, nonetheless, on the contrary, on the one hand...on the other hand..., otherwise, regardless, still, though, yet*

To indicate to readers that a sentence contains an example: *for example, for instance, indeed, in fact, of course, specifically, such as, to illustrate*

To help readers see cause and effect: *accordingly, as a result, because, consequently, for this purpose, hence, so, then, therefore, thus, to this end*

To make clear to readers the spatial relations among objects you are describing: *above, adjacent to, behind, below, beyond, closer to, elsewhere, far, farther on, here, in the background, near, nearby, opposite to, there, to the left, to the right*

To concede that your arguments are open to question: *although it is true that, granted that, I admit that, it may appear that, naturally, of course*

To show that sentences are summarizing or concluding: *as a result, as I have argued, as mentioned earlier, consequently, in any event, in conclusion, in other words, in short, on the whole, therefore, thus, to summarize*

USING THE LINKING WORDS AND PHRASES, REPETITION, AND PARALLELISM, TO BUILD COHERENCE

The paragraph below shows how each sentence connects to the next through repetition of words and phrases, as we noted on page 173—but we also show how coherence is additionally built through linking words and parallelism.

You can see that only a few linking words are used; too many linking words can fragment a paragraph, so, generally, writers use only a few but combine them with the other strategies we listed on page 173 to link sentences.

"war"

War is used in four out of the seven sentences of this paragraph, helping keep the paragraph unified around its topic of how the Civil War changed the U.S. without destroying it.

It is a remarkable fact about the United States that it fought a civil war without undergoing a change in its form of government. The Constitution was not abandoned during the American Civil War; elections were not suspended; there was no coup d'état. The war was fought to preserve the system of government that had been established at the nation's founding—to prove, in fact, that the system was worth preserving, that the idea of democracy had not failed. This is the meaning of the Gettysburg Address and of the great fighting cry of the north: "Union." And the system was preserved; the union did survive. But in almost every other respect, the United States became a different country. The war alone did not make America modern, but the war marks the birth of a modern America.

parallelism

This sentence has three clauses, each of which has the same structure; the clauses are linked with semicolons. This structure shows that the three ideas have equal weight.

"in fact"

In fact precedes an explanation here and emphasizes the explanation. In this way, *in fact* indicates that the words following it amplify the words that precede it.

"This"

This refers to "that the system was worth preserving, that the idea of democracy had not failed." The pronoun carries those concepts into the next sentence, linking them.

"And"

And indicates to readers that the sentence it begins adds information to the sentence before it.

"But"

But signals to readers that there will be a change from what the preceding sentences were arguing.

SHAPING PARAGRAPHS FOR
AUDIENCE AND PURPOSE
PARAGRAPHS THAT DEVELOP

WHAT DOES "DEVELOPMENT" MEAN FOR PARAGRAPHS?

No matter its specific purpose, all writing is meant to move readers: It can move them from knowing nothing about a proposal in an upcoming election to understanding why some people are against the proposal, or it might move them out of daily routines into stopping to savor the pleasures of breathing.

If writing is to move readers, it has to begin with ideas familiar to them and then, from paragraph to paragraph and within paragraphs, develop those ideas in new or unexpected directions.

Effective paragraphs thus start with a sentence that grows out of the preceding paragraph—and then each following sentence develops or adds to the idea that is the focus of the first sentence.

You can shape this development from the familiar to the unfamiliar in many ways; in the next pages, we describe patterns—moving from simpler to more complex—for developing paragraphs.

The simpler kinds of paragraphs (such as description, definition, and narrative) usually appear near the beginning of a composition because they help writers lay out the ideas and terms at stake. Later, when a writer is trying to persuade readers to make particular connections among ideas, the more complex kinds of paragraphs (classification and division, comparison and contrast, cause and effect, syllogistic, and analogical) are more useful.

→ Because introductory and concluding paragraphs have very specific stylistic functions, we discuss them in Part 6 on style; see pages 232–235.

PARAGRAPHS THAT DESCRIBE

Descriptive paragraphs give details about people, places, or things. They serve two functions. First, because they appeal to our senses, they make what is being described more immediate and so they engage readers' attention. Second, such paragraphs help writers set the scene: They provide the background within which discussions, controversies, and experiments occur. Because they engage readers and set the scene, writers often use descriptive paragraphs at the very beginning of writing—but whenever writers need to make a scene clear or describe a situation that affects their arguments, they can use descriptive paragraphs.

▪ ▪ ▪

> DARK NIGHT in the mountains and no drums beating. No flute music like birdsong from the forest above the village–the men controlled the flutes and this was women's business, secret and delicious, sweet revenge. In pity and mourning but also in eagerness the dead woman's female relatives carried her cold, naked body down to her sweet-potato garden bordered with flowers. They would not abandon her to rot in the ground. Sixty or more women with their babies and small children gathered around, gathered wood, lit cooking fires that caught the light in their eyes and shone on their greased dark skins. The dead woman's daughter and the wife of her adopted son took up knives of split bamboo, their silicate skin sharp as glass. They began to cut the body for the feast.
>
> New Guinea was the last wild place on earth. Its fierce reputation repelled explores.

The paragraph above is the first paragraph of a book about certain neurological diseases. The writer's descriptions appeal to ears and eyes, and they also describe skin sensations. Attention to a range of senses helps writers make descriptions as vivid as possible.

▪ ▪ ▪

> the Peppermill. Especially Flowers.
>
> As a rock star, he's a strange case: A crushworthy frontman and a bit of a peacock, he's given to showy, flamboyant stage performances. But in person, he's shy and sweet, a married, practicing Mormon (who enjoys the occasional beer or cigarette). When he talks about Vegas, he constantly ends up talking about his roots. "Vegas is my hometown, and it's turned into a place that's really sentimental to me," he says. "I think a lot of people can identify with that."
>
> The son of parents who hooked up in a Vegas trailer park when

The paragraph above appeals to readers' expectations and emotional senses by using concrete adjectives and nouns (*crushworthy*, *flamboyant*, *shy*) and by using words spoken by the person being described.

PARAGRAPHS THAT DEFINE

If you are unsure whether your readers will understand a particular term or concept, give a definition. If you use a term or concept special to a discipline or field, chances are you will need to define it for a general audience. And if the term or concept is central to your argument, then defining it allows you and your readers to be in agreement about its meaning.

Because writers and readers need to develop a shared understanding of terms and concepts if discussion and argument are to be possible, definitions of new or contested terms usually comes early in a text or early in a section that first uses the term or concept.

Sometimes a one-sentence definition is all you need—but if a term or concept is complex or central to your purpose, then use a whole paragraph to build a detailed definition.

■ ■ ■

The paragraph to the right comes from a book arguing that food in the United States is now a petroleum product because of how crops and livestock are raised. This paragraph comes from a chapter in which the author describes Joel Salatin's farm in Virginia. The author uses this farm as an example of how crops and livestock can be raised without petroleum.

Notice how the first sentence gives a general definition of **grass farmer** (which itself includes a quick definition of **keystone species**). The following sentences add further detail and description—and use the words of an expert to support the definition being offered.

meat and milk) than anyone had ever thought possible.

Grass farmers grow animals—for meat, eggs, milk, and wool—but regard them as part of a food chain in which grass is the keystone species, the nexus between the solar energy that powers every food chain and the animals we eat. "To be even more accurate," Joel has said, "we should call ourselves sun farmers. The grass is just the way we capture the solar energy." One of the principles of modern grass farming is that to the greatest extent possible farmers should rely on the contemporary energy of the sun, as captured every day by photosynthesis, instead of the fossilized sun energy contained in petroleum.

For Allan Nation, who grew up on a cattle ranch in Mississippi, doing so is as much a matter of sound economics as environ-

TIP: ABOUT USING DICTIONARY DEFINITIONS

Except when they are comparing definitions given by dictionaries, or want to comment on the shortcomings of a dictionary definition, few published writers quote from dictionaries when they need to define terms. Instead, they quote experts, people who know what a term means in practice. This gives the writer's words more authority.

PARAGRAPHS THAT NARRATE

Paragraphs that narrate tell stories. Stories personalize issues. When we hear the fortunes—or misfortunes—of others, we imagine ourselves in those situations. We know what feelings must be involved and might feel them ourselves. Stories can thus build emotional connections—positive or negative—between readers and topics.

Because stories are always about the experiences of one person or a few people, rarely can they stand alone as evidence: Readers will question a writer's attempts to generalize from limited experience to a broad claim. But stories can be useful in introductory or concluding paragraphs (of a whole essay or just a section) to engage readers emotionally with a topic or to make the topic memorable.

To write a narrative paragraph, tell what happened, in order. Include details—where the event took place, who was involved—but keep the narrative focused on your purpose: What is the main idea or feeling you want readers to remember?

(Note that stories based on real experiences are more effective than made-up stories; readers will not accept made-up stories as evidence because such stories are not real.)

▓ ▓ ▓

Death Nap

THE DANGERS OF TILTING BACK THE FRONT SEAT–DON'T DO IT!

By Emily Bazelon

Posted Friday, Sept. 7 2007, at 4.24 PM ET

A couple of weeks ago, I was sleeping in the front passenger seat of our car when it slammed into the vehicle in front of us. We were on the highway coming home from a family trip. The other three people in our car weren't hurt. But I'd reclined my seat, and my seat belt, which was riding high, left a long welt around my rib cage and along my stomach. As it turned out, I had internal bleeding from a lacerated spleen and three cracked ribs. I spent the next two days in intensive care.

I've recovered nicely, thank you. But the more I thought about my accident, the more I wondered whether I'd inadvertently done myself in by tilting my car seat back—as I do on just about every long drive. We worry a lot about car seats and

The paragraph to the left introduces an article on the dangers of sitting in a tilted-back front seat of a car. The author's own story makes the topic real—and scary. In the paragraphs that follow in the article, the writer describes what she learned about tilted front seats through research and offers much more evidence than her own experience to argue that the dangers of riding in a reclined front car seat ought to be more well known.

PARAGRAPHS THAT GIVE EXAMPLES

If you write, *No wonder people don't watch television news—there are so many commercials!*, readers might respond, *Sure, sure....* But imagine you wrote this:

No wonder people don't watch television news anymore—there are so many commercials! Last night, for example, I counted 12 commercials during one thirty-minute local newscast and 15 during a thirty-minute national newscast.

Examples give readers vivid, concrete evidence, and so give them reason to consider the situation you are discussing.

→ The evidence you offer as examples can be of different kinds; see pages 106–107.

■ ■ ■

feet of their mothers for nearly all of their first eight years of life, after which young females are socialized into the matriarchal network, while young males go off for a time into an all-male social group before coming back into the fold as mature adults.

When an elephant dies, its family members engage in intense mourning and burial rituals, conducting weeklong vigils over the body, carefully covering it with earth and brush, revisiting the bones for years afterward, caressing the bones with their trunks, often taking turns rubbing their trunks along the teeth of a skull's lower jaw, the way living elephants do in greeting. If harm comes to a member of an elephant group, all the other elephants are aware of it. This sense of cohesion is further enforced by the elaborate communication system that elephants use. In close proximity they employ a range of vocalizations, from low-frequency rumbles to higher-pitched screams and trumpets, along with a variety of visual signals, from the waving of their trunks to subtle anglings of the head, body, feet and tail. When communicating over long distances—in order to pass along, for example, news about imminent threats, a sudden change of plans or, of the utmost importance to elephants, the death of a community member—they use patterns of subsonic vibrations that are felt as far as several miles away by exquisitely tuned sensors in the padding of their feet.

This fabric of elephant society, Bradshaw and her colleagues concluded, had effectively been frayed by years of habitat loss and poaching, along with

The paragraph above comes from a newspaper magazine article about a breakdown in the social structures of elephant groups. Elephants are performing violent acts against other animals, other elephants, and humans; young elephants suffer from what looks to researchers like post-traumatic stress syndrome. To argue that we should therefore treat elephants differently than we currently do, the writer needs readers to think of elephants as complex beings deserving of our sympathies, respect, and awe.

This paragraph lists examples of concrete elephant behaviors, shaped to encourage readers to think of elephants differently.

PARAGRAPHS THAT USE ANALOGY

If you wish explain to small children why cars need gasoline, you can talk with them about eating: Children probably understand that they need to eat because food gives them energy—so they can understand that cars need gasoline because otherwise the cars won't run. This explanation is an analogy: It uses a concept an audience already understands to explain a concept they don't.

Science writing for popular audiences uses analogies frequently, because the writing's purpose is usually to explain complex processes and concepts to people who don't have a technical background; using analogies that draw on an audience's experiences bridges their unfamiliarity.

You can use paragraphs based on analogies when you need to make a complex concept or process seem simpler. In addition, when you use an analogy, whatever associations your audience has with the more well-known concept will shape their attitudes toward the new or more complex concept. With the above analogy of food and gasoline, for example, it is likely that, because the audience probably likes food, they will think gasoline is a good thing. If you did not want the children to think in such generous ways toward cars or gasoline, the analogy could get you into trouble later.

→ For more on using and evaluating analogies, see pages 100-101.

The paragraph to the right draws on an audience's basic understanding of what computers are in order to help them understand how and why humans can be physically but not socially adept, as with conditions like autism (which, as you can see, is what the paragraph following the example is about).

individual, they later expect the individual to approach the character that helped it and to avoid the one that hurt it.

Understanding of the physical world and understanding of the social world can be seen as akin to two distinct computers in a baby brain, running separate programs and performing separate tasks. The understandings develop at different rates: the social one emerges somewhat later than the physical one. They evolved at different points in our prehistory; our physical understanding is shared by many species, whereas our social understanding is a relatively recent adaptation, and in some regards might be uniquely human.

That these two systems are distinct is especially apparent in autism, a developmental disorder whose dominant feature is a lack of

PARAGRAPHS THAT DIVIDE

Paragraphs that define can easily become or lead into paragraphs that divide: A definition establishes a criterion that names what something is (or is not); once you have done that, you can use the criterion to categorize and divide.

Academic writing often hinges on such categorization or division because such categorization or division is analysis. Analysis allows us to name and so to sort through the components of a process or event. We do that to learn what happened or to learn what stands in our way of accomplishing what we desire.

Paragraphs that divide are often followed by paragraphs that compare and contrast—because it is possible to compare and contrast two objects, processes, or events only when we can see that the objects, processes, or events are divided, or different.

(The opposite kind of paragraph—a paragraph that unites—is also central to academic work. Just as it is important to show that what had seemed the same is really different, it helps us when we can see that what had seemed different is really the same.)

■ ■ ■

Danah Boyd, working on her PhD at Berkeley and a Fellow at the Berkman Center for Internet and Society at the Harvard Law School, researches how young people use social networking software like MySpace and Facebook. In a recent blog article she uses sociologist Nalini Kotamraju's definition of "class" to consider differences between MySpace and Facebook. Kotamraju argues that in the United States class isn't about money but rather about social connection: who you know is going to shape your life and what you can do more than how much much money you make. Based on that distinction, Boyd argues that the difference between who uses Facebook and who uses MySpace is one of class: Facebook is where the "goodie two shoes, jocks, athletes, or other 'good' kids" go, while MySpace

> is still home for Latino/Hispanic teens, immigrant teens, burnouts, alternative kids, art fags, punks, emos, goths, gangstas, queer kids, and other kids who didn't play into the dominant high school popularity paradigm.

Boyd argues that marketers and the military have figured out this distinction and are making decisions on it; Boyd hopes that teachers and social workers will figure this out, too, in order to talk with young people about how cultural structures and decisions shape individual lives.

In the paragraph to the left, the writer summarizes part of another writer's arguments about youth culture. The summary shows how the original writer—Danah Boyd—starts with a definition of **class**. She then uses that definition to show a division: Many people had thought that all social networking sites that use profiles are the same, but Boyd shows how they are divided, or different.

By using the definition to show a division in an area that had seemed the same throughout, Boyd can point to problems we might not otherwise see.

PARAGRAPHS THAT BLEND ORGANIZATIONS

Depending on your arguments, paragraphs can get complex: Writers need them to perform multiple functions.

(Keep in mind, though, that even when paragraphs blend several kinds of organizations, the paragraph will still have one main function in the overall argument of which it is a part: It needs to move the argument forward one step.)

■ ■ ■

The example to the right comes from a newspaper editorial, published on Labor Day, in which writer Mike Rose argues that we should "honor the brains as well as the brawn of American labor."

In this paragraph, Rose lists examples of the mental work that different kinds of blue-collar work require.

But this paragraph is not only examples. The examples ground Rose's argument that we need to unite rather than divide: We need to see that blue-collar and white-collar work have much in common.

Rose thus combines examples and analysis—unifying disparate elements—in this one paragraph.

beauty salons and restaurants, auto factories and welding shops. And I've been struck by the intellectual demands of what I saw.

Consider what a good waitress or waiter has to do in a busy restaurant. Remember orders and monitor them, attend to an ever-changing environment, juggle the flow of the work, make decisions on the fly. Or the carpenter: To build a cabinet, a staircase, or a pitched roof requires complex mathematical calculations, a high level of precision. The hairstylist's practice is a mix of scissors technique, knowledge of biology, aesthetic judgment, and communication skills. The mechanic, electrician, and plumber are trouble-shooters and problem-solvers. Even the routinized factory floor calls for working smart. Yet we persist in dividing labor into the work of the hand and the work of the mind.

Distinction between blue collar and white collar do exist. White-collar work, for example, often requires a large investment of time and

TIP: MANY MORE KINDS OF PARAGRAPHS

In the last few pages, we have described some of the most used paragraphs. But there are also paragraphs that classify, that explain processes, that show cause and effect, and that function in other ways depending on a writer's particular purposes. As you read others' writing, try to classify their paragraphs, and to determine why they used a particular kind of paragraph when they did; such observations will not only help you expand your tool kit of kinds of paragraphs but will also help you strengthen your own argumentative choices.

VISUAL ORGANIZATION

As our chart on page 143 suggests, written and visual texts share similar overall organization: They can both be analyzed for their overall conceptual framework, their major elements, and their detailed elements.

Just as with written texts, we will consider the conceptual frameworks and major elements of visual texts in these pages; in Part 6 we will consider the detailed elements of visual texts.

■ ■ ■

We'll start here by discussing the major elements of visual texts that mix words and visual pieces, and then we'll consider the organizational frameworks that are built from them.

MAJOR ELEMENTS OF TEXTS THAT MIX WORDS, PICTURES, AND OTHER VISUAL PIECES

You might have been taught about paragraphs so long ago that you don't realize you are creating major organizational elements as you write. When you work with texts that mix words and visual elements, you similarly have to create (or at least choose) the elements you will organize.

When you work with photographs, paintings, drawings, charts, and graphs, your choices shape readers' and viewers' possible responses.

→ If in your composition you use a photograph, painting, drawing, chart, diagram, graph, or table made by someone else, you need to cite the source; see pages 389-395 for formatting such citations in MLA style, and pages 436-437 for APA style.

PHOTOGRAPHS

Use photographs to document how a person, place, or object looks or looked (because of digital technologies, however, you might need to assure readers that photographs you use have not been manipulated).

Use photographs to create emotional connections between readers and a topic: Seeing a person or place encourages readers to feel physically, and hence emotionally, closer than words.

When you use photographs, keep in mind that how the elements within a photograph are organized or cropped affects how readers respond. In the two photographs to the left, one creates a more intimate relation between viewer and photographed subject than the other because of how it has been cropped.

PAINTINGS AND DRAWINGS

Kehinde Wiley composed the painting to the left. Wiley asks Black men to look at paintings of saints from the Renaissance and Baroque periods and to choose poses from the paintings; Wiley then paints the men in those poses.

Paintings—and drawings—show a composer's imagination. Like photographs, paintings and drawings are arranged to direct your visual attention and shape your attitude toward the subject.

Photographs, because they come out of cameras, seem more direct and less abstract than paintings or drawings. Use paintings and drawings, then, when you need to present or illustrate abstractions.

PHOTOGRAPHS, PAINTINGS, DRAWINGS—AND WORDS

How would you respond to the family photograph above if it were titled "The Scientist as a Girl, with Her Family"? What if it were titled "From the W.E.B. Du Bois albums of photographs of African Americans in Georgia exhibited at the Paris Exposition Universelle in 1900"? What would you think about the Wiley portrait if our writing didn't tell you that its pose was derived from a Renaissance painting?

When words are not attached to a photograph, painting, or drawing, viewers use their own experiences to make associations with or interpretations of the text; when words are added—as a title or explanation—the words limit how freely a viewer can interpret or make associations and instead start to shape the viewer's interpretation.

BUILDING VISUAL ORGANIZATIONS

Print texts have a clear beginning, a clear order to follow, and a clear end. Films and videos have linear organization similar to print, but one-page visual texts (posters, flyers, each page in a newsletter or brochure) do not. To build visual organizations with one-page texts, construct visual relationships among the elements.

MAKE SOME ELEMENTS STAND OUT

Organizing visual text requires making obvious which elements are most important and should be seen first, and which should be seen second and third. Elements are made to stand out—and be what is first seen—through contrast, placement, and leaving some space unemphasized.

Which movie flyer to the left would catch your eye on a campus wall? What do your eyes see in each flyer?

With the top flyer, you probably see a mass of text; no part stands out. With the second, your eyes are probably caught first by the rhinoceros and the big words at the bottom; then you notice the text at the upper right. The second flyer immediately tells you what it is about and perhaps piques your interest enough that you move close to read the details—which the flyer composer knew you would read if you were pulled in by the rhino.

Contrast

The second flyer works because the bottom words are so big compared to the words at the top right. Create contrast by giving elements **very** different sizes, colors, or styles.

Placement

Western reading patterns accustom our eyes to moving left to right and top to bottom, as well as to page centers. If you organize page elements so that the biggest element is at the top left or overlaps the center, you double its visual emphasis and so make it even more eye attracting.

Unemphasized Space (or "White Space")

White space is the design term for space on a page that only appears unused. But white space (which can be any color; **white space** comes from white paper) makes visual organization possible. Areas of a visual composition cannot be emphasized if every bit of space is full. Leaving some spaces empty allows the parts that are full to stand out.

GROUP ELEMENTS

When you group visual elements or make them similar (and sometimes you do both at once), you create a page that feels unified and coherent to viewers—for all the same reasons that we gave for unified and coherent paragraphs on page 172.

Also, elements that are grouped or similar can create a background against which other elements can stand out.

Group Elements

When several elements on a page serve the same function—giving the time, date, and location information about an event, for example, or serving as the eye-catching elements—group them close to each other. A viewer's eyes see and so understand that they belong together.

You can see this in the rhinoceros movie flyer to the left, where the rhinoceros and the big words are overlapped to make one element. The words at the top right of the flyer are also grouped: A viewer can quickly see that information about the movie is in one place.

▩ ▩ ▩

Grouping can happen at the level of headings in a text, too. Compare the two text boxes to the right. The top box looks as though it contains seven different bits of text, because there is the same amount of space above and below each line of the bold, all-capitol-letter text.

The second box has more space above the bold text and none underneath; this groups the bold text with the words underneath. The grouping makes very obvious to a viewer that the bold text serves as titles for the words underneath.

Notice, too, how the second box looks as though it contains only four elements instead of seven.

The components of color are hue, saturation, and brightness:

HUE

Hue describes what many of us just think of as color: When you name the hue of a color, you describe it as red or blue or yellow or green...

SATURATION

Saturation describes how much hue is present in a color. Vivid pink is highly saturated, while pastel pink is not.

BRIGHTNESS

Brightness describes how light or dark a color is.

The components of color are hue, saturation, and brightness:

HUE
Hue describes what many of us just think of as color: When you name the hue of a color, you describe it as red or blue or yellow or green...

SATURATION
Saturation describes how much hue is present in a color. Vivid pink is highly saturated, while pastel pink is not.

BRIGHTNESS
Brightness describes how light or dark a color is.

UNIFY ELEMENTS THROUGH REPETITION

The boldness of a typeface can repeat the boldness of a line elsewhere on a page; the shape of a box on the page can repeat the shape of the page. If the title of a presentation being advertised on a flyer is "Four Aspects of Educational Success," the flyer could have four photographs about education on it.

When you repeat the elements of a composition, whether visual or written, the resulting organization will be unified and coherent for your audience.

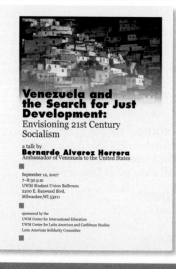

Venezuela and the Search for Just Development: Envisioning 21st Century Socialism

Bernardo Alvarez Herrera
Ambassador of Venezuela to the United States

September 12, 2007
7–8:30 p.m
UWM Student Union Ballroom
2200 E. Kenwood Blvd.
Milwaukee, WI 53211

sponsored by the
UWM Center for International
Education
UWM Center for Latin
American and Caribbean
Studies
Latin American Solidarity Committee

The top flyer to the left has sufficient contrast, expected placement, and appropriate grouping to enable viewers easily to see the major elements of the flyer. But the elements still do not seem as though they belong together. Each grouping is in a different typeface, and the elements seem randomly placed horizontally.

The redesign of the flyer, below left, adds a photograph to the top to make the title even more visually engaging. But notice, too, what is now repeated in the new flyer's organization:

- Only two typefaces are used: a big bold one at the top and for the speaker's name, and a more traditional serifed typeface repeated for everything else.

→ See page 260 to learn about the typeface classifications of serif and sans serif.

- The typefaces are modern typefaces, repeating the concept of the twenty-first century mentioned in the talk's title.

- The left alignment is repeated for all the text elements.

- A gray square is repeated down the left side of the composition, helping separate the type groups.

- The gray of the square repeats the gray and the rectangular shapes of the buildings in the photograph.

ALIGN ELEMENTS

Aligning each element of a visual composition with at least one other element will help a layout look coherent and unified. Elements are aligned when you can draw straight lines along the edges of elements:

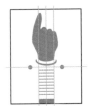  

The top flyer at right has sufficient contrast, expected placement, and appropriate grouping and typefaces to enable viewers to see the major elements of the flyer; it also has a photograph appropriate to the presentation topic.

But the bottom flyer feels still more unified and coherent because the composition is now organized around two (imaginary) vertical lines, one on the left and one on the right.

Notice that the title of the presentation stretches between both the lines, as do the bottom lines of text; this reinforces the unity the alignment brings.

(Notice also that the design repeats the photograph twice, first at the top and then smaller and flipped upside down at the bottom; notice also how the two photographs are aligned, a form of repetition.)

TIP: PHOTOGRAPHIC INTEREST

You've probably noticed in each redesigned flyer that a photograph or illustration is added. Photographs—especially of people—attract eyes. If added to a composition and placed to have contrast, eyes will be drawn to start there.

ORGANIZATION FOR ORAL PRESENTATIONS

If they need help remembering where they are in a printed text, audiences can look back over the pages and paragraphs they hold in their hands; audiences for oral presentations cannot do this.

When you develop oral presentations, therefore, your biggest consideration about organization should be helping your audience hear and remember the parts of your presentation: If they can remember the organization, they will remember the main points and argument attached to that organization.

REPEAT...AND KEEP IT BRIEF

- As our advice above and to the right suggests, repeating your purpose and main points in your introduction, as you move from paragraph to paragraph, and in your conclusion helps audiences follow your arguments. Repeat similar words as you repeat.

- Pare it down. These days, when we rarely receive instruction in how to listen, audiences usually benefit from straight-forward, focused presentations.

TIP: AN ORGANIZATIONAL FUNCTION FOR VISUAL AIDS

If you use visual aids such as slides, overheads, or handouts during your presentation, include an opening screen or page that sketches or outlines the overall organization of the presentation; this will help keep your audience oriented.

As you move through the parts of your presentation, use screens that name the parts as you move into them, again to help keep your audience oriented.

THE PARTS OF AN ORAL PRESENTATION

Like papers, oral presentations have the basic structure of introduction, body, and conclusion. But as you prepare, use strategies that make the organization audible to your audience.

INTRODUCTION

You can start with an anecdote, quotation, or another attention-getting strategy (just as with introductory paragraphs, as discussed on pages 234–235)—but then explicitly and clearly tell your listeners what your presentation is about and describe the parts that make up its structure. You want your audience to hear your purpose and organization clearly and several times so that they will remember them.

Vary the sentence patterns you use to describe your purpose and organization, so that you keep your audience engaged (→ see pages 508–525 about sentence patterns)—but then repeat the same or similar noun phrases to describe your purpose and organization so that audiences remember them well (→ see pages 477 and 510 on noun phrases).

BODY

Choose an easy-to-remember structure and plan to keep your audience aware of each movement you make from one point to the next.

Easy-to-remember structures have few parts: In a five- to ten-minute presentation, audiences will be able to remember three to five steps in an argument. Easy-to-remember structures are:

- *Chronological.* Audiences can easily follow presentations that present events in the order in which they occurred.

- *Logical.* Use your thesis statement (→ as we describe on pages 154–155) to organize the body into three parts: one for the warrant, one for the reason, and one for the claim.

- *Problem-Solution.* Describe the problem and then argue for the solution you favor.

- *Comparative.* If you are recommending one approach to a problem over another, first present the approach you least favor and then the one you want audiences to remember.

Keeping your audience aware of your movement from one point to the next involves phrases like the following:

- My third point is…

- Now that I have described the problem, let me tell you what I think the best solution is.

- I've described what microcredit is, so let me tell you why economists think it is so important.

- Finally… or In conclusion…

  → The phrases on page 174 can help you move your audience from one point to the next.

CONCLUSION

Remind your audience of your argument and main points. If you can find one that fits well with your purposes, use an anecdote, story, or quotation to end memorably, so that your listeners hold on to your talk.

HINTS & TIPS FOR ORGANIZING TEXTS

BE WARY OF SETTLING ON AN ORGANIZATION TOO QUICKLY

If you want to produce writing that is smart, complex, and creative, you have to let your writing direct you. Although you have a thesis statement and a statement of purpose, and although they can help you give a rough shape to your writing before you sit down to write, it is in writing that you really test out and find the ideas you want.

All experienced writers will tell you of times that, in working out an argument in writing, they came to different or more focused conclusions than they had originally planned. Because they listened to their words, and followed the logic of their initial ideas or of new evidence, their writing had to take on new organizations.

So don't try to force an organization on your ideas; listen to your ideas and the directions they take you. You can always reorganize a paper once you have found a new or shifted argument.

CHECKING ORGANIZATION THROUGH AN AFTER-THE-FACT OUTLINE

Once you are confident in your arguments and know that your conclusion is exactly what you want (→ see pages 232–233), check back over all your other paragraphs: Does each logically follow what precedes it and lead to what comes next?

Experienced writers often make outlines for their papers *after* they have a first (or later) draft:

- Summarize each paragraph in one sentence. (If you cannot summarize a paragraph in a sentence, then you probably need to break the paragraph into two or more new paragraphs.)

- List the paragraph summaries in order.

- Does this outline step you logically from the introduction to the conclusion? If not, you may need to add, take out, or clarify paragraphs to have different summaries.

HOW OTHERS CAN HELP YOU CHECK ORGANIZATION

When you have a draft, cut it apart so that each paragraph is on its own piece of paper. Shuffle the pieces of paper and give them to someone else; ask the other person to tape the paragraphs back into a whole, leaving out any paragraphs that don't make sense or marking any places where it is impossible to tell what should come next.

Sometimes the other person will hand you back something with a clearer order, and sometimes you will learn where you need to make clarifications, additions, or subtractions.

PART 5
DRAFTING A PAPER, CONNECTING WITH AUDIENCES

CONTENTS

WHERE ARE WE IN THE PROCESS FOR COMPOSING?

Understanding your project

Getting started

Asking questions

Shaping your project for others
Thinking in depth about audience
Developing a statement of purpose

Drafting a paper
Writing a rough draft

Getting feedback
Receiving feedback to drafts
Developing a revision plan

Revising

Polishing

ARE YOU READY TO USE THE NEXT PAGES OF THIS BOOK?

NO...
Are you running through possible topics in your mind?
Have you just found some sources that finally seem just right?
Are you figuring out your thesis statement?
If any of these is your situation, then, no, you are not ready for the next pages.

Only when you have solid research in support of a narrowed topic and when you also have a thesis statement that follows from that research are you ready to draft a paper with as few frustrations and as much pleasure and ease as possible.

→ For help with narrowing a topic, see pages 28–33.

→ For help with researching a topic, see pages 34–73.

→ For help with a thesis statement, see pages 96-97, 138-139, and 152-155.

YES.
Do you have a thesis statement and have you used it to figure out the main parts of your argument?
The next pages will help you move from a thesis statement to a statement of purpose, which will help you build on the thesis statement's logic so you can shape your composition for your particular audience.

UNDERSTANDING YOUR AUDIENCE

THE CONCERN

You know what you are writing about. For example, in Parts 2–4 we have followed Riley's development of ideas for writing about how microcredit loans change women's lives in developing countries. As you saw, Riley put together a thesis statement: *Women who receive microcredit without discussion support groups and classes in economics won't know how to change the community conditions that encourage poverty; therefore, microcredit should only be offered with such support.* **But who needs to know this? For whom does this argument matter, and why?**

Through her research, Riley has accumulated some supporting evidence for her thesis, but what of that evidence will be most persuasive? Into what order should she put her evidence? What tone of voice should she use in her writing?

Riley can answer these questions only if she has some sense of who will read her writing and why.

Riley can say, *I am writing to people who know about microcredit and think it's always good*—but that level of understanding of audience is vague; it does not help her make the choices posed by the questions above.

How can Riley develop a more discerning and useful sense of her readers so that she can make specific choices about her writing?

ADDRESSING THE CONCERN

Experienced writers will tell you that understanding their audiences is the most important step in composing writing that achieves its purposes.

Concrete and persuasive writing grows out of thinking about what your readers believe and why. For example, if Riley is writing to people who think microcredit is good, she needs to ask, *Why do they think microcredit is good? What do they think is good about it? Why haven't they heard about some of the questionable sides of microcredit? Just what do they know about it, at all?*

There is also another important question Riley has to ask, a question that any writer has to ask when addressing an audience that might not know about the topic: *Why should my readers care?*

Those questions suggest further research as well as decisions a writer like Riley has to make about readers. Riley has to research her readers—and their beliefs and opinions—because if she is going to be persuasive about microcredit, she will have to address what matters to her readers about the lives of women in developing countries.

Riley needs to develop a thicker characterization of her audience, so she needs to think about her audience as concretely as possible. If she can think of them as real, living, breathing people with emotions and attitudes toward events, then she can write to them almost as though she would talk with them, taking into consideration their opinions, thoughts, and feelings.

■ ■ ■

Whether you are writing a business memo, composing a flyer about your band, or producing a research website on the Gilded Age in the United States, taking some steps to help you think about your audiences more concretely will help you produce more effective writing.

Following, we suggest strategies for thinking about your audience in depth. Here are the steps we follow:

**general observations
about an audience's
shared characteristics**

▼

**observations
about what audiences
know, think, and feel about a topic**

▼

**developing
a statement of purpose**

CHARACTERISTICS YOUR AUDIENCE MIGHT SHARE

You can begin thinking about your audience by considering their general characteristics and how those characteristics can affect the attitudes they might have toward your topic.

YOU MIGHT THINK YOU ALREADY KNOW YOUR AUDIENCE...

You are writing a paper for your classmates (which, as you know, also means you are writing for your teacher). Or perhaps you are writing a memo to your boss proposing new procedures.

In each case, you think you know these people. After all, you live and work with them; you spend considerable time in varying degrees of contact.

But do you know their concerns and opinions on your topic? Do you know *why* they hold those concerns and opinions?

If your writing is to catch and hold these readers' attention, you need to give time to what they think about your topic, and why they think those things.

...OR MAYBE YOU DON'T KNOW THEM AT ALL

You are writing a letter to the editor of your city's newspaper. You are putting together a grant application for a nonprofit organization. You are composing webpages for a new business.

In such cases, you probably don't know your audiences. Newspaper audiences are broad; people from diverse positions make grant decisions; businesses try to reach wide audiences. How do you shape your writing in these cases?

Even when you are writing to audiences with whom you are not in regular contact, you can still make judgments, based on the information you do have, about why the audiences will read what you offer and how their concerns and opinions will shape their reading.

READERS' GENERAL CHARACTERISTICS

No matter how much or how little you know about your readers, use what you do know to help you compose.

Step through the following general characteristics, asking how they might impinge on readers' responses to your warrant, evidence, and claim:

- ❏ age
- ❏ ethnicity
- ❏ level of education
- ❏ sexual orientation
- ❏ upbringing
- ❏ place of work
- ❏ gender
- ❏ language
- ❏ able-bodiness
- ❏ class
- ❏ place of living
- ❏ other characteristics that might matter, given your thesis

If you know your audience well, you can focus on the characteristics they have in common, such as age or place of living. If your audience is a general audience, or if you do not know your audience, step through these characteristics to consider which matter most.

TIP: USING CARE WITH AUDIENCE CHARACTERISTICS

To define someone just by age, ethnicity, level of education, gender, or class—or even to define based on all the characteristics above—is to miss the complex mix of experiences and culture that shapes each of us. The characteristics above are just a beginning to help you think about how readers *might* respond. You can never know for sure how a person's particular life will affect his or her responses.

FOR EXAMPLE...

Riley writes about her readers, in general:

> I guess both the age and gender of my classmates might matter as I write about microcredit. The women in class are probably more likely to care, because I am writing about women. Only one or two people in class that I know of have kids, and people who don't have children might not sympathize with women trying to make a small living for their families or get an education for their children. (I wonder how many people in class know that in other countries you often have to pay for K-12 education?)
>
> And if someone hasn't traveled, or has had a nice middle-class life, they might not understand the social and economic issues of poverty...?
>
> I guess I am going to need to work hard at showing why we should all care. What can I write to make that happen?

FOR EXAMPLE...

You are writing a letter to the editor of your local paper about a proposed wind power plant that a power company wants to install on land that was once a farm. You live nearby, and are concerned about the potential noise of the plant and an increase in traffic. Are people who do not live as close to the farm going to think your concerns are simply selfish? Are people looking to bring jobs to the area going to think your concerns are only about the niceties of life instead of the essentials, like jobs?

WHAT DO PEOPLE KNOW, THINK, AND FEEL ABOUT THE ISSUE?

The attitudes people have toward an issue can shape how committed they are to their positions.

READERS AS PEOPLE WITH OPINIONS AND ATTITUDES

Move your focus from general characteristics to what people feel about a topic or issue. Talk to potential readers, asking about

❑ what they know of the topic.

❑ their emotional responses to the topic.

❑ how they have learned what they know of the topic.

❑ personal connections they might have to the topic.

❑ values/beliefs/commitments related to the topic.

❑ questions they might have about the topic.

❑ their self-identity as it connects them to the topic. How do they see themselves connected to the topic because of their specific relations to others? That is, does it matter that a reader is a mother, a daughter, unemployed, a Republican or a leftist, rich or not, a boss or a worker, a student or a teacher, ambitious or laid back, or…?

❑ recent events—locally, nationally, or internationally—that might shape their responses to the topic.

If you cannot talk directly with readers, ask yourself the same questions, imagining how people with different backgrounds would respond.

FOR EXAMPLE…

If you were writing to argue that it might be time to build more nuclear power plants in the United States, you might learn that many people are opposed. You might learn that most people learned about the science of nuclear power in high school textbooks; they also learned about nuclear power from reading newspapers and magazines about cancer rates following Chernobyl and how people can no longer live in that community because of radiation. And, silly as it may seem, all the science fiction movies people have seen about mutations do underlie general perception, further adding to the general emotional climate of fear and uncertainty around nuclear power.

In addition, people who have children are perhaps more resistant to nuclear power because they do not want their children to be in danger. On the other hand, businesspeople (or children of businesspeople) might be more concerned about the future costs of power because of how those costs affect their ability to keep their businesses running.

These observations can help writers understand that, for most readers these days, making decisions about nuclear power is not simply a matter of coolly weighing numeric, scientific evidence; it is also about fear of mutations, cancer, and the destruction of communities. This tells writers that they probably should not compose a list of facts but will have to address people's emotional concerns about radiation and its potential long-term effects.

FOR EXAMPLE…

Riley writes about what she learns from her classmates:

I didn't realize how little the people in my class know nothing about microcredit and the lives of women in developing countries. Maybe they know a little bit from having seen something on TV. If they <u>do</u> know something about it, they don't think they need to worry about it because it happens in other countries and involves people with very different lives.

But I know that microcredit organizations work in the U.S., too, because they are needed here—so maybe I can make my research interesting because it does apply here—and so maybe I can shape my writing to help readers think about the economic conditions of <u>their</u> own lives.

AND! When I talk to men in class about microcredit, they at first think it is just a women's issue. It doesn't concern them. But almost all the guys care deeply for their mothers and respect the work their mothers do to take care of their families— so maybe I can help the guys connect to my writing by encouraging them to think about how the women who receive microcredit loans are often mothers?

STARTING TO WRITE FOR AN AUDIENCE
DEVELOPING A STATEMENT OF PURPOSE

MOVING FROM A THESIS STATEMENT TO A STATEMENT OF PURPOSE

A thesis statement, as we described in Part 3 of this book, is a short statement summarizing the logic of your argument.

→ See pages 96–97.

Because humans respect logic but are also, well, human, writers also must consider more than just the potential logic of their words. You need to consider how your writing will be emotionally persuasive to a particular audience and how your readers will construct a sense of you the writer— your authority, believability, and general character—based on your words. (→ See pages 86–89 for more on these strategies of pathos and ethos.) A statement of purpose helps you do this.

A statement of purpose weaves together the logical purpose of a thesis statement with what a writer learns about audience from doing the thinking and research we have described on the preceding pages.

A statement of purpose is not itself a formal piece of writing. Instead, it is thinking-on-paper, a way to help you consider what you really want your readers to think, feel, or do as they read your writing and when they are done reading it.

FOR EXAMPLE…

This thesis statement is for a research paper:

> We can build new nuclear power plants in the United States to help take care of our energy needs and reduce reliance on foreign oil because nuclear power plants have become safer and more reliable.

One possible statement of purpose from that thesis statement is this:

> My audience is a general audience, of different ages and backgrounds. They've heard or read about Chernobyl, Three Mile Island, and the government's tests in Utah in the 1950s. They've seen science fiction movies. So they're likely to start reading with some real fears, that nuclear energy, not carefully handled, can result in horrible children's cancers, as in Chernobyl. They also probably have some fears grounded in speculation, from movies.
>
> Because of those fears, I doubt I can change their minds completely—but I'm hoping to persuade them just to look again at nuclear power. I believe recent developments might put them more at ease.
>
> My readers also share concerns that might encourage them to be more open. They are concerned about how current energy sources—oil and coal—affect the environment. They are concerned about the costs of power production and use. So if I can show how nuclear power might just be cleaner and less expensive, they are likely to look at it again.
>
> Should I start by addressing their fears, or should I start by talking about a form of energy that's cleaner and less expensive?

WHAT YOU CAN LEARN FROM A STATEMENT OF PURPOSE

A statement of purpose helps you make these decisions about your writing:

ETHOS

Because his statment of purpose to the left helps this writer realize he needs to encourage others to accept something they feared in the past, he needs to have a careful tone of voice in his writing and admit that he doesn't have all the answers. If he came across as a know-it-all, how do you think his readers would likely respond?

PATHOS

This writer now understands that, because he is trying to shift people's thinking about something that has frightened them, he needs to acknowledge the fear and not pretend that it doesn't exist. If he made fun of the fear, or made it sound as though only stupid people are afraid, chances are he'd lose his audience.

EXAMPLES AND EVIDENCE THAT WILL BE USEFUL, GIVEN THE AUDIENCE

This writer now understands that he needs to give many—and very credible—examples and evidence to persuade his readers that nuclear power might be cleaner and less expensive than oil or coal.

HOW MUCH MORE RESEARCH TO DO

This writer has done enough research to understand that he needs to do more: He needs to find the credible sources—probably impartial academic sources and not industry sources—that will help him provide the examples and evidence his audience will need.

HOW TO WRITE A STATEMENT OF PURPOSE

To prepare,

- You need to have a thesis statement that you've developed following the guidelines on pages 96–97 and 138–139.

- You need to have thought about your audience in the ways we've described on pages 196–201.

- Set aside some time (thirty minutes to one hour) when you can be relaxed and write without being distracted.

To write a statement of purpose, write in response to the following questions:

- Who, to the best of your ability to describe them, are your readers? What do they know—or not—about your topic?

- Given what you know about your audience, are they likely to accept your warrant with little discussion? What sort of immediate responses are they likely to have to your evidence and claim in your thesis statement?

- When they finish reading your writing, what would you like them to think, feel, or do?

- What sort of shifts—in emotion, in opinion—is your audience going to have to make, if you are to persuade them to reconsider their likely initial response to your topic, so that they have the response you hope they will when finished reading?

A statement of pupose is informal writing, but helps you move from writing-to-learn to writing-to-communicate (→ see pages 18–19). A statement of pupose saves you time by helping you make important decisions about your writing before you start it, before you get yourself too tied down to a first draft.

(→ see pages 18–19)

TIP: JUST WHAT CAN YOU ACHIEVE WITH WRITING?

Have you ever had your mind changed **completely** on a topic (especially a controversial topic like abortion, gun control, gay marriage, or genetic engineering) by reading one article written by someone you don't know? Chances are your answer is **No**.

Most often, when we change our minds completely on such topics—or on almost any topic—it's the result of extended conversations with people we know and trust.

The writing of strangers—even of respected, experienced writers—might give us a little nudge to reconsider a position, but it will rarely change our minds completely.

When you are writing a statement of purpose, therefore, keep your purpose within reach. Don't expect to *convince my readers that gun control is bad* or *make my readers finally understand how harmful our dependence on oil is*. Instead, using verbs like the following in your statement of purpose will help you design achievable purposes:

inform	**suggest**
recommend	**consider**
acknowledge	**propose**
ask	**reflect**
attempt	**understand**

FOR EXAMPLE...

Here is Riley's thesis statement:

Women who receive microcredit without discussion support groups and classes in economics won't know how to change the community conditions that encourage poverty; therefore, microcredit should only be offered with such support.

Here is her statement of purpose.

My audience is others in class—and, of course, my teacher. From talking with the others in class, I know that even if they have heard about microcredit, they don't know much about it. They've maybe heard of the man who started microcredit, Muhammad Yunus of Bangladesh, and how he won the Nobel Peace Prize in 2006. They've also only heard good things about microcredit. Unless I make my topic interesting to them, they're probably not going to have much interest.

But when they are finished reading, I'd like my readers to be informed about what microcredit is and to understand how it's way more complicated than just giving people small loans. I also want them to care about the women who need the loans, so that they can make good decisions about donating money to a microcredit organization if they want or about working with one.

I'm interested in this because I got all caught up in all the stories about microcredit when I first read about it: It was exciting to read about something that seemed so simple but that could make such huge differences in people's lives. But then as I was doing more research I realized that all the promises people were making about microcredit mostly really weren't coming true. They weren't coming true because people's lives are so much more complex than just some money can fix. It's whole communities that need "fixing."

So that's why it seems like it's so important that the loans be accompanied by support groups and classes, so that the women can really make the differences in their lives that seems possible.

I wonder if I write my paper in the way that I learned about microcredit (first, how good it seems to be and then telling about the problems and why the problems exist), then maybe my readers will get caught up in it the way I did. All those stories of all those women going from having almost nothing to having their own businesses can suck you in, I think.

If I did that, it might just move my readers from caring about the women and their stories to caring about what doesn't always work with microcredit. Then I can describe what needs to happen to make it work.

A ROUGH DRAFT

WHAT IS A ROUGH DRAFT?

A rough draft is a testing ground. Written with the expectation that it can be strengthened through feedback from others and revision, it is an attempt to shape a coherent argument.

Successful writers write rough drafts, often many rough drafts. Such writers do not expect that any piece of writing will be finished in one sitting.

Instead, they allow themselves time to produce writing they know will be rough but that is necessary to help them figure out their final thoughts. Even though these writers have a pretty good idea of what they want to write before they sit down (by having developed a thesis statement and then a statement of purpose), they know that as they write, their ideas might shift or that they'll write something that doesn't quite do what they want it to.

TIP: HOW DO YOU FIND YOUR STARTING WORDS?

If you have prepared your thesis state-ment and statement of purpose, you should have a good idea of what your paper needs to include…but if you are stuck about how to start your writing, look at the suggestions for different kinds of introductions in Part 6.
See pages 234–235.

Pick any of the kinds of introductions that catches your fancy; the point now is to get started writing; you can always change an introduction later if the work of the draft or feedback suggests a more appropriate introduction.

ARE YOU READY TO WRITE A FULL ROUGH DRAFT?

You are not ready to write a full rough draft until you

❑ have a thesis statement and have gathered good evidence in support of the reasons for your thesis's claim.

❑ have a statement of purpose that helps you understand how to shape your thesis for your particular readers.

PREPARING TO WRITE A DRAFT

- Review any notes you have taken from your sources.
- Keep your sources (or copies of your sources) nearby so that you can check that you are summarizing, paraphrasing, or quoting according to academic conventions.

  → See pages 298–309 on how to summarize, paraphrase, and quote in academic papers.

- Set up your writing area so that you will have few distractions.
- Arrange your time so that you have at least an hour, but preferably two or three hours, to write at any one sitting.
- Do not expect to complete a five- to seven-page draft in one sitting. Plan for at least two or three different times that you will write.

USING YOUR THESIS STATEMENT TO ARRANGE THE MAJOR PARTS OF YOUR DRAFT

→ See pages 152–155 in Part 4 for suggestions on how to use your thesis statement to arrange the parts of your draft.

WHILE WRITING

- Don't stop the flow of your ideas by fixating on grammar or spelling; instead, focus on writing your argument. Because this is a draft, you will have time later to revise and edit.

  → If English is not your home language, however, see the advice on pages 449 and 454 for working on drafts.

- If you get stuck in your writing, you have at least three options:

  1 Get up and walk away; come back to the writing later, after you've had a chance to rest, go for a walk, chat with some friends, or otherwise refresh your mind.

  2 Start rereading your writing from the beginning to see if this sparks your thinking.

  3 Review your thesis statement and statement of purpose to see if you have covered all that you know you need to cover; if you've missed anything, start writing about it.

- If you summarize, paraphrase, or quote (→ see pages 298–309) any source, be sure to include the expected in-text citation in the format you are using. Also be sure to put any such sources into a running bibliography list at the end of your draft.

  → For **MLA style**, see pages 328–394.

  → For **APA style**, see pages 395–438.

  → For **CSE style**, see pages 439–443.

  → For **CMS style**, see pages 444–448.

STARTING TO WRITE FOR AN AUDIENCE
A ROUGH DRAFT

Riley has produced a rough draft for an assignment that asks for a five- to seven-page paper. She is using this draft just to get her ideas onto paper, to see how they look, and to get a sense of how her ideas will work for her readers.

We've indicated some of her initial choices, as well as places she is not yet sure of her choices—and we've indicated where in this book she can look for further assistance.

As you read Riley's draft, look for how she starts to develop her argument. It's not as clear as it could be in this draft, but it is starting to take shape. Also look for how she's addressing the concerns of her readers, as she came to understand them through developing a statement of purpose.

→ Riley's polished revision of this draft is on pages 330–341.

Title

After you read the draft, return here: Do you think Riley's title accurately prepares a reader for what is to come?

Opening quotation

Will this quotation encourage readers to care for the women who receive microloans, as Riley hopes?

Introduction

Does this introductory paragraph help readers understand clearly and easily what is to follow?

→ Pages 234–235 give suggestions for introductions that meet academic expectations.

Do you think this paragraph engages readers sufficiently with Riley's warrant?

Transitions

Do you think readers will understand why Riley moves from her introductory paragraph to this sentence?

→ See pages 236–237 for information on how to write transitions that help readers follow your arguments.

A long quotation

Riley has correctly followed the standard punctuation format for quotations that take more than five lines.

→ See the information on block quotations on page 302 to learn how to punctuate long quotations

But this quotation will seem too long to practiced readers of academic texts. Riley should paraphrase and summarize at least some of this passage.

→ See pages 306–309 for information on summarizing and paraphrasing.

And will readers know who Dr. Yunus is?

ROUGH DRAFT
Money Makes the World Go Round

Says Nyamba Konate, a USAID microloan beneficiary, "I can now ensure that my children go to school, and I can better support my husband by buying food and stocking it to get us through the difficult rainy season." ("Microloans and Literacy")

Everyone wants poverty to go away, and microloans have been described as one way to do this.

A Google search with "microloan" gets over 2,000,000 hits, many to organizations that offer very small loans to people who otherwise would not qualify for traditional bank loans. The websites tell stories of the changes microloans can make in the lives of poor women all over the world. But anyone who thinks microloans are always good has obviously not read enough.

Grameen Bank was the first to give microcredit.

The inspiration for Grameen Bank came to Dr. Yunus during a trip to the village of Jobra in Bangladesh during the devastating famine of 1974. He met a woman who was struggling to make ends meet as a weaver of bamboo stools. She needed to borrow to buy materials, but because she was poor and had no assets, conventional banks shunned her, and she had to turn instead to local moneylenders whose extortionate rates of interest consumed nearly all her profits.

Dr. Yunus, then a professor of rural economics at Chittagong University, gave the woman and several of her neighbors loans totalling $27 from his own pocket. To his surprise, the borrowers paid him back in full and on time. So he started traveling from village to village, offering more tiny loans and cutting out the middlemen. Dr. Yunus was determined to prove that lending to the poor was not an "impossible proposition," as he put it.

When he later formalized the loan-making arrangement as the Grameen Bank in 1983, the bank adopted its signature innovation: making borrowers take out loans in groups of five, with each borrower guaranteeing the others' debts. Thus, in place of the hold banks have on wealthier borrowers who do

1

Fragment

→ See pages 466–469 for how
to recognize and fix sentence fragments.

A paragraph that does too much

This paragraph covers a lot of problems with micro-credit—and so is hard for readers to follow. Look at Riley's final draft on pages 330–341 to see how this paragraph is clearer when it is broken up into several smaller paragraphs, each focused on one particular point.

Logos: giving evidence

In this (too) long paragraph, Riley makes many assertions about the ways microcredit can go wrong—but she offers sources to support only two of the assertions. Each of the sentences in this paragraph makes a small claim, and should have a source connected to it.

→ Riley's final draft on pages 330–341 shows how to use sources as evidence in support of claims you want to make in your writing.

A quotation without introduction or attribution

Rarely in academic writing do writers use quotations without introducing them.

→ Page 305 has suggestions for weaving quotations into your writing.

Never in academic writing do writers use quotations without an attribution.

→ See pages 342–351 for how to give the expected attributions for quotations in MLA style (which Riley uses here). (See pages 410–413 for APA style, page 439 for CSE, and page 445 for CMS.)

Explaining terms

It seems clear by now that Riley's paper is focusing on microloans—but has she written this explicitly in any part of the paper? Has she defined *microloan*?

not pay their debts—foreclosure and a low credit rating—Grameen depends on an incentive at least as powerful for poor villagers, the threat of being shamed before neighbors and relatives. (Giridharadas and Bradsher)

Almost everyone talks about how good microloans are. As though poverty as we know it will end. Women will be liberated.

But one writer says that most studies of microcredit programs "find very small increases in income for quite large numbers of borrowers; in only a very small number of cases are there significant income increases" (Mayoux 39). It most often benefits women who are not at the lowest levels of poverty, while the poorest of the poor lose ground. Microcredit also doesn't last long because the borrowers often can't use their loans for anything but tonight's dinner or an emergency. Or maybe the women do work that doesn't make much money, like selling home-made food on the streets, cleaning the houses of others, or working at home. So women are still stuck at home or in small jobs. Meaning their communities will still be poor. "Bangladesh and Bolivia are two countries widely recognized for having the most successful microcredit programs in the world. They also remain two of the poorest countries in the world." And the loan often added to what women have to do in a day. When women use their loans to make and sell food or other stuff, they do this on top of running households and taking care of children sometimes they have to pull their children out of school to help out, in order to stay on top of the loan to pay it back (Cheston 25). And rather than learning how to use and work with the loan money themselves, a lot of women give their loans to men in their families because they live in communities where men are supposed to make money decisions. Because of this the men sometimes get mad and are both verbally and physically violent against women.

Why are women supposed to be liberated by microloans? The United Nations says

> Women's access to microfinance not only benefits women but also their families and communities, by generating:
> – Increased income, awareness, and bargaining power for women;
> – Increased resources available to the family for investment in nutrition and education;
> – Growth in local economies through local increases in women's spending;

2

Explaining terms

Do you think Riley can count on her readers knowing what FINCA is? If you are ever in doubt whether readers will understand a term you are using, explain it—and always spell out abbreviations the first time you use them.

→ See pages 556 and 590–591 for information on using abbreviations.

More long quotations

Academic readers will often accept one or two quotations of this length, but you can see that Riley's paper is full of them: It looks as though her writing simply strings together the words of others. Riley needs to shorten her quotations, or to paraphrase and summarize them, to show readers that she has really thought through and made her own sense of these ideas.

→ See pages 306–309 for information on summarizing and paraphrasing.

Building ethos by using the authority of others

Riley is quoting someone named Susy Cheston here; the quotation suggests that Susy Cheston knows quite a bit about women and microloans—but why should readers trust her? If Riley explains who Susy Cheston is by including Cheston's title or explaining why Cheston has authority to speak on this topic, Riley's readers are more likely to accept the authority of this quotation and so to accept that Riley has authority, too.

→ Page 303 includes information about how to give a title to or explain the authority of someone you are quoting.

Helping readers check sources

To check a source, readers usually need the name of the person(s) responsible for the words (so that they can find the source in the bibliography list at the end of the paper) and a page number. Because the name of the person who wrote these words preceded this quotation, Riley needs only to give a page number here.

→ See pages 342–351 for how to show the sources of your quotations and evidence in MLA style (which Riley uses here). (See pages 410–413 for APA style, page 439 for CSE, and page 445 for CMS.)

and
— An expanded view in the larger society of social and economic norms that
relate to women.

FINCA says that it lends primarily to women because

Seventy percent of the world's poor are women, largely because of their
limited access to education or to productive resources like land and credit.
Another worldwide trend is an increase in woman-headed households, in
which a mother provides the sole support for her children. Most victims of
severe poverty are children. According to UNICEF, at least half of the 12
million children aged five or younger who die each year, die from malnutrition
associated with severe poverty. The most direct way to improve childrens'
survival and welfare is to strengthen their own mothers' ability to take care of
them. ("Frequently Asked Questions")

Microloans are supposed to help women be confident taking care of their own
money and taking part in their communities. They are expected to use any money
they earn from their loans for their families. Because the families are supposed to
improve, their communities are supposed to improve, too.

Research supports this, some. Susy Cheston says that:

According to research by microfinance impact assessment specialist Suzy
Salib-Bauer of Sinapi Aba Trust, an Opportunity International microfinance
institution (MFI) in Ghana, 42 percent of mature clients (those in the program
two years or more) had an improvement in their poverty level—either moving
from "very poor" to "poor" or from "poor" to "non-poor" status, as measured by
a standard household asset and income index. ASHI, an MFI in the
Philippines that exclusively targets poor women, found that 77 percent of
incoming clients were classified as "very poor"; after two years in the program,
only 13 percent of mature clients were still "very poor." (23)

Another writer describes a program that

had an important positive impact on a large number of women members.
Over one third of the sample had been able to begin market work with a loan,
and the loans had enabled women to keep marginal businesses afloat in
family crises without recourse to moneylenders. Access to loans was also
estimated to have led to increased earnings for a quarter of all the sampled

3

Logos: helping readers with summaries and transitions

Riley helps readers by ending this paragraph with a summary of the main point of her paragraph.

→ Pages 236–237 have suggestions for helping readers stay oriented in your writing.

Conclusions: a place for pathos

Riley has mostly used this last paragraph to summarize and restate her main argument, using some pathos. Academic readers expect this in essays. But what they don't expect in a conclusion is new information, such as Riley's comment about MacIsaac's report. (Riley has also not included MacIsaac in the Works Cited list.)

→ Pages 232–233 contain ideas for shaping conclusions to academic writing.

Making a works cited list

For a rough draft, it is alright to start a Works Cited listing on the same page as the rest of the paper. For a final draft, however, the Works Cited listing should start on its own page in MLA format.

→ See pages 352–394 for help in constructing a Works Cited list in the MLA format.

Enough sources?

There are many places in Riley's paper where she has made assertions without offering any evidence—so she should probably have more sources than she shows here.

Enough different kinds of sources?

Some readers will note that these sources are all websites, and will not approve—even though the websites are of different kinds: a journal article published by the U.S. Department of State, a website for a respected nonprofit organization, an article from the *New York Times*, and a United Nations report.

You need to judge whether your audience will accept only webpages as sources. If an assignment does not have a clear policy about using only webpages, ask.

women, often through enabling them to switch jobs and trades to more lucrative ones. Some had diversified their activities, adding a second line of work or a secondary job. For other women the loan kept them out of further debilitating debt through diversion of the loan in times of major stress events such as illness, flood, death or desertion of husband and enabling them to carry out their ritual responsibilities necessary to maintaining social status. (Mayoux 39)

So no one is wrong to think that microloans can have positive effects in the lives of women.

Microloans have helped some women. But anyone who believes microloans will cure the world is way off. MacIsaac has written a report that shows how microloan programs ought to work. If we really honestly do want to end poverty, we must help women be in big business. We must help them make their own decisions. We must give them what will help them deal with the family and community stuff that stands in the way of them getting ahead, and so we must give them support groups and economic classes in addition to the microloans.

Works Cited

Cheston, Susy. "Women and Microfinance: Opening Markets and Minds." *Economic Perspectives: An Electronic Journal of the U.S. Department of State* 9.1. Feb. 2004. Web. 29 May 2010.

"Frequently Asked Questions." *FINCA*. Web. 28 May 2010.

Giridharadas, Anand, and Keith Bradsher. "Microloan Pioneer and His Bank Win Nobel Peace Prize." *New York Times* 13 Oct. 2006. Web. 28 May 2010.

Mayoux, Linda. "From Vicious to Virtuous Circles? Gender and Micro-Enterprise Development." *United Nations Research Institute for Social Development*. 1995. Web. 20 May 2010.

"Microloans and Literacy Are Contributing to Food Security in Poor Upper Guinea." *USAID Africa Success Stories*. 2005. Web. 20 May 2010.

4

RECEIVING FEEDBACK TO A DRAFT

See Riley's paper, revised to account for this and other feedback, on pages 330–341.

To the right is feedback Riley received from her teacher, with Riley's notes in response.

The feedback summarizes this particular reader's understanding of Riley's argument; now Riley can understand whether readers are hearing what she hopes they will hear.

Receiving such feedback can be hard if you've put a lot of effort into writing: You might not want to hear that you have more work to do. But it's important to know how to receive feedback, because feedback is what helps you strengthen your writing so that it communicates what you want.

Read feedback as soon as you get it but then put it aside for a day or two. Read it again with a little distance, and you'll be in a better position to understand it.

Feedback is what most helps you move your words from writing-to-learn to writing-to-communicate (→ see pages 18–19).

When you receive feedback, keep in mind:

- The feedback of others helps you become a stronger writer. Only by hearing how others read and understand do you learn how your words communicate.

- If readers do not understand your argument, or believe it to be other than you intended, don't blame the readers. If readers miss or misinterpret your argument, ask them why they see the argument they do. Ask readers to go through your writing sentence by sentence, explaining out loud what they understand, so you can learn the particular effects your words have—and so you can learn how to revise your words to do what you hope.

→ To learn more about revising a paper, see Part 6, beginning with pages 220–221.

Riley—

This is a fine start: I can see that the paper is building an argument that, even though many people believe microloans always have positive results and that they can make big changes in the world, microloans won't solve poverty and don't necessarily help women.(Given that so many people think microloans are good — as you note in your writing — it's probably important that you acknowledge that there are good results for microloans; don't just make them sound all bad.) Your paper provides strong evidence for the shortcomings of microloans: you have done your rsearch!

Darn. She isn't seeing the argument that I want to make with my thesis statement...

I sometimes get a little lost in the argument the paper makes, though.

Most importantly, I wonder about the order of the paragraphs. After the introduction, your paper gives a history of microloans, and then describes how they are bad and then how they are good. Why discuss the bad before the good? Also, I often have trouble understanding why the paper moves from one paragraph to the next; I think your paper could provide more direct transitions in order to help readers.

WHY did I talk about the bad first? Does this make me sound biased to readers?

OK—I need to work on transitions...

Finally, one last thing I noticed: the paper ends with a call for women who receive microloans also to be helped with support groups and to be given business classes. I have to tell you that, for me as a reader, this comes out of the blue. The paper offers no evidence that support groups and business classes overcome the problems the paper describes, and so as a reader I can't help but feel unsatisfied with this recommendation. Could the argument about microloans stand without it?

Is my original thesis statement too ambitious for a 5 to 7-page paper? I just don't think I have room to show how microloans can be problems AND how to solve those problems...

I look forward to seeing your revisions of this. You should take confidence from the strengths of this draft so that, as you revise, you focus on the matters I've suggested above.

Riley writes notes in the margins to help her think about this feedback.

Please come talk if you have any questions.

Thanks! Professor Maathai

RESPONDING TO THE WRITING OF YOUR PEERS

When you are asked to respond to someone else's writing, consider the following:

WHAT IS THE MOST USEFUL, RESPECTFUL FEEDBACK YOU'VE EVER RECEIVED?

Keep a collection of useful feedback, and analyze what makes it useful. This will not only help you give good feedback to others, but will help you develop a stronger eye for reading your own words.

WHAT KIND OF FEEDBACK DOES THE WRITER NEED?

Perhaps the writer only needs help checking grammar and spelling—but perhaps the writer needs feedback on the order of ideas, in which case for you to correct spelling is useless because the words you correct might go away in the revision. If a writer asks for help and does not specify what kind, ask. (By asking, you also help the writer to articulate what the writing needs.)

HAVE YOU READ TWICE BEFORE RESPONDING?

Take notes during a first reading, while you get a sense of what the writer is trying to do. Then reread, looking for what in the writing most supports what the writing is trying to do, and for the parts that aren't as supportive. Then write comments.

HAVE YOU PRIORITIZED YOUR FEEDBACK?

You know how unhelpful it is to get a long, unordered list of feedback. When you are preparing feedback for another, pick the two to five most important observations you have—the observations that you think will most help the writer revise toward the best paper—and present only those.

Dear Riley,

I liked how your paper starts with those words from a woman talking about her family. Right away you give me a sense of real people (but I guess I wish there was even more sense of people as the paper goes on).

I also like how you are teaching me something new about microloans. I knew a little bit about them before, and only knew good things, so I like learning how they might not be so perfect. I think you are starting to give enough evidence to persuade me that they are not always perfect.

As I read the paper, I felt a little like the writing was jumping from one concern to the next too quickly. For example, in the long paragraph on page 2, the writing starts by talking about how only certain women benefit from the loans, but then goes on to talk about how men can be bad to women because of the loans. Maybe that paragraph could be broken up, so that those different points could each get more focus? And maybe more transitions between paragraphs would help me understand better as a reader why the argument is moving me from one point to the next.

I hope these comments are helpful. Let me know.

Aaron

Do tell writers what you like about their writing, and why

Writers (like any person) need to know what they do well. When we have a sense of what we do well, it gives us a ground on which we can stand as we start developing our other abilities.

If you are asked to give feedback to the main argument, say first what you think the main argument is

You may be seeing a different main argument from what the writer intends, and the writer needs to know; the writer can then reshape the argument to fit the original intention, or can reshape it to pull out what you see. But if you give feedback on a different argument than what the writer intends, the writer will be revising at cross (and confusing) purposes.

Respond by talking about how you read

All writers need help understanding how others understand their words, and so a good way to give feedback is to say something like, "The first sentence of this paragraph made me think that what would follow would be about x, but instead it was about y—so I got confused." This is much more helpful to writers than, "This paragraph was confusing."

Respond to the writing, not the writer

Respond with "This introduction didn't help me understand what the paper was about," not with "You can't do introductions well." The first response helps a writer understand what revisions are needed; the second just makes the writer feel incompetent and will get in the way of helping the writer improve.

Give reasons for your comments

If instead of, "I get lost in this paragraph," you say, "In this paragraph you started out writing about the effects of video game violence on children but then you ended by writing about television cartoons, and I couldn't see what connected those two ideas," you give the writer information useful for revision. (And if you work to articulate feedback in this way, you'll find it easier to look at your own writing just as carefully; teachers of writing often talk about how useful to their own writing it is to have to formulate feedback to people in their classes.)

HINTS & TIPS FOR CONNECTING WITH READERS

ASK FOR FOCUSED FEEDBACK TO YOUR WRITING

Because getting feedback from readers is the main way to strengthen your writing, getting useful feedback is crucial. But giving good feedback is a learned skill, and many readers won't automatically know how to give you useful feedback.

When you are ready for feedback, tell readers what you need: For example, ask them to focus on your argument and to try to tell you what your thesis statement is. Or ask them to read the argument to see if you offer enough evidence, or if your transitions help them understand why you move from one paragraph to the next.

Choose only one or two areas for them to focus on in their reading.

BE SURE YOU UNDERSTAND FEEDBACK

If you hear something you don't understand from a reader, ask for clarification. If you don't understand feedback, it can't help you.

GET FEEDBACK FROM YOURSELF

Put your writing aside for at least several hours to get some distance from it, and then reread it. Reread it once to see if your thesis seems sufficiently developed, read it again to check your transitions, and so on.

You need to learn to be your own audience, because the paper you turn in is yours. You have the final responsibility for it.

Explore these topics online:

Peer response

www.mycomplab.com

TIP: CONNECTING WITH DIFFERENT KINDS OF AUDIENCES

Pages 194–199 of Part 5 help you think about any kind of audience for which you might compose, and pages 146–155 help you think about drafting a paper specifically for academic audiences.

To help you draft compositions for workplace or popular audiences, Part 4 contains suggestions on the organizations of such compositions.

→ See pages 156–169.

PART 6
REVISING
WITH STYLE

CONTENTS

WHERE ARE WE IN THE PROCESS FOR COMPOSING?

Understanding your project

Getting started

Asking questions

Shaping your project for others

Drafting a paper

Getting feedback

Revising
Paying attention to style—to the effects for your audience of your individual sentences and words

Polishing

ARE YOU READY TO USE THE NEXT PAGES OF THIS BOOK?

NO...
Are you struggling to begin a draft of a paper?
If this is your situation, then, no, you are not ready for the next pages.

What follows in the next pages is about how to revise your writing to make it as effective as possible for your particular audience, given your word, sentence, and paragraph choices.

→ For help with drafting a paper, see pages 200–213.

YES.
Are you working on a draft about which you feel pretty confident?
What follows will help you consider how your word, sentence, and paragraph choices are likely to strike your readers.

REVISING YOUR WRITING

→ See Riley's revised paper on pages 330–341.

WHAT IS REVISION?

To revise, you focus on your argument and how well readers understand your argument. At this stage of the composing process, you might need to move paragraphs around, find new evidence and write new paragraphs to hold that evidence, rewrite your introduction, or move your conclusion so that it becomes your introduction. (Often, after developing a first draft, it is with the conclusion that a writer can finally state what the paper is really about.)

You will most strengthen your writing if you don't get distracted by grammar, spelling, and mechanics now but instead let yourself be open to large changes.

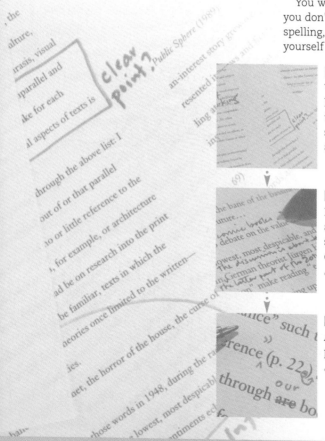

REVISING

When you revise, you attend to large-scale persuasive aspects of a text: organization and style. You start revising once you have close to a full draft.

EDITING

In editing, you attend to sentences and other large details: Are sentences readable? Have you documented all your sources?

→ See pages 452–453 for more on editing.

PROOFREADING

A proofreader checks spelling, punctuation, and other mechanics.

→ See pages 454–455 for more on proofreading.

TO REVISE, ASK YOURSELF:

- Am I clear about my argument? Can I state it as a thesis statement?
  ⟶ See pages 96–97, 138–139, and 152–155.

- Did I offer well-supported and accurate evidence for each of my claims?
  ⟶ See pages 98–107.

- Have I been fair and respectful toward the differing positions one could take on my arguments?
  ⟶ See pages 108–123.

- Will my readers understand the purpose of each paragraph?
  ⟶ See pages 176–183.

- Can I say why my paragraphs are ordered as they are? Can I describe the steps of my argument?
  ⟶ See pages 152–155.

- Will my writing engage readers?
  ⟶ See pages 224–259.

- Does my introduction engage readers with my argument and initial concerns?
  ⟶ See pages 234–235.

- Have I given appropriate emphasis to the main parts of my arguments?
  ⟶ Look through Part 6 for pages checked for helping with emphasis.

- Do my transitions help readers move from one paragraph to the next?
  ⟶ See pages 236–237.

- Does my conclusion sum up my argument and end memorably for readers?
  ⟶ See pages 232–233.

PART 3

PART 4

PART 6

DEVELOPING A REVISION PLAN

→ See Riley's revised paper on pages 330–341.

After you receive feedback to a draft, make time to develop a revision plan for yourself. A revision plan is informal, just for you.

To the right, Riley's plan lays out how she understands the feedback she received and how she plans to respond.

The feedback you receive from others, as well as the list on page 221, can help you determine how to focus your revision efforts.

REVISING, NOT EDITING OR PROOFREADING

Notice that in her revision plan Riley doesn't mention anything about spelling or grammar: That's because revising is about focusing on your argument and how well readers understand those arguments, not on the details of spelling and grammar.

→ When you are ready to edit and proofread, see pages 450–455.

TIP: GO TO THE WRITING CENTER!

If your school has a Writing Center, the staff will be happy to help you at any stage of your writing process—but know that visiting them while you are working on revising is a particularly smart move.

Writing Center staff are well trained in helping writers clarify and strengthen drafts. After you have a first draft, talking with someone in your Writing Center will help you speed your process and focus on the most important revision steps you can make.

Explore these topics online:

Revision

www.mycomplab.com

Given the feedback I've received from Professor Maathai and others in class, I don't think I really got across the main point of my thesis statement. I don't think I was able to say enough to persuade people that microloan programs have their best chances of working when the women who receive the loans get classes in economics and business and have lots of time to talk with other women about their experiences and problems. Maybe I need to revise my thesis, to argue just that people shouldn't expect microloans to solve poverty and liberate women because of all the problems with microloans.

→ See Riley's draft on pages 206–213.

→ See the feedback she received on pages 214–217.

Given all the feedback I've gotten, I also need to

- Experiment with different arrangements of the parts of my paper, to see which most help people understand that microloans don't do what most people think.

Organization and arrangement

→ See Part 4.

- Have more sources to support my claims about microloans.

Working with sources

→ See Parts 2 and 3.

- Figure out, still, how to get readers to care more: I still don't think I've got enough examples or am presenting stuff in ways that suck people in.

Working with examples

→ See Part 4.

- Work out, like above, how to make my introduction more compelling.
- Experiment with my tone of voice, so that it's not so choppy.
- Work on the transitions between my paragraphs.

Introductions, tone of voice, transitions, and other matters of style

→ See Part 6.

REVISING, STYLE, AND AUDIENCE

TWO ASPECTS OF REVISION

As we mentioned a few pages back, when you revise, you attend to large-scale persuasive aspects of a text:

1 ORGANIZATION. Are your paragraphs arranged so that readers understand why one paragraph follows the next? Can they follow the steps of your argument?

→For more on working with paragraphs and the arrangements of paragraphs, see pages 152–155 and 176–183.

2 STYLE. Here in Part 6 we help you revise your writing so that it is clear, concise, coherent, puts emphasis on the points where you want emphasis, and engages your readers.

Style is not about being fancy; it is about the detailed choices you make to design your ideas for your audience.

We focus on style here, in these pages about revision, because—once you have the organization of your argument in place—it is through attending to the paragraphs, sentences, and words of your writing that you can be most persuasive.

ALL COMMUNICATIONS HAVE STYLE

In a book about the senses we read:

One scent can be unexpected, momentary, and fleeting, yet conjure up a childhood summer beside a lake in the Poconos, when wild blueberry bushes teemed with succulent fruit and the opposite sex was as mysterious as space travel; another, hours of passion on a moonlit beach in Florida, while the night-blooming cereus drenched the air with thick curds of perfume and huge sphinx moths visited the cereus in a loud purr of wings; a third, a family dinner of pot roast, noodle pudding, and sweet potatoes, during a myrtle-mad August in a midwestern town, when both of one's parents were alive.

On a webpage describing the work of two scientists, we read:

In 1991 Axel and Buck discovered a family of roughly 1,000 genes that encode the odorant receptors of the olfactory epithelium, a patch of cells on the wall of the nasal cavity. The olfactory epithelium contains neurons that send messages directly to the olfactory bulb of the brain. When an odor excites a neuron, the signal travels along the nerve cell's axon and is transferred to the neurons in the olfactory bulb.

Both paragraphs describe the sense of smell. The paragraphs differ because the writing is aimed at two different audiences:

- The first paragraph is for a general audience. The paragraph is the opening of a chapter; it leads into passages that contain somewhat technical information. The style of the paragraph suggests to the readers that even though what the chapter covers is somewhat technical, readers will still enjoy it because the information will be detailed, sensuous, and concrete.

- The second paragraph, as you could tell, was written by scientists for scientists. Individual words are not defined, because the writer assumes the reader knows them. The sentences are much shorter than in the first example, and they focus on describing processes as directly as possible, with few adjectives.

Although the second paragraph may not seem to have much style, many choices went into it, choices about individual words, the length of sentences, and the grammatical construction of the sentences.

OVERALL STYLE—AND FINELY DETAILED STYLE

The example paragraphs probably enable you to imagine the source of each: The first paragraph comes from a book full of fine and luscious descriptions; the second comes from a short, to-the-point, descriptive piece of writing. Notice, then, that style is about:

- **The overall feel a piece has for a reader.** Does the piece feel lush and detailed, or quick and precise? In what contexts and for what purposes will audiences expect writing like the first example paragraph or like the second?

- **The feel of words, sentences, and paragraphs.** The overall style of a piece is built from the choices you make at the level of words and sentences. We've already pointed out the differences in sentence length and word choice between the two examples; what other differences can you see between the two?

STYLE IN WRITING

STYLING FOR CLARITY, CONCISION, COHERENCE, EMPHASIS, AND ENGAGEMENT

If you construct your writing to be clear, concise, coherent, emphatic, and engaging, you will have writing that works for present-day readers in most contexts. Your readers may not be able to name those five values, but in the United States we are in a culture that desires information to come quickly and easily as well as with some pleasure. (Or, to look at it in another way, no one likes having to work hard for boring information.)

If you are to construct writing that has these values, you need to know your purposes in writing. To decide how to style a sentence or paragraph, you need to ask how your choices will help your readers understand your purposes.

CLARITY

Clarity comes from a Latin word that means *clear*, as when the air is clear on a bright day. When you strive for clarity in writing, you shape sentences to help your readers see what is most important, quickly and easily.

CONCISION

Being concise means getting to the point. To be concise in writing, use as few words as possible. Concision supports clarity.

COHERENCE

When writing is coherent, it feels as though all its parts belong together. Readers see connections between the parts of a writing, and can easily grasp the overall purpose of the writing.

EMPHASIS

To persuade others to listen to your concerns, you need to make your purposes clear and you need to offer reasons. Some reasons will be more persuasive to your audience than others, and so the following pages offer strategies for emphasizing the parts of writing that you want your audience most to notice and remember.

Keep in mind, when you want to emphasize specific parts of your writing, that you cannot emphasize every single word or phrase. That would be like yelling continually at your audience—and, as you know, when someone yells at you continually, you stop listening. Instead, emphasis is when someone has been talking in a regular tone for a while and only now and then raises (or lowers) her voice.

ENGAGEMENT

Humans are lively, energetic, social beings. We like to tell jokes. We like to hear about odd events in the lives of others. We need to learn the practical details of living well and healthily. We need to learn how others live with the sorrows of death and pain.

We learn best from each other when our minds are active and engaged.

Writing that helps readers feel and understand someone else's delight or sorrow will be more effective than writing that doesn't. Writing that helps readers understand concretely and comfortably how to put together a stereo system will be more effective than writing that doesn't. Writing that helps readers understand the consequences of a melted polar ice cap is much more likely to bring readers to action than writing that just lists sterile facts.

■ ■ ■

The following pages discuss strategies you can use—with your own choices of individual words and your own constructions of sentences and paragraphs—to shape your writing to include all these values.

Because style is present in all levels of writing, we divide the following pages into the following order:

PARAGRAPHS

SENTENCES

WORDS

STYLE IN WRITING
STYLES READERS EXPECT IN DIFFERENT SETTINGS

To the right are samples of writing on the same topic but aimed at different kinds of audiences.

Underneath each sample we note the stylistic features readers generally expect in writing for these different audiences and contexts.

ACADEMIC WRITING

Today nearly every job requires good performances on more than one task. Employees have to deal with several simultaneous demands, and good job performance is therefore linked to good multitasking performance. This holds true for many jobs, as shown by data from the Occupational Information Network (O*NET; cf. Peterson, Mumford, Borman, Jeanneret, & Fleishman, 1999) and other job analyses (e.g., Maschke & Goeters, 1999, for airline pilots). In terms of personnel selection, therefore, it would appear to be essential to identify future employees with adequate multitasking abilities.

Bühner, M., et al. (2006). Working memory dimensions as differential predictors of the speed and error aspect of multitasking performance. *Human Performance, 19,* 253–275.

1 Uses technical terms: *good multitasking performance, personnel selection.*

2 Has long noun phrases: *several simultaneous demands, adequate multitasking abilities.*

3 Has long sentences.

4 Uses verbs that refer to unchanging conditions (such as mental or bodily states): *is ... linked, requires.*

5 Has an element of doubt: *nearly every job, it would appear.*

6 Has a neutral tone.

7 Shows respect for the ideas and work of others by citing names and sources.

WORKPLACE WRITING

Meyer offers the following tips to reduce workplace stress:

- Set aside time for mindful work. Ignore or turn off your email signal and don't answer your phone so you can focus on the project at hand. Multi-tasking can make us less productive and it may be helpful to set aside time for focused effort each day.

- Revisit timelines. Assess whether your timelines are realistic. Working toward deadlines you cannot meet is self-defeating. Readjust the timeline when necessary.

Illinois Manufacturers' Association. (2007, August 29). HR Memo. Retrieved from Web site: http:// www.ima-net.org/ library/hrmemo/ hr082907.cfm

1 Mixes popular words and expressions (*don't, set aside time*) with technical terms appropriate to the particular workplace (*timelines, deadlines*).

2 Has few long noun phrases; instead, if nouns are modified, it is usually with one adjective.

3 Has short sentences.

4 Uses crisp, active verbs: *ignore, revisit*.

5 Makes confident and direct recommendations, with explanations.

6 Has a confident tone.

7 Cites sources as needed.

POPULAR WRITING

Recently I poked fun at those New Age marvels we call the multi-taskers. If you missed it, the salient point was this: Laboratory experiments prove that multi-tasking is, contrary to all hype, hugely inefficient.

Balzar, J. (2003, April 27). One thing at a time, please. *Los Angeles Times*.

1 Mixes popular words and expressions (*hype, marvels*) with technical terms and formal vocabulary (*salient, Laboratory experiments*).

2 Has few long noun phrases; instead, if nouns are modified, it is usually with one adjective.

3 Has shorter sentences.

4 Uses verbs that refer to actions: *poked fun, missed*.

5 Can make confident and wide-ranging claims: *multi-tasking is ... hugely inefficient*.

6 Can have a playful, even sarcastic, tone.

7 Doesn't cite sources in the text.

STYLING PARAGRAPHS

What is on this page will help you style your writing for:

- ☐ CLARITY
- ☐ CONCISION
- ☐ COHERENCE
- ☑ EMPHASIS
- ☑ ENGAGEMENT

In Part 4 we discussed the expectations readers have about paragraph organization; we also discussed the different functions paragraphs can perform. (→ See pages 176–183.)

In the next pages, we consider smaller-scale decisions you can make about paragraphs: How do you keep readers engaged and at the same time help them follow your argument?

■ ■ ■

Here are some strategies for composing engaging paragraphs:

VARY SENTENCE LENGTH

If every sentence in a paragraph is the same length, readers might fall into a lulling rhythm and stop paying attention. The paragraph below shows—with the last sentence a contrast to all that precedes—one possible strategy for keeping such rhythms from developing:

In the Web 2.0 model, we have thousands of services scrutinizing each new piece of information online, grabbing interesting bits, remixing them in new ways, and passing them along to other services. Each new addition to the mix can be exploited in countless new ways, both by human bloggers and by the software programs that track changes in the overall state of the Web. Information in this new model is analyzed, repackaged, digested, and passed on down to the next link in the chain. It flows.

VARY SENTENCE PATTERNS

In Part 9 we describe the four patterns of sentences. (→ See pages 508–509.) Varying a paragraph's sentence patterns can keep readers engaged:

In the thirties, Harold Gray's comic strip *Little Orphan Annie* had 47 million readers. Then it languished until the 1970s when Martin Charnin thought it would make a good stage musical. It did. For the film, fresh songs and scenes were added, and 8,000 girls auditioned for the part of Annie. Director John Huston wanted "a girl who can sing, dance and act, with tons of personality, so that for two hours audiences won't take their eyes off her." Aileen Quinn's high spirits in the role have caused children to say, after seeing the film, that they too want to be orphans.

You don't have to use all four patterns in every paragraph you write; just be aware that, if a paragraph's sentences are sounding repetitive to you, varying the patterns is one solution.

VARY SENTENCE ORDER

In English, readers expect sentences to have the order of subject-verb-object. (→ See pages 510–511.) Because this expectation is so widespread, you can create emphasis in a paragraph by reversing the word order of a sentence. Just be careful to do this infrequently, only when you want to create special emphasis. The following paragraph would be less strong if the first sentence were *Potential homebuyers should check basements first.*

Basements are where potential homebuyers should go first. The most expensive home repairs come up from weak and shaky foundations, and after you buy a house you do not want the surprise of thousands of dollars in bills for digging out and replacing the stone or cement block that is supposed to support your house. Only a detailed inspection by a foundation specialist can tell you whether a crack results from simple settling or the foundation breaking in two.

VARY PARAGRAPH LENGTH

Audiences expect different paragraph lengths, depending on medium and genre. For example, because many people are still becoming accustomed to reading online, paragraphs in online genres such as newspapers are often much shorter than paragraphs in print, only two or three sentences each. Paragraphs in academic genres, on the other hand, can extend over a page or two in a twenty-page paper. (In a paper shorter than ten pages, readers expect paragraphs to be shorter than a whole page.)

In general, all the paragraphs in any text will be of similar length, just long enough to develop and make clear the concept the writer needs to make at that point in the composition. But when you want to emphasize one point, you can use a paragraph that is much shorter than the others. Readers will see visually and through a change in reading rhythm that what the short paragraph discusses is important.

CONCLUDING PARAGRAPHS

What is on this page will help you style your writing for:

☑ CLARITY

☐ CONCISION

☑ COHERENCE

☑ EMPHASIS

☑ ENGAGEMENT

Why talk about concluding paragraphs before introductory paragraphs?

Because you cannot have a shining, strong introductory paragraph until you know the exact end toward which that paragraph points readers.

FUNCTIONS OF CONCLUDING PARAGRAPHS FOR READERS

1 Concluding paragraphs are logical: They sum up the arguments of the paper.

2 Concluding paragraphs carry emotional weight: Because readers read them last, concluding paragraphs are often what readers remember most.

TIP: FUNCTIONS OF CONCLUDING PARAGRAPHS FOR WRITERS

Once they are drafted, concluding paragraphs provide surprisingly useful suggestions to writers about revising.

→ See page 266.

STRATEGIES FOR CONCLUDING

As you write, you cannot separate the two functions of concluding paragraphs. As you read the following examples, look for how they mix functions, but also try to imagine what preceded the conclusion; a strong conclusion should enable you to do that.

RESTATING OR SUMMARIZING YOUR ARGUMENT

Provide a crisp summary, not a rote repetition. You can include a question, quotation, or recommended action:

In sum, the globalization of English does not mean that if we English-speakers just sit back and wait, we'll soon be able to exchange ideas with anyone else anywhere: We can't count on much more than a very basic ability to communicate. Outside of certain professional fields, if English-speaking Americans hope to exchange ideas with people in a nuanced way, we should do as people elsewhere are doing: become bilingual.

RECOMMENDING ACTION

The following conclusion recommends specific actions its audience can take:

The problem at hand is so huge it requires a response like our national mobilization to fight—and win—World War II. To move our nation off of fossil fuels, we need inspired, Churchillian leadership and sweeping statutes à la the Big War or the Civil Rights Movement. So, frankly, I feel a twinge of nausea each time I see that predictable "10 Things You Can Do" sidebar in a well-meaning magazine or newspaper article. In truth, the only list that actually matters is the one we should all be sending to Congress *post haste*, full of 10 muscular clean-energy statutes that would finally do what we say we want: rescue our life-giving Earth from climate catastrophe.

(Note: In the examples of introductory paragraphs on page 235 is the introduction that leads to this conclusion.)

SUGGESTING MORE QUESTIONS FOR RESEARCH

Suggestions about the conduct of technical writing courses must remain suggestions and not firm recommendations, until we know more about engineers' composing processes. Additional research on composing might reveal how Nelson, his firm, and his subdiscipline are and are not typical. It might show how his composing habits are more efficient or less efficient than those of his colleagues. It might suggest that some tasks call for very different composing habits and skills than others, or it might imply that technical writers should develop several composing styles to fit different composing situations. One thing seems certain, however: Only when more research is completed will teachers know how to better prepare students for the kinds of writing they will do at work.

REFLECTING ON HOW YOUR WRITING HAS AFFECTED YOU

Using your own voice pulls readers closer, making your observations more compelling.

In the interviews I conducted for this paper, I learned that men and women learn to be men and women by experiencing all the photographs, movies, magazine covers, and popular songs that portray what men and women are supposed to be and do. I've also learned how the simplest of tossed-off sentences can shape someone's sense of what's proper behavior. I heard how a teacher's comments are remembered for a long time. As an education major, it's that last observation I will carry with me, to help me think about the responsibilities I'll be taking on.

INTRODUCTORY PARAGRAPHS

What is on this page will help you style your writing for:

- ☑ CLARITY
- ☐ CONCISION
- ☐ COHERENCE
- ☑ EMPHASIS
- ☑ ENGAGEMENT

FUNCTIONS OF INTRODUCTORY PARAGRAPHS FOR READERS

1 Introductory paragraphs engage readers with the topic.

2 Introductory paragraphs focus readers' attention on the particular aspects of the topic that matter to you.

WHAT TO AVOID

- **Introductions that are broad and vague.** *From the beginning of time, humans have …* or *Life is amazing.* If you see similar phrases in your introduction, make your introduction more focused by stating as explicitly as you can what matters to you in this writing.

- **Starting with a dictionary definition.** Readers will think you are not confident enough about your own arguments to put them in your own words.

- **Excuses.** Don't make excuses about not being an expert. Readers don't expect experts to be writing college papers; instead, they expect well-researched arguments that acknowledge other possible positions.

TIP: WHAT'S YOUR DISCIPLINE?

Writers in the humanities frequently do not explicitly state their thesis; instead, they develop it over the writing. Writers in the sciences and social sciences are expected to be explicit about their thesis and to announce the structure of their papers.

If you have any questions about what is appropriate for an assignment, ask your teacher.

STRATEGIES FOR INTRODUCING

You can explictly state why readers should care about a topic, or you can engage them indirectly through how you talk about a topic. You can state your thesis directly or imply it.

BE DIRECT AND EXPLICIT

In the following pages I will argue that, even though many people consider microcredit capable of ending poverty, it instead can exacerbate poverty, especially for women and for the most poor.

USE A QUOTATION

In the 1820s, Fanny Trollope, that perceptive, sharp-tongued traveller, described North America as "a vast continent, by far the greater part of which is still in the state nature left it, and a busy, bustling, industrious population, hacking and hewing their way through it." That hewing, hacking, and shooting was to cause a lot of environmental damage.

USE A QUESTION

Millionaire Steve Fossett has been missing since last Monday, when he took off from a Nevada airstrip on a short flight. Rescue crews have yet to find the famous adventurer or his plane, but according to news reports, they've discovered at least *six uncharted wrecks* across a 17,000-square-mile swath of the Sierra Nevada—or nearly one a day since the search began. Why are there so many undocumented crash sites around the Sierra Nevada?

MAKE A SUPRISING CLAIM

Strange but true: Energy-efficient light bulbs and hybrid cars are hurting our nation's budding efforts to fight global warming.

MAKE A COMPELLING CLAIM

The rate of bipolar disorder diagnoses in children and adolescents seen as outpatients by physicians shot up dramatically between 1994 and 2003, raising new concerns about possible overdiagnosis of this severe mood disorder among young people.

PAINT A VISUAL PICTURE

Lady, an Australian shepherd mix who had been lounging in a sunny window seat at the Bothell Regional Library, pricked up her ears and wagged her tail when she saw 10-year-old Nicholas Goodman. When he sat down next to her with the book *Down in the Subway* and started to read aloud, she leaned against him, eyes closed, and appeared to listen intently. Her expression never changed, not even when Nicholas stumbled over tricky words like "guava."

That's the whole idea behind "Reading with Rover," a summer program for children at the Bothell and Kenmore branches of the King County Regional Library System.

TIP: HOW LONG?

In five- to ten-page papers, an introduction, like a conclusion, should rarely take up more than two-thirds of a page. A longer introduction will have readers wondering, midway through, when the paper starts; a longer conclusion will have readers wondering if a new paper or argument is starting.

STYLING PARAGRAPHS
TRANSITIONS BETWEEN PARAGRAPHS

What is on this page will help you style your writing for:

- CLARITY
- CONCISION
- COHERENCE
- EMPHASIS
- ENGAGEMENT

In Part 4, we discussed creating coherence within paragraphs; here we discuss creating coherence **between** paragraphs.

Most writers need to learn how to provide transitions between paragraphs, but learning how to do this will help your writing be confident and effective. When you use the strategies we discuss here, you tell readers why one paragraph follows another; you enable readers to follow and so better understand your arguments.

STRATEGIES FOR BUILDING TRANSITIONS

- Repeat crucial words, phrases, or concepts from one paragraph to the next.
- Repeat crucial concepts by using synonyms.
- Use the linking words listed on page 174 to show relationships between the paragraphs.

LINK THE LAST SENTENCE OF ONE PARAGRAPH TO THE FIRST SENTENCE OF THE NEXT

In constructing transitions from one paragraph to the next, choose the most important words, phrases, or concepts of the last sentence of a paragraph; and then weave those words, phrases, or concepts into the first sentence of the next paragraph.

The paragraphs to the right use the strategies above to build transitions.

ozone in Mexico City have exceeded the country's air-quality standards 284 days per year, on average. Geography doesn't help: Mexico City lies on a broad basin ringed by tall mountains that can block the movement of air masses that might clear out pollution.

Furthermore, the city's rapid spread in recent decades has aggravated its pollution problems. Mexico City now covers about 1,500 square kilometers—about 10 times as much as it occupied just 50 years ago.

In this example, the writer uses the first paragraph to discuss connections between pollution in Mexico City and the city's geography; in the second paragraph, he turns to discussing how the city's size contributes to its pollution problems. **Furthermore** tells readers that additional information is being added, and **city** and **pollution** carry the topic from one paragraph to the next.

■ ■ ■

still-unawakened self, a collective psyche dangerously out of balance, and this awareness united many of the poets in an effort to support and produce a poetry of protest whose fundamental aim was not to destroy the establishment but to rethink it, heal it, render it more flexible and self-aware.

The work of Allen Ginsberg paved the way for this sensibility by claiming the right of the self to be what it has to be and write the poetry it has to write; but Ginsberg also went a step further "to insist" as James E. Mersmann points out in his

In this example's first paragraph, the writer describes poets' general desires in the mid-twentieth century; in the second paragraph, he turns to discussing how one poet helped shape those desires. Note how **this sensibility** summarizes and repeats the description of poets' desires, thus linking the two paragraphs.

■ ■ ■

the same thing he does, you do it using plain words without instruments. Words are like music. Well-reasoned thoughts, conveyed with well-chosen words, can touch us deeply as a moving symphony or a driving drum beat.

But Maggie Simpson doesn't possess language and doesn't speak. In the twentieth century, philosophers concerned with humanity's place in the universe have turned to the relationship between words and thoughts. How do we think if

In this example, the writer argues first that words matter in communication; in the second paragraph, the discussion shifts to focus on a character who doesn't use words. **But** signals this shift to readers. The two paragraphs are still strongly connected by the repetition of concepts concerning words and language.

PASSIVE VOICE

What is on this page will help you style your writing for:

- ☐ CLARITY
- ☐ CONCISION
- ☐ COHERENCE
- ☑ EMPHASIS
- ☑ ENGAGEMENT

Passive voice is a feature of individual sentences, and we define it in Part 9 (→ see page 465).

Even though passive voice is a feature of sentences, we discuss it here because it is in paragraphs that passive voice has its largest effects. Readers will rarely notice the use of passive voice in one or two sentences within several paragraphs or sections; when a whole paragraph is in passive voice, however, what readers take from the paragraph will be affected because the whole sense of the paragraph is affected.

In addition, as we point out to the right, writing some sentences in passive voice can constrain your other sentences.

PASSIVE VOICE IN SCIENTIFIC AND TECHNICAL WRITING

By using passive voice, writers can shift readers' focus away from who performs an action to the object acted upon. Because science writing is meant to be objective—that is, to imply that the actions (experiments, surveys, observations) being described could be performed by anyone—scientific writing often uses passive voice:

The behavior of fiber reinforced polymer (FRP) strengthened reinforced concrete beams subjected to torsional loads has not been well understood, compared to other loads. Interaction of different components of concrete, steel, and FRP in addition to the complex compatibility issues associated with torsional deformations have made it difficult to provide an accurate analytical solution. In this paper an analytical method is introduced for evaluation of the torsional capacity of FRP-strengthened RC beams. In this method, the interaction of different components is allowed by fulfilling equilibrium and compatibility conditions throughout the loading regime while the ultimate torque of the beam is calculated similarly to the well-known compression field theory. It is shown that the method is capable of predicting the ultimate torque of FRP-strengthened RC beams reasonably accurately.

PASSIVE VOICE—OR NOT?—IN WRITING FOR NONSCIENTIFIC AUDIENCES

Compare this paragraph—

During the last couple weeks, American snouts have increased dramatically in my garden and the surrounding area. But that is nothing like the masses that were recorded farther south in Texas a few weeks ago. An estimated 7.5 million snouts were reported in the Alamo area of the Lower Rio Grande Valley on September 5. And there is a chance that our numbers will continue to build over the next few weeks, at least until the really cold weather sets in.

—with this:

In the last few weeks, I thought American snouts had taken over my garden. On September 5, however, observers farther south in Texas recorded numbers that make my garden seem empty: They saw almost 7.5 million snouts in the Alamo area of the Lower Rio Grande Valley. And until the cold weather sets in, these small butterflies might very well overwhelm us with their numbers.

When they wish to sound scientific—which requires longer and less direct grammatical constructions—writers often carry the patterns of passive voice into their other sentences, making all of them longer and more complex than they need to be.

If an occasional passive voice sentence supports your purposes, be alert to keeping your other sentences in the active voice.

STYLING SENTENCES

Style is all about how you connect with audiences in order to achieve your purposes.

On the next pages, we consider sentence style from two angles:

1 How do you construct sentences with the grammatical structures that readers expect in a formal, academic style of writing?

2 How do you construct sentences that readers want to read and that help you make your points?

Perhaps you think these two angles are really the same. After all, if sentences have the structures audiences expect, doesn't that mean readers will want to read them? Doesn't that mean the sentences will help writers make their points?

Consider this paragraph:

I must be real. Hear what I'm saying. We ain't going nowhere, as the boys in the hood be saying. Nowhere. If you promote all the surviving Afghans to the status of honorary Americans, Mr. President, where exactly on the bus does that leave me. When do I get paid. When can I expect my invitation to the ranch. I hear Mr. Putin's wearing jingle-jangle silver spurs around his dacha. Heard you fixed him up with an eight-figure advance on his memoirs. Is it true he's iced up to be the Marlboro man after he retires from Russia. Anything left under the table for me. And mine.

[Order Single Font] [Order Font Package]

That paragraph breaks just about every rule one can imagine for formal writing. The writer uses periods instead of question marks. There are sentence fragments. The writer uses what some would call **colloquial phrasing**.

The paragraph's writer is John Edgar Wideman, who has won many prestigious awards for his writing and has taught writing at the university level. The paragraph comes from an essay, "Whose War," that appeared in the highly respected collection *The Best Essays of 2003*.

Given what he understood about his purposes—questioning the U. S. government's use of resources in the opening years of the twenty-first century—Wideman chose to write as he did. He chose to go against expectations of formal writing so that his essay would stand out, so that his essay would convey anger and frustration, so that his essay would read as though it were being spoken, passionately.

■ ■ ■

Wideman chose to break expectations because he was in a position to do so. He was in a position to do so both because he is a practiced writer who knows and can use the expectations and standards of formal writing when he wants, and also because he is a well-known writer. Because he is a well-known writer, others know that he usually does write in more expected formats, and that he must therefore have had his reasons for writing differently.

As you are styling your sentences, then, keep in mind the expectations of your readers, in regard to your words and to you. Will your readers expect a formal piece? Do your readers know you well enough to know that, if you break expectations, it is because you chose to do so? If you break expectations, how do you let readers know that you did so for a reason?

■ ■ ■

On the next pages, we offer angles for learning the expectations readers have for formal, academic writing.

Learn these well so that you can use them but also so that you can modify them as your purposes demand.

ACADEMIC SENTENCES

All academic writing will have the stylistic features listed below:

What is on this page will help you style your writing for:

☑ CLARITY

☑ CONCISION

☑ COHERENCE

☐ EMPHASIS

☐ ENGAGEMENT

CHECKLIST FOR FORMAL, ACADEMIC SENTENCES

❏ Your sentences have positive structures.

→ See page 243 to learn about sentences without double negatives.

→ See page 243 to learn about sentences that are positive rather than negative.

❏ Each sentence fits one of the four sentence patterns.

→ See pages 508–509.

❏ You use no sentence fragments—except, rarely, for emphasis.

→ See pages 466–469.

❏ Your sentences do not shift among grammatical forms.

→ See pages 472–473 to learn about shifts in person and number.

→ See pages 462–463 to learn about shifts in verb tense.

→ See page 465 to learn about shifts in voice.

→ See page 464 to learn about shifts in direct and indirect discourse.

→ See page 464 to learn about shifts in levels of formality.

❏ Your sentences are easy to read.

→ See pages 244–245.

SENTENCES DO NOT USE DOUBLE NEGATIVES

In formal writing, convention requires using only one negative in a sentence.

NEGATIVES: *barely hardly neither no not never none nothing scarcely*

Sometimes there will be more than one way to fix a double negative:

INCORRECT Bob did not have no solution for the problem.
          NEGATIVE   NEGATIVE

CORRECT Bob had no solution for the problem.
         NEGATIVE

CORRECT Bob did not have a solution for the problem.
         NEGATIVE

Sometimes only one solution will be obvious:

INCORRECT Nobody said nothing about how to make quotations in a paper.
          NEGATIVE   NEGATIVE

CORRECT Nobody said anything about how to make quotations in a paper.
         NEGATIVE

SENTENCES ARE POSITIVE, NOT NEGATIVE

The following two sentences are both grammatically correct—but the second sentence is easier to read and understand because it presents its information in a straightforward, positive manner.

Classic gangster films were not without a message, showing audiences that if a gangster's life had no order, it was because society had no order.

Classic gangster films had a message, showing audiences that the chaos of a gangster's life mirrored the chaos of society.

TIP: READ!

Formal, academic writing—even in scientific disciplines—leaves considerable room for working with style. Reading widely respected writers in a discipline is the best way to learn the leeway you have.

TIP: WHERE TO FOCUS?

You are probably already in good control of several of these features of academic sentences. Ask someone who is familiar with your writing—a teacher or someone in your Writing Center—which of these features needs your attention, and then focus your attention just on those.

STYLING SENTENCES
SENTENCES THAT ARE EASY TO READ

What is on this page will help you style your writing for:

- ☑ CLARITY
- ☑ CONCISION
- ☑ COHERENCE
- ☐ EMPHASIS
- ☑ ENGAGEMENT

Easy-to-read sentences have the following six qualities:

SENTENCES ARE NOT WORDY

Due to the matter of the final report, which was turned in after the due date, I did not acquire the grade I hoped for in class and now therefore I appeal for a second chance to succeed.

Because of a late final report, I failed the class; I hope to retake the class.

Wanting to sound formal or legal, writers stretch for long phrases and a complex vocabulary; the resulting sentences are often stilted and hard to read.

Those who study writing know that writers' language gets wordy and awkward precisely when writers are trying hard, perhaps because of a challenging or emotionally touchy project (like a grade appeal). If you have taken on a project that makes you nervous, or if you are worried about wordiness, ask a trusted reader to look over your writing.

SENTENCES AVOID EXPLETIVES

An expletive can be a swear word, but it can also be a phrase that adds length but no meaning to a sentence, such as *There is ...*, *There are ...*, or *It is necessary ....*

Using one or two such phrases in several pages of writing is not a disaster, but learn to be on the lookout for expletives and replace them:

If we are to end global warming, one thing that is necessary is that people get out of their cars and walk.

To end global warming, people need to get out of their cars and walk.

SENTENCES USE FEW PREPOSITIONAL PHRASES

One argument of the parents from the neighborhood was that all parks in the city should be child-friendly.

Neighborhood parents argued that all city parks should be child-friendly.

Too many prepositions block readers from seeing your ideas.

When you can, convert prepositional phrases into adjectives (which you then place before the noun being modified):

the girl with red hair
the red-haired girl

the ambition of the senator
the senator's ambition

SENTENCES USE FEW RELATIVE PRONOUNS

The relative pronouns *who, which, whom, whose,* and *that* can slow readers:

Childhood is the audience sector which is most exposed to media seduction.

Childhood is the audience sector most exposed to media seduction.

Children who are breast-fed usually have stronger immune systems.

Breast-fed children usually have stronger immune systems.

If you can remove a relative pronoun without upsetting your sentence, do so, or try changing a relative clause (*who are breast-fed*) into an adjective.

SENTENCES FOCUS ON ACTION

A carefully chosen active verb can make sentences come alive for readers:

The never-ending war brought on a reduction in the morale of citizens.

The never-ending war demoralized citizens.

New parking regulations caused great confusion among the commuters.

New parking regulations confused the commuters.

SENTENCES AVOID NOMINALIZATIONS

When you change a verb or adjective into a noun, you nominalize the verb or adjective:

difficult ➜ difficulty

destroy ➜ destruction

investigate ➜ investigation

analyze ➜ analysis

Nominalizations shift a sentence's focus from verbs and adjectives to abstract nouns—and thus deaden sentences.

Change nominalizations back to verbs or adjectives to enliven sentences:

In this paper I give an analysis of the difficulty of the task of the crash investigation of the space shuttle.

In this paper I analyze the difficult task of those who investigated the space shuttle crash.

My observation was of the locals' table in a busy local restaurant.

I observed the locals' table in a busy local restaurant.

USING COORDINATION AND SUBORDINATION

What is on this page will help you style your writing for:

- ☑ CLARITY
- ☐ CONCISION
- ☑ COHERENCE
- ☑ EMPHASIS
- ☐ ENGAGEMENT

When you have two ideas to express to readers, do you want the ideas to have equal weight in their minds, or is one idea less important than the other?

When the ideas are equal, they are **coordinate**.

When one idea is less important than another, it is **subordinate**.

As you build sentences with independent clauses, you relate the clauses through coordination or subordination.

Both coordination and subordination are signs of formal, academic writing.

TO COORDINATE OR TO SUBORDINATE?

It's up to you: What understanding do you want readers to have of a sentence?

For example, if you want readers to consider knitting's traditional role to be equal to its more recent role, use *coordination*:

Knitting has traditionally been a domestic activity for women, but in the last decades it has been turned into a fine art.

Knitting has traditionally been a domestic activity for women; however, in the last decades it has been turned into a fine art.

If, however, you want to emphasize the recently growing importance of knitting over its past role, use *subordination*:

Although knitting has traditionally been a domestic activity for women, in the last decades it has been turned into a fine art.

→ To learn more about independent and dependent clauses, see pages 469, 510–511, and 517.

→ To learn more about conjunctions, see pages 502–505.

THE PATTERN

COORDINATION

There are two patterns for building a sentence that uses coordination:

1 independent clause + **,** + coordinating conjunction + independent clause + **●**

COORDINATING CONJUNCTIONS: *and but for nor or so yet*

Stone is bad insulating material, but it makes a tight wall that radiates stored heat for hours.

2 independent clause + **;** + conjunctive adverb + independent clause + **●**

CONJUNCTIVE ADVERBS: *consequently furthermore however moreover otherwise therefore thus nevertheless*

With normal communication channels cut down during the war in Bosnia, the only news came by word of mouth; consequently posters became a cheap and easy way to spread information.

THE PATTERN

SUBORDINATION

There is one pattern for building a sentence that uses subordination, but you can reverse its order:

independent clause + **,** + subordinating conjunction + dependent clause + **●**

OR

subordinating conjunction + dependent clause + **,** + independent clause **●**

SUBORDINATING CONJUNCTIONS: *after although as because before if since that though unless until when where whether which while who whom whose*

After she placed a doily on top of a cupcake, my grandmother would sift sugar on top to make a lacy pattern.

My grandmother would sift sugar on top of a cupcake to make a lacy pattern, after she had placed a doily on top of the cupcake.

PARALLELISM

If you want readers to see similarities between two or more ideas, use sentence structure: Parallel grammatical form makes the ideas look and sound similar. Readers will take that similarity away with them.

Would you prefer to go swimming, biking, or kayaking?

First we heard whispers, then giggles, then screams of laughter.

Under the eclipse's brief, false night, birds will cease their singing, cows will head for the barn, and people will get weak in the knees.

Parallelism can set up a rhythm that engages readers: As they read, they fall into the rhythm and thus into the movement of your ideas.

What is on this page will help you style your writing for:

☐ CLARITY

☐ CONCISION

☑ COHERENCE

☑ EMPHASIS

☑ ENGAGEMENT

CERTAIN KINDS OF WORDS AND PHRASES HELP IN BUILDING PARALLELISM

You use **coordinating conjunctions** (*and*, *but*, *or*, *nor*, *for*, *so*, and *yet*) to join words or phrases that have equal importance—and you can use them to build parallel structures:

I may still have a young man's body, but now I have an old man's heart.

Correlative conjunctions (*both ... and*, *either ... or*, *neither ... nor*, *not only ... but also*, and *whether ... or*) function similarly, so also be sure the words or phrases following each part of these conjunctions have parallel structures:

The town council will decide whether to grant the zoning variance or to sue the owner over the structure.

→ See page 502 to learn about coordinating conjunctions and page 503 to learn about correlative conjunctions.

Build parallelism by repeating the same grammatical structure in a list of words, prepositional phrases, sentences, or any other grammatical unit.

She finished the work by not eating, drinking, or sleeping.
PARTICIPLE   PARTICIPLE   PARTICIPLE

My sister liked to eat chocolate and to avoid broccoli.
PREPOSITION + VERB + NOUN   PREPOSITION + VERB + NOUN

Empty stores are signs of a fading past; empty schools are a sign of a fading future.
"Empty"+ NOUN + "are a sign of a fading"+ NOUN   "empty"+ NOUN + "are a sign of a fading"+ NOUN

One way to check that you are building parallelism is to stack the parts on top of each other, to see that they follow the same grammatical structure:

For your final draft, pay close attention to proofreading your words,
being sure you've cited all sources,
and formatting your works cited list.

TIP: AVOIDING FAULTY PARALLELISM

Faulty parallelism, a common writing error, occurs when a writer builds a list that does not have parallel grammatical structures:

If you have trouble sleeping, try cutting out coffee after lunch, getting rid of the TV in your room, and to fall asleep at the same time every night.

Fix this by making all the parts of the list have the same grammatical structure:

If you have trouble sleeping, try cutting out coffee after lunch, getting rid of the TV in your room, and falling asleep at the same time every night.

STYLING SENTENCES
FIGURATIVE LANGUAGE

What is on this page will help you style your writing for:

- ☐ CLARITY
- ☐ CONCISION
- ☐ COHERENCE
- ☑ EMPHASIS
- ☑ ENGAGEMENT

When you want readers to understand or remember a crucial concept, use figurative language. *Figurative language* refers to a range of strategies that make concepts stand out.

FIGURATIVE COMPARISONS

As we said when we discussed analogy in Part 3 (→ see pages 100–101), you can help readers understand new or complex ideas by describing the ideas in terms readers already know. Similarly, you can make ideas more vivid—and so more memorable—with unexpected comparisons.

COMPARISONS TO MAKE NEW IDEAS FAMILIAR

This passage uses concepts of building blocks and atoms to explain mathematical concepts:

Prime numbers, such as 17 and 23, are those that can be divided only by themselves and 1. They are the most important objects in mathematics because, as the ancient Greeks discovered, they are the building blocks of all numbers—any of which can be broken down into a product of primes. (For example, $105 = 3$ x 5 x 7.) They are the hydrogen and oxygen of the world of mathematics, the atoms of arithmetic.

TIP: HOW MUCH?

Like spice, figurative language works best in small quantities. Because figurative language can heighten readers' attention to important points in your writing, using it a lot would diffuse its effects.

COMPARISONS TO MAKE IDEAS MEMORABLE

Microsoft is a middle-aged company struggling to figure out how to dance with the teenagers, and its body simply can't keep up with its intentions, no matter how correct they may be.

The passage could instead read, *Microsoft is having trouble attracting young audiences*—but would that have created such a funny picture in your head?

Michael Ondaatje's *The English Patient* is a novel whose nervous system connects books, visual art, and war.

By giving the novel it discusses a **nervous system**, the example above compares the novel to a living being, giving it a vibrancy it wouldn't otherwise have.

"Goya's Last Works," at the Frick, isn't large, but neither are grenades.

The one little word **grenades**—emphasized by its placement as the last word of the sentence—suggests that the exhibit of paintings being described is explosive and even somehow dangerous.

"I think of her as the human embodiment of Wal-Mart," said Kevvy Schlaucher, a 25-year-old engineer from Calgary, Canada, who used to watch the show with his mother. "The Oprah Empire is everywhere. She makes sure you don't get out of the system."

Saying that Oprah Winfrey's empire is a big business is not as memorable as making you hold her and Wal-Mart in your head at the same time.

FIGURATIVE PATTERNS

Experiments with familiar language patterns can make memorable sentences:

On Monday, engineers repaired the ruptured 17th Street Canal levee in New Orleans and floodwaters receded a bit as some suburban residents, carrying suitcases and heavy hearts, briefly returned to their homes and sifted through the sodden debris.

When you read **carrying suitcases and**..., you might expect the next words to be **backpacks** or **boxes**. **Heavy hearts** can slow your reading, making palpable the residents' emotions.

Experiment with any language pattern, such as those of conjunctions:

All day I keep the Shabbos. This means I do not turn on a light or tear paper or write or bathe or cook or sew or do any of the hundred kinds of work involved in building the Holy Temple.

The **or**'s stretch out the list of actions to emphasize the number of items.

Just as you can multiply conjunctions, you can also take them away:

I smiled. We smoked. We looked up at the stars. We shook from cold.

Grammatical disconnection and emotional disconnection between people are shown by a lack of conjunctions.

TIP: NEED INSPIRATION?

Listen to country-western music. Figurative language abounds there, sometimes funny, sometimes not, as when Julie Roberts sings, "Men and mascara always run."

STYLING WORDS

Compare these two sentences:

What did the first settlers of Easter Island eat when they were not eating the local equivalent of maple syrup?

What did the first settlers of Easter Island eat when they were not glutting themselves on the local equivalent of maple syrup?

Which sentence gives you a clearer and sharper sense of action? Why? When might you use one sentence rather than the other?

Compare these two sentences:

The Canadian Rangers protect the Canadian Arctic, an area of Precambrian earth covered with 1,000-year-old Inuit settlements and ice.

The Canadian Rangers protect the Canadian Arctic, an old hunk of Precambrian earth, ice carpeted and spotted with Inuit settlements dating back 1,000 years.

The differences are subtle—but the second sentence (we think) asks you to think about the Canadian Arctic as a familiar, almost living, piece of the earth.

In what writing contexts would the second sentence be appropriate for shaping an audience's relations to the topic?

■ ■ ■

In the following pages we offer strategies to help you make your words as vivid and concrete as your purposes demand.

TIP: WHAT ARE YOUR MOST USED WORDS?

Go to www.wordle.com and follow the instructions to paste in an essay. You will see, in a pleasing way, the words you use most—which might show that you are emphasizing topics you don't mean to or are not offering readers enough variety.

The dictionary defines cancer as "A malignant growth of cells caused by their abnormal and uncontrolled division." Chances are, however, that you cannot read *cancer* without some fear; it's possible you read the word with memories of someone close to you who has had cancer.

The definition of *cancer* is what we call the **denotation** of the word. The denotation of any word is simply its analytic definition, what we can count on most anyone else knowing.

Connotation, on the other hand, is what individuals bring to a word because of their personal or cultural background. Connotation describes the ideas or mental pictures that come to people's minds— unbidden from their memories and experiences—when they hear a word.

As you choose words, consider what associations—the ideas and mental pictures—your readers are likely to have. Do you want your readers to have positive or negative associations?

Most importantly—and especially if you are writing for an audience you do not know very well—you want to avoid using words that will have associations opposite to those that will help you achieve your purposes.

DICTIONARY DEFINITIONS & ASSOCIATIONS WITH WORDS

What is on this page will help you style your writing for:

- ☑ CLARITY
- ☐ CONCISION
- ☐ COHERENCE
- ☐ EMPHASIS
- ☑ ENGAGEMENT

TIP: FIND A READER

To be sure your word choices do not encourage readers to think of connotations that will undermine your purpose, have people from your audience read drafts of your writing.

STYLING WORDS
THE NAMES WE USE

What is on this page will help you style your writing for:

☑ CLARITY

☐ CONCISION

☐ COHERENCE

☐ EMPHASIS

☑ ENGAGEMENT

If the problem were called *Atmosphere cancer* or *Pollution death,* the entire conversation would be framed differently.

The writer of the above sentence is discussing **global warming**, and argues that we might, as individuals and as a culture, be less sanguine about global warming if the concept had been named more compellingly.

The words used to name a condition, a syndrome, or a place carry considerable weight through their connotations (→ discussed on page 253). Consider how the following terms ask readers to think about the person or position named:

pro-choice	pro-abortion
right-wing	conservative
heterosexual	straight
gun rights	gun control
affirmative action	racial preferences
illegal alien	undocumented immigrant

Readers respond to the names you use based on how they interpret the names. Someone in favor of affirmative action, for example, will likely be less amenable to writing that uses *racial preferences*.

TIP: KNOW YOUR AUDIENCE

Ask people from your audience about any terms you are considering so that you can learn how they respond. This will help you decide which terms help you make the arguments you desire.

Jump. Giggle. Estimate. Play. Clarify.
Balance. Sing. Compare. Interpret.

These are action verbs: They name actions readers can imagine themselves taking. (This is connotation at work again.) Because action verbs encourage readers to imagine doing what a sentence describes, action verbs help readers connect with writing.

Action verbs describe concrete actions and so clarify what is going on:

He is enjoying performing.

He revels in performing.

The second sentence uses an action verb instead of **is**. **Revels** carries associations of energetic delight, and so will likely convey that emotion to readers.

Here are other examples:

The wasp put her stinger through the roach's exoskeleton and directly into its brain.

The wasp slipped her stinger through the roach's exoskeleton and directly into its brain.

The second sentence helps a reader understand more precisely what the wasp did—and makes the wasp's action scarier and more compelling.

STYLING WORDS
ACTION VERBS

What is on this page will help you style your writing for:

- ☑ CLARITY
- ☐ CONCISION
- ☐ COHERENCE
- ☑ EMPHASIS
- ☑ ENGAGEMENT

TIP: **REPLACING "IS"**

When you want your writing to connect with readers, underline every use of **is** (including its variations, such as **are** and **was** and **will be**) in your writing, and if you see more than a few, replace those words with action verbs.

CONCRETE NOUNS

What is on this page will help you style your writing for:

☑ CLARITY

☐ CONCISION

☐ COHERENCE

☐ EMPHASIS

☑ ENGAGEMENT

When you hear the word **it**, what picture comes into your head? Any?

In the sentence *After he ordered his lunch he had to wait 30 minutes for it to be delivered,* **it** clearly refers to **his lunch**—and readers can make concrete connections with the word. But when you read the sentence below, what associations can you make with the **It** at the beginning?

It is wasteful of their energies if full-grown orangutans move randomly through trees looking for food.

It in the sentence above refers to nothing. Here is a revised sentence:

Full-grown orangutans can't afford to lumber along randomly through the trees, hoping to blunder upon food.

The replacement of **is wasteful** with **can't afford to** and the movement of **full-grown orangutans** to the front of the sentence make this sentence concretely descriptive and thus clearer and more engaging.

When you want readers to have concrete (and hence compelling) pictures in their heads about what you are writing, start your sentences with words that refer to specific people, animals, or objects.

TIP: REPLACING "IT IS"

Sometimes you need to use **it is** (or **there are**). But when you want your writing to connect with readers, underline every use of **is**, **it is**, and **there are**, and if you see more than a few, replace those phrases with concrete nouns and verbs.

Playing with fire. No place like home. Have a field day. From bad to worse. Bad hair day. Like a breath of fresh air.

Clichés are phrases that once stood out because they were—at one time—new and funny or compelling. Because they were new and stood out, however, people used them, and used them … and used them until they stopped being new and compelling.

Because clichés have been used so much, they have become just part of language—and so they come to mind easily when you are writing. Readers will notice them, however, and because they've seen them before, the writing will seem tired and boring.

CLICHÉS

What is on this page will help you style your writing for:

- ☑ CLARITY
- ☐ CONCISION
- ☐ COHERENCE
- ☑ EMPHASIS
- ☑ ENGAGEMENT

TIP: TO CATCH AND FIX CLICHÉS

To catch clichés, read your writing aloud; you can often hear clichés.

To fix clichés, be clear about your purpose: You need to explore wording that carries the meaning and emotion of your purpose. For example, instead of *His proposal was dead as a doornail*, you could write *His proposal received no response* or, more emotively, *Given how little attention others gave his proposal, he might as well never have spoken.*

TIP: CLICHÉS IN A NEW LANGUAGE

If you are not writing in your home language, clichés can be hard to hear because you are not familiar enough with them in the new language. Ask someone who grew up with your new language to read your writing and identify—and explain—clichés.

JARGON

What is on this page will help you style your writing for:

- ☑ CLARITY
- ☑ CONCISION
- ☐ COHERENCE
- ☐ EMPHASIS
- ☑ ENGAGEMENT

Jargon can describe the specialized language of an organization or a profession; it can also describe fancy-sounding words someone else uses that you don't understand. Jargon, then, is useful when you are writing to those inside your profession and need to be precise; it is bad to use outside the profession because readers can't follow your writing.

To a reader immersed in computer culture, this probably makes sense:

In architecting our software, build systems, and engineering processes, we have given considerable thought to how our code will be able to evolve alongside the Mozilla code, without forking it.

Most readers know **architect** and **fork** as nouns, not verbs, and probably do not know what a **build system** or **Mozilla** is. A general audience is more likely to understand:

In developing our software and engineering processes, we have considered how our code will be able to evolve alongside the existing code with which it must work—without making a mess.

TIP: KNOW YOUR AUDIENCE

If you are writing for people who share a vocabulary, use that vocabulary to be precise. If you do not know your audience, err on the side of caution: Use only words almost anyone would understand. Check this by having someone else read your writing.

As far as we can see, it is a fact that there are a whole lot of ways you can end up with way too many words in your sentences and, as a result of the too many words, make your readers bored or make it too hard for them to figure out your purpose.

When we see sentences like the above, it is usually a sign that the writer isn't sure what to say and is fumbling for a way to say it; sometimes people write like that when they aren't confident.

The sentence above is characterized by both empty words (words that add nothing to the purpose of the sentence) and redundant words (words that repeat uselessly what has already been said).

If we modify the sentence, we can end up with this, which is more concise and hence clearer for readers:

There are many ways to have too many words in a sentence, boring your readers and getting in the way of their understanding.

To compose focused sentences, ask yourself, *What is it exactly that I want readers to take from this sentence?*

What is on this page will help you style your writing for:

- ☑ CLARITY
- ☑ CONCISION
- ☐ COHERENCE
- ☐ EMPHASIS
- ☑ ENGAGEMENT

TIP: **REREAD**

Put your writing aside for a while, and then reread it: Looking at your writing anew will help you see where you have used more words than you need. You can also ask others to read it, to help you find the sentences that need tightening to clarify your points.

STYLE IN VISUAL TEXTS

TYPOGRAPHY
SERIF AND SANS SERIF TYPEFACES

Knowing this major distinction between kinds of typefaces will help you choose typefaces to fit your purposes.

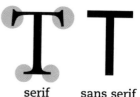

serif   sans serif

Serif is a French word meaning **tail**, and it describes typefaces that have little swashes (circled above) added to the ends of letters. **Sans** is French for **without**; thus **sans serif** typefaces have no serifs.

Serifed typefaces generally look more classical or old-fashioned than sans serif typefaces. Audiences in the United States are accustomed to seeing serifed typefaces in long sections of text that are meant to be readable.

DECORATIVE TYPEFACES

Typefaces that look like this are called "**DECORATIVE.**" They are not easy to read in anything but short phrases and so they are most often used for short pieces of text like titles and headers. OCCASIONALLY A PARTICULAR PURPOSE JUSTIFIES USING THEM FOR BLOCKS OF TEXT YOU WANT PEOPLE TO READ, BUT ONLY OCCASIONALLY.

SOME NOTES ON USING TYPEFACES

Since the invention of the printing press in the fifteenth century, conventions for the use of type in different genres have developed.

- Academic and other texts that are meant to be serious or formal almost always use one size of a single, serifed typeface throughout. For example, teachers might expect you to use the typeface Times in 12-point type for papers; at most, then, you would use the plain, italic, and bold versions of the Times typeface.

    Occasionally, writers will use a second typeface in such writings: A plain, sans serifed typeface such as Helvetica or Arial, in its bold version, can provide sufficient contrast for headings, as described to the right.

- Visual unity, a value of many genres, underlies the number of typefaces experienced visual designers use. Even in genres that have considerable wiggle room in choice of type—genres such as posters or brochures—designers most often use only two or three typefaces: one for the title or main head, another for the information or body text, and perhaps a third if there is another text function that needs to be visually differentiated.

HEADINGS

When you chunk a text by inserting headings, you allow readers to better see the sections of your text. This can help readers both comprehend and remember your arguments.

- Headings should be short, taking up only one line, so that readers can see them at a glance.

- Headings should have space above them so that readers see a heading as part of the text that follows it.

- The typeface of a heading should be different (in size, thickness, or style) from the typeface used in the body of the text, again so that readers can see and read the heading easily.

To create a conservative look in a heading
Use a bold version of the typeface you use for the body of text.

To create a more modern look in a heading
Use a sans serif typeface heading with a serifed typeface for the body of the text. Usually, you will have to use a bold version of the sans serif typeface to create an easy-to-see contrast between the heading and the body.

NOTE: Unless a heading is very short, use upper- and lowercase letters. Using only uppercase letters is hard to read for more than just a few words.

COLOR

COLOR TERMINOLOGY

To use color in support of your purposes, you need to know why you are choosing one color over another—and to do that, you need to know color terminology.

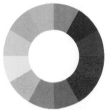

Hue

Hue describes what many of us think of as color. When you name the hue of a color, you say whether it is red or blue or yellow or ....

Brightness

Brightness (sometimes also referred to as **value**) describes how light or dark a color is. In the bar above, the color at the extreme left has no brightness; the color at the extreme right is as bright as it can be.

Saturation

Saturation describes how much of a hue is present in a color. In the bar above, the colors at the far left are unsaturated; they have no blue in them. As you move to the right in the bar above, the color becomes more saturated: It has more blue.

Hue, saturation, and brightness are present in all colors. In the examples above, the leftmost color is red-hued, with as much saturation and brightness as possible. The middle color is not very bright, but is still a fairly saturated red hue. The color on the right has a hue of blue, is fairly bright, but is not very saturated.

Color connotations

Colors and color combinations have connotations just as words do (→ see page 253). For example, we often associate bright red, blue, and yellow with childhood, while combinations of highly saturated red and green or orange and blue will remind some of concert posters from the 1960s.

When you choose colors to use in composing, keep in mind that the connotations we have with certain colors will be affected by the shape of the color and what is around it. For example, blue can suggest cold when used with **ice** or **winter**, but warmth and relaxation when used with **Caribbean summer afternoon**.

USING COLOR

CHOOSING HARMONIOUS COLORS

- Choose colors close to each other on the color wheel:

Colors next to each other—or one step apart—will be harmonious.

- Choose one color that supports your purpose, and then increase or decrease its saturation or brightness to create a set of harmonious colors to use:

- Choose a range of different hues, but give each the same brightness and saturation:

COLOR AND TYPE

Type is easiest to read when there is as much contrast as possible between the color of the type and the color of the background. The contrast between the colors can be a contrast in hue, saturation, or brightness.

STRONG CONTRAST
WEAK CONTRAST

STRONG CONTRAST
WEAK CONTRAST

STRONG CONTRAST
WEAK CONTRAST

STRONG CONTRAST
WEAK CONTRAST

Sometimes, however, you can create a very strong contrast in hue, but if the colors are very saturated and very bright, they can hurt our eyes rather than be easy to read:

STRONG CONTRAST BUT HARD TO READ.

STRONG CONTRAST BUT HARD TO READ.

STYLE IN ORAL PRESENTATIONS

In oral presentations, the main component of style is you: Your voice and gestures will be your main strategies for creating emphasis and engagement.

CONNECTING WITH AN AUDIENCE

Public speaking might make you anxious. In addition to remembering to breathe deeply before and during a talk, making eye contact with people in your audience and even addressing them directly can help you relax. These actions are also style decisions.

As you prepare, decide how to connect with your audience. Few presentation contexts and purposes require formality. Rather, in almost all circumstances, you can engage your audience—and thus encourage their generosity toward your arguments—by asking them questions, speaking directly to them while looking into their faces, or smiling.

SPEAKING STYLES

Your voice—its volume, speed, and tone—gives you a wonderful range of style choices while you speak. To take advantage of your voice, have your presentation organized in time so you can practice often: Seek a conversational style and avoid reading.

Identify the presentation parts (words or sentences) you wish to emphasize. Then experiment with different ways of saying those parts. Exaggerate volume and tone, playfully, and make yourself laugh. This will help you relax—but will also help you find what works best for the real presentation.

BODY LANGUAGE

For most presentations, you need to use your body language—expressions and gestures—to put your audience at ease and to emphasize the major points of your presentation.

Look over what you have written for your presentation, and decide what facial expressions (and where) support your arguments. In the past, audiences expected almost theatrical gestures and expressions; now, simple smiles, frowns, nods, or occasional head shakes are enough.

Similarly, current audiences do not expect grand hand gestures. You will make audiences uncomfortable if you nervously wring your hands, but you can instead keep your hands clasped in front of or behind you, placed on the lectern, or holding your notes.

Do check over your words, seeing where a gesture will emphasize what needs emphasizing. And then practice.

Practicing your presentation over and over will help you make your body language relaxed and friendly.

USING VISUAL SUPPORTS

Visual supports can be slide presentations (using software like PowerPoint or Keynote), overheads, handouts, or physical objects.

Use visual supports to help your audience see the main points of your presentation.

Use objects that help you demonstrate procedures you are discussing or that illustrate your main points: A stretched-out plastic bag holding the amount of trash an average American throws out in one day will make the point about our resource use much more strongly than a spoken statistic.

Whatever your visual aids, practice with them. You need to be able to use them comfortably so that your audience focuses on the points you are making rather than on your trying to use a projector. Also, using visual aids slows down a presentation; if you have a time limit, practicing with your visuals will help you stay within that time limit.

PARALLELISM IN ORAL PRESENTATIONS

Apply to the paragraphs you will speak the same guidelines for building parallelism in sentences that we described on pages 248–249. Paragraphs that use parallelism create rhythmic and emotionally compelling paragraphs, as in this Convocation Address by Nikki Giovanni:

We are Virginia Tech.

The Hokie Nation embraces our own and reaches out with open hearts and hands to those who offer their hearts and minds. We are strong, and brave, and innocent, and unafraid. We are better than we think and not quite what we want to be. We are alive to the imaginations and the possibilities. We will continue to invent the future through our blood and tears and through all our sadness.

We are the Hokies.

We will prevail.

We will prevail.

We will prevail.

We are Virginia Tech.

HINTS & TIPS
FOR CONCLUDING PARAGRAPHS

USING CONCLUDING PARAGRAPHS TO HELP YOU REVISE

You are writing your first draft. You type the last period for the last sentence, and breathe deeply: You are done.

But, no, wait, sorry: You are not done, not if you want the strongest possible writing. Definitely take a deep breath and leave your paper for a while—but come back several hours or a day later.

For writers, the first draft of a conclusion provides crucial information:

- Often, a conclusion is when you realize what your argument really is. Experienced writers know that a first draft is only a beginning, and that often they don't know what they really want to argue until that first attempt at a conclusion. Sometimes writers use the concluding paragraph of a first draft—because it is often a succinct and passionate statement of an argument—as the first paragraph of the next draft.

- If you do feel that the concluding paragraph is an accurate and strong statement of your argument, go back through the rest of the paper to ask yourself: Do all the other paragraphs lead up to and support the conclusion?

- Because most writers intuitively know that concluding paragraphs should include a little passion, they include passion—but often there is no passion in the rest of the writing, and so the conclusion will seem abruptly out of place to readers. When you finish a conclusion, check that its emotional tone is supported by the rest of the writing, just as you check to make sure its logical claims are likewise supported.

- Use the concluding paragraph to help you make your introductory paragraph as strong and engaging as possible. Knowing the end point where you want to take readers, what might be the most effective starting point?

- Once you have a strong conclusion that satisfies you, revise your introduction—as well as the body of your paper—to use some of the same words and phrases as your conclusion: This will help give your whole paper pleasing coherence for your readers.

PART 7
WRITING FOR DIVERSE AUDIENCES

CONTENTS

If You Grew Up Speaking a Language Other Than English...
Look for boxes colored like this one throughout Part 9 for additional strategies to help you with some of the idioms and conventions of written English, including:

WHERE ARE WE IN THE PROCESS FOR COMPOSING?

Understanding your project

Getting started

Asking questions

Shaping your project for others

Drafting a paper

Getting feedback

Revising
Varieties of English
Writing for global audiences
Inclusive language uses

Polishing

ARE YOU READY TO USE THE NEXT PAGES OF THIS BOOK?

NO...
Are you figuring out your thesis statement?
Are you beginning the first draft of a paper?
If this is your situation, then, no, you are not ready for the next pages.

What follows in the next pages will help you fine-tune your writing for a range of audiences. It is not worth your time to do such fine-tuning until you are confident in a draft of your writing.

→ For help with narrowing a topic, see pages 28–33.

→ For help with researching a topic, see pages 34–73.

→ For help with a thesis statement, see pages 96–97, 138–139, and 152–155.

YES.
Are you working on a draft about which you feel pretty confident?
What follows will help you shape your writing to be generous toward a wide range of readers.

VARIETIES OF ENGLISH

> **"** I been thru a lot of struggles to get where I'm at today.

I've struggled to accomplish what I have.

"

■ ■ ■

> **"** My brother was into skydiving and he got me hooked on this stuff.

My brother, who is a skydiving fan, introduced me to the sport.

"

Some would react negatively to the top statement in each set above, saying, "That's not good English." By *good English*, they mean what is often called *Standard English*, represented by the second statement in each set above. Standard English—and its grammatical rules and patterns—is what is taught in schools and used in many formal situations.

Standard English is a historical accident: It resulted from the language practices of those who were economically and politically advantaged at the time people were thinking that grammar and English usage should be standardized.

LANGUAGE STANDARDIZATION AND LANGUAGE VARIETY

That we assign *good* or *bad* to different statements reflects two opposite tendencies in language use:

1
LANGUAGE STANDARDIZATION

Languages tend to become standardized in formal practice. In any language, one set of grammatical practices and speaking patterns will be favored more than others, as we noted on the page to the left.

Some argue that such standardization supports wider communication among speakers of different varieties of a language. Standard forms of language are thus often used in the media (think of how network television news reporters speak or of the writing in big-city newspapers) and in schooling, which is often meant to provide people from different backgrounds with a common culture and an ability to speak across their differences.

2
LANGUAGE VARIETY

Because of a language's use in different contexts for different purposes, different varieties of a language develop. In their daily use, people who fix cars will tend to use different sets of words than people who treat diseases. Different occupations can become so specialized—as law has, for example—that they have their own language patterns.

Similarly, different communities of people will shape local vocabularies and grammars. For example, the Gullah people, who live on islands off the southern states of North Carolina south to Florida, hold on to African words and speech patterns; these words and patterns have been brought into and have changed English in the area.

Depending on the influence that different groups have, and how much they interact with others, their words and language patterns can be accepted into the standard variety of a language, as the words of computer programming—*interface*, *platform*, and *input*—have become part of our day-to-day talk.

VARIETIES OF ENGLISH
ACADEMIC ENGLISH

> " … by the time I came to the United States as a … student in foreign and second language education …, I was not competent in writing in my second language. Although I had no trouble expressing myself in English, I was not familiar with the standards of academic writing. I remember the first assignment I had in an education course…. I spent hours and hours composing the essay, and yet, with great disappointment, the paper turned out to be a Chinese composition in English, although the instructor did not comment on this. "

In the words above, Chinese student Jun Liu describes his struggles to learn to write papers in academic English. What he describes is common for all writers entering a new writing context, whether or not their first language is English.

Every time you are asked to write a document you haven't written before, there is a learning curve. You have to learn the textual conventions, style preferences, and reader expectations unique to the new context. These new exigencies may seem challenging and uncomfortable at first, but you carry some basic tools with you from all your previous reading and writing instruction that can be adapted for the new context.

Following are some principles of academic writing and some strategies to help you tackle new academic writing contexts.

THE ORGANIZATION OF ACADEMIC WRITING IN ENGLISH

→ See pages 144–155 for information about the organizational features of academic writing across disciplines.

UNDERSTANDING HOW WRITING IS ORGANIZED IN A NEW DISCIPLINE

When you need to write for a discipline or academic area new to you, analyze writing of the kind you need to produce. Ask teachers or those who write in the area to give you sample texts they consider effective *and* well written. Use the following strategies to understand what makes this type of writing successful.

- Look for background information. What kind and how much background information is provided before the writer launches into the argument?

- Look for supporting evidence. What kinds of supporting evidence are provided? How is this supporting information used?

- Where in the document does the main argument appear?

- How is the text organized? How does the writer signal this organization? With headings? With transitional phrases?

- Are headings standard from one document to another or are they author-created? What function do they serve? If they are standard headings, what information appears in each section of the document?

- Are ideas repeated? If so, which ideas and where does the repetition appear?

- How does the writer make important information stand out? Bullet points? Numbering? Headings? Bold text?

THE STYLE OF ACADEMIC WRITING IN ENGLISH

→ See pages 228–229 and 242–243 for information about the stylistic features of academic writing across disciplines.

UNDERSTANDING HOW WRITING IS STYLED IN A NEW DISCIPLINE

Analyze writing of the kind you need to produce, and then use the questions below to help you understand—and be able to reproduce—the style.

- What is the tone of the text? Is the vocabulary formal or informal? Does it use words that are subjective and judgmental or objective?

- Is the text simple and direct or more dense and involved? To determine this, look at the length of sentences.

- Does the writer rely more on noun phrases and technical terms or on a variety of verbs?

- When the writer uses the verb **to be**, is it followed by adjectives or complex noun phrases?

- Are there parts of the text in which the writer uses more informal language and a more personal style? If so, in what sections?

ENGLISH AS A GLOBAL LANGUAGE

> ❝ I became boring.
> **I became bored.** ❞

> ❝ I will climb machine to the junction. I cannot trek.
>
> **I will ride my motorcycle to the junction. I can't walk the short distance.** ❞

The two examples above show English used in different countries. In the first set of sentences, Singaporean English contrasts with what some consider to be Standard English; the second set starts with Nigerian English.

As transportation and communication technologies bring once-distant communities in touch through commerce and culture, language standardization and language variation shape English.

Standardization steps in because businesses now operate worldwide and because media are on a twenty-four-hour, worldwide news cycle. Some believe the use of one language can ease this communication. English has taken on that role, in most cases being the language of business, science, and to some extent, the Internet.

English has taken on this role not because it is a superior language but simply because of accidents of history: English happened to be in the right place at the right time. And, possibly, English will be displaced by another language at some time in the future when it is no longer politically or economically advantageous.

Language variation is also at work. Because English has been adopted in so many countries, many varieties of English have emerged, such as Singaporean English, Nigerian English, Indian English, Caribbean English, Malaysian English, and so on. Language experts refer to these varieties as *world Englishes*. Each group of new English users changes the grammar and vocabulary of what we think of as **Standard English** to reflect their culture and needs—just as, starting in the sixteenth century, people in the British colonies (including what is now the United States) changed English as it was spoken and written in England.

WRITING FOR A GLOBAL AUDIENCE

Globalization in markets, science, and media has meant that texts produced for business or technical purposes—reports, advertisements, business plans—are translated between languages. Sometimes, as the following example shows, the translation process creates problems:

Original meaning: Sexual harassment is your concern.

Translation into another language: Make sexual harassment your business.

Whatever the final result, the globalization of communication is influencing the language of writing. When writers of business or technical reports produce a document, they must take into account the translation process their texts will undergo.

TO ENSURE ACCURACY AND EASE OF TRANSLATION

- Use clear (not simple) sentence structures. For example, this sentence is difficult to translate:

The rapid level of increase in entry of women into the workforce has changed people's shopping patterns from daily shopping to weekly or monthly.

Easier to translate is this sentence:

Because more women have entered the workforce, people no longer shop daily, but weekly or monthly.

- Use straightforward vocabulary. Avoid idioms and vague word choice that might create confusion.

The *italicized words* in the following text will be difficult to translate because they are idiomatic or make cultural references that are not shared outside the United States:

Recently I *poked fun* at those *New Age marvels* we call the multi-taskers. If you missed it, the salient point was this: Laboratory experiments prove that multi-tasking is, contrary to *all hype*, hugely inefficient.

- Anticipate vocabulary that might have multiple meanings and cause translation difficulties.

For example, **concern** in the sexual harassment example on the left causes difficulty because it has two potential meanings: **business concern** and **problem**.

WRITING ENGLISH WHEN ENGLISH IS NOT YOUR HOME LANGUAGE

WRITING AS A SECOND LANGUAGE

We learn to speak as we grow up in the comfort and informality of home. Without thinking about it, we imitate what we hear those around us saying, and our families teach us informally while we eat or work together.

But we learn to write through formal instruction. In the United States, the first five or six years of school focus on the basics of writing; in other countries, the amount of time given to writing instruction varies.

Given that learning to write is so formalized and separated from learning to speak, it is as though writing is a second language for everyone.

Anytime we move from one writing context to another—whether we move from texting a friend to writing a school essay or from writing in a home language to writing in English—we have to shift how we write. From any previous learning experience, we carry some knowledge of how to shape writing, but in new contexts and with a new language, we have to attend carefully to textual conventions, style preferences, and reader expectations that are unique to the new context. All of these can be learned.

> Because I had not learned to write more than a paragraph in English before, I had much to learn in the first-year composition class I took during that first semester. In the first class, the teacher told us that there are some rules in English composition we have to follow, but that if we follow the rules, anybody can write a reasonably good composition. The teacher's statement sounded like God's blessing to me, as I was already struggling with the quantity of writing requirements in other classes. The *rules* I learned in the composition class included the concepts of unity and cohesion, which have since helped my English writing a great deal.
>
> I also learned several effective patterns of paragraph development such as *cause and effect* or *comparison and contrast*. Although I later learned that not all writers of English follow such rules and patterns, these rules were truly helpful for a new writer like me.
>
> Another important thing I learned in the first-year composition class was the idea of writing as a process. I learned that a good end product can only be achieved through a long revising process. I had never learned such things either in my previous English or Japanese classes in Japan.
>
> —Miyuki Sasaki

MULTILINGUAL WRITERS WRITING IN ENGLISH

If English is your second or third language, you may feel at a disadvantage when you use English to communicate in writing—but having already mastered writing in a second or third language is an advantage to you in several ways:

- You are comfortable gathering ideas and putting them together in an extended text.
- You have experience with successfully writing for various audiences and purposes in the other languages in which you write.
- You can draw on vocabulary and language resources from two or three languages.

Especially when gathering and thinking through ideas, you might find it more comfortable to gather ideas and plan your text in your first language.

Also, writing involves turning unformed ideas into concrete words and sentences. That means all writers must translate ideas into words, a difficult process even if the language you speak in is the language in which you are most comfortable writing.

If you know a second or third language, use it to help you put your thoughts into words. Later, as you are drafting, you can find the English equivalents for those words. Doing this will make the process of composing more efficient and will lessen the frustration of **word hunting**.

IF YOU GREW UP SPEAKING A LANGUAGE OTHER THAN ENGLISH…

If English is your second or third or more language, look for boxes colored like this one throughout Part 9 of this book. In those boxes, you will find ideas and strategies for editing and proofreading your work that can help you learn some of the conventions and styles unique to written English.

USING INCLUSIVE LANGUAGE

> My name is Jane Takagi-Little. Little was my dad, a Little from Quam, Minnesota. Takagi is my mother's name. She's Japanese. Hyphenation may be a modern response to patriarchal naming practices in some cases, but not in mine. My hyphen is a thrust of pure superstition. At my christening, Ma was stricken by a profound Oriental dread at the thought of her child bearing an insignificant surname like Little through life, so at the very last minute she insisted on attaching hers. Takagi is a big name, literally, comprising the Chinese character for "tall" and the character for "tree." Ma thought the stature and eminence of her lofty ancestors would help equalize Dad's Little. They were always fighting about stuff like this.
>
> "It doesn't mean anything," Dad would say. "It's just a name!," which would cause Ma to recoil in horror. "How can you say 'justa name'? Name is very first thing. Name is face to all the world."

This passage from Ruth L. Ozeki's novel *My Year of Meats* describes how the main character comes to be named and, in so doing, describes how we use words to shape our relations with those who may have grown up in cultures different from ours. Jane's mother is alert to the social weight of words, of how the words we use to describe ourselves—and others—shape how we are seen and treated by others. She insists that her daughter carry a name that gives her importance and so respect in the eyes of others.

This matter of how we are named comes up elsewhere in Ozeki's novel, as in the following exchange:

> Then, at the pancake breakfast where we had been filming, a red-faced veteran from WWII drew a bead on me and my crew, standing in line by the warming trays, our plates stacked high with flapjacks and American bacon.
>
> "Where are you from, anyway?" he asked, squinting his bitter blue eyes at me.
>
> "New York," I answered.
>
> He shook his head and glared and wiggled a crooked finger inches from my face. "No, I mean where were you **born?**"
>
> "Quam, Minnesota," I said.
>
> "No, no … **What** are you?" He whined with frustration.
>
> And in a voice that was low, but shivering with demented pride, I told him, **"I … am … a … fucking … AMERICAN!"**

Neither the questioning man nor Jane comes across well in Ozeki's writing, both insistent, neither willing to back off. It is precisely because our identities—the words we use to describe who we are—carry so much weight that this scene in the novel matters.

But Jane's position is the one with which Ozeki asks us to sympathize, in the end, because Jane, in spite of her expletives, is defending herself. The man wants to judge her based only on how she looks.

Instead, Jane insists on naming herself, on choosing to be seen through a word that belies the assumptions the man wants to make.

Who does not want the right to be known by a name that speaks truthfully to and respectfully of one's background and experiences?

■ ■ ■

It is important, then, that we grant each other the right to choose the names by which we are called and understood by others.

When others write or talk about us using names we believe do not reflect our backgrounds or experiences accurately or respectfully—or when they write or talk about us in ways we believe to be disrespectful—they show us either that they have made mistakes about us or that they do not see us as worthy of the same respect that they expect for themselves.

When we write about others, it would seem only right that we grant the same respect to them. If your readers feel excluded because of your word choices, because of how you refer to them, then they will either stop reading or they will read your words with a hostile, sad, or distanced attitude, thus undermining your purpose in writing.

Writing that connects with readers connects because readers feel respected by the writing. When you write, it is not about you. It is about your readers, and about giving them the same respect and courtesy you believe you deserve.

HOW DO YOU SHOW RESPECT TO YOUR READERS?

Here are general guidelines:

- **Ethnicity, gender, sexual orientation, age, religion, and mental and bodily ability are sensitive characteristics in our time. Anytime in your writing you refer to one of these areas, check that your word choice is both necessary and respectful of those to whom you are referring.** Educate yourself about why these issues are sensitive, because knowing the reasons behind these issues will help you make good decisions about how to write.

How we refer to each other will shape how we think of and treat each other. How are the following sentences likely to affect a reader's attitude toward the people being described?

Given how she finished the race before so many others who had two real legs, you would almost think she was a real athlete.

A pert woman in a short leather skirt, the prime minister spoke about the financial relations between our countries.

He has two children and a daughter adopted from China.

Equally important, how are readers likely to think about the person who wrote these sentences?

- **Have you referred to people by the names they have chosen for identification?** If you are writing a description of a person you have interviewed, for example, ask the person what terms to use. Avoid using names that people find offensive; again, ask if you are unsure or do not know.

As political and social changes affect our lives, the names people prefer may change; you will have to ask or do research to stay current. Members of a group may disagree about their preferred name; you can acknowledge this in your writing.

- **Do you refer to a person's characteristics only if your purpose requires it?** Imagine that the following sentences began newspaper articles about speeches given on a college campus.

The speaker, a cute blonde, talked at length about world hunger.

The speaker, a feisty old guy, lectured on parenting mishaps.

From his wheelchair, the speaker argued against current tax policies.

Do the descriptions in the sentences help you learn about the content of the speeches? Do they have anything to do with the speeches?

The descriptions turn our attention away from the speeches and from the hard work done by the speakers, instead asking us to focus on qualities of the speakers that are incidental to their abilities as serious speakers.

- **Have you made assumptions about the lives of others based on your own experiences?** Only one team wins in a big sporting event, but different people experience that win differently: One set of fans will be jubilant and one will be frustrated. It is the same with elections, judicial cases, and world happenings: While everyone might agree on the facts of the outcome, different people, because of their different backgrounds, will respond differently.

   This is also true of reading. You might read one set of words and think they are just fine, but the person across the table from you might be annoyed, hurt, or angered by the same words.

   If you have a lot in common with others, you can make some predictions about their responses to different events, but in all cases, if you find yourself writing statements like these—

Who could possibly believe that?

All reasonable people will take this action.

Only an uninformed person could respond in this way.

—then you are making assumptions based on your own particular experiences and beliefs. You should not be surprised when some or many readers are turned off by how you characterize those who believe differently from you.

- **Have you avoided stereotyping?** Stereotyping happens when you focus on only one of a person's characteristics, with that characteristic being a negative or limited belief about a group.

Just like a man!

He's acting like an old lady!

What else could you expect from a teenage girl?

- **Have you expected one person's experience to represent everyone's?** To expect one woman to be an expert about the lives of all other women can result in creating stereotypes—just as asking one African American man to speak for all African Americans, or for one teenager who is a lesbian to speak about the lives of all teenagers or all lesbians, or for one Christian to speak about the lives of all Christians.

In the following pages are guidelines for specific areas of inclusive language.

TIP: **FOLLOWING THESE SUGGESTIONS WON'T FIX EVERYTHING**

The word choice issues we discuss on these pages matter—but keep in mind that they work together with the tone of voice you use, the attitude you convey, and the other positions you consider in your writing to give your readers an overall sense of your fairness and integrity.

USING INCLUSIVE LANGUAGE
INCLUDING ALL ETHNICITIES

"ETHNICITY" OR "RACE"?

More and more, scientists argue that *race*—as a genetic basis for categorizing humans—does not exist. We have tended to define someone's race based on the physical appearance of the person, but people may have similar physical appearances (such as skin color) because their ancestors grew up far apart although in similar physical environments; even though two people might look alike, their genetic differences might be so considerable that they share little common heritage.

Because there is controversy over *race*, and because *race* focuses our attention on physical characteristics, we have found it generally better—when we must refer to others through such lenses—to use the term *ethnicity*.

Ethnicity refers to heritage and culture: Ethnic groups tend to come into being because of a people's common ancestry, language, or religion.

TIP: CONSIDERING "RACE"

For centuries, in this country as in many others, the idea of *race* was used to justify the unequal treatment of different peoples. We need to keep this historical fact in mind because, sadly, it is still shaping people's relationships and livelihoods. Therefore, unless you are writing about *race* as a topic, use *ethnicity* to encourage your readers to enact more thoughtful and more accurate relationships.

CHECKING YOUR WRITING

- **Have you referred to a person's ethnicity or national origin only when it is relevant to your argument?**

- **Have you used names that people from an ethnicity prefer for themselves?** As political and social changes affect people of different ethnicities, the names they prefer may change; you will have to ask or do research to find currently preferred names. Members of a group may disagree about their preferred name for different reasons; you can acknowledge this in your writing.

  Learn the names that people find offensive so that you do not inadvertently use them; these are often names that other cultures assigned or used in the past.

- **Have you assumed that your readers share the same ethnicity or experiences as you?** Unless you are writing to people who have precisely the same background as you do, be careful not to assume that your readers hold the same beliefs as you. This can be hard since much of what we believe, think, and feel is implicit; when in doubt, ask someone not of your ethnicity and who has grown up differently from you to read what you have written, to be sure that you are not inadvertently attributing to your readers qualities or beliefs that you hold because of your particular upbringing.

- **Have you been as specific as you can in naming an ethnic group?** The more specific you can be about an ethnicity, the less likely you are to slip into stereotyping. For example, use *Ojibwa* or *Cherokee* instead of *American Indian;* use *Bahraini* or *Saudi* instead of Arab.

- **Have you used hyphens in multiword names?** In current usage, you should write (for example) *Japanese American* rather than *Japanese-American* because the hyphen implies both dual citizenship (which may not be the case) and that one is not completely American. In the nonhyphenated form, such as *Swedish American*, the first word is an adjective modifying the second word, emphasizing the second word but also holding on to the particular experiences that the first word conveys.

- **Have you avoided phrases that use ethnically tied terms?** You may have grown up with phrases that seem to you just part of language, such as *Latin lover* or *Jewish mother*—but these terms stereotype people. They imply that all people of that ethnicity share some set of broadly defined (and often derogatory) characteristics.

- **Have you capitalized the names of ethnicities?** For example, write *Polish American* or *Filipino American*.

- **Have you checked that any adjectives you put before the name of an ethnic group are appropriate?** To write that someone is (for example) *a quiet American* can imply that Americans are loud.

Because language is social and is therefore continually changing, these usages can change. Keep your ears open to stay current so that your writing is always respectful.

USING INCLUSIVE LANGUAGE
INCLUDING ALL GENDERS

SEXISM

Language is sexist when it implies that women are not only different from men but also somehow inferior.

CHECKING YOUR WRITING TO AVOID SEXISM

- **Anytime you have described someone's gender—or used descriptive terms that are culturally gender-related—ask yourself if the description is necessary.** One way to check this is to rewrite the sentence, changing the gender. For example, if you have written, *The musician, a pretty redheaded girl, played the Bach concertos effortlessly* but would not write, *The musician, a pretty redheaded boy, played the Bach concertos effortlessly*, then change the original sentence to, simply, *The musician played the Bach concertos effortlessly.*

- **Have you used unequal terms to refer to men and women in equal positions?** If, for example, you are writing about the presidents of two countries, it is incorrect to write *Mrs. Halonen and President Bush*; instead, write *Presidents Halonen and Bush.* Similarly, *man and wife* puts the woman in a subordinate position; *husband and wife* treats both with equal respect. If you write *the girls' team*, then refer to the boys' team as *the boys' team*; to call one team *the team* and the other *the girls' team* is to imply that the first team is the standard and the second is a deviation.

- **Have you used *man*, *men*, *he*, or *him* to refer to a group of people that might include women?** Some argue that these words are always inclusive of both men and women, but look at these sentences:

On this form, everyone should add the name of his husband or wife.

When pregnant, men ought to aim for more sleep.

Pantyhose fit properly if a man feels a slight cling at his waist.

Because these words are not inclusive, revise any such uses so that your words don't exclude the women in your audience.

To revise:
Substitute gender-neutral nouns for *man* or *men* or words that include them. For example, instead of *chairman*, use *chairperson*.

Make a sentence plural so that you can change *he* and *him* to the gender-neutral *they* and *them*: *Everyone should bring his own umbrella* can become *All visitors should bring their own umbrellas.*

- **Have you avoided stereotyped uses of occupations?** The sentences *Each computer programmer has his own style of coding* and *A teacher can have a tremendous impact on her students* imply that these occupations are the domain of one gender only. Make the sentences plural to avoid the stereotypes: Write, *All computer programmers have their particular styles of coding* and *Teachers can have a tremendous impact on their students.*

- **Have you used any words that stereotype behavior according to gender?** If you are describing a group made up only of women or only of men, check that your sentences do not use words that belittle some members.

You can check this by rewriting the sentence for the other gender. For example, if you've written, *The women were gossiping about the senatorial candidate,* see if *The men were gossiping about the senatorial candidate* sounds right. If it does not, then change the original sentence to *The women were discussing the senatorial candidate.*

- **Have you used salutations that include all members of an audience?** Do not start a letter with *Dear Sirs* if you do not know your audience; you can start with *To whom it may concern* or *Dear Colleagues,* or you can leave off the salutation.

INCLUDING ALL ABILITIES

> It is recommended that the word disability be used to refer to an attribute of a person, and handicap to the source of limitations. Sometimes a disability itself may handicap a person, as when a person with one arm is handicapped in playing the violin. However, when the limitation is environmental, as in the case of attitudinal, legal, and architectural barriers, the disability is not handicapping—the environmental factor is. … Thus, prejudice handicaps people by denying access to opportunities; inaccessible buildings surrounded by steps and curbs handicap people who require the use of a ramp.

ABLEISM

The American Psychological Association's language use guidelines, extracted above, acknowledge what people with disabilities have been working to counteract: People with disabilities are often seen as defined by their disabilities. For example, the expressions a *crippled woman* or *wheelchair-bound* focus our attentions not on the people, their intelligence, and their abilities but rather on their disability—a form of prejudice called **ableism**.

CHECK YOUR WRITING TO AVOID ABLEISM

- **Have you emphasized the person, not the disability?** This practice, known as *person-first language*, is called for by the 1990 Americans with Disabilities Act (ADA). This practice asks us to use language that treats all people as possessing a complex and wide range of strengths, abilities, and skills. To practice person-first language, describe the person before you describe the disability. For example, write, *person who has AIDS* rather than *AIDS sufferer*, or *child who uses a wheelchair* rather than *wheelchair-bound child*. Also, use adjectives rather than nouns to describe someone with a disability. To call someone *a mute*, *a cripple*, or *an epileptic* is to imply that the person is completely swallowed up by the disability; to say, *a child who cannot speak*, *a doctor with an amputation*, or *a musician who has epilepsy* starts to let the person—who has many other characteristics besides the disability—come forward.

- **When you refer to someone's disability in your writing, is it necessary to your purpose?** As with sexist and ageist writing, try rewriting the passage in question without the reference; if your purpose is still clear, then omit the reference.

- **Have you avoided asking your readers to think of the person as deserving only of sympathy?** If you use emotional words to describe someone with a disability (*the poor child with the limp* or *the helpless quadriplegic*), you are asking your readers to see the person as incapable of doing anything but passively accepting our concern.

- **Have you used *disability* and *handicap* according to accepted uses?** The quotation at the top of this page describes how to use these terms.

- **Does your writing emphasize that people with disabilities contribute widely and in multiple ways to their communities?**

USING INCLUSIVE LANGUAGE
INCLUDING ALL AGES

AGEISM

In some other cultures, gray hair and wrinkles are respected as signs of the knowledge and understanding that can come with a long life. In the United States, however, most people now want to stay young; one result is that older people can be stereotyped as frail, rigid, reactionary, and incompetent—or as soft, kindly, and powerless. Meanwhile, young people are often stereotyped as reckless, selfish and self-absorbed, unambitious, sex-crazed, and lazy.

If you think about all the people you know who are younger than you and all the people who are older than you, however, your experiences ought to give you many counter-examples to these stereotypes. Ageism, the stereotyping of people because of their age, is therefore—like racism and sexism—a form of prejudice because it shapes our understanding of others in negative, limiting, and rarely true ways.

CHECKING YOUR WRITING TO AVOID AGEISM

- **Have you referred to the age of a person only when your purpose requires it?** To check the necessity of referring to age in your writing, try taking it out; if your readers can still understand your purpose, then remove the reference. If, for example, in an article about poker you have written, *Ms. Jucovy, who is 63, won the final pot,* change the sentence to *Ms. Jucovy won the final pot* and ask others to read the article. If they still understand your article, then stay with the second version.

- **Have you used ageist terms to describe others?** Terms to avoid for people who are older include the following: *geriatrics, over the hill, ancient, old-timers, matronly, well-preserved.*

  Terms to avoid for young people include the following: *punk, gangbanger, juvie.*

- **Have you used terms that patronize people because of their age?** Treat older—and younger—people with the same respect, using the same titles. The standard in Anglo culture in the United States, then, is not to call an old man *Grandpa* (unless he really is your grandfather) or to refer to an older woman as *Honey, Dear,* or *Auntie*: These terms imply a level of familiarity you wouldn't assume with people of other ages.

- **Don't refer to older people as "our seniors" or "our elders."** The use of *our* implies that the group of people being discussed is the writer's property or possession instead of individual humans.

- **Have you referred to older people as the vital, interesting, productive people they are?** People who are retired do not share any common characteristic other than retirement: Some retire in their forties, and others retire in their seventies; some retire from one career to take up another while others take on active volunteer work. The more you learn about what a range of older people does, the more you are likely to write respectfully, fairly, and accurately about them.

INCLUDING ALL SEXUAL ORIENTATIONS

HETEROSEXISM

To write as though all readers have the same sexual orientation is to risk losing their attention and respect just as much as writing as though all readers are male, European American, or of one age risks losing their attention and respect.

CHECK YOUR WRITING TO AVOID HETEROSEXISM

- **When you refer to someone's sexual orientation in your writing, is it necessary to your purpose?** If you would not write, *The heterosexual engineer was fluent with both the aesthetic and the technical aspects of design,* then do not write, *The gay engineer was fluent with both the aesthetic and the technical aspects of design.*

  As we have similarly recommended on previous pages, if you are unsure about the appropriateness of including references to sexual orientation in your writing, remove the references. If readers still understand your purpose, then you can omit the references.

- **Have you used *sexual orientation* rather than *sexual preference*?** To write *sexual preference* is to imply that sexuality is the result of conscious choice, a view that neither scientific research nor the reported experiences of lesbians, gays, or heterosexuals support.

- **Have you used terms that those you are describing themselves prefer?** Currently, *gay* is the preferred term for homosexual men and *lesbian* is the preferred term for homosexual women; people whose sexual orientation includes both men and women prefer *bisexual. Transgendered* is preferred for those whose sex is not congruent with their gender identity.

Homosexual emphasizes sexuality over relationships and in the past has been associated with mental illness and criminality. It has also been used primarily to refer to male sexuality, and thus erases lesbians from the discussion. Many people thus avoid using *homosexual.*

Keep in mind that, in the twenty-first century, *lesbian* and *gay* are primarily about communities of people rather than sexual activity. This is important because some people have sex with others of the same gender but do not consider themselves *lesbian* or *gay.*

If you have any concerns about the terms you are using, ask and do research. As with all your writing, ask a range of people to read what you write, to be sure none feel pushed away by your word choices.

- **Have you avoided assuming heterosexuality?** In a manual for a large corporation, the sentence *All employees are encouraged to bring their wives to these yearly events* is a problem because it assumes that all the employees are married heterosexual males. In contrast, *All employees are encouraged to bring their partners or significant others to these yearly events* includes employees of all genders and sexual orientations as well as those who are not married.

USING INCLUSIVE LANGUAGE
INCLUDING ALL RELIGIONS
EXCLUSIONARY LANGUAGE ABOUT RELIGION

While there is no name for language that promotes one religion over others, religion is just as sensitive in our time as any of the other aspects of people's identities we have discussed. As with other aspects of identity, our beliefs about deities and religions matter deeply to each of us. Therefore, as with the other aspects of identity we have discussed, the main guideline for writing when you want to build common ground with a wide audience is to respect others' beliefs as you would want yours respected.

CHECK YOUR WRITING TO AVOID RELIGIOUS DISCRIMINATION

- **Have you referred to someone's religion only when it is central to your purpose?** Whenever you include a reference to someone's religion in your writing, try taking it out and having others read your writing. If your readers still understand your purpose, then leave the reference out. We recommend this not because we believe that religion should be excluded from all writing but rather because, given the weight of religious beliefs in people's lives, particular care is warranted.

- **When you write about religion in general, have you used terms that reflect a range of religions?** For example, if you are writing about how varying communities construct special buildings for religious observances, you should not write, *All over the world, people build churches for practicing their religions*; instead, write, *All over the world, people build mosques, temples, churches, and other specially named buildings for their religions*. Similarly, be alert to the names religions use for their members and leaders. *Rabbi, priest, reverend, imam,* and *bishop* are only some of the possibilities. Doing a little research helps you show your respect for your readers.

- **Have you avoided assuming your readers hold the same religious beliefs as you?** Many who believe in a deity do not belong to an established church, and many do not believe in a deity; the names of deities in different religions are different. If you are trying to reach a broad audience—locally or globally—be careful that any references you include about your own faith and religion do not imply that everyone else does or should believe as you do.

- **Have you used the terms the people you are describing use for their beliefs?** When you want your writing to be read by a wide audience, be careful about your use of terms like *cult* instead of *religion*, or *myth* instead of *religious belief*. If you need to describe religious practices and beliefs, do research. Have a range of others read your writing to be sure it is respectful.

- **Have you acknowledged the broad beliefs held by people in the same religion?** When you write about a religion, do not assume all its members hold the same beliefs. Catholics, for example, hold a range of views on abortion, the death penalty, birth control, and the status of women. The same is true of Muslims, Jews, Baptists, and the members of any other religion you can name, on any topic.

USING AN ESL DICTIONARY

There are English-English dictionaries specifically designed to support learning English as a new language. Such dictionaries have special features to help you learn the subtleties of the language; below is a sample excerpt from such a dictionary:

entry word

This dictionary color-codes each entry word. Not only does this help you see the words being defined, but in this dictionary, pink tells you a word is a noun; blue tells you it is a verb.

frequency information

These codes tell you that the word "card" is one of the top 1,000 words used in spoken English and one of the top 2,000 words used in written English; you can look through the dictionary to learn the most commonly used words.

pronunciation

This phonetic transcription tells you how the word is pronounced.

part of speech

n: noun
v: verb
adj: adjective
adv: adverb
prep: preposition

usage categories

The highlighted words tell you that the use of this word shifts in different categories.

definitions

ESL dictionaries provide definitions in easier-to-understand language than other dictionaries do.

sample sentences

Sample sentences can be more useful to you than definitions because they show a word in use and help you remember usage patterns.

frequency use of definition

The numbers before the categories indicate that the categories are listed by frequency of use.

card[1] S1 W2 / kaɪd $ kaɪrd / n

1 INFORMATION [C] a small piece of plastic or paper containing information about a person or showing, for example, that they belong to a particular organization, club etc: *Employees must show their **identity cards** at the gate.* | *I haven't got my **membership card** yet.*

2 MONEY [C] a small piece of plastic, especially one that you get from a bank or shop, which you use to pay for goods or get money: *Lost or stolen cards must be reported immediately.* | *a £10 phone card* | *Every time you use your store card, you get air miles.* → CHARGE CARD, CHEQUE CARD, CREDIT CARD, DEBIT CARD

3 GREETINGS [C] a piece of folded thick stiff paper with a picture on the front, that you send to people on special occasions: **birthday/Christmas/greetings etc card** *a Mother's Day card*

4 HOLIDAY [C] a card with a photograph or picture on one side, that you send to someone when you are on holiday; ▤ postcard: *I sent you a card from Madrid.*

5 STIFF PAPER [U] *BrE* thick stiff paper; → **card-board**: *Cut a piece of white card 12 x 10cm.*

6 FOR WRITING INFORMATION [C] a small piece of thick stiff paper that information can be written or printed on: *a set of recipe cards* | *a score card*

count and noncount nouns

C: count noun
U: noncount noun
→ See pages 489–490 to learn about this important distinction between kinds of nouns.

PART 8
DOCUMENTING

pressure to ackr
of composing [...].
material. It makes writing, li
musical, graphic, handicraft, engin
literally fashions the world. (697)

perhaps more than George and Trir

he language of design ("Available

ell with our view of social life and

societies" (20). What this changi

h again the New L

CONTENTS

WHERE ARE WE IN THE PROCESS FOR COMPOSING?

Understanding your project

Getting started

Asking questions

Shaping your project for others

Drafting a paper

Getting feedback

Revising
Integrating sources

Polishing
Documenting sources

ARE YOU READY TO USE THE NEXT PAGES OF THIS BOOK?

NO...

Are you figuring out if you have the most relevant and credible sources?
Are you beginning the first draft of a paper?
If this is your situation, then, no, you are not ready for the next pages.

What follows in the next pages will help you integrate the words of others into your writing, according to standard academic expectations.

→ For help with checking the relevance and credibility of your sources, see pages 124–137.

→ For help with a draft, see pages 200–213.

YES.

Are you working on a draft about which you feel pretty confident?
Are you working with the sources you know are most useful for your argument?
What follows will help you shape your writing to be generous toward a wide range of readers.

RESEARCHING ETHICALLY

When others recognize that something legally belongs to you and that you can use it as you desire, that thing is considered your property.

When you hear **property** you probably think of land or buildings, which, legally, are considered to be **real property**; **personal property**, on the other hand, consists of objects you can move with you. Both real and personal property are things that can be touched.

Intellectual property refers to things you cannot touch: ideas. When someone invents, writes, draws, composes, or performs something, that person's intellectual property isn't in the particular object—the thing invented or the book written—but in the ideas that make the invention or book possible.

There are two kinds of intellectual property: **industrial property**, which is inventions and trademarks like company logos, and **creative property**, which is literary and artistic works. **Creative property** is covered by copyright laws.

Copyright law developed over several hundred years, in a push-pull process between individual authors, musicians, and other creators of culture and those who publish and distribute what the creators make. Copyright gives legal protection to creators so that they have control over how what they make gets used by others.

Plagiarism occurs when someone uses another's creative property without the other's consent or knowledge. This can involve using a part of another's work or passing off the whole as one's own. Plagiarism is unethical and can be illegal.

→ See pages 292–295 for more on plagiarism.

SHARED CULTURE, ACADEMIC RESEARCH, AND FAIR USE

If we had to pay the inventor every time we used certain inventions—such as speech or writing—we would probably have no culture. The same goes for some ideas: If we had to pay someone every time we told a fairy tale, sang an old lullaby, or repeated the story of George Washington chopping down the cherry tree, we would have no shared experiences to bind us as a culture. In recognition of this, it is the law that after a set number of years, creators' copyright control over their productions passes into what is called the **public domain**. When a creative production is in the public domain, others can use it freely, as when the Disney Company makes a movie about Pocahontas or the Little Mermaid.

But academic research—in all the disciplines of the sciences, social sciences, and the humanities—cannot wait the length of time it takes for ideas to pass into the public domain. Academic research depends on being able to use and build on the ideas of others *now*, as does artistic development. In recognition of such conditions, there is a doctrine in U.S. copyright law called **fair use**.

FAIR USE

Fair use is a doctrine in copyright law that allows certain uses of other's copyrighted material without needing permission. Fair use does not specify exactly how much of another's work one may use; instead, four factors are considered, in legal cases, to help determine if a use is fair:

1 **The purpose and character of the use.** Is the use commercial or for nonprofit and educational purposes (such as criticism, parody, or art)? Fair use is meant to support public, not personal, enrichment. If the use transforms the copied work, making something new of it, that is also more likely to be considered fair use.

2 **The nature of the copyrighted work.** Generally, uses of published nonfiction works are considered to benefit the public—and not harm the rights of a copyright holder—more so than uses of unpublished or fictional works.

3 **The amount and substantiality of the portion used in relation to the copyrighted work as a whole.** The less one copies, the more likely the copying is to be considered fair use.

4 **The effect of the use upon the potential market for or value of the copyrighted work.** If the use will not cause the copyright holder to lose income, it is more likely to be considered fair use.

The doctrine of fair use underpins academic uses of the words of others—as in research writing—which is what we discuss in this part of this book.

TIP: IS IT FAIR USE?

Fair use protects most academic uses of intellectual property—but as soon as you use that property for personal gain or commercial uses, the use is no longer protected.

WHY CITE AND DOCUMENT SOURCES?

CONSIDERING PLAGIARISM—AND HOW TO AVOID IT

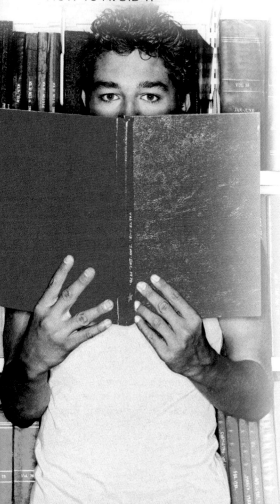

Do you want to live and work in communities—school districts, neighborhoods, cities, countries—where people respect each other and each other's ideas, and where people try to persuade you and each other based on the best possible evidence?

If you do, some of your part in shaping such communities is knowing cultural expectations for showing respect in spoken or written deliberations—even when you disagree. Your part is understanding how to determine and use the best possible evidence while letting others know where that evidence comes from so that they can judge and check it.

To cite is to name the people from whom you drew your ideas; **to document** is to record where—print or online books, journals, or newspapers—you found the ideas.

Many people think that using, citing, and documenting sources is only for academic writing. There are certainly academic conventions for doing such work—and helping you learn those conventions is a large part of the following pages. But these conventions exist because people who write academic papers, no matter what discipline, want to be sure that they are using the best possible evidence and that they are making that evidence available to others to check—and doing all this ethically, acknowledging the origins of the ideas (as we discussed on pages 290–291).

Citing and documenting sources shows that you want to take part in ongoing cultural and academic deliberations while being respectful of the research and thinking others have done before you. It shows that you want others to understand where your good reasons and thinking come from.

WHAT IS PLAGIARISM?

Plagiarism is using the ideas or words of others without acknowledgment, as though they were your own.

Plagiarism can happen inadvertently: While doing research, you might take notes or copy some text from a webpage and, in the rush to finish a paper, you lose track of where the words came from and put them straight into your paper. Plagiarism can also happen when you don't have enough confidence in your own ideas or the quality of your research to take your own positions; you let the words of others stand in for your words.

Whether plagiarism is inadvertent, purposeful, or the result of not enough confidence, it is considered wrong in the United States. It can cause you to have to redo an assignment, to fail an assignment or a class, or to be expelled from school. It stops you from learning how to have confidence in presenting your ideas in ways others will respect; it also stops you from developing your own ideas and learning.

PLAGIARISM—OR MISUSE OF SOURCES?

Sometimes students and other novice writers are accused of plagiarism because they did not cite all their sources or did not cite their sources conventionally. This can happen when writers are inexperienced with or simply do not know the conventions.

To avoid this happening to you, here are steps you can take:

- If you receive an assignment that asks you to use sources, be sure you know what citation style your teacher wants you to use. If an assignment does not specify a style, ask.

- Ask your teacher or someone in a Writing or Learning Center to look at a draft of your writing: Are you using citation styles as conventions ask?

- Pay close attention to the conventions as they are presented in this handbook. The conventions are detailed, and can seem tedious to learn, but the conventions are detailed precisely because it is a cultural practice in the United States to be very careful with the words and ideas of others.

CULTURAL ATTITUDES TOWARD THE WORDS AND IDEAS OF OTHERS

In some cultures, using the words of respected authorities and knowing when others are using them, without mentioning the source, are signs of being educated. In some cultures, students use the words of their teachers and other authorities as their own to indicate that they have learned what they were supposed to. In the United States, however, concern for the value of property—and a belief that words and ideas can be individual property (→ see pages 290–291)—has led to a valuing of and the development of conventions for acknowledging uses of others' words or ideas.

WHAT WORDS AND IDEAS DON'T NEED TO BE CITED

You don't need to cite sources when the ideas you are using are

- **Common and shared knowledge.** Most people will accept without question that there are seven days in a week or that the capital of Maryland is Annapolis. To be sure whether you need to give a source, ask yourself if everyone in your audience will know. If the answer is **yes**, then you can write without citing a source. If you're unsure if what you are writing is common knowledge, find and cite a source for it.

- **Facts that are available in a wide range of sources.** If every encyclopedia or newspaper article you check states that Joan of Arc died in 1431 or that somewhere between 22 and 26 inches of snow fell in upstate New York on Monday, then you can include these facts in your writing without citing any source for the facts.

- **The results of your own field research.**

WHAT WORDS AND IDEAS ALWAYS NEED TO BE CITED

Cite the origins of ideas and words you use in writing or oral presentations if the words and ideas are

- **Someone else's exact words** that you copied from a book, website, or interview.

- **Your paraphrase or summary of someone else's words or ideas.** (→ See pages 306–309 on paraphrasing and summarizing.)

- **Facts not known or accepted by everyone in your audience.** For example, while global climate change is accepted by almost all scientists, many nonscientific audiences are still unsure about the details. If you are writing to a nonscientific audience, you should provide sources for any evidence you offer that the climate is changing.

- **Photographs, charts, graphs, or illustrations.** Give the source—and permission you have received from the text's copyright holder, if possible—for any visual object you place into writing or a webpage. Do this even if you made the object, to calm any concerns readers might have.

HOW TEACHERS TRY TO PREVENT OR RECOGNIZE PLAGIARISM

Teachers have developed ways both to avoid and to detect plagiarism. Teachers help you avoid plagiarism by asking you to develop research projects through notes, drafts, and revisions so that they can see and encourage the progress of your ideas. (Teachers who ask you to do this will therefore be curious if you abandon a topic at the last moment and turn in a final paper on a new topic.) Some software programs can check papers online against existing writing to recognize if writers have used words from others; this software is controversial because it is not always accurate and can impinge on students' privacy and intellectual property rights.

TIPS FOR AVOIDING PLAGIARISM

The best way to avoid plagiarism is to have integrity toward your sources and toward yourself as a researcher: *Respect the words and ideas of others as you would like your own words and ideas respected.*

Your work habits can help you: If you take notes carefully and record your research, you will know when you are using the words and ideas of others.

- Keep a working bibliography of all sources you might use. This will help you have at hand the information you need when you need it so that you can cite sources as others expect.

  → To learn about working bibliographies, see pages 76–77.

- If you record someone else's words because you might use them later, mark that they are someone else's words; this will help keep you from inadvertently using those words as though they were yours.

  If you copy words from a webpage into your notes, color-code the notes or put quotation marks around them; always record the information you need for citing the words.

  → See pages 322–327 for the information you need to record to cite webpages.

If you record words from print sources, put quotation marks around them immediately and record the source information.

  → See pages 312–321 for the information to record to cite print texts.

- If you work online, take advantage of websites like diigo.com or citeulike.org to track your sources. Similarly, make copies of print sources you might use so that you can check—after you've finished your writing—that you have cited with integrity.

- Understand how to quote, summarize, and paraphrase.

  → See pages 298–309.

- Understand how to cite the words of others in your text.

  → For MLA in-text citations, see pages 345–351 for APA, see pages 410–413; for CSE, see page 439; for CMS, see pages 444–448.

- Understand how to build an appropriate and accurate Works Cited page.

  → For sample sets of MLA Works Cited pages, see pages 340–341 and 354–355; for a sample APA References list, see pages 408–409.

TIP: HOW TO CHECK THAT YOU HAVE CITED ALL YOUR SOURCES

When your writing is very close to finished, give it to a friend (one who is a careful reader) with two different colored highlighters. Ask the friend to mark your paper, highlighting your ideas in one color and the ideas of everyone else in the other color. If your friend highlights the ideas correctly, then your paper should be good to go. If not, you need to add citations and other indications—as we show later in these pages—so that it is clear when the ideas and words in your paper are not your own.

There are four facets to
CITING AND DOCUMENTING

1

USING OTHERS' WORDS IN YOUR WRITING BY QUOTING, SUMMARIZING, OR PARAPHRASING

Quoting is using others' exact words; summarizing is reporting the main idea of someone else's words, without details; paraphrasing is putting others' ideas into your own words.

QUOTING
"We started making videos to send home that showed what our life here was like," says Wright in an e-mail from his Antarctic base.

SUMMARIZING
Pollan's book tells us about the origins of four meals from widely different sources, asking us to question how our eating habits embed us in social, economic, political, and ecological webs.

PARAPHRASING
Sabido describes how he wants his telenovelas to reach his audience's limbic brain, which governs emotions.

→ To learn more about quoting, summarizing, and paraphrasing, go to pages 298–309.

2

COLLECTING THE CITATION INFORMATION YOU NEED FOR ANY SOURCE YOU USE

Anytime you quote, summarize, paraphrase, or otherwise use any kind of source (including photographs, drawings, charts, and graphs) in your writing, you need to give readers information about the source.

For different sources you need to collect different information.

→ To learn the information to collect, see pages 312–328.

→ To determine the kinds of sources you have, see pages 44–53.

→ For help figuring out if the kinds of sources you are using are right for your arguments, see pages 42–43.

THE STYLES OF CITATIONS
There are four styles for citing sources: MLA, APA, CMS, and CSE. Each style is used by a different set of disciplines. As we note on the opposite page, we devote separate pages of this book to each of these styles; see the section on a style to learn who uses it.

3

CREATING IN-TEXT CITATIONS FOR YOUR SOURCES

When you use the words or ideas of someone else, provide information to help readers find those words themselves. Each style provides ways for you to give this information.

MLA STYLE

Monroe reminds us that there is no generic access to computers: Access at home is not the same as access at work or school (19–20, 26–27).

APA STYLE

Whalen (1995) analyzed how the talk of operators responding to emergency 911 calls was organized in part by the task of filling in required information on a computer screen with a specific visual organization.

4

CREATING WORKS CITED LISTS, REFERENCES LISTS, AND BIBLIOGRAPHIES

Each style has its own name for the list of sources at the end of a piece of writing, but all of them require writers to list all the sources used in their writing.

APA STYLE

Panofsky, E. (1970). *Meaning in the visual arts*. Harmondsworth, England: Penguin.

CSE STYLE

20. Latchman DS. From genetics to gene therapy: the molecular pathology of human disease. London: Bios Scientific Publishers; 1994. 362 p. (UCL molecular pathology series).

Because each style for in-text citations and works cited lists is different, we provide separate sections for each style.

→ The **MLA style** for in-text citations is described on pages 342–351; the style for the list of works cited at the end of a paper is described on pages 352–394.

→ The **APA style** for in-text citations is described on pages 410–413; the style for the list of references at the end of a paper is described on pages 426–451.

→ The **CSE style** for in-text citations is described on page 439; the style for the list of references at the end of a paper is described on pages 439–443.

→ The **CMS style** for in-text citations is described on pages 444–445; the style for the list of references at the end of a paper is described on pages 446–448.

QUOTING, SUMMARIZING, AND PARAPHRASING

DECIDING WHETHER TO QUOTE, SUMMARIZE, OR PARAPHRASE

Whenever you quote, summarize, or paraphrase others' words, you show readers that you are engaging with the ideas of others; you show readers that you are working to make sense of and build on available ideas and information. This is a hallmark of academic writing, as well as of any deliberative writing, writing that is about considering with others the choices we might make as citizens and community members.

The chart below can help you decide when to use one method rather than another for incorporating the words and ideas of others into your writing.

QUOTING

- emphasizes the exact words being used, which helps you emphasize ideas you want to highlight because they support your arguments or provide important counter-positions.

- carries the authority of the person being quoted into your writing.

- can bring vibrant and memorable language into your writing.

SUMMARIZING

- focuses readers on the main points of an argument you are using to support your own purposes.

- shows that you are considering extended arguments made by others.

PARAPHRASING

- allows you to modify language your readers might not understand (technical language, for example) into language they will.

- allows you to bring in the opinions of others if their ideas are not presented succinctly or in memorable ways.

→ When you quote, paraphrase, and summarize, you have to show the sources for the words and ideas you are using. Each citation style handles this differently. For the MLA style, see pages 352–394; for the APA style, see pages 414–438; for the CSE style, see pages 439–443; for the CMS style, see pages 444–448.

EXAMPLE PASSAGE

So that we can best explain how to follow the conventions of quoting, paraphrasing, and summarizing, here is a passage to which we will refer on the following pages. The passage is from the article "You're not studying, you're just...," by Ravi Purushotma, published in the journal *Language Learning & Technology* in January 2005. (Note that **L2** means *second language*.)

Perhaps the most successful innovation in game designs is the development of modern massively multiplayer online games—MMOGs. In these games, rather than playing within a pre-programmed environment, players exist as characters in a virtual world formed through their interactions with other live players on the Internet. The unparalleled success of these games should be of interest to anyone trying to understand adolescent motivation and attention. In stark contrast to the high school language teacher sometimes struggling to receive 30 minutes worth of homework from students, the alarming success of MMOGs has prompted the establishment of government organizations to control their use and psychological addiction (Yee, 2002) after a set of players neglecting to break for food collapsed following up to 84 hours straight at their keyboards (Farrell, 2002; Gluck, 2002). Makers of the popular online game *Everquest* (commonly referred to as "Evercrack" for its addictive properties) found the average player spends over 20 hours a week playing the game ("Everquest or Evercrack?," 2002).

While it might be nice to get teens to spend 20 hours a week solely on their Spanish homework, we should consider the educational potential for leveraging the phenomenal ability of MMOGs to capture the attention of adolescent audiences and bring them into a manipulatable world with players from all over the planet. Some studies have reported success at integrating MOOs, the historical predecessor to modern MMOGs, into the language classroom (Von der Emde, Schneider, & Kötter, 2001), although the educational potential for MMOGs is only just beginning to be examined (Coleman, 2004; Squire & Jenkins, in press). Simply by having such an international population together in a virtual community based on communicative interaction, motivated players have access to countless native L2 speakers and tasks to discuss with them—though much could be done to extend this possibility to encourage shy learners to find and interact with players speaking their L2. For example, in a game like *The Sims Online*—the MMOG version of *The Sims*—players begin by choosing a city to live in, finding a house, then chatting with and getting to know their roommates. Besides merging international editions to form bilingual versions, another almost effortless modification game designers could make to interest language learners would be to create incentives and ways in which players could find and partner with native speakers of their L2 trying to learn their L1. This would not only provide the above-mentioned benefits of playing a bilingual game, but also provide learners with an L2 native from whom to learn about culture and language while performing a series of entertaining tasks requiring communicative exchanges. Alternatively, teachers could collaborate with classes in other countries and assign their students L2 speaking roommates.

→ This long journal quotation uses the APA style for in-text citations; see pages 410–413.

QUOTING THE WORDS OF OTHERS

Here is one way to use the words of the journal excerpt on page 299:

> Because of the "addictive qualities" of massively multiplayer online games (MMOGs), a researcher of uses of digital technologies for language learning, Ravi Purushotma, argues that teachers ought to use such games "to capture the attention of adolescent audiences and bring them into a manipulatable world with players from all over the planet" (86).

When you quote the words of others, it is as though you invite the words to speak for you: You bring both the sense of speaking and the authority of the speaker into your writing.

Because of this, use the exact words of others in your writing when those words add something to your argument that you cannot provide with your own words.

- Use words from those whom your readers are likely to recognize either by name, work, or affiliation. This will give readers more reason to accept your points.

- Quote words that will be funny, poignant, striking, or otherwise memorable for your readers. This will help readers better remember your points.

- When in your writing you are considering the positions of people with whom you disagree, it can be useful to quote their words. This shows your audience that you are being fair by letting others speak for themselves.

THE PARTS OF QUOTING WELL

Here is the example of quoting from the journal article excerpt on page 000. We repeat the example from the opposite page—with color coding—to show the many conventions that readers of more formal texts have come to expect:

Because of the " addictive qualities " of massively multiplayer online games (MMOGs), a researcher of uses of digital technologies for language learning, Ravi Purushotma, argues that teachers ought to use such games " to capture the attention of adolescent audiences and bring them into a manipulatable world with players from all over the planet " (86).

The points to the right can be a checklist for when you quoting another's words, to be sure you follow the conventions.

It is a convention that all direct quotations are indicated by quotation marks.
→ See page 302 for details on using quotation marks.

The words you are quoting should be the exact words, with no changes.
→ Sometimes, however, you will need to modify the words you are quoting—perhaps to shorten the quotation, to give an explanation readers might need, or to correct spelling; see page 303.

Using a title or affiliation of the person you are quoting, or the source of the quote, can help your audience understand why they should pay attention to this person.
→ See page 303 for ways to do this.

It is a fairly consistent convention to give the name of the person(s) responsible for the words you are quoting.
→ See page 303 for ways to do this.

Signal to your readers that you are quoting the words of others with the verb you choose to introduce the quoted words; use these verbs to weave the quotation into your writing.
→ See pages 304–305 for a list of signal words and for hints on weaving others' words into your own writing.

Each citation style specifies how to reference the page or paragraph of a citation's source. Readers can then find the exact place from which you drew your cite.
→ For MLA style, see pages 342–351.
→ For APA style, see pages 410–413.
→ For CSE style, see page 439.
→ For CMS style, see pages 445–448.

USING QUOTATION MARKS

Quotation marks are an immediately visible indicator to readers that you are using someone else's exact words—and there are many conventions regarding their use.

→ See pages 570–579 for the specific details of using quotation marks. Pay particular attention to using quotation marks with other punctuation; this is an area where many people lose track of the details.

WHEN WORDS YOU QUOTE CONTAIN THEIR OWN QUOTATION MARKS

Suppose you want to quote these words, from marketing author and blogger Seth Godin, on how the name *Global Warming* shapes how we talk about environmental change:

If the problem were called "Atmosphere cancer" or "Pollution death" the entire conversation would be framed in a different way.

The U.S. convention for quoting words that are already within quotation marks is to change the double quotation marks to single quotes:

As marketing author Seth Godin suggests, the general public might be more alarmed about global warming if "the problem were called 'Atmosphere cancer' or 'Pollution death.'"

Notice how this use of quotations means that the passage ends with a single quotation mark followed immediately by a double quotation mark.

WHEN NOT TO USE QUOTATION MARKS

If your quotation will take up more than four lines in your paper, make it into a **block quotation**. Introduce the quotation as you would any other, but:

- Make the quotation its own paragraph.
- Indent the paragraph from the left margin of your writing (but don't additionally indent the first line).
- Put the parenthetical information at the end of the quotation, following the style you have been asked to use.
- Put the parenthetical information outside the punctuation mark that ends the quotation.
- Follow a long quotation with words of your own.

Marie Vassiltchikov, a Russian refugee, worked in Berlin during World War II with a group that tried to kill Hitler. Her diaries give the only eyewitness account. In her diaries she also describes the night bombings of Berlin; after one such bombing, a friend of hers stopped by:

During the night's raid (which I had described as "nothing serious") his driver had been killed and he himself had been buried in the cellar of his house, which had caved in; he had only managed to crawl out in the morning. He announced—and this is typical for our times!—that he had just bought one hundred oysters. (121)

Another time she tries on a new hat while buildings burn around her. Her diaries give a sense of how people try to hold on to what's normal during horrible times.

WHEN AND HOW TO MODIFY THE WORDS YOU ARE QUOTING

IF YOU NEED TO REMOVE WORDS FROM A QUOTATION

If you need to remove words to emphasize the main information, use an ellipsis punctuation mark:

In a recent article on tapeworms, science writer Carl Zimmer describes how some tapeworms called monogeans that live inside fish "give birth to offspring without releasing them from their bodies. Their offspring mature inside them and give birth as well .... A monogenean may contain twenty generations of descendents inside its body!"

→ See page 567 for more on using ellipses.

IF YOU NEED TO ADD AN EXPLANATORY COMMENT TO A QUOTATION

Put the explanation in square brackets:

Leslie Collins (1976: 620) notes that "over 1000 women leaders were killed in China in 1927 by [members of a center-right political party opposed to the Communists]; many of [the women] were not Communists but simply active participants in the women's movement."

→ See page 561 for more on using brackets.

WHEN THERE IS AN OBSOLETE SPELLING OR A MISSPELLING IN THE WORDS YOU ARE QUOTING

If you are quoting an old text in which the spelling differs from what current readers expect, use the original spelling; including the words' date or providing an explanatory preface will help readers understand:

"Terrour," reasoned Thomas Churchyard in 1579, "made short warres."

USING TITLES, AFFILIATIONS, OR SOURCES

If you know that your readers know the person you are quoting, then you probably do not need to explain who the person is. But if you think your readers won't know why it is worth quoting a particular person, introduce the person with a title, affiliation, or other relevant information such as the source of the quotation so that readers understand the authority behind the person's words.

As Professor of English Diana George argues...

In her article in *Neurological Studies of the Eye*, Doctor Binti Musa has explained...

USING THE NAME OF THE PERSON BEING QUOTED

When you cite someone for the first time, giving the full name of the person is a convention in formal writing. It is a way of acknowledging that ideas are always connected to thinkers.

The sports historian James Riordan suggests that after the revolutionary stirrings of 1905, factory owners introduced soccer to their workers "as an attempt to encourage a form of civil loyalty and to divert their employees from revolutionary and other disruptive actions" (27).

In later references to that person, use the person's last name:

Riordan believes that the factory owners' strategies were largely successful.

Not:

James believes that the factory owners' strategies were largely successful.

SIGNALLING THAT YOU ARE QUOTING: CHOOSING AN INTRODUCTORY VERB AND WEAVING IN THE WORDS OF OTHERS

It is a convention to introduce others' words with phrases that

- signal to readers that you are about to quote.
- weave the quoted words into your writing so that they fit the structure of your own sentence.

CHOOSING SIGNALLING VERBS

Many verbs signal to readers that they are about to read quoted words; at right, we list many of them for you to choose.

Note, however, that the verb you choose not only signals that you are about to quote another's words; your verb choice can also signal to readers your position about the quoted words. Consider the examples below, looking at how they ask you to think about what Paulk says.

In his article about interior design in the computer game *The Sims*, Charles Paulk says that the Sims are "hard-wired social climbers" (n.p.).

In his article about interior design in the computer game *The Sims*, Charles Paulk charges that the Sims are "hard-wired social climbers" (n.p.).

In his article about interior design in the computer game *The Sims*, Charles Paulk complains that the Sims are "hard-wired social climbers" (n.p.).

SIGNALLING VERBS

acknowledges	adds	admits
advises	agrees	analyzes
answers	argues	asks
asserts	believes	charges
claims	comments	complains
concedes	concludes	concurs
condemns	confirms	considers
contends	criticizes	declares
denies	describes	disagrees
disputes	emphasizes	explains
expresses	finds	holds
illustrates	implies	insists
interprets	lists	maintains
notes	objects	observes
offers	opposes	points out
predicts	proposes	refutes
rejects	remarks	replies
reports	responds	reveals
says	shows	speculates
states	suggests	thinks

WEAVING QUOTED WORDS INTO YOUR WRITING

Anytime you quote, watch that:

- Your own words weave together with the quoted words to make a sentence that is **logical**.

  "Poverty is more than a problem of economics," Farah claims, because it is also a public health problem.

  The words that follow the quotation do not explain why Farah thinks poverty is a public health problem. Here is a fix:

  "Poverty is more than a problem of economics," Farah claims, because it is also a public health problem: Poverty can adversely affect how the brain functions and so affect how people are able to live with each other.

- Your own words weave together with the quoted words to make a sentence that is **grammatical**.

  If poverty can "literally damage our brains," as Farah asserts, then it "directly affecting the biological substrate of who we are and what we can become."

  Because the verb forms used above are inconsistent, the sentence is ungrammatical. Here is a fix:

  If poverty can "damage our brains," as Farah asserts, then it damages also "the biological substrate of who we are and what we can become."

TIPS: FOR QUOTING

- Papers composed completely or mostly of quotations would be viewed by most readers as potentially interesting experimental writing. For more formal writing, there are no hard-and-fast conventions for how many quotes are acceptable—but even though quotations can memorably and powerfully support your points, do not use so many that they lose their strength. Check your drafts with readers to see if they think you are using too many (or too few) quotations.

- To ensure that you are respecting the words of others, make it a part of your final proofreading of any writing to check your quotations against the originals.

- Anytime you quote the words or ideas of others, ask yourself if you are being honest to the other person's intent and meaning. Build thoughtful and respectful communities by using the words and ideas of others as you would want them to use your words and ideas.

SUMMARIZING THE WORDS OF OTHERS

A summary condenses the main points of someone else's words and ideas. When you summarize, you leave out illustrations, examples, and details not necessary for your arguments: Go for the main points.

Here is a summary of the journal article excerpted on page 299:

In an article in *Language Learning & Technology*, Ravi Purushotma argues that the addictive qualities of massively multiplayer online computer games make them highly appropriate for engaging adolescents in learning a second language.

Notice that this summary:

- Is much shorter than the original.
- Tells whose ideas are being summarized.
- Indicates where this information was found.
- Focuses on the excerpt's main point, drawing on information from throughout the excerpt.

Notice what this summary *does not* do:

- The summary's words do not repeat the exact words used in the excerpt (although it is fine to use a short quotation in a summary).
- The summary does not include any statistics, facts, or commentary from the article (although you might include such information in the following sentences or paragraphs if it were necessary to support your own developing arguments).

AVOIDING PLAGIARISM IN SUMMARIES

This summary—

To appeal to the motivation of adolescents, Ravi Purushotma argues, language teachers should take advantage of the phenomenal ability of computer games to capture adolescent attention (86).

—takes most of its words and phrases directly from the original article; even though the author of the article is named and a page number is given, this is still plagiarism. Here is a revision, another possible summary, that does not plagiarize:

To appeal to adolescents, Ravi Purushotma argues, language teachers can draw on "the phenomenal ability" of computer games to appeal to such audiences (86).

Notice that the words taken directly from the excerpt have quotation marks around them and the page number is cited. Synonyms have been used in place of the original authors' words, to avoid any possibility of accidentally plagiarizing their words.

→ See pages 342–351 for how to cite pages in MLA style, pages 410–413 for APA style, page 439 for CSE style, and pages 445–448 for CMS style.

TIP: HOW TO SUMMARIZE TO AVOID PLAGIARISM

- Read the piece you want to summarize several times, jotting down the ideas and points that stick out for you—using your own words. (Use a thesaurus to look up synonyms for important terms.)

- Without looking at the piece, try to say out loud what you think the main point of the piece is. (This is easier to do if you can say it out loud to someone else.)

- Write down what you said, and check it against the piece to be sure you are accurate.

TIP: SUMMARIZING WELL

- A summary should always be considerably shorter than the original.

- Weave summaries into your writing using the same sorts of introductory phrases and strategies you use with quotations. (→ See pages 304–305.)

- Use the same sorts of strategies for alerting readers to the authority of the authors of the piece you are summarizing as you use for quotations. (→ See page 303.)

- A summary should be truthful to the ideas of the piece being summarized and focus on main points instead of details, facts, and examples.

QUOTING, SUMMARIZING, AND PARAPHRASING
PARAPHRASING THE WORDS OF OTHERS

A paraphrase is about as long as the original passage, but it is a restatement of the original in your own words. You paraphrase when you do not want to quote someone else's words, perhaps because you already have used many quotations or because the original words are not memorable or need modification so that your audience will understand them.

Here is a passage from the journal article excerpted on page 299:

> Besides merging international editions to form bilingual versions, another almost effortless modification game designers could make to interest language learners would be to create incentives and ways in which players could find and partner with native speakers of their L2 trying to learn their L1. This would not only provide the above-mentioned benefits of playing a bilingual game, but also provide learners with an L2 native from whom to learn about culture and language while performing a series of entertaining tasks requiring communicative exchanges.

Here is a paraphrase of the passage:

> Purushotma suggests that if game designers want to make their software more useful to adolescent language learners, they could design games that encourage the language learners to play alongside and talk with native speakers of the language being learned; in the process of solving game tasks together, the language learners would also learn about culture from a native.

Notice that this paraphrase:

- Retells in new words all the points of the passage's sentences.
- Makes the passage more accessible to a nonspecialist audience, often a reason for paraphrasing.
- Is more detailed than a summary would be: Summaries tend to be about whole arguments; paraphrases are usually of parts of arguments.

AVOIDING PLAGIARISM IN PARAPHRASES

This paraphrase—

Purushotma argues that the extreme success of some massively multiplayer online games should interest anyone trying to get the attention of adolescents: In contrast to high school language teachers trying to get their students to do half an hour of homework, computer games have been so successful at attracting teenagers for long periods of time that some governments are trying to control their use.

—is plagiarism because:

- It repeats, overall, the grammatical and sentence structures of the original; it also repeats the order of the sentences.
- It simply removes a few words from the original, rearranges a few others, and replaces some words with synonyms.

TIP: HOW TO PARAPHRASE TO AVOID PLAGIARISM

- Read several times the passage you want to paraphrase.
- On a piece of paper, break the passage up into its parts: What are the main points of the passage?
- Without looking at the passage or your notes, write down what you understand the passage to be communicating.
- Check your writing against the original to be sure you have the main ideas and have not inadvertently used the same words and structures in the original.

TIP: PARAPHRASING WELL

- A paraphrase is usually about as long as the original.
- Weave paraphrases into your writing using the same sorts of introductory phrases and strategies you use with quotations. (⇒ See pages 304–305.)
- Use the same sorts of strategies for alerting readers to the authority of the authors of the piece you are paraphrasing as you use for quotations. (⇒ See pages 303.)
- The point of a paraphrase is to present the ideas of another as you think that writer wants others to understand them—so don't offer your interpretation or any comments until after you have finished a full and honest paraphrase.

There are five kinds of
SOURCES and each requires different citation information.

1
PRINTED BOOKS

For the purposes of academic documentation, the category of printed books includes the following:

- edited collections and anthologies
- novels
- graphic novels
- computer documentation and software instructions bound like books
- conference proceedings
- textbooks and handbooks

→ See pages 312–315 to learn what you need to find for documenting books.

2
PARTS OF PRINTED BOOKS

If you are summarizing, paraphrasing, or quoting from any of the following—

- an essay in a book that contains essays written by different authors (and this could include one story in a collection of graphic stories, for example)
- a single chapter in a book that is written by the same author as the book
- an article in a reference collection
- one poem in a collection of one author's poems
- one poem in a collection of many authors' poems
- the preface, introduction, foreword, or afterword in a book

—then you need to find the same information you would find for the book in which you found the part you are citing, as well as additional information.

→ See pages 316–317 to learn what additional information to find to cite a part of a book.

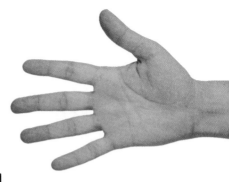

3

PRINT PERIODICALS

Periodicals are printed regularly: every day, every week, every month, four times a year, or on some other schedule. Every issue of a periodical has the same name and similar formatting.

If you are summarizing, paraphrasing, or quoting from any of the following print materials—

- a newspaper or newsletter
- a letter to the editor
- an editorial
- a popular journal, such as a magazine published once a month or even weekly
- an academic journal
- an article on microfilm
- a government booklet, pamphlet, or brochure
- a comic book that is published in a series

—then you are working with a periodical.

→ See pages 318–321 to learn what information to find in order to cite print periodicals.

4

WEBPAGES

If you are documenting an article in an online database,

→ See pages 326–327 to learn what information to find to create a citation.

For documenting any other kind of webpage,

→ See pages 322–325 to learn what information to find to create a citation.

→ To determine the kind of webpage you are using, see pages 49–53.

5

EVERYTHING ELSE...

If you wish to cite a source other than the four kinds listed here,

→ See pages 366–367.

COLLECTING CITATION INFORMATION FROM PRINTED BOOKS

Most often, you find a book's citation information in two places:

- On the Title page, which is usually the second or third page of a book and has the title, the author's name, and the name and location of the publisher.
- On the Copyright page, which usually is the back of the Title page. (In some books, this information is on the very last page.)

No matter what citation style you use, record the five pieces of information described on the next page, some of which you will use for in-text citations and all of which you will use for the works cited section of your paper. All the styles require this same information; they just use it differently.

YOU MIGHT ALSO NEED...

→ See page 388 for the additional information you need for dissertations, translations, multiple-volume series, and second (or later) editions.

→ See page 387 for the additional information you need if the book you are using is a collection of essays or articles written by different authors; a chapter in a reference work; a poem in an anthology.

Girls Make Media

Mary Celeste Kearney

Routledge
Taylor & Francis Group
New York · London

Routledge is an imprint of
Taylor & Francis Group, an informa business

Title page

Published in 2006 by
Routledge
Taylor & Francis Group
270 Madison Avenue
New York, NY 10016

Published in Great Britain by
Routledge
Taylor & Francis Group
2 Park Square
Milton Park, Abingdon
Oxton OX14 4RN

© 2006 by Taylor & Francis Group, LLC
Routledge is an imprint of Taylor & Francis Group

Printed in the United States of America on acid-free paper
10 9 8 7 6 5 4 3 2 1

International Standard Book Number-10: 0-415-97278-7 (Softcover)
International Standard Book Number-13: 978-0-415-97278-9 (Softcover)
Library of Congress Card Number 2005029586

Library of Congress Cataloging-in-Publication Data

Copyright page (detail)

☐ **BOOK'S TITLE**

Record the book's title exactly as it appears on the Title page of the book, including punctuation (also record the subtitle if there is one). If the book's title is not in English, copy it exactly, including any punctuation.

☐ **AUTHOR'S NAME**

Record the author's name exactly as it appears on the Title page of the book.

→ See pages 314–315 for what to record in cases of no or multiple authors, if a company or organization is listed, or if the author is described as an editor.

☐ **PUBLISHER'S NAME**

Record the publisher's name exactly as it appears on either the Title or the Copyright page. (For the sample to the left, you would record *Routledge*; the other corporate information is not used in citations.)

☐ **PLACE OF PUBLICATION**

Record the city and state, or the city and country if the book was not published in the United States. If you cannot find a place of publication, make a note of this. If more than one place is listed, use the first.

☐ **DATE OF PUBLICATION**

Record the year listed on the Copyright page (sometimes it is also on the Title page). If no year is listed, record that there is no date. Record the latest date if more than one is listed.

WHAT TO DO WHEN THERE IS NO SINGLE PERSON LISTED AS AUTHOR

- ☐ **If you cannot find an author's name,** make a note of this.

- ☐ **If there is not a person's name but instead the name of a government organization,** record the information exactly as it appears.

- ☐ **If there are two or three author names listed,** record them all exactly as they appear, in the order they appear. For the example below, you would record, *Bowker, Geoffrey C., and Susan Leigh Star*.

Sorting Things Out
Classification and Its Consequences

Geoffrey C. Bowker
Susan Leigh Star

- ☐ **If there are more than three authors**

  → See pages 369–371 to record this information in the MLA format.

  → See pages 421–422 to record this information in the APA format.

  → See page 442 to record this information in the CSE format.

  → See page 447 to record this information in the CMS format.

Images of an Era: the American Poster 1945-75

National Collection of Fine Arts   Smithsonian Institution   **Washington, D.C.** 1975
Distrubuted by The MIT Press   Cambridge, Massachusetts   London, England

---

Aesthetic Computing

edited by Paul Fishwick

THE

ELEMENTS

OF STYLE

by
WILLIAM STRUNK, JR.

*With Revisions, an Introduction, and
a New Chapter on Writing*

by E. B. WHITE

If no person's name is listed but there is instead the name of an organization or business, you have what is called a corporate author. Record the name exactly as it appears on the Title page. For example, for the book above, you would record and cite "National Collection of Fine Arts."

If the person listed on the Title page is described as an editor (as on the left), record the person's name and that the person is the editor. (If more than one person is listed, record the names just as you would record multiple authors' names, as described on page 314.)

If the book has an author listed as well as the name of someone who revised that person's work (as to the left), record the name of the author as well as the name of the person who revised the book, indicating that the second person did a revision.

COLLECTING CITATION INFORMATION WHEN YOU ARE CITING PART OF A PRINTED BOOK

When you are citing a part of a book—

- a poem in an anthology
- one essay or article from an edited collection of essays or articles
- a chapter in a reference work
- the preface, foreword, introduction, or afterword to a book

—collect the same information you would for a book, as shown on pages 312–315, as well as the following:

❏ The name of the person(s) who wrote the part of the book you are citing

❏ Its title

❏ Its page number(s)

On the following pages we show you where to find this information.

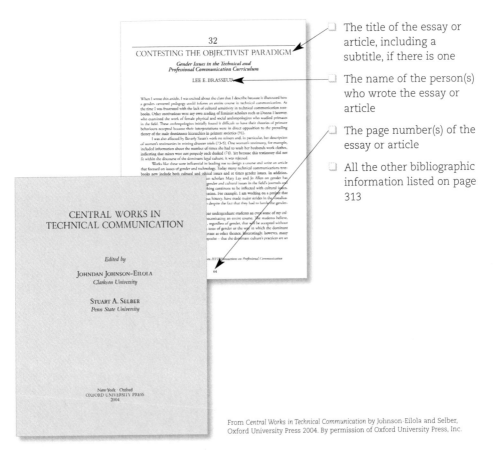

From *Central Works in Technical Communication* by Johnson-Eilola and Selber, Oxford University Press 2004. By permission of Oxford University Press, Inc.

ONE ESSAY OR ARTICLE IN AN EDITED COLLECTION OF ESSAYS OR ARTICLES

For the Introduction shown above you would record:

Brasseur, Lee E. "Contesting the Objectivist Paradigm: Gender Issues in the Technical and Professional Communication Curriculum." *Central Works in Technical Communication*. Editors Johndan Johnson-Eilola and Stuart A. Selber. New York: Oxford UP, 2004. pp. 64–80.

(Note that we had to find some of this information on other pages in this book, and that this is not the final format for a works cited page.)

COLLECTING CITATION INFORMATION WHEN YOU ARE CITING PRINTED PERIODICALS

The six pieces of information listed to the right are used by every citation style, with some minor shifts.

IF YOU ARE WORKING WITH THE FOLLOWING...

you will need to record some additional or different information:

❏ if you are citing a letter to the editor, an editorial, a published interview, a review (of a book, movie, CD, performance, or anything else), or a microfilm, **record the kind of publication** (that is, along with all the other information listed to the right, record **letter to the editor** or **review**).

❏ a daily newspaper; see page 320.

❏ a periodical that is published every week or every other week; see page 321.

→ See pages 46–47 for descriptions of different kinds of periodicals and how they can be useful for different projects.

WHAT DO "VOLUME," "ISSUE," AND "NUMBER" MEAN?

An **issue** is probably what comes to your mind when you hear **magazine** or **journal**: It is the paper-bound collection of articles that comes out once a week, once a month, or seasonally.

Often, after a year, organizations that publish magazines or journals will bind together all the issues published in that year. The bound-together set of issues is the **volume**.

When you look at the Table of Contents page of a magazine or journal and see Volume 25, Issue 8, what that means is that the periodical has been published for 25 years, and that you are looking at the eighth issue published in that year.

Sometimes, instead of **issue**, you'll see **number**: This is just another way of referring to **issue**.

The Black Collegian article image showing "Brittany was Here! My Global Study Experience in Dubai"

TITLE OF ARTICLE

Record the title exactly as it appears. If the title is not in English, copy it exactly, including the punctuation.

AUTHOR'S NAME

Record this exactly as it appears. In some periodicals, the author's name is at the end of the writing.

PERIODICAL NAME

Record the name exactly as it appears on the periodical's Table of Contents or in the header or footer.

PAGE NUMBERS

Record the page numbers for all the pages, even if the article is not on sequential pages. The example to the left is on pages 62–63, but you might have an article that goes from pages 72–75 and from 120–123; record all the pages.

DATE OF PUBLICATION

Record the exact date: It may be a month and year, two months, or a specific day. The date can appear in a page header or footer, but it is always on the Table of Contents. In this example, the date is *2006*.

VOLUME AND ISSUE NUMBER

Record the volume and issue number from the Table of Contents. Sometimes this information is at the top of the page, but it might be at the bottom or on a second page. Look carefully—but know that some periodicals do not include this information. Record what you can find.

A DAILY NEWSPAPER

Daily newspapers do not have volume and issue numbers; instead, they have dates. They also often have sections labeled by letters of the alphabet, so that page numbers might be **A12** or **J3** instead of simply **12** or **3**.

When you record citation information for a daily newspaper, record the same information as for any other periodical article (as shown on page 319), but record the full date (day, month, and year) listed and the section letter for the pages.

In addition, if what you are citing is a letter to the editor or an editorial, record that information.

For the letter to the editor shown below, here is what you would record:

Vocke, Timothy L. "Sheboygan Judge Did the Right Thing." Letter to the Editor. Milwaukee Journal Sentinel. 23 September 2007. page 5J.

- Newspaper name; if a local (not national) newspaper does not include the city name in its title, record the city name as well.

- Date (day, month, and year)

- Page number(s), including any letters that designate the section of the newspaper. If the article is on multiple pages, record all of its pages, even if they are not sequential.

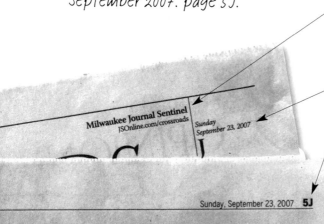

Milwaukee Journal Sentinel
JSOnline.com/crossroads
Sunday
September 23, 2007

Sunday, September 23, 2007 **5J**

CHILD ENTICEMENT CASE

Sheboygan judge did the right thing

The Journal Sentinel Editorial Board's claim that a judge needs to explain his decision in overturning a jury's conviction in a child enticement case is complete nonsense ("A nonsense ruling," Sept. 21).

Sheboygan County Circuit Judge Timothy Van Akkeren made his decision; disagree with it if you like, but he has already explained it completely by rendering it.

It is his job to decide cases the best that he can and

A PERIODICAL THAT IS PUBLISHED EVERY WEEK OR EVERY OTHER WEEK

Different citation styles require different information for periodicals that are published every week or every other week. To be sure that you will have the information you need, record every item listed for periodical articles (as shown on page 319) when you are citing a periodical that is published every week or every other week. When you create your citations, you may or may not need what you have recorded, but you will be prepared if you have recorded everything.

For the article shown below, here is what you would record:

Barry, Patrick. "Curry Powder: An Age-Old Seasoning Could Help Combat Alzheimer's." *Science News*. Volume 172, Number 11, 15 September 2007. pages 167–168.

- Date (day, month, and year)
- Volume and issue numbers
- Page number(s). If the article is on multiple pages, record all of its pages, even if they are not sequential.

SEPTEMBER 15, 2007   PAGES 161-176   VOL. 172, NO. 11

the stem of consciousness
ing antimatter

SCIENCE NEWS
THE WEEKLY NEWSMAGAZINE

CURRY POWER

An age-old seasoning could help combat Alzheim

BY PATRICK BARRY

magine that you're living 3,000 years ago in a village in what's now southern India. When you get sick or injured, you visit the healer, who most likely is a practitioner of the herbal medicine called ayurveda. For whatever ails you, you'll probably get a treatment that includes a bit of bright, yellow-orange powder, the spice turmeric.

If you have a scrape, the healer will put turmeric on it. Indigestion? Turmeric. Jaundice? Turmeric. "Nervous weakness"? That's right—turmeric.

The powder comes from a broad-leafed plant that thrives in the hot, rainy climates of southern Asia. Its pinecone-shaped stalks of white, pink, and yellow flowers smell faintly of mango, and its bulbous roots

Alzheimer's disease involves the steady det in the brain, leading to dementia. A leading th ease arises when a small protein in the brain g called plaques. In this scenario, these plaqu by triggering inflammation, a state of heigh activity that can damage the body's own cell duce free radicals, which cause oxidative da

"We looked at [curcumin] and said, 'Y thing which is anti-inflammatory," says C curcumin was also a better antioxidant th said, 'This thing has got all these propertie test it," against Alzheimer's.

Those experiments and subsequent v have shown that, in addition to its anti-in idant properties, curcumin has several effe dem to protect other ways. "If [molecular] ta

COLLECTING CITATION INFORMATION WHEN YOU ARE CITING WEBPAGES

For the purposes of citation, there are two kinds of websites:

• Databases of journals
• All others

We start by looking at all the other kinds of webpages because this work requires collecting less information than when you cite an article you found through an online database.

→ To determine the kind of webpage you are using, see pages 49–53.

ALL WEBPAGES EXCEPT THOSE FROM DATABASES

To the right we list the seven pieces of information you should try to collect for most webpages you cite. Because webpages can be so different, on the two following pages we show some examples of what to do when you can't find all seven pieces of information.

For the website shown to the right, here is a way to record the information you would collect. *What we show is not the final format for a citation*, but will help you keep track of a website in a running list.

Zinn, Lennard. "Tech Talk: Real Bikes for Real People." VeloNews. 3 Oct. 2006. Inside Communications. 5 June 2007. <http://www.velonews.com/tech/report/articles/10960.0.html>.

URL

Record the whole URL. (But if you are getting information for an article from a database, see pages 326–327.)

WEBSITE NAME

If there is a name for the overall webpage or website, record it exactly.

TITLE OF ARTICLE YOU ARE CITING/ TITLE OF WEBPAGE

Record the title exactly as it appears on the webpage, with its punctuation.

AUTHOR'S NAME

Record this exactly.

PUBLICATION DATE

This can be near the author's name, at the end of the text you are citing, or at the bottom of the page. If you find only a year, record that. If you find nothing, note that, too.

SPONSORING ORGANIZATION

If there is a company or organization that sponsors the information on the page, copy the name exactly. If this information is not obvious at the top of the page, look at the bottom of the page.

DATE ACCESSED

Record the date on which you visited the webpage. If readers visit later, they can then see if the information has changed.

TIP: LOOK EVERYWHERE!

The information listed to the right could be anywhere on a webpage. If some of this information is not included on a webpage, leave it out of your final citation.

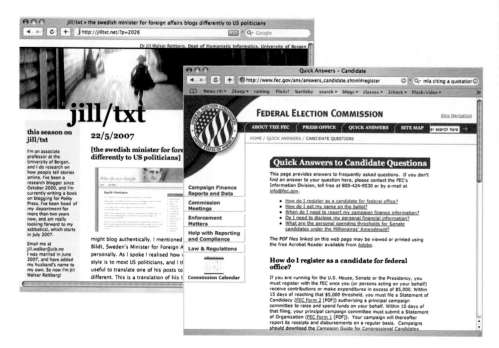

INDIVIDUAL'S WEBSITE OR BLOG

Sometimes a personal website or blog will have a sponsoring organization, but often it won't, as with the website above. Note that the website does have a name, different from the entry, and that you can find the writer's name (at both top and side) and that the date is given in European format, with the day of the week coming before the month. Here is what you would record:

Rettberg, Jill Walker. "The Swedish Minister for Foreign Affairs Blogs Differently to U.S. Politicians." jill/txt. 5 May 2007. 27 May 2007 <http://jilltxt.net/?p=2026>.

GOVERNMENT WEBSITE

This website gives no date; in such cases, it is a good idea to note that the date you record for accessing the site is the access date, as shown below.

"How do I register as a candidate for federal office?" U.S. Federal Election Commission. Accessed 10 Nov. 2007. <http://www.fec.gov/ans/answers_candidate.shtml#register>.

NONPROFIT ORGANIZATION

This webpage does not give an individual writer for the article being cited, and the sponsoring organization is the same as the website name, so record the following:

"Automakers Summer Prescription for American Drivers: Higher Gas Prices, More Pollution." Union of Concerned Scientists. 24 May 2007. 26 June 2009. <http://www.ucsusa.org/news/press_release/automakers-summer-0034.html>.

ONLINE PERIODICAL

Here is what you record for an article like the above, where the website and the sponsoring organization are the same:

Miller, Laura. "Panic in the Pages." Rev. of The Ten-Cent Plague, by David Hajdu. Salon.com. 25 Mar. 2008. 15 May 2009 <http://www.salon.com/books/review/2008/03/24/hajdu/>.

CITATION INFORMATION FOR DATABASES OF JOURNALS

Because it is often easier and more convenient to find relevant and credible journal articles through online databases than through print searches, more and more researchers are having to learn how to cite these sources.

When you cite an article that you found through an online database, you need to collect the same information you would for a print article—but you also need to collect information about the database, as we show on the next page.

→ See pages 58–65 to learn how to use online databases.

FIRST, collect the same information as you would for a print article; this will usually be in one place on the page the database provides about the article, as in the example to the right.

- ❑ **THE NAME(S) OF THE AUTHOR(S)**
- ❑ **THE TITLE OF THE ARTICLE**
- ❑ **THE NAME OF THE PERIODICAL**
- ❑ **THE PUBLICATION DATE**
- ❑ **THE VOLUME AND ISSUE NUMBERS**
- ❑ **THE ARTICLE'S PAGE NUMBERS**

—but note that some databases will give you the article as a pdf and some will not. *When the article is a pdf,* the page numbers will be the same anywhere, and so you can copy the page numbers exactly as they are given. *When the article is **not** a pdf,* or when you see a list like the example to the right, copy only the first page number, however it is presented. (The *p17, 24p* in the information to the right means that the article starts on page 17 in the journal and is 24 pages long.)

For the article shown on the right, you would record what is shown below.

Vespia, Kristin M. "A National Survey of Small College Counseling Centers: Successes, Issues, and Challenges." _Journal of College Student Psychotherapy_ 22.1 (2007): 17. database: EBSCOhost. accessed 2 August 2009. doi: 10.1300/J035V22n0103

THEN, collect information about the database and your use of it, being aware that MLA and APA citation tyles require different information:

☐ **MLA: THE NAME OF THE DATABASE**
This is usually at the top left.

☐ **MLA: THE DATE OF ACCESS**

☐ **APA: THE DOI**
The digital object identifier (→ see page 434) is usually listed down the page; if you cannot find it, look for a "stable url."

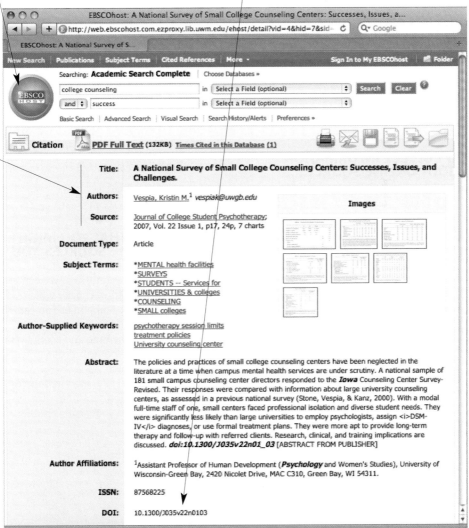

HINTS & TIPS FOR COLLECTING CITATION INFORMATION

COLLECT IT NOW!

If there is any possibility that you might use a source, record its citation information immediately.

Nothing will vex you more than having to try to find a source at the last minute, as you are putting the finishing touches on a paper.

DO COLLECT INFORMATION ABOUT ONLINE SOURCES

Even though you can bookmark webpages and go back to them later, two problems will confront you if you do not collect citation information immediately:

- You have to wade through all your other bookmarks to find the ones you want.

- The information on the page might have changed from when you first visited it.

If you are publishing your paper online, you might think that you do not need to provide a works cited list because you can provide links directly to the webpages you cite. But many readers will still want to see the full list, in one place, of all your citations—and, because websites can change (or disappear), a citation will reference when you saw the site.

KEEP ALL YOUR SOURCE INFORMATION IN ONE PLACE

Get in the habit of having a notebook or folder or single online document in which you keep track of all your sources.

You want to be able to put together your final, formal list of works cited all at once, and you want to be able to check your in-text citations all at once.

IF YOU KNOW THE STYLE EXPECTED FOR YOUR FINAL PAPER, PUT YOUR SOURCES INTO THAT FORMAT RIGHT AWAY

This will save you time when you are finishing your paper.

→ For MLA style, see pages 352–394.

→ For APA style, see pages 414–437.

→ For CSE style, see pages 439–443.

→ For CMS style, see pages 445–448.

KEEP IN MIND THAT YOU MIGHT NOT USE ALL THE SOURCES YOU COLLECT

Until you have the absolute, final version of a paper, you will not know exactly which sources you will need. Sometimes you can become attached to a source, or to all your sources, because of the time and energy you put into researching—but this doesn't mean you will need the source.

Remember that you cite only the sources that you quote, paraphrase, summarize, or otherwise reference in your writing.

PART 8
MLA
DOCUMENTATION

MLA DOCUMENTATION

329

GUIDE TO MLA DOCUMENTATION MODELS

Explore these topics online!
DK Han
online
Documentation
www.mycomplab.com

A PAPER IN MLA FORMAT

ture Theory, 24).

Mitchell's book is an argument that neither of the t...

...osed sets has any necessary precedence over the other.

...o find understandings between word and image tha...

...of a simple dichotomous opposition. For example,...

...ds of iconoclasm—rejection of images—in Marx a...

Mitchell argues that images contain more than th...

...to them by those he labels iconoclasts; instead, he...

...image as having a dialectical nature, containing bot...

...valence—as object in the world, as representation,...

...evice, as figure—most of all as a Janus-faced embl...

...or of history, and a window beyond it" (*Iconology*, 2...

The particular dichotomies Mitchell lists are pre...

...reans and their list, quoted by Aristotle, of the ten...

...goreans believed shaped all existence—

limit and the absence of limit

odd and even

The Modern Language Association, an organization of scholars and teachers of languages and literature, publishes the *MLA Handbook for Writers of Research Papers*, which is now in its seventh edition and from which we take the formatting used here. The MLA style is used primarily in English studies, comparative literature, languages, literary criticism, and other humanities fields.

To the right is a paper in MLA style, showing MLA conventions for formatting, for how sources are quoted and cited, and for how sources are listed at the end. In the following pages we show you how to attend to the details that go into such formatting.

FORMATTING

To format in MLA style, use the margins we have shown in blue to the right and:

- Double-space the paper throughout.
- Put your name at top right of every page.
- Center the title above the paper's body on the first page.
- Use a readable typeface like Times or Arial in a readable size, such as 12 point.

Opening quotations

Riley has added more quotations than she had in her original draft (→ see pages 206–213), to help readers understand why microloans matter.

Defining terms

Notice that Riley has defined *microloan*—and how quickly she is able to do this.

Providing signposts to readers

In this paragraph, Riley gives readers a sense of what is to come. Such paragraphs are like road maps: They help readers understand how a paper's parts fit together. Because readers don't have to figure this out, such paragraphs help readers focus on and understand the paper's argument.

Riley M. Savage

Professor Lynch

UN2001

17 Dec. 2009

Do Microloans Cure Women's Poverty?

In Afghanistan, under the Taliban regime, Estorai ran her home-based beauty parlor in secret, fearing reprisals for violating the ban against cosmetics. Today, with FINCA loans, her business is flourishing and Estorai is determined her daughter will receive the education she needs to succeed in the new Afghanistan. ("Change for the Better in Afghanistan")

Says Nyamba Konate, a microloan beneficiary, "I can now ensure that my children go to school, and I can better support my husband by buying food and stocking it to get us through the difficult rainy season." ("Microloans and Literacy")

"Miriam began operating her own taxi business a few years ago with the help of microloans. . . . Miriam and her husband were able to build a home, and now put the profits towards their children's education and saving for the future. Miriam even purchased a computer for her daughter, which helps with her university studies and also allows her to offer desktop publishing services to other students and community members." ("Improving Lives")

Google "microloan" and you'll get over two million results. Many results link to organizations that offer very small loans—called "microloans"—to people who do not qualify for traditional bank loans. The websites tell stories like the ones above, about the positive changes microloans make in poor women's lives worldwide, including the United States.

In this paper, I question what microloans are capable of doing. After giving a brief history and explaining how microloans work, and then describing the claims many make for microloans, I show how different critics question the purposes and potentials of

The paper to the right is the final draft of Riley's paper, which we've shown developing from Part 2 through Part 5 of this book.

→ Pages 78–79 in Part 2 show Riley's initial research on the topic of microcredit.

→ Pages 138–139 in Part 3 show how Riley developed a thesis statement.

→ Pages 154–155 in Part 4 show how Riley used her thesis statement to figure out the arrangement of her paper and what to include in her paragraphs.

→ Throughout Part 5, you can see how Riley developed a statement of purpose for her paper by analyzing her audience.

→ Pages 206–213 and 223 show Riley's first draft and revision plan. Look for differences between the two drafts to learn choices you can make to strengthen your writing.

Summarizing

This paragraph was a long quotation in Riley's first draft. By summarizing the quotation, Riley keeps her readers focused on the points important to her argument—and also then has more room to make her arguments.

Transitions between paragraphs

By repeating concepts and words from the end of one paragraph at the beginning of the next, Riley helps readers see how her ideas connect from one paragraph to the next.

→ See pages 236–237 about transitions between paragraphs.

Asking questions

Riley focuses the purpose of her paper further by asking whether the microloan system works for borrowers. Questions also challenge readers to answer them, and so can increase their engagement. (Asking questions can be overdone, however; in a paper of this length, two to three questions will seem reasonable to readers.)

Using the words of others to make your point

Riley wants to show that many people expect microloans to end poverty and change the status of women. Because she makes this point using the words of the Nobel Peace Prize Committee—a group that should have considerable authority with readers—her readers are likely to accept her point about people's expectations about microcredit.

Explore these topics online:

Sample MLA and APA papers
www.mycomplab.com

microloans for women. I consider how microcredit could be offered to poor women so that their communities really are enriched and the women join the global economy in ways that make sense to them and not just to the people who make the loans.

Microcredit originated in Bangladesh. In the 1970s, Muhammad Yunus, an economics professor at a Bangladeshi university, started making very small loans to villagers so they could buy supplies for their small businesses; Yunus had learned that traditional banks would not give loans to the villagers. Eventually, out of Yunus's loan-making came the Grameen Bank. The Bank makes loans to groups of five villagers, who are responsible for each other's debts. Because of the groups, villagers have repayment incentive: "the threat of being shamed before neighbors and relatives" (Giridharadas and Bradsher).

The successes of Grameen Bank led to many other organizations following the same pattern: Loans are made to a small group, each member of which is responsible that all repay their loans. In addition, Grameen started another pattern, of loan recipients meeting regularly to learn community-building habits. For the loanmakers, this system seems to work: The repayment rate on microloans through microenterprise organizations is at least 95% ("Microenterprise Quick Facts"). But does the system work for borrowers?

The "microloan" Google search described at the beginning of this paper brings up, in addition to microloan organization websites, many newspaper and magazine articles. Almost all the writing celebrates the microloan movement's successes, describing—as in my opening quotations—how women in poor communities turn small loans into small businesses, have enough money to send their children to school, and sometimes even start providing jobs for others. These writings also often show the same expectations about microloans as the Nobel Peace Prize committee did when they gave the 2006 prize to Yunus and the Grameen Bank: The Committee wrote that "Lasting peace can not be achieved unless large population groups find ways in which to break out of poverty" and that "Microcredit has proved to be an important liberating force in societies where women in particular have to struggle against repressive social and economic conditions"

Supporting your claims

By quickly citing all these sources in addition to the Nobel Peace Prize Committee, Riley has probably provided enough support for her claim that many people expect microloans to end poverty and change the status of women.

Notice that, because she is referring to an overall argument made by each of these sources, she does not need to refer to page numbers of specific parts of the sources.

Summarizing and paraphrasing

This is another paragraph that, in the rough draft, was composed of long quotations. Compare this draft and the rough draft (→ see page 210) to see how Riley used summary and paraphrase to make the argument hers.

Spelling things out

In her original draft, Riley didn't explain what *FINCA* meant (→ see page 211). Notice here how she gives the full name of the organization and then puts the abbreviation in parentheses. (Notice too that throughout this draft she explains the background of the people she cites, to give readers reason to take their words seriously.)

TIP: **MLA STYLE QUOTATIONS**

As you read the paper to the right, look closely at how Riley integrates the words of others into her writing, always making clear when she is using the words or ideas of others.

Note also how she follows the MLA style for showing the authors and titles of cited works and for showing page numbers of sources in parentheses. This style has been designed to keep the parenthetical citations as unobtrusive as possible so that readers can read easily.

→ See pages 344–351 to learn how to do such in-text citations.

Being careful with your claims

Riley is not arguing that microloans are always and everywhere bad; instead, she acknowledges that they often do benefit women and their families. Academic writing is characterized by such attempts at being careful in arguments and taking into account evidence that shows issues to be gray rather than starkly black or white.

("Nobel Peace Prize"). Again and again in writings about microcredit those two themes emerge: Microcredit will help poor populations break out of poverty and it will be women who do this by using microloans to help themselves and their families. From the Nobel Peace Prize Committee to *New York Times* opinion pieces (Bajaj; Freid; Kristof; Temes), from bills passed in the U.S. Congress (Smith) to articles in environmental magazines (Kelly), those two claims are repeated over and over.

Why are women so important as beneficiaries of microloans? In its early years, the Grameen Bank loaned money almost equally to men and to women—but more recently its loans go overwhelmingly to women (Rahman, slide 9). Another well-known microfinance organization, the Foundation for International Community Assistance (FINCA), says that it lends primarily to women because

> Most victims of severe poverty are children. According to UNICEF, at least half of the 12 million children aged five or younger who die each year die from malnutrition associated with severe poverty. The most direct way to improve childrens' survival and welfare is to strengthen their own mothers' ability to take care of them. ("Frequently Asked Questions")

2" for indented quotations

The United Nations has put out a "Guide for Best Practices" in microcredit, which argues that women's "access to microfinance not only benefits women but also their families and communities" because it not only improves women's economic lives but also improves women's places in society (Burjorjee, Deshpande, and Weidemann 7). Microloans are supposed to help women gain confidence in taking part in local economies and asserting themselves in their communities, and any income they get from the loans is expected to be applied to their families and so to the betterment of their communities.

The anecdotes that begin this paper, like the others that appear in almost every source I've mentioned so far, suggest that, to some extent, microloans do help women make their—and their children's—lives better. There has been some research to support these claims. For example, Susy Cheston, an official with the aid organization Opportunity International, provides evidence that, in one program in the Philippines,

A transition paragraph

Riley uses words she quoted earlier to return to her main questions and keep her readers aware of how and why she is moving from one paragraph to the next.

Focused paragraphs

In her first draft, this paragraph and the next were all one (→ see page 209). By turning back to her thesis statement (→ see page 203), Riley was able to break the original paragraph into two. Each of the paragraphs now focuses on one specific point about how microloans work.

When you quote words that you found quoted

Riley found the words about Bangladesh and Bolivia quoted in a journal article. She decided to use the exact words, so she has to show that she found them in that article. Putting *qtd. in* before the in-text citation to the source indicates that she is doing this.

"77 percent of incoming clients were classified as 'very poor'; after two years in the program, only 13 percent of mature clients were still 'very poor'" (23). Another writer, in a paper written for the United Nations Research Institute for Social Development, describes how women in India use loans to start work in local markets and keep their families and small businesses going in hard times (Mayoux 39). So no one is wrong to think that microloans can have positive effects in the lives of women.

But can those effects really "liberate women" and help "large population groups . . . break out of poverty" as the Nobel Prize committee suggested? Many do not think so, given the evidence.

For example, in terms of poverty, the writer of the paper for the United Nations Research Institute for Social Development, quoted above, says, immediately after the passage I summarized, that most studies of microcredit programs "find very small increases in income for quite large numbers of borrowers; in only a very small number of cases are there significant income increases" (Mayoux 39). In addition, studies also find that microcredit benefits women who are not at the lowest levels of poverty; the poorest of the poor may, in fact, get poorer trying to repay (MacIsaac 11-12; Mayoux 40-44). The benefits from microcredit also don't last long because borrowers often can't use loans for anything but immediate need (MacIsaac 15; Mayoux 41) or the borrowers take up work where they make only a little bit of money and where they gain no economic clout (Feiner and Barker; Roy). Under such conditions, women's positions within the overall economy do not change, meaning that their communities are unlikely to "break out of poverty." Even though microcredit has been in existence for over twenty years, Robert Pollin, co-director of the Political Economy Research Institute at the University of Massachusetts, pointed out in 2006 that "Bangladesh and Bolivia are two countries widely recognized for having the most successful microcredit programs in the world. They also remain two of the poorest countries in the world" (qtd. in Cockburn 9).

And what of women being liberated by microcredit? Using the loan often adds to, rather than changes, women's daily work: When women use their loans to make and sell

Using and referring to multiple sources

From her original audience analysis (→ see page 203), Riley knew she needed to give lots of evidence that microloans have problems. In this paragraph she shows that she has done her research and that she has lots of support for her claims. Notice that she doesn't have to quote the words of the people she cites; instead, she summarizes their points and uses the parenthetical documentation at the end of the sentences to list the sources. (When you do this, put semicolons between the sources.)

Getting to the claim

Compare these last two paragraphs to the last paragraph of Riley's original draft (→ see page 213). By having used her thesis statement to help her organize her writing (→ see page 155), Riley can now address her thesis statement's claim in this next-to-last paragraph. Prior to this, she has offered much evidence that microloans are problematic when money is just given to women; here, then, she can make her claim explicit. If her prior evidence has been sufficient, readers should be prepared to accept Riley's claims; do you think Riley has offered enough prior evidence?

Concluding

Compare this last paragraph to the last paragraph of Riley's original draft (→ see page 213). Riley no longer brings in new evidence but instead summarizes her claim and ends with a pathos appeal to future possibility.

food or other items, it is on top of running their households and taking care of their children, and sometimes they have to pull their children out of school to work in order to repay loans (Cheston 25; MacIsaac 13). And rather than learning about money use themselves, a significant number of women give their loans to male relatives because in their communities, men are supposed make economic decisions (Cowen; MacIsaac 13; Mayoux 25). For the same reasons, when women do use their loans, it can lead to both verbal and physical violence against them from their families (MacIsaac 22; Mayoux 24; Rahman, slides 23-24).

There is no question that microloans have helped some women, as all the anecdotes on all the organizational websites and in many writings show—but the evidence does not support the grand hopes for microloans that many hold. There are studies indicating what approaches to microcredit seem to work best for helping women take advantage of the potentials of microloans (Burjorjee, Deshpande, and Weidemann; MacIsaac). These studies acknowledge the problems I've noted about microloans, and, in response, acknowledge that women have to be given support in addition to loans. When women take part in regular support groups where they talk about how to use money and make economic decisions—and where they can talk about family and social circumstances—they gain both knowledge and confidence; they learn they have support for making decisions about money. In addition, when they are given information about economics and building businesses, and when they are provided mentoring, they are in a better position to understand possibilities for and consequences of their decisions.

As I have described, there has been much good that has come from microcredit. But if we truly do want to end poverty, we cannot just give loans to women. We must also help women learn how to operate within the larger economy, help them make their own decisions, and give them resources for dealing with the familial and community structures that stand in the way of their confidence and abilities.

Works Cited

Bajaj, Vikas. "Out to Maximize Social Gains, Not Profit." *New York Times*. New York
    Times, 9 Dec. 2006. Web. 22 Nov. 2007.

Burjorjee, Deena M., Rani Deshpande, and C. Jean Weidemann. *Supporting Women's
    Livelihoods: Microfinance That Works for the Majority: A Guide to Best Practices*.
    New York: United Nations Capital Development Fund/Special Unit for Microfinance,
    2002. Print.

"Change for the Better in Afghanistan." *FINCA*. FINCA International, July 2007. Web. 20
    Nov. 2007.

Cheston, Susy. "Women and Microfinance: Opening Markets and Minds." *Economic
    Perspectives: An Electronic Journal of the U.S. Department of State* 9.1 (2004):
    23-26. Web. 19 Nov. 2007.

Cockburn, Alexander. "The Myth of Microloans." *Nation* 6 Nov. 2006: 9. Print.

Cowen, Tyler. "Microloans May Work, but There Is Dispute in India over Who Will Make
    Them." *New York Times*. New York Times, 10 Aug. 2006. Web. 19 Nov. 2007.

Feiner, Susan F., and Drucilla K. Barker. "Microcredit and Women's Poverty." *Dollars
    and Sense* Nov.-Dec. 2006: 10-11. Print.

Freid, Joseph P. "From a Small Loan, a Jewelry Business Grows." *New York Times*.
    New York Times, 12 Nov. 2006. Web. 19 Nov. 2007.

"Frequently Asked Questions." *FINCA*. FINCA International, n.d. Web. 20 Nov. 2007.

Giridharadas, Anand, and Keith Bradsher. "Microloan Pioneer and His Bank Win Nobel
    Peace Prize." *New York Times*. New York Times, 13 Oct. 2006. Web. 19 Nov. 2007.

"Improving Lives: Miriam Carolina Mejía, Juticalpa, Honduras." *Global Partnerships*.
    Global Partnerships, 2007. Web. 21 Nov. 2007.

Kelly, Sean. "Banking on Women: Microcredit in
    Northern Ghana." *Natural Life*
    May-June 2007: 34-35. Print.

TIP: MLA STYLE WORKS CITED
There are lots of fine details for
formatting and arranging these pages.
→ See pages 354–355 to learn how to forma
and arrange an MLA Works Cited list.

Kristof, Nicholas D. "You, Too, Can Be a Banker to the Poor." *New York Times*. New York
Times, 27 Mar. 2007. Web. 21 Nov. 2007.

MacIsaac, Norman. "The Role of Microcredit in Poverty Reduction and Promoting
Gender Equity: A Discussion Paper." *Canadian International Development Agency*.
Strategic Policy and Planning Division, Asia Branch Canadian International
Development Agency, 12 June 1997. Web. 18 Nov. 2007.

Mayoux, Linda. "From Vicious to Virtuous Circles? Gender and Micro-Enterprise
Development." *United Nations Research Institute for Social Development*. United
Nations Research Institute for Social Development, 1995. Web. 18 Nov. 2007.

"Microenterpise Quick Facts." *Economic Perspectives: An Electronic Journal of the U.S.
Department of State* 9.1 (2004): n. pag. Web. 16 Nov. 2007.

"Microloans and Literacy Are Contributing to Food Security in Poor Upper Guinea."
USAID Africa Success Stories. USAID, 2005. Web. 24 Nov. 2007.

Norwegian Nobel Committee. *Nobel Peace Prize for 2006*. Oslo: Norwegian Nobel
Institute, 13 Oct. *Norwegian Nobel Committee*. Web. 22 Nov. 2007.

Rahman, Aminur. "Microfinance and Gender-Based Violence: Experience from the
Grameen Bank Lending." Slide program. *Canadian International Development
Agency*. Canadian International Development Agency, 9 Nov. 2004. Web.
24 Nov. 2007.

Roy, Ananya. "Against the Feminization of Policy." *Woodrow Wilson International Center
for Scholars*. Woodrow Wilson International Center for Scholars, Nov. 2002. Web.
23 Nov. 2007.

Smith, Christopher H. "Microcredit Loans Are Critical Tools for Helping the World's Poor."
Economic Perspectives: An Electronic Journal of the U.S. Department of State 9.1
(2004): n. pag. Web. 17 Nov. 2007.

Temes, Peter. "Bridgeport v. Bangladesh." *New York Times*. New York Times, 1 July
2007. Web. 20 Nov. 2007.

MLA DOCUMENTATION FOR IN-TEXT CITATIONS

ture Theory, 24).

Mitchell ... makes an argument ... either of the tw...

...osed sets has any necessary precedence over the other, a...

o find understandings between word and image that...

of a simple dichotomous opposition. For example, i...

nds of iconoclasm—rejection of images—in Marx an...

, Mitchell argues that images contain more than the...

l to them by those he labels iconoclasts; instead, he w...

image as having a dialectical nature, containing bot...

yvalence—as object in the world, as representation, a...

device, as figure—most of all as a Janus-faced embl...

ror of history, and a window beyond it" (*Iconology*, 2...

The particular dichotomies Mitchell lists are pres...

goreans and their list, quoted by Aristotle, of the ten p...

hagoreans believed shaped all existence—

> limit and the absence of limit
> odd and even

The MLA style comes from the Modern Language Association, which is an organization of scholars and teachers of languages and literature. The *MLA Handbook for Writers of Research Papers* is now in its seventh edition, published in 2009. The MLA style is used primarily in English studies, comparative literature, foreign-language, literary criticism, and humanities fields.

PURPOSES OF IN-TEXT CITATIONS

The overall purpose of an in-text citation is to help readers see your cited sources for themselves. People who value the free exchange of ideas—who want to think for themselves—want to trace the sources of your ideas.

In-text citations also help give your writing authority: When readers see that your sources are respected and well established, they are more likely to take your writing seriously.

Stemming from these overall purposes, in-text citations in the MLA style have two more focused purposes:

1 In-text citations are guides to the Works Cited page: By giving authors' names or the title of a reference, they help readers learn from the Works Cited list where you found the words and ideas that you quote, paraphrase, or summarize.

2 By giving a page number, in-text citations also tell readers exactly where in a source to find the words or ideas being referenced.

natural to today's student cohort, there's nothing innate about knowing how to apply their skills to the processes of democracy.

Although there is nothing innate about such knowledge, David Buckingham argues that this knowledge is necessary for young people because "to become an active participant in public life necessarily involves making use of modern media" (5) and eng
technologies provides a "bas
media production in the fut
amplification of global econ

the quoted person's name

page number of the quoted piece

full information of the source's publication

Works Cited

Barry, Lynda. "Common Scents." *One Hundred Demons*. Seattle: Sasquatch, 2002. Print.

Berger, John. *The Success and Failure of Picasso*. London: Penguin, 1965. Print.

Buckingham, David. *Media Education: Literacy, Learning, and Contemporary Culture*. Cambridge, UK: Polity, 2004. Print.

Clark, T. J. *The Painting of Modern Life: Paris in the Art of Manet and His Followers*. Rev. ed. Princeton: Princeton UP, 1999. Print.

HOW IN-TEXT CITATIONS FUNCTION

In an in-text citation in the MLA style, as shown above, the writer gives—at a minimum—the name of the person being quoted and the page number from which the quotation comes.

- A reader can use the quoted person's name to find full information about the source's publication in the Works Cited list at the end of the paper.

- The reader can then use the page number from the body of the paper to find the exact passage being cited.

THE BACK-AND-FORTH OF CREATING IN-TEXT CITATIONS

In composing a research paper, you move back and forth between creating in-text citations and a Works Cited list. Here is one way to create these essential parts of a research paper:

- Whenever you weave a citation into your paper, put the basic information for the citation into the body of your writing. → See pages 344–351.

- As soon as you weave a citation into your paper, add the source to the Works Cited list. → See pages 352–394 to learn about MLA Works Cited lists.

- Because you may have to make some adjustments to your in-text citations after your Works Cited page is complete, always leave time to double-check your citations against your Works Cited. You will need to make such adjustments if, for example, you use two or more sources from the same author or use sources by authors who have the same last name. → See pages 354–355 to learn what to do about these conditions.

IN-TEXT CITATIONS IN THE MLA STYLE

Whether you are citing books or electronic sources, in-text citations in the MLA style generally contain:

1

The name of the author of the words or ideas being quoted, summarized, or paraphrased.

The author's name can appear within the sentence containing the quoted words, or it can appear within parentheses at the end of the sentence.

2

The page number(s) of or some other reference to the words or ideas being cited.

The number of the page from which quoted words come goes at the end of the sentence, in parentheses.

In her article on two nineteenth-century women preachers, Patricia Bizzell argues that "a conjunction between the female sex and moral activism is traditional in Methodism" (379).

One writer on nineteenth-century women preachers argues that "a conjunction between the female sex and moral activism is traditional in Methodism" (Bizzell 379).

PUNCTUATION IN MLA IN-TEXT CITATIONS

- The parentheses that contain page numbers go at the end of the sentence, followed by the punctuation that ends the sentence.

- When you put an author's name in the parentheses with the page number, put a single space between the name and the page number.

- If the words you are quoting run across several pages, cite them like this: (23-25).

- If the words you are quoting are from several nonsequential pages, cite them like this: (45, 76).

VARIATIONS ON THE PATTERN

What if you run into one of the following cases?

→ No author is named for the source.
See page 346.

→ There is no page number (for example, you are citing a brochure or a webpage).
See page 346.

→ Your Works Cited contains two or more sources by the same author.
See page 347.

→ Your Works Cited contains sources by two authors with the same last name.
See page 347.

→ The work you are citing has two or three authors.
See page 348.

→ The work you are citing has four or more authors.
See page 348.

→ The work you are citing has a corporate author or is a government document.
See page 349.

→ See page 315 for what **corporate author** means.

→ You are quoting words that another writer quoted.
See page 349.

→ You are citing part of an edited collection or anthology.
See page 349.

→ Your sentence references a whole source (such as a whole book or webpage).
See page 349.

→ You are citing an encyclopedia or dictionary.
See page 350.

→ Your sentence references two or more sources.
See page 350.

→ You are citing a novel.
See page 350.

→ You are citing a short story.
See page 351.

→ You are citing a sacred text, such as the Bible or Koran.
See page 351.

→ You are citing lines from a play.
See page 351.

→ You are citing lines from a poem that is divided into parts or that has line numbers.
See page 351.

VARIATIONS ON THE PATTERN

NO AUTHOR IS NAMED

If you cannot find a named author, use the title of the work instead:

To "watch the rejects crash and burn" is why we watch *American Idol,* according to *Rolling Stone* magazine ("Idol Worship").

→ See page 369 for the corresponding Works Cited listing.

→ If you find the name of a company or government organization as author, see pages 370–371.

THERE IS NO PAGE NUMBER

If you cite a source that has no page number, give a paragraph or part number if there is one; otherwise, give just the name of the author.

The World Health Organization identifies obstetric fistulas as a global problem, estimating that over two million women suffer from them, with 50–100 thousand new cases each year.

For the example above, readers will look in the Works Cited for a listing under *World Health Organization.*

→ See page 355 for the corresponding Works Cited listing.

The pamphlet accompanying the Museum of Modern Art's exhibit "The Changing of the Avant-Garde" argues that architecture following World War II was influenced by "Pop culture, the first stirrings of the information age, and the radical politics of the 1960s."

The words preceding the citation make clear that the source is a pamphlet; readers won't expect a page number, and will look in the Works Cited for an entry under *Museum of Modern Art.*

→ See page 371 for the corresponding Works Cited listing.

YOUR WORKS CITED CONTAINS TWO OR MORE SOURCES BY THE SAME AUTHOR

When you use two or more works by the same author, indicate which work you are referencing each time, to help your readers. You can do this by giving the work's name in your sentence or in the in-text citation.

If you give the name in the in-text citation, do not use the complete name of the work cited, to save space; instead, use the title's first main noun. These citations are for the first work cited from one author:

That meat from grass-fed cows is more nutritious than that from corn-fed cows is one of Pollan's arguments in *The Omnivore's Dilemma* (68).

That meat from cows fed on grass is more nutritious than that from corn-fed cows is just one of the many arguments Pollan makes (*Omnivore* 68).

Here is how a second work is cited:

By the end of *The Botany of Desire*, Pollan knows how commercial potatoes are raised and cannot bring himself to eat one given to him as a gift (235).

Because his research shows just what chemicals go into a commercial potato, Pollan cannot bring himself to eat one given to him as a gift (*Botany* 235).

→ See page 355 for how these two citations appear in the Works Cited listing.

When you put an author's name, the work's title, and a page number into the citation, there is a comma between the author's name and the title, and a space between the title and the page number.

YOUR WORKS CITED CONTAINS SOURCES BY TWO AUTHORS WITH THE SAME LAST NAME

So that readers can find the right citation in your Works Cited list, either use authors' full names in your sentences or use each author's first initial and full last name in the parenthetical citation. (If both authors have the same first initial, use their full first names instead.)

Here are examples from the same paper using authors' full names:

Richard Rorty argues that our understanding of what knowledge is has changed over two hundred years: We ought no longer to think of our minds as "mirrors" that directly and only reflect what is already in the world.

Amélie Oksenberg Rorty shows how Aristotle's *Rhetoric* brings together understandings of situations in which people communicate, the psychology of audiences, the character of communicators, the structures of communication, and politics.

Here are examples that avoid ambiguity through their parenthetical citations:

Some philosophers argue that our understanding of what knowledge is has changed over the last two hundred years: We ought no longer to think of our minds as "mirrors" that directly and only reflect what is already in the world (R. Rorty).

Aristotle's *Rhetoric* brings together understandings of situations in which people communicate, the psychology of audiences, the character of communicators, the structures of communication, and politics (A. Rorty).

→ See page 355 for how these two citations appear in the Works Cited listing.

THE WORK YOU ARE CITING HAS TWO OR THREE AUTHORS

List the names in the same order as they are given in the source.

For two names, use **and** between the names, whether you use the names in your sentence or in parentheses at the end of a sentence:

As "much an activist as an analytical method" is how Moeller and Moberly describe McAllister's approach to computer games.

As "much an activist as an analytical method" is how two online reviewers describe McAllister's approach to computer games (Moeller and Moberly).

→ See page 369 for the corresponding Works Cited listing.

With three names, put commas between the names:

DeVoss, Cushman, and Grabill draw our attention to "the institutional and political arrangements" that make new media compositions possible (16).

A recent article draws our attention to "the institutional and political arrangements" that make new media compositions possible (DeVoss, Cushman, and Grabill 16).

→ See page 369 for the corresponding Works Cited listing.

THE WORK YOU ARE CITING HAS FOUR OR MORE AUTHORS

If the work you cite has four or more authors, you can list each author's name (following the same guidelines as for two or three authors). You can also use only the first author's name, followed by the expression **et al.** **Et al.** is Latin for **and others**. When you use **et al.**, put a period after **al**.

What happens when a ninth-grade World Literatures class is offered at high honors level for all students, without tracking? Fine, Anand, Jordan, and Sherman offer a two-year study of such a class in "Before the Bleach Gets Us All."

What happens when a ninth-grade World Literatures class is offered at high honors level for all students, without tracking? Fine et al. offer a two-year study of such a class in "Before the Bleach Gets Us All."

When a ninth-grade World Literatures class is offered at high honors level for everyone, without tracking, students "who never expected to be seen as smart" come to see themselves as capable and sharp, and "questions of power are engaged" (Fine et al. 174, 175).

→ See page 370 for the corresponding Works Cited listing.

THE WORK YOU ARE CITING HAS A CORPORATE AUTHOR OR IS A GOVERNMENT DOCUMENT

Use the name of the corporation or government office in full, unless there is a common shortened form of it. (If the name is long, including it in the sentence will read less awkwardly than including it within the parentheses.)

In a pamphlet published by the U.S. Dept. of the Interior, the Keweenaw National Historic Park is described as giving a "view of the birth of an industrialized society" in the United States.

Because the writer explains that the quotation comes from a pamphlet, readers will not expect a page number; they will look in the Works Cited for a listing under *United States. Dept. of the Interior.*

→ See page 371 for the corresponding Works Cited listing.

YOU ARE QUOTING WORDS THAT ANOTHER WRITER QUOTED

Use the expression *qtd*. **in** (for *quoted in*) before the source reference to show where you found the quoted words.

Elizabeth Durack, a blogger, argues that *Star Wars* "and other popular media creations take the place in modern America that culture myths like those of the Greeks or Native Americans did for earlier peoples" (qtd. in Jenkins 153).

Readers will look for the corresponding Works Cited listing under *Jenkins*.

YOU ARE CITING PART OF AN EDITED COLLECTION OR ANTHOLOGY

Use the name of the author who wrote the words you quote, not the name of the collection's editor. For example, if you are citing an article by Tania Modleski in a collection edited by Amelia Jones, use Modleski's name in your in-text citations:

Tania Modleski's article "The Search for Tomorrow in Today's Soap Operas" examines the different pleasures women find in soap opera narratives.

One researcher has argued that women find many different pleasures in soap opera narratives (Modleski).

→ See page 369 for the corresponding Works Cited listing.

YOUR SENTENCE REFERENCES A WHOLE SOURCE

Sometimes you will want to refer to a whole source in your writing, not just part of it. In such cases, do not reference page numbers; instead, you can include the author's name and the name of the work in your writing, or just reference the source in the parentheses at the end of the sentence.

Oliver Sacks's *Seeing Voices* is an argument that sign languages are indeed real languages, so that when people who are deaf learn to sign, they gain the same neurological benefits as people who can hear gain when they learn to speak.

An increase in childhood sports injuries seems related to increased competition (Gorman).

→ See page 379 for the corresponding Works Cited listing.

YOU ARE CITING AN ENCYCLOPEDIA OR DICTIONARY

If you cite a section of a reference work that has a named author, then set up your citation and Works Cited entry just as you would for a part of a book, starting with the author's name.

If you cite a section of a reference work that does not list an author, put the section into your Works Cited list alphabetically, by the title. Because such sections are usually arranged in alphabetical order, you do not need to give a page number; readers can easily find what you are referencing without the page number.

Mad cow disease, the popular name given to bovine spongiform encephalopathy (a fatal neurological disorder of cattle), appears to be transferable to humans, in whom it is called Creutzfeldt-Jacob disease; mad cow disease is spread when cows are fed processed remains of other cattle who have the disease ("Bovine Spongiform Encephalopathy").

→ See page 374 for the corresponding Works Cited listing.

YOUR SENTENCE REFERENCES TWO OR MORE SOURCES

There are two ways you can include more than one source.

First, if your sentence refers to the different sources in different parts of the sentence, put a citation after each reference:

While some research finds a link between violent games and aggressive behavior in children (Provenzo 12), many recent studies challenge the idea of a direct connection between gaming and real-world behaviors (Jones 144).

Second, if multiple sources support your point, put them all into the parentheses, separated by semicolons:

Although there is agreement that hundreds of languages were spoken in the Americas before Europeans arrived, there is disagreement over the number of linguistic families into which all those languages fit (Crystal 403-08; Wade 113-18).

CITING LITERARY WORKS

Because literary works—novels, poems, plays—come in many editions, someone who wishes to find the original words in the source may look in a different edition—so giving only page numbers will not help.

NOVELS

In addition to the page number, give the chapter or part number:

At the end of *The Yacoubian Building*, it is hard to tell whether Al Aswany wants us to see hope or futility for Egypt in Busayna and Zaki's marriage, when old Zaki starts dancing with the young woman, "raising his arms aloft amid the joyful laughter" (246, part 2).

SHORT STORIES

Because short stories *are* short, you can give just the page number:

In Lahiri's story "Interpreter of Maladies," the Indian family that lives in the United States need guidebooks to visit their old country—but even so it is lost to them, so that it is "no longer possible to enter the temple, for it had filled with rubble years ago" (57).

A SACRED TEXT, SUCH AS THE BIBLE OR KORAN

Give the chapter and verse of the words you quote, separated by periods. You can use common abbreviations for chapters in the Bible.

The sermon took as its starting point the theme of love: "Love is patient and kind; love is not jealous or boastful; it is not arrogant or rude" (New Jerusalem Bible, 1 Cor. 13.4-5).

When you include a sacred text in your Works Cited list, include the name of the edition you are using.

LINES FROM A PLAY

Instead of page numbers, include the act, scene, and line numbers of the lines, separated by periods.

Claudius recognizes that his prayers are in vain when he concludes that "words without thoughts never to heaven go" (*Hamlet* 3.3.98).

Readers should know from the context that *Hamlet's* author is Shakespeare.

→ See page 355 for the corresponding Works Cited listing.

LINES FROM A POEM THAT IS DIVIDED INTO PARTS OR THAT HAS LINE NUMBERS

Give the part and line numbers (and most often you will have to count the line numbers):

In the middle of his long poem "Sphere," about how life is in the movement from big to small and back again, A. R. Ammons gives this small metaphor: "crush a bug and the universe goes hollow / with hereafter" (80.1-2).

If the poem is not divided into parts, give only the line numbers. The first time you reference a poem, include "lines" in the parentheses; afterward, just include the line numbers. For example, this sentence starts a short essay on a poem:

Like the poet Barbara Ras, I too would like "to write myself out of grief, dig out / to a place washed by heaven-haunted light" (lines 1-2).

This sentence would come later:

Ras's poem shows, however, that writing is a momentary distraction and perhaps no comfort; she ends the poem with "I am left / writing into emphatic wet matter and the singular pain / of missing my mother" (22-24).

→ See page 375 for the corresponding Works Cited listing.

MLA DOCUMENTATION FOR WORKS CITED

Mitchell's

osed sets has any necessary

to find understandings between word and image that

The following pages show you how to format the Works Cited list at the end of any research project—and how to create the individual citations that make up the list.

of a simp **THE PATTERN**

nds of icor

Three elements make up any citation in the Works Cited of an MLA-style paper:

Author's Name. *Title of Text.* Publication information.
    1   2   3

, Mitchell

The publication information about a text includes where and when the text was published; it also includes the medium of the text: Was the text printed or online, or was it a movie, interview, map, or something else?

d to them

For example, here is a citation for a book:

Treichler, Paula. *How to Have Theory in an Epidemic: Cultural Chronicles*
     1   2

image as

of AIDS. Durham: Duke UP, 1999. Print.
       3

(Note the indenting in the example: This is standard when formatting your list of Works Cited, as we describe on pages 000–000.)

lyvalence—

device, as figure—most of all as a Janus-faced embl

ror of history, and a window beyond it" (*Iconology*, 2

The particular dichotomies Mitchell lists are pr

goreans and their list, quoted by Aristotle, of the ten

hagoreans believed shaped all existence—

limit and the absence of limit

odd and even

As you work with MLA citations, keep in mind the following words from the authors of the *MLA Handbook*, seventh edition:

> While it is tempting to think that every source has only one complete and correct format for its entry in a list of works cited, in truth there are often several options for recording key features of a work. . . . You may need to improvise when the type of scholarly project or the publication medium of a source is not anticipated by this handbook. Be consistent in your formatting throughout your work. (129)

TO MAKE MLA WORKS CITED LISTS

1 **MAKE AN INDIVIDUAL LISTING
FOR EACH WORK
YOU ARE CITING**

Do you know the kind of source you have?
YES   **NO** ···➤ Go to page 46.

Have you collected the expected citation information for your source?
YES   **NO** ···➤ Go to page 310.

Go to the page with the citation pattern for the kind of source you have.

PRINT PERIODICAL	**ONLINE PERIODICAL**	**WEBPAGE**	**BOOK**	**PART OF BOOK**	**OTHER**
Page 356.	Page 358.	Page 360.	Page 362.	Page 364.	Page 366.

- Follow the pattern to construct your listing part by part, starting with the author, moving on to the title, and so on.
- If a part of your citation varies from the pattern, follow the page references to see the format for the variation.

2 **CONSTRUCT YOUR WORKS CITED PAGE**
When you have all your individual citations, put them together into the Works Cited page.

➔ See page 354 for how to format the Works Cited page.

A WORKS CITED PAGE IN MLA FORMAT

The last page or pages in a paper written in MLA style will look like the page to the right.

On the following pages we show you how to make the individual listings that go on such a page, which is formatted following these conventions:

❏ Put the listing at the very end of the paper.

❏ The Works Cited starts on its own page.

❏ Use the same margin measurements as the rest of the paper (→ see page 331).

❏ Number each Works Cited page at the top right of the page (as you do each page in the MLA format; → see page 331). The number on the first page follows the number of the last page of the paper. For example, if the last page of the paper is 8, the first page of the Works Cited will be 9.

❏ **Works Cited** is centered at the top of the page.

❏ The listings are arranged alphabetically——by the author's last name. (If a listing starts with the title of a source, place it into the whole list alphabetically, using the first letter of the title. If the title begins with **A**, **An**, or **The**, alphabetize by the second word of the title.)

❏ If you list two or more sources by the —— same author, alphabetize them by the source titles. List the author only once; start all subsequent entries with three hyphens and a period.

❏ If you have two authors with the same —— last name, alphabetize by the first name.

❏ Double-space the entries.

Explore these topics online:

Documentation

www.mycomplab.com

Works Cited

Bauby, Jean-Dominique. *The Diving Bell and the Butterfly*. Trans. Jeremy Leggatt.
New York: Knopf, 1997. Print.

King Lear. By William Shakespeare. Dir. Trevor Nunn. Perf. Ian McKellen. Guthrie
Theater, Minneapolis. 14 Oct. 2007. Performance.

"The Melody of Murder." *The Avenger*. 3 Aug. 1945. *RadioLovers*. Bored.com, 4 June
2007. Web. 11 Apr. 2009.

Pollan, Michael. *Botany of Desire: A Plant's-EyeView of the World*. New York: Random,
2001. Print.

---. *The Omnivore's Dilemma: A Natural History of Four Meals*. New York: Penguin,
2006. Print.

Rorty, Amélie Oksenberg. "Structuring Rhetoric." *Essays on Aristotle's* Rhetoric. Ed.
Amélie Oksenberg Rorty. Berkeley: U of California P, 1996. 1-33. Print.

Rorty, Richard. *Philosophy and the Mirror of Nature*. Princeton: Princeton UP, 1979.
Print.

Shakespeare, William. *Hamlet*. Ed. A. R. Braunmuller. New York: Penguin Classics,
2001. Print.

World Health Organization. *The World Health Report 2005: Make Every Mother and
Child Count*. Geneva: World Health Organization, 2005. *World Health
Organization*. Web. 13 Mar. 2009.

Use hanging indentation

So that readers can scan the alphabetical list easily and quickly, indent by 1/2 inch all lines underneath the first.

NOTE!

Only list in your Works Cited those sources you cited in your paper. Do not include sources that you read but did not cite.

FOR PERIODICALS IN PRINT
(JOURNALS, MAGAZINES, OR NEWSPAPERS)

1 ARE YOU SURE YOU ARE WORKING WITH A PRINT PERIODICAL?
See page 46 to check.

2 DO YOU HAVE ALL THE NEEDED INFORMATION FOR YOUR CITATION?
See pages 318–321 to check.

3

THE PATTERN

Here is a sample citation for an article from an academic journal in the MLA format:

Omoniyi, Tope. "Hip-hop through the World Englishes Lens: A Response to Globalization." *World Englishes* 25.2 (2006): 195-208. Print.

Author's Name.	"Title of Article."
The pattern for an author's name is on page 368.	The pattern for the article name is on page 372.
WHAT TO DO WHEN YOU HAVE:	**WHAT TO DO WHEN YOU HAVE:**
• no author named: page 369	• a title in a language other than English: page 375
• one author: page 369	• a letter to the editor: page 377
• two or three authors: page 369	• an editorial: page 377
• four or more authors: page 370	• a published interview: page 377
• a corporation or business is listed as the author: page 370	• a review: page 375
• a government author: page 371	• a government document: page 377

Periodical Volume.Issue (Date): Pages. Medium.

If the journal name begins with A or *The*, you can leave out that word.

Italicize the journal name (or underline it if you are not working on a computer).

If you are citing a local (not national) newspaper, see the example on page 379.

The pattern for the volume and issue numbers and date is on page 378.

WHAT TO DO WHEN YOU HAVE:

- no issue number: page 379

- only a date: page 379

- a daily newspaper: page 379

- a weekly or biweekly journal or magazine: page 379

- a monthly or seasonal journal or magazine: page 379

The pattern for page numbers is on page 380.

WHAT TO DO WHEN YOU HAVE:

- an article in a journal that is paginated by volume: page 380

- an article that does not have sequential page numbering: page 380

It is part of the MLA style to include the medium of the source you are referencing: for all sources on paper, put **Print.** at the end of your citation.

MLA WORKS CITED
FOR ARTICLES FROM ONLINE SCHOLARLY JOURNALS AND DATABASES

1 ARE YOU SURE YOU ARE WORKING WITH A DATABASE OR SCHOLARLY JOURNAL?
See page 52 to check.

2 DO YOU HAVE ALL THE NEEDED INFORMATION FOR YOUR CITATION?
See pages 326–327 to check.

3 FOLLOW THE PATTERN TO THE RIGHT.

The citation formats for articles from online databases and from scholarly journals are almost the same: The only difference is that the citation for articles from databases includes the name of the database.

Here is a citation for an article from an online scholarly journal:

> Schaffner, Spencer. "Urban Literacy Center Manifesto." *Kairos* 12.3 (2008): n. pag. Web. 23 May 2009.

Here is a citation for a full-text article retrieved from an online database:

> Forman, Richard T. T., and Lauren E. Alexander. "Roads and Their Major Ecological Effects." *Annual Review of Ecology and Systematics* 29 (1998): 207-31. JSTOR. Web. 8 Aug. 2006.

Notice how each citation consists of two major parts: There is information about the article that is given exactly as though the article were in print, following the pattern on pages 356–357; then there is the information about the online source of the article.

FOR ARTICLES FROM ONLINE SCHOLARLY JOURNALS

Citation of article as on pp. 356–357. Medium. Date accessed.

Start this citation by citing the article exactly as you would cite a print article—although do not include *Print* at the end.

Include the page numbers as they appear in the article, unless:

- If the pages are not continuous (for example, if the article's pages are numbered 27, 32, 47), give the first page number followed by a plus sign: **27+**.

- If there are no page numbers, put **n. pag.** where the page numbers would usually go in a citation.

It is part of the MLA style to include the medium of the source you are referencing: for all database sources put **Web.** in your citation before the date accessed.

Put the day first, then the month (abbreviated as shown), then the year:

5 Jan. 2006	28 Feb. 2008
19 Mar. 2007	4 Apr. 2010
1 May 2006	11 June 2008
22 July 2009	17 Aug. 2011
22 Sept. 2007	31 Oct. 2006
10 Nov. 2006	25 Dec. 2012

FOR ARTICLES FROM ONLINE DATABASES

Format the citation exactly as for the pattern above for articles from scholarly journals, but add the name of the database, in italics, as shown below.

Citation of article as on pp. 356–357. *Name of Database*. Medium. Date accessed.

Give the name of the database exactly as it appears on the webpage, using the same capital-ization and including *The* if it is used in the name.

FOR WEBPAGES

OTHER THAN ARTICLES YOU FIND IN DATABASES AND SCHOLARLY JOURNALS

1 ARE YOU SURE THIS ISN'T A DATABASE OR SCHOLARLY JOURNAL?
See page 49 to check.

2 DO YOU HAVE ALL THE NEEDED INFORMATION FOR YOUR CITATION?
See pages 322–325 to check.

3

THE PATTERN

Author's Name. "Webpage Title." Title of Website.

The pattern for an author's name is on page 368.

WHAT TO DO WHEN YOU HAVE:

- no author named: page 369
- one author: page 369
- two or three authors: page 369
- four or more authors: page 370
- a corporation or business is listed as the author: page 370
- a government author: page 371

This is the title of the webpage itself, which is often different from that of the website within which the page exists.

The pattern for presenting the titles of webpages is the same as for titling articles; see page 372.

For help determining the title of either a webpage or a website, see pages 384–386 and 322–325.

The pattern for giving the title of a website is on page 384.

WHAT TO DO WHEN YOU HAVE:

- a personal website: page 385
- a blog: page 385
- an online newspaper: page 386
- a popular magazine, online: page 386
- a webpage with no apparent affiliation (that is, you can find no name of a website): page 386

YOU MAY NEED TO ADD INFORMATION HERE...
If you are citing an advertisement, chart, map, graph, performance, interview, or video that has been posted online, you will need to add here the additional information about the medium of your source. See pages 389–394.

Here is a citation for an article from an online journal in the MLA format:

Carroll, Jon. "Soul Resident." *SFGate*. San Francisco Chronicle, 21 Jan. 2009. Web. 21 Jan. 2009.

Publisher, Publication Date. Medium. Date accessed.

If there is a company or organization associated with the website, give its name exactly as it appears on the webpage, using the same capitalization and including *The* if it is used in the title.

If you cannot find any sponsoring organization listed, put **N.p.**

Follow the same formatting for this date as for the date accessed, shown to the right.

If there is no date listed, put **n.d.**

WHAT TO DO WHEN YOU HAVE:

• a date for the last time the page was revised: page 385

It is part of the MLA style to include the medium of the source you are referencing; for all web-pages, put **Web.** in your citation before the date accessed.

Put the day, then the month (abbreviated as shown), then the year:

5 Jan. 2006
27 Feb. 2008
19 Mar. 2007
1 Apr. 2006
1 May 2006
11 June 2008
22 July 2009
17 Aug. 2006
22 Sept. 2007
31 Oct. 2006
10 Nov. 2006
3 Dec. 2008

Put the URL for the website here ...
If you know that your readers won't be able to find a source without a URL, put the URL here, after the Date Accessed information. See pages 385, 386, and 394 for examples.

FOR BOOKS

1 ARE YOU SURE YOU ARE WORKING WITH A BOOK?
See page 48 to check.

2 DO YOU HAVE ALL THE NEEDED INFORMATION FOR YOUR CITATION?
See pages 312–315 to check.

3

THE PATTERN

Here is a citation for a book, in the MLA format:

> Berger, John. *About Looking*. New York: Vintage, 1992. Print.

Author's Name. *Title of the Book.*

The pattern for an author's name is on page 368.

WHAT TO DO WHEN YOU HAVE:

• no author named: page 369

• one author: page 369

• two or three authors: page 369

• four or more authors: page 370

• a book revised by a second author: page 370

• an edited collection: page 370

• a corporation or business listed as the author: page 370

• a government author: page 371

• a pamphlet without an author: page 371

• a pseudonym in place of an author's name: page 371

• the preface, introduction, foreword, or afterword to a book: page 371

The pattern for the title is on page 372.

WHAT TO DO WHEN YOU HAVE:

• a book: page 374

• a title that is in a language other than English: page 375

• a religious text: page 375

• a title of another text mentioned within the main title: page 376

Place of Publication: Publisher, Year. Medium.

The pattern for the place of publication is on page 381.

WHAT TO DO WHEN:

- the book was published in another country: page 381
- this information is missing: page 381

YOU MAY NEED TO INCLUDE ADDITIONAL INFORMATION HERE...

- if the book is translated from another language: page 387
- if the book is a published or unpublished dissertation: page 388
- if the book is part of a multivolume series: page 388
- if the book is a second (or later) edition: page 388

From the publisher's full name, you can leave off information such as *Press* or *Company*. Instead of *University Press* put *UP*: for example, *Oxford UP*.

WHAT TO DO WHEN YOU HAVE:

- a book that has been republished: page 383
- a book published before 1900: page 383
- a book with no publication date: page 383

If you find more than one copyright date for a book, list the most recent.

It is part of the MLA style to include the medium of the source you are referencing: for all sources on paper put **Print.** at the end of your citation.

FOR PARTS OF BOOKS

ESSAYS FROM EDITED COLLECTIONS; POEMS FROM ANTHOLOGIES; ARTICLES FROM REFERENCE BOOKS; PREFACES, INTRODUCTIONS, FOREWORDS, OR AFTERWORDS TO BOOKS

1 ARE YOU SURE YOU ARE WORKING WITH PART OF A BOOK?
See page 48 to check.

2 DO YOU HAVE ALL THE NEEDED INFORMATION FOR YOUR CITATION?
See pages 316–317 to check.

3

THE PATTERN

Here is a citation for a book, in the MLA format:

Blanchard, Drew. "Idle." *Best New Poets 2006*. Ed. Eric Pankey. Charlottesville: Samovar, 2006. 74-75. Print.

Author's Name. "Article Title." *Title of the Book.* Editor's Name.

The pattern for an author's name is the same as for the books shown on page 368.	The pattern for titles of parts of books is on page 373.	The pattern for the book's title is the same as when you cite a whole book, shown on page 372.	First, put *Ed.* (even if you have multiple editors) after the title of the book.

WHAT TO DO WHEN YOU HAVE:

- no author named: page 369
- one author: page 369
- two or three authors: page 369
- four or more authors: page 370
- a corporation or business is listed as the author: page 370
- a government author: page 371

WHAT TO DO WHEN YOU HAVE:

- an essay or a chapter in a book: page 374
- an article from a reference book: page 374
- a poem or short story in a book: page 375
- the preface, introduction, foreword, or afterword to a book: page 376

WHAT TO DO WHEN YOU HAVE:

- a book: page 374
- a title that is in a language other than English: page 375
- a religious text: page 375
- a title of another text mentioned within the main title: page 376

Then put the full names of the editor or editors exactly as they are printed on the title page of the book.

Place of Publication: Publisher, Year. Pages. Medium.

The pattern for the place of publication is on page 381.

WHAT TO DO WHEN:

- the book was published in another country: page 381
- publication information is missing: page 381

From the publisher's full name, you can leave off information such as *Press* or *Company*. Instead of *University Press* put *UP*: for example, *Oxford UP*.

It is part of the MLA style to include the medium of the source you are referencing: for all sources on paper, put **Print.** at the end of your citation.

Put the number of the article or essay's first page, then a hyphen, and then the number of the article or essay's last page. If there is only one page, put only that number. Add a period after the numbers.

If you find more than one copyright date for a book, list the most recent.

WHAT TO DO WHEN YOU HAVE:

- a book that has been republished: page 383
- a book published before 1900: page 383
- a book with no publication date: page 383

MLA WORKS CITED
FOR OTHER KINDS OF TEXTS

In addition to books, periodicals, and webpages, there are many other kinds of texts you can use to support your writing. The list on these pages does not include all the possibilities—but it comes close. If you find a source you want to use that is not listed in these pages, follow the basic pattern of all the citations by listing as much information as you can about an author, the title of the piece, and where and when it was published. You may also need to specify the kind of text it is. Look at the samples for these kinds of texts to see the pattern.

SOUND RECORDING
page 390

SOFTWARE
page 390

MAP, GRAPH, CHART
(print or online)
page 390

CD-ROMS
page 389

A PUBLIC TALK
(a presentation at a professional conference or a speech, debate, or lecture)
page 391

ADVERTISEMENTS
(print or online)
page 389

FILM OR VIDEO
(print or online)
page 391

CARTOON OR COMIC STRIP
(print or online)
page 392

PAINTING, DRAWING, SCULPTURE, OR PHOTOGRAPH
(print or online)
page 393

MUSICAL COMPOSITION
page 392

PERFORMANCE
(musical, dramatic, dance, poetic, or other artistic performance)
page 392

TELEVISION OR RADIO PROGRAM
page 393

ONLINE SOURCES OTHER THAN THOSE WE'VE ALREADY MENTIONED
page 394

BROADCAST INTERVIEW
page 392

AN INTERVIEW YOU CONDUCT
page 390

MLA WORKS CITED
Author's Name

Note that the pattern for author names is consistent across citations for all texts in all media.

Author's Name. "Article Title." *Periodical*
Volume.Issue (Date): Pages. Medium.
PERIODICALS IN PRINT—go back to page 356

Author's Name. "Article Title." *Periodical*
Volume.Issue (Date): Pages. *Name of Database*. Medium. Date Accessed.
ARTICLE FROM ONLINE DATABASE—go back to page 358

Author's Name. "Article Title." *Periodical*
Volume.Issue (Date): Pages. Medium. Date Accessed.
ARTICLE FROM ONLINE SCHOLARLY JOURNAL—go back to page 358

Author's Name. "Webpage Title." *Website Title*.
Publisher, Publication Date. Medium. Date Accessed.
ARTICLE FROM OTHER WEBPAGES—go back to page 360

Author's Name. *Book Title*. Place of Publication: Publisher, Year. Medium.
BOOK—go back to page 362

Author's Name. "Article Title." *Book Title*. Editor's Name. Place of Publication: Publisher, Year. Pages. Medium.
PARTS OF BOOKS—go back to page 364

THE PATTERN

The first author listed is always written with the last name first, then a comma, and then the first name.

Last Name, First Name.

Singh, Amardeep.

If the writer you are citing uses a middle name or initials, those follow the first name. Sometimes a writer will use only initials.

Phelps, Louise Wetherbee.

Mitchell, W. J. T.

If what you are citing has more than one author, the additional names should be listed after the initial author, with the first name first and the last name last. List the authors in the order in which they are listed in the book.

Phelps, Louise Wetherbee, and Janet Emig.

Fine, Michelle, Lois Weis, Linda Powell Pruitt, and April Burns.

Note that, in a citation, there is a period after the author's name or the list of authors' names.

→ Here we show how authors' names appear in individual citations for a range of sources; on pages 354–355 we show you how to create a full Works Cited list out of individual citations.

NO AUTHOR NAMED

If you cannot find an author's name, start the citation with the title of the book or article.

ONE AUTHOR

TWO AUTHORS

In these citations, the first author appears with last name first; all following authors' names are listed starting with their first names.

THREE AUTHORS

In these citations, the first author appears with last name first; all following authors' names are listed starting with their first names.

Electronic Text Center. U of Virginia Lib., 11 July 2007. Web. 15 May 2009.
TEXT AND IMAGE ARCHIVE, ONLINE

"Idol Worship." *Rolling Stone* 8 Feb. 2007: 7. Print.
MAGAZINE ARTICLE, NO AUTHOR LISTED

Ultimate Visual Dictionary. Rev. ed. New York: Dorling Kindersley, 2002. Print.
REFERENCE WORK

Brodkey, Linda. *Writing Permitted in Designated Areas Only*. Minneapolis: U of Minnesota P, 1996. Print.
BOOK

Modleski, Tania. "The Search for Tomorrow in Today's Soap Operas." *The Feminism and Visual Culture Reader*. Ed. Amelia Jones. London: Routledge, 2003. 294-302. Print.
CHAPTER, IN EDITED BOOK

Flint, Julie, and Alex de Waal. *Darfur: A Short History of a Long War*. London: Zed, 2006. Print.
BOOK

Moeller, Ryan M., and Kevin Moberly. Rev. of *Game Work: Language, Power, and Computer Game Culture*, by Ken S. McAllister. *Kairos* 10.2 (2006): n. pag. Web. 2 Feb. 2009.
REVIEW, ONLINE
REVIEW, OF BOOK

DeVoss, Dànielle Nicole, Ellen Cushman, and Jeffrey T. Grabill. "Infrastructure and Composing: The When of New-Media Writing." *CCC* 57.1 (2005): 14-44. Print.
ARTICLE, IN ACADEMIC JOURNAL

Joyce, Justin A., Dwight A. McBride, and Melvin Dixon. *A Melvin Dixon Critical Reader*. Jackson: Mississippi UP, 2006. Print.
BOOK

Wittig, Rob, Scott Rettberg, and William Gillespie. "&Now Conference Review." *Electronic Book Review*. Dept. of English, U of Illinois, Chicago, 26 July 2005. Web. 2 Feb. 2009.
REVIEW, ONLINE
REVIEW, OF CONFERENCE

FOUR OR MORE AUTHORS

You can write out the names of all the authors, following the pattern described earlier for multiple authors—or you can give only the name of the first author listed. All the other authors are then represented by *et al.*, which is a Latin abbreviation meaning *and others*.

Fine, Michelle, Bernadette Anand, Carlton Jordan, and Dana Sherman. "Before the Bleach Gets Us All." *Construction Sites*. Ed. Lois Weiss and Michelle Fine. New York: Teachers College, 2000. 161-79. Print.
CHAPTER, IN EDITED BOOK

Imus, Anna, et al. "Technology: A Boom or a Bust? An Understanding of Students' Perceptions of Technology Use in the Classroom." *Inventio* 6.1 (2004): n. pag. Web. 1 Mar. 2009.
ARTICLE, IN ONLINE ACADEMIC JOURNAL

A BOOK REVISED BY A SECOND AUTHOR

The second author is considered to be an editor:

Strunk, William. *Elements of Style*. Ed. E. B. White. 4th ed. Boston: Allyn, 2000. Print.
BOOK

→ On page 315 you can see the Title page of a book revised by a second author.

A CORPORATE AUTHOR

Start the citation with the name of the corporate author exactly as it is listed in the source (but omit *A*, *An*, or *The*).

Museum of Modern Art. *The Changing of the Avant-Garde: Visionary Architectural Drawings from the Howard Gilman Collection*. New York: Museum of Modern Art, 2002. Print.
PAMPHLET

AN EDITED COLLECTION

Put *ed.* (or *eds.*, for multiple editors) after the names that begin the citation.

NOTE!

If you are citing only a piece from an edited collection and not the whole collection, create the citation following the pattern shown on pages 364–365.

ONE EDITOR

Le Faye, Deirdre, ed. *Jane Austen's Letters*. 3rd ed. Oxford: Oxford UP, 1995. Print.
BOOK, EDITED

TWO EDITORS

If the book has more than two editors, follow the pattern for a book with multiple authors.

Hocks, Mary, and Michelle Kendrick, eds. *Eloquent Images: Word and Image in the Age of New Media*. Cambridge: MIT P, 2003. Print.
BOOK, EDITED

A GOVERNMENT AUTHOR

Start the citation with the country name, then give the name of the government organization responsible for the publication, exactly as it appears in the publication.

United States. Dept. of the Interior. *Keweenaw*. Washington: GPO, 2002. Print.
BROCHURE

United Nations. Development Program. *Beyond Scarcity: Power, Poverty, and the Global Water Crisis*. New York: United Nations, 2006. Print.
REPORT

(**GPO** stands for **Government Printing Office** and is a standard abbreviation you can use. Documents from the United Nations start with **United Nations**.)

A PAMPHLET WITHOUT AN AUTHOR

Renoir Lithographs. New York: Dover, 1994. Print.
PAMPHLET

A PSEUDONYM IN PLACE OF AN AUTHOR'S NAME

Start the citation with the pseudonym, then put the author's real name in brackets.

LeCarré, John [David Cornwell]. *The Russia House*. New York: Knopf, 1989. Print.
BOOK

THE PREFACE, INTRODUCTION, FOREWORD, OR AFTERWORD TO A BOOK

Put the name of the person who wrote the preface, introduction, foreword, or afterword in the author's name position.

After that, put **Preface**, **Introduction**, **Foreword**, or **Afterword**. Then put the book's title, followed by the name of the person responsible for the book (preceded by **By** if the person is the author or **Ed.** if the person is the editor).

At the end of the citation, give the page numbers of the cited part.

Zizek, Slavoj. Afterword. *The Politics of Aesthetics*. By Jacques Rancière. Trans. Gabriel Rockhill. London: Continuum, 2004. 67-79. Print.
AFTERWORD, BOOK
BOOK, TRANSLATED

> ### NOTE!
>
> In these examples, we show citations with what is called *hanging indentation*: The first line of a citation sticks farther into the left margin than the other lines. This is the standard form of indenting for MLA Works Cited lists. A hanging indent of one-half inch makes the list easier to read.
>
> Also keep in mind that—in a formal paper—your Works Cited list will be double-spaced.

MLA WORKS CITED
Titles

Note how the patterns for titles are consistent across citations for all kinds of texts in all kinds of media.

Author's Name. "Article Title." *Periodical* Volume.Issue (Date): Pages. Medium.
PERIODICALS IN PRINT—go back to page 356

Author's Name. "Article Title." *Periodical* Volume.Issue (Date): Pages. *Name of Database*. Medium. Date Accessed.
ARTICLE FROM ONLINE DATABASE—go back to page 358

Author's Name. "Article Title." *Periodical* Volume.Issue (Date): Pages. Medium. Date Accessed.
ARTICLE FROM ONLINE SCHOLARLY JOURNAL—go back to page 358

Author's Name. "Webpage Title." *Website Title*. Publisher. Publication Date. Medium. Date Accessed.
ARTICLE FROM OTHER WEBPAGES—go back to page 360

Author's Name. *Book Title*. Place of Publication: Publisher, Year. Medium.
BOOK—go back to page 362

Author's Name. "Article Title." *Book Title*. Editor's Name. Place of Publication: Publisher, Year. Pages. Medium.
PARTS OF BOOKS—go back to page 364

THE PATTERN

BOOK TITLES

Follow these steps to build the pattern:

1 Capitalize all the words of the title except for

articles (*a, an, the*)

prepositions (*to, at, by, for, from, in, of, with, between*)

conjunctions (*and, but, for, or*)

the word **to** when it is part of an infinitive (as in **to read** or **to write**)

2 Capitalize the first word and the last word even if the words are one of the exceptions above.

3 Italicize the whole title.

4 Put a period after the title. (If the title ends with a question mark or exclamation point, use that instead.)

The Title of the Book.

Crow Lake.

The Diving Bell and the Butterfly.

If the book has a subtitle, put the subtitle after a colon and capitalize it as you would the title:

Scribbling the Cat: Travels with an African Soldier.

The Quick and the Dead: Artists and Anatomy.

A Country Doctor's Casebook: Tales from the North Woods.

→ Many full citation examples follow, on pages 374–377.

→ Here we show how titles of works appear in individual citations for a range of sources; on pages 354–355 we show you how to create a full Works Cited list out of individual citations.

TITLES OF PARTS OF BOOKS, PERIODICAL ARTICLES, AND WEBPAGES

Follow these steps to build the pattern:

1 Capitalize the title, following the same guidelines for a book title.

2 Put quotation marks around the title.

3 Put a period after the last word of the title but inside the final quotation mark. (If the title ends with a question mark or exclamation point, use that.)

4 Follow the pattern below for finishing the title, depending on the source.

PARTS OF BOOKS

Put the title of the whole book after the title of the part of the book you are citing.

"The Title of the Part of the Book." *The Title of the Book.*

"The New Dionysianism." *The Sticky Sublime.*

"Meno." *The Collected Dialogues of Plato.*

"Pointers for Pets." *Living with the Animals.*

JOURNAL ARTICLES

Put the name of the journal after the article name.

"The Article." *Journal Name*

"Will the Next Election Be Hacked?" *Rolling Stone*

"What if It's (Sort of) a Boy and (Sort of) a Girl?" *New York Times*

"A Bookling Monument." *Kairos*

WEBPAGES

Put the name of the website after the name of the webpage.

"The Article." *Website Name.*

"Project Description." *The Nora Project.*

"My Favorite Mozart." *Marginal Revolution.*

"Pictures Without Bias: How to Avoid Discrimination in Visual Media." *Center for Media Literacy.*

→ For working with the titles of websites (as opposed to webpages), see pages 384–386.

A BOOK

Lawson, Mary. *Crow Lake*. New York: Delta Trade, 2002. Print.
BOOK

Petherbridge, Deanna, and Ludmilla Jordanova. *The Quick and the Dead: Artists and Anatomy*. Berkeley: U of California P, 1997. Print.
BOOK

Sharp, Lesley A. *The Possessed and the Dispossessed: Spirits, Identity, and Power in a Madagascar Migrant Town*. Berkeley: U of California P, 1993. *eScholarship Editions*. Web. 22 Sept. 2008.
BOOK, ONLINE

AN ESSAY OR CHAPTER IN A BOOK

Makhan, Jha. "Island Ecology and Cultural Perceptions: A Case Study of Lakshdweep." *Lifestyle and Ecology*. Ed. Baidyanath Saraswati. New Delhi: Indira Gandhi National Centre for the Arts, 1998. N. pag. *Kalasampada*. Web. 30 June 2008.
ESSAY, IN ONLINE BOOK

Plato. "Meno." *The Collected Dialogues of Plato*. Ed. Edith Hamilton and Huntington Cairns. Trans. W. K. C. Guthrie. Princeton: Princeton UP, 1961. 353-85. Print.
ESSAY, IN EDITED BOOK

Van Proyen, Mark. "The New Dionysianism." *The Sticky Sublime*. Ed. Bill Beckley. New York: Allworth, 2001. 165-75. Print.
ESSAY, IN EDITED BOOK

AN ESSAY IN AN ONLINE COLLECTION

Badger, Meredith. "Visual Blogs." *Into the Blogosphere: Rhetoric, Community, and Culture of Weblogs*. Ed. Laura J. Gurak, Smiljana Antonijevic, Laurie Johnson, Clancy Ratliff, and Jessica Reyman. U of Minnesota, June 2004. Web. 23 Sept. 2008.
ESSAY, IN ONLINE COLLECTION

AN ARTICLE FROM A REFERENCE BOOK

Reference works rarely give the name of the person who wrote the article. Put the article's title in quotation marks at the beginning of the entry.

"Islam." *The New York Public Library Desk Reference*. 1989. Print.
ARTICLE, IN REFERENCE BOOK

"Bovine Spongiform Encephalopathy." *Encyclopædia Britannica Online*. Encyclopædia Britannica, 2007. Web. 25 Feb. 2007.
ARTICLE, IN ONLINE REFERENCE BOOK

A POEM OR SHORT STORY IN A BOOK

Ras, Barbara. "Where I Go When I'm Out of My Mind." *One Hidden Stuff*. New York: Penguin, 2006. 19-20. Print.
POEM, IN BOOK BY ONE AUTHOR

Mông-Lan. "Trail." *The Best American Poetry 2002*. Ed. Robert Creeley. New York: Scribner's, 2002. 108-17. Print.
POEM, IN EDITED COLLECTION

Mina, Hanna. "On the Sacks." *Literature from the "Axis of Evil."* Trans. Hanadi Al-Samman. New York: New, 2006. 179-206. Print.
SHORT STORY, IN EDITED BOOK
SHORT STORY, TRANSLATED

In this example, note that the date of the book's original publication follows the book's title.

Woolf, Virginia. "Monday or Tuesday." *A Haunted House*. 1921. N. pag. *Bartleby.com: Great Books Online*. Web. 17 Feb. 2009.
SHORT STORY, IN ONLINE BOOK

A REVIEW

Davies, Sam. Rev. of *Electroma*, dir. Thomas Bangalter and Guy-Manuel de Homam-Christo. *Sight & Sound* 17.8 (2007): 62. Print.
REVIEW, OF MOVIE

Stephens, Dana. "The Metaphysics of David Cronenberg's *Violence*." Rev. of *Eastern Promises*, dir. David Cronenberg. *Slate*. Washington Post Newsweek Interactive, 13 Sept. 2007. Web. 14 Sept. 2008.
REVIEW, ONLINE
REVIEW, OF MOVIE

A TITLE THAT IS IN A LANGUAGE OTHER THAN ENGLISH

Note that the citations follow the capitalization conventions of the original language.

Baudelaire, Charles. *Les Fleurs du mal*. Paris: Pocket, 2000. Print.
BOOK OF POETRY, TITLE IN LANGUAGE OTHER THAN ENGLISH

Doreau, Delphine. "Merci à tous ceux qui ont fait coucou hier." *Non Dairy Diary*. N.p., 10 Aug. 2007. Web. 11 Apr. 2009.
BLOG ENTRY, TITLE IN LANGUAGE OTHER THAN ENGLISH

Tapia, Rosa. "'Mia o de Naiden.' La Reescritura de la Violencia en 'Pasion de Historia' de Ana Lydia Vega." *Hispanic Review* 75.1 (2007): 47-60. Print.
ARTICLE, IN ACADEMIC JOURNAL
ARTICLE, TITLE IN LANGUAGE OTHER THAN ENGLISH

A RELIGIOUS TEXT

If you are not citing a particular edition of a religious text such as the Bible or the Koran, you do not need to include it in the Works Cited list at the end of your paper.

A TITLE OF ANOTHER TEXT MENTIONED WITHIN THE MAIN TITLE

If you are citing the title of a book that contains the title of another book, the embedded title should not be italicized or enclosed in quotation marks.

Kummings, Donald D. *Approaches to Teaching Whitman's* Leaves of Grass. New York: MLA, 1991. Print.
BOOK

If you are citing a journal article, and the title contains the title of a book, italicize the book title.

Froula, Christine. "Out of the Chrysalis: Female Initiation and Female Authority in Virginia Woolf's *The Voyage Out*." *Tulsa Studies in Women's Literature* 5.1 (1986): 63-90. Print.
ARTICLE, IN ACADEMIC JOURNAL

If you are citing a part of a book, and the title contains the title of still another work, put the embedded title within single quotation marks.

Gruber, Sibylle. "'I, a Mestiza, Continually Walk Out of One Culture and into Another': Alba's Story." *Feminist Cyberscapes: Mapping Gendered Academic Spaces*. Ed. Kristine Blair and Pamela Takayoshi. Stamford: Ablex, 1999. 105-32. Print.
CHAPTER, IN EDITED BOOK

A BOOK'S PREFACE, INTRODUCTION, FOREWORD, OR AFTERWORD

The person who wrote the preface, introduction, foreword, or afterword is the author. After that name, put the appropriate word (not italicized): *Preface*, *Introduction*, *Foreword*, or *Afterword*.

Then put the title of the book, followed by the name of the person responsible for the book (preceded by **By** if the person is the author or by **Ed.** if the person is the editor).

At the end, give the page numbers for the cited part.

Zizek, Slavoj. Afterword. *The Politics of Aesthetics*. By Jacques Rancière. Trans. Gabriel Rockhill. London: Continuum, 2004. 67-79. Print.
AFTERWORD, IN BOOK
AFTERWORD, TRANSLATED

A LETTER TO THE EDITOR

Put **Letter.** after the title of the letter.

A city name follows the local newspaper name because the name does not identify the city.

McDonald, Mary. "Pandemic Prep." Letter. *Scientific American* Mar. 2006: 14. Print.
LETTER TO THE EDITOR

Coté, Cynthia. "Hancock is OK." Letter. *MiningGazette.com*. Daily Mining Gazette [Houghton, MI], 18 Aug. 2007. Web. 19 Aug. 2007.
LETTER TO THE EDITOR, ONLINE

AN EDITORIAL

Put **Editorial.** after the title of the editorial.

Schulte, Margaret F. Editorial. *Frontiers of Health Services Management* 24.1 (2007): 1. Print.
EDITORIAL, UNTITLED

Nasibu, Charles. "Africa's Weapons of Mass Destruction." Editorial. *Independent* 16 Aug. 2007: 1. Print.
EDITORIAL, TITLED

"Failure Is Not an Option." Editorial. *JSOnline*. Milwaukee Journal Sentinel, 16 Sept. 2007. Web. 31 May 2008.
EDITORIAL, ONLINE
EDITORIAL, NO AUTHOR NAMED

A PUBLISHED INTERVIEW

An interview is considered published when it is presented on a page or screen. Start with the name of the person interviewed. If you have the name of the person who conducted the interview, follow the pattern in the entry for Satrapi.

Robbins, Trina. Interview with Michelle Garcia. *Bitch* Fall 2002: 60+. Print.
INTERVIEW, PUBLISHED
INTERVIEW, UNTITLED

Satrapi, Marjane. Interview with David Welsh. "Marjane Satrapi Returns." *Powells.com*. Powell's Bookstore, 17 Sept. 2004. Web. 21 Apr. 2008.
INTERVIEW, ONLINE

A GOVERNMENT DOCUMENT

Montana. Dept. of Fish, Wildlife, and Parks. "2007 Montana Fishing Regulations." Helena: State of Montana, 2007. Print.
GOVERNMENT DOCUMENT, STATE
GOVERNMENT DOCUMENT, REVISED EDITION

United States. Federal Trade Commission. "The Truth about Cellphones and the National Do Not Call Registry." 15 Apr. 2005. *Federal Trade Commission*. Web. 27 Nov. 2006.
GOVERNMENT DOCUMENT, FEDERAL
GOVERNMENT DOCUMENT, ONLINE

Periodical Volume, Issue Number, and Date

When periodicals were first printed, publishers developed a pattern of binding a full year's set into one volume. This made finding and referring to any particular issue easy: One could find the volume first, and then the article in the volume by its issue number or date.

Author's Name. "Article Title." *Periodical*
Volume.Issue (Date): Pages. Medium.
PERIODICALS IN PRINT—go back to page 356

Author's Name. "Article Title." *Periodical*
Volume.Issue (Date): Pages. *Name of Database*. Medium. Date Accessed.
ARTICLE FROM ONLINE DATABASE—go back to page 358

Author's Name. "Article Title." *Periodical*
Volume.Issue (Date): Pages. Medium. Date Accessed.
ARTICLE FROM ONLINE SCHOLARLY JOURNAL—go back to page 358

THE PATTERN

VOLUME AND ISSUE NUMBERS, AND DATE

The volume number goes directly after the name of the periodical; there is a space but no punctuation between the two. If there is an issue number, put a period after the volume number and then the issue number.

The date follows, in parentheses.

Volume Number.Issue Number (Date)

5.2 (2004)

27.11 (1976)

→ Here we show how periodical volume numbers and dates appear in individual citations for different sources; on pages 354–355 we show you how to bring together individual citations like these to create a full Works Cited list for the end of any MLA-style research paper.

| **EXAMPLE** | French, R. M. "Using Guitars to Teach Vibrations and Acoustics." *Experimental Techniques* 29.2 (2005): 47-48. Print. |
| | ARTICLE FROM PRINT JOURNAL |

WHEN THERE IS NO ISSUE NUMBER

The volume number and date give readers enough information for finding the source.

Ostrow, Saul. Rev. of *Sharp? Monk? Sharp! Monk! Bomb* 100 (2007): 15. Print.

REVIEW, OF SOUND RECORDING, IN JOURNAL
REVIEW, IN JOURNAL

WHEN THERE IS ONLY A DATE

Many popular magazines list dates, not volume numbers.

Birnbaum, Charles A. "Cultivating Appreciation." *Dwell* Sept. 2007: 196+. Print.

ARTICLE, IN POPULAR MAGAZINE

A DAILY NEWSPAPER

Because daily newspapers don't have volumes and issues, they are cited only with the date—which does not have parentheses around it.

"Rethinking Abstinence." Editorial. *Bangor Daily News* 17 Sept. 2007: 8. Print.

EDITORIAL, NO AUTHOR NAMED

Rozek, Dan. "Girls' Squabble over iPod Over: And in the End, Neither Will Get Music Player." *Chicago Sun-Times* 10 Nov. 2006: 3. Print.

NEWSPAPER ARTICLE

A WEEKLY OR BIWEEKLY JOURNAL OR MAGAZINE

Do not give the volume and issue numbers even if they are listed. Do not put parentheses around the date.

Gorman, Christine. "To an Athlete, Aching Young." *Time* 18 Sept. 2006: 60. *Expanded Academic ASAP*. Web. 25 Feb. 2007.

ARTICLE, IN WEEKLY JOURNAL, RETREIVED
FROM ONLINE DATABASE

Schlei, Rebecca. "Faithful Comrade: A Monumental Affair." Rev. of *Loving Frank*, by Nancy Horan. *Shepherd Express* 6 Sept. 2007: 48. Print.

REVIEW, OF BOOK, IN WEEKLY JOURNAL

A MONTHLY OR SEASONAL JOURNAL OR MAGAZINE

Do not give the volume and issue numbers even if they are listed. Do not put parentheses around the date.

Fallows, James. "Macau's Big Gamble." *Atlantic* Sept. 2007: 96-105. Print.

REVIEW, OF BOOK, IN MONTHLY MAGAZINE

Page Numbers for Articles from Periodicals

EXAMPLES

French, R. M. "Using Guitars to Teach Vibrations and Acoustics." *Experimental Techniques* 29.2 (2005): 47-48. Print.
BI-MONTHLY MAGAZINE

Watts, Steven. "Walt Disney: Art and Politics in the American Century." *Journal of American History* 82.1 (1995): 84-110. Print.
SCHOLARLY JOURNAL

AN ARTICLE IN A JOURNAL THAT IS PAGINATED BY VOLUME

Include both the volume and the issue number as well as the page numbers when you cite articles from scholarly journals, even if the journal is paginated by volume.

Bizzell, Patricia. "Frances Willard, Phoebe Palmer, and the Ethos of the Methodist Woman Preacher." *Rhetoric Society Quarterly* 36.2 (2006): 377-98. Print.
ARTICLE, IN ACADEMIC JOURNAL
ARTICLE, IN JOURNAL PAGINATED BY VOLUME

AN ARTICLE THAT DOES NOT HAVE SEQUENTIAL PAGE NUMBERING

In newspapers and magazines, articles are often broken across nonsequential pages. In such cases, give the number of the first page, followed by +.

Lenzer, Jean. "Citizen, Heal Thyself." *Discover* Sept. 2007: 54+. Print.
ARTICLE, IN POPULAR MAGAZINE

THE PATTERN

PAGE NUMBERS FOR ARTICLES FROM PERIODICALS

Place a colon after the date of the periodical and then put the page number or numbers. Follow the page numbers with a period.

Even if you refer to only a small portion of an article, give the page numbers for the entire article.

: xx-xx.

| : 52. | : 721-86. | : 237-58. |
| : B5. | : 21-28. | : 237-358. |

(Note that if the ending page is above 100, you list only the last two digits of the page number unless more are necessary for clarity.)

Place of Publication

Note how the pattern for listing the place of publication for a text is consistent across citations for all kinds of texts in all kinds of media.

Author's Name. *Book Title.* Place of Publication: Publisher, Year. Medium.
BOOK—go back to page 362

Author's Name. "Article Title." *Book Title.* Editor's Name. Place of Publication: Publisher, Year. Pages. Medium.
PARTS OF BOOKS—go back to page 364

THE PATTERN

Put the city of publication after the title of the book, followed by a colon; you do not need to mention a state or country.

Place of Publication:

Boston:

Santa Monica:

Calumet:

If more than one place of publication is listed, use the first one.

EXAMPLES

Bourriaud, Nicolas. *Relational Aesthetics.* Dijon-Quetigny: Les Presses du Réel, 2004. Print.
BOOK PUBLISHED IN ANOTHER COUNTRY

Eisner, Will. *Graphic Storytelling and Visual Narrative.* Tamarac: Poorhouse, 1996. Print.
BOOK

Harris, Stephen L. *Agents of Chaos: Earthquakes, Volcanoes, and Other Natural Disasters.* Missoula: Mountain, 1990. Print.
BOOK

Howes, David. "Sensory Basket Weaving 101." *NeoCraft: Modernity and the Crafts.* Ed. Sandra Alfoldy. Halifax: Press of the Nova Scotia College of Art and Design, 2007. 216–24. Print.
ESSAY IN EDITED COLLECTION

Yanagi, Soetsu. *The Unknown Craftsman: A Japanese Insight into Beauty.* Tokyo: Kodansha, 1989. Print.
BOOK PUBLISHED IN ANOTHER COUNTRY

A WORK WITHOUT PUBLICATION INFORMATION

If you find a book that does not include complete information about the place of publication, use the abbreviation **n.p.** (an abbreviation for *no publication information*).

→ On these pages, we show how the place of publication appears in individual citations for a range of sources; on pages 354–355 we show you how to bring together individual citations like these to create a full Works Cited section that goes at the end of any MLA-style research paper.

Year of Publication

Note how the pattern for listing the year of publication for a text is consistent across citations for many kinds of texts in many kinds of media.

Author's Name. *Book Title.* Place of Publication: Publisher, Year. Medium.
BOOK—go back to page 362

Author's Name. "Article Title." *Book Title.* Editor's Name. Place of Publication: Publisher, Year. Pages. Medium.
PARTS OF BOOKS—go back to page 364

THE PATTERN

Put a comma after the publisher's name, then put the year of publication, followed by a period.

, Year of Publication.

, 2002.

, 1996.

, 2012.

If you find more than one copyright date for a book, use the most recent date.

EXAMPLES

Davis, Neil. *The Aurora Watcher's Handbook.* Fairbanks: U of Alaska P, 1992. Print.
BOOK

González-Crussi, F. *On Seeing: Things Seen, Unseen, and Obscene.* New York: Overlook Duckworth, 2006. Print.
BOOK

→ On these pages, we show how the publication dates of books appear in individual citations for a range of sources; on pages 354–355 we show you how to bring together individual citations like these to create a full Works Cited section that goes at the end of any MLA-style research paper.

A BOOK THAT HAS BEEN REPUBLISHED

A republished book has been previously published by a different publisher or published in a different form (as when a hardback book is republished as a mass-market paperback).

For such books, use the pattern for book entries but insert the original publication date after the book's title; put the republished edition's date at the end.

If the republication adds material such as an introduction, add this to the citation: Put it after the original publication information.

If the republished book has a new title, put it and the publication date, then put **Rpt. of** (for *reprint of*) and the original title and publication information.

Johnson, Steven. *Emergence: The Connected Lives of Ants, Brains, Cities, and Software.* 2001. New York: Touchstone-Simon, 2002. Print.

BOOK, REPUBLISHED WITH THE SAME TITLE

Isherwood, Christopher. *The Last of Mr. Norris.* New York: New Directions, 1945. Rpt. of *Mr. Norris Changes Trains.* London: Hogarth, 1935. Print.

BOOK, REPUBLISHED WITH DIFFERENT TITLE

A BOOK PUBLISHED BEFORE 1900

For a book published before 1900, you do not need to list a publisher's name.

Whitman, Walt. *Leaves of Grass.* Brooklyn, 1855. Print.

BOOK, PUBLISHED BEFORE 1900

Nightingale, Florence. *Notes on Nursing: What It Is, What It Is Not.* 1860. *Internet Archive.* Web. 21 Nov. 2008.

BOOK, PUBLISHED BEFORE 1900
BOOK, ONLINE

A BOOK THAT HAS NO PUBLICATION DATE

If a book does not list a date of publication on its Copyright page, put the abbreviation **n.d.** (for *no date*) where the year of publication usually goes in a citation.

Baudrillard, Jean. *Simulations.* New York: Semiotext(e), n.d. Print.

BOOK, NO PUBLICATION DATE

Website titles

Webpages are almost always part of larger websites. When you cite a webpage, you must also cite the website of which it is a part—just as when you cite an article or essay, you also cite the book in which you found the article or essay.

In their capitalization, website titles function just like the titles of books.

In their placement, website titles are like book titles when you are citing part of the book: You place the website title after the title of the webpage being cited.

Author's Name. "Webpage Title." *Website Title.* Publisher, Publication Date. Medium. Date Accessed.

ARTICLE FROM OTHER WEBPAGES—go back to page 360

▨ ▨ ▨

Because of the similarities we've just listed, we could have included information on website titles on the preceding pages. But because citing websites is still new to many, and because there are so many possible variations in websites, we are focusing on them here.

THE PATTERN

WEBSITE TITLES

Take the title exactly as you find it on the website, and follow these steps to build the pattern:

1 Capitalize all the words of the title except for

articles *(a, an, the)*

prepositions

conjunctions *(and, but, for, or)*

the word **to** when it is part of an infinitive (as in **to read** or **to write**)

2 Capitalize the first word and the last word even if the words are one of the exceptions above.

3 Italicize the whole title.

4 Put a period after the title. (If the title ends with a question mark or exclamation point, use that instead.)

The Title of the Website.

Electronic Book Review.

Google.

ScientificAmerican.com.

The Institute for the Future of the Book.

We Make Art, Not Money.

PeaceWomen across the Globe.

→ Many full citation examples follow, on pages 385–386.

→ On these pages, we demonstrate how to include titles for individual citations for a range of sources; on pages 354–355 we show you how to bring together individual citations like these to create a full Works Cited section that goes at the end of any MLA-style research paper.

A PERSONAL WEBSITE

If you are citing a personal website that has a title, include it in italics and add the publisher of the site (use **N.p.** if no publisher's name is listed).

If a personal website does not have a title, use the generic label "home page" instead. A URL is included in this citation because readers would not be able to find the site without it.

El-Sayed, Najib M. Home page. *The El-Sayed Laboratory*. El-Sayed Laboratory. Web. 23 June 2008.

PERSONAL WEBSITE

Mullis, Kary. Home page. 2004. Web. 1 Jan. 2009 <http://www.karymullis.com/>.

PERSONAL WEBSITE

A BLOG

The general pattern for a blog entry is:

Author's Name. "Title of Blog Entry." *Name of Blog*. Sponsoring organization, Date posted. Web. Date accessed.

If you can't find a publisher or sponsor listed (look at the bottom of the page, usually), use **N.p.** Include a URL for the site only if you think a reader would not be able to find the website without one.

Ifill, Sherrilyn. "Right and Wrong." *Blackprof.com*. Blackprof.com, 15 Feb. 2009. Web. 16 Feb. 2009.

BLOG, GROUP

Mueller, Derek. "Everything Inventive Is Good for You." *Earth Wide Moth*. N.p., 13 Feb. 2009. Web. 16 Feb. 2009.

BLOG BY ONE PERSON

AN ONLINE SCHOLARLY JOURNAL

Scholarly journals published online are cited much like print journals. Many online journals do not use page numbers; use **n. pag.** instead. Include the medium of publication (**Web**) and the date you accessed the site.

Sorapure, Madeleine. "Between Modes: Assessing Student New Media Compositions." *Kairos* 10.2 (2006): n. pag. Web. 25 June 2008.

ARTICLE, IN ONLINE SCHOLARLY JOURNAL

Metinides, Enrique. Interview with Daniel Hernandez. *Journal of Aesthetics and Protest* 5 (2007): n. pag. Web. 5 Aug. 2008.

INTERVIEW, IN ONLINE SCHOLARLY JOURNAL

AN ONLINE NEWSPAPER

Benjamin, Mark. "Want a Water Study? Dig Deep." *Fresno Bee.*
Fresno Bee, 17 Sept. 2007. Web. 17 Apr. 2009.
NEWSPAPER ARTICLE, ONLINE

Sukma, Rizal. "Managing Disasters Should Be Government's
Top Priority." *Jakarta Post.* Jakarta Post-PT Bina Media
Tenggara, 18 Sept. 2007. Web. 18 Feb. 2009.
NEWSPAPER ARTICLE, ONLINE

A POPULAR MAGAZINE, ONLINE

Shepherd, Julianne. "The Making of Keyshia Cole's 'Let It Go.'"
Vibe. Vibe Media Group, 25 June 2007. Web. 1 July 2008.
ARTICLE, IN POPULAR MAGAZINE, ONLINE

"Man Dies from Three-Day Gaming Binge." *Time.* Time, 17 Sept.
2007. Web. 15 Feb. 2009.
ARTICLE, IN POPULAR MAGAZINE, ONLINE
ARTICLE, IN POPULAR MAGAZINE, NO AUTHOR

A WEBPAGE WITH NO APPARENT AFFILIATION

Jodi.org. N.p., n.d. Web. 15 Mar. 2008.
<http://404.jodi.org/index.html>.
WEBSITE

You might find yourself
needing to cite a webpage that
is not a personal home page
and that provides no
information about itself other
than its URL.

The example citation shown
is for an art project.

TIP: LINE BREAKS AND URLS

To assist readers in correctly retyping a URL when they want to find a source you've cited,
be sure that URLs break only after slashes when you enter them in your Works Cited list.

Do this:

<http://www.jsonline.com/story/
index.aspx?id=662796>

Not this:

<http://www.jsonline.com/story/in
dex.aspx?id=662796>

Additional Information

Books are published under varying circumstances. On these pages, we show how to handle citations for several circumstances that occur frequently.

→ On pages 354–355 we show you how to bring together individual citations like these to create a full Works Cited section that goes at the end of any MLA-style research paper.

AN ARTICLE, ESSAY, OR POEM FROM AN EDITED COLLECTION

In this case, in addition to all the information listed on pages 000–000, you also need to include

- the title of the text
- the title of the collection
- the name of the editor or editors (preceded by **Ed.** to help readers distinguish between the author and the editor)
- the article's page numbers

Author's Name. "Title of Text." *Title of Collection*. Ed. Editor's Name. Place of Publication: Publisher, Year of Publication. Page numbers of the article. Medium.

Lebowitz, Fran. "Pointers for Pets." *Living with the Animals*. Ed. Gary Indiana. Boston: Faber, 1994. 61-64. Print.
ESSAY, IN EDITED BOOK

Van Proyen, Mark. "The New Dionysianism." *The Sticky Sublime*. Ed. Bill Beckley. New York: Allworth, 2001. 165-75. Print.
SHORT STORY, IN EDITED BOOK

A BOOK OR ARTICLE TRANSLATED FROM ANOTHER LANGUAGE

In addition to all the information listed on pages 000–000, also include:

- the name of the translator or translators, preceded by **Trans.** (for **Translated by**).
- the article's page numbers (if you are citing an article).

The translator's name comes after the title of the book or after the names of any editors.

Author's Name. *Title of Book*. Trans. Translator's Name. Place of Publication: Publisher, Year of Publication. Medium.

Bauby, Jean-Dominique. *The Diving Bell and the Butterfly*. Trans. Jeremy Leggatt. New York: Knopf, 1997. Print.
BOOK, TRANSLATED

Grossman, David. *See Under: Love*. Trans. Betsy Rosenberg. New York: Washington Square, 1989. Print.
BOOK, TRANSLATED

Plato. "Meno." *The Collected Dialogues of Plato*. Ed. Edith Hamilton and Huntington Cairns. Trans. W. K. C. Guthrie. Princeton: Princeton UP, 1961. 353-85. Print.
ESSAY, IN EDITED BOOK
ESSAY, TRANSLATED

A PUBLISHED OR UNPUBLISHED DISSERTATION

If you are citing a published dissertation, follow the pattern for a book but add the abbreviation **Diss.** to make clear that the source is a *dissertation*. Include the name of the university that granted the degree as well as the date of the degree in addition to the publication date.

If the dissertation is unpublished, put its title in quotation marks instead of *italicizing* it.

Arola, Kristin L. *Invitational Listening: Exploring Design in Online Spaces*. Diss. Michigan Technological U, 2006. Ann Arbor: UMI, 2006. Print.

DISSERTATION, PUBLISHED

Babior, S. L. "Women of a Tokyo Shelter: Domestic Violence and Sexual Exploitation in Japan." Diss. UCLA, 1993. Print.

DISSERTATION, UNPUBLISHED

PART OF A MULTIVOLUME SERIES

If you need to cite only one part of a multivolume set, list only the volume to which you are referring.

If you need to refer to two or more parts of a multivolume set, give the total number of volumes in the work (**2 vols.**) following the title.

Since the two volumes in the second example were published over several years, the complete date range is included.

Rothenberg, Jerome, and Pierre Joris, eds. *Poems for the Millennium: The University of California Book of Modern & Postmodern Poetry*. Vol. 1. Berkeley: U of California P, 1995. Print.

BOOK, PART OF MULTIVOLUME SERIES, A PART

Rothenberg, Jerome, and Pierre Joris, eds. *Poems for the Millennium: The University of California Book of Modern & Postmodern Poetry*. 2 vols. Berkeley: U of California P, 1995-98. Print.

BOOK, PART OF MULTIVOLUME SERIES, COMPLETE

IF THE BOOK IS A SECOND (OR LATER) EDITION

Put the number of the edition, followed by *ed.* after the title of the book.

Lynch, Patrick J., and Sarah Horton. *Web Style Guide: Basic Principles for Creating Web Sites*. 2nd ed. New Haven: Yale UP, 2001. Print.

BOOK, SECOND OR LATER EDITION

For Other Kinds of Texts

You can use almost any kind of published or online text as support or evidence for your arguments—and you need to cite any text you use as support or evidence.

→ These examples continue on pages 390–394.

→ On pages 354–355 we show you how to bring together individual citations like these to create a full Works Cited section that goes at the end of any MLA-style research paper.

CD-ROMS

Because they are usually published only once, like books, the citation format of CD-ROMs follows that of books, except that the medium is **CD-ROM**.

If instead of an author you find an editor or compiler, cite that information, with the appropriate abbreviation (**ed.** or **comp.**). If you cannot find any of this information, cite what you do find.

Blue, Carroll Parrott, Kristy H. A. Kong, and the Labyrinth Project. *The Dawn at My Back: Memoir of a Black Texas Upbringing*. Los Angeles: Annenberg Center for Communication, 2003. CD-ROM.
CD-ROM, THREE OR MORE AUTHORS

Three Winters in the Sun: Einstein in California. Los Angeles: Annenberg Center for Communication, 2005. CD-ROM.
CD-ROM, NO AUTHOR

ADVERTISEMENTS

Give the name of the product or company advertised, followed by **Advertisment**. End with the publication information for the kind of medium where you found the advertisement.

Goin' Home: A Tribute to Fats Domino CD Set by Vanguard Records. Advertisement. *Nation* 1 Oct. 2007: 40. Print.
ADVERTISEMENT, IN JOURNAL OR MAGAZINE

PETA. Advertisement. KTRK, Houston, 18 Sept. 2007. Television.
ADVERTISEMENT, ON TELEVISION

TIP: **THERE IS NO ONE PERFECT CITATION FOR THESE TEXTS**
Don't let anxiety about creating *the perfect citation* slow you down. A citation's purpose is to help readers find the source being cited, should readers so desire. If you provide as much information as you can, given what is suggested for the different texts, and you format the texts in the order suggested, your citations will fulfill their purpose.

SOUND RECORDINGS

To cite commercial recordings, start with the name of the person(s) you reference in your writing: the performer or band, the composer, or the conductor. Then give the title of the recording, the artist (if not mentioned at the beginning of the citation), the manufacturer, and the date.

To cite only one song, put it (within quotation marks) after the artist's name.

Bach, J. S. *The Goldberg Variations*. Perf. Simone Dinnerstein. Telarc, 2007. CD.

SOUND RECORDING, ENTIRE ALBUM

Black Francis. *Bluefinger*. Cooking Vinyl, 2007. CD.

SOUND RECORDING, ENTIRE ALBUM

Simone, Nina. "Please Don't Let Me Be Misunderstood." *The Lady Has the Blues*. Tomato Records, 2003. CD.

SOUND RECORDING, ONE SONG

SOFTWARE

Cite software as you would a book without a named author (→ see page 369), putting the medium at the end. If there is a publisher, put the name and date of publication; for software you have downloaded, give the download date.

Encyclopaedia Britannica 2008 Ultimate. Encyclopaedia Britannica, 2008. CD-ROM.

SOFTWARE

Firefox. Version 2.0.0.7. 22 Sept. 2007. Digital file.

SOFTWARE, DOWNLOADED

MAP, GRAPH, CHART

Cite a map, graph, or chart as you would a book or an article without a named author—but include **Map.**, **Graph.**, or **Chart.** after the title.

"Choose Your Weapon: The Global Arms Trade." Chart. *International Networks Archive*. Dept. of Sociology, Princeton U, n.d. Web. 12 Apr. 2007.

CHART, ONLINE

Milwaukee by Bike. Map. Milwaukee: Bicycle Federation of Wisconsin, 2005. Print.

MAP

AN INTERVIEW YOU CONDUCT

Give the name of the person interviewed, the kind of interview (**Personal interview.**, **Telephone interview.**, or **E-mail interview.**), and the date.

Bok, Hillary. E-mail interview. 24 Feb. 2011.

INTERVIEW, CONDUCTED BY YOU

A PUBLIC TALK

For presentations, speeches, debates, or lectures, give the speaker's name, the presentation title (in quotation marks), the sponsoring organization (if there is one), the place, and the date. End with **Address, Lecture, Keynote Speech,** or **Reading,** as appropriate.

Cooper, Marilyn. "The Animal Who Writes." Penn State Conference on Rhetoric and Composition. State College, PA. 10 July 2007. Keynote Speech.
PRESENTATION AT A PROFESSIONAL CONFERENCE

Trimble, Virginia. "Astrophysics Meets the Millennium." LIGO Public Lectures. Richland, WA. 11 Nov. 2003. Lecture.
LECTURE

FILM OR VIDEO

Begin with the film or video name, then list the director(s), the distributor, and the year of release. If your purpose suggests it, include the names of any writers, performers, or producers before the distributor.

If you saw the film or video in a theater or on broadcast television, end with **Film.** If you saw it on DVD, end with **DVD.**

(Notice, too, that you include—after the English title—the original title of a film was made in another country.)

If, in citing the film or video, you comment on the part played by a particular person, start the citation with that person's name. (**Perf.** abbreviates *performer*.)

The Longest Day. Dir. Ken Annakin, Andrew Marton, Bernhard Wicki, and Darryl F. Zanuck. Twentieth Century-Fox, 1962. Film.
FILM, SEEN IN THEATER

Terminator Salvation. Dir. McG. Warner Bros., 2009. Film.
FILM, SEEN IN THEATER

Fantoche (two times). Animatorblu. *BLU/blog*. 15 Sept. 2007. Web. 10 Nov. 2009.
VIDEO, ONLINE

Groundhog Day. Dir. Harold Ramis. Sony, 1993. DVD.
FILM, ON DVD

Pan's Labyrinth [El Laberinto del fauno]. Dir. Guillermo del Toro. New Line, 2006. DVD.
FILM, ON DVD
FILM, FOREIGN

Newman, Paul, perf. *The Price of Sugar*. Dir. Bill Haney. Uncommon Productions, 2007. Film.
FILM, FOCUS ON ACTOR OR DIRECTOR

TIP: FINDING INFORMATION ABOUT FILMS

You can find this information at the Internet Movie Database (IMDB; www.imdb.com). Within IMDB the director and release date are close to the top of a movie's webpage; to find the distributor (the company responsible for getting the movie into consumers' hands), scroll down to "Company," then click "More." Use the most recent distributor within the United States for the medium you are citing.

CARTOON OR COMIC STRIP

If you have only an author's name or a title, start with what you have; otherwise, give both the name and then the title. Follow that with **Cartoon.** or **Comic Strip.** End with the full publication information for the source where you found the cartoon or comic strip. (If the source's date matters to your argument, put it after the title.)

Carlson, Stuart. Cartoon. *Milwaukee Journal Sentinel* 23 Sept. 2007: 2J. Print.

CARTOON, IN NEWSPAPER

"The Last Rail Split by 'Honest Old Abe.'" Cartoon. 1816. *Explore History*. HarpWeek, 17 May 2006. Web. 15 Apr. 2009.

CARTOON, ONLINE
CARTOON, NO KNOWN AUTHOR

Chapman, Hank, writer. "The Last Tattoo!" Comic strip. Art by Fred Kida. 1952. *Arf Museum*. Ed. Craig Yoe. Seattle: Fantagraphic, 2007. 60-64. Print.

COMIC STRIP, IN BOOK
COMIC STRIP, REPRINTED

Horne, Emily, and Joey Comeau. "A Softer World." Comic strip. *A Softer World*. N.p., 15 Sept. 2007. Web. 11 Apr. 2009.

COMIC STRIP, ONLINE
COMIC STRIP, TWO AUTHORS

MUSICAL COMPOSITION

Begin with the composer's name, followed by the work's title. (If you cite a composition that is identified by a number, do not italicize it or put quotation marks around it.)

Price, Florence. *Mississippi River Suite*. Chicago: KOCH Classics, 1940. Print.

MUSICAL COMPOSITION

Sibelius, Jean. Symphony no. 7 in C major. Copenhagen: Wilhelm Hansen, 1980. Print.

MUSICAL COMPOSITION

BROADCAST INTERVIEW

For interviews you see on television or hear on the Internet or on the radio, follow the same pattern as for print interviews (→ see page 377).

Salzmann, Marc. Interview with Jonathan Mann. "Awaiting *Halo 3*." *CNN.com*. Cable News Network, 24 Sept. 2007. Web. 24 Sept. 2007.

INTERVIEW, ONLINE VIDEO

Harper, Ben. Interview with David Dye. "Transcending Genre." *Natl. Public Radio*. Natl. Public Radio, 7 Sept. 2007. Web. 12 Sept. 2007.

INTERVIEW, ONLINE RECORDING

PERFORMANCE

To cite a musical, dramatic, dance, poetic, or other artistic performance, start with the title (unless you can name the performers). End with the performance's location and date.

King Lear. By William Shakespeare. Dir. Trevor Nunn. Perf. Ian McKellen. Guthrie Theater, Minneapolis. 14 Oct. 2007. Performance.

PERFORMANCE, THEATRICAL

Of Montreal. Ogden Theater, Denver. 12 Nov. 2007. Performance.

PERFORMANCE, MUSICAL

TELEVISION OR RADIO PROGRAM

Start with the name of the particular episode you are citing, then give the program title. List the writer (using **By**), the director (**Dir.**), or the Host; also list the performers (**perf.**) if appropriate for your use of the source. Give the name of the network and then the call letters of the station on which you saw or heard the broadcast. (If the station is local, give the city name). End with the show's broadcast date.

"Homer's Phobia." *The Simpsons*. By Ron Hauge. Dir. Mike B. Anderson. Fox. WITI, Milwaukee, 16 Feb. 1997. Television.
TELEVISION PROGRAM

"Babysitting." *This American Life*. Host Ira Glass. Public Radio International. WNMU, Marquette, 1 June 2001. Radio.
RADIO PROGRAM

"The Melody of Murder." *The Avenger*. 3 Aug. 1945. *RadioLovers*. Bored.com, 4 June 2007. Web. 11 Apr. 2009.
RADIO PROGRAM, ONLINE

PAINTING, DRAWING, SCULPTURE, OR PHOTOGRAPH

Put the artist's name first, then the title of the work, its date, and its medium. If you are citing artwork from a museum, give the museum's name and place.

For artwork you find reproduced in a magazine or online, do not put the artwork's medium, but do put **Print** or **Web** where you would in any other citation for a print or online source. If you are citing artwork you found in a publication, give the full publication information.

For a personal photograph that has not been published or exhibited, give a descriptive title, tell who took the photograph, and give its date.

Bastien-Lepage, Jules. *Joan of Arc*. 1879. Oil on canvas. Metropolitan Museum of Art, New York.
PAINTING, IN MUSEUM

Bennett, Henry Hamilton. *Lone Rock with Canoe, Wisconsin Dells*. c. 1880. Photograph. Milwaukee Art Museum, Milwaukee.
PHOTOGRAPH, IN MUSEUM
DATE APPROXIMATED

Todd, Mark. *Man in the Moon. Raygun* Nov. 1994: n. pag. Print.
PHOTOGRAPH, IN MAGAZINE

Bruegel, Pieter, the Elder. *The Triumph of Death*. c. 1562. Museo Nacional del Prado, Madrid. Web. 28 May 2009.
PAINTING, ONLINE

Clown. 2007. Nelson-Atkins Museum of Art, Kansas City. Web. 12 Jan. 2008.
PHOTOGRAPH, ONLINE
PHOTOGRAPH, PHOTOGRAPHER UNKNOWN

Big Snowfall, Upper Peninsula. Personal photograph by Dennis Lynch. 18 Oct. 1992.
PHOTOGRAPH, PERSONAL

ONLINE SOURCES OTHER THAN THOSE ALREADY MENTIONED

TO CITE E-MAIL, give the writer's name and the subject line, then put **E-mail to** followed by the recipient's name. End with the message's date.

Taylor, Sarah. "Arkansas Attorney Firing." E-mail to Kyle Sampson. 16 Feb. 2007.

E-MAIL

TO CITE A LISTSERV POSTING, give the writer's name and the subject line. Then put **Online posting** followed by the date of the posting and the list's name. End with the message's date, the date you accessed it, and a URL or the list's e-mail address.

Spinuzzi, Clay. "Re: Google, Tech Comm, and Professionalism." Online posting. Association of Teachers of Technical Writing, 10 Sept. 2007. Web. 12 Sept. 2007. <attw-l@lyris.ttu.edu>.

LISTSERV POSTING

TO CITE AN ONLINE SYNCHRONOUS DISCUSSION (such as a MOO, MUD, chat, or IM), you can decide to cite the whole discussion or only one contribution.

To cite the whole discussion, give the event title, a description of the event and its date, the forum in which the discussion took place, the date you accessed the discussion, and the URL.

To cite one person's contribution, follow the same format as above, but put the name of the person first. (Although the MLA has not yet caught up with some of the indexing possibilities of online texts, you can help your readers in cases like this by going beyond what the MLA format asks: giving the time *and* date of the listing.)

"MOO: The Second Decade." Online discussion. *Computers and Writing Conference Online 2005*. 8 June 2005. Web. 12 July 2006. <http://www.accd.edu/sac/english/lirvin/encore/ CW2005/ TranscriptC&W2005.htm>.

ONLINE SYNCHRONOUS DISCUSSION, WHOLE DISCUSSION

MaxoidLittleL. "Chat Transcript." Online discussion. *The Sims2 Community*. 16 Aug. 2007, 5:00:57 PM. Web. 1 Jan. 2008. <http://thesims2.ea.com/community/chat_08_16_07.php>.

ONLINE SYNCHRONOUS DISCUSSION, SINGLE ENTRY

APA DOCUMENTATION

GUIDE TO APA DOCUMENTATION MODELS

ABOUT THE DIFFERENT CITATION STYLES

Current United States conventions for citing others' work developed since the end of the nineteenth century, when a University of Chicago Press proofreader put together a guideline sheet to help authors format their writing. This sheet eventually grew into a book, published in 1906.

Because scholarly writing builds on others' ideas, and because scholars' reputations require them to add knowledge to their disciplines, scholars show where their work is new and where it builds on—or refutes—what preceded them. What came to be *The Chicago Manual of Style*, therefore, not only included guidelines for spelling and mechanics but also standards for how scholars should cite others' work.

Over time, as different disciplines became more distinct and as publishing technologies become more complex with microfilm (for example), other groups came to believe that *The Chicago Manual of Style* did not address their particular needs. These days, there are a number of different published conventions for how a writer should cite the works of others.

In this part of the handbook, we consider the four style conventions you are most likely to encounter in college:

MLA

This is the style of the Modern Language Association, which is an organization of scholars and teachers of languages and literature. *The MLA Handbook for Writers of Research Papers* is now in its seventh edition, published in 2009. The MLA style is used primarily in English studies, comparative literature, foreign-language, literary criticism, and humanities fields.

APA

The American Psychological Association publishes the *Publication Manual of the American Psychological Association*, which is now in its sixth edition, published in 2010. The style's title might suggest that only psychologists use it, but APA style is also used in disciplines such as business, economics, sociology, nursing, social work, and criminology. APA style was developed for researchers to report research results, and—in line with twentieth-century beliefs about the objectivity of scientific research—this style encourages writing in the third person or passive voice; it also encourages straightforward presentation of data, tables, charts, and graphs.

CHICAGO MANUAL OF STYLE

The Chicago Manual of Style (CMS), now in its fifteenth edition (published in 2003), is used by writers in the arts and humanities—especially in history. Among its other recommendations, CMS presents two systems for documenting sources, numbered endnotes or author-date, but it is usually endnote style that CMS advocates prefer.

CSE

This style used to be called CBE, after the Council of Biology Editors, which developed it. Because this style has become so widespread in the sciences, the CBE changed its name in 2000 to the Council of Science Editors (CSE). In 2006, the CSE published a new and expanded seventh edition of its style guide, *Scientific Style and Format*. CSE documentation style is used by authors working in the natural and applied sciences.

A PAPER IN APA FORMAT

To the right are the title page and abstract page in APA style, showing APA conventions for formatting. The next pages show the rest of the paper, showing how sources are quoted and cited, and how sources are listed at the end.

FORMATTING

To format in APA style, use the margins we have shown in blue to the right and:

- Double-space the paper throughout, including with titles and quotations.
- The "preferred" typeface for APA papers is Times, in 12 point size. Use the same typeface throughout the whole paper.

Running Head

At the top left of every page put a running header, as shown to the right. On the title page, start with a *Running head:* followed by your title in all capital letters. The title in the running header should be no more than fifty characters; if you have a title that has two phrases separated by a colon (for example, "Smiles, Speech, and Body Posture: How Women and Men Display Sociometric Status and Power"), only put the part of the title before the colon into the running head.

Title page

Without bolding or italicizing, center this information on your page, approximately half-way down: your paper's title, your name, and your institution. (In a paper to be published, you would also include an "author note"; see the APA *Publication Manual* if you need to insert this information.)

Abstract

The APA requires this page for papers going to publication; if your teacher requests you include it, put it on a separate page (following the title page and numbered 2); abstracts average between 150–250 words, but can be shorter. An abstract is a summary of the paper, reporting (without evaluation) what was studied, why it was studied, and the results of the study.

1"

1"

1"

Nonverbal Power Displays by Doormen

Christine Wysocki

University of San Diego

Abstract

This paper reports the results of a study conducted by a research team into the nonverbal behavior of doormen and security personnel at eight establishments within the city limits of San Diego. The initial hypothesis was that doormen are likely to speak with strong, stern voices, have a large physical appearance, use direct body orientations, and adopt or adapt various artifacts that signal or exert the power necessary to establish and maintain their authority and control over approaching patrons. The results of the study mostly confirmed the initial hypothesis, with two exceptions: the doormen did not uniformly employ a strong, stern tone of voice, and the doormen did not use the advantage of a higher plane of orientation in order to establish and maintain relations of power.

The body of your paper...

...will begin on the page numbered 3, if your teacher has asked you to include an abstract; otherwise it will begin on page 2. Note that the running header appears on every page of your paper.

Repeat your title

Put your title, centered, before you begin the body of your paper. Do not bold or italicize it.

Inroducing your work

In a longer paper in APA format, you would have a section labeled "Introduction." In a shorter paper, readers will assume your first paragraphs are an introduction.

THE CONTENT OF THE INTRODUCTION: How does your research relate to others' research?

In an APA paper the introduction lays out the problem under consideration, saying why the problem is worth addressing and how it relates to previous research—which you can see here as Christine first gives other research to situate her own work and then states this paper's specific focus.

Citing multiple sources

→ See page 412 for how to cite multiple sources together in a parenthetical citation.

Indent the first line of every paragraph $1/2$″ from the left edge of your text

This means that the first line will be $1 1/2$″ from the left edge of the page.

Defining terms

If there is any possibility your audience won't understand a term you use, define the term.

Quoting words from a source

→ See pages 300–305 for how to weave the exact words of a source into your writing.

→ See pages 411–413 for how to cite a direct quotation in APA style.

Nonverbal Displays by Doormen

According to some researchers, nonverbal cues may contribute up to sixty-five percent of what we understand in any communication exchange (Knott, 1979). Even before people speak, they transmit nonverbal messages, so that verbal and nonverbal communication are always entwined in any given situation. Understanding the roles the nonverbal—or what is often referred to as "paralanguage"—plays in overall communication can help us to become better communicators.

Although people control only a part of the nonverbal messages they send, it is possible to extend the conscious control one has of what one nonverbally projects—the nonverbal signals one sends—in any given situation. In other words, those who seek to project an image of power can learn to take on certain behaviors and appearances in order to affect others.

This paper reports on a study of a group of people, doormen at nightclubs, whose work necessitates that they project an image of power. By providing security and deciding who enters a club, doormen need others to accept their judgments quickly and not to challenge their authority. Through observations and interviews, this study examines the nonverbal behaviors doormen use, and do not use, to do their jobs.

The perceived or actual social distances between individuals can influence the role of power in interactive behaviors (Carney & LeBeau, 2005; Dunbar & Burgoon, 2005; Dunbar & Abra, 2008). For example, a principal and a teacher will interact differently together than will a principal and a student. If the means by which someone exerts power is studied and understood, power becomes less of an unknown variable, and nonverbal behaviors become easier to decode.

Among the paralanguage aspects of interactive behavior in the nonverbal development of power that have been already been studied are vocal tones, haptics, physical appearance, body orientation, and use of artifacts and space.

Vocalics, or the delivery of audible sound, involves rate of speech, tone, volume, accent, and use of pauses. For example, when men and women interact, who spends the most time talking is an "indicator of high power," with the strength of the correlation being "unusually high" for men (Cashdan, 1998, p. 214).

Signalling coherence

Notice how Christine has used expressions like "also" and "finally" to show that these paragraphs are all on the related topic, how power can be shown nonverbally.

Notice, too, how she has repeated "power" in different expressions in order to help her readers see her focus.

→ See pages 172–175 for strategies for creating coherence in and across paragraphs.

THE CONTENT OF THE INTRODUCTION: What is your hypothesis?

After you have introduced the problem on which your paper focuses, and have provided background for it, you state your hypothesis or the main question guiding your research.

THE METHOD SECTION

In this section you describe in detail how you conducted your study. You give this information so readers can evaluate the appropriateness of your approach, which then enables them to judge the validity of your results.

Decscribe in detail who or what you studied, by characteristics, number, and place where you performed your study. When you describe the characteristics of a group, emphasize the characteristics that might bear on your results.

Formatting heads

→ See page 406 for the APA's style for formatting the different levels of headings in a paper.

Physical appearance can also be used to amplify power: one's body type and shape in and of themselves indicate power. For example, facial expression plays a role in identifying and discerning power and dominance (Krumhuber, Manstead, & Kappas, 2007), and, again, research suggests men are less likely to smile in a public setting thus influencing the power they project (Cashdan, 1998).

Power relations are also present in bodily orientation—or proxemics. If a person moves close to another, or violates another's personal space, the other can become stressed and react in a variety of ways, including but not limited to, increased anxiety, discomfort, and aggressiveness (May, 2000). Likewise, standing in the center of a small space, such as a doorway, or blocking others' access to a destination signals to others that movement is not possible without negotiation or struggle (Nadler, 1986). Perceived power can also be influenced by posture and the plane of interaction: elevation provides the most power, followed by postural orientation and rank (Schwartz, Tesser, & Powell, 1982). Conversely, as Tiedens and Fragale's study (2003) on body orientation mimicry and posture shows, a complimentary (open/closed versus closed/closed) posture results in higher likeability and an easing of power relations.

Finally, what one wears or carries—considered as artifacts—can also convey power. For example, wearing a uniform can deliver authority to the wearer. In addition, since "people are conditioned [in our society] to regard with awe anything printed," if the uniform is labeled in some way, its authority can be enhanced (Cohen, 1980, p. 58).

Based on this initial research, we hypothesize that, to establish and maintain their authority and control over approaching patrons, doormen are likely to speak with strong, stern voices; have a large physical appearance; use direct body orientations; and use various artifacts that signal or exert power.

Method

Three research methods were used in the collection of data.

The first method was based on a series of observations conducted by four researchers at eight establishments in the city of San Diego. The eight establishments studied were Pacific Beach

Passive voice

Because the APA style reports research that any researcher anywhere ought to be able to replicate, the identity of the person doing the research is not supposed to matter—and so passive voice is frequently used to put emphasis on what was done rather than on who did it.

→ See pages 238–239 for more on passive voice.

THE RESULTS SECTION

In this section you summarize the data you collected and whatever analysis you performed that supports your conclusions. If you have results that run counter to your initial hypothesis, be sure to mention this.

The value of accuracy

Careful reporting of counts and numbers is a hallmark of APA style because one goal of the APA's Ethics Code is to "ensure the accuracy of scientific knowledge" (http://www.apa.org/ethics).

Use left alignment for the body of the paper

Do not justify the body of the paper; instead, the right edge of the text will be "ragged."

Bar & Grill, The Field, Cabo Cantina, Typhoon, Tavern, The Marble Room, Stingaree, and Sandbar. The researchers unobtrusively observed doormen at these different locations and recorded in detail the interactions between doormen and patrons. Data was collected about the doormen's use of vocal tones, haptics, physical appearance, body orientation, and use of artifacts. Researchers did not initially inform the subjects of the study in order to ensure the greatest degree of objectivity.

The second method of data collection consisted of staged interactions between the researchers and the doormen at the eight establishments. This method specifically provided insights into the ways the doormen used nonverbal actions to establish and act on their authority, and it allowed for a more direct collection of data.

The last method of data collection was face-to-face interviews conducted with individual doormen at four of the different establishments. The interviewers gathered data about the degree to which doormen were cognitively aware of their behaviors in establishing power.

Results

Based on our observations, we drew the following conclusions.

In terms of vocal tones, four out of five of the doormen used softer vocal tones with females. Speaking with men, six out of eight doormen used more stern, stronger, and deeper vocal tones.

In their physical appearance, five out of eight of our subjects were taller than six feet. It was observed that doormen also responded to patrons depending on whether patrons were perceived as a possible threat due to physical stature and gender: Doormen tended to address the male member of a male-female couple, and were more courteous to men whose height was closer to, or taller than, theirs.

The body orientation of doormen was shown through how six doormen stood on the same level as the patrons, while only one sat on a stool and one stood on a raised platform.

In their use of artifacts, all doormen wore some sort of attire that signified the particular establishment they worked for. Half of the sample wore jackets with writing that announced their position (ex. "STAFF" or "SECURITY"), and the other half wore all-black clothing. Three out of

Each table and figure begins on a new page

If you include any tables or figures (illustrations of any kinds) in your paper, put them at the top of a new page. (Christine's research project is small enough that no tables or figures are necessary to help explicate the research or results.)

Capitalize after a colon

APA style asks that you capitalize the first letter of any independent clause that follows a colon.

THE DISCUSSION SECTION

In this section you evaluate and interpret the implications of your results, in light of your initial hypothesis. Notice how Christine quickly notes here how the research findings run counter to their initial hypothesis.

Also discuss here anything in the results that seem particularly significant, or that suggest unresolved or new problems to be studied, as Christine does on the next page. (If what you have to discuss is short and straightforward, you can combine it with the Results section, labeling the new setion "Results and Discussion.")

the four that wore black attire worked at eating establishments. Almost all of our subjects held some sort of artifact, usually a flashlight, to convey their position of authority. In addition, it was observed that the more formal a person's dress, the more courteously the doormen responded and the more likely the patron was to be admitted into the establishment.

Based on our interviews, we learned the following. The first interviewee expressed that his height, which is greater than six feet, was his most powerful asset. Interviewee two made a distinction between the varied types of establishments for which he works, noting that each demands a different level or kind of power to be employed: The classier (downtown) establishment where he is employed expects a more steady, "stalwart," display of power, whereas the more informal (beach) establishment where he also works is "laid-back" and expects a "less rigid" display of power. Interviewee three said his "muscle tone" is more useful than "a strong voice" or artifacts such as a flashlight for maintaining authority and order. Interviewee four explained that he works at a low-key, less trafficked establishment that allows him to use "personal interaction" and direct eye contact as his main way to exert power.

Discussion

Study results demonstrate that the voice—the vocal tones—in doormen varied with the gender of the patrons. Notably, a variation in vocalics did not play a role in the establishment of authority or relations of power, but verbal tones did vary from gender to gender. This finding is contrary to the initial hypothesis that doormen would regularly exert stronger and deeper vocal tones when dealing with patrons. Observations regarding the second factor studied, physical appearance, show that doormen are usually taller than six feet and have a mesomorphic frame. Regarding body orientation, doormen often stood in a manner that made them appear larger, and thus more powerful, than they actually are. Lastly, in regard to artifacts, doormen (with already noted exceptions) typically held or used some sort of object to signify and increase their sense of power. Common artifacts include boundary ropes, ID card scanners, flashlights, and VIP guest lists. It is important to note that they all wore distinct outfits or uniforms while working, suggesting that this aspect of authority has unusual weight in the overall maintenance of power.

What is still to learn?

As we noted on page 404 about the "Discussion" part of an APA style paper, it is important to note at the end of a paper what new research the current research suggests. Noting what might appear as shortcomings of the current research is not an admission of having done anything wrong but is rather a way of indicating what was learned and what more could be learned.

TIP: FORMATTING HEADINGS IN APA STYLE

Although in a 5–7 page paper you might not need to use headings, the chart below shows you how to format headings according to the APA guidelines.

Level of heading	Format
1	Centered, Bold, Uppercase and Lowercase
2	Flush left, Bold, Uppercase and Lowercase
3	Indented 1/2", bold, lowercase, ending with a period.
4	*Indented 1/2", bold, italicized, lowercase, ending with a period.*
5	*Indented 1/2", italicized, lowercase, ending with a period.*

The aggregate of data revealed four different tactics—nonverbal displays of power—used by the doormen: vocalics (specifically, tonal variation), physical stature, body orientation, and the possession or wielding of artifacts. Two aspects of the initial hypothesis for this study should be discussed. First, the idea that "doormen are highly likely to exert strong vocal tones" was not born out by the study (though the idea that "they will have a large physical appearance, use direct body orientations, and adopt artifacts that signal or exert power" seems to be correct). Second, the idea that doormen will use the advantage of a higher "plane or orientation" (standing upon a higher threshold) also was not born out by the study.

Beyond what was accomplished by this reasearch project, a further study should be considered to encompass factors that were not included or were ruled out by the choice of methods. The number of doormen present at each site was not a part of this study, and neither was an exact measurement of the "proxemics" affecting doormen-patron interactions. Vocalic tactics also could be more carefully distinguished and measured. And finally, and perhaps most important to our understanding of how these interactions work, the positions and perspectives of patrons should be included; a further study is also suggested that would focus on the gender of patrons relative to the doormen's development of nonvocal power. These and other possible lines of research would not only help to solidify or confirm the results of this study but might alter or clarify the parameters within which the study was conducted.

A REFERENCES PAGE IN APA FORMAT

The last page or pages in an APA-style paper will look like the page to the right, which is from Christine Wysocki's paper that we've annotated on the preceding pages.

Format the References following these conventions:

❑ Put the References page at the very end of the paper, starting on its own page.

❑ Use the same margin measurements as the rest of the paper (→ see page 399).

❑ Put the running header and page number on each Reference List page at the top (as you do every APA-formatted page; → see page 396). The number on the first page follows the number of the last page of the paper. For example, if the last page of the paper is 7, the first page of the References will be 8.

❑ **References** is centered at the top.

❑ The listings are arranged alphabetically by the author's last name. (If a listing starts with the title of a source, place it into the whole list alphabetically, using the first letter of the title. If the title begins with **A**, **An**, or **The**, alphabetize by the second word of the title.)

❑ If you list two or more sources by the same author, order them by the date, with the earliest first. If there are second authors, alphabetize by the second author's name.

❑ Double-space the entries.

→ See pages 414–437 for how to create the individual entries.

Explore these topics online:

Sample MLA and APA papers
www.mycomplab.com

References

Carney, D., Hall, J., & LeBeau, L. (2005). Beliefs about the nonverbal expression of social power. *Journal of Nonverbal Behavior, 29*(2), 105-123. doi:10.1007/s10919-005-2743-z

Cashdan, E. (1998). Smiles, speech, and body posture: How women and men display sociometric status and power. *Journal of Nonverbal Behavior, 22*(4), 209-228. Retrieved from http://www.springer.com/psychology/personality+&+social+psychology/journal/10919

Cohen, H. (1980). *You can negotiate anything*. New York, NY: Bantam Books.

Dunbar, N., & Abra, G. (2008). Observations of dyadic power in interpersonal interaction. *Conference Papers—International Communication Association*. Retrieved from http://www.icahdq.org/

Dunbar, N., & Burgoon, J. (2005). Perceptions of power and interactional dominance in interpersonal relationships. *Journal of Social & Personal Relationships, 22*(2), 207-233. doi:10.1177/0265407505050944

Knott, G. (1979). Nonverbal communication during early childhood. *Theory Into Practice, 18*(4), 226. Retrieved from http://ehe.osu.edu/tip/

Krumhuber, E., Manstead, A., & Kappas, A. (2007). Temporal aspects of facial displays in person and expression perception: The effects of smile dynamics, head-tilt, and gender. *Journal of Nonverbal Behavior, 31*(1), 39-56. doi:10.1007/s10919-006-0019-x

May, S. (2000). Proxemics: The hula hoop and use of personal space. *Communication Teacher, 14*(2), 4-5. Retrieved from http://www.tandf.co.uk/journals/titles/17404622.asp

Nadler, L. (1986). Body politics/nonverbal behavior and social psychology/nonverbal behavior. *Communication Education, 35*(3), 324. Retrieved from http://www.tandf.co.uk/journals/titles/03634523.asp

Schwartz, B., Tesser, A., & Powell, E. (1982). Dominance cues in nonverbal behavior. *Social Psychology Quarterly, 45*(2), 114-120. Retrieved from http://www.asanet.org/cs/social_psychology_quarterly

Tiedens, L., & Fragale, A. (2003). Power moves: Complementarity in dominant and submissive nonverbal behavior. *Journal of Personality & Social Psychology, 84*(3), 558-568. doi:10.1037/0022-3514.84.3.558

Use hanging indentation

So readers can scan the list easily and quickly, indent by 1/2 inch all lines underneath the first.

APA DOCUMENTATION FOR IN-TEXT CITATIONS

IN-TEXT CITATIONS IN APA STYLE

Whether you are citing books, periodicals, or electronic sources, in-text citations in the APA style generally contain these three elements:

1
The **name of the author** of the words or ideas being quoted, summarized, or paraphrased. The name can appear within a sentence containing quoted words, or it can appear in parentheses at the sentence's end.

2
The **date** when the source being cited was published.

3
The **page number(s)** of or some other reference to the cited words or ideas. The number of the page from which quoted words come goes at the end of the sentence, in parentheses; **p.** goes before the page number.

These three elements can be arranged in one of these two ways:

In her article on two nineteenth-century women preachers, Bizzell (2006) argues that "a conjunction between the female sex and moral activism is traditional in Methodism" (p. 379).

One writer on nineteenth-century women preachers argues that "a conjunction between the female sex and moral activism is traditional in Methodism" (Bizzell, 2006, p. 379).

→ Pages 411–413 list variations on this pattern for APA in-text citations.

PUNCTUATION IN APA IN-TEXT CITATIONS

- The parentheses that contain page numbers go at the end of the sentence, followed by the punctuation that ends the sentence.
- When you include an author's name in the parentheses with the year and page number, put a comma between each element.
- If the words you are quoting run across several pages, cite them like this: **(pp. 23–25)** (**pp.** stands for **pages**).
- If the words you are quoting are from several nonconsecutive pages, cite them like this: **(pp. 45, 76)**.

VARIATIONS IN THE APA PATTERN OF IN-TEXT CITATIONS

→ There is no page number (for example, you are citing a brochure or a webpage).
See page 411.

→ No author is named for the source.
See page 411.

→ The work has two authors.
See page 411.

→ The work has three, four, or five authors.
See page 412.

→ The work has six or more authors.
See page 412.

→ The work has a group or corporate author or is a government document.
See page 412.

→ See page 315 for what "corporate author" means.

→ You are citing an electronic source such as a webpage or e-mail.
See page 412.

→ You are citing two or more sources in one sentence.
See page 412.

→ Your References list contains two or more sources by the same author.
See page 413.

→ You are citing a classical work, sacred text, or other work with no date listed.
See page 413.

→ Your References list contains sources by two authors with the same last name.See page 413.

THERE IS NO PAGE NUMBER

Give a paragraph or part number if possible; otherwise, give only the name of the author.

The World Health Organization (2006) identifies obstetric fistulas as a global problem, estimating that over two million women suffer from them, with 50 to 100 thousand new cases each year (para. 64).

Readers will look in the References for a listing under *World Health Organization*.

NO AUTHOR IS NAMED

If there is no author, use the work's title:

To "watch the rejects crash and burn" is why we watch *American Idol*, according to *Rolling Stone* magazine ("*Idol* Worship," 2007).

→ See page 421 for the corresponding References list entry.

→ If you find that a government or corporate organization is the author, see page 422.

THE WORK HAS TWO AUTHORS

List the names in the same order as they are given in the source. Use *and* between the names in the body of your paper, but use an ampersand (&) in parenthetical references:

As "much an activist as an analytical method" is how Moeller and Moberly (2006) describe McAllister's approach to computer games.

As "much an activist as an analytical method" is how two online reviewers describe McAllister's approach to computer games (Moeller & Moberly, 2006).

→ On page 421, you can see the References list citations for the samples on these two pages.

THE WORK HAS THREE, FOUR, OR FIVE AUTHORS

In the first citation, list each author's name. Afterward, list only the first author's name followed by *et al.* (*Et al.* is Latin for *and others*.) Put a period after *al*.

What happens when a ninth-grade World Literatures class is offered at the high honors level for all students, without tracking? Fine, Anand, Jordan, and Sherman (2000) offer a two-year study of such a class.

Later in the same paper:

As a result of their study, Fine et al. (2000) argue that students "who never expected to be seen as smart" come to see themselves as capable and sharp (pp. 174, 175).

THE WORK HAS SIX OR MORE AUTHORS

Include only the first author's name, followed by *et al*. *Et al*. is Latin for *and others*. Put a period after *al*.

Statistical data can be useful but is "easily misinterpreted" (Walpole et al., 2006, p. 217).

Walpole et al. (2006) argue that statistical data is useful but "easily misinterpreted" (p. 217).

THE WORK HAS A GROUP OR CORPORATE AUTHOR OR IS A GOVERNMENT DOCUMENT

To cite a work by an association, government agency, or corporation, write out the group's name:

When organizing catalogs, librarians typically follow guidelines established by the American Library Association (2004).

When organizing catalogs, librarians typically follow established guidelines (American Library Association, 2004).

YOU ARE CITING A WEBPAGE OR E-MAIL

Many such sources have no page numbers. If your source includes paragraph numbers, use that number, preceded by *para*.

Some researchers have suggested the concept of "virtual wives" to describe the new role of technology in personal life (Clark-Flory, 2007, para. 12).

If paragraphs are not numbered, cite the nearest main heading and then count to the paragraph you are citing:

Some researchers have suggested the concept of "virtual wives" to describe the new role of technology in personal life (Clark-Flory, 2007, Introduction section, para. 1).

Readers cannot access other's personal e-mails, so do not include them in your References List. Cite them only in your text.

Austin's famous Congress Avenue bats first appeared in 1980 (E. C. Lupfer, personal communication, March 17, 2003).

YOU ARE CITING TWO OR MORE SOURCES IN ONE SENTENCE

If you need to cite two or more sources in a single reference, list the sources in alphabetical order by each author's last name. Separate the entries with a semicolon.

The language used to describe issues of race and ethnicity often shapes the way people respond to calls for diversity or social justice (Adams, 2000; Fletcher, 2007).

Adams (2000) and Fletcher (2007) argue that language plays a vital role in shaping the way people respond to calls for diversity and social justice.

YOUR REFERENCES LIST CONTAINS TWO OR MORE SOURCES BY THE SAME AUTHOR

To help readers, indicate which work you are referencing at the specific point in your text. Do this by giving the date of the work in your sentence or in the in-text citation.

Here is a citation for the first work cited from one author:

That meat from cows fed on grass is more nutritious than that from corn-fed cows is just one of the many arguments Pollan makes (2006, p. 211).

That author's second work is then cited:

Because his research shows just what chemicals go into a commercial potato, Pollan cannot bring himself to eat one given to him as a gift (2001, p. 98).

YOU ARE CITING A CLASSICAL WORK, SACRED TEXT, OR OTHER WORK WITH NO DATE LISTED

Use the author's name followed by a comma and **n.d.** for **no date**.

Early in its history, rhetoric was defined as the use of the available means of persuasion (Aristotle, n.d.).

You can also use the date of translation, if known, preceded by **trans.**

Early in its history, rhetoric was defined as the use of the available means of persuasion (Aristotle, trans. 1954).

If you are citing passages from a sacred text like the Bible or the Koran, you do not need a References List entry. The first time you cite the work, identify the version you use.

John 11:7 (Revised Standard Version)

YOUR REFERENCES LIST CONTAINS SOURCES BY TWO AUTHORS WITH THE SAME LAST NAME

Include the authors' initials in your citations so readers know which citation to check in the References List. Here are examples from the same paper, using the authors' initials:

R. M. Rorty (1979) argues that we ought no longer to think of our minds as "mirrors" that directly and only reflect what is already in the world.

A. O. Rorty (1996) shows how Aristotle's *Rhetoric* brings together understandings of situations in which people communicate, the psychology of audiences, the character of communicators, the structures of communication, and politics.

These examples avoid ambiguity in their parenthetical citations:

Some philosophers argue that our understanding of what knowledge is has changed over the last two hundred years: We ought no longer to think of our minds as "mirrors" that directly and only reflect what is already in the world (R. M. Rorty, 1979).

Aristotle's *Rhetoric* brings together understandings of situations in which people communicate, the psychology of audiences, the character of communicators, the structures of communication, and politics (A. O. Rorty, 1996).

THE PURPOSES OF IN-TEXT CITATIONS IN APA STYLE

Although APA style uses a slightly different format for in-text citations than the MLA style uses, the reasons for using in-text citations are the same.

→ See page 342 to learn the purposes of in-text citations.

APA DOCUMENTATION FOR REFERENCES LIST ENTRIES

The following pages show you how to format entries in the References List that goes at the end of any APA-style paper. The essential pattern is shown here:

THE PATTERN

Four elements make up any citation in the Reference List of an APA-style paper:

Author's Name. (Date of Publication). *Title of text*. Publication information.
    1   2   3   4

The publication information about a text includes who published a text and where. For example, here is a citation for a book:

Treichler, Paula. (1999). *How to have theory in an epidemic: Cultural*
    1   2   3

chronicles of AIDS. Durham, NC: Duke University Press.
                                       4

(Note the indenting in the example: This is standard when formatting your list of References, as we describe on pages 408–409.)

In distinguishing among the kinds of sources to be cited, the APA distinguishes between periodicals and nonperiodicals. (Nonperiodicals are books and any other kind of source not printed on a regular schedule.) We follow the same distinction in the pages that follow.

Note that when you cite a book, periodical, or webpage, the format of the citation—the capitalization of the title of a book, the inclusion of a periodical's doi, or the listing of a URL—tells a reader what kind of text you are citing. When you cite a text that isn't a book, periodical, or webpage, you may also need to indicate what kind of text it is.

TO MAKE APA REFERENCES LISTS

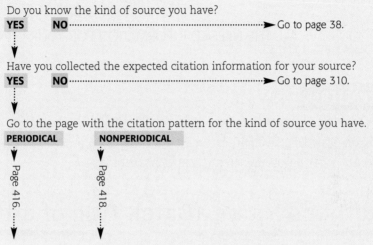

1   MAKE AN INDIVIDUAL LISTING FOR EACH WORK YOU ARE CITING

Do you know the kind of source you have?

YES   **NO** ···➤ Go to page 38.

Have you collected the expected citation information for your source?

YES   **NO** ···➤ Go to page 310.

Go to the page with the citation pattern for the kind of source you have.

PERIODICAL   **NONPERIODICAL**

Page 416.   Page 418.

- Follow the pattern to construct your listing part by part, starting with the author, moving on to the title, and so on.
- If a part of your citation varies from the pattern, follow the page references to see the format for the variation.

2   CONSTRUCT YOUR REFERENCES

When you have all your individual citations, put them together into the References page.

→ See page 438 for how to format the References.

FOR PERIODICAL SOURCES

1 ARE YOU SURE YOU ARE WORKING WITH A PERIODICAL?
See page 46 to check.

2 DO YOU HAVE ALL THE NEEDED INFORMATION FOR YOUR CITATION?
See pages 318–321 to check.

3

THE PATTERN

Here is a sample APA citation for an article from a periodical, followed by a detailed pattern

Atkinson, M. (2006). Straightedge bodies and civilizing processes. *Body and Society, 12*(1), 69–95. doi: 10. 1177/1375034X06061194

Author's Name. (Date). Title of article.

The pattern for an author's name is on page 420.

WHAT TO DO WHEN YOU HAVE:

• no author named: page 421

• one author: page 421

• two to six authors: page 421

• more than six authors: page 422

• two or more works published by the same author in the same year: page 422

• a government author: page 422

• a corporate author: page 423

• a work signed *Anonymous*: page 423

The pattern for the article title is on page 427.

WHAT TO DO WHEN YOU HAVE:

• a letter to the editor: page 429

• a review: page 421

The pattern for year of publication is on page 424.

WHAT TO DO WHEN YOU HAVE:

• a monthly magazine article: page 425

• a daily newspaper article: page 425

WHAT COUNTS AS A PERIODICAL?

A periodical is a publication that is published at regular intervals: every week, every month, every season. Journal, magazine, or newspaper articles, *including when they are published online,* are periodicals.

Periodical Name, Volume(Issue), Pages. doi:

If the periodical name begins with *A* or *The*, you can leave off those words.

Italicize the journal name.

DOI:

Included a digital object identifier if one is assigned. See page 434.

The pattern for the volume and issue numbers is on page 432.

WHAT TO DO WHEN YOU HAVE:

- no issue number: page 433
- only a date: page 433
- a daily newspaper: page 433
- a weekly or biweekly journal or magazine: page 433

Give the inclusive page numbers: **37–52** or **121–145**.

If you cite a newspaper article, put **p.** (for single page articles) or **pp.** (for multipage articles) before the page numbers: **p. J3** or **pp. C2–C5**. If the pages are discontinuous, put a comma between the numbers: **pp. B1, B4**.

FOR NONPERIODICAL SOURCES

1 ARE YOU SURE YOU ARE WORKING WITH A NONPERIODICAL?
See page 48 to check.

2 DO YOU HAVE ALL THE NEEDED INFORMATION FOR YOUR CITATION?
See pages 312–317 to check.

3

THE PATTERN

Here is a sample APA citation for a nonperiodical, followed by a detailed pattern.

Berger, J. (1992). *About looking*. New York, NY: Vintage.

Author's Name. (Year). *Title*.

The pattern for an author's name is on page 420.

WHAT TO DO WHEN YOU HAVE:

- no author named: page 421
- one author: page 421
- two to six authors: page 421
- more than six authors: page 422
- an edited collection: page 422
- a government author: page 422
- a corporate author: page 423
- a work signed *Anonymous*: page 423

The pattern for titles is on pages 426–427.

WHAT TO DO WHEN YOU HAVE:

- an essay or chapter in a book: page 428
- an essay in an online collection: page 428
- an article from a reference book: page 428

Put the year in parentheses, followed by a period. If you have no publication date, put **n.d.** (for **no date**) inside the parentheses, without quotation marks.

WHAT COUNTS AS A NONPERIODICAL?

The category of nonperiodical includes books, parts of books (like essays and chapters in books), films, videos, CDs, audio recordings, and reports—*including when they are published online.*

Place of Publication: Publisher.

The pattern for the place of publication is on page 430.

WHAT TO DO WHEN:

• the state is not listed: page 431

• the book was published in another country: page 431

IF YOUR SOURCE IS ONLINE:

The pattern for online sources is on pages 434–435.

From the publisher's full name, you can leave off words such as **Press** or **Company**.

Note that a colon precedes the publisher's name and that a period follows it.

YOU MAY NEED TO INCLUDE ADDITIONAL INFORMATION IN YOUR CITATION IF...

• you are citing a report from the Educational Resources Information Center (ERIC): page 429

• the work is translated: page 429

• a book is a second (or later) edition: page 429

• the work is in more than one volume: page 429

• the work is a review: page 429

• you are citing software, visual sources like charts or photographs, film and television shows, interviews, conference papers, or sound recordings: pages 436–437

AUTHOR'S NAME

Note how the patterns for author names are consistent across citations for all kinds of texts in all kinds of media.

Author's Name. (Date). Title of article. *Periodical Name, Volume*(Issue), Pages. Online information (if necessary).

PERIODICAL—go back to page 416

Author's Name. (Year). *Title.* Place of Publication: Publisher. Online information (if necessary).

NONPERIODICAL—go back to page 418

THE PATTERN

The first author listed is always written with the last name first, then a comma, and then the initials.

Last Name, Initials.

Singh, A. R.

If an author's first name includes a hyphen, include that hyphen with the initials.

Chen, K.-H.

If a work you are citing has more than one author, the additional names should be listed in the order in which they are given in the source. All authors are cited last name first. Use an ampersand (&) before the last author's name.

Phelps, L. W., & Emig, J.

Fine, M. T., Weis, L., Pruitt, L. P., & Burns, A.

Note that, in a References List entry, there is a period after the author's name or the list of authors' names.

→ On these pages, we show you how authors' names appear in individual citations for a range of sources; on page 438 we show you how to bring together individual citations like these to create a full References list that goes at the end of any APA-style research paper.

NO AUTHOR NAMED

If you cannot find an author's name, start the entry with the name of the book or article.

Idol worship. (2007, February 8). *Rolling Stone*, *1016*, 7.
MAGAZINE ARTICLE

Ultimate visual dictionary (Rev. ed.). (2002). New York, NY: Dorling Kindersley.
REFERENCE WORK

ONE AUTHOR

Pollan, M. (2006). *The omnivore's dilemma: A natural history of four meals*. New York, NY: Penguin.
BOOK

Xavier, J. (2007, June 11). Timo Veikkola (Nokia): A vision for the future. Message posted to http://julianax.blogspot.com /2007/06/timo-veikkola-nokia-vision-of-future.html
BLOG POSTING

Fletcher, M. A. (2007). At the corner of progress and peril. In K. Merida (Ed.), *Being a black man: At the corner of progress and peril*. New York, NY: Public Affairs.
ESSAY, IN EDITED BOOK

TWO TO SIX AUTHORS

In References List entries, include the names of up to six authors. Separate names and initials with commas and use an ampersand (&) before the last author.

Levitt, S. D., & Dubner, S. J. (2006). *Freakonomics: A rogue economist explores the hidden side of everything*. New York, NY: HarperCollins.
BOOK

Moeller, R. M., & Moberly, K. (2006). [Review of the book *Game work: Language, power, and computer game culture*]. *Kairos, 10,* 2. Retrieved from http://english.ttu.edu/kairos /10.2/binder.html?reviews/moeller_moberley/index.html
REVIEW, ONLINE
REVIEW, OF BOOK

DeVoss, D. N., Cushman, E., & Grabill, J. T. (2005). Infrastructure and composing: The when of new-media writing. *CCC, 57,* 14–44.
ARTICLE, IN ACADEMIC JOURNAL

Fine, M., Anand, B., Jordan, C., & Sherman, D. (2000). Before the bleach gets us all. In L. Weiss & M. Fine (Eds.), *Construction Sites* (pp. 161–179). New York, NY: Teachers College Press.
CHAPTER, IN EDITED BOOK

MORE THAN SIX AUTHORS

If you need to cite a source by seven or more authors, list only the first six names and abbreviate the rest as *et al.* **Et al.** is not italicized and always includes a period after *al.* (**Et al.** is Latin for *and others*.)

Nash, G. B., Jeffrey, J. R., Howe, J. R., Frederick, P. J., Davis, A. F., Winkler, A. M., et al. (2006). *The American people: Creating a nation and society* (7th ed.). New York, NY: Longman.
BOOK, MORE THAN SIX AUTHORS

TWO OR MORE WORKS PUBLISHED BY THE SAME AUTHOR IN THE SAME YEAR

If you need to cite two or more works by the same author that have the same year of publication, list the works in alphabetical order by title, and use lowercase letters (*a*, *b*, *c*, etc.) following the year to distinguish the works.

Helfand, G., & Walker, C. J. (Eds.). (2001a). *Mastering APA style: Instructor's resource guide. Washington,* DC: American Psychological Association.
BOOK

Helfand, G., & Walker, C. J. (Eds.). (2001b). *Mastering APA style: Student's workbook and training guide.* Washington, DC: American Psychological Association.
BOOK

Note that your in-text citations would also need to include the lowercase letters so that readers know which source you are referring to.

A GOVERNMENT AUTHOR

National Center for Educational Statistics. (2005). *Comparative indicators of education in the United States and other G8 countries: 2004.* Washington, DC: U.S. Department of Education Center for Educational Studies.
REPORT

U. S. Department of Health and Human Services. (2002). Mental health aspects of terrorism. Retrieved from http://mentalhealth.samhsa.gov/publications/allpubs /KEN-01-0095/default.asp
ARTICLE FROM GOVERNMENT WEBSITE

AN EDITED COLLECTION

Adams, M. (Ed.). (2000). *Readings for diversity and social justice: An anthology on racism, sexism, anti-semitism, heterosexism, classism, and ableism.* New York, NY: Routledge.
BOOK, EDITED

NOTE!
If you are citing only a piece from an edited collection and not the whole collection, create the citation following the pattern *An Essay or Chapter in a Book* shown on page 428.

A CORPORATE AUTHOR

A corporate author is an organization, corporation, association, or government agency. Start your citation with the name of the corporate author exactly as it is listed in the source (but omit *A*, *An*, or *The*).

American Library Association. (2004). *Anglo-American cataloguing rules* (2nd ed.). Chicago, IL: Author.
BOOK

American Counseling Association. (2007). *Basic facts about clinical depression* [Brochure]. Alexandria, VA: Author.
BROCHURE

Employee Benefit Research Institute. (2007). *How are retirees doing financially in retirement?* (Issue Brief No. 302). Washington, DC: Author.
REPORT FROM A PRIVATE ORGANIZATION

WORK BY ANONYMOUS AUTHOR

If the work is signed *Anonymous*, use *Anonymous* as the author's name. If no author is named, list the source by its title.

Anonymous. (2007). How to be an anarchist. Retrieved from WikiHow: http://www.wikihow.com/Be-an-Anarchist
WIKI POSTING

NOTE!

In the examples on these pages, we show the citations with what is called *hanging indentation*: The first line of a citation sticks farther into the left margin than the other lines. This is the standard form of indenting for APA citations; your teacher might also ask you to double-space the citations.

If you do not have access to a computer, underline the titles of books and periodicals instead of italicizing them.

If the paper on which you are working will be read online, always italicize the titles; if you underline them, the titles will look like links to other webpages.

See pages 420–437 for specific instructions on how to format individual citations in your References List.

DATE OF PUBLICATION

Note how the pattern for listing the year of publication for a text is consistent across citations for many kinds of texts in many kinds of media.

Author's Name. (Date). Title of article. *Periodical Name*, *Volume*(Issue), Pages. Online information (if necessary).
PERIODICAL—go back to page 416

Author's Name. (Year). *Title.* Place of Publication: Publisher. Online information (if necessary).
NONPERIODICAL—go back to page 418

THE PATTERN

Place the copyright date or year of publication in parentheses, followed by a period.

(Year of Publication).

(2007).

If you find more than one copyright date for a book, use the most recent one.

For monthly magazines, newspapers, and newsletters, give the year followed by the month.

(2006, July).

Include the day for periodicals published daily, like newspapers.

(2007, August 23).

→ On these pages, we show you how the publication dates appear in individual citations for a range of sources; on page 438 we show you how to bring together individual citations like these to create a References list that goes at the end of any APA-style research paper.

WHAT TO DO WITH A BOOK THAT HAS BEEN REPUBLISHED

A republished book is one that has been previously published by a different publisher or published in a different form.

For such books, use the standard pattern for book entries, and insert the original publication date at the end.

Johnson, S. (2002). *Emergence: The connected lives of ants, brains, cities, and software*. New York, NY: Touchstone-Simon. (Original work published 2001)

BOOK, REPUBLISHED

WHAT TO DO WITH A BOOK THAT HAS NO PUBLICATION DATE

If a book does not list a date of publication on its copyright page, put the abbreviation *n.d.* (for *no date*) where the year of publication usually goes in a citation.

Baudrillard, J. (n.d.). *Simulations*. New York, NY: Semiotext(e).

BOOK, NO PUBLICATION DATE

MAGAZINE ARTICLE

For magazines and other monthly periodicals, include the month of publication following the year.

Ehrenreich, B. (2000, April). Maid to order: The politics of other women's work. *Harper's*, 59–70.

ARTICLE, MAGAZINE

NEWSPAPER ARTICLE

For newspapers and other daily periodicals, include the month and day of publication following the year.

Lipton, E. (2007, September 2). Product safety commission bears heavy scrutiny. *Austin American Statesman*, p. A11.

ARTICLE, NEWSPAPER

APA DOCUMENTATION FOR REFERENCES LIST ENTRIES
TITLES

Note how the patterns for titles are consistent across citations for all kinds of texts in all kinds of media.

Author's Name. (Date). Title of article. *Periodical Name, Volume*(Issue), Pages. Online information (if necessary).
PERIODICAL—go back to page 416

Author's Name. (Year). *Title.* Place of Publication: Publisher. Online information (if necessary).
NONPERIODICAL—go back to page 418

→ On these pages, we show you how the publication dates appear in individual citations for a range of sources; on page 438 we show you how to bring together individual citations like these to create a References list that goes at the end of any APA-style research paper.

THE PATTERN

BOOK TITLES
Follow these steps to build the pattern:

1 Capitalize only the first word of the title and the first word of the subtitle.

2 Capitalize any proper nouns within a title.

3 Italicize the whole title. If you are not using a computer, underline the title.

4 Put a period after the title. (If the title ends with a question mark or exclamation point, use that instead.)

The title of the book.

Crow Lake.

The diving bell and the butterfly.

If the book has a subtitle, put the subtitle after a colon and capitalize its first word.

Scribbling the cat: Travels with an African soldier.

The quick and the dead: Artists and anatomy.

A country doctor's casebook: Tales from the north woods.

TITLES OF PARTS OF BOOKS, PERIODICAL ARTICLES, AND WEBPAGES

Follow these steps to build the pattern:

1 Capitalize only the first word of the title and the subtitle.

2 Do not italicize or put quotation marks around the title.

3 Put a period after the last word of the title. (If the title ends with a question mark or exclamation point, use that instead.)

4 Follow the pattern below for finishing the title, depending on the source.

PARTS OF BOOKS

For a chapter in an edited book, list the title of the chapter first, followed by the word *In* and the editor's name, followed by the title of the book.

The title of the chapter. In Editor's name (Ed.), *The title of the book.*

At the corner of progress and peril. In K. Merida (Ed.), *Being a black man: At the corner of progress and peril.*

JOURNAL ARTICLES

Put the name of the journal—in italics—after the article name. (If you are not using a computer, underline the journal's title.)

The article. *Journal Name*

Will the next election be hacked? *Rolling Stone*

Animal magnetism and curriculum history. *Inquiry*

WEBPAGES

Put the name of the website—in italics—after the name of the webpage. (If you are not using a computer, underline the webpage's title.)

The article. *Website name.*

Project description. *The Nora Project.*

Pictures without bias: How to avoid discrimination in visual media. *Center for Media Literacy.*

A BOOK

Lawson, M. (2002). *Crow Lake*. New York, NY: Delta Trade.
BOOK

Petherbridge, D., & Jordanova, L. (1997). *The quick and the dead: Artists and anatomy*. Berkeley, CA: University of California Press.
BOOK

A WEBSITE

Austin City Connection: The Official Web Site of the City of Austin. (n.d). *Childhood Lead Poisoning Prevention Program*. Retrieved from http://www.ci.austin.tx.us /health/education.htm
WEBSITE, ENTIRE SITE

AN ESSAY OR CHAPTER IN A BOOK

Makhan, J. (1998). Island ecology and cultural perceptions: A case study of Lakshdweep. In B. Saraswatie (Ed.), *Lifestyle and ecology*. New Delhi: Indira Gandhi National Centre for the Arts. Retrieved from http://www.ignca.nic.in /cd_08012.htm
ESSAY, IN ONLINE BOOK

Plato. (1961). Meno (W. K. C. Guthrie, Trans.). In E. Hamilton & H. Cairns (Eds.), *The collected dialogues of Plato* (pp. 353–385). Princeton, NJ: Princeton University Press.
ESSAY, IN EDITED BOOK
ESSAY, TRANSLATED

Van Proyen, M. (2001). *The new Dionysianism*. In B. Beckley (Ed.), The sticky sublime (pp. 165–175). New York, NY: Allworth.
ESSAY, IN EDITED BOOK

AN ESSAY IN AN ONLINE COLLECTION

Badger, M. (2004, June). Visual blogs. In L. J. Gurak, S. Antonijevic, L. Johnson, & J. Reyman (Eds.), *Into the blogosphere: Rhetoric, community, and culture of weblogs*. Retrieved from http://blog.lib.umn.edu/blogosphere/ visual_blogs.html
ESSAY, IN ONLINE COLLECTION

AN ARTICLE FROM A REFERENCE BOOK

Reference works rarely give the names of the people who wrote the articles. Put the title in place of the author in these cases.

Islam. (1989). In *The New York public library desk reference*.
ARTICLE, IN REFERENCE BOOK

Bovine spongiform encephalopathy. (2007). In *Encyclopedia Britannica*. Retrieved from Encyclopedia Britannica Online: http://www.search.eb.com/eb/article-9002739

ARTICLE, IN ONLINE REFERENCE BOOK

APA PATTERN FOR REFERENCES
ADDITIONAL INFORMATION

Sources are published—and cited—under varying circumstances. On these pages, we show you patterns for how to handle citations for several circumstances that occur frequently.

→ On these pages, we show you how the publication dates appear in individual citations for a range of sources; on page 438 we show you how to bring together individual citations like these to create a References list that goes at the end of any APA-style research paper.

REPORT FROM THE EDUCATIONAL RESOURCES INFORMATION CENTER (ERIC)

If you are doing research in the field of education, you are likely to find and use reports available through ERIC. These sources are usually numbered; provide this ERIC number in parentheses at the end of the reference entry.

Polette, N. (2007). *Teaching thinking skills with picture books, K-3*. Portsmouth, NH: Teacher Ideas Press. (ERIC Document Reproduction Service No. ED497152)
REPORT, FROM ERIC

A WORK WITH A TRANSLATOR

Burgat, F. (2008). *Islamism in the age of al-Qaeda* (P. Hutchinson, Trans.). Austin, TX: University of Texas Press.
BOOK, TRANSLATED

A BOOK IN A SECOND OR LATER EDITION

Rubenstein, J. M. (2004). *The cultural land-scape: An introduction to human geography* (8th ed.). Upper Saddle River, NJ: Prentice Hall.
BOOK, IN A SECOND OR LATER EDITION

WORK IN MORE THAN ONE VOLUME

Goldman, B. A., & Mitchell, D. F. (2007). *Directory of unpublished experimental mental measures* (Vol. 9). Washington, DC: American Psychological Association.
BOOK, MULTIVOLUME

A BOOK REVIEW

Julius, A. (2007, September 2). A people and a nation [Review of the book *Jews and power*]. *New York Times Book Review*, p. 27.
REVIEW, OF BOOK

AN ABSTRACT

Lacy, E., & Leslie, S. (2007). Library outreach near and far: Programs to staff and patients of the Piedmont Healthcare System. *Medical Reference Services Quarterly*. Abstract obtained from Library, Information Science & Technology Abstracts database.
ABSTRACT, JOURNAL ARTICLE

LETTER TO THE EDITOR

Delaney, J. (2007, August 28). Helping the world's sexually abused children [Letter to the editor]. *Washington Post*, p. A12.
LETTER TO THE EDITOR

APA DOCUMENTATION FOR REFERENCES LIST ENTRIES
PLACE OF PUBLICATION

Note how the pattern for listing the place of publication for a text is consistent across citations for all kinds of texts in all kinds of media.

Author's Name. (Year). *Title.* Place of Publication: Publisher. Online information (if necessary).

NONPERIODICAL—go back to page 418

THE PATTERN

Put the city and state of publication after the title of the book, followed by a colon.

Place of Publication:

Boston, MA:

Cambridge, UK:

Santa Monica, CA:

Calumet, MI:

If more than one place of publication is listed, use the first one.

EXAMPLE

Jackson, L. (2002). *Twentieth-century pattern design: Textile and wallpaper pioneers.* Princeton, NJ: Princeton Architectural Press.

Merrell, F. (1991). *Unthinking thinking: Jorge Luis Borges, mathematics, and the new physics.* West Lafayette, IN: Purdue University Press.

Wardlow, G. D. (1998). *Chasin' that devil music: Searching for the blues.* San Francisco, CA: Miller Freeman.

→ On these pages, we show you how the publication dates appear in individual citations for a range of sources; on page 438 we show you how to bring together individual citations like these to create a References list that goes at the end of any APA-style research paper.

WHEN TO MENTION THE STATE

A majority of books are published in major cities whose states most readers already know: Boston, Chicago, New York, San Francisco, and so on.

In APA style, include both the city and state (or country) in all references.

Eisner, W. (1996). *Graphic storytelling and visual narrative*. Tamarac, FL: Poorhouse.
BOOK

Hargittai, I., & Hargittai, M. (1994). *Symmetry: A unifying concept*. Bolinas, CA: Shelter Publications.
BOOK

Harris, S. L. (1990). *Agents of chaos: Earthquakes, volcanoes, and other natural disasters*. Missoula, MT: Mountain Press.
BOOK

WHEN THE BOOK WAS PUBLISHED IN ANOTHER COUNTRY

In APA style, include both the name of the city and the name of the country.

Yanagi, S. (1989). *The unknown craftsman: A Japanese insight into beauty*. Tokyo, Japan: Kodansha.
BOOK

Bourriaud, N. (2004). *Relational aesthetics*. Dijon-Quetigny, France: Les Presses du Réel.
BOOK

PERIODICAL VOLUME AND ISSUE

When periodicals were first printed, publishers would bind a sequential set of issues into one volume; eventually the pattern developed of binding a full year's set into one volume. This makes finding and referring to any particular issue easy: One can find the volume first, and then the article in the volume by its issue number or date.

Author's Name. (Date). Title of article. *Periodical Name*, *Volume*(Issue), Pages. Online information (if necessary).
PERIODICAL—go back to page 416

VOLUME AND ISSUE NUMBER

The volume number, italicized, follows the name of the periodical; there is a comma between the two. If there is an issue number, put it in parentheses immediately after the volume number. Issue numbers are not italicized.

Volume(Issue)

5(2)

27(11)

EXAMPLES

French, R. M. (2005, March/April). Using guitars to teach vibrations and acoustics. *Experimental Techniques, 29*(2), 47–48.

Watts, S. (1995, June). Walt Disney: Art and politics in the American century. *The Journal of American History, 82*(1), 84–110.

→ On these pages, we show you how the publication dates appear in individual citations for a range of sources; on page 438 we show you how to bring together individual citations like these to create a References list that goes at the end of any APA-style research paper.

WHEN THERE IS A VOLUME AND AN ISSUE NUMBER

If a journal paginates each issue separately, include the issue number in your References List entry.

Baker, B. (2007). Animal magnetism and curriculum history. *Inquiry*, *37*(2), 123–158.

ARTICLE IN A JOURNAL PAGINATED BY ISSUE

WHEN THERE IS NO ISSUE NUMBER

The volume number and date give readers enough information for finding the source.

Lawrence, R. (2000). Equivalent mass of a coil spring. *Physics Teacher*, *38*, 140–141.

ARTICLE IN A JOURNAL PAGINATED BY VOLUME

WHEN THERE IS ONLY A DATE

Many popular magazines do not list volume numbers, just a date.

Birnbaum, C. A. (2007, September). Cultivating appreciation. *Dwell*, 196+.

ARTICLE, IN POPULAR MAGAZINE

A DAILY NEWSPAPER

Because daily newspapers don't have volumes and issues, they are cited only by the date.

Rethinking abstinence. (2007, September 17). [Editorial]. *Bangor Daily News*, p. 8.

EDITORIAL, NO AUTHOR
NEWSPAPER ARTICLE, NO AUTHOR

Rozek, D. (2006, November 10). Girls' squabble over iPod over: And in the end, neither will get music player. *Chicago Sun-Times*, p. 3.

NEWSPAPER ARTICLE

A WEEKLY OR BIWEEKLY JOURNAL OR MAGAZINE

Gorman, C. (2006, September 18). To an athlete, aching young. *Time*, *168*(12), 60. Retrieved from Expanded Academic ASAP database.

ARTICLE, IN WEEKLY JOURNAL, RETRIEVED FROM ONLINE DATABASE

If a weekly or biweekly journal or magazine doesn't have volume and issue numbers, cite only the date.

Schlei, R. (2007, September 6). Faithful comrade: A monumental affair [Review of the book *Loving Frank*]. *Shepherd Express*, 48.

REVIEW, OF BOOK, IN WEEKLY JOURNAL

FOR ONLINE TEXTS

Because one purpose of reference lists is to enable readers to find the sources used by a writer, the APA recommends that References list entries for online sources include all the same information, in the same order, as for print sources—with the addition at the end of the citation of as much information as needed to enable readers to find electronic sources.

THE APA GIVES TWO OPTIONS FOR INCLUDING RETRIEVAL INFORMATION FOR SOURCES:

1 GIVE THE SOURCE'S DOI.

DOI stands for **digital object identifier**. The DOI system was developed by a group of international publishers to help readers find sources: The publishers recognized that URLs can change and shift, and so are not stable enough to ensure readers can find sources. These publishers instead developed a system where publications are given unique identifying numbers—the DOI—that provides a persistent link to the online source.

You can find DOIs at the top of journal articles or in the long citation information provided by databases. (→ See pages 326–327 on finding DOIs.)

To put a DOI into a reference list citation, create the citation as you would following the patterns on pages 416–419, then put **doi:** and then the DOI.

For example:

> Berke, J. H., & Schneider, S. (2007). Nothingness and narcissism. *Mental Health, Religion, and Culture, 10*(4), 335-351. doi:10.1080/13694670600722452

You can also use CrossRef.org to find DOIs for many sources.

2 GIVE THE SOURCE'S URL.

As you find and track sources, copy a source's URL from your browser and paste it into your running entry list (→ see pages 76–77) so that you record the exact URL.

When you put the URL into your reference list, create the citation as you would following the patterns on pages 416–419, then put **Retrieved from:** and then the URL.

For example:

> Moeller, R. M., & Moberly, K. (2006). [Review of the book *Game work: Language, power, and computer game culture*]. *Kairos, 10*(2). Retrieved from http://english.ttu.edu /kairos/10.2/binder.html?reviews/moeller_moberley/index.html

For periodical sources with no DOI, give the url for the home page of the journal. As you enter URLs into reference lists, take care your word processor does not automatically hyphenate them: This can "break" the URL, since a reader will try to use the hyphen as part of the URL, which won't work. Instead, if you have a long URL and need to break it across lines, break it before a slash or other hyphenation.

CITING AN ENTIRE WEBSITE

Austin City Connection: The Official Web Site of the City of Austin. (n.d). *Childhood Lead Poisoning Prevention Program*. Retrieved from http://www.ci.austin.tx.us /health/education.htm

WEBSITE

CITING ONLINE ARTICLES

Lieberman, J. E. (2005, November/December). Coming clean. *Psychology Today*, *38*(6), 8. Retrieved from www.psycholo-gytoday.com

ARTICLE, ONLINE VERSION OF PRINT SOURCE

When you cite articles from databases, give either the DOI for the article or find the stable URL provided by the database (⟶ see pages 326–327); you do not need to provide the database name.

Clark-Flory, T. (2007, August 10). Roundup: Virtual wives, non-ironic feminism and more. *Salon.com*. 1-1. Retrieved from http://www.salon.com/mwt/broadsheet/2007/08/10/roundup

ARTICLE, ONLINE ONLY

Franzen, L., & Smith, C. (2009). Acculturation and environmental change impacts dietary habits among adult Hmong. *Appetite*, *52*(1), 173-183. doi: 10.1016/j.appet.2008.09.012

ARTICLE, FROM DATABASE

CITING E-MAIL

Because personal e-mail cannot be retrieved by your readers, the APA says not to include it in a References List (⟶ see page 412 on in-text citations for e-mail). For retrievable postings—discussion groups, mailing lists—use the format shown to the right.

McLaughlin, B. (2007, September 4). Webinar for enviromental benchmarking survey. Message posted to AAUP-L mailing list, archived at http://ucp.uchicago.edu/mailman /listinfo/aaup-l

DISCUSSION GROUP OR MAILING LIST POST

CITING BLOGS AND WIKIS

Include a retrieval date for sources that are updated frequently.

Xavier, J. (2007, June 11). Timo Veikkola (Nokia): A vision for the future. Message posted to http://julianax.blogspot.com/2007/06/timo-veikkola-nokia-vision-of-future.html

BLOG POSTING

Wiki. (2007, 25 October). Retrieved October 28, 2007, from Wikipedia: http://en.wikipedia.org /wiki/Wiki

WIKI POSTING

CITING PART OF AN ONLINE DOCUMENT

Sales, L. (2005). Part II. In *Hurricane Katrina: Reporter's diary*. Retrieved from http://www.abc.net.au/news/newsitems/200509/s1460732

ONLINE DOCUMENT, PART

FOR OTHER KINDS OF SOURCES

You may need to create references for other types of sources, including visual and multimedia sources. In APA style, a note or identifying description usually helps clarify the type of source you are citing.

As the examples on these two pages show, you can help readers by describing the medium of a source that is not usual:

Author's Name. (Year). *Title*. [Medium]. Place of Publication: Publisher. Online information (if necessary).

NONPERIODICAL—go back to page 418

As the examples on these two pages show, you can put here in a citation **Chart**, **CD**, **Computer software**, **Television series**, **Episode**, **Motion picture**—whatever information will help readers know the kind of source you are citing if it is not a print or online alphabetic text.

SOFTWARE

Cite software as you would a book without a named author (→ see page 421)—but include **Computer software** in brackets after the title. If there is a publisher, include the name and date of publication; for software you have downloaded, give the date of the download and the URL.

PsychMate (Version 2.0) [Computer software]. (2007). Philadelphia, PA: Psychology Software Tools.

SOFTWARE

SOUND RECORDING

Camera Obscura. (2009). Away with Murder. On *My Maudlin Career* [CD]. London: 4AD Records.

MUSIC OR AUDIO RECORDING

VISUAL SOURCES

Fruitrich, C., & Ward, S. (2007). Groups' Goodwill helps [Chart]. USATODAY.com. Retrieved from http://www.usatoday.com /news/snapshots/25anniversary/goodwill.htm
CHART, ONLINE

Cubitt, C. (2006). *Church*. Katrina: A gallery of images. Retrieved from http://www.claytoncubitt.com/publish/katrina
PHOTOGRAPH, ONLINE

Adams, A. (ca. 1930). *Factory Building, San Francisco*. Santa Fe, NM: Museum of Fine Arts.
PHOTOGRAPH

CONFERENCE PAPER PRESENTATION

Use this format if you need to cite a conference presentation or similar lecture or speech that has not been published.

Kleinberg, S. L. (2005, June). *The changing face of Texas in the twenty-first century: Perspectives on the new immigration*. Paper presented at Gateway on the Gulf, a Humanities Texas Institute for Texas Teachers.
PRESENTATION OR LECTURE

AN INTERVIEW YOU CONDUCT

Because it does not consider an unpublished interview to be data that someone can check, the APA says not to include such an interview in the References List. You may, however, give an in-text citation for the interview:

> Some music composers believe digital technologies slow down their composing processes because they offer so many options (M. Boracz, personal communication, October 18, 2007).

FILM AND TELEVISION

Gibney, A. (Director). (2005). *Enron: The smartest guys in the room* [Motion picture]. United States: Magnolia.
FILM, VIDEOTAPE, OR DVD

Hanson, H. (Writer), & Yaltanes, G. (Director). (2005, September 13). Pilot [Television series episode]. In B. Josephson & H. Hanson (Producers), *Bones*. New York: Fox Broadcasting.
TELEVISION SHOW OR SERIES

TIP: FINDING INFORMATION ABOUT FILMS

The *Internet Movie Database* (http://www.imdb.com) gives you access to all the information you need for citing films.

SAMPLE REFERENCE LISTINGS

The sample listings below are for the in-text citations shown on pages 420–437. Note that:

❏ The listings are arranged alphabetically by the author's last name. (If a listing starts with the title of a source, place it alphabetically in the list by the first letter of the title. If the title begins with **A**, **An**, or **The**, alphabetize by the second word of the title.)

❏ If you list two or more sources by the same author, arrange them by the year of publication, earliest first. If the sources are published in the same year, arrange them alphabetically by title.

❏ If you have two authors with the same last name, alphabetize by the first name.

References

Anonymous. (2007). How to be an anarchist. Retrieved January 29, 2008, from WikiHow: http://www.wikihow.com/Be-an-Anarchist

Idol worship. (2007, February 8). *RollingStone, 1016*, 7.

Moeller, R. M., & Moberly, K. (2006). [Review of the book *Game work: Language, power, and computer game culture*]. *Kairos, 10*(2). Retrieved from http://english.ttu.edu/ kairos

Pollan, M. (2001). *The botany of desire: A plant's-eye view of the world*. New York, NY: Random House.

Pollan, M. (2006). *The omnivore's dilemma: A natural history of four meals*. New York, NY: Penguin.

Rorty, A. O. (1996). Structuring Rhetoric. In A. O. Rorty (Ed.), *Essays on Aristotle's rhetoric* (pp. 1–33). Berkeley, CA: University of California Press.

Rorty, R. M. (1979). *Philosophy and the mirror of nature*. Princeton, NJ: Princeton University Press.

U. S. Department of Health and Human Services. (2002). Mental health aspects of terrorism. Retrieved from http://mentalhealth.samhsa.gov/publications/allpubs/ KEN-01-0095/default.asp

World Health Organization. (2005). *The world health report 2005: Make every mother and child count*. Retreived from http://www.who.int/whr/2005/whr2005_en.pdf

CSE DOCUMEN- TATION

[2] J. Allan: Automatic hypertext

[4] R. Hammwöhner / R. Kuhlen: Se
Information Science, 20(3), 175-184.

[5] R. Hammwöhner / M. Rittberg
Management, 33(2), 243-254. 1997

[6] Z. Zhang: Experiemnteller Aufbau
Hypertext-System (KHS). Master Thesis
Feb.,1995.

[7] M. Agosti / J. Allan: Introduction to
construction of hypertext. Information Proce

[8] R. Aßfalg: Integration eines offenen Hy
Web. Hartung-Gorre Verlag: Konstanz. 1996

[9] R. Furuta / C. Plaistant / B. Scheinerman:
1(2), 179-195, 1989.

[10] M.H. Chignell et al.: The HEFTI model
991.

] P. Thistlewaite: Automatic construction and
Management, 33(2), 161-174. 1997

This style used to be called CBE, after the Council of Biology Editors, which developed it. But because this style has become so widespread in the sciences, the CBE changed its name in 2000 to the Council of Science Editors (CSE).

In 2006, the CSE published a new, seventh, edition of their style guide, *Scientific Style and Format*. CSE documentation style is used by authors in the the life sciences, physical sciences, and mathematics.

The citation system advocated by the seventh edition of the CSE manual is known as **the citation-name system**. In this system, writers must create their list of references before they can insert their in-text citations—and so to the right we discuss the reference list before we discuss the in-text citation format.

CSE REFERENCES

In the citation-name system, writers complete the list of references and then create the in-text citations. The reference list (called **References**, **Cited References**, **Literature Cited**, or **Bibliography**) is arranged alphabetically by author and then numbered:

References

1. Amann RI, Ludwig W, and Schleifer KH. Phylogenetic identification and in situ detection of individual microbial cells without cultivation. Microhi01 Rev. 1995;59:143-169.

2. Barns SM, Fundyga RE, Jeffries MW, and Pace NR. Remarkable arched diversity detected in a Yellowstone National Park hot spring environment. Proc Natl Acad Sci USA. 1994;91:1609-1613.

3. Dojka, MA, Harris JK, and Pace NR. Expanding the known diversity and environmental distribution of an uncultured phylogenetic division of bacteria. Appi Environ Microbiol. 2000;66:1617-1621.

→ See pages 440–441 for information on how to format CSE style references.

CSE IN-TEXT CITATIONS

The numbers alphabetically assigned to these end references are then used for in-text references, regardless of the sequence in which the works appear in the text:

> Early studies[2] used molecular methods to reveal remarkable microbial diversity in the sediment of Yellowstone hot springs.

or:

> Early studies (2) used molecular methods to reveal remarkable microbial diversity in the sediment of Yellowstone hot springs.

In order to avoid ambiguity, citation numbers appear immediately after the relevant word, title, or phrase rather than at the end of a sentence. Usually, the citation number appears as superscript, but it can also be set in parentheses. Set the citation number with one space both before and after, except when followed by a punctuation mark. This spacing makes the citation number easier to see.

When there are several in-text citations occurring at the same point in the text, put them in numerical order so that a reader can find them easily in the list of references. Separate the numbers by commas; if the numbers are consecutive, they can be joined by a hyphen:

> Researchers have studied brucellosis for the better part of a century [3,5,16-18,43], finding that ...

CSE REFERENCES

FOR BOOKS

Number. Author's Name. Title of the book. City of Publication (State): Publisher; Year.

19. Stewart J. Calculus. Boston (MA): Brooks/Cole; 2002.

FOR ARTICLES FROM PERIODICALS

Number. Author's Name. Article title. Periodical. Date;Volume(Issue):Pages.

17. Richie DJ, Lappos VJ, Palmer PL. Sizing/optimization of a small satellite energy storage and attitude control system. JOSR. 2007 Jul-Aug;87(52):940-952.

FOR ONLINE SOURCES AND ELECTRONIC MEDIA

Number. Title of source [Kind of electronic medium]. Edition. Place of Publication: Publisher; date of publication [date updated; date cited]. Notes.

44. WebElements: chemistry nexus [Internet]. Sheffield (UK): University of Sheffield; c1993-2007 [cited 2007 Jun 18]. Available from: http://www.webelements.com/nexus/

When you cite a book, periodical, or webpage, the format of the citation—the punctuation of the title of a book, the inclusion of a periodical's issue number, or the listing of a URL—tells a reader what kind of text you are citing. When you cite a text that isn't a book, periodical, or webpage, indicate what kind of text you are citing, in brackets after the title (as in the pattern for online sources).

→ See pages 442–443 for more sample CSE references.

DETAILS OF THE PATTERNS

AUTHOR'S NAME

An author's name is listed last name first, with initials for first and middle names. If there are two initials, they are not separated by space or periods. A period separates the author's name from the title.

TITLES OF BOOKS AND PARTS OF BOOKS

1. Capitalize only the first word and any proper nouns.

2. Do not italicize or underline book titles.

3. Put a period after the title.

JOURNAL TITLES

Journal titles in CSE are always abbreviated according to ISO (International Organization for Standardization). For example, the full title of the journal in the example numbered 17 to the left is the **Journal of Spacecraft and Rockets**. The CSE manual has guidelines for abbreviations. Your school's library has this manual.

DATES

If a date is not given in any of the usual places (copyright page, etc.) but it can be discerned from other information in the publication, set the date in brackets [2002]. If only a copyright date is available, use that with a **c** for **copyright** (c1962). If there is a publication date and a copyright date, with more than three years between them, give both dates (2007, c1962). If there is no date of publication, use the words **date unknown** in brackets: [date unknown]. With a website, the copyright or publication date will be a span of years. In this case, use a hyphen (c1993-2007). For multiple years of publication, separate the years by a hyphen (2004-2005).

ONLINE SOURCES AND ELECTRONIC MEDIA

References for Internet sources and electronic media do not differ significantly from what is required for print sources. There is still an author or organization who is responsible for the content, a title, a place of publication, and a date of publication. Additional information will be the URL and access date, and with some media, technical information.

Always put the medium (Internet; CD-ROM; DVD) in brackets after the title.

CSE also notes dates of updates (which are most applicable to websites) and dates accessed for Internet sources. In some cases, a date of update will not be provided, but you should always note the date of access, especially for materials that change frequently, such as a blog or wiki.

In a CSE citation, notes include URLs as well as technical information.

CSE SAMPLE REFERENCES

NO AUTHOR NAMED
Start with the work's title.

8. Handbook of geriatric drug therapy. Springhouse (PA): Springhouse; c2000.

MORE THAN ONE AUTHOR

17. Sebastini AM, Fishbeck DW. Mammalian anatomy: the cat. 2nd ed. Burlington (NC): Carolina Biological; 2005.

A CORPORATION OR ORGANIZATION AS AUTHOR
Start with the abbreviated name of the corporate author as it appears in the source.

3. Center for Chemical Process Safety. Guidelines for safe and reliable instrumented protective systems. Indianapolis (IN): Wiley; 2007.

AN EDITED BOOK
Put *editor* or *editors* after the name(s) at the start.

2. Brockman J, editor. What we believe but cannot prove: today's leading thinkers on science in the age of certainty. New York (NY): HarperCollins; 2006.

A GOVERNMENT AUTHOR
GPO stands for *Government Printing Office.*

6. US Government Printing Office. Style manual. Washington (DC): GPO; 2000.

AN ESSAY OR CHAPTER IN A BOOK

8. Feynman RP. The making of a scientist. In: Leighton R, editor. Classic Feynman: All the adventures of a curious character. New York (NY): Norton; 2006. p. 13-19.

A REVISED OR LATER EDITION OF A BOOK
Add the edition after the title.

22. Tufte ER. The visual display of quantitative information. 2nd ed. Cheshire (CT): Graphics Press; 2001.

AN ONLINE BOOK

7. Ebert D. Ecology, epidemiology, and evolution of Parasitism in Daphnia [Internet]. Bethesda (MD): National Library of Medicine (US), National Center for Biotechnology Information; 2005 [cited 2007 Sep 4]. Available from: http://www.ncbi.nlm.nih.gov/entrez/query.fcgi?db=Books

AN ARTICLE IN A DAILY NEWSPAPER

24. Revkin AC. Cooking up a fable of life on melting ice. New York Times. 2007 Jul 22;Sect. 2:11.

A VOLUME IN A SERIES

The series information goes in parentheses at the end.

9. Honjo T, Melchers F, editors. Gut-associated lymphoid tissues. Berlin (Germany): Springer-Verlag; 2006. (Current Topics in Microbiology and Immunology; vol. 308).

A TECHNICAL REPORT

Include the performing and/or sponsoring organization. (The example shows the performing organization [the group that performed the research], the University of Washington Department of Statistics; the sponsoring group funded the research.)

14. Krivitsky P, Handcock M, Raftery AE, Hoff P. Representing degree distributions, clustering, and homophily in social networks with latent cluster random effects models. Seattle (WA): University of Washington Department of Statistics; 2007. No. 517. Available from: http://www.stat.washington.edu/www/research/reports/

Note: Often, the very end of the citation acknowledges the funding; for example: *(Sponsored by the Nuclear Regulatory Commission)*. The report number goes at the end of the citation (before the URL if there is one). If there is a contract number, include it.

A CONFERENCE PRESENTATION

Include the location and dates.

2. Braun F, Noterdaeme JM, Colas L. Simulations of different Faraday screen configurations for the ITER ICRH Antenna. In: Ryan PM, Rassmussen D, editors. Radio frequency power in plasmas: 17th topical conference on radio frequency power in plasmas; 2007 May 7-9; Clearwater (FL). Melville (NY): American Institute of Physics; 2007. p. 175-178.

A JOURNAL PAGINATED BY VOLUME

8. Gradstein FM, Og JG. Geologic time scale 2004—why, how, and where near! Lethaia. 2004;(37):175-181.

AN ONLINE ARTICLE

24. Spiesel S. Can a rollercoaster really scare you to death? And more. Slate [Internet]. Aug 28 [cited 2007 Sep 3]. Available from: http://www.slate.com/id/2172960/fr/flyout

A WEBPAGE

5. DNA Interactive [Internet]. Cold Spring Harbor (NY): Cold Spring Harbor Lab; c2003 [cited 2007 Aug 12]. Available from: http://www.dnai.org/

AN ONLINE DATABASE

3. Catalysts and catalysed reactions [Internet]. London (UK): RSC Publishing. 2002 [updated 2007 Aug; cited 2007 Sep 5]. Available from: http://pubs.rsc.org/Publishing/CurrentAwareness/CCR/CCRSearchPage.cfm

A BLOG POSTING

4. Diganta [screen name]. Pushing the limits of speciesism. In: Desicritics. org [Web log]. [posted 2007 Jun 18; cited 2007 Sep 2].

CHICAGO MANUAL OF STYLE DOCUMENTATION AND IN-TEXT CITATIONS

The **Chicago Manual of Style** (CMS) is now in its fifteenth edition (published in 2003). It is used by writers in the arts and humanities, especially history.

Rather than using the author and date in-text citation format of MLA and APA, most CMS advocates prefer the footnote or endnote style of citation. In this style, a superscript number is placed after any quotation, paraphrase, or summary. These numbers are consecutive throughout the text, and correspond either to a footnote set at the bottom of the page or to endnotes that come at the end of the text.

Because CMS notes provide full bibliographic information for the sources cited, writers do not need to provide a **Works Cited** or **References** listing—although they can.

---

[12] Wang, 84. On the increasi
the Qing, see the articles by El
to ban Western Chamber, see
Change and Dissemination," A

[13] Jin's claim is echoed by
kenkyu," 107. Wang Ji-si, howe
a convenient discussion of the
Hargett in the Indiana Compani
H. Nienhauser (Bloomington: In

CMS IN-TEXT CITATIONS AND FOOTNOTES

Here is a sample sentence containing a quotation as it would appear in the body of a paper with a superscript number at its end, and the footnote to that sentence, linked by the number. (This sample is numbered 12 because there are eleven source references before it.)

> In *Marriage, a History*, Stephanie Coontz states that, "whether it is valued or not, love is rarely seen as the main ingredient for marital success."[12]
>
> 12. Stephanie Coontz, *Marriage, a History: From Obedience to Intimacy or How Love Conquered Marriage* (New York: Viking, 2005), 18.

SUBSEQUENT NOTE ENTRIES

After the first reference to a book or other source, CMS conventions say that writers should put into a footnote the following:

- the author's last name
- the title of the work (or a shortened version if the title is long)
- a page number

Some writers, however, use only the author's name and the page number if there will be no ambiguity as to which source is being cited. The footnote could thus read

10. Coontz, *Marriage*, 99.

Or

10. Coontz, 99.

If a reference is to the same work as in the preceding note, you can use the abbreviation **Ibid.** (**Ibid.** is a shortened form of the Latin word **ibidem**, which means **in the same place**.)

11. Ibid., 103.

BIBLIOGRAPHY

If the writer of these sample citations were to include a bibliography listing at the paper's end, the citation would be:

Coontz, Stephanie. *Marriage, a History: From Obedience to Intimacy or How Love Conquered Marriage*. New York: Viking, 2005.

(Notice, in this case, that the listing has the same formatting as MLA style.)

→ See pages 446–448 for more sample CMS footnotes.

CMS SAMPLE REFERENCES

BOOKS

For a footnote:

16. J. H. Plumb, *The Italian Renaissance* (New York: Mariner Books, 2001), 86.

In the bibliography:

Plumb, J. H. *The Italian Renaissance*. New York: Mariner Books, 2001.

AN ESSAY OR CHAPTER IN A BOOK

For a footnote:

8. F. J. Byrne, "Early Irish Society (1st–9th Century)," in *The Course of Irish History*, eds. T. W. Moody and F. X. Martin (Lanham, MD: Roberts Rinehart, 2002), 55.

In the bibliography:

Byrne, F. J. "Early Irish Society (1st–9th Century)." In *The Course of Irish History*, eds. T. W. Moody and F. X. Martin, 43–60. Lanham, MD: Roberts Rinehart, 2002.

ARTICLES FROM PERIODICALS (JOURNALS, MAGAZINES, OR NEWSPAPERS)

For a footnote:

13. Valerie A. Kivelson, "On Words, Sources, and Historical Method: Which Truth About Muscovy?" *Kritika: Explorations in Russian and Eurasian History* 3, no. 3 (2002): 490.

In the bibliography:

Kivelson, Valerie A. "On Words, Sources, and Historical Method: Which Truth About Muscovy?" *Kritika: Explorations in Russian and Eurasian History* 3, no. 3 (2002): 487–99.

A JOURNAL ARTICLE RETRIEVED FROM ELECTRONIC DATABASE

The citation should follow the same form for a journal, but the URL for the article is included.

For a footnote:

23. Bryon MacWilliams, "Yale U. Press Strikes Deal with Russian Archive to Open Stalin's Papers to Scholars," *Chronicle of Higher Education* 53, no. 44 (July 2007), http://web. ebscohost.com.ezproxy.lib.utexas.edu/ehost.

In the bibliography:

MacWilliams, Bryon. "Yale U. Press Strikes Deal with Russian Archive to Open Stalin's Papers to Scholars." *Chronicle of Higher Education* 53, no. 44 (July 2007), http://web.ebscohost. com.ezproxy.lib.utexas.edu/ehost.

ONLINE SOURCES (OTHER THAN DATABASES)

For a footnote:

4. Chris Johnson, "Statement from Human Rights Campaign President Joe Solmonese on Recent ENDA Developments," *Human Rights Campaign*, September 28, 2007, http://www.hrcbackstory.org/2007/09/state-ment-from-.html.

In the bibliography:

Johnson, Chris. "Statement from Human Rights Campaign President Joe Solmonese on Recent ENDA Developments." *Human Rights Campaign*, September 28, 2007, http://www.hrcbackstory.org/2007/09/state-ment-from-.html.

NO AUTHOR NAMED

Start the citation with the work's title.

For a footnote:

    4. *Broad Stripes and Bright Stars* (Kansas City, MO: Andrews McMeel, 2002), 15.

In the bibliography:

Broad Stripes and Bright Stars. Kansas City, MO: Andrews McMeel, 2002.

TWO OR THREE AUTHORS

In a footnote, put all of the authors' full names. For subsequent references, give the authors' last names only. In the bibliography, give full names.

For a footnote:

    2. Larry J. Reynolds and Gordon Hutner, eds., *National Imaginaries, American Identities: The Cultural Work of American Iconography* (Princeton, NJ: Princeton University Press, 2000), 56.

In the bibliography:

Reynolds, Larry J., and Gordon Hutner, eds. *National Imaginaries, American Identities: The Cultural Work of American Iconography*. Princeton, NJ: Princeton University Press, 2000.

FOUR OR MORE AUTHORS

In a footnote, give the name of the first author listed, followed by **and others**. List all the authors in the bibliography.

For a footnote:

    3. James Drake and others, *James Drake* (Austin: University of Texas Press, 2008), 40.

In the bibliography:

Drake, James, Bruce Ferguson, Steven Henry Madoff, and Jimmy Santiago Baca. *James Drake*. Austin: University of Texas Press, 2008.

A CORPORATE AUTHOR

Start with the name of the corporate author as it appears in the source.

For a footnote:

    5. Brady Center to Prevent Gun Violence, *Guns and Hate: A Lethal Combination* (Washington, DC: Brady Center to Prevent Gun Violence, 2009).

In the bibliography:

Brady Center to Prevent Gun Violence. *Guns and Hate: A Lethal Combination*. Washington, DC: Brady Center to Prevent Gun Violence, 2009.

A GOVERNMENT AUTHOR

List the full agency or department name as author.

For a footnote:

    11. Central Intelligence Agency, *The World Fact Book 2007* (Washington, DC: Potomac Books, 2007), 136.

In the bibliography:

Central Intelligence Agency. *The World Fact Book 2007*. Washington, DC: Potomac Books, 2007.

AN EDITED BOOK

Put **ed.** (or **eds.** for multiple editors) after the names that begin the citation.

For a footnote:

    14. J. Peter Burkholder and Claude V. Palisca, eds., *Norton Anthology of Western Music*, Vol. 1, *Ancient to Baroque* (New York: Norton, 2005), 550.

In the bibliography:

Burkholder, J. Peter, and Claude V. Palisca, eds. *Norton Anthology of Western Music*. Vol. 1, *Ancient to Baroque*. New York: Norton, 2005.

continued on the next page

CMS SAMPLE REFERENCES, continued

AN ARTICLE FROM A REFERENCE BOOK

Well-known reference materials are not usually listed in a CMS bibliography, so you need to know only the footnote format. Start with the name of the reference work, and then list its edition. Put *s.v.* (*sub verba*, Latin for *under the word*) and then put the title of the entry you are citing in quotation marks:

9. *Riverside Dictionary of Biography*, 2004 ed., s.v. "Aaron, Hank (Henry Lewis)."

AN ARTICLE FROM AN ONLINE REFERENCE

The access date should be included in the citation only for sources that are frequently updated, such as Wikis. (And, as with reference works in print, there should be no listing in the bibliography.)

26. Wikipedia, s.v. "Deadwood, South Dakota," http://en.wikipedia.org/wiki/Deadwood%2C_South_Dakota (accessed September 4, 2007).

A RELIGIOUS TEXT

Citations for religious texts appear in the notes, but not in the bibliography.

12. Qur'an 18:16–20.

AN E-MAIL

If you reference e-mails in the text of your paper, you do not need to provide a note. E-mails are not listed in a CMS bibliography.

In an e-mail message to the author on November 6, 2006, Jason Craft noted….

If you do need to include a footnote:

24. Jason Craft, e-mail message to author, November 6, 2006.

A WEBPAGE

For a footnote:

19. New York Historical Society, "Galleries," New York Divided: Slavery and the Civil War, http://www.slaveryinnewyork.org/tour_galleries.htm (accessed September 2, 2007).

In the bibliography:

New York Historical Society. "Galleries." New York Divided: Slavery and the Civil War. http://www.slaveryinnewyork.org/tour_galleries.htm (accessed September 2, 2007).

A BLOG POSTING

When you give the URL for a blog entry, give the *permalink* to the entry rather than the URL of that blog so a reader can go directly to the entry without having to scroll through the entire blog.

For a footnote:

8. Dooce [Screen name], "The Labor Story, Part 2," In the Dooce Blog, comment posted July 27, 2009, http://www.dooce.com/2009/07/27/labor-story-part-two (accessed August 3, 2009).

In the bibliography:

Dooce Blog. "The Labor Story, Part 2." http://www.dooce.com/2009 /07/27/labor-story-part-two.

PART 9
EDITING AND PROOFREADING YOUR WORK

CONTENTS

WHERE ARE WE IN THE PROCESS FOR COMPOSING?

Understanding your project

Getting started

Asking questions

Shaping your project for others

Drafting a paper

Getting feedback

Revising

Polishing Editing and proofreading

ARE YOU READY TO USE THE NEXT PAGES OF THIS BOOK?

NO…

Are you are moving around the parts of a draft, making major revisions? Are you clarifying the purposes of your paragraphs?

If any of these questions describes your situation, then, no, you are not ready for the next pages.

Until you have a solid draft, editing and proofreading will get in the way of you making needed revisions. Put your focus where your paper most needs it—on revising—and come back to Part 9 when you have a draft that is settled in the organization and style of its parts.

→ For help with revising, see pages 220–223.

→ For help with paragraphs, see pages 170–183 and 230–273.

YES.

Do you have a draft that is solid, with no need to clarify organization or paragraph functions?

You are ready to do the last polishing steps on your writing.

IF YOU GREW UP SPEAKING A LANGUAGE OTHER THAN ENGLISH…

Don't wait until a paper is finished to edit and proofread. Instead, once you have a full draft, do a little editing. If you leave all the language work until the end, you may not have enough time or you may find it too overwhelming and discouraging.

EDITING AND PROOFREADING

WHAT ARE REVISING, EDITING, AND PROOFREADING?

As you write a paper, you move through stages of development. In the initial stages, you are finding and arranging ideas and then arranging them into an overall argument. Once you have a full first draft, you move into the middle stage of writing—revision—and then into the later stages of writing—editing and proofreading.

REVISING

When you revise, you attend to large-scale persuasive aspects of a text: organization and style. You start revising once you have close to a full draft.

→ See pages 220–223 for more on revising.

EDITING

When your overall argument is solid and unlikely to change, you focus on editing. In editing, you attend to sentences and other large details: Are sentences readable? Have you documented all your sources?

PROOFREADING

A proofreader checks spelling, punctuation, and other mechanics. While you can pay attention to these details throughout the development of a paper, you also want to do this *as your very last step*: Whenever you revise or edit, you can make mistakes, and you want to be sure to catch them once and for all.

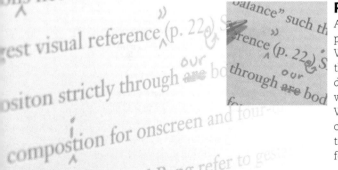

REVISING

- Am I clear about my argument? Can I state it as a thesis statement?
    → See pages 96–97, 138–139, and 152–155.

- Did I offer well-supported and accurate evidence for each of my claims?
    → See pages 98–107.

- Have I been fair and respectful toward the differing positions one could take on my arguments?
    → See pages 108–123.

- Will my readers understand the purpose of each paragraph?
    → See pages 176–183.

- Can I say why my paragraphs are ordered as they are? Can I describe the steps of my argument?
    → See pages 152–155.

- Will my writing engage readers?
    → See pages 224–259.

- Does my introduction engage readers with my argument and initial concerns?
    → See pages 234–235.

- Have I given appropriate emphasis to the main parts of my arguments?
    → Look through Part 6 for pages checked for helping with emphasis.

- Do my transitions help readers move from one paragraph to the next?
    → See pages 236–237.

- Does my conclusion sum up my argument and end memorably for readers?
    → See pages 232–233.

EDITING

- Are my sentences easy to read?
- Will my sentences engage readers?
- Are my sentences grammatically appropriate for my audience and purpose? Does each sentence make sense on its own?
- Have I integrated my quotations of others' work into my writing—while making it clear when I am using the ideas or words of others?
- Have I documented my sources according to expected conventions?
- Have I checked my writing to remove all possible biased references to others?

→ Pages 452–453 go into more detail on these editing steps.

PROOFREADING

- Is every word spelled and capitalized according to convention?
- Did I leave out any words?
- Have I used the right word?
- Is my punctuation conventional?
- Are my quotations punctuated according to convention?

→ Pages 454–455 go into more detail on these proofreading steps.

HOW TO EDIT

EDITING IS ABOUT SENTENCES

Effective editing creates sentences that move, delight, and persuade readers.

Like all crafts, editing asks time, patience, persistence, and practice from you. Learning to edit can be frustrating because sentences have so many details—but those details also allow creativity and experimentation.

Don't let the length of the list to the right daunt you. Start at the beginning and move step by step, doing as much as you can when you can; for each paper you write, focus on a few of the listed items. Over time, these features can become intuitive to you, and you will find pleasure and satisfaction in shaping sentences that build the relations you want with others.

TIPS: EDITING

- Leave yourself time to edit. As you schedule writing time for a paper, aim to finish writing and revising at least a day before a paper is due: You want to put a paper aside for a while in order to change your mindset to the close and relaxed attentions sentences require.

- To understand how readers hear your sentences, read your writing aloud to yourself or a friend—or ask another to read it to you.

- Ask your teacher to help you determine the aspects of sentence style and grammar that challenge you. Focus on those aspects when you edit.

- Edit systematically: Choose one or two elements from the list to the right, and go through your writing sentence by sentence, paying attention to only those elements.

Explore these topics online:

Revision

www.mycomplab.com

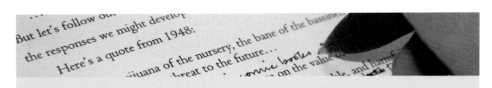

TO EDIT, ASK YOURSELF:

Are my sentences easy to read? Will my sentences engage readers?
❏ Do my sentences have all the qualities that make them easy to read? See pages 244–245.

❏ Are my verbs active? Are my nouns concrete? See pages 255–256.

❏ Have I avoided clichés and jargon? See page 257–258.

Are my sentences grammatically appropriate for my audience and purpose? Does each sentence make sense on its own?
❏ A sentence's subject and verb agree in person and number. See pages 456–459.

❏ Verb tenses are used according to academic conventions. See pages 460–461.

❏ The tenses of verbs change only when necessary. See pages 462–463.

❏ The voice and level of formality in sentences is consistent. See pages 464–465.

❏ Have I checked for sentence fragments, run-ons, and comma splices, to be sure I've only used them if I can justify them rhetorically? See pages 466–471.

❏ In any sentence that uses a pronoun, the pronoun has a clear antecedent with which it agrees in person and number. See pages 472–473.

❏ Modifiers in sentences are placed so readers can tell easily what is being modified. See pages 474–475.

Have I integrated quotations of others' work into my writing—while making it clear when I am using the ideas or words of others?
❏ See pages 298–309.

Have I documented my sources according to expected conventions?
❏ Pages 329–395 show documentation in the MLA style; APA style is on pages 396–438 and 439–443; and CMS style is on pages 444–448.

Have I checked my writing to remove all possible biased references to others?
❏ See pages 276–287.

HOW TO PROOFREAD

PROOFREADING IS ABOUT PUNCTUATION AND INDIVIDUAL WORDS

Proofreading puts the final shine on your writing. Like that last look in the mirror before you step out with someone important to you, proofreading checks that all the details are in place.

Like that last look in the mirror, then, proofreading requires that you know what details to check. The list to the right offers you the details readers expect in formal, academic writing.

IF YOU GREW UP SPEAKING A LANGUAGE OTHER THAN ENGLISH...

Start proofreading as soon as you have any writing that seems solid to you; don't wait until the paper is finished. If you leave all the proofreading until the end, you may not have enough time or you may find it too overwhelming and discouraging.

If you know someone whose proofreading abilities you respect, ask that person to proofread and to note each change (and reason for change) while you watch and listen.

TIPS: PROOFREADING

- Leave yourself time to proofread. You need fresh eyes to see where you have left a word out that your brain fills in for you.

- If you work on the computer, proofread on screen but then also proofread a paper copy so that you see your paper differently.

- Proofread more than once. Each time focus on one of the elements to the right. If you know the elements that cause you trouble, move through them from most to least important.

- Proofread line by line, using a blank sheet of paper to cover the rest of the paper so that you stay visually focused.

- When you are checking spelling, move backwards through your paper, word by word: you will see your words out of order and so are more likely to see misspellings.

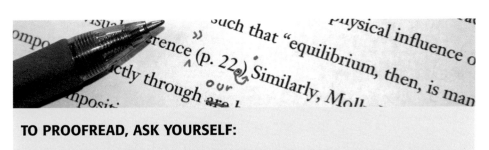

TO PROOFREAD, ASK YOURSELF:

Is every word spelled and capitalized according to convention? Are the other mechanics of my paper appropriate for my purpose and context?

❑ For spelling, see pages 586–587.

❑ For capitalization, see pages 588–259.

❑ For other details of mechanics, see pages 585 and 590–593.

Did I leave out any words?

Only careful proofreading, following the approaches in the Tip box to the left, can help you find where you might have inadvertently left out a word.

Have I used the right word?

Wrong words result from two things: a spellchecker suggests a replacement word that is incorrect (*their* instead *there*, or *to* instead of *too*) or you are not yet familiar enough with the conventions of formal writing or of a discipline to know the expected word.

❑ To catch wrong words of the first kind, use spellcheckers carefully (⟶ see page 587) and proofread carefully, following the approaches in the Tip box to the left.

❑ To catch wrong words of the second kind, find someone who knows your audience's expectations, and ask that person to read while looking for any such words.

Is my punctuation conventional?

❑ Check that you have apostrophes where needed in possessives and in contractions. See page 569.

❑ Do you have commas before coordinating conjunctions in compound sentences? See pages 540–541.

❑ Do you have commas after nonessential information at the beginning of a sentence? See pages 543–546.

Are my quotations punctuated according to convention?

❑ See pages 532–533; pages 578–579 contain a chart to help you punctuate quotations conventionally.

EDITING AND PROOFREADING
SUBJECT-VERB AGREEMENT

In sentences that fit with academic expectations, the subject has the same person and number as the verb.

To determine whether your writing meets this expectation, you need to determine a sentence's subject and its verb, to see if they agree.

The information to the right will help you figure this out.

THE PATTERN

SUBJECTS AND VERBS AGREE IN PERSON AND NUMBER.

correct
He loves me.
third person, singular   third person, singular

incorrect
He love me.
third person, singular   second person, singular

correct
We are addicted to oil.
first person, plural   first person, plural

incorrect
We is addicted to oil.
first person, plural   third person, singular

correct
The senator and her brothers are going to jail.
third person, plural   third person, plural

incorrect
The senator and her brothers is going to jail.
third person, plural   third person, singular

HOW TO EDIT FOR SUBJECT-VERB AGREEMENT: PERSON

1 Identify a sentence's subject (see below).

2 Determine the subject's person: Is it first, second, or third person? (→ See page 458.)

3 Find the sentence's verb, and identify its person: Is it first, second, or third person? (→ See pages 496–497.)

4 Do the subject and verb have the same person?

YES? Your sentence is fine.

NO? Use the information on pages494–497 to create the appropriate form of the verb.

HOW TO EDIT FOR SUBJECT-VERB AGREEMENT: NUMBER

1 Identify a sentence's subject (see below).

2 Determine the subject's number: is it singular or plural? (→ See pages 458–459.)

3 Find the sentence's verb, and identify its number: Is it singular or plural? (→ See pages 496–497.)

4 Are the subject and verb the same number?

YES? Your sentence is fine.

NO? Use the information on pages 494–497 to create the appropriate verb.

1 IDENTIFYING A SENTENCE'S SUBJECT

The information on pages 512–513 can help you identify the subject of a sentence.

Sentences that contain prepositional phrases, however, can confuse writers trying to identify the subject because they add nouns to the sentence in addition to the subject. The following steps will help you identify the subject.

1 Underline any prepositional phrases (→ see pages 500–501) or other descriptive phrases that come before the verb.

The boy <u>with the gloves</u> dances particularly well.
The record <u>that he set for driving across country</u> is thirty-one hours.

2 Rewrite the sentence *without* the phrases you underlined. This should put the subject next to the verb.

The <u>boy</u> dances particularly well.
The <u>record</u> is thirty-one hours.

Help with subject-verb agreement continues on the next page…

2 DETERMINING THE SUBJECT'S PERSON

Use the grid below to determine the person of the subject you've identified.

	singular	plural
First person	I	we
Second person	you	you
Third person	he, she, it	they
	All nouns are also third person:	
	woman, cat	women, cats
	The President of the United States	
	furniture, justice	

3 DETERMINING WHETHER THE SUBJECT IS SINGULAR OR PLURAL

Use the information about the plurals of nouns on page 482 to help you determine the number of the subject. Keep an eye out, however, for the following kinds of subjects, whose number might not be immediately obvious.

COMPOUND SUBJECTS JOINED BY *and*

Compound subjects joined by *and* are usually plural:
Leela and Joe work on their homework together.

There are exceptions:

• If the compound subject names what we consider to be one object or activity—as with *peanut butter and jelly* or *drinking and driving*—it is singular. (Company names using *and* are also singular, as with a law firm named **Black and Bland**.)

• If the compound subject refers to the same person or thing, then it is singular:
  My best friend and advisor is my father.

• If the compound subject is preceded by *each* or *every*, then it is singular:
  Each dog, cat, and pet ferret is to be registered.
  Every girl and boy deserves health insurance.

COMPOUND SUBJECTS JOINED BY *or, nor, either… or,* OR *neither… nor*

The number of the subject is determined by the noun closest to the verb:

A dog or crows get into our garbage every week. Because *crows* is closest to the verb and is plural, the subject of this sentence is plural.

Crows or a dog gets into our garbage every week. Because *a dog* is closest to the verb and is singular, the subject of this sentence is singular.

SUBJECTS THAT USE INDEFINITE PRONOUNS

The indefinite pronouns (→ see page 485) *anybody, anyone, anything, each, everybody, everyone, everything, nobody, no one, someone, somebody,* and *something* are singular:

Everyone in my class is late with homework! • Everything has gone wrong.

The indefinite pronouns *both* and *many* are plural:

Both motorcycles were broken. • Many have visited our town.

The indefinite pronouns *all, any, none,* and *some* can be singular or plural, depending on the noun or pronoun to which they refer:

SINGULAR	All my money goes to rent.	Some of his dinner was overcooked.
PLURAL	All my nieces go fishing.	Some of his books were lost.

COLLECTIVE NOUNS

Nouns referring to collections of people—*audience, class, committee, crowd, family, group, public, team*—are usually singular because the collection is usually described as acting as one.

The audience was delighted by the performance.

When such a nouns refers to its members acting individually, however, it is plural:

The audience were looking at each other.

CLAUSES AND PHRASES

When a sentence's subject is a clause or a phrase, the subject is singular:

What frustrates me is my math homework.

Going to the dentist makes me nervous.

If the verb is a form of *be* and the subject complement (→ see page 515) is plural, then the verb is plural even if the subject is singular:

What frustrates me are inconsiderate drivers.

WATCH OUT FOR THIS!

Phrases like *along with, in addition to,* and *together with* can sound as though they build compound nouns—but they do not.

Hasan, together with Kim, is driving to Appleton. The subject of this sentence is *Hasan; together with Kim* is an adjectival phrase.

EDITING AND PROOFREADING
ACADEMIC VERB TENSES

Because verb tenses (→ see pages 494–497) convey so much information, writers use them to show relationships among the events about which they write. In turn, readers understand verb tenses as signals that help them understand the relationships and order of events.

The descriptions below focus on verb tenses in academic writing. Look at different types of writing—lab reports, summaries and responses to literature, research proposals—to learn what verb tenses tend to be used in each type of writing.

THE SIMPLE PRESENT
is used to...

- describe the present situation.
  Conservationists at the Masai Mara work hard to protect the wildebeest from poachers.

- generalize.
  Studies show that chronic stress contributes to heart attacks and other diseases.

- describe the contents of a book, movie, or other text.
  In his thesis, "Intimate Relationships with Artificial Partners," Levy conjectures that robots will become so human-like that people will fall in love with them.

THE PRESENT PROGRESSIVE
is used to...

- describe actions in progress at the moment of speaking.
  Women are dying from complicated pregnancies and childbirth at almost the same rate they were in 1990.

- compare two present actions. One action is described in simple present, the other in present progressive.
  Children with strict parents follow rules when under supervision, but when their parents are not watching they often engage in reckless actions.

THE PRESENT PERFECT

is used to...

- describe actions begun in the past but not completed.
  The once vanished gray wolf has made a comeback in the Northern Rockies.

- describe actions begun at an unspecified past time.
  Over half of adolescents have tried alcohol and drugs at least once.

- introduce a topic.
  Once a disease of the Western world, breast cancer has become a global concern.

THE SIMPLE PAST

is used to...

- describe completed events or states.
  Charles M. Schulz drew "Peanuts" for nearly half a century.

- report past research or events, summarize lab or research results, and to give narrative examples.
  Steven C. Amstrup of the United States Geological Survey led a recent exhaustive study of polar bears.

THE PAST PERFECT

is used to...

- compare two past events. The past perfect signals the event that happened first.
  The protesters were demanding the freedom and democracy for which their parents had fought.

THE SIMPLE FUTURE

is used to describe...

- intentions and promises.
  In this paper I will explore the relations between media portrayals of men and men's body images.

- predictions.
  American employers will hire 270,000 fewer IT workers this year than they did in 2003.

TIP: HOW TO EDIT FOR ACADEMIC VERB TENSES

1 Underline or highlight each sentence's main verb. The main verb has a subject. Each sentence should contain a complete verb phrase: **Main verb** or **Helping verb + Main verb.**

2 Identify the tense of the verb. See pages 494–497 for help in identifying the tense.

3 For each sentence, ask if your verb tense signals your desired meaning.

SHIFTS IN VERB TENSES

THE PATTERN

CONSISTENT VERB TENSES CREATE COHERENCE

If you shift verb tenses in a sentence, you shift from one sense of time to another. Readers can be confused by shifts in verb tense because they might not know if the actions of a sentence happened in the past, present, or future.

incorrect Jenna sent me a letter about her Botswana trip; she says many companies
simple past tense   simple present tense
are coming to start uranium mining.

correct Jenna sent me a letter about her Botswana trip; she said many companies
simple past tense   simple past tense
are coming to start uranium mining.

A CONSISTENT TENSE FOR WRITING ABOUT FICTION

When you are summarizing the plot or describing the actions of fiction, write as though the events are happening in an eternal present, and put all descriptions in present tense.

In Colette's novels *Cheri* and *The Last of Cheri*, the character Léa works hard to appear and act young at the start but by the end she is gray-haired and stout.

BUT SOMETIMES YOU NEED TO CHANGE TENSES...

Because writing often involves describing relations among events that occured at different times, you sometimes need to change tenses, as this example shows:

A new study offers some relief to parents who worry that their children will never eat anything but chocolate milk, Gummi vitamins, and the occasional grape. Researchers examined the eating habits of 5,390 pairs of twins between eight and eleven years old and found children's aversions to trying new foods are mostly inherited. The message to parents: It's not your cooking, it's your genes.

Present tense
The present tense verbs describe how a study can ease parental worries now.

Past tense
The past tense verbs describe the actions that had to have taken place before the study could be useful now, in the present.

Future tense
The future tense describes parents' fears about their children's future actions.

USING PRESENT PERFECT AND PAST PERFECT TO INDICATE TIME DIFFERENCES

Writers can show relationships between actions or states by shifting from simple or progressive present tense to present perfect; they can also shift from simple or progressive past tense to past perfect. The perfect tenses signal that the action or state they describe occurred before the action or state in the other tense.

Present perfect maintains a present focus; past perfect maintains a past focus.

SWITCHING TENSES WHEN THE TIME FOCUS IS THE PRESENT

The homeless can be roughly divided into two groups: those who have had homelessness forced upon them and want nothing more than to escape it, and those who have chosen it for themselves and now accept it, or in some cases, embrace it.

Present tense   **Present perfect tense**

This sentence focuses on a present distinction; for that distinction to be possible, however, the people being described had to have become homeless in the past.

SWITCHING TENSES WHEN THE TIME FOCUS IS THE PAST

In 1965, a new drug was introduced that is responsible for much of the homeless problem we see today. The drug is Thorazine. Before it was introduced, people diagnosed with mental illness, particularly schizophrenia, had been considered incurable and had been confined to mental institutions.

Past progressive tense

Past perfect tense

This sentence focuses on a distinction that occured in the past. The writer uses the past progressive tense to describe how a drug was introduced in the past; the writer then uses the past perfect tense to show conditions that happened even further in the past than the drug.

TIP: HOW TO EDIT FOR SHIFTS IN VERB TENSES

1 Using different color pens, highlight each verb tense in its own color.

2 Where you see shifts, ask whether readers will understand why the tense shifts.

3 If needed, do one of the following:

- Add words or time expressions that signal a tense shift.
- Change one verb to present or past perfect to indicate that an action or state occurred prior to another.
- Change the tense of the verb to maintain a consistent time focus.

→ See pages 494–497 for help naming verb tenses.

EDITING AND PROOFREADING
SHIFTS IN GRAMMATICAL FORMS

Shifts occur when a sentence begins with one grammatical form but ends with another. The conventions of formal, academic writing call for none of these shifts.

SHIFTS BETWEEN DIRECT AND INDIRECT DISCOURSE

When you quote someone's words directly, you are using *direct discourse*:

Harriet's sister asked, "Are you going to the store without me?"

In *indirect discourse*, you report what someone else said:

Harriet's sister wanted to know if we were going to the store without her.

A convention of formal written English is not to shift from one of these forms to another in a sentence:

Harriet's sister wanted to know are we going to the store without her.

SHIFTS IN LEVELS OF FORMALITY

Even in academic writing, there are levels of formality. Convention says to choose one level and stay with it.

FORMAL WRITING

Coltrane's saxophone playing is tender but has a searching quality, and this searching is perhaps the most salient characteristic of both his work and his life.

LESS FORMAL WRITING

Saxophones can whisper or shriek, breathe warmth or spit fire, and a quick listen to John Coltrane's 1965 album, *Transition*, will disabuse anyone of the misimpression that the saxophone is limited to that canned sound you heard during the credits of *L.A. Law*.

MIXED LEVELS

Coltrane's saxophone playing is tender, but there is a searching quality to it and sometimes his changes can really bug a listener.

TIP: PURPOSEFUL SHIFTS

Sometimes shifts are required if you are to make the meaning you want in a sentence. To be sure that you use shifts only when necessary, follow this rule: When you are checking your writing and find any of the shifts we have described on these pages, remove the shift unless you can give a solid reason why the shift is necessary.

SHIFTS IN VOICE

THE PATTERN

Is the subject of a sentence performing an action or being acted upon? When the subject is performing an action, the sentence is in *active voice*; when the subject is being acted upon, the sentence is in *passive voice*.

ACTIVE VOICE

Jade fed the macaw.
subject

We caught and ate some of the mice that came into our camp.
subject

PASSIVE VOICE

The macaw was fed by Jade.
subject

Who ate the mice? The sentence doesn't say...

Some of the mice that came into our camp were caught and eaten.
subject

Active voice uses active verbs, which convey movement and energy (→ see page 255). Passive voice uses forms of *be*, and can also need a preposition before the noun that explains who performed the action—and so passive sentences tend to be wordy and slower to read.

The passive voice is useful, however, when a writer wants to avoid naming who performed an action—as in the sentence above about the mice. Scientific and technical writing often uses passive voice because it can seem fact-based and objective. Writers present their research and conclusions without attribution, so the writing appears to be unshaped by individual bias.

→ For more on uses of active and passive voices, see pages 238–239.

MIXED VOICE

When writers mix active and passive voice together, the resulting sentences are often wordy and awkward.

Jade fed the macaw even though it had been fed earlier by David.

When we had no food, some of the mice that came into our camp were caught and eaten.

CONSISTENT VOICE

Sentences with consistent voice are both easier to understand and have more direct movement than the mixed voice sentences. In formal written English, readers expect consistent voice:

Jade fed the macaw even though David had fed it earlier.

When we had no food, we caught and ate the mice that came into our camp.

SENTENCE FRAGMENTS

A sentence fragment is an incomplete sentence.

And hid under the steps.

Because Vered said so.

Where I watched my father sleep.

A capital letter and appropriate punctuation do not turn a string of words into a sentence. A sentence, grammatically, is an independent clause, which we describe on page 517.

Your brother hid under the steps.

Vered said so.

In the hospital I watched my father sleep.

TIP: FINDING SENTENCE FRAGMENTS

If you are uncertain whether a phrase is a sentence or not, try saying it aloud with *I believe that...* in front of the phrase. If the result sounds odd to you, it probably is a fragment, and worth checking with the steps to the right.

STEPS FOR DETERMINING IF YOU HAVE A SENTENCE—OR A FRAGMENT

Apply each of the three steps below to a sentence to be sure it is not a fragment.

Identify the sentence you think might be a fragment:

	EXAMPLE 1 **Danced in the streets.**	EXAMPLE 2 **The computer on the desk.**	EXAMPLE 3 **Unless there is old wiring in the house.**	EXAMPLE 4 **Nevertheless, they plotted.**
1 Is there a subject? → See pages 512–513.	**NO, there is no subject. THIS IS A FRAGMENT.**	**YES**, there is a subject: *The computer*. Move to the next step.	**YES**, there is a subject: *there*. Move to the next step.	**YES**, there is a subject: *they*. Move to the next step.
2 Is there a predicate? → See pages 512–515.		**NO, there is no predicate. THIS IS A FRAGMENT.**	**YES**, there is a predicate: *is*. Move to the next step.	**YES**, there is a predicate: *plotted*. Move to the next step.
3 Do the words make up a dependent clause without an attached independent clause? → See page 469.			**YES, this is a dependent clause with no attached independent clause. THIS IS A FRAGMENT.**	**NO. THIS IS A SENTENCE.**
	→ To fix fragments that lack subjects, see page 468.	→ To fix fragments that lack predicates, see page 468.	→ To fix fragments that are dependent clauses, see page 469.	

FIXING FRAGMENTS THAT LACK SUBJECTS

Fix fragments that lack subjects with one of the following two approaches:

ADDING A SUBJECT TO A FRAGMENT

These phrases are fragments because they lack subjects:

Danced in the street.

Sensing their delight in winning.

To add a subject, ask *Who is doing the action?* and then give that information:

Mary and Elaine danced in the street.

Christa was sensing their delight in winning. [OR] Christa sensed their delight in winning.

As with the second example, note that you may have to modify the verb when you add a subject.

JOINING A FRAGMENT TO A SENTENCE

Often people inadvertently write fragments in longer descriptions:

Mary and Elaine won the guitar contest last June. They were so happy they threw a party. Danced in the street.

The **danced in the street** fragment can be joined to the sentence before it with a coordinating conjunction:

Mary and Elaine won the guitar contest last June. They were so happy they threw a party and danced in the street.

→ We discuss coordinating conjunctions on page 502 and pages 540–541.

FIXING FRAGMENTS THAT LACK PREDICATES

Fix fragments that lack predicates with one of the following two approaches:

ADDING A PREDICATE TO A FRAGMENT

These phrases are fragments because they lack predicates:

The computer on the desk.

Only the lonely.

To add a predicate, ask *What is happening to the objects named the fragment?*—and then give that information:

The computer on the desk was broken.

Only the lonely know how I feel tonight.

JOINING A FRAGMENT TO A SENTENCE

Just as with fragments that lack subjects, fragments without predicates often occur when people write descriptions:

Nobody was out walking after midnight. Only the lonely.

The **only the lonely** fragment can be joined to the sentence before it by making it into the subject:

Only the lonely were out walking after midnight.

Or you can use a conjunction to join the fragment to the end of the sentence:

Nobody was out walking after midnight, except for the lonely.

→ We discuss conjunctions on pages 502–505.

FIXING FRAGMENTS THAT ARE DEPENDENT CLAUSES WITHOUT ATTACHED INDEPENDENT CLAUSES

This fragment type is a common problem for those learning to write formal prose.

THE PATTERN

DEPENDENT CLAUSES

To recognize these fragments, you need to be able to recognize dependent clauses. Dependent clauses begin in two ways:

- with one of the *subordinating conjunctions*, which we list on page 504.

  rather than build a road

  although we lived under the Nazi regime for only one year

  when the people of this part of Peru were building their cities

- with one of the *relative pronouns*, which we describe on page 486.

  who regularly sat in hot tubs   *whom* he had met in high school

Anytime you see a phrase that begins with a subordinating conjunction or a relative pronoun, it cannot stand on its own; each gray text above is a fragment.

Fix fragments that are dependent clauses with one of the following approaches:

JOIN SUBORDINATE CLAUSE FRAGMENTS TO INDEPENDENT CLAUSES

Rather than build a road, they installed a tram over the trees.

Although my family lived under the Nazi regime for only one year, I will never forget the fear and humiliation I experienced that year in Vienna.

When the people of this part of Peru were building their cities, there was only one other urban complex on earth.

REMOVE THE SUBORDINATING CONJUNCTION TO MAKE A SENTENCE

Note that this gives you two sentences, separated by a period:

We lived under the Nazi regime for only one year. I will never forget the fear and humiliation I experienced that year in Vienna.

INSERT A CLAUSE BEGINNING WITH A RELATIVE PRONOUN INTO AN INDEPENDENT CLAUSE

All the men who regularly sit in hot tubs showed signs of infertility.

Talib Kweli began recording with Mos Def, whom he had met in high school.

RUN-ON SENTENCES

Run-on sentences result when you put two independent clauses together with unconventional or no punctuation.

→ See page 517 to learn about independent clauses.

Run-on sentences have two varieties:

FUSED SENTENCES

A fused sentence has no punctuation between its two independent clauses:

> Flower was one of the meerkats on the Animal Planet documentary series *Meerkat Manor* she died after being bitten by a cobra.

COMMA SPLICES

A comma splice puts a comma between its two independent clauses:

> Flower was one of the meerkats on the Animal Planet documentary series *Meerkat Manor*, she died after being bitten by a cobra.

Explore these topics online:

Punctuation: Commas

www.mycomplab.com

TIP: FINDING COMMA SPLICES

In your paper, look for longer sentences that have a comma roughly in the middle. When you find such a sentence, ask these two questions:

1 On either side of the comma is there an independent clause? (→ See page 517 to learn about independent clauses.)

2 Is there a coordinating conjunction immediately after the comma? (→ See page 502 for a list of coordinating conjunctions.)

If you answer **YES** to #1 and **NO** to #2, then you have a comma splice, and need to fix it with one of the strategies on the opposite page.

ONE WAY COMMA SPLICES HAPPEN

Conjunctive adverbs (see page 505) imply a logical relation between the two independent clauses they join. When writers use conjunctive adverbs, they can hear the logic—but miss that they are working with two independent clauses that can't be joined with a comma.

> Corporations expect their employees to move in response to the corporations' needs, consequently, employees tend not to live where they grew up.

GIVING RUN-ON SENTENCES CONVENTIONAL PUNCTUATION

Five strategies help you convert run-on sentences into expected academic forms.

1 MAKE THE TWO INDEPENDENT CLAUSES INTO TWO SENTENCES

Flower was one of the meerkats on the Animal Planet documentary series *Meerkat Manor*. She died after being bitten by a cobra in South Africa.

This is the easiest strategy: Put a period between the two independent clauses. (Be sure to capitalize the first letter of the second sentence.)

2 JOIN THE INDEPENDENT CLAUSES WITH A SEMICOLON OR COLON

Flower was one of the meerkats on the Animal Planet documentary series *Meerkat Manor*; she died after being bitten by a cobra.

Corporations expect their employees to move in response to the corporations' needs; consequently, employees tend not to live where they grew up.

In less formal writing, you can also join independent clauses with a dash.

→ See page 459 to learn about joining independent clauses with semicolons.

→ See page 555 to learn about joining independent clauses with colons.

3 JOIN THE INDEPENDENT CLAUSES WITH A COMMA AND A COORDINATING CONJUNCTION

Flower was one of the meerkats on the Animal Planet documentary series *Meerkat Manor*, but she died after being bitten by a cobra.

The coordinating conjunctions are **and**, **but**, **or**, **nor**, **for**, **so**, and **yet**; we describe coordinating conjunctions on pages 502 and 540–541.

4 MAKE ONE OF THE INDEPENDENT CLAUSES INTO A DEPENDENT CLAUSE

Flower, who was a meerkat on the Animal Planet documentary series *Meerkat Manor*, died after being bitten by a cobra.

→ Page 469 discuss dependent clauses.

5 RESTRUCTURE THE TWO INDEPENDENT CLAUSES INTO ONE INDEPENDENT CLAUSE

Flower, one of the meerkats on the Animal Planet documentary series *Meerkat Manor*, died after being bitten by a cobra in South Africa.

You might be able to turn one of the independent clauses into a phrase that you can then place next to the word it modifies.

PRONOUN REFERENCE AND AGREEMENT

TO USE PRONOUNS CONVENTIONALLY, YOU HAVE TO KNOW ABOUT ANTECEDENTS

The person or thing to which a pronoun refers is its antecedent.

In the sentences below, the antecedent is underlined.

The dog wasn't gray; it was black.

Marina came prepared: She brought her toolbox.

Computers change time: They speed it up.

Jamshed and I worked and then we ate lunch.

TIP: HOW TO EDIT FOR PRONOUN REFERENCE AND AGREEMENT

- Circle every pronoun in your paper.
- Search for the pronoun's antecedent.
- If you *can't* find an antecedent, insert one beforehand or change the pronoun to a noun.
- If the pronoun could have two different antecedents, edit the sentence to clarify the antecedent, as we show to the right.
- If you *can* find an antecedent, be sure it and your pronoun agree in number and person.

PRONOUN REFERENCE

Check your writing for sentences in which a pronoun could have two antecedents. Revise the sentences to remove the ambiguity.

Marisa told Gretel that she had passed the class after all.

Marisa told Gretel, "I passed the class after all."

After Mabel put the book in her bag, she couldn't find it.

After Mabel put it in her bag, she couldn't find the book.

PRONOUN AGREEMENT

Pronouns must agree in person, number, and gender with their antecedents.

THE PATTERN

AGREEMENT IN NUMBER

incorrect If a person wants to be a good citizen, they should vote.
third person, singular   *third person, plural*

correct **If people want to be good citizens, they should vote.**
third person, plural   *third person, plural*

AGREEMENT IN PERSON

incorrect Mental health providers must understand the hidden impacts
third person, plural

of trauma on families; if you don't treat children, you can harm
    second person, plural   *second person, plural*

their development.

correct **Mental health providers must understand the hidden impacts**
third person, plural

of trauma on families; if they don't treat children, the children's
    thirdd person, plural

development can be harmed.

Note that, with the second example, you might need to revise a sentence in order to keep the pronoun reference clear when you fix pronoun agreement.

Use this chart to help you track that you are using pronouns of the same number and person in your sentences.

	singular number	plural number
First person	I, me, my	we, us, our
Second person	you, your	you, your
Third person	he, she, it, one, anyone	they, them, their
	him, her, his, her, its	

GRAMMAR
MISPLACED AND DANGLING MODIFIERS

Modifier is the collective name for adjectives, adjectival phrases, adverbs, and adverbial phrases.

Modifiers make writing concrete and engaging—if readers can tell what words are being modified. Unfortunately, writers can easily put modifiers in odd places, which is why we offer the following suggestions.

PUT MODIFIERS CLOSE TO THE WORDS THEY MODIFY

In this sentence—

Covered in chocolate icing, my friends will love this cake.

—the friends sound like people we should approach with spoons in hand. When the adjectival phrase *covered in chocolate icing* is moved closer to the noun it is meant to modify, the result—

My friends will love this cake covered in chocolate icing.

—is clearer about the icing's location.

You are most likely to produce such slips when you write sentences with several modifiers. The following sentence has two modifiers (**all over Europe** and **passing close to earth**) placed to make it sound as though Europe passed close to earth in 1577:

The Great Comet of 1577 was viewed by people all over Europe passing close to earth.

When **passing close to earth** is moved closer to the noun phrase it should modify, the sentence is clearer:

Passing close to earth, the Great Comet of 1577 was viewed by people all over Europe.

TIP: HOW TO CHECK MODIFIERS

Modification slips are easy to produce as you write—and easy to fix. Fixing them requires finding them, however, and finding them takes time and careful reading.

To check your modifiers:

1 Underline every modifier in your writing and then draw a line from each to the word it modifies.

2 Move modifiers that are far from the words they modify closer to those words.

3 If the underlined word is a limiting modifier (→ see page 475), is it placed so that the sentence means what you desire it to?

4 If you cannot find a noun to which the modifier refers, you have a dangling modifier. Choose one of the options on the opposite page to fix the dangling modifier.

PAY PARTICULAR ATTENTION TO LIMITING MODIFIERS

Limiting modifiers are words such as *almost*, *even*, *hardly*, *just*, *nearly*, *not*, *only*, and *simply*. They can be placed almost anywhere in a sentence, which makes them dangerous: Their placement can change a sentence's meaning.

For example, this sentence says that Luther thought about donating his collection, but didn't:

Luther almost donated his entire collection of LPs to the auction.

This sentence says that Luther **did** donate a large part of his collection:

Luther donated almost his entire collection of LPs to the auction.

Check each instance of limiting modifiers in your writing to be sure your sentences say what you want.

MOVE DISRUPTIVE MODIFIERS

Modifiers are disruptive when they disrupt a sentence's grammatical elements. In the first sentence below, a long phrase creates a distracting pause for readers between the sentence's subject and predicate:

Palenquero, although its grammar is so different that Spanish speakers cannot understand it, is thought to be the only Spanish-based Creole language in Latin America.

Moving the phrase makes the sentence easier to read:

Although its grammar is so different that Spanish speakers cannot understand it, Palenquero is thought to be the only Spanish-based Creole language in Latin America.

FIX DANGLING MODIFIERS

A modifier **dangles** when it cannot logically modify anything in its sentence. For example, unless the writer of this sentence has an unusual dog—

Reading a book, my dog rested her head on my knee.

—the sentence describes an impossible situation because the position of the modifier *reading a book* implies that the dog can read.

In addition, the person we assume is reading is not made explicit as a noun in this sentence. Because there is no such noun, the sentence cannot be fixed by moving the modifier closer to the nonexistent noun.

Because dangling modifers cannot be fixed by being moved, there are two other options for fixing them:

1 Revise the dangling modifier to make explicit the noun that is to be modified:

As I was reading a book, my dog rested her head on my knee.

2 Revise the sentence so that there is a noun to be modified:

Reading a book, I was warmed when my dog rested her head on my knee.

GRAMMAR

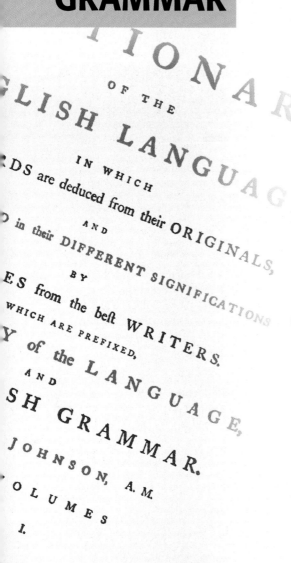

WHAT IS GRAMMAR?

The grammars that appear in handbooks and textbooks attempt to capture language patterns that develop as humans talk and write. Not only do grammars change as times change but they shift among groups of people.

The grammar we present in the next pages is **the grammar of academic American English writing**. You may have grown up into this pattern if you grew up where people write and read a lot. You may have grown up where other patterns—other grammars—of English are used. You may have grown up in another language.

No matter what your language background, studying the current patterns in academic American English writing can help you move between different grammar communities and help you decide how you want to shape the words you use to reach others.

■ ■ ■

The illustration to the right shows the basic parts—and how they build—of English sentences.

Like any illustration, it is not perfect, but it is accurate enough for you to see how sentences are broken down into clauses, subjects and predicates, noun and verb phrases, and then the parts of speech.

You can also move from the bottom up, to see how words—the parts of speech—come together to form phrases and then subjects and predicates and then clauses and finally sentences.

The nineteenth-century Society for the Diffusion of Really Useful Knowledge published and distributed widely *The Penny Magazine* and *The Penny Cyclopedia*, because its members were worried about the reading practices of working-class audiences.

SENTENCES
are made of...

The nineteenth-century Society for the Diffusion of Really Useful Knowledge published and distributed widely *The Penny Magazine* and *The Penny Cyclopedia*

because its members were worried about the reading practices of working-class audiences.

CLAUSES, of which there are two kinds,
both of which are made of...

The nineteenth-century Society for the Diffusion of Really Useful Knowledge

its members

SUBJECTS,
which are made of...

published and distributed widely *The Penny Magazine* and *The Penny Cyclopedia*

were worried about the reading practices of working-class audiences.

PREDICATES,
which are made of...

The nineteenth-century Society for the Diffusion of Really Useful Knowledge

The Penny Magazine and *The Penny Cyclopedia*

its members

the reading practices of working-class audiences

NOUN PHRASES,
which can be made of...

NOUNS: Society, Diffusion, Knowledge, members, *Magazine, Cyclopedia,* practices, audiences
PRONOUNS: its
ARTICLES: the
ADJECTIVES: nineteenth-century, Useful, working-class
ADVERBS: Really
CONJUNCTIONS: and
PREPOSITIONS: of

published and distributed widely

were worried

VERB PHRASES,
which can be made of...

VERBS: published, distributed, worried
HELPING VERBS: were
ADVERBS: widely
CONJUNCTIONS: and

Nouns, pronouns, articles, adjectives, adverbs, conjunctions, prepositions, and verbs, taken all together, are referred to as

THE PARTS OF SPEECH.

GRAMMAR
PARTS OF SPEECH

The parts of speech are the most basic units of sentences: The parts of speech are the individual words of sentences, named according to the functions they serve in sentences.

The illustration to the right gives a quick introduction to the parts of speech; on the following pages, we go into the parts of speech in more detail.

■ ■ ■

Keep in mind that identifying a word as a particular part of speech depends on how the word is used in a sentence. In the following sentences—

I fish for my dinner.

There aren't many fish in this lake.

I do not like to bait fish hooks.

—the word **fish** serves first as a verb, then as a noun, and then as an adjective.

■ ■ ■

There is one part of speech that we do not mention in the illustration because it does not show up much in academic writing. This kind of word usually stands alone as a sentence:

INTERJECTIONS

Explore these topics online:

Grammar: Parts of Speech

www.mycomplab.com

Words that describe the person, place, thing, or idea being discussed are **NOUNS.**

Words that describe what the person, place, thing, or idea is doing are **VERBS.**

Alice walks.

She walks.

A certain kind of noun that refers back to an earlier mentioned noun is a **PRONOUN.**

Words that give more details about nouns are **ARTICLES** and **ADJECTIVES.**

Words that give more detail about how an action is done (where, when, or in what manner) are **ADVERBS.**

The smiling woman walked happily yesterday.

Words that allow us to talk about more than one noun or action at a time are **CONJUNCTIONS.**

Alice and Chuck walk and talk.

Words that allow us to describe how the actors and actions in a sentence are placed in space or time are **PREPOSITIONS.**

After saying good-bye, Alice walked into the store.

Prepositions are always the first words of phrases; those phrases can tell us more about nouns (in what shape was Alice?), in which case they are **ADJECTIVAL PREPOSITIONAL PHRASES**...

Out of breath, Alice leaned against the wall .

... or those phrases can tell us more about verbs (where did Alice lean?), in which case they are **ADVERBIAL PREPOSITIONAL PHRASES.**

GRAMMAR—PARTS OF SPEECH
NOUNS

Nouns name people, animals, places, things, and ideas or concepts.

Most nouns are **common nouns**; when a noun names a particular person or place, then it is called a **proper noun** and is capitalized.

PEOPLE

ANIMALS

common noun	person	woman	dog
proper noun	Philip Andrews	Doctor Lincoln	Champion Frida

Singular nouns name one person, object, or idea (as in all the examples above). **Plural nouns** name more than one. Most nouns become plural when you add **-s** to the end, but some nouns have irregular plural forms, as in the examples to the right.

common noun plural	people	women	dogs

→ See page 482 to learn more about making nouns plural.

PLACES

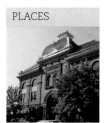

THINGS

IDEAS OR CONCEPTS

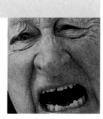

building

leaf

religion

emotion

City Hall

Ficus repens

Buddism

buildings

leaves

religions

emotions

IF YOU GREW UP SPEAKING A LANGUAGE OTHER THAN ENGLISH…

→ English differentiates between two kinds of nouns—count and noncount nouns—that challenge many writers. See pages 489–490.

MAKING NOUNS PLURAL

In English, a noun's ending usually indicates whether it is singular or plural.

If you have any questions about a noun's plural form, a dictionary will show you the plural form.

PLURAL ENDINGS

SINGULAR	PLURAL
-s	
a boy	the boys
the site	many sites
freedom	seven freedoms
my radio	their radios
father-in-law	fathers-in-law

If a noun ends in an *-o* preceded by a **vowel**, it usually takes an *-s* to make it plural.

With compound hyphenated words, add *-s* to the main noun, even if that noun is not at the end of the word.

-es	
a box	six boxes
my church	our churches
one potato	two potatoes

Nouns that end in *-s, -sh, -ch*, and *-x* add *-es* to become plural.

If a noun ends in an *-o* preceded by a **consonant**, it usually takes an *-es* to make a plural.

-ies	
the summary	several summaries
a boundary	the boundaries

Nouns that end in *-y* lose the *-y* and add *-ies* to become plural.

-ves	
my life	our lives
a calf	six calves

Nouns that end in *-f* or *-fe* replace the *-f* or *-fe* with *-ves* to become plural.

other endings	
one medium	the media
the analysis	the analyses
one criterion	three criteria
his child	his children

Sometimes the plurals of words that derive from other languages take their plural form from the original language.

changed form	
one man	many men
a mouse	three mice

Words that have been in use since the beginning of language often change their forms to make plurals.

no change	
one moose	two moose
one deer	many deer

Many names for large animals keep the same form in both singular and plural.

MAKING NOUNS POSSESSIVE

A possessive noun comes before another noun, and its possessive form indicates possession of or other close association with the noun it precedes.

POSSESSIVES USING SINGULAR NOUNS

Add **-'s** to the end of the noun even if the noun ends in **-s**:

a cell's wall	Magnolia's cupcakes	my life's story
Luis's award	the grass's height	a potato's texture

With nouns ending in **-s**, you can leave off the **-'s** and simply use an apostrophe if pronouncing the words would be awkward:

Jesus's sayings	**Jesus' sayings**
Aesops's stories	**Aesops' stories**

POSSESSIVES USING PLURAL NOUNS

If the plural noun does not end in **-s**, add **-'s**.

the children's choir	the media's analysis	the deer's diseases

If the plural noun *does* end in **-s**, add only an apostrophe.

a bakers' dozen	the Kennedys' compound	the grasses' heights
the boxes' interiors	many potatoes' textures	our lives' stories

POSSESSIVES USING COMPOUND NOUNS

The last word in a compound noun becomes possessive, following the above guidelines:

a NASCAR driver's car	the school nurse's office
the fathers-in-law's meeting	some swimming pools' depths

POSSESSIVES USING TWO OR MORE NOUNS

If the object in question is owned jointly by the nouns, make the last noun possessive:

Abbott and Costello's "Who's on first?" routine was developed in the 1930s.

If each of the two nouns has possession, make both possessive:

Abbott's and Costello's lives had very different endings.

TIP: LEARN THE DIFFERENCE BETWEEN PLURALS AND POSSESSIVES

Both plurals and possessives usually add an **-s** at the end of a noun. The difference is that possessives always have an apostrophe; plurals do not.

PRONOUNS

Pronouns can take the place of nouns in many different ways. Sentences like these—

Tara put Tara's hat on the shelf. The hat had been given to Tara by Tara's sister. Tara sat down and poured a cup of coffee for Tara. Tara is usually a very patient person. Tara burned Tara's tongue on the coffee because Tara was too tired to wait for the coffee to cool.

—can be made much simpler and less awkward with pronouns:

Tara put her hat, which her sister had given her, on the shelf. She sat down and poured herself a cup of coffee. Tara, who is usually a very patient person, burned her tongue on the coffee because she was too tired to wait for it to cool.

PERSONAL PRONOUNS   I, me, he, him, she, her, it   we, our, they, their

Personal pronouns refer to specific people or things. In writing, you must first name the person or thing; then you can refer to the person or thing later with a pronoun:

Jasper finished work and then he walked to the store. (*he* and *him* are masculine.)

Jenna came prepared: She brought her briefcase. (*she* and *her* are feminine.)

The dog wasn't gray; it was black. • Sara and Lia walked to the beach where they ate lunch.

Jamshed and I worked for a while, and then we ate lunch.

The person or thing to which the pronoun refers is called the pronoun's **antecedent**. (Notice that *I* does not have an antecedent; readers will understand the person to whom *I* refers.)

→ In formal and academic English, a pronoun agrees in person, number, and gender with its antecedent. To learn more about this common problem for writers of formal and academic English, see pages 472–473.

INTERROGATIVE PRONOUNS who, which, what

We use interrogative pronouns to ask questions about people, places, things, or ideas. When we build such questions, there is a noun implied by the question.

Who climbed the stairs? (That is, someone climbed the stairs. *Who* was that someone?)

Which man spoke to you? • Which people were there?

Who ate the pies? • What animals are most popular as pets in the United States?

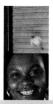

POSSESSIVE PRONOUNS   my, mine, his, her, its   our, their

Possessive pronouns indicate close relationship or ownership. As with personal pronouns, you need to make clear to readers the person or thing for which the pronoun is standing in. (Again, as with **I**, the antecedent of **my** is understood.) Like adjectives, possessive pronouns tell us about the noun they precede: They tell us who **possesses** the noun.

Eva lost her backpack. • The dog leaned into my hand—its nose was cold! • My opinion is unsettled.

Jonathan and Mack got on the same train even though their destinations varied.

INDEFINITE PRONOUNS   one, each, every, another, anybody, none, no one, neither, either, both, few, some, many, most, all

Indefinite pronouns exist to help us communicate when we do not want to or cannot be specific about people or things. Indefinite pronouns function as adjectives, telling readers something about the noun they precede: They give readers a rough—indefinite—idea about the noun, not specifiying, for example, exactly which person or how many did something.

One could climb the stairs. • Each woman brought a book.

Few people complained. • Some dogs like to swim. • Most homes here are old.

DEMONSTRATIVE PRONOUNS   this, that   these, those

These pronouns help us be specific about a person or object we want to discuss.

This woman is my friend. • That dog belongs to Mavis.

These people went to the museum. • Those buildings are on Washington Street.

In the examples above, the demonstrative pronouns function like adjectives, telling readers exactly what person or thing is meant. Below, the pronouns function like nouns:

This is the most important issue of our time: Are we running out of oil?

That is my best pen. • Those who care for others will themselves be cared for.

RECIPROCAL PRONOUNS   each other, one another

Use reciprocal pronouns when you want to show people or objects acting on each other.

The survivors helped one another. • The dogs chased each other.

RELATIVE PRONOUNS   who, whoever, whom, which, that, what, whatever

Relative pronouns allow us to combine sentences that are about the same person, place, thing, or idea. Using them, we can help readers see the connections between two sentences:

The man was tired. The man climbed all the stairs. • **The man who climbed all the stairs was tired.**

(The single sentence implies more strongly than the two separate sentences that the man was probably tired because he climbed the stairs. Note that *who* replaces *The man*.)

The buildings burned. The buildings were old. • **The buildings that burned were old.**

(The single sentence implies more strongly than the two separate sentences that the buildings burned because they were old. Note that *that* replaces *The buildings*.)

■ ■ ■

Relative pronouns function as the first words of clauses (page 477) that give additional information about a noun. Clauses made with relative pronouns are called **dependent clauses** (page 469) because they are not sentences by themselves; to make a sentence with such a dependent clause, join it to an **independent clause** (page 517):

DEPENDENT CLAUSE: who climbed all the stairs • **INDEPENDENT CLAUSE:** The man was tired.

SENTENCE: The man who climbed all the stairs was tired.

→ For more on using relative pronouns, see pages 469 and 520–521.

REFLEXIVE PRONOUNS   myself, oneself, himself, herself,   ourselves, themselves
itself

Reflexive pronouns refer back to the person or thing performing an action, to emphasize who did the action.

Mark cut himself. • **Luisa made herself dinner.** • **The men took themselves out of the race.**

IF YOU GREW UP SPEAKING A LANGUAGE OTHER THAN ENGLISH...

→ See pages 472–473 about choosing the correct pronoun for the noun to which you are referring.

ADJECTIVES

With adjectives, we can describe the specific qualities of people, places, objects, and ideas.

WHICH ONE? WHAT KIND?

Adjectives allow us to specify exactly which people, places, objects, or ideas we are discussing.

She wore red shoes. • The green ones are comfortable.

HOW MANY?

Adjectives help us say how many people, places, objects, or ideas are at stake.

Four of these potatoes will feed three people.

HOW DO THEY COMPARE?

Adjectives help us specify which people, places, objects, or ideas we mean by allowing us to make comparisons.

Please hand me the smallest book.

The larger of the two books contains less information than the smaller.

PLACEMENT OF ADJECTIVES

1 Adjectives usually come before the nouns they modify:

Use only the sharpest tools to prune your bushes. • Last night we saw a brilliant green aurora.

There is no biological reason for this condition.

The jubilant procession danced through the narrow streets.

2 Adjectives come after the verbs *appear*, *be*, *feel*, *look*, *seem*, *smell*, *sound*, and *taste*:

She was not at her sharpest. • The frog looked a brilliant green in the sun.

The reason is purely biological. • The team sounded jubilant after their win.

→ See pages 474–475 to learn how to avoid some problems writers often have with placing adjectival phrases.

IF YOU GREW UP SPEAKING A LANGUAGE OTHER THAN ENGLISH...

→ Pages 536–537 describe how to place adjectives and how to order multiple adjectives.

GRAMMAR—PARTS OF SPEECH
ARTICLES
Articles are a special kind of adjective. There are three articles: *a*, *an*, and *the*.

indefinite articles: *a, an*

a and *an* have the same function: They are used when a noun refers to an unfamiliar or unspecific person, animal, place, thing, or idea.

◼ ◼ ◼

Use indefinite articles before nouns when you are making general statements:

A computer is useful for homework. • **A birthday happens only once a year.**

Also use indefinite articles before nouns when you are not writing about a particular person or thing of its kind:

An hour passes quickly when you are focused on your work. (It could be any hour of the day.)

◼ ◼ ◼

Use *a* before nouns (or adjectives placed before nouns) that begin with a consonant sound; use *an* before nouns (or adjectives placed before nouns) that begin with a vowel sound.

A knife is useful on a camping trip. • An octopus is an unusual pet.

Note that *h* and *u* can sometimes sound like vowels and sometimes like consonants at the beginning of words. Use the sound of the word following the article to determine whether to use *a* or *an*:

An honest person returned my wallet. • A history book was on the table.

the definite article: *the*

the is used when your reader or listener will know or be able to figure out exactly which person, animal, place, thing, or idea you are describing.

◼ ◼ ◼

To decide whether to use the definite or indefinite article, consider the context in which you are writing or speaking. If you know for sure that your readers or listeners will know the exact person or thing to which you refer, use *the*:

The rosebush needs water. (If you are standing in your yard speaking with neighbors, and there is only one rosebush, everyone will know exactly which rosebush you mean.)

ARTICLES AND NOUNS
COUNT AND NONCOUNT NOUNS

Knowing this distinction between kinds of nouns can help you decide which article (if any) to use with a noun.

Count nouns refer to objects that exist distinctly as countable units: dogs, chairs, words, toes, plates, books, glances. Count nouns refer to what you can perceive with your senses.

COUNT NOUN singular a woman   the dog   his emotion

COUNT NOUN plural women   dogs   emotions

Noncount nouns cannot be counted. Noncount nouns name what can't be cut into parts: They can name abstractions (justice, anger, education, weather) and can name collections of objects (furniture, silverware, rice, coffee).

NONCOUNT NOUN justice   weather   anger

IF YOU GREW UP SPEAKING A LANGUAGE OTHER THAN ENGLISH...

Count and noncount nouns are a feature of English that differs considerably from some other languages, so you may want to pay particular attention to how they work.

USING ARTICLES WITH COUNT AND NONCOUNT NOUNS

Singular count nouns *always* need an article or another adjective (**this**, **that**, **my**, **each**) in front of them. The five sentences below use singular count nouns; notice how every single one has an article or other adjective before it.

ARTICLE OR OTHER ADJECTIVE	SINGULAR COUNT NOUN

A snowstorm hit our town this week.

That dog ate a toy.

The teacher gave an apple to each child.

His emotion showed on his face.

Does a monkey see itself in a mirror?

Plural count nouns do not need articles—but can have other adjectives.

PLURAL COUNT NOUN

or

ADJECTIVE	PLURAL COUNT NOUN

Dogs don't eat toys often, do they?

How did we come to associate teachers with apples?

Emotions show on bodies and faces.

Our winters have big snowstorms.

Do nonhuman animals such as monkeys, dolphins, crows, or ants experience subjective feelings?

Noncount nouns are the only kind of noun that can stand alone without an article. Because they cannot be counted, they cannot be used with quantifiers (*one*, *two*, *many*) or made plural. Use **much** (not *many*), **little** (not *few*), **amount of** (not *number of*) in front of these nouns.

NONCOUNT NOUN

Privacy is under attack online.

You can study emotion in psychology.

Do you prefer rice, bread, or pasta?

The amount of homework is killing me!

PROOFREADING FOR ARTICLES

Here are two common mistakes in writing—and advice for proofreading for them.

MISSING "a" OR "an"

Underline all singular nouns that appear in your writing without an article or adjective. Decide whether the noun is countable or uncountable. (Many nouns can be either, depending on their contexts.)

❑ If what you've underlined is a noncount noun, it does not need *a*, *an*, or an adjective in front of it.

❑ If what you've underlined is a count noun, it must be marked in some way:

If it refers to an indefinite or unspecified person, place, or thing, add *a* or *an*:

When I was young, I used an abacus instead of a calculator in math class.

If a noun is used as a representative of a class of nouns rather than of a particular individual member of that class, add *a* or *an*:

An abacus is a Chinese counting device.

If the noun refers to *all* members of the group or is general, make the noun plural and use no articles.

For some math problems, abacuses work as well as calculators.

MISSING "the"

As we mentioned on page 488, we use *the* when we know readers will understand exactly what object is meant by a noun we use. To be sure you have used *the* when you should, underline all singular nouns that appear without an article or adjective. If the noun fits one of the three categories described below, it is "specific," so put *the* before it.

1 *Shared knowledge.* For example, because two people who live together can be expected to know that they have children, one could send this e-mail to the other:

Can you pick up the kids from school on your way home?

(Can you pick up kids would mean Pick up some kids, any kids…!)

2 *Second mention.* When a singular count noun is used more than once, readers will know what is meant by the second reference—and so *the* goes before its later uses:

Depo-Provera, a contraceptive, may first mention **cause serious side effects. Some drug companies, however, have promoted** second mention **the contraceptive outside the U.S. with no warnings about its side effects.**

3 If a noun is followed by a relative clause or a prepositional phrase that modifies it, and *if there is a count noun in the clause or phrase*, put *the* before the count noun:

He described the ways in which the sound ◄ of music calms him.

prepositional phrase

→ See pages 479 and 500–501, and 516 to learn more about prepositional phrases.

VERBS

Verbs describe what the nouns of a sentence do in time. Verbs are about actions (whether of body or of mind) or about states of being in the present, past, or future.

AT THE PRESENT TIME: The man runs. • The man is running.

IN THE PAST: The man ran. • The man was running.

IN THE FUTURE: The man will run.

AT THE PRESENT TIME: The woman thinks. • The woman is thinking.

IN THE PAST: The woman thought. • The woman was thinking.

IN THE FUTURE: The woman will think.

AT THE PRESENT TIME: The dog plays. • The dog is playing.

IN THE PAST: The dog played. • The dog was playing.

IN THE FUTURE: The dog will play.

IN ENGLISH, VERBS CHANGE THEIR FORMS TO INDICATE:

TIME (OR TENSE).
Some tenses are shown on the preceding page.

→ For more on the tenses of English verbs, see pages 494–497.

WHO IS DOING THE ACTION (OR BEING ACTED ON).
This is called the person of the verb.

first person:	I run.	I was thinking.	We will play.
second person:	You run.	You were thinking.	You will play.
third person:	She runs.	He was thinking.	It will play.

→ The person of the verb has to agree with the verb form; see pages 456–459.

HOW MANY PEOPLE ARE DOING THE ACTION.
This is called the number of the verb.

singular:	I am thinking.	You, Kris, forgot.	She has run.
plural:	We are thinking.	You three forgot.	They have run.

→ The number of the verb has to agree with the verb form; see pages 456–459.

VOICE.
There are two voices:

active: The person, animal, place, object, or idea named by the noun is performing the action described by the verb: **You run.** • **She will play.**

passive: The person, animal, place, object, or idea named by the noun has the action of the verb performed on it: **The record was played.** • **The store was run by two sisters.**

→ For more on the voice of English verbs, see pages 238–239 and 465.

MOOD.
There are three moods:

indicative: The indicative mood states facts, opinions, and questions: **The song plays for twenty minutes.**

imperative: The imperative mood is for commands and requests: **Run!** • **Please think.** • **Play!**

subjunctive: The subjunctive mood is for wishes and hypothetical situations: **I wish we could play.** • **Were he to think, he might pass the class.**

THE TENSES OF ENGLISH VERBS

The examples below show the tense forms for the first person singular forms of the regular verb **talk** and the irregular verbs **begin** and **be**.

THE PATTERNS

SIMPLE TENSES

In the present, the simple tense describes actions taking place at the time a sentence is written or spoken, or for actions that occur regularly. The simple past describes actions that were completed in the past. The simple future describes actions that have not yet begun.

PRESENT	I talk.	I begin.	I am.
PAST	I talked.	I began.	I was.
FUTURE	I will talk.	I will begin.	I will be.

PROGRESSIVE TENSES

The progressive tenses describe actions that continue—or will continue—over time.

PRESENT	I am talking.	I am beginning.	I am being.
PAST	I was talking.	I was beginning.	I was being.
FUTURE	I will be talking.	I will be beginning.	I will be being.

PERFECT TENSES

The perfect tenses describe actions that have been (or will have been) completed.

PRESENT	I have talked.	I have begun.	I have been.
PAST	I had talked.	I had begun.	I had been.
FUTURE	I will have talked.	I will have begun.	I will have been.

PERFECT PROGRESSIVE TENSES

The present perfect progressive tense describes an action that began in the past, continues in the present, and may continue into the future. The past perfect progressive tense describes a stretched-out action that was completed before some other past action; this tense usually appears in sentences that describe the other past action (→ see pages 460–461). The future perfect progressive tense describes a stretched-out action that will occur before some specified future time.

PRESENT	I have been talking.	I have been beginning.	I have been being.
PAST	I had been talking.	I had been beginning.	I had been being.
FUTURE	I will have been talking.	I will have been beginning.	I will have been being.

→ To learn more about these tenses and how they are used in academic English writing, see pages 460–461.

FORMING THE TENSES OF ENGLISH VERBS, PART 1

Except for the verb *be*, all English verbs have five forms.

	BASE FORM	–S FORM	PRESENT PARTICIPLE	PAST FORM	PAST PARTICIPLE
REGULAR VERB	walk	walks	walking	walked	walked
IRREGULAR VERB	sing	sings	singing	sang	sung
IRREGULAR VERB	ride	rides	riding	rode	ridden

THE BASE FORM

The base form is how you find a verb in a dictionary, and it is the form from which all the verb's tenses are built. If you place **to** in front of the base form, you make what is called **the infinitive**.

THE -s FORM

This form is the third person singular present tense of any verb.

THE PRESENT PARTICIPLE

The present participle, made by adding **-ing** to the base form, is used with a helping verb to construct the progressive tenses of any verb. (Note that if a verb's base form ends in **-e**, the **-e** is dropped before the **-ing** is added.)

The present participle can also be used as an adjective: **Let sleeping dogs lie**.

THE PAST FORM

The past form is used for the simple past tense. Because English has been formed from so many other languages, many frequently used verbs have irregular past forms. A dictionary will show you the past form of any verb.

THE PAST PARTICIPLE

With a helping verb, the past participle is used to construct the perfect tenses of any verb. For regular verbs, the past participle is the same as the past form; for irregular verbs, you will need to check a dictionary to learn the past participle.

MAIN VERBS AND HELPING VERBS

In the patterns to the left, note that—except for the simple present and simple past—verb tenses are constructed from a main verb and a helping verb, as shown on page 496.

The main verb is one of the five forms of a verb described above; a helping verb is one of the forms of the irregular verbs **be**, **have**, and **do**.

→ In addition to the helping verbs **be**, **have**, and **do**, there is another kind of helping verb. To learn about these modal auxiliary verbs, see page 497.

FORMING THE TENSES OF ENGLISH VERBS, PART 2

The pattern chart to the right shows all the verb forms for the tenses shown for one regular verb. (Look in the dictionary for the past form and participle forms of irregular verbs.)

THE PATTERN

VERB FORMS WITH SUBJECTS

	singular	plural

SIMPLE PRESENT

Only the third person singular changes to the *-s* form.

first	I ask.	We ask.
second	You ask.	You ask.
third	She/He/It asks.	They ask.

SIMPLE PAST

All persons and numbers use the past form of the verb.

I/We/You/You/She/He/It/They asked.

SIMPLE FUTURE

All persons and numbers use *will* + the simple form of the verb.

I/We/You/You/She/He/It/They will ask.

PRESENT PROGRESSIVE

Use the appropriate simple present form of *be* + the present participle.

first	I am asking.	We are asking.
second	You are asking.	You are asking.
third	She/He/It is asking.	They are asking.

PAST PROGRESSIVE

Use the appropriate simple past form of *be* + the present participle.

first	I was asking.	We were asking.
second	You were asking.	You were asking.
third	She/He/It was asking.	They were asking.

FUTURE PROGRESSIVE

All persons and numbers use *will be* + the present participle.

I/We/You/You/She/He/It/They will be asking.

PRESENT PERFECT

Use the appropriate simple present form of *have* + the past participle.

first	I have asked.	We have asked.
second	You have asked.	You have asked.
third	She/He/It has asked.	They have asked.

PAST PERFECT

All persons and numbers use *had* + the past participle.

I/We/You/You/She/He/It/They had asked.

FUTURE PERFECT

All persons and numbers use *will have* + the past participle.

I/We/You/You/She/He/It/They will have asked.

PRESENT PERFECT PROGRESSIVE

All persons and numbers use *have been* + the present participle.

I/We/You/You/She/He/It/They have been asking.

PAST PERFECT PROGRESSIVE

All persons and numbers use *had been* + the present participle.

I/We/You/You/She/He/It/They had been asking.

FUTURE PERFECT PROGRESSIVE

All persons and numbers use *will have been* + the present participle.

I/We/You/You/She/He/It/They will have been asking.

THE FORMS OF HELPING VERBS

BASE FORM	PRESENT SINGULAR	PLURAL	PARTICIPLE	PAST SINGULAR	PLURAL	PARTICIPLE
be	I am You are He/She/It is	We are You are They are	being	I was You were He/She/It was	We were You were They were	been
have	I have You have He/She/It has	We have You have They have	having	I had You had He/She/It had	We had You had They had	had
do	I do You do He/She/It does	We do You do They do	doing	I did You did He/She/It did	We did You did They did	done

MODAL HELPING VERBS

Helping verbs also include the verbs called modals, whose form never changes: **can**, **could**, **may**, **might**, **must**, **ought to**, **shall**, **should**, **will**, **would**. Modals help us express abilities, possibilities, necessity, intentions, requests, or obligation.

ABILITY, POSSIBILITY, REQUEST: You could have gone running with us last night. • Can you play with our band this weekend?

POSSIBILITY, REQUEST: May I think a little longer about it? • Conrad might run in the race.

OBLIGATION: You must think about a vacation. • The senator really ought to run harder in this election.

INTENTIONS: I shall play over the weekend. • You should run over to school. • Jamshed will practice his violin every day.

VERB TENSES IN ACADEMIC WRITING

Certain verb tenses are used most frequently and in certain ways in academic writing in English: see pages 460–461.

Additionally, verb tenses remain consistent (with a few exceptions) within formal English writing: see pages 462–463.

IF YOU GREW UP SPEAKING A LANGUAGE OTHER THAN ENGLISH...

How verb tenses change and how they are used differs considerably from language to language, so—no matter what your home language—pay particular attention to the information about verbs on these pages and on pages 460–461.

ADVERBS

Adverbs are most often used to show when, how, or where the action of a verb takes place. Adverbs can also modify adjectives or other adverbs.

ADVERBS OF TIME

Adverbs of time describe when something happened; they can also describe for how long and how often something happens.

She wants food now.

He slept all winter.

She plays sometimes.

ADVERBS OF MANNER

Adverbs of manner describe how something happened. Adverbs of manner are usually formed by adding **–ly** to the end of an adjective.

He shook wildly.

He rolls the ball happily.

She rested lazily.

She waited patiently.

ADVERBS OF PLACE

Adverbs of time describe where or the direction in which something happened.

He walked forward.

She worked uphill.

She sat down.

He jumped high.

PLACEMENT OF ADVERBS

Adverbs generally follow the verb or the object.

She drives carefully. • She drives the car carefully.

The older children stayed behind. • The number of scholarships has dropped considerably.

CREATING EMPHASIS WITH ADVERBS OF MANNER

When using adverbs of manner, they generally go after the verb or object, as we noted above—unless you want to emphasize the manner in which something is done. In such cases, you can place adverbs of manner before the verb.

The lion carefully approached the elephants. • The man repeatedly claimed his innocence.

For even more emphasis, you can start a sentence with an adverb of manner.

Proudly she accepted his diploma.

Belatedly the soldiers received their new protective bodywear.

ADVERBS OF TIME

Adverbs of time that express how often something happens are usually placed before the verb. (If there is a helping verb with the main verb, the adverb goes between the two.)

Small refinements in energy production are rarely considered newsworthy.

An issue decided in the past can always be discussed again.

Physicians often change their decisions about management of cancer patients based on results of PET scans.

When an adverb tells the exact number of times something happens, it usually goes at a sentence's end.

The city's alternative newspaper is published weekly.

A new drug for preventing hip fractures in older people is taken once a year.

→ See pages 474–475 to learn how to avoid some problems writers often have with placing modifying phrases, which can be adverbial.

PREPOSITIONS

Prepositions help us express a relationship in time or space between (usually) two nouns in a sentence.

Prepositions start prepositional phrases:

on the Web   in Asia and Europe

at almost the speed of light   to the first year of parenthood

Prepositional phrases serve as adjectives or adverbs within sentences:

Would you put your health records on the Web? (In this sentence, *on the Web* is an adverbial prepositional phrase.)

My cellphone works in Asia and Europe. (In this sentence, *in Asia and Europe* is an adverbial prepositional phrase.)

Einstein's special theory of relativity describes the motion of particles at almost the speed of light. (In this sentence, *at almost the speed of light* is an adjectival prepositional phrase.)

Anna and Otto wrote a guide to the first year of parenthood. (In this sentence, *to the first year* is an adjectival prepositional phrase—and so is *of parenthood*.)

Prepositions functioning like adverbs can go anywhere in a sentence, depending on the emphasis you want. Prepositions that function like adjectives generally go right after the noun they modify.

IF YOU GREW UP SPEAKING A LANGUAGE OTHER THAN ENGLISH…
PREPOSITIONS ARE IDIOMATIC

Certain verbs are followed by certain prepositions: **He was listening to music. We rely on each other.** Checking a verb in the dictionary will tell you which prepositions follow it.

Similarly, certain nouns and adjectives are followed by certain prepositions: **He has an interest in anthropology. She puts emphasis on the importance of rules.** Again, checking nouns and adjectives in the dictionary will tell you which prepositions follow them.

PREPOSITIONS DESCRIBING RELATIONSHIPS IN TIME

The prepositions *at*, *on*, and *in* are conventionally used for certain time relations:

TIME WITH at

- exact time: at 3 p.m., at midnight
- meal times: at dinner, at breakfast
- parts of the day, when no article is used for the part of the day: at night, at daybreak, at noon (*compare:* in the morning, in the evening)
- age: At 21 you are legally considered a full adult.

TIME WITH on

- days of the week: on Monday, on Tuesdays
- parts of the day, when the day is named: on Friday evening, on Saturday morning
- dates: on July 28th, on September 22nd

TIME WITH in

- seasons: in spring, in summer
- months: in April, in November, in the third month
- years: in 2056, in 1956
- durations: in ten minutes, in four days, in a month

PREPOSITIONS DESCRIBING RELATIONSHIPS IN SPACE

at, by, in, on show an object's settled position or position after it has moved	I arrived at the Baghdad airport. An old power plant sat unused by the school. In this town most people work at the call center. They carry their children on their backs.
to, onto, into show the direction of movement toward a point, surface, or area	They brought their babies to the clinic. She placed the crown onto his head. Walking into his office is like walking into a zoo.
by, along, through show the direction of movement next to or past a point, surface, or area	We drove by the ocean. From their castles along the Rhein River, German princes could regulate river traffic. Omero Catan, a salesperson from New York, drove the first car through the Lincoln Tunnel after waiting in line for 30 hours.
from, out of show the direction of movement away from a point, surface, or area	The *joropo* is a waltzy musical form from Venezuela. After the airplane crashed, she had to walk out of the jungle.

CONJUNCTIONS

Conjunctions connect words or groups of words. There are four kinds of conjunctions, each of which helps you express different kinds of relations between the words you are connecting.

THE PATTERN

COORDINATING CONJUNCTIONS

Coordinating conjunctions can connect nouns (including pronouns), adjectives, adverbs, prepositions, clauses, and sentences.

Use a coordinating conjunction when you want a reader to see that the words you are connecting have equal—coordinate—emphasis. The coordinating conjunctions, together with the relations they show, are

and	addition	Jacob and Ali went to the store. Loretta cooked and ate dinner.
for	cause	The dog is wet, for she swam. I am hungry, for I forgot to eat.
but, yet	contrast	Jacob went to the store, but Ali stayed home. Loretta cooked dinner, yet she did not eat right away.
or	choice	Jacob or Ali can go. • Loretta can cook dinner or eat out.
so	effect	I am hungry, so I will eat. The dog is wet from the rain, so I will dry her.
nor	exclusion	José doesn't swim, nor do I.

To connect individual words—such as nouns (including pronouns), adjectives, adverbs, and prepositions—**or phrases** use this pattern:

WORD OR PHRASE	COORDINATING CONJUNCTION	WORD OR PHRASE

To connect sentences, use this pattern:

INDEPENDENT CLAUSE	**,**	COORDINATING CONJUNCTION	INDEPENDENT CLAUSE	**.**

CORRELATIVE CONJUNCTIONS

Correlative conjunctions are like coordinating conjunctions in that they help you give equal emphasis to the words you are connecting—but correlative conjunctions come in two parts, and readers always expect to see both parts:

both...and, not only...but also
addition

Both Miguel and Rav are on vacation.
She did both her English and her math work.

either...or, whether...or
choice

I could hire either Paul or Shawna.
I want either to go out for dinner or to sleep.
Either you will eat at home, or you will go out.

just as...so
equality

Just as the smell of the air brought back memories, so too did the taste of the bread bring back memories.

neither...nor
exclusion

Neither this car nor that is running.
Neither will Omi go out, nor will she stay in!

To connect individual words—such as nouns (including pronouns), adjectives, adverbs, and prepositions—**or phrases**, use this pattern:

CORRELATIVE CONJUNCTION, PART 1	WORD OR PHRASE	CORRELATIVE CONJUNCTION, PART 2	WORD OR PHRASE

To connect sentences, use this pattern:

CORRELATIVE CONJUNCTION, PART 1	INDEPENDENT CLAUSE		CORRELATIVE CONJUNCTION, PART 2	INDEPENDENT CLAUSE	
		,			**.**

SUBORDINATING CONJUNCTIONS

These conjunctions join two sentences. The sentence following the conjunction is
subordinate to—less emphasized than—the other sentence.

as, because, since cause or reason	I am angry because she told lies. Since you left, our group has no women.
so that effect or result	He packs a lunch so that he can save money. So that you can travel, you must get a passport.
if, even if, provided that, unless condition	You couldn't get in even if you wanted. If you want, he can bake the cake.
although, even though, though contrast	He took the test even though he had not studied. Although she was tired, she went out.
where, wherever location	Nan sings wherever there is karaoke. Wherever Heather goes, laughter follows.
after, before, once, since, until, when, whenever, while time	She went to the movies after she had dinner. While it rains, the city cannot fix the road.

Putting a subordinating conjunction in front of a sentence turns the sentence into a
dependent clause.

When you put the dependent clause at the beginning of a sentence, put a comma
after it:

SUBORDINATING CONJUNCTION	INDEPENDENT CLAUSE	**,**	INDEPENDENT CLAUSE	**.**

When you join two sentences by putting a subordinating conjunction between them, you
need no comma:

INDEPENDENT CLAUSE	SUBORDINATING CONJUNCTION	INDEPENDENT CLAUSE	**.**

CONJUNCTIVE ADVERBS

Independent clauses can be joined with a semicolon and conjunctive adverb to show the relationships listed here:

also, besides, furthermore, moreover	addition	We don't need a car; besides, we can't afford one. The city repaved our street; moreover, they put up a new sign.
however, instead, likewise, nevertheless, nonetheless, otherwise, similarly, still	comparison and contrast	We could eat; otherwise, we should go home. Their team went into the game with a three point advantage; nonetheless, they lost.
accordingly, consequently, hence, then, therefore, thus	result or summary	The jury found her not guilty; thus, she was freed. She went home with a migraine; consequently, she missed the lecture.
finally, meanwhile, next, now, then	time	The first expedition set out; meanwhile, the second expedition gathered its equipment.

When you use conjunctive adverbs, start with an independent clause followed by a semicolon; then, put the conjunction (followed by a comma) and then put the second independent clause.

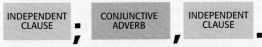

THERE ARE 4 SENTENCE FUNCTIONS.

With sentences, we can…

1

MAKE STATEMENTS

These kind of sentences are called **DECLARATIVE SENTENCES**, and they are the main kind of sentence you will see in all writing, including academic.

Lyle sits hunched over on the tailgate.

In the fifth and sixth centuries, Ireland was the center of high culture in Europe.

In the last years of his life, Ray began to manifest a strange relationship with snow.

Between the end of the Civil War and the turn of the century, the controversy in American life about who women were and ought to be played itself out in popular self-improvement manuals that offered condensed versions of academic and practical subjects including the principles of elocution, oratory, and composition.

2

ASK QUESTIONS

These are **INTERROGATIVE SENTENCES**, and they matter in all writing. In academic writing, authors often use questions to set up the problems they want to address.

What should we do now?

How can an experiment be "wrong"?

How lethal was the flu of 1918?

Will all broadband infrastructures be privately owned?

What is it like to live in a cell in one of the most notorious prisons in the country?

Why is it that people have such strange attitudes toward images, objects, and media? Why do they behave as though pictures were alive, as if works of art had minds of their own, as if images had a power to influence human beings, demanding things from us, persuading, seducing, and leading us astray?

3

COMMAND

These are **IMPERATIVE SENTENCES.** They tell someone to do something. You also find them in instruction sets and manuals.

Go home.

Put down the weapon and raise your hands.

Watch out that the temperature of the beaker's contents does not rise about 275°.

In a large saucepan over low heat, warm the oil until hot but not smoking. Add the curry paste. It should just sizzle; if it spits and pops wildly, remove the pan from the heat for a moment.

(Note that imperative sentences have an implied subject: It is as though every imperative sentence begins with the implied word **You**.)

4

BE EMOTIONAL

These are **EXCLAMATORY SENTENCES.** Exclamations are expressions of strong feeling. Writers often use exclamatory sentences when they are describing the speech of others. These sentences end with exclamation points.

Anthrax!

When we were little, how we loved to be scared silly!

If the electrons are not seen, we have interference!

THERE ARE 4 SENTENCE PATTERNS.

It is out of these four patterns that all American English sentences are built.

1

SIMPLE SENTENCES

are used in all writing:

Dogs bark.

Jumping dogs bark loudly.

She and I were going to the park.

An autumn wind gusts up to thirty miles an hour.

He pointed to a pile of smooth bricks.

They giggle and laugh.

Simple sentences are the building blocks of the other kinds of sentences, so it is important that you have a good understanding of them because the other kinds of sentences are much used in academic and formal writing. (Notice, too, that simple sentences are neither necessarily short nor uninformative even though they are called **simple**.)

➔ GO TO PAGE 510.

2

COMPOUND SENTENCES

join two simple sentences:

Dogs bark and cats meow.

She and I went to the exhibit, but everyone else went swimming.

An autumn wind gusts up to thirty miles an hour; a winter wind can gust up to fifty miles an hour.

I am not worried about getting lost in the woods; besides, the point of wilderness is to lose yourself in it.

Compound sentences are important in academic and other kinds of formal writing because they help you express a range of relationships among the elements of your sentences.

➔ GO TO PAGE 518.

➔ The parts out of which sentences are built are words, which we discuss in the Parts of Speech pages beginning on page 478.

3

COMPLEX SENTENCES

allow you to express complicated relations among the elements you are describing. These sentences are also very important in academic and other kinds of formal writing.

Those who want to learn more should come to the Friday-evening classes.

In this chapter I examine the development of Piaget's thought, which has three main features.

Although his mother remarried after his father died, she was soon abandoned by her second husband.

I argue that James's use of metaphor is not so straightforward when one considers it in light of his family background.

→ GO TO PAGE 520.

4

COMPOUND-COMPLEX SENTENCES

As their name suggests, compound-complex sentences result when you combine a compound sentence with a complex sentence. These sentences tend to be long, and are used almost exclusively in academic writing.

Much contemporary writing is stuffed with casual references to consumer products, and, after the next two generations of people grow up, this writing will be incomprehensible.

Chinese mathematical thought was always profoundly algebraic instead of geometrical, and in the Sung and Yuan dynasties of the twelfth to fourteenth centuries A.D., the Chinese school led the world in the solution of equations; thus the triangle we now call Pascal's was already old in China in 1300 A.D.

→ GO TO PAGE 524.

DK Online Handbook
online
DK Hand

Explore these topics online:

Grammar: Sentences

www.mycomplab.com

SIMPLE SENTENCES

Two words can make a sentence. The first word names a person, place, thing, or idea; the second word describes what that person, place, thing, or idea is, was, or will be doing.

THE BASIC PATTERN

PERSON, PLACE, THING, OR IDEA + ACTION = SIMPLEST SENTENCE

NOUN	VERB
Sylvia	swam.
Water	glistens.
Dogs	barked.
You	smile.
Happiness	is.
SUBJECT	**PREDICATE**
INDEPENDENT CLAUSE	

You can add descriptions to the nouns and verbs in the most basic sentences:

ADDING TO THE BASIC PATTERN

NOUN AND DESCRIPTION + VERB AND DESCRIPTION = SENTENCE

NOUN PHRASE	VERB PHRASE
The woman	swam slowly.
Blue water	glistens lightly.
A dog	barked loudly.
You	smile widely.
Our happiness	stays still.
SUBJECT	**PREDICATE**
INDEPENDENT CLAUSE	

To the nouns and verbs in the most basic sentences you can also add objects, which are the persons or things acted on by the subject.

ADDING TO THE BASIC PATTERN

NOUN PHRASE ➕ **VERB PHRASE** ➕ **OBJECT (NOUN PHRASE)** ⹀ **SENTENCE**

The woman	quickly walks	her barking dog.
An irritated man	slapped	a whiny mosquito.
The chair legs	dented	the floor.
The wind	easily moves	the lake water.
She	shifted	her weight.
You	warily watch	the changing weather.
I	make	the bed.
Our happiness	fills me.	

SUBJECT   PREDICATE

INDEPENDENT CLAUSE

→ To learn more about nouns, see pages 480–486.

→ To learn more about verbs, see pages 492–497.

→ To learn more about subjects, see pages 512–513. To learn more about predicates, see pages 512–515. To learn more about objects, see pages 514–515.

→ A subject and predicate together are a clause (page 477); when they can stand alone as a sentence, they are independent clauses (page 517).

→ The words that help us say descriptive things about nouns are called adjectives (page 487). Articles are the words *a*, *an*, and **the**, and are a special kind of adjective (pages 488–491).

→ The words that help us say descriptive things about verbs are called adverbs (pages 498–499).

→ When nouns and verbs have descriptive words added to them, as above, they are called (respectively) noun phrases (page 477) and verb phrases (page 477).

SUBJECTS & PREDICATES

To move from writing simple sentences to writing compound, complex, and compound-complex sentences, writers need to understand about subjects and predicates.

SUBJECTS

Subjects are the word or words in a sentence that name who or what is performing some action. Subjects can be composed of one word (in which case it is always a noun) or multiple words (in which case they are some combination of nouns and articles, conjunctions, and/or adjectives).

> Yang smiles.
>
> Michael and the new student went to lunch together.
>
> Their sad songs filled the valley and echoed in the air.

SUBJECT

➡ To learn more about the kinds of words that make up subjects, see pages 480–486 for nouns, pages 488–491 for articles, page 487 for adjectives, and pages 502–505 for conjunctions.

SUBJECT-VERB AGREEMENT

➡ In formal English, the subject of a sentence agrees with the verb in person and number. To learn how this works, see pages 456–459.

PREDICATES

Predicates are the word or words in a sentence that describe the action taken by the subject. Predicates can be made of one word (in which case it is always a verb) or multiple words (in which case they are some combination of verbs and adverbs, conjunctions, or noun phrases that are objects).

> Yang smiles.
>
> Michael and the new student went to lunch together.
>
> Their sad songs filled the valley and echoed in the air.

PREDICATE

➡ To learn more about the kinds of words that make up predicates, see pages 492–497 for verbs, pages 498–499 for adverbs, pages 514–515 for objects, page 477 for noun phrases, and pages 502–505 for conjunctions.

COMPOUND SUBJECTS & PREDICATES

You can use the patterns on the preceding pages to build more detailed sentences. One way to do this is to use a kind of word called a **conjunction** to build:

SUBJECTS THAT DESCRIBE MORE THAN ONE PERSON, PLACE, THING, OR IDEA

You can substitute any of the following subjects for any of the noun phrases in the simple sentence patterns on the preceding pages (as long as you make the verb agree):

Sylvia **and** Luisa walk.

Neither the air **nor** my heart moved.

Dogs **or** coyotes barked last night outside my window.

Paul, Tonio, **and** I make the beds.

SUBJECT PREDICATE

The subjects above are called **compound subjects** because they are compounded out of multiple nouns.

→ Note that the form of the verb sometimes has to change when you change the subject of a sentence; see pages 456–459 and 482–486.

PREDICATES THAT DESCRIBE MORE THAN ONE ACTION

You can substitute any of the following predicates for any of the verb phrases in the simple sentence patterns on the preceding pages (as long as the subject and predicate agree in number):

Sylvia walks **or** runs.

My heart jumped **and** stilled.

The dogs **both** barked **and** snored loudly.

Paul makes the bed **and** sweeps the floor.

SUBJECT PREDICATE

The predicates above are called **compound predicates** because they are made of multiple predicates.

→ To learn more about conjunctions, see pages 502–505.

MORE ON PREDICATES

As we described on the preceding page, a predicate always contains a verb (see pages 492–497 to learn more about verbs). The verb in a predicate can be one of three kinds:

- a verb that takes objects
- a verb that does not take objects
- a linking verb

VERBS THAT TAKE OBJECTS

Objects can be parts of predicates. Objects are the nouns or nouns phrases that describe the person, place, thing, or idea affected by the verb's action. Verbs that take objects are called **transitive verbs**.

She smelled the roses.

Jamieson interviewed a variety of experts.

Neanderthals were cooking shellfish in Italy about 110,000 years ago.

There are two kinds of objects: **direct objects** and **indirect objects**. The examples above all show direct objects.

Indirect objects only appear in sentences that have direct objects. Indirect objects answer the questions *For whom was this action carried out?* or *To whom was the object given?*

	indirect objects	direct objects
He gave	me	water.
Mark read	his son	a story.
The carpenter will build	us	new bookshelves.

An indirect object usually comes between the verb and the direct object.

Indirect objects do not follow prepositions (→ see pages 500–501). Sentences with indirect objects (like the examples above) can be rewritten with prepositions—

He gave water to me.

Mark read a story to his son.

The carpenter will build new bookshelves for us.

—but then the indirect object becomes the object of the preposition before it and is no longer an indirect object.

VERBS THAT DON'T TAKE OBJECTS

Verbs that don't take objects or subject complements (see below) are **intransitive verbs.**

Meredith left. • Margarete complained. • The train arrived.

Intransitive sentences can have **adverbs** (see pages 498–499) or adverbial phrases following the verb, but these modify the verb; they are not objects:

Meredith left sadly. • Margarete complained about her haircut. • The train arrived two hours late.

LINKING VERBS

Linking verbs "link" a noun to a fuller description.

Eric is happy.

Communication overload may be sapping your productivity.

The words following a linking verb are a **subject complement**: the subject complement fills out (or **complements**) what readers know about the noun. The subject complement in a sentence can be a noun, noun phrase, or pronoun—

"Why Did I Get Married" is the big screen adaptation of Tyler Perry's stage play.

—or it can be an adjective—

The process was difficult for everyone involved.

Linking verbs are usually a form of the verb *be* (see page 497) but can also be verbs such as *appear*, *become*, *feel*, *look*, *make*, *seem*, *smell*, *sound*, or *taste*:

The cheese smelled stinky but delicious.

> **TIP: DOES A VERB TAKE A DIRECT OBJECT, NO OBJECT, OR A SUBJECT COMPLEMENT?**
> A dictionary entry will tell you.
>
> **TIP: SOME VERBS CAN BE BOTH TRANSITIVE AND INTRANSITIVE**
> She moved the furniture to her new house.
>
> Molecules and ions moved through the cell membrane.
>
> In the first sentence above, **moved** functions as a transitive verb, with **the furniture** as its direct object. In the second sentence, **moved** functions as an intransitive verb; **through the cell membrane** is an adverbial phrase. A dictionary entry can help you learn about such verbs and how to use them.

USING PREPOSITIONAL PHRASES TO MAKE MORE DESCRIPTIVE SUBJECTS AND PREDICATES

Prepositions are kinds of words that allow you to say more precisely where a noun is in space or time or where the action of a verb takes place. Prepositions do this by being the first word of **prepositional phrases**, which show where one noun is in relation to another or where the action of a verb takes place relative to some noun. Prepositional phrases thus allow you to make subjects and predicates that can be very descriptive.

MORE DESCRIPTIVE SUBJECTS

As parts of subjects, prepositional phrases function like adjectives, telling your readers more about the nouns you are using:

The dog on the sidewalk was barking.

The air in the tent shimmered.

Paul, on the telephone, sounds less serious.

Children at school tend to be quieter.

SUBJECT PREDICATE

MORE DESCRIPTIVE PREDICATES

As parts of predicates, prepositional phrases function like adverbs, telling your readers more about the action being described by the verb, such as where or when the action takes or took place:

Sylvia walks into the store.

My heart jumped at the sound of your voice.

The dogs hid underneath the table.

Paul makes the bed over the course of the day.

SUBJECT PREDICATE

→ To learn more about prepositions, see pages 500–501.

→ To learn more about adverbs, see pages 498–499.

INDEPENDENT CLAUSES

Consider what *independent* and *dependent* mean: Something that is independent can stand alone; something that is dependent cannot.

Independent clauses can be sentences, and dependent clauses cannot.

THE PATTERN

AN INDEPENDENT CLAUSE CAN STAND ALONE AS A SIMPLE SENTENCE

SUBJECT + PREDICATE = INDEPENDENT CLAUSE

Nazila bikes.

Dogs and coyotes bark in the lonely night.

The cell was large and unevenly shaped.

The fast growth of cities causes trouble for mapmakers.

When an independent clause stands by itself, it is a simple sentence. When it is combined with dependent clauses (as we show on the next pages), you build complex sentences.

→ For help with subjects and predicates, see pages 512-516.

GRAMMAR—SENTENCES
COMPOUND SENTENCES
Compound sentences are made up of two or more simple sentences joined by punctuation or conjunctions—or both punctuation and conjunctions.

THE FUNCTION OF COMPOUND SENTENCES
When you write with compound sentences, your sentences can show readers more complex relations among events than simple sentences allow. Compound sentences show up frequently in academic writing.

Because compound sentences are made up of two independent clauses joined together, they show that the writer wants to give equal emphasis to both clauses.

PATTERN ONE

MAKING COMPOUND SENTENCES USING PUNCTUATION

INDEPENDENT CLAUSE **;** INDEPENDENT CLAUSE **=** COMPOUND SENTENCE

Cecelia walks; Martha bikes.

I was sleeping; you were reading.

Dogs bark; coyotes howl.

The cell was large; it could attach to the molecule.

You jump; he leaps; we all dance.

This pattern implies that the events described in the joined independent clauses happened at the same time and are of equal importance.

→ To learn more about using semicolons to join two independent clauses, see page 549.

MAKING COMPOUND SENTENCES USING CONJUNCTIONS

INDEPENDENT CLAUSE , CONJUNCTION + INDEPENDENT CLAUSE =
COMPOUND SENTENCE

Cecelia walks, and Martha bikes.

I was sleeping, while you were reading.

Dogs bark, but coyotes howl.

The cell was large, but it could attach to the molecule.

This pattern uses **coordinating conjunctions**.

→ To learn more about coordinating conjunctions and the relations they can help you build between independent clauses, see page 502.

MAKING COMPOUND SENTENCES USING PUNCTUATION AND CONJUNCTIONS

Some kinds of conjunctions take the following pattern for joining independent clauses (note the comma after the conjunction):

INDEPENDENT CLAUSE ; CONJUNCTION , INDEPENDENT CLAUSE
= COMPOUND SENTENCE

Cecelia walks; meanwhile, Martha bikes.

I slept; instead, you read.

It rained while we were there; moreover, it was cold.

She was found innocent; accordingly, she will go free.

This pattern uses **conjunctive adverbs**.

→ To learn more about conjunctive adverbs, see page 505.

COMPLEX SENTENCES

Complex sentences combine one independent clause with one dependent clause.

THE FUNCTION OF COMPLEX SENTENCES

Complex sentences show readers more complex relations among events than simple sentences allow because the sentences are made of two clauses, one of which—the independent clause—will always have more emphasis than the other.

PATTERN ONE

COMPLEX SENTENCES WITH DEPENDENT ADJECTIVE CLAUSES

RELATIVE PRONOUN + PREDICATE = ADJECTIVE CLAUSE

who was biking

which was in the street

that hid under the bushes

whose shape kept changing

Adjective clauses allow you to give additional information about subjects, and so they help you write expressive sentences. Adjective clauses are inserted into independent clauses to make **THE FIRST KIND OF COMPLEX SENTENCE**:

The woman who was biking is my sister.

The bicycle, which was in the street, is missing.

The cell whose shape kept changing has been identified.

→ To learn more about relative pronouns, see page 486.

→ To learn more about the punctuation of adjective clauses when you weave them into independent clauses, see pages 542–546. Pay close attention to this; punctuating adjective phrases can cause writers trouble.

WATCH OUT FOR THIS!

Adjective clauses can look like independent clauses because they have a similar structure to sentences: There is a word and then a predicate. But, in formal English, relative pronouns cannot take the place of nouns—and so adjective clauses cannot stand alone as sentences.

NOT SENTENCES

who was biking

which was in the street

that hid under the bushes

whose shape kept changing

→ The phrases above are fragments of sentences that can be turned into sentences. To learn more about sentence fragments, see pages 466–471.

SENTENCES

<u>Mary was biking.</u>

<u>The bicycle was in the street.</u>

<u>The woodchuck hid under the bushes.</u>

<u>The cell's shape kept changing.</u>

SENTENCES

Sometimes, if you put a question mark on the end of an adjective clause—and you capitalize the first letter of the relative pronoun—you can make interrogatory sentences out of adjective clauses:

Who was biking?

Whose shape kept changing?

When you do this, you are changing the function of the pronoun, and so you are changing the type of the pronoun, from a relative pronoun to an interrogative pronoun.

→ To learn more about interrogative pronouns, see page 484.

COMPLEX SENTENCES WITH ADVERB CLAUSES

SUBORDINATING CONJUNCTION + <u>SUBJECT</u> + <u>PREDICATE</u> = **ADVERB CLAUSE**

after it rains

although she was biking

before it was in the street

when it hid under the bushes

while the cell's shape changed

Adverb clauses help writers express complex ideas—and so they are important in academic writing. You can combine adverb clauses with independent clauses to make sentences that express subtle relationships, as in the examples below. Add adverb clauses to independent clauses to make **THE SECOND KIND OF COMPLEX SENTENCE:**

After it rains, we will go for a bike ride.

Although she was biking, she wore her high-heel shoes.

The bicycle was in the garage before it was in the street.

The woodchuck was safe when it hid under the bushes.

While the cell's shape changed, it could not be identified.

→ To learn more about subordinating conjunctions, see page 504. Try to recognize the pattern and don't worry about names: If the word at the beginning of a clause isn't a noun or pronoun, it is likely a subordinating conjunction or correlative adverb—and the clause is therefore a dependent clause.

→ Notice that adverb clauses can come at the beginning or the end—and even in the middle—of sentences. Sometimes the conventions of written English require commas around the clauses. To learn more about the punctuation of adverb clauses when you weave them together with independent clauses, see pages 542–546. Pay close attention to this; punctuating adverb phrases can cause writers trouble.

Adverb clauses are not independent clauses, so they cannot stand alone as sentences.

NOT SENTENCES

after it rains

although she was biking

before it was in the street

when the woodchuck hid under the bushes

while the cell's shape changed

→ The phrases above are fragments of sentences that can be turned into sentences. To learn more about sentence fragments, see pages 466–471.

SENTENCES

When you need to make an adverb clause into a sentence, you can attach it to an independent clause, as shown in the pattern box on page 522. You can also remove the subordinating conjunction:

It rains.

She was biking.

It was in the street.

The woodchuck hid under the bushes.

The cell's shape kept changing.

COMPOUND-COMPLEX SENTENCES

Compound-complex sentences are a sure sign of academic writing. Writers who know how to compose and mix compound and complex sentences into compound-complex sentences are writers who can build sentences for the widest range of contexts and purposes.

THE PATTERN

Compound-complex sentences have at least two independent clauses and at least one dependent clause, in any order.

INDEPENDENT CLAUSE + **INDEPENDENT CLAUSE** + **DEPENDENT CLAUSE** = **COMPOUND-COMPLEX SENTENCE**

The clauses can be joined together in any of the ways we have described for compound and complex sentences. Look back over the preceding pages for compound and complex patterns to see how they add up in the examples below.

Because compound-complex sentences are made up of many parts, they tend to be long. Because they characterize academic writing, we have taken our examples from essays in various academic disciplines.

In his essay, Tolman proposed that rats who were able to find food in a maze weren't simply reacting to a conditioned behavioral stimulus but the rats had generated a cognitive map of the overall environment.

The compound-complex sentence above consists of:

- A complex sentence containing a dependent adjective clause.
- The conjunction **but**.
- A simple sentence.

Below is a compound-complex sentence made of:

- A simple sentence.
- The conjunction **and**.
- A complex sentence containing a dependent adverb clause.

> The American colonies were initially as jealous of their autonomy as the Cherokee chiefdoms, and their first attempt at amalgamation under the Articles of Confederation in 1781 proved unworkable because it reserved too much autonomy for the ex-colonies.

Can you see the parts making up this compound-complex sentence?

> We readily recognize people's distinctive handwriting when they put addresses on envelopes, and our signatures remain a key way in which we can identify ourselves during a variety of transactions.

PUNCTUATION

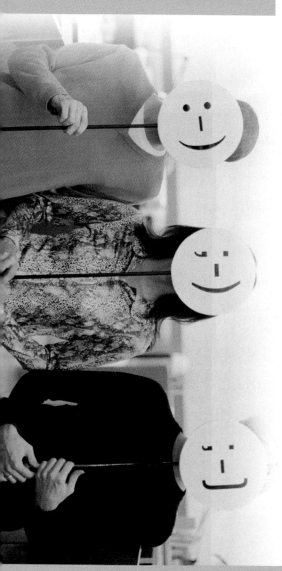

Before writing, there was no punctuation: People simply spoke, not thinking of what they said as being words, much less as being divided up by punctuation. People simply put sounds together in different orders, and they understood each other.

After the invention of writing, it was still many centuries before punctuation (or even spaces between words) was invented. What seems to have given rise to punctuation was the need for speakers to read printed words aloud to listeners, as in churches. Imagine reading this passage aloud if you hadn't had time to figure out the passage beforehand:

most punctuation marks are composed to be seen but not heard these subtle often understated devices are quite important however for they are the meter that determines the measure within the silent voice of typography punctuation directs tempo pitch volume and the separation of words periods signify full stops commas slow the reader down question marks change pitch quotation marks indicate references

Punctuation is thus an important part of writing to communicate: It shows readers how you are shaping your ideas, where you are putting emphasis, and when you are using others' words.

There is considerable room for you to choose how to punctuate in order to reach the audiences for whom you write—but the information in the following pages will help you make informed decisions.

THERE ARE TWO MAIN DIVISIONS OF PUNCTUATION MARKS:

PUNCTUATION THAT GOES WITHIN SENTENCES

- commas
- semicolons
- colons
- parentheses
- dashes
- brackets
- hyphens
- slashes
- quotation marks
- apostrophes

PUNCTUATION THAT GOES AT THE END OF SENTENCES

- periods
- exclamation points
- question marks

AND...

There is another form of punctuation that is not really a mark and that you might not think of as punctuation, but—like all punctuation—it is very important for helping readers understand where sentences begin and end:

CAPITALIZATION

Punctuation, then, is a matter of care. Care for words, yes, but also, and more important, for what the words imply. Only a lover notices the small things: the way the afternoon light catches the nape of a neck, or how a strand of hair slips out from behind an ear, or the way a finger curls around a cup. And no one scans a letter so closely as a lover, searching for its small print, straining to hear its nuances, its gasps, its sighs and hesitations, poring over the secret messages that lie in every cadence. The difference between "Jane (whom I adore)" and "Jane, whom I adore," and the difference between them both and "Jane—whom I adore—" marks all the distance between ecstasy and heartache.

PICO IYER,
"In Praise of the Humble Comma"

COMMAS
have four main uses.

1

USING COMMAS TO MAKE NUMBERS, PLACE-NAMES, AND DATES CLEAR

To learn how and when to use commas in sentences like the following—

Virginia's population was 1,000,000 in 1830. It took eighty more years for it to reach its second million (2,061,612 in 1910).

If you visit Emily Dickinson's house in Amherst, Massachusetts, you won't see anything that truly belonged to Emily Dickinson.

Abraham Lincoln was shot the night of April 14, 1865, and died the following morning.

→ GO TO PAGE 530.

2

USING COMMAS TO HELP INDICATE WHEN YOU ARE QUOTING (EXACTLY) THE WORDS OF SOMEONE ELSE

To learn how and when to use commas in sentences like the following—

"Hello," she said, "can I help you with that?"

"The real problem with having a robot to dinner," argues Ellen Ullman, "is pleasure."

—or to learn about the following kinds of sentences (in which you aren't quoting someone else's words directly)—

She asked if she could help me.

Ellen Ullman has argued that pleasure (or the lack of it) is why people don't have robots to dinner.

→ GO TO PAGE 532.

3

USING COMMAS TO SEPARATE WORDS THAT ARE PARTS OF LISTS IN SENTENCES

To learn how and when to use commas in sentences like the following—

At lunch I ate potato chips, a peanut butter and jelly sandwich, a banana, two cupcakes, and some barbecued eel.

The stinking, reeking water roiled down the street.

She caught a cab, her breath, and then the flu.

He was livid, he was angry, and he was mad.

→ GO TO PAGE 534.

4

USING COMMAS TO BUILD SENTENCES THAT CONTAIN MULTIPLE PARTS

To learn how and when to use commas in sentences like the following—

To hear him tell it, the bananas were not exactly conducive to a happy stomach.

Her father, who was born in Saudi Arabia, always longed for the hottest days in August.

Can you bring me the ladder, which is in the backyard?

You'd think it would be enough that she earned A's in all her classes, but my roommate, a biomechanical engineering major, also wanted to have the highest GPA on campus.

He looked up at me, and he burst into tears.

→ GO TO PAGE 538.

Explore these topics online:

Punctuation: Commas

www.mycomplab.com

WHEN SHOULDN'T YOU USE COMMAS? → GO TO PAGE 547.

COMMA USE 1
USING COMMAS TO MAKE NUMBERS, PLACE-NAMES, AND DATES CLEAR

NUMBERS

When you are writing numbers, use commas to separate the digits in numbers higher than 999.

1,000 (but 999)

2,304,504

$87,000,000,000

Note that the commas separate the long numbers into groups of three, *moving from the right to the left.*

Here are examples of commas in numbers in sentences:

How had 9,125 relatively uneventful days passed so quickly, and how might I slow the days ahead?

In 1889 more than 3,000,000 acres in the Indian Territory, now Oklahoma, were opened to non-Indian homesteaders, so that a territory that had held virtually no non-Indians in 1880 had 730,000 in 1900.

Here is comma use with large numbers when money is at issue:

On the $65,000,000 bond sale, Morgan and Belmont made a perfectly legal profit somewhere between $1,500,000 and $16,000,000; no one outside the banks knew exactly how much.

BUT!

In the examples above, notice that there are no commas in numbers that represent years. It is also conventional not to use commas in street addresses:

20419 West Second Street

PLACE-NAMES

When you mention a location and the larger place of which it is a part—such as a neighborhood in a city, a city in a state, a state or province in a country—separate the two place-names with commas:

Neighborhood, city: **Algiers, New Orleans**

City, state: **Houghton, Michigan**

State, country: **Oregon, United States**

Province, country: **Tangier, Morocco**

In sentences:

In 1948, Adrian Piper, an artist and philosopher, was born in Harlem, New York City.

Fela Kuti was born in Abeokuta, Nigeria, to a middle-class family.

To finish his Ph.D. at the University of California, Davis, he had to figure out how to put a rattlesnake on a leash.

■ ■ ■

To put a multiline address—

Habitat for Humanity/Metro Jackson
P.O. Box 55634
Jackson, MS 39296-5634

—onto one line in your writing, put commas between the sections:

Please send your donations to Habitat for Humanity/Metro Jackson, P.O. Box 55634, Jackson, MS 39296-5634.

Note that there is no comma between the state and the zip code.

DATES

There are three common formats for written dates in the United States, only one of which requires a comma:

1
February 17, 1951

When you include a full date in this order—month, day, year—put a comma after the day:

On January 26, 1950, the Constitution of India was adopted and gave many powers to the individual states.

2
17 Feb. 1951

This format is for citing online sources in the MLA style:

Hayden, Teresa Nielsen. "Yo, Wocky Jivvy, Wergle Flomp." *Making Light.* N.p., 29 June 2005. Web. 18 Feb. 2006.

→ See pages 359 and 361 for more information on this use of dates.

3
February 1951

If you are writing only the month and year, you do not need a comma between them:

In February 1912 La Follette delivered an angry, rambling, and—according to some—drunken speech at an important dinner for newspaper publishers, extinguishing whatever slender chances he had had for gaining the Republican nomination.

COMMA USE 2

USING COMMAS TO HELP INDICATE WHEN YOU ARE QUOTING (EXACTLY) THE WORDS OF SOMEONE ELSE

When you embed someone else's spoken or written words into your own, use commas to separate the words you are quoting from the phrases that signal you are quoting:

"I've got to sing," he said, hoarsely.

WHEN YOU **DON'T** BREAK UP THE SENTENCES YOU ARE QUOTING

You can put quoted words at the beginning or at the end of a sentence.

"Keep the hard hat on," she said to me when we parked.

As the poet W. H. Auden put it, "The chances are that, in the course of his lifetime, the major poet will write more bad poems than the minor."

In the first case, notice that the comma goes **inside** the quotation mark and **before** the *she said* phrase. In the second case, the comma goes **after** the (equivalent of the) *she said* phrase, **before** and **outside** the quotation mark.

WHEN YOU **DO** BREAK UP THE SENTENCES YOU ARE QUOTING

You can break up the words of others for effect:

"Why," asks Jonathan Burt, "should the rat be such an apt figure for horror and the target of so much hatred and loathing?"

Note that the first comma goes **inside** the quotation marks and **before** the (equivalent of the) *he said* phrase; the second comma goes **after** the (equivalent of the) *he said* phrase, **before** and **outside** the quotation mark.

WHEN YOU DON'T QUOTE A WHOLE SENTENCE

These examples use no comma before the quoted words because the quoted words are not sentences.

In describing his cityscapes of Paris, Fox Talbot says that photography "chronicles whatever it sees," noting the complex and jumbled array of chimney pots and lightning rods.

She finally cobbled together some mumbo jumbo about a "man from the West" who would "walk on water" to the "East."

WHEN YOU QUOTE SEVERAL SENTENCES

The following example starts in the usual way, with a comma following *observed*—but notice that there are two complete sentences being quoted, separated by a period.

The cop observed, "In the older generations we didn't even drink a beer. If your mom and dad smelled a beer on you, oh my God, you might have to stay in for a year."

In the next example, because the **he said** words break up the sentences being quoted, the **he said** has a comma before it:

"It was the sociological nadir of the American spirit," a Pepsi executive recalled. "Protests. Woodstock. Drugs. A surly and sullen generation occupying the dean's office, burning it down—whatever it was. It was all that sixties stuff."

WHEN YOU DON'T QUOTE WORDS EXACTLY

When you refer to something that someone else said but don't use the person's exact words, you are using **indirect quotation**. In indirect quotation, you do not use quotation marks or commas. Very often, **that** introduces the words that are being indirectly quoted.

INDIRECT QUOTATION:

Mr. Quiring has told me that essays and stories generally come, organically, to a preordained ending that is quite out of a writer's control.

DIRECT QUOTATION:

In class, Mr. Quiring said, "Essays and stories come to a preordained ending organically—completely out of a writer's control!"

→ See pages 298–309 for help in thinking about how and why to incorporate the words of others in your academic writing.

→ See pages 578–579 for more information on using quotation marks to punctuate quotations.

COMMA USE 3
USING COMMAS TO SEPARATE WORDS THAT ARE PARTS OF LISTS IN SENTENCES

In official grammar terms, a list of words—such as **dogs, tables, justice, snow,** and **imagination**—is referred to as a series.

THE PATTERN

1

If you are listing only two nouns, verbs, adjectives, phrases, or clauses in a sentence, here is the pattern to follow:

| | **and** | |

For example:

She ran and dove into the water.

or

The audience sing-along was flaccid and unenthusiastic.

2

If you are combining **three or more** nouns, verbs, adjectives, phrases, or clauses, here is the pattern to follow:

| | **,** | | **, and** | |

For example:

She grinned, ran, and dove into the water.

or

The audience sing-along was short, flaccid, and unenthusiastic.

This pattern can be expanded to include any number of items:

In the past week we had rain, hail, snow, and a desire for springtime.

USING COMMAS IN LISTS OF INDIVIDUAL NOUNS

When you list only two nouns in a sentence, no comma is necessary:

A hat and gloves are necessary for winter.

We find ourselves entering a realm of fantasy and paradox.

When you make a list of three or more nouns, put a comma after each item in the list—except the last:

A hat, gloves, and boots are necessary for winter.

After spending the bulk of the afternoon talking with patients who had no idea what year, month, or day it is, I myself felt rather disoriented.

Mr. Armstrong pleased most of the audience; he has timing, charisma, and plenty of eyeliner—and he's not afraid to sweat.

The player is then set loose in a huge, colorful fantasy world with cities, plains, oceans, mountains, forests, rivers, jungles, deserts, and (of course) dungeons.

Other writers who scholars have argued had temporal lobe epilepsy include Tennyson, Lear, Poe, Swinburne, Byron, de Maupassant, Molière, Pascal, Petrarch, Dante, Teresa of Avila, and Saint Paul.

USING COMMAS IN LISTS OF INDIVIDUAL VERBS

When you list only two verbs in a sentence, no comma is necessary:

The infant burped and grinned.

I learned to shovel coal and haul clinkers at an early age.

When you make a list of three or more verbs, put a comma after each item in the list—except the last:

On that rooftop, she sees, imagines, and remembers.

Lawrence North High School basketball center Greg Oden passes, blocks, shoots, scores, rebounds, and smiles.

→ The ability to use commas as we describe on these pages is important in building parallelism, which is a form of list building. See pages 248–249 to learn about parallelism.

COMMA USE 3 continued

USING COMMAS IN LISTS OF PHRASES AND CLAUSES

As with nouns and verbs, when you list three or more phrases or clauses, use a comma between each.

Furious, Buffmeier walked through the front door, exited to the back, crossed the parking lot, and went into his shack.

Gilligan's work emphasizes relationships over rules, connection over isolation, caring over violence, and a web of relationships over hierarchy.

The Egyptians mummified their dead in a complex process that involved pulling the brain through the nostrils with an iron hook, washing the body with incense, and, in later dynasties, covering it with bitumen and linen.

BUT!

Use semicolons—and not commas—between a series of phrases that themselves contain commas:

The four common principles that ran through much of this thought through the end of the Cold War were a concern with democracy, human rights, and, more generally, the internal politics of states; a belief that American power can be used for moral purposes; a skepticism about the ability of international law and institutions to solve serious security problems; and, finally, a view that ambitious social engineering often leads to unexpected consequences and thereby undermines its own ends.

USING COMMAS IN LISTS OF INDIVIDUAL ADJECTIVES

When you put together **two or more adjectives**, you have to decide two things:

1

whether or not to use a comma between them

AND

2

whether to use **and** between them.

WHEN TO USE A COMMA OR "AND" IN LISTS OF ADJECTIVES

Use a comma or **and** to separate two adjectives if you can change their order without changing the meaning of the sentence. For example, the meaning of

He was a thin, dapper fellow who preferred a suit and vest to ordinary clothes.

isn't changed when it is written as

He was a dapper, thin fellow who preferred a suit and vest to ordinary clothes.

or as

He was a thin and dapper fellow who preferred a suit and vest to ordinary clothes.

In these examples, **thin** and **dapper** are called **coordinate adjectives**, the name for adjectives whose order can be changed without the meaning of the sentence changing.

WHEN TO USE NEITHER A COMMA NOR "AND" IN LISTS OF ADJECTIVES

If you cannot rearrange the adjectives in a sentence without changing the meaning of the sentence, do not put a comma between them, *no matter how many adjectives you are using*:

The prize for my banana costume was a radio designed to look like a box of frozen niblets corn.

This sentence doesn't have a comma between **frozen** and **niblets** because, in the United States, we would not say **niblets frozen corn** or **niblets and frozen corn**.

Here is another example:

Three huge gray whales swam by.

Because **three** is describing how many **huge gray whales** this writer saw, **three** goes before the other adjectives.

Adjectives that cannot be rearranged are called **noncoordinate adjectives**, and they do not have commas between them.

WHEN TO USE A COMMA AND "AND" IN LISTS OF ADJECTIVES

When you have three adjectives whose order can be changed without changing the meaning of the sentence, use the same pattern as with lists of nouns, verbs, phrases, and clauses. Put a comma after each of the adjectives except the last:

Reappropriate.com is a political, current-events, and personal blog written from the perspective of a loud and proud Asian-American woman.

We have come to know zero intimately in its mathematical, physical, and psychological embodiments.

WHEN SHOULDN'T YOU USE COMMAS IN A LIST OF WORDS?

Sometimes writers want to emphasize the length of time that goes into a series of actions, so they link the words or phrases of a series with **and** or **or**:

Instead, we arrange the platters of food and remove bread from the oven and fill cups with grape juice and wine.

The example at the left is correct, as is the example below (which creates a quicker sense of the time involved in all the actions):

Instead, we arrange the platters of food, remove bread from the oven, and fill cups with grape juice and wine.

COMMA USE 4

USING COMMAS TO BUILD
SENTENCES THAT CONTAIN
MULTIPLE PARTS

Here is a paragraph of simple sentences:

There was a racist bombing of a church in Alabama. This happened in 1963. *ID* magazine published an article about race in industrial design. The article discussed only one female African American designer. Her name is Madeleine Ward.

Here are those sentences joined into one:

In 1963, in response to a racist bombing of a church in Alabama, *ID* magazine published an article about race in industrial design, but the article discussed only one female African American designer, Madeleine Ward.

The ideas are more tightly woven together in the single sentence, and (some would argue) the single sentence suggests more strongly than the individual sentences that something is wrong with the magazine article if it discusses only one female African American designer.

If you decide that the audience and purpose motivating your writing require using sentences like the single-sentence example, then your sentences will need commas. When you write such sentences, which complicate the basic subject-verb-object structure, commas set off the sentence's parts and help readers see and better understand how the sentence's parts relate to each other.

There are two patterns for building such sentences:

1

USING COMMAS TO ADD ONE SENTENCE ONTO THE END OF ANOTHER

To learn how and when to use commas in sentences like the following—

Her body seems distracted, but her mind is not.

Every limb was broken, and he ended up a triple amputee.

Music has got to be useful for survival, or we would have gotten rid of it years ago.

Will I get a second chance, or am I supposed to remain a suspect for the rest of my life?

One woman in each tent started dinner, and the other finished securing the tent and sleds for the night.

St. Sebastian was condemned to be shot by arrows, but a tradition says that he survived this torment only to be stoned to death.

→ GO TO PAGE 540 TO SEE THIS PATTERN.

2

USING COMMAS TO ADD ADDITIONAL INFORMATION TO THE MAIN IDEA OF A SENTENCE

To learn how and when to use commas in sentences like the following—

A parrot that cannot talk or sing is, we feel, an incomplete parrot.

Kudos are due to Dwyane Wade, who pretty much single-handedly won the NBA Finals.

Without raising his voice above a murmur, this artist-thinker gives the condition of exile an existential, universalist weight.

The freshwater vertebrates, originally found in the slow waters of East India, are fast replacing the lab rat as a prime model for studies in genetics and development.

→ GO TO PAGE 542 TO SEE THIS PATTERN.

→ The kinds of sentences we discuss here are part of the style of most academic and other nonfiction writing; see pages 517–525 to learn about other aspects of these kinds of writing.

PATTERN 1

USING COMMAS TO ADD ONE SENTENCE ONTO THE END OF ANOTHER

When you combine two sentences, the convention of written English is to put a comma and then a coordinating conjunction between the two:

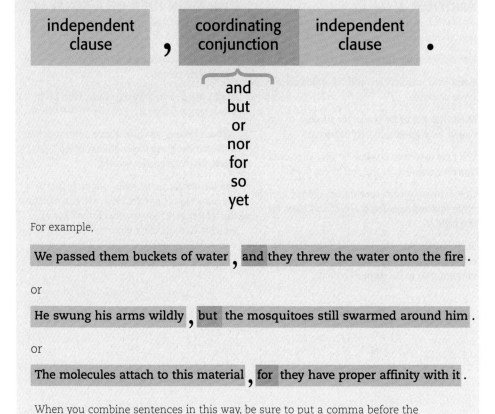

| independent clause | **,** | coordinating conjunction | independent clause | **.** |

and
but
or
nor
for
so
yet

For example,

We passed them buckets of water **,** and they threw the water onto the fire .

or

He swung his arms wildly **,** but the mosquitoes still swarmed around him .

or

The molecules attach to this material **,** for they have proper affinity with it .

When you combine sentences in this way, be sure to put a comma before the coordinating conjunction.

Here are more examples. Note how each follows this pattern:

independent clause + **,** + coordinating conjunction + independent clause •

I tried to draw him out, but it saddens Hugh to discuss his childhood monkey.

The sweaters I've made aren't impressive specimens, but they've taught me a lot.

Part of Goldstein's work was concerned with the effects of brain damage, and he found that, whenever there was extensive damage, there tended to be an impairment of abstract-categorical capacity.

Twenty years later there were 3,000 factory hands at Baldwin, and by 1900 there were more than 8,000.

Several selective pressures may act similarly and simultaneously on trees, so it is difficult to tease apart the contributions those pressures make to tree evolution.

It sounds like something you'd read on a movie poster, but sometimes the sins you haven't committed are all you have to hold on to.

Like most Kenyans, I was not taught about my culture or about the things my parents learned from their parents in school, yet I was taught about the American Revolution, Niagara Falls, and the Second World War.

BE CAREFUL...

If you were to take these sentences—

In this section I focus on fluorescent biological samples.

The techniques may be applied to material science.

—and combine them without using a coordinating conjunction—

In this section I focus on fluorescent biological samples, the techniques may be applied to material science.

—you would have **a comma splice**. Writing teachers notice comma splices—so if you have been making this error without knowing it, now is the time to learn how to keep your writing teacher smiling at you.

Here is the version that will make a writing teacher put away the red pen:

In this section I focus on fluorescent biological samples, but the techniques may be applied to material science.

You can avoid comma splices by following the pattern shown on these two pages, joining two sentences with a comma and a coordinating conjunction.

→ There are other strategies for mending comma splices; see pages 466–471.

→ For more on coordinating conjunctions, see page 502.

PATTERN 2

USING COMMAS TO ADD ADDITIONAL INFORMATION TO THE MAIN IDEA OF A SENTENCE

You can add additional information to a sentence at the beginning, middle, or end.

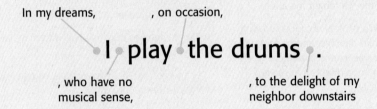

In my dreams,   , on occasion,

I play the drums .

, who have no   , to the delight of my
musical sense,   neighbor downstairs

You can add the suggested insertions (some of which are adjective phrases, some adverb phrases) to the sentence above to build the following:

In my dreams, I play the drums.

I, who have no musical sense, play the drums, to the delight of my neighbor downstairs.

I play, on occasion, the drums.

Notice the pattern of comma use around the inserted information:

- When you add information at the **beginning of a sentence**, put a single comma after what you add.
- When you add information in the **middle of a sentence**, put a comma before and a comma after what you add.
- When you add information at the **end of a sentence**, put a comma before what you add.

WHAT DO WE MEAN BY ADDITIONAL (OR "NONESSENTIAL") INFORMATION?

Each of the additions to the sentence *I play the drums* to the left brings something new to the sentence, but if you took away all the additions, you would still understand the basic idea of the sentence.

If you can remove information from a sentence without harming a reader's ability to understand the main point, then the information is additional.

In the following pages, we will refer to such additional information as **nonessential**, because that is the official grammatical term.

If you can remove a phrase from a sentence without changing the basic meaning of the sentence, separate the phrase from the rest of the sentence with commas.

NONESSENTIAL INFORMATION AT THE BEGINNING OF A SENTENCE

These examples show ways you can start a sentence with a nonessential phrase. Notice the comma in each:

Unlike many other producers who step to the mic, Kanye is also an extremely talented emcee who flexes a relaxed but focused flow that's never short on clever lyrics.

At the time of her husband's assassination, Mary Todd Lincoln had already buried two young sons.

Because data are always ambiguous, it can be years before physicists feel confident enough to publish potentially controversial results.

As unions waxed stronger after 1886, the number of strikes to enforce union rules grew steadily.

Once upon a time, I was one of those nerds who hung around Radio Shack and played with LEDs, resistors, and capacitors.

Even in the harsh penal environment of early America, some colonies had laws against feeding lobsters to inmates because it was thought to be cruel and unusual, like making people eat rats.

If you use only one or two introductory words, you can omit the comma:

On Wednesday we conduct the experiment.

COMMA USE 4 continued

NONESSENTIAL INFORMATION IN THE MIDDLE OF A SENTENCE

Short interjections of words can add a conversational tone to writing; these interjections remind readers that a person wrote the words, so interjections can help writers build relations with their readers. Put a comma before and after such interjections:

Dirt, it seems, is an important ingredient in particle physics experiments.

Some sequels, as we all know, are better than the originals.

Let me clarify two points that will, I hope, make clear our disagreement.

■ ■ ■

When you use explanatory words and phrases such as **though** and **for example**, they should be set off by commas:

Once I'm awake, though, I tend to lie there wondering if I've made a terrible mistake.

Among Plains tribes, for example, certain forms of design knowledge, such as quill embroidery and beadwork, are sacred.

BUT!

Do not put a comma after **though** if the word introduces a phrase:

Though she had already been executed, Joan of Arc was acquitted on July 7, 1456.

■ ■ ■

The following sentences have phrases that come after nouns (very often names) and that explain what the noun is; put a comma before and after all such phrases:

Aunty Lau, an accomplished weaver, teaches Hawaiian culture in the schools.

My son, who is eleven, has a memory like wet cement.

Lascelles Brown, an athletic Jamaican butcher who had briefly dabbled in boxing, first got interested in bobsledding after seeing the 1993 Disney film *Cool Running*, based on Jamaica's 1988 Olympic team.

Scissors, a mundane object to which we are introduced in kindergarten, are a sophisticated tool requiring opposable thumbs and some dexterity.

The Space Shuttle, on track and on schedule, came into view just after 5:53 Pacific time.

Nature, when abused, may react eventually like a tiger whose tail has been pulled.

We know from research that dogs, even kennel-raised puppies, do much better than generally more brilliant wolves or human-like chimpanzees in responding to human cues in a food-finding test.

The nouns or noun phrases set apart by commas in the sentences above are called **appositives**; an appositive gives additional information about the noun it follows.

STEPS FOR DECIDING IF INFORMATION IS ESSENTIAL OR NOT

1

For a sentence about which you are unsure, describe to yourself exactly what is most important to you in the sentence: *What exactly is it that you want your readers to take away from your sentence?*

EXAMPLE 1

Your sentence emphasizes some events that took place in New York City.

EXAMPLE 2

Your sentence focuses readers' attentions on society's responses to women who died in the Vietnam War.

2

Identify in the sentence the information that may or may not be essential.

All of this took place in New York City, which is cruelly, insanely expensive.

This website is dedicated to women who died in the Vietnam War.

3

Remove the information you identified in step 2.

All of this took place in New York City.

This website is dedicated to women.

4

Ask yourself this question about the shortened sentence: *Does it give your readers exactly what you want them to take from the sentence?*

If you are writing this sentence to emphasize that the events you are describing took place in New York City and not to emphasize the cost of being in New York City, the answer is **yes**.

If you are writing this sentence to focus readers' attentions on society's responses to women who died in the Vietnam War and not on all women, the answer is **no**.

5

If the answer is **yes**, then the information you identified in step 2 is nonessential, and should be separated from the rest of the sentence with commas.

If the answer is **no**, then the information you identified in step 2 is essential and should not be separated with commas.

YES? Use commas:

All of this took place in New York City, which is cruelly, insanely expensive.

NO? DON'T use commas:

This website is dedicated to women who died in the Vietnam War.

NONESSENTIAL INFORMATION AT THE END OF A SENTENCE

These examples show some of the many ways you can end a sentence with a nonessential phrase. Notice where the comma is in these examples:

I used to play that song over and over in the dark when I was nine, the year I really became aware of my own existence.

Ray has exceptionally large glasses, like an underwater mask, as if he never knows when he'll have to do some welding or shield himself from a solar eclipse.

Shani Davis stood out as a rare African American in a mostly white sport, supported by a single mother who helped bulldoze any barriers she sensed were in front of him.

Knitting is a skill that has come in handy throughout my life, mostly because I am so afflicted with the Protestant work ethic that I can't bear to watch television unless I am doing something productive with my hands.

Dogs are said to be the first domestic animals, displacing pigs for primal honors.

TIP: IF YOU ARE NOT SURE WHETHER INFORMATION IS ESSENTIAL OR NONESSENTIAL, REVISE THE SENTENCE TO SAVE YOURSELF ANY WORRY

In the following sentence, is the phrase *seeing how quickly glaciers are melting* essential or nonessential?

Scientists seeing how quickly glaciers are melting say we cannot ignore global warming.

You could make arguments in either direction for the phrase, meaning that the sentence will be ambiguous for its readers and hence potentially confusing.
   Moving and rewording the phrase in question can remove the ambiguity:

When they see how quickly glaciers are melting, scientists say we cannot ignore global warming.

Sometimes, rewording the sentence can help you create the sense you want your readers to understand:

Those scientists who see how quickly glaciers are melting are the most emphatic that global warming is occurring now.

WHEN NOT TO USE COMMAS

We list here kinds of sentences in which people are often tempted to use commas—but for which the conventions of formal writing say not to.

BEFORE INFORMATION ESSENTIAL TO A SENTENCE

I am writing about the woman, who was nominated for president by the Republican Party in 1964. *delete*

I am writing about the woman who was nominated for president by the Republican Party in 1964.

Read the sentence without the part following the comma; if the sentence loses the meaning you want it to have, then you **do not** need the comma.

→ For more information on making this decision, see page 545.

BETWEEN TWO CLAUSES THAT ARE NOT INDEPENDENT CLAUSES   *delete*

Some people look at war, and see nothing but violence and chaos.

Some people look at war and see nothing but violence and chaos.

→ If you need help determining whether you are writing independent clauses, see pages 469 and 517–525.

BEFORE "THAN"

Some scientists argue that there is no clearer indication of global warming, than Greenland's melting glaciers.   *delete*

Some scientists argue that there is no clearer indication of global warming than Greenland's melting glaciers.

BETWEEN A SENTENCE'S VERB AND ITS SUBJECT OR OBJECT

Everything good*, is bad for you.*   *delete*
Everything good is bad for you.

One of the dominant themes in American science policy this past year was*, how we can maintain a competitive edge in a global*   *delete* economy.
One of the dominant themes in American science policy this past year was how we can maintain a competitive edge in a global economy.

If you include more than one word in a subject, it can be tempting to put a comma after it because you might read the sentence out loud with a pause after the subject—which can suggest that a comma should go there. The same temptation can happen with long objects: If you were reading it out loud, you would probably pause before the object. But in writing, the convention is not to put commas in these places.

BEFORE OR AFTER PARENTHESES

delete
A political career*,* (or a legal one) is the surest ticket to a historical legacy.
A political career (or a legal one) is the surest ticket to a historical legacy.

or

A political career, or a legal one, is the surest ticket to a historical legacy.

The convention is to use parentheses or commas around parenthetical comments, but not both.

AFTER A SUBORDINATING CONJUNCTION

delete
Although*,* scientists no longer consider Pluto to be a planet, many still seek that little celestial body in their telescopes.
Although scientists no longer consider Pluto to be a planet, many still seek that little celestial body in their telescopes.

→ Page 504 lists and explains subordinating conjunctions.

BEFORE THE FIRST ITEM IN A LIST, OR AFTER THE LAST ITEM

delete
E-mail spammers endure*,* legal harassment, exclusion from polite society, and the disgust of nearly every computer user.
E-mail spammers endure legal harassment, exclusion from polite society, and the disgust of nearly every computer user.

delete
Many accidents of geography, history, and biology*,* created our lopsided world.
Many accidents of geography, history, and biology created our lopsided world.

→ See pages 534–537 for the conventional uses of commas with lists.

SEMICOLONS have two main uses.

1

USING SEMICOLONS TO SEPARATE THE ITEMS IN A LIST WHEN THE ITEMS ARE COMPLEX

Usually, we use commas to build lists—

I need a hat, gloves, and boots for winter.

—but in a complex sentence, commas might not be of help to readers:

Istanbul's steep hills and harbor views remind you of San Francisco, its overcrowded streets recall Bombay, its transportation facilities evoke Venice, for you can go many places by boats, which are continually making stops.

Instead, with semicolons separating the items, it is easier to see the separate items:

Istanbul's steep hills and harbor views remind you of San Francisco; its overcrowded streets recall Bombay; its transportation facilities evoke Venice, for you can go many places by boats, which are continually making stops.

If you build a list using items that contain their own punctuation, use semicolons to separate the items:

As the leech began to suck, it released several substances into his ear: an anticoagulant, which prevented his blood from clotting; a vasodilator, which opened his vessels, increasing blood flow; and a spreading factor, which moved these chemicals quickly into tissue farthest from the bite, liquefying any hardening blood.

2

USING SEMICOLONS TO JOIN TWO SENTENCES

Be sure you have two complete sentences (that is, independent clauses), and then join them with a semicolon. The first letter of the word following the semicolon is not capitalized, unless it is a proper noun.

The father didn't move out; he just moved to a different bedroom.

The ceiling, freshly painted, was luminous as the sky; I almost thought I could smell the paint.

My fears were powerful and troubling and annoyingly vague; I couldn't establish exactly what it was that frightened me.

The highway went for miles between high mud walls and canebrakes; the black tracery of date palms rose above them, against the brilliant night sky.

You can use semicolons to join multiple sentences:

Work made people useful in a world of economic scarcity; it staved off the doubts and temptations that preyed on idleness; it opened the way to deserved wealth and status; it allowed one to put the impress of mind and skill on the material world.

→ To be sure you are joining complete sentences, read about independent and dependent clauses, pages 517–523.

COLONS
have three main uses. 1

USING COLONS IN CERTAIN CONVENTIONAL PATTERNS.

To learn how and when to use colons in writing situations like the following—

Dear Senator Gonzaga:

The experiment took place at 3:22 P.M.

Her article is titled "Concrete: A Hard History."

New York: Longman, 2008.

→ GO TO PAGE 552.

2

USING COLONS TO PREPARE READERS FOR INFORMATION AT THE END OF A SENTENCE.

To learn how and when to use colons in sentences like the following—

He brought along his equipment: some collecting jars, a microscope, and his lunch.

The shops gave the street a strange air: They all looked alike from the outside.

→ GO TO PAGE 554.

3

USING COLONS TO LINK TWO SENTENCES.

To learn how and when to use colons in sentences like the following—

In April, Stefano and his team completed preliminary research on the medicinal leech: They found morphine in its head region, which contains the leech's salivary glands.

→ GO TO PAGE 555.

TIP: CHOOSING HOW MUCH EMPHASIS YOU WANT TO GIVE

The next three punctuation marks—colons, parentheses, and dashes—have some overlaps in their uses: Each of these punctuation marks can be used to emphasize parts of a sentence.

For you to decide which punctuation mark to use in your writing, you have to decide how much emphasis you want to give. Look at the examples here and on the following pages, where words are set off by colons, parentheses, or dashes, in order to determine the level of emphasis you want your words to have.

COLON USE 1

USING COLONS IN CERTAIN CONVENTIONAL PATTERNS

SALUTATIONS

In formal or business letters, colons are used after the greeting at the beginning of the letter:

Dear Sir or Madam:

Dear Dr. Lucchesi:

Dear Ms. Poole:

BUT!

In the past, it was acceptable to start any business letter with *Dear Sirs:*—but now, with more women than ever before in workplaces, you cannot know the gender of the person opening a letter you send. It is better to write "Dear Sir or Madam:"

MEMO HEADINGS

In workplaces, memos (less formal than letters) are often used to inform others of the progress of a project, or of meetings or other events. The top of a memo will usually look like this:

To: The members of the Research Committee

From: Ralph Bunker

Re: Next Steps

(**Re:** means **regarding**; think of it as being like the subject heading of an e-mail.)

TIME

When you are writing the time of day, use a colon between the hour, the minutes, and the seconds (if you include them):

12:32 P.M.   4:50:32 P.M.

I awoke just before the alarm went off, at 5:59:59 A.M.

Similarly, when you are recording the duration of an event, such as a race or experiment, use colons between the hour, minutes, and seconds:

She ran her first mile in 4:35 and her second in 4:50.

Sometimes, however, you need to spell out the time:

The cells separated after 2 hours and 35 seconds.

Otherwise, it might be unclear to readers whether you are describing the time of day or the duration you are recording:

The cells separated after 2:35.

BETWEEN TITLE AND SUBTITLE

When you are writing the title of any communication—book, article, movie, television show—that has a subtitle, put the title, then a colon, then the subtitle:

"Katherine Dunham: Dancing Queen"

Wind: How the Flow of Air Has Shaped Life, Myth, and the Land

Fibroids: Women Seek Answers, Treatment

To learn whether to italicize a title or put it in quotation marks, see pages 572 and 585.

MLA WORKS CITED LISTINGS

When you are putting together a listing of the works you have cited in a paper, put a colon after the name of the city where the book was published, and then put the name of the publisher:

Le Faye, Deirdre, ed. *Jane Austen's Letters*. 3rd ed. Oxford: Oxford UP, 1995. Print.

Mông-Lan. "Trail." *The Best American Poetry 2002*. Ed. Robert Creeley. New York: Scribner, 2002. 108–17. Print.

Monroe, Barbara. *Crossing the Digital Divide; Race, Writing, and Technology in the Classroom*. New York: Teachers College Press, 2004. Print.

→ For fuller explanation of how to punctuate MLA citations, see pages 356–365.

BIBLE VERSES

If you cite verses from the Bible, put a colon between the chapter and the verse:

Matthew 6:5

Deuteronomy 5:17

Psalm 46:9

COLON USE 2

USING COLONS TO PREPARE
READERS FOR INFORMATION AT
THE END OF A SENTENCE

Use a colon at the end of a sentence to
introduce an explanation:

If the three prongs of the suburban American
dream are family, job, and house, there is a
ghostly, underdiscussed consequence:
yardwork.

In a year full of big blockbusters and heavy
message films, *Wallace & Gromit: The Curse of
the Were-Rabbit* offered audiences something
altogether different: pure fun.

The networked information economy holds out
the possibility of reversing two trends in cultural
production central to the project of control:
concentration and commercialization.

Use a colon to introduce an example:

Writers ought to consider how the defense and
commercially tied history of computers has
shaped the thinking encouraged by the design
of the software we use for writing: How many
word processing or webpage composing
software packages do you know that encourage
scribbling, doodling, or writing outside the
margins?

Use a colon to introduce a list:

I improvised with my equipment: fashioning
together a hook and a line, making my own
harpoons, or gathering up cast-off pieces of net
from the fishermen.

→ When you put a list at the end of a sentence,
punctuate it just as you would any other list;
see pages 534–537.

COLON USE 3
USING COLONS TO LINK TWO SENTENCES

→ Use colons to link sentences only when the sentences meet the criteria to the right; for other cases, join sentences using the punctuation described on pages 502–505 and 549.

WHEN THE SECOND SENTENCE EXPLAINS OR SUMMARIZES THE FIRST

If you are joining two sentences where you could lead into the second sentence with *for example* or *that is*, use a colon between the two:

Her illness confined her to a sofa, and so she did the one thing she could think to do on a sofa: She started writing.

There's a reason that freedom of the press was enumerated in the First Amendment: It's more fundamental to our liberty than even guns.

The late nineteenth century witnessed a dramatic increase of women doctors in the United States: Their numbers rose from 200 or fewer in 1860 to 2,423 in 1880 to more than 7,000 by 1900.

It is the style of some journals—and the preference of some teachers—that the sentence following the colon start with a capital letter.

WHEN THE SECOND SENTENCE IS A QUOTATION

If you use a sentence to introduce a quotation, use a colon between them:

In order to write today's novel, movie, or song, I need to use and rework existing cultural forms, such as story lines and twists. This characteristic is known to economists as the "on the shoulders of giants" effect, recalling a statement attributed to Isaac Newton: "If I have seen farther it is because I stand on the shoulders of giants."

PARENTHESES
have four main uses.

1

USING PARENTHESES TO EXPLAIN ABBREVIATIONS

Through use, titles—of organizations, laws, or objects—can be abbreviated into acronyms. Acronyms are usually composed of the first letters of the title's main words, as *United States of America* becomes USA.

If you are writing about something that has an acronym, don't assume that your readers know the acronym. The first time you mention the organization, law, or object, put the acronym in parentheses following the full name. After that, use the acronym:

The builders followed the Americans with Disabilites Act (ADA) to construct the building's entry; the ADA requires that all buildings be accessible to people with a range of abilities.

Depending on the species of plant and the level of volatile organic compounds (VOC) present in your house, a plant for every ten square feet should provide adequate air filtration. Plants such as English ivy and philodendrons do an excellent job of absorbing VOCs.

San Francisco's Museum of the African Diaspora (MoAD) has a different goal than many other museums: The staff of MoAD work to put together exhibitions that represent the global impact of Africans—in South America, Central America, Europe, and Asia.

2

USING PARENTHESES FOR NUMBERS IN LISTS

If you are including a numbered list in your writing, use parentheses to indicate the steps:

The steps for checking writing that you think is done are (1) edit for readability, (2) check spelling, (3) check grammar, (4) proofread.

The networked information economy improves the practical capacities of individuals along three dimensions: (1) It improves their capacity to do more for and by themselves; (2) it enhances their capacity to do more in loose commonality with others, without being constrained to organize their relationship through a price system or in traditional hierarchical models of social and economic organization; and (3) it improves the capacity of individuals to do more in formal organizations that operate outside the market sphere.

Note the punctuation above: If the steps are short, put a comma before each number; otherwise, put a semicolon.

3

USING PARENTHESES FOR IN-TEXT CITATIONS

Readers of academic writing expect—whenever a writer quotes another's words—that the writer will give them information for finding those words in the original source. Providing this information involves giving the name of the author being quoted as well as the number of the page from which the words come (readers can then look to the essay's list of works cited to find the information for finding the cited work):

In Carruther's argument, a sacred book's bejeweled cover signifies to readers that one's memory, tied to the book, was "a storehouse, a treasure-chest, a vessel, into which the jewels, coins, fruits, and flowers of text are placed" (246). By the twelfth century the same books could also appear in "cheap and decorative binding" (Foot 118).

Note that, if the author's name is included as part of a sentence, it is not noted in the parentheses; otherwise, the name goes into the parentheses with the page number.

To be an academic writer yourself, you need to learn these conventions.

> → The example above is for the MLA citation style, about which there is more on pages 342–395. For the APA style, see pages 396–438.

4

USING PARENTHESES TO ADD INFORMATION

You can use parentheses to insert comments or additional information into a sentence. When you do this, you are adding **parenthetical remarks** to the sentence. Many writers do this to add humor to a sentence:

Sometimes in the morning Mrs. Murrow asks me if I heard the cobras singing during the night. I have never been able to answer in the affirmative, because in spite of her description ("like a silver coin falling against a rock"), I have no clear idea of what to listen for.

This afternoon, Johnny Depp is wearing a white undershirt tucked into gray tweed slacks hiked a tad too high (in the style of certain retirement-aged Italian gentlemen).

You can also use parenthetical information to add dates, definitions, a url, or anything else you think will help readers understand:

Katherine Dunham's dance piece "Southland" (1951), which was a protest against lynching and depicted a lynching on stage, created a lot of controversy in America.

Traditionally, a hysterectomy (removal of the uterus) was the primary way to treat fibroids, and it remains the only permanent cure.

DASHES
have four main uses.

1

USING A DASH TO EMPHASIZE INFORMATION AT THE END OF A SENTENCE

Sometimes writers want to put particular emphasis on a word or phrase. Should you choose to do this, using a dash to set off a word or phrase at the end of a sentence helps to emphasize that word or phrase:

I stood in my empty room. In place of the bed was—shame?

She danced a bit by herself in the corner to a wailing Brenda Lee record, but it was obvious she couldn't dance—she had the white girl's embarrassing habit of brandishing an invisible tambourine.

One woman whispered something to her friend, who responded to the whisper by twisting around in her chair to peer at me—the pair were so unsubtle that I tossed them a decidedly impertinent wave.

2

USING DASHES TO INDICATE A RESTATEMENT OR A CHANGE IN TONE

To make writing sound conversational, and to add particular emphasis to phrases that might otherwise sound out of place because of the explanation or emotion they provide, writers will use dashes:

The wall-to-wall carpet—roughly the color of brains—was frayed and worn.

Sisters in black habits and a doctor in white—no, there were two doctors—hurried among those who waited.

It dawned on him that he knew plenty of Americans—he was one himself—who held apparently contradictory beliefs, such as faith in both medicine and prayer.

"The Making of Americans" was a work that Stein evidently had to get out of her system—almost like a person having to vomit—before she could become Gertrude Stein as we know her.

3

USING DASHES TO SET OFF EXPLANATORY INFORMATION

Sometimes writers use dashes to put more emphasis on infomation, which could also be set off by commas:

A jay can store up to five acorns—depending on their size and his—in his throat.

When the explanatory information itself contains commas, writers use dashes instead of commas to set off the information so that readers will have no confusion:

Markets full of live animals—rabbits, chickens, lambs, and cows—were part of our lives.

Here is the sentence with commas instead of dashes; notice that you have to tease apart the commas to decide what is explanatory and what is not:

Markets full of live animals, rabbits, chickens, lambs, and cows, were part of our lives.

4

USING DASHES TO SHOW HESITATION IN SPEECH

When writers are transcribing speech or are trying to emulate speech for readers, they use dashes to show where a speaker has hesitated or changed direction in mid-sentence:

On the witness stand, Michael Eisner responded to a lawyer's question by saying, "I think you're getting into an area that—that—I just want to say that this is ill-advised...."

TIPS: FINE POINTS OF DASHES

- You can use dashes to give a slowed-down, conversational tone to your writing, but they can also make writing seem very informal. If you use dashes frequently, they can break up the flow of writing so much that readers have trouble following.
- Keep in mind these differences between hyphens and dashes: Hyphens are shorter than dashes, and hyphens are used in between words and parts of words; dashes are used between phrases and sentences.

[BRACKETS
have two main uses.] 1

USING BRACKETS INSIDE PARENTHETICAL COMMENTS

Sometimes writers need to put parenthetical information inside other parenthetical information. When this is the case, the convention is to put the embedded information inside brackets instead of inside another set of parentheses:

(For further discussion, see Abdo [2000] and Burgat [2003].)

Khubz marquq (also called *lavash tannour* [mountain bread]) is a flat bread with a slightly tangy taste.

2

USING BRACKETS TO INSERT INFORMATION INTO A QUOTATION

Anytime writers use the words of someone else, the words are removed from their full context; sometimes, then, writers have to fill in some information or change a few words so that readers can understand the quotation.

If writers need to do this in the middle of a quotation, the convention is to put the changed or added information inside brackets so that readers can see where the original has been changed. For example, here are words as they were originally spoken by Anthony B. Pinn, a professor of Humanities and Religion at Rice University in Houston:

What you get with mega-churches is a kind of caricature of the social gospel thrust. In terms of the hard issue of social justice, such churches tend to be theology-lite.

Here is how a magazine article quoted those words, in order to fit them to its needs:

What you get with mega-churches is a … caricature of the social gospel thrust. In terms of … social justice, [they] tend to be theology-lite.

➜ If you need to leave words out of quotations, use ellipses, a punctuation mark explained on pages 566–567, to show the omissions.

■ ■ ■

To figure out whether you need to add or modify the information in a quotation, ask yourself if your readers will understand a quotation exactly as it is written. If not, modify the quotation in the smallest way you can while still helping your readers.

For example, imagine that the words in brackets below contained someone's name (which was in the original quotation); would the quotation make sense?

In Field's most recent novel, *The Lawyer's Tale*, Harry Cain asks his private eye to dig up dirt on an opponent. Harry "didn't want to commit extortion if he could avoid it," Fields writes. "But he had to get a message to [the opponent] that would change his mind."

Here is a quotation in which the bracketed words are used to explain a term that comes from the British educational system:

Miss Lee reports that "the other day a child in the reception class [kindergarten] in Myatt Gardens told me a story about September 11."

Without the bracketed information, would you have known what a *reception class* is?

With quotations, then, notice how you can use brackets to replace a term that readers might not know with familiar information or to add explanatory information.

HY [ ]
PHENS have three main uses.

1

USING HYPHENS TO BREAK WORDS AT THE END OF LINES

If you are using a typewriter, you need to know about hyphens in order to fit part of a word at the end of a line when you run out of space for the whole word. Watch the lines as you type them, and—if you need to break a word—break it after a syllable and put a hyphen at the end of the line. (If you are unsure, check a dictionary to learn where the syllables break in a word.)

Like almost every other recent documentary on a politically charged topic, *Crude* does not pretend to neutrality.

Poets use hyphens to create wordplay:

when sunsnap
sheet-
back-
boys-
slip
pinned
to shade

If you are writing with a word processing program on a computer, the computer will automatically break words at syllables and insert hyphens at the end of lines.

2

USING HYPHENS FOR CLARITY

A precise reader sees considerable difference between these two sentences:

He was a big city man.

He was a big-city man.

The first is about a man from the city who is big; the second is about a man from a big city. When using two words as an adjective, put a hyphen between them if you wonder whether others will read your words as you intend.

■ ■ ■

When you use the prefixes *re-*, *anti-*, and *pre-* with verbs, use a hyphen between the prefix and the verb if, without the hyphen, a different meaning is made.

I resent her letter.

I re-sent her letter.

■ ■ ■

Use hyphens if the first word of a compound word you are making begins with the same letter as the second:

doll-like   non-native

3

USING HYPHENS IN COMPOUND WORDS

Compound words are made when writers put together any two (or more) other words to make one new word:

Operating on an off-the-shelf Linux-based computer, MooBella's fresh-on-the-spot system changes the blueprint of traditional ice-cream vending machines, which spit out months-old bars.

In the above sentence, the compound words are *off-the-shelf*, *Linux-based*, *fresh-on-the-spot*, *blueprint*, *ice-cream*, and *months-old*.

The longer a compound word has been in use, the more likely it won't have a hyphen in it (think of **bathtub**, **earthquake**, **bookshelf**, or **website**); conversely, the newest compound words will most likely have hyphens in them. (Some writers who want to sound cool make up compound words; you'll find new compound words in blogs and science fiction writing.)

■ ■ ■

TIP: U.S. HYPHENS

In the United States, it is customary **not** to put spaces around hyphens or dashes: write **nineteenth-century**, not **nineteenth - century**.

Some compound words, however, do conventionally keep their hyphens:

In Rochester, Dr. Bonnez's solution was to approach veterinarians treating dairy cows, which grow grapefruit-sized warts loaded with virus. He still has a block of 20-year-old cow warts in his freezer.

When compound words are used as adjectives before nouns—such as **20-year-old** and **grapefruit-sized** above or in the term **nineteenth-century art**—they tend to be hyphenated.

To be safest, check a dictionary: Because our uses of compound words are time-sensitive, it is wise to check whether a compound word is in the dictionary. If you cannot find the word in a dictionary, put hyphens in it.

■ ■ ■

When you write out numbers between 21 and 99, a hyphen is conventional:

twenty-three

one hundred twenty-three

one thousand two hundred and ninety-four

SLASH / SLASHES
have three main uses.

1

USING SLASHES IN PAIRED TERMS

There are some terms in English that are hard to separate:

on/off switch	and/or
a pass/fail class	yes/no
an either/or situation	

It is the preferred convention for writing in Humanities disciplines **not** to use such terms, but sometimes a slash is the only way to give readers the sense you intend:

If we consider all writing as a form of quotation—as blogs invariably include a mix of "original" text and text copied from other weblogs or sites—students (and teachers) learn to question the "original"/"copied" dichotomy.

If you need to use a slash to indicate two terms that are inseparably bound together, do not put spaces on either side of the slash.

■ ■ ■

A sentence like the following—

Each person brought his own tent and sleeping bag.

—implies there were only male campers present. Many writers have recognized that such sexist choices in writing affect women readers negatively—but English does not have a singular pronoun that includes both women and men. How then should you work with such a sentence?

The conventions that have emerged say not to use *he/she* or *he or she* because these are awkward solutions:

Each person brought his/her own tent and sleeping bag.

Each person brought her or his own tent and sleeping bag.

Instead, you can make the subject of the sentence plural (and then adjust the verb and objects) or modify the sentence to do away with the problem:

The campers brought their own tents and sleeping bags.

Each camper was responsible for bringing a tent and a sleeping bag for personal use.

→ See pages 282–283 for more on avoiding sexist writing.

2

USING SLASHES TO INDICATE LINE BREAKS IN POEMS YOU ARE QUOTING

Poets consider carefully where to stop one line of a poem and start another: Their choices shape how readers respond. Because these line breaks matter, be careful to reproduce line breaks when you quote poems.

In the MLA style, this is easy to do if you are quoting four or more lines of the poem: Reproduce the lines exactly as they appear on the page.

→ See pages 302 and 335 for quoting four or more lines in MLA style.

If, however, you need to quote three or fewer lines, the following example shows the convention. Here are lines from a poem by Charles Simic:

**Like the sound of eyebrows
Raised by a villain
In a silent movie.**

Here is a quotation using those lines:

Simic can create striking metaphors, as in these lines from "The Wooden Toy," where the toy is quiet, "Like the sound of eyebrows / Raised by a villain / In a silent movie."

Note that there is a space on either side of each slash.

3

USING SLASHES WITH DATES AND FRACTIONS

DATES

In informal and business writing in the United States, the convention is to write dates with slashes, giving the month, day, and year:

11/10/56   10/31/2009

Note that there are no spaces around the slashes, and that you can use two or four digits for the year. In Europe, the day comes before the year, which can lead to confusion in cross-continent communication; if you are corresponding with someone from a European country, you can avoid confusion if you use the form for dates expected in academic and other formal writing:

November 10, 1956

October 31, 2009

FRACTIONS

Put a slash between the two numbers of a fraction:

1/2   2/3   15/16

There are no spaces between the numbers and the slash.

ELLIPSES...
have two main uses.

1

USING ELLIPSES TO SHOW A PAUSE OR AN INTERRUPTION IN SPEECH THAT YOU ARE QUOTING

Because readers cannot hear words that you quote but can only see your transcription of them on a page, use ellipses to signal, visually, where someone you are quoting paused:

In an interview with Powells.com's Dave Weich, chef and writer Anthony Bourdain said: "I knew already that the best meal in the world, the perfect meal, is very rarely the most sophisticated or expensive one... Context and memory play powerful roles in all the truly great meals in one's life."

Put a space after the ellipsis.

In contexts less formal than the academic one, writers sometimes use ellipses to show hesitation or surprise; the following sentence, for example, comes from a science magazine for general audiences:

In the grand tradition of linking raunchy music with irresponsible sexual activity comes a new study touting a link between sexual risk taking and listening to... gospel music.

→ You can also use dashes to show hesitation in speech that you are quoting; see page 559.

2

USING ELLIPSES TO SHOW THAT YOU HAVE OMITTED WORDS FROM A QUOTATION

IN A PROSE QUOTATION

If you need to drop words from a sentence you are quoting, use ellipses.

Here are George Lucas's original words from an interview:

> When I was younger, I had a collection of history books that I was addicted to, a whole series about famous people in history from Ancient Greece and Alexander the Great, up to the Civil War—the Monitor and the Merrimac. I think they were called "Landmark" books, and I collected a whole library of them. I used to love to read those books. It started me on a lifelong love of history.

Here is one way to quote those words:

> When I was younger, I had a collection of history books that I was addicted to, a whole series about famous people in history from Ancient Greece and Alexander the Great, up to the Civil War … I collected a whole library of them. I used to love to read those books. It started me on a lifelong love of history.

Put a space before and a space after the ellipsis.

IN A QUOTATION OF POETRY

Sometimes when you are quoting poetry, you need to emphasize several lines while omitting others. If you ever need to quote a passage from which you must drop one or more lines, use a line of periods, with a space between each, to show where you have dropped the lines; make the line of periods be approximately as long as the other lines in the poem.

In "Elegy for Thelonius," Yusef Komunyakaa brings Thelonius Monk back to life:

> damn the alley cat
> wailing a muted dirge
> off Lenox Ave.
> Thelonious is dead.
>
> . . . .
>
> Let's go to Minton's
> & play "modern malice"
> till daybreak. Lord,
> there's Thelonious
> wearing that old funky hat
> pulled down over his eyes.

APOSTROPHES
have three main uses. 1

USING APOSTROPHES TO MAKE PLURALS OF CERTAIN WORDS

Use an apostrophe to make plurals of lower-case letters; if you do not use an apostrophe, readers might confuse the plural with a word or think you have made a mistake:

Is it "cross your is and dot your ts," or is it the other way around?

Is it "cross your i's and dot your t's," or is it the other way around?

Use an apostrophe to make plurals of uppercase letters if the addition of an **-s** without an apostrophe would make a word:

She earned As throughout school but could never rise above an entry-level position.

She earned A's throughout school but could never rise above an entry-level position.

Otherwise:

He never earned higher than Cs or Ds in school, yet he's a well-known newscaster.

2

USING APOSTROPHES TO MAKE CONTRACTIONS

Apostrophes show where letters have been taken out of a contraction:

I am	=	I'm
I would	=	I'd
you are	=	you're
she is	=	she's
he is	=	he's
it is	=	it's
we are	=	we're
we have	=	we've
they are	=	they're
do not	=	don't
did not	=	didn't
cannot	=	can't

One odd pattern to learn:

will not	=	won't

I'm sure that we didn't leave the window open, but shouldn't we go back and check?

We've got time; he won't expect us until late.

TIP: LEARN THE DIFFERENCE BETWEEN *it's* AND *its*

it's = it is

its = the possessive form of the pronoun it

It's going to rain. (It is going to rain.)

Democracy can be said to be its own biggest threat. (its is a stand-in for *democracy's*)

3

USING APOSTROPHES TO MAKE POSSESSIVES

When readers see a word ending with an apostrophe and the letter **s**, they usually assume that the word is a possessive.

This blog's message is "Stop Buying Crap."

Discovery Channel's new reality television show is *Last One Standing*.

The New Mexico Spaceport Authority's design for Spaceport America—the world's first public launching and landing site for space vehicles—includes a passenger terminal and a hangar big enough for seven craft.

→ To learn more about the possessive case, see page 483.

TIP: PROOFREADING FOR APOSTROPHES

Circle every word in your paper that ends in **s**. Ask the following about each word:

- Are you using the word to show possession? Then there should be an apostrophe before the s: *The president's words* or *A voter's decision*.

- Is the word a contraction? Check it against the list to the left to make sure it has an apostrophe in the expected place.

- Is the word a plural? Then it doesn't need an apostrophe.

QUOTATION MARKS
have six main uses.

1

USING QUOTATION MARKS FOR TITLES OF SHORT WORKS

For sentences like the following—

The radio is playing The Romantics' "That's What I Like About You."

→ GO TO PAGE 572.

2

USING QUOTATION MARKS TO INDICATE YOU ARE USING A WORD AS A WORD

For sentences like the following—

And by "malignant" and "addictive" I do not mean evil or hypnotizing.

→ GO TO PAGE 573.

5

USING QUOTATION MARKS TO INDICATE DIRECT QUOTATION

For sentences like the following—

David Foster Wallace believes that "fiction writers as a species tend to be oglers" (21).

→ GO TO PAGE 576.

6

USING QUOTATION MARKS TO INDICATE SPEECH

For sentences like the following—

The woman at Macy's asked me, "Would you be interested in full-time elf or evening and weekend elf?"
I said, "Full-time elf."

→ GO TO PAGE 577.

Words go here.

3

USING QUOTATION MARKS TO INDICATE TECHNICAL TERMS AND WORDS FROM OTHER LANGUAGES

For sentences like the following—

"Malar" means relating to the cheek.

The pub's advertisement promised "ceol agus craic," which, as we happily found out, means "music and good times."

→ GO TO PAGE 574.

4

USING QUOTATION MARKS TO SHOW IRONY

For sentences like the following—

To quantify the "benefit" side of the equation, a dollar amount is assigned to each saved human's life.

Barbies are marked as "ethnic," or foreign, only to the extent that they differ from the original doll.

→ GO TO PAGE 575.

QUOTATION MARKS USE 1

USING QUOTATION MARKS FOR TITLES OF SHORT WORKS

Use quotation marks to indicate the name of a show or exhibition—

"Goya's Last Works," at the Frick, isn't large, but neither are grenades.

—the titles of poems and musical pieces—

I had to study why Van Halen moved (certain) people as much as the Beatles, but, folks, they did, in the same way Whitman did. "Hot For Teacher" is "Song of Myself" with crappier words but much better lead guitar.

—and the titles of essays—

"The Making of Americans" was a work that Stein evidently had to get out of her system—almost like a person having to vomit—before she could become Gertrude Stein as we know her.

—or the titles of almost any work that is not book length.

→ Information on how to indicate the titles of book-length works is on page 585.

Words go here.

QUOTATION MARKS USE 2

USING QUOTATION MARKS TO INDICATE YOU ARE USING A WORD AS A WORD

Sometimes, writers need to refer to a word as a word. If ever you need to do this, put quotation marks around the word:

"Doctor" comes from the Latin word *docere*, "to teach."

The term "preservation" usually comes up in reference to buildings, not to the graffiti that covers them.

His student asked him how to use "until" according to English conventions.

Franziska often spews repetitive insults using the word "fool."

→ The use of quotation marks for this function goes back to the days of typewriters. With computers, italics can replace quotation marks; see page 585 on using italics.

→ Because quotation marks are almost always woven with other punctuation, it is tricky to use them as academic readers and readers of published work expect. On pages 532–533 and 578–579 we go over the little but important details of using quotation marks in expected ways.

Words go here.

QUOTATION MARKS USE 3

USING QUOTATION MARKS TO INDICATE TECHNICAL TERMS AND WORDS FROM OTHER LANGUAGES

Use quotation marks to indicate technical terms and words from other languages:

Ringed seals, ivory gulls, and other birds and mammals whose lives are ice-oriented are called "pagophylic."

During the thirteenth century, the Dutch instituted a "wind brief," a tax paid to the lord or king over whose fields the wind blew before reaching a mill.

Consider, for example, a form of creativity that seems strange to many Americans but that is inescapable within Japanese culture: "manga," or comics.

As I explain in the pages that follow, we come from a tradition of "free culture"—not "free" as in "free beer" (to borrow a phrase from the founder of the free software movement), but "free" as in "free speech," "free markets," "free trade," "free enterprise," "free will," and "free elections."

→ The use of quotation marks for this function goes back to the days of typewriters. With computers, italics can replace quotation marks; see page 585 on using italics.

→ Because quotation marks are almost always woven with other punctuation, it is tricky to use them as academic readers and readers of published work expect. On pages 532–533 and 578–579 we go over the little but important details of using quotation marks in expected ways.

Words go here.

QUOTATION MARKS USE 4

USING QUOTATION MARKS TO SHOW IRONY

Writers sometimes want to distance themselves from words: They need to use particular words, as in the examples below, but want to show that they don't agree with the word choice. In such cases, writers can put quotation marks around the words.

Look, for example, at how novelist Janet Frame, in her autobiography, uses quotation marks to let readers know how she feels about the sincerity of the women who visited her mother after her sister's death:

They sat patting and arranging their "permanent" waves.

Here are sentences from scientists commenting on how others have characterized scientific practice:

How can an experiment be "wrong"?

The problem I am posing here is not one of individual morality, of individual scientists doing "dirty" work or "clean" work; rather, the problem is institutional.

In each case, the quotation marks let readers know that the writers question the characterizations of experiments and other scientific work contained in the punctuated words.

→ Because quotation marks are almost always woven with other punctuation, it is tricky to use them as academic readers and readers of published work expect. On pages 532–533 and 578–579 we go over the little but important details of using quotation marks in expected ways.

Words go here.

QUOTATION MARKS USE 5

USING QUOTATION MARKS TO INDICATE DIRECT QUOTATION

Over the centuries, conventions have developed in different languages for indicating to readers that writers are quoting the words of others. In English, quotation marks—placed on either side of the words being quoted—have become the expected way of doing this, even if a writer is quoting only one word from someone else:

Fukasawa's approach to designing electronic gadgets, based on over 25 years' experience, has been called "anti-technical" because it dispenses with unnecessary buttons, displays, and other high-tech signifiers.

A comparison to make a point is Sarah Vowell's claim that "Going to Ford's Theatre to watch the play is like going to Hooter's for the food."

At the time the Wright brothers invented the airplane, American law held that a property owner owned not just the surface of his land, but all the land below, down to the center of the earth, and all the space above, to "an indefinite extent, upwards."

→ Because quotation marks are almost always woven with other punctuation, it is tricky to use them as academic readers expect. On pages 532–533 and 578–579 we go over the details of using quotation marks in expected ways.

Words go here.

QUOTATION MARKS USE 6

USING QUOTATION MARKS TO INDICATE SPEECH

When you wish to suggest to your readers that the words you are writing were spoken out loud by someone else, quotation marks are the customary strategy in English:

"He was going to write the definitive book on leeches," she says. "It was his primary ambition in life."

"Reading ability is a proxy for intelligence in American culture," said Dr. Sally E. Shaywitz of Yale University School of Medicine, a pediatrician who is an expert on dyslexia.

"You have to listen to music before you go out on a mission and get real hyped," says Sgt. Junelle Daniels, a twenty-five-year-old generator mechanic from Miami who is gearing up for a second deployment to Iraq. "If not, you start thinking, 'What if? What if this happens? What if that happens?' You start to get the fear."

Note that indicating speech is sometimes the same as indicating a direct quotation.

→ Because quotation marks are almost always woven with other punctuation, it is tricky to use them as academic readers and readers of published work expect. On pages 532–533 and 578–579 we go over the little but important details of using quotation marks in expected ways.

→ In academic writing, any time you quote someone else, the expectation is that you will give a source of the quotation; see pages 292–328 for how to do this.

Words go here.

USING QUOTATION MARKS AND OTHER PUNCTUATION WHEN YOU INCLUDE OTHERS' WORDS IN YOUR WRITING

To quote others' words in the patterns that readers of academic and other formal texts expect, pay close attention to these details in the examples below:

- The use of a comma or period at the end of the quotation. (And note that, whether a comma or period is used, it is included inside the quotation mark.)
- The capitalization of the words at the beginning of the quotation

THE PATTERN	QUOTING A COMPLETE SENTENCE
AT THE BEGINNING OF YOUR WRITING	"Most of what we teach is wrong," said Johndan Johnson-Eilola.
IN THE MIDDLE OF YOUR WRITING	Johndan Johnson-Eilola said, "Most of what we teach is wrong," while speaking at a recent conference.
AT THE END OF YOUR WRITING	Johndan Johnson-Eilola said, "Most of what we teach is wrong."
WITH IN-TEXT CITATION (MLA STYLE)	Johndan Johnson-Eilola said, "Most of what we teach is wrong" (77).

→ For more on in-text citations, see pages 342–351 for MLA style; pages 410–413 for APA style; page 439 for CSE style; page 445 for CMS style.

→ If your quotation will take up more than four lines in your paper, use different conventions for embedding it in an academic paper; see page 302.

→ See page 304 for help with choosing the words to use to introduce or explain the words you are quoting.

QUOTING PARTS OF A SENTENCE

"A natural sense of geometry" is innate in babies, argues cognitive psychologist Elizabeth Spelke.

All babies have "a natural sense of geometry," argues cognitive psychologist Elizabeth Spelke.

Cognitive psychologist Elizabeth Spelke argues that all babies have "a natural sense of geometry."

All babies have "a natural sense of geometry," argues cognitive psychologist Elizabeth Spelke (qtd. in Talbot 92).

If you are quoting only part of a sentence, don't capitalize the first word, unless the quoted words start your sentence.

Note also that the quoted words in these examples do not have commas before them.

QUOTING A SENTENCE ENDING WITH A QUESTION MARK OR EXCLAMATION POINT

"Why did wealth and power become distributed as they are now, rather than in some other way?" Jared Diamond asks at the beginning of his book.

Jared Diamond asks, "Why did wealth and power become distributed as they are now, rather than in some other way?" at the beginning of his book.

At the beginning of his book, Jared Diamond asks, "Why did wealth and power become distributed as they are now, rather than in some other way?"

"Why did wealth and power become distributed as they are now, rather than in some other way?" Jared Diamond asks at the beginning of his book (15).

NOTE: If you are quoting a sentence that ends with an exclamation point, the punctuation pattern is the same as when the sentence ends with a question mark.

PERIODS
have two main uses.

1

USING PERIODS WITH SOME ABBREVIATIONS

Abbreviations are shortenings of words.

Mon.	Mr.	Jr.	Co.
etc.	Inc.	Dr.	St.

are shortenings of

Monday, Mister, Junior, Company,

etcetera, Incorporated, Doctor, Street

These abbreviations are made of the first letter of the word and the last letter, or are truncated versions of the words (**Mon.** for **Monday** or **Co.** for **Company**). When an abbreviation is made this way, it will most likely have a period after it.

■ ■ ■

When you abbreviate a name—

John Fitzgerald Kennedy

Mary Francis Kennedy Fisher

—the custom is to use a period:

John F. Kennedy

M. F. K. Fisher

■ ■ ■

Some abbreviations—

a.m.   r.s.v.p.   U.N.I.C.E.F.

—are the first letters of word series:

ante meridiem (Latin for **before noon**)

respondez, s'il vous plait (French for **Please respond**)

United Nations International Children's Emergency Fund

When an abbreviation is made this way, it is becoming common not to use periods:

am   rsvp   UNICEF

The U.S. Postal Service supports using no periods in state abbreviations and requests that we abbreviate state names this way:

MI   CA   RI   AK

If you have any hesitations about whether to use periods in an abbreviation, check your dictionary.

■ ■ ■

If an abbreviation is of names—

W. J. T. Mitchell

—put a space after each period. If an abbreviation is of other words, do not put spaces after the periods.

2

USING PERIODS TO END SENTENCES THAT MAKE STATEMENTS OR COMMANDS

There are four kinds of sentences (→ pages 506–507); two of them, declarative and imperative sentences, conventionally are indicated by ending with periods.

The following are declarative sentences, which make statements:

Water buffalo do not exist in Africa.

Smaller species of exploding ants are more likely to combust than larger ones.

Neil Burger's movie *The Illusionist*, based on a short story by Steven Millhauser, is a delicate film, almost a fairy tale.

Though armed with a sharp, venom-coated barb on their tail, stingrays use the weapon only defensively, and attacks on humans are extremely rare.

The following are imperative sentences, which make commands:

Mix the sliced pears and walnuts together.

Fasten your seat belt by sliding the metal notch into the buckle.

Use a period after most abbreviations.

TIP: FINE POINTS OF USING PERIODS

• If a sentence ends with an abbreviation, do not put another period at the end of the sentence; let the abbreviation's period end the sentence:

The basic genre that World of Warcraft belongs to is called the massively multiplayer online game, or M.M.O.

• If you put a complete sentence *inside* parentheses, end the sentence with a period inside the parentheses.

She told me to walk as far as the corner. (At least, I think that's what she said.)

Do not put such parenthetical comments within other sentences; the example below is not customary usage in formal writing:

She told me (At least, I think that's what she said.) to walk as far as the corner.

If parentheses contain less than a complete sentence, do not give them any end punctuation:

The toxins are mostly made up of 5-nucleotidase and phospho-diesterase, which are cytotoxins (which kill cells and tissue) and result in local necrosis (tissue death).

→ Using periods with quotation marks requires careful attention. See pages 578–579.

QUESTION MARKS ?
have two main uses.

1

USING QUESTION MARKS TO END SENTENCES THAT ARE QUESTIONS

Of the four functions that sentences can have (➡ pages 506–507), asking questions is one; sentences that ask questions are called interrogatory sentences:

What is education?

Have you ever browsed a sperm bank catalog?

You bought the CD or DVD, and that means you own it, right?

If prisons are meant to make troubled men and women into citizens, he wondered, might there be a social cost to bad prison design?

BUT!

The examples above are **direct questions**; there are also **indirect questions**, in which a writer describes someone else asking a question, without direct quotation. *These end with a period, not a question mark:*

I heard her ask whether the mail had arrived.

He asked how the test had gone.

2

USING QUESTION MARKS TO SHOW DOUBT ABOUT DATES AND NUMBERS

Ir you have doubts about a date or quantity, or if your sources describe doubt about a date or quantity, put **(?)** after the date or quantity.

In this photograph, Reynolds is seen with his mother in 1928(?).

Witness reports put the number of people trapped in the building at 180(?).

➡ Using question marks with quotation marks requires careful attention. See pages 578–579

EXCLAMATION POINTS
have one main use.

1

USING EXCLAMATION POINTS TO INDICATE TO READERS THAT A SENTENCE CARRIES EMOTIONAL WEIGHT

It is customary in written American English to put a single exclamation point after a sentence when the sentence is an exclamation—

Yikes! Oh no!

—a strong command—

Help!

Don't touch that burner!

Don't go beyond the perimeter!

—or is meant by its writer to encourage a strong emotional response in a reader—

Each treehouse is built in two main pieces: the playhouse and the log. The log is a real, old, fallen tree that we hollow out using a chainsaw!

Age is absolutely no barrier in today's world. In fact, some 30 percent of students today are "non-traditional," meaning us, of course! Your age is not an issue unless you choose to make it one; don't!

In academic writing, exclamation points are almost nonexistent because academic writing is meant to appeal primarily to reason. In most other kinds of writing, the exclamation point is also rare, because people who grow up into American English tend to think that exclamation points are a sign of youth or silliness—especially when several sentences in a row have them or when a single sentence ends in many of them.

There are exceptions: In blogs, for example, writers sometimes use them excessively, as a self-conscious indication that they know exclamation points are dangerous but still potent:

It's not that we know we aren't writing well—and so tack on some exclamations!!!—it's that we know what we're saying doesn't deserve to be written at all.

→ Using exclamation points with quotation marks requires careful attention. See pages 578–579

→ Many interjections use exclamation points. See page 478.

MECHANICS

In academic writing, convention determines spelling, capitalization, italicizing and underlining, and abbreviations and numbers. When you attend to these details of writing (which you should do as the last step of writing), you make few decisions; instead, you follow the conventions of English writing that have developed over time.

In the next pages, we discuss the following aspects of mechanics:

- using italics and underlining
- spelling
- capitalizing
- abbreviating
- using numbers

USING ITALICS AND UNDERLINING

Italic type

Italic type was developed during the Italian Renaissance, and over time, those who used printing presses developed specific uses for it.

Until computers were developed, those who didn't have access to printing presses but who instead used typewriters—like most college students—could not use italic type. A convention developed to use underlining wherever a printer would use italics.

If you cannot use italics as we discuss below, use underlining.

FOR THE TITLES OF BOOKS AND OTHER LONG PUBLICATIONS

Use italics for the titles of books, magazines, journals, newspapers, websites, feature films, radio and television shows, book-length poems, comic strips, plays, operas and other musical performances, ballets and other dance performances, paintings, sculptures, pamphlets, and bulletins.

Marilyn's book will be titled *The Animal Who Writes*.

Little Nemo was a popular comic strip of the early twentieth century.

(Quotation marks are used for shorter publications; see page 572.)

FOR FOREIGN TERMS

The environmental studies professor, who is from Pakistan, was first educated in a *madrassah*, or Muslim school.

China is shifting resources away from state-directed scientific research into initiatives designed to stimulate *zizhi chuangxin* (indigenous innovation).

You do not need to italicize commonly used foreign expressions and abbreviations:

cum laude, e.g., et al., ex officio, i.e., in vitro, vice versa, vis-à-vis

FOR SCIENTIFIC NAMES IN LATIN

It is conventional to put the Latin names of organisms in italics.

Foot-and-mouth disease (*Aphtae epizooticae*) is a highly contagious and sometimes fatal viral disease of cattle and pigs.

The Bengal Tiger is *Panthera tigris tigris* and the Siberian Tiger is *Panthera tigris altaica*.

FOR REFERRING TO WORDS AS WORDS

When you need to discuss a word in its functions as a word, you can italicize it. (In this case, if you cannot italicize, use quotation marks.)

The English articles are *a*, *an*, and *the*.

FOR EMPHASIS

Do this sparingly. This kind of visual emphasis works only when it can stand out against large passages that receive no visual emphasis.

Sacks said, "I didn't just care for these patients. I *lived* with these patients."

MECHANICS
SPELLING

In Shakespeare's time, spelling was not standardized: *Been* was spelled *beene*, *bene*, or *bin*—and *Shakespeare* was spelled *Shakspere*, *Shaksper*, *Shakespere*, and *Shackspeare*. As governments grew and required standardized documents—and as printing presses replaced scribes for reproducing documents—people came to expect that a word would be spelled the same way every time it appeared on a page.

In our time, then, it is an expected sign of formal documents that the words are all spelled according to conventions that have developed over time and that are recorded in dictionaries.

SPELLING RULES? CHECK A DICTIONARY!

Spelling is the attempt to put spoken language into consistent patterns on the page, using just the twenty-six characters of the English alphabet. Because English developed out of many different languages, the spelling of a word often results from an attempt in the past to use the English alphabet to translate sounds made in other languages.

English spelling can therefore be vexing, even if your home language is English. There are some spelling rules for English, but all have considerable exceptions and variations, and many people find them confusing.

The best advice we can give you when you are trying to spell a word is to use a dictionary.

USING SPELL CHECKERS

Spell checkers only check spelling; they cannot tell if you are using the wrong word or have made other mistakes.

To use spell checkers well, follow these steps:

1 After you have a complete and edited draft, use a spell checker to catch obvious spelling errors.

2 Use the items listed below under *What spell checkers miss* to find specific kinds of mistakes.

3 Proofread the whole text at least one more time, using any of the strategies we describe on pages 454–455.

WHAT SPELL CHECKERS MISS

- **Incorrect words that are spelled correctly.** In the sentence "He might loose his job," all the words are spelled correctly, but **loose** should be **lose**. The Glossary shows many words that are commonly confused.

- **Homonyms.** *Peace* and *piece* are homonyms: They are words that are spelled differently but sound the same. When writing quickly, it is easy to use a homonym in place of the word you want. The Glossary in this book contains some common homonyms.

- **Possessives used as plurals—and vice versa.** If you are writing about more than one dress, it is easy to write *dress's* instead of *dresses*.

  → See page 483 to learn about possessives.
  → See page 482 to learn about plurals.

- **Pronouns that don't match their antecedents.** For example, *If a person wants to write well, you have to write a lot* should be *If you want to write well, you have to write a lot*.

  → See pages 472–473 to learn about pronouns and antecedents.

- **Words that are missing.** A spell checker will not catch when you have left a word out of a sentence. Reading your work out loud, slowly, will help you hear if you have left out any words.

- **Misspelling someone's name.** Spell checkers rarely check for proper nouns because there are so many of them. Misspelling the name of an author or major figure about whom you are writing is not only embarrassing, but readers can also interpret this as a sign you were not paying close and careful attention while you were writing. Anytime you use a proper noun, check its spelling by looking up the name in a newspaper, magazine, or biographical dictionary.

MECHANICS
CAPITALIZING WORDS

Conventionally, capital letters are used for:

THE FIRST WORDS OF SENTENCES

We must become spies on behalf of justice.

A combination of ego and gin stood between me and my ability to learn from my mistakes.

THE FIRST WORD IN A DIRECT QUOTATION

She said, simply, "No."

Roddy Doyle wrote, "One thing about my life, it has a great soundtrack."

Chris Magnus, Chief of Police in Richmond, California, has said, "There's a mentality among some people that they're living some really violent video game."

DAYS, MONTHS, AND PUBLIC HOLIDAYS

On Tuesday, we'll be home late.

Is spring break in February or March?

My family could celebrate Hanukkah, Christmas, and Kwanzaa.

NAMES OF PEOPLE

Capitalize first and last names, whether you use one or both.

Heidi worked until the early morning.

Li Templeton was my roommate.

Thomas Pynchon begins his novel *Gravity's Rainbow* with the sentence, "A screaming comes across the sky."

NAMES OF CITIES, STATES, AND COUNTRIES

Capitalize these names when they are nouns and when they are adjectives.

My cousins were visiting from San Salvador, El Salvador.

Seattle has changed since I was born there.

Have you ever been to Arkansas?

The Waifs are an Australian band.

NAMES OF ORGANIZATIONS

My brother belonged to Habitat for Humanity.

On the twenty-fifth of May 2007, the Social Democratic Party walked out of the Croatian Parliament after being accused of posting videos on YouTube.

"Doctors Without Borders" is the English name for the organization started in France, *Médecins Sans Frontières*.

PROFESSIONAL TITLES

Whether they are spelled out or abbreviated, capitalize all professional titles.

It was Colonel Peacock in the kitchen with the knife.

Dr. Jack operated on my mother.

Professor Yunus won the Nobel Prize.

Surgeon General Joycelyn Elders said, "When hope dies, moral decay can't be far behind."

TITLES OF ARTWORKS

The artworks can be paintings, sculptures, photographs, musical compositions, and songs.

Art historians do not know who posed for *The Mona Lisa*.

I wish I knew all the words to that Mose Allison song "Your Mind Is on Vacation, But Your Mouth Works Overtime."

Many people think Dali's painting *The Persistence of Memory* should be titled *The Limp Watches*.

TITLES OF BOOKS AND OTHER WRITINGS

Arundhati Roy's book, *The God of Small Things*, won the Booker Prize.

"The Moral Equivalent of War" is an essay by William James.

⟹ See page 572 to learn when to use quotation marks around titles; see page 585 to learn when to italicize titles.

ABBREVIATIONS

TITLES

Dr. and *St.* (*Saint*) are abbreviated before a name but not after.

…said Dr. Robert Cantu.

…said Robert Cantu, a doctor specializing in neurosurgery.

Prof., *Sen.*, *Gen.*, *Capt.*, and other titles can be abbreviated when placed before a full name (i.e., first and last names, or initials and last name) but not before the last name when it is given alone:

Sen. Hattie Wyatt Caraway
Sen. H. W. Caraway
Senator Caraway

Put academic and professional titles—*Sr.*, *Jr.*, *J.D.*, *Ph.D.*, *M.F.A.*, *R.N.*, *C.P.A.*—after names. (The periods are often left out of abbreviated titles.)

Ralph Simmons, Ph.D., will speak.

COMPANY NAMES

If a company name contains an abbreviation, write the name as the company does:

Charlie and the Chocolate Factory, distributed by Warner Bros. Studios, is based on a novel by Roald Dahl.

MEASUREMENTS

In a paper's body, spell out measurement units such as *foot*, *percent*, *meter*—but abbreviate them in charts, tables, and graphs.

HMS Titanic was 883.75 feet long and 92.5 feet wide.

TIP: MAKING ABBREVIATIONS PLURAL AND POSSESSIVE

To make an abbreviation plural, put **-s** after it.

Analysts estimate that more than 6,000 PCs become obsolete in California every day.

To make an abbreviation possessive, put **'s** after it.

IBM's earning forecast was grim.

TIP: ABBREVIATIONS IN DIFFERENT DISCIPLINES

Different disciplines—mathematics, social sciences—use abbreviations differently. The advice we offer on these pages is general, so if you are writing for a specific discipline, ask someone familiar with the field (or a reference librarian) for help in learning the field's conventions.

PLACE-NAMES

Spell out the names of continents, rivers, countries, states, cities, streets, and so on, except in these three cases:

1 Use **D.C.** when referring to Washington, D.C.

Citizens of Washington, D.C., have no voting representation in Congress.

2 Use U.S. as an adjective, not as a noun:

U.S. soldiers

soldiers from the United States

3 To put a full address in a sentence, write it as you would on an envelope, using the state's postal abbreviation.

Please send your applications to Habitat for Humanity International, 121 Habitat St., Americus, GA 31709.

Otherwise, spell out the state name:

Habitat for Humanity International's head office is in Americus, Georgia.

DATES

Spell out months and days of the week.

"Statistically, you are more likely to have an accident on Monday, November 27, than any other day of the year," the insurance official said.

For dates, these abbreviations are customary:

399 B.C.   399 B.C.E.

1215 C.E.   A.D. 1215

B.C. (*Before Christ*), **B.C.E.** (*Before the Common Era*), and **C.E.** (*Common Era*) are placed after the year. **A.D.** (*Anno Domini,* "Year of Our Lord") goes before the year. **B.C.E.** and **C.E.** are currently the most favored abbreviations.

TIMES

The conventional abbreviations for time of day are **A.M.** or **a.m.** for *before noon* and **P.M.** or *p.m.* for *afternoon*.

ACRONYMS

An acronym is a word formed by the initial letters of a phrase or title.

PC   *personal computer*
NPM   *National Poetry Month*
BBC   *British Broadcasting Corporation*

If you use an acronym that readers might not know, spell it out first, put the acronym in parentheses, and then use the acronym for all later references.

Folding At Home (FAH) is Stanford University's distributed computing project to study and understand protein folding, protein aggregation, and related diseases. So far, almost 500,000 users have donated processing time to FAH's projects.

LATIN EXPRESSIONS

Some Latin expressions, commonly used in academic writing, appear only as abbreviations:

cf.   *compare*   e.g. *for example*
et al. *and others*   etc. *and so forth*
i.e.   *that is*   n.b. *note well*

IN DOCUMENTING SOURCES

Different documentation styles use different abbreviations for words like **anonymous**, **editor**, or **no date**. Check the style manual you are using for any abbreviations you need to use.

→ See page 580 for how to use periods with abbreviations.

MECHANICS
NUMBERS

WRITING NUMBERS

Spell out numbers that can be expressed in one or two words (and note the hyphen). Give the numerals for longer numbers.

seven	178
sixty-one	1,347
forty-one dollars	$77.17
twenty-two years	250 years
ninety people	2,200 people
ten miles	352 miles

Spell out any number that precedes another number expressed in numerals; otherwise readers might have trouble understanding the numbers. (For example, in the first sentence below, it is possible to see the two numbers as 10,250.)

The game is run from 10 250 gigabyte servers.

The game is run from ten 250 gigabyte servers.

WRITE OUT NUMBERS THAT BEGIN SENTENCES

19% of survey respondents knew when the U.S. Constitution was written.

Nineteen percent of survey respondents knew when the U.S. Constitution was written.

Except: Sentences can begin with a year:

1787 is the year the U.S. Constitution was written.

USE NUMBERS CONSISTENTLY IN WRITING

If you spell numbers out or use numerals in a series, do so consistently.

Walsh notes that on average there are between 10,000 and fifteen thousand avatars in Second Life at any given time.

Walsh notes that on average there are between 10,000 and 15,000 avatars in Second Life at any given time.

DATES AND TIMES

Use numerals for dates and times.

On July 22, 1929, Alvin Macauley, president of Packard Motor Company, was on the cover of *Time* magazine.

President John F. Kennedy was shot and killed on November 22, 1963, at 12:30 p.m.

PAGES AND OTHER PARTS OF BOOKS

Use numerals for pages, chapters, and other book divisions.

In his book *The Uses of Disorder*, Richard Sennett defines adulthood as the time when people "learn to tolerate painful ambiguity and uncertainty" (108).

Chapter 3 of John Stuart Mill's *On Liberty* is titled, "On Individuality, as one of the elements of well-being."

ADDRESSES AND PHONE NUMBERS

Use numerals for addresses and phone numbers.

Grauman's Chinese Theatre is located at 6801 Hollywood Boulevard in Hollywood. For showtimes, call (323) 464-8111.

DECIMALS AND PERCENTAGES

Use numerals for percentages and use the percentage sign (%).

By one estimate, 26% of all electric-cable breaks and 18% of all phone-cable disruptions are caused by rats.

(If the percentages come at the beginning of a sentence, however, spell out both the number and the percentage sign, as shown in the U.S. Constitution example on the preceding page.)

SCORES AND STATISTICS

Use numerals for scores and statistics.

The average age of the most frequent game buyer is 38 years old. In 2007, 92% of computer game buyers and 80% of console game buyers were over the age of 18.

The home run hit by New York Giants outfielder Bobby Thomson to win the National League pennant at 3:58 p.m. on October 3, 1951, is called the "Shot Heard 'Round the World." The Giants won the game 5 to 4, defeating the Dodgers in their pennant playoff series, two games to one.

TIP: NUMBERS IN DIFFERENT DISCIPLINES

Different disciplines—mathematics, social sciences—use numbers differently. The advice we offer on these pages is general, so if you are writing for a specific discipline, ask someone familiar with the field (or a reference librarian) for help in learning the field's conventions.

GLOSSARY OF GRAMMATICAL TERMS AND USAGE

In this glossary, we provide definitions of grammatical terms (shown in **blue**) and guidelines for usage. We also list homonyms (words that are spelled differently but sound the same) and other words that writers can easily confuse.

As you use this glossary, just as you use this handbook, keep in mind that the guidelines for usage are not strict rules but are, rather, academic and professional conventions developed over time. When you follow these conventions, your writing is more likely to be perceived by readers as academic and professional.

One further note: In academic and professional writing, words considered colloquial, nonstandard, or informal (as we label them in this glossary) are usually avoided by writers.

a/an   **A** and **an** are indefinite articles because they indicate general objects (*a book, an apple*) rather than specific objects (*the president*). **A** is used when the following word begins with a consonant (*a tire*); **an** is used when the following word begins with a vowel sound (*an hour, an orange*).

a lot/alot   **A lot** and **alot** are often used in informal writing to mean *many* or *much*. It is better to use *many* or *much* instead of **a lot** in academic writing. **Alot** is nonstandard.

accept/except/expect   **Accept** is a verb meaning "to receive." **Except** is usually used as a conjunction or preposition meaning "other than," but it can also be used as a verb meaning "leave out." **Expect** is a verb meaning "to regard something as likely."

active voice   In a sentence or clause in active voice, the subject of the clause or sentence performs the action. See **passive voice** also. (See pp. 238–239 and p. 493.) *We installed a new operating system on the computer.*

ad/add   **Ad** is a shortened form of *advertisement*; **add** is a verb meaning "to join or combine."

adjective   An adjective is a word that modifies a noun or pronoun. (See p. 487.) *I like salty snacks.*

adjective clause   An adjective clause is a subordinate clause that modifies a noun or pronoun. Adjective clauses are also called relative clauses because they begin with a relative pronoun. (See p. 486.) *The park allows only dogs that are on leashes.*

adverb   An adverb is a word that modifies a verb (*talk quietly*), another modifier (*very inexpensive*), or a whole clause or sentence (*Fortunately, we had an umbrella*). (See pp. 498–499.)

adverb clause   An adverb clause is a subordinate clause that modifies a verb, another modifier, or a whole clause or sentence. (See pp. 522–523.) *We did not leave until all of the trash had been picked up.*

advice/advise   **Advice** is a noun meaning "an opinion." **Advise** is a verb meaning "to give an opinion or advice."

affect/effect   **Affect** is usually used as a verb meaning "to influence," and **effect** is a noun meaning "a result." Sometimes **affect** is used as a noun meaning "an emotional state or feeling" and sometimes **effect** is used as a verb meaning "to bring about."

agreement   Agreement refers to the correspondence of one word to another in gender, number, or person. For example, a verb should agree with its subject (The <u>mechanic knows</u> how to fix the engine) and a pronoun must agree with its antecedent (The <u>factory workers</u> are on strike for <u>their</u> benefits). (See pp. 456–459 on subject-verb agreement.)

all ready/already   **All ready** is an adjective phrase meaning "ready to go." **Already** is an adverb that means "before" or "previously."

all right/alright   **All right** means "acceptable" and is all right to use in academic writing. **Alright** is considered nonstandard.

all together/altogether   **All together** means "in one place" or "in unison." **Altogether** means "entirely."

allude/elude   **Allude** means "to refer to." **Elude** means "to escape."

allusion/illusion   An **allusion** is an indirect reference to something. An **illusion** is a false or misleading impression.

among/between   Use **between** when referring to two objects; use **among** when referring to three or more objects.

amount/number   **Amount** is used for quantities of things that can be measured but not counted, such as *energy*. **Number** is used for quantities of things that can be counted, such as *bananas*.

an   See **a/an**.

antecedent   An antecedent is the noun or pronoun referred to by a pronoun. (See p. 484.) In the following sentence, "Betty" is the antecedent of "her." <u>Betty</u> was on <u>her</u> way to pick up <u>her</u> grandchildren.

any more/anymore   **Any more** means "no more." **Anymore** means "now." Both are used in negative constructions. (I don't want to hear any more lies; I don't believe you anymore.)

anybody/any body/anyone/any one   **Anybody** and **anyone** are indefinite pronouns that have the same meaning. **Any body** and **any one** are usually followed by the noun each modifies (*any body of water, any one incident*).

anyway/anyways   **Anyway** is used to support a point that was just made and is the correct form, but the nonstandard **anyways** is often used in informal writing and conversation.

apt/liable/likely   **Apt** and **likely** are interchangeable, but apt specifically means "having a tendency to." *He is apt to make mistakes like that.* **Liable** means "in danger of" and is best used only in contexts describing a dire situation. *You are liable to start a fire if you light a match near a gas tank.*

article   Articles are always followed by a noun. *A, an,* and *the* are articles. (See pp. 488–491.)

as/like   Use **as** instead of **like** before dependent clauses, which contain a noun and a verb (He ran as if his life depended on it). Use **like** before a noun or pronoun (He ran like a cheetah).

assure/ensure/insure   **Assure** means "promise," **ensure** means "make certain," and **insure** means to "arrange for compensation in case of damage." These words are often used incorrectly in place of each other.

at/where   Using **at** with **where** is unnecessary and makes writing seem wordy. *We are right at where we started.*

auxiliary verb   See **helping verb**.

awful/awfully   **Awful** is an adjective that means "awe inspiring" but it is more commonly used to mean "really bad." **Awful** and the adverb form **awfully** should not be used interchangeably, and they do not require intensifiers such as "very" or "extremely." *We heard an awful sound and were frightened awfully.*

awhile/a while   **Awhile** is an adverb and **a while** is a pairing of an article and noun. Consequently, **awhile** cannot be used as the object of a preposition (**a while**, however, can), and **a while** cannot be used to modify a verb. *We waited <u>awhile</u> because Mario said he would be back in <u>a while</u>.*

bad/badly   **Bad** should be used only as an adjective; **badly** is the adverb. *I sing badly.*

being as/being that   Both **being as** and **being that** are colloquial and should not be used in academic writing.

beside/besides   **Beside** means "next to." **Besides** means "except." *No one, besides Mary, would sit beside Archie.*

between   See **among/between**.

bring/take   **Bring** describes movement from a more distant location to nearby. **Take** describes movement away from. *Bring me that box so I can take it with me to work.*

but/however/yet **But, however,** and **yet** can all be used to indicate a contrast. Using them together in the same sentence will make it wordy.

can/may In academic writing, **can** indicates the ability to do something, while **may** indicates permission to do something. Informally, these words are often used interchangeably.

capital/capitol A **capital** is the main governmental city of a state or country. *Annapolis is the capital of Maryland.* A **capitol** is the building in which government bodies meet. *The senator gave a press conference on the steps of the capitol.*

case Case is the form of a noun or pronoun that indicates its function. Nouns change case only to show possession. (See p. 483.) *I wrote a letter outlining my concerns* (subject). *He wrote a letter to me outlining his concerns* (object of preposition). *The letter's purpose was clear* (possessive noun).

censor/censure To **censor** is to ban or silence. To **censure** is to reprimand publicly.

cite/sight/site **Cite** is a verb meaning to "reference specifically." **Sight** is used as a verb meaning "to view" and as a noun meaning "vision." **Site** is usually used as a noun to mean "location," but it can also be used as a verb to mean "to locate."

clause A clause is a group of words containing a subject and a verb. A **main** or **independent clause** can stand alone as a sentence (see p. 517), but a **subordinate** or **dependent clause** acts as a part of speech and cannot stand alone (see pp. 520–523).

comma splice A comma splice occurs when two independent clauses are joined incorrectly by a comma. (See pp. 470–471.) *Jose did not approve of our choice, he wanted to hire the other candidate* (incorrect). *Jose did not approve of our choice; he wanted to hire the other candidate* (correct).

common noun A common noun names a general person, place, or thing. Common nouns are not capitalized unless they are the first word of a sentence. (See pp. 480–481.) *Did Johnny Depp portray a pirate in that movie?*

complement/compliment To **complement** something is to complete it. To **compliment** is to flatter. Because they are spelled so similarly, they are often confused.

complex sentence A complex sentence is a sentence that contains at least one subordinate clause attached to an independent clause. (See pp. 520–523.) *Despite the heat, we had a really good time at the festival.*

compound sentence A compound sentence contains at least two main clauses. (See pp. 518–519.) *We ate dinner* and *then we went for a walk.*

compound-complex sentence A compound-complex sentence contains at least two independent clauses and a subordinate clause. (See pp. 524–525.) *Even though my parents are both Italian, I have not visited Italy* and *I do not speak the language.*

conjunction A conjunction is a word that links and relates parts of a sentence. (See pp. 502–505.) *Eric arrived late, but the movie had not started yet.* See **coordinating conjunction**, **correlative conjunction**, and **subordinating conjunction**.

conjunctive adverb A conjunctive adverb is an adverb (such as *however, besides, consequently,* or *therefore*) that relates two main or independent clauses. (See p. 505.) *Our car is broken; consequently, we had to carpool with the neighbors.*

conscience/conscious **Conscience** is a noun meaning "a sense of right or wrong." **Conscious** is an adjective meaning "awake."

continual/continuous **Continual** is an adjective meaning "recurring." **Continuous** is an adjective meaning "constant." *That continual noise is a continuous bother.*

coordinating conjunction A coordinating conjunction is a word (such as *and, but, or, for, nor, yet,* and *so*) that links two grammatically equal parts of a sentence. (See p. 502 and pp. 540–541.) *I brushed my teeth and went to bed.*

correlative conjunction Correlative conjunctions are two or more words (*neither…nor, either…or, not only…but also*) that work together to link parts of a sentence. (See p. 503.) *Not only were we excited, but we were also a little bit afraid.*

could of **Could of** is often used in informal writing, but *could have* is more appropriate.

count noun A count noun names things that can be counted. (See pp. 489–490.) *goats, shoes, computers*

criteria/criterion A **criterion** is a singular noun that means "a measure" or "a condition." **Criteria** is the plural form of **criterion**.

dangling modifier   A dangling modifier does not have a clear connection to the word it modifies. (See pp. 474–475.) *Spicier than expected, she spat out the soup.*

data/datum   **Datum** is a singular noun that refers to a piece of information or a fact. **Data** is the plural of **datum**, and although it is often used as a singular noun, it should be treated as a plural noun and take a plural verb.

declarative   A declarative sentence is a statement. (See p. 506.) *The measurements were incorrect.*

dependent clause   See **subordinate clause**.

differ from/differ with   To **differ from** means "to be unlike." To **differ with** means "to disagree with."

different from/different than   **Different from** is preferred in academic writing to **different than** except in situations where **different from** would be wordy.

direct object   A <u>direct object</u> is the noun, pronoun, or noun clause naming the person or thing that takes the action of a <u>transitive verb</u>. (See pp. 514–515.) *The chef <u>threw</u> <u>the meatloaf</u> in the trash.*

discreet/discrete   **Discreet** is an adjective meaning "careful" or "prudent." **Discrete** is an adjective meaning "separate."

disinterested/uninterested   **Disinterested** is an adjective that means "impartial." It is often used incorrectly in place of **uninterested**.

double negative   A double negative is the use of two negatives to convey one negative idea. It should be avoided in academic writing. (See p. 243.) *I <u>don't</u> have <u>no</u> time to go with you.*

due to the fact that   **Due to the fact that** is a wordy substitute for **because**.

each other/one another   **Each other** should be used for two things; **one another** should be used for more than two things.

effect   See **affect/effect**.

elicit/illicit   **Elicit** is a verb that means "to bring out." **Illicit** is an adjective that means "unlawful." These words are often incorrectly used in place of each other.

emigrate from/immigrate to   **Emigrate** is a verb meaning "to leave one's country." **Immigrate** is a verb that means "to settle in another country."

ensure   See **assure/ensure/insure**.

etc.   **Etc.** is an abbreviation for the Latin *et cetera* and is used to shorten a list of items. **Etc.** is mostly used in informal writing.

every body/everybody/every one/everyone   **Everybody** and **everyone** are both collective nouns referring to all parties under discussion. **Every body** and **every one** are both adjective-noun combinations that refer to individuals within the larger group.

except   See **accept/except/expect**.

except for the fact that   **Except for the fact that** is a wordy substitute for *except that*.

expect   See **accept/except/expect**.

expletive   *There* and *it* are expletives, or "dummy subjects" that are used to fill a grammatical slot in a sentence. (See p. 244.) *It is very clear.*

farther/further   **Farther** refers to distance, while **further** refers to time or another abstract concept.

fewer/less   **Fewer** is used for things that can be counted, while **less** is used for things that cannot be counted.

fragment   A fragment is a group of words that is capitalized and punctuated like a sentence but lacks a subject and predicate. Fragments are used in some forms of writing, such as fiction and advertising copy, but they are usually not acceptable in academic writing. (See pp. 490–493.) *A representative who cares.*

further   See **farther/further**.

gender   Gender is the classification of nouns or pronouns as masculine and feminine. (See p. 473.)

good/well   **Good** can be used only as an adjective, while **well** can be used as both an adjective and an adverb. *His last album was <u>good</u>. He sings <u>well</u>. Is your mother <u>well</u>?*

hanged/hung   **Hanged** is a verb that specifically refers to an execution. **Hung** is used in all other instances. *In the past, criminals were often hanged. The noose hung from the gallows.*

have/of   **Have**, rather than **of**, should be used after auxiliary or helping verbs such as *could, should, would, might,* and so on.

he/she; s/he   Academic audiences prefer writing that is gender inclusive (unless a distinction of gender is necessary). (See pp. 282–283.)

helping verb   Helping verbs are also known as auxiliary verbs. These verbs (forms of *be, do,* and *have*) join with other verbs to indicate tense and mood. Modal verbs can also be used as helping verbs. (See p. 495 and p. 497.) *By Friday, she had collected enough signatures to be listed on the ballot.*

herself/himself/myself/yourself   These *–self* pronouns refer to or intensify nouns or other pronouns. They are often used colloquially in place of personal pronouns, but not usually in academic writing.

hopefully   **Hopefully** is an adverb that is often used to modify a sentence, but it is considered nonstandard.

if/whether   **Whether** is clearer than **if** when you are posing an alternative. *Whether your vote matters depends on the integrity of the electoral process.*

illusion   See **allusion/illusion**.

immigrate   See **emigrate from/immigrate to**.

impact   **Impact** is used as a noun referring to a violent collision and, less commonly, as a verb meaning "to collide violently." The use of **impact** as a noun to mean "an effect" or as a verb to mean "to have an effect on" is prevalent, but it is considered nonstandard.

imperative   An imperative sentence expresses a command. The subject of an imperative sentence is often implied. (See p. 507.) *Be quiet!*

implicit   See **explicit/implicit**.

imply/infer   **Imply** is a verb meaning "to suggest." **Infer** is a verb meaning "to conclude."

in regards to   **In regards to** is a wordy substitute for *regarding*.

incredible/incredulous   **Incredible** is an adjective that means "unbelievable." **Incredulous** is an adjective used to mean "not believing." *Our incredulous minds could not fathom the incredible sight before us.*

independent clause   An independent—or main—clause is a group of words with a subject and predicate that can stand alone as a sentence. (See p. 517.)

indirect object   An indirect object is a noun, pronoun, or noun phrase that names the person or thing that is affected by the action of a transitive verb. (See pp. 514–515.) *The waiter served us fresh coffee.*

interjection   An interjection is a word that expresses strong emotion. (See p. 478.) *Ouch! That hurt!*

interrogative   An interrogative sentence asks a question. (See p. 506.) *What did you do this weekend?*

intransitive verb   An intransitive verb does not take an object. (See pp. 514–515.) *I just wanted to participate.*

irregardless/regardless   **Irregardless** is often used as a substitute for **regardless**, but using **irregardless** in that way is considered nonstandard.

irregular verb   An irregular verb does not take *–ed* or *–d* to form its past tense or past participle. (See pp. 495–497.) *slept, swam*

it is my opinion that   **It is my opinion that** is a wordy substitute for *I believe that*.

its/it's   **Its** is the possessive form of **it** and does not take an apostrophe. **It's** is the contraction of *it is*. *As the fish swam, its fins undulated. It's a sad day when the Cubs lose.*

-ize/-wise   The suffix **-ize** turns a noun or an adjective into a verb (*motorize*). The suffix **–wise** turns a noun or an adjective into an adverb (*clockwise*).

kind of/sort of/type of   These three constructions are used to classify things. Informally or colloquially they are used to mean *somewhat* or *rather*. *That kind of soup makes me rather queasy.*

knew/new   **Knew**, a verb, is the past tense of "to know." **New** is an adjective meaning "fresh, not seen before."

lay/lie   **Lay** is a verb that means "to place," and it takes a direct object. **Lie** means "to recline" or "to position" and does not take a direct object.

leave/let   **Leave** and **let** are interchangeable only when followed by "alone." **Leave** means "go" and **let** means "allow."

less   See **fewer/less**.

lie   See **lay/lie**.

linking verb   A linking verb connects a subject to a complement. (See p. 515.)

literally   **Literally** means "actually" or "just as the words say." It is often used colloquially to intensify a word.

loan/lone   A **loan** is money that is borrowed; **lone** is an adjective meaning "single, isolated."

loose/lose   **Loose** is an adjective meaning "not tight." *His pants were so loose he couldn't walk.* **Lose** is a verb meaning "to misplace" or "to be defeated." *Don't lose your homework.*

lots/lots of   **Lots** and **lots of** are often used as substitutes for *many*, but they are considered nonstandard.

main clause   See **independent clause**.

may/can   See **can/may**.

may be/maybe   **May be** is a verb phrase. **Maybe** is an adverb.

media/medium   **Medium** is a singular noun referring to a means of conveying information. **Media** is the plural of **medium** and takes a plural verb. *The media portray…*

might of   See **have/of**.

modifier   A modifier is a word, phrase, or clause that describes another word. Modifiers are adjectives (see p. 487), adverbs (see pp. 498–499), adjective clauses (see pp. 520–521), and adverb clauses (see pp. 522–523).

must of   See **have/of**.

noncount noun   A noncount noun names things that cannot be counted. (See pp. 489–490.) *electricity, history, peace*

nonrestrictive modifier   A nonrestrictive modifier is not essential to the meaning of the word, phrase, or clause it modifies and should be set off by commas or other punctuation. (See pp. 543–545.) *My uncle, Misha, used to work on Wall Street.*

noun   A noun names a person, place, or thing. (See pp. 480–483.)

number   See **amount/number**.

object   An object is the receiver of an action within a sentence, clause, or phrase. (See pp. 510–511.)

OK/O.K./okay   **OK**, **O.K.**, and **okay** are all okay for informal writing but are less okay in academic writing.

owing to the fact that   **Owing to the fact that** is a wordy substitute for *because*.

parallelism   Parallelism is the practice of putting similar elements in a sentence in a similar grammatical pattern. (See pp. 248–249.) *His resume stated that he had trained and supervised employees, analyzed and evaluated software, and organized and maintained records.*

parts of speech   There are eight parts of speech, or groups of words classified by their grammatical functions and meanings: nouns, pronouns, verbs, adjectives, adverbs, prepositions, conjunctions, and interjections. (See pp. 478–505.)

passed/past   **Passed**, a verb, is the past tense of "to pass." **Past** is a noun or adjective, describing something that happened prior to the present moment.

passive voice   Passive voice is indicated by a clause with a transitive verb that is acting upon the subject. (See pp. 238–239 and p. 493.) *The issue was called to our attention by the maintenance crew.*

peace/piece   **Peace** is a state of harmony. A **piece** is a part of something.

people/persons   Use **people** to refer to a general group, unless it is necessary to emphasize individuals within the group. In that case, use **persons**.

per   The Latin word **per** means "for each." It is best used in familiar phrases such as *miles per gallon*.

phenomena/phenomenon   **Phenomenon** is a singular noun meaning "observable fact" or "unusual event." The plural form of **phenomenon** is **phenomena**, which takes a plural verb. *Among the phenomena that were discussed were alien abductions and reincarnation.*

phrase   A phrase is a group of words that does not contain both a subject and a predicate. (See pp. 511–516.) *A lovely day*

plenty   **Plenty** is often used as a colloquial substitute for *very*.

plus   **Plus** is often used incorrectly to join clauses or sentences. It is better to use *and, also, moreover, furthermore*, or another conjunctive adjective instead.

possessive case   The possessive case indicates ownership. (See p. 483.) *my lunch, his shoes, Tran's car*

precede/proceed   **Precede** and **proceed** are both verbs, but precede means "come before" and proceed means "continue."

predicate   The predicate is the part of a clause that expresses the action or tells something about the subject. The predicate includes the verb and its complements, objects, and modifiers. (See pp. 512–516.)

prejudice/prejudiced   *Prejudice* is a noun meaning "bias." **Prejudiced** is an adjective meaning "biased" or "intolerant."

preposition   A preposition is a part of speech that shows relationships or qualities. (See pp. 500–501.)

prepositional phrase   A prepositional phrase is a phrase formed by a preposition and its object. A prepositional phrase includes the modifiers of the object. (See p. 516.)

pretty   **Pretty** is often used as a colloquial substitute for *very*. Avoid using **pretty** to mean *very* in academic writing.

principal/principle   **Principal** can be a noun, meaning "the head of a school" or it can be an adjective, meaning "the most important element." **Principle** is a noun meaning "a rule or standard."

pronoun   A pronoun is a part of speech that stands for other nouns or pronouns. Classes of pronouns include: **possessive pronouns**, **personal pronouns**, **demonstrative pronouns**, **indefinite pronouns**, **relative pronouns**, **interrogative pronouns**, **reflexive pronouns**, and **reciprocal pronouns**. (See pp. 484–486.)

pronoun case   Pronouns that act as the subject of a sentence are in the **subjective case** (*I, you, he, she, it, we, they*). Pronouns that act as direct or indirect objects are in the **objective case** (*me, you, him, her, it, us, them*). Pronouns that indicate ownership are in the **possessive case** (*my, your, his, her, its, our, their*). (See pp. 484–486.)

proper noun   A proper noun is a noun that names a particular person, place, thing, or group. Proper nouns are capitalized. (See pp. 480–483.) *Anthony Bourdain, Dublin, Yom Kippur*

question as to whether/question of whether   These phrases are both wordy substitutes for *whether*.

raise/rise   The verb **raise** means "lift up" and takes a direct object. The verb **rise** means "get up." It does not take a direct object.

real/really   **Real** is an adjective, while **really** is an adverb. These words are often used incorrectly in place of each other.

reason is because   **Reason is because** is often used to explain causality. *Reason is* and *is because* are less wordy.

reason why   **Reason why** is a redundant construction that should be avoided in academic writing. Instead of *The reason why he went to Malaysia is for work,* you can write, *He went to Malaysia for work.*

relative pronoun   A <u>relative pronoun</u> initiates <u>clauses</u>. *That, which, what, who, whom,* and *whose* are relative pronouns. (See p. 486.) *The woman <u>who makes those funny, furry purses</u> will have a booth at the fair.*

restrictive modifier   A restrictive modifier is essential to the meaning of the word, phrase, or clause it modifies. Unlike a nonrestrictive modifier, it is not set off by punctuation. (See pp. 543–545.) *My uncle <u>who lives in Canada</u> is visiting next week.*

rise/raise   See **raise/rise.**

run-on sentence   A run-on sentence occurs when two main clauses are fused together without punctuation or a conjunction. (See pp. 470–471.) *I don't like Wednesdays they are too far away from the weekend.*

sentence   A sentence is a grammatically independent group of words that contains at least one independent clause. (See pp. 506–525.)

set/sit   The verb **set** means "to put" and it takes a direct object. **Sit** means "to be seated" and does not take a direct object.

shall/will   **Shall** is very formal, and is most often used in first person questions, while **will** can be used in the future tense with all persons.

should of   See **have/of.**

simple/simplistic   Although it is often used as such, **simplistic** is not a synonym of *simple.* **Simplistic** means "crude" or "unsophisticated," while **simple** means "easy."

since   **Since** most commonly refers to time, but it can also be used as a synonym of *because.* Keep in mind, though, that some readers prefer that **since** not be used as a synonym of *because.*

sit/set   See **set/sit.**

some time/sometime/sometimes   **Some time** refers to a period of time, while **sometime** refers to an unspecified time. **Sometimes** means "occasionally."

somebody/some body; someone/some one **Somebody** and **someone** are indefinite pronouns that mean the same thing. **Some body** and **some one** are adjective-noun combinations.

sort of See **kind of/sort of/type of.**

subject A subject is a noun, pronoun, or noun phrase that identifies what the clause is about and is connected to the predicate. (See p. 512.)

subject-verb agreement See **agreement.**

subjunctive mood The subjunctive mood expresses a wish, a condition contrary to fact, a recommendation, or a request. (See p. 493.)

subordinate A subordinate relationship is a relationship of unequal importance, in either grammar or meaning. (See pp. 246–247.)

subordinate clause A subordinate clause, also called a dependent clause, is a clause that cannot stand alone but must be attached to a main clause. (See pp. 520–524.)

subordinating conjunction A subordinating conjunction is a word that introduces a subordinate clause. Some subordinating conjunctions are *after, although, as, because, before, if, since, that, unless, until, when, where,* and *while.* (See p. 504.)

such **Such** means "of the previous kind" (*such behavior, such praise*), but it is often used informally as a synonym for *very.*

sure **Sure** is often used as an adverb to mean *certainly,* but it is more properly used as an adjective.

sure and/sure to; try and/try to **Sure to** and **try to** are correct; do not add *and* after *sure* or *try.*

take See **bring/take.**

than/then **Than** is a conjunction expressing difference. *I would rather watch a movie than go out tonight.* **Then** is an adverb expressing time. *First we went to church, then we went shopping.*

that/which **That** introduces a restrictive or essential clause, while **which** is usually used to introduce nonrestrictive or nonessential clauses.

their/there/they're **Their** is a possessive pronoun (see p. 485); **there** is most commonly used as an expletive (see p. 244); and **they're** is a contraction of *they are* (see p. 569).

to/too/two **To** is a preposition, while **too** is an adverb. **Two** is a number.

transition A transition is a word or phrase that notes movement from one unit of writing to another. (See pp. 236–237.)

transitive verb A transitive verb is a verb that takes a direct object. (See pp. 514–515.)

try and/try to See **sure and/sure to.**

unique If something is **unique,** it is one of a kind and can't be compared to anything else. Consequently, it is not necessary to use words such as *most* to modify **unique.**

usage/use/utilize **Utilize** and **usage** are often used in informal writing as synonyms for **use.**

verb A verb is a word that shows action or characterizes a subject in some way. (See pp. 492–497.)

well/good See **good/well.**

weather/whether **Weather** is a noun, describing whether it is sunny, raining, hot, or cold outside. **Whether** is a conjunction that can mean "if" or can introduce a set of opinions.

which/that See **that/which.**

who/whom **Who** is the subject pronoun, while **whom** is the object pronoun. *Who is that in the yard? With whom did you dance?*

who's/whose **Who's** is a contraction of *who is,* while **whose** is a possessive. *Who's there? Whose shoes are those?*

will/shall See **shall/will.**

-wise/-ize See **-ize/-wise.**

would of See **have/of.**

you **You** is primarily used to directly address the reader, but it is often used informally to refer to people in general.

your/you're **Your** and **you're** are not interchangeable. **Your** is the possessive form of *you. Your conscience will rest easier after you vote.* **You're** is the contraction of *you are. You're a citizen, and so you are expected to vote.* (See p. 483 on possessives; see p. 569 on contractions.)

CREDITS

PHOTOS

All photos not credited below are courtesy of the author.

Part 1: Opener: Masterfile RF; 2 Stone/Allstock/Getty Images; 4 RF fotosearch; 6 top, Vicky Kasala; 6 bottom, Stone/Allstock/Getty Images.

8 Stockbyte/Getty Images; 9 top left, Image Bank/Getty Images; 9 top center, Stone/Allstock/Getty Images; 9 top right, Esbin Anderson/Omni Photo Communications, Inc.; 9 center left, ImageState/International Stock Photography, Ltd.; 9 center right, Stockbyte; 9 bottom, AP/Wide World Photos; 12 Stockbyte/Getty Images.

Part 2: Opener: photolibrary.com; 18 Stockbyte/Getty Images; 19 top, Stone/Allstock/Getty Images; 19 bottom left, The Stock Connection; 19 bottom right, Jeff Greenberg/PhotoEdit, Inc.; 20 Michael Newman/PhotoEdit, Inc.; 24 Stockbyte/Getty Images; 26 Photo Disc/Getty Images; 28 David Young-Wolff/PhotoEdit, Inc.; 29 Peter Arnold, Inc.; 34 Dex Images; 38 Taxi/Getty Images; 46 top, Stockbyte/Getty Images; 46 middle, ©Time Magazine/Getty Images; 46 bottom, Copyright 2005 Rolling Stone. Photograph by James Dimmock; 54 Stone/Allstock/Getty Images; 74 Colin Young/Wolff/PhotoEdit, Inc.; 76 Michelle Bridwell/PhotoEdit, Inc.; 78 Taxi/Getty Images.

Part 3: Opener: photolibrary.com; 82 Allstock/Getty Images; 87 right, ©2002 Donna Tartt. Cover courtesy Alfred A. Knopf, Random House, Inc. All rights reserved; 89 right ©2002 Donna Tartt. Cover courtesy Alfred A. Knopf, Random House, Inc. All rights reserved; 91 right, ©2002 Donna Tartt. Cover courtesy Alfred A. Knopf, Random House, Inc. All rights reserved; 94 Dag Sundberg/Getty Images; 101 National Archives; 123 The Mayor's Office to Combat Domestic Violence, New York City; 124 Taxi/ Getty Images; 138 Stockbyte/Getty Images.

Part 4: Opener: Stone/Allstock/Getty Images; 142 Six-Cats Research, Inc. 143 top row, left: Jeff Greenberg/PhotoEdit, Inc.; 143 top row, middle: Friedrich Stark/Das Fotoarchiv; 143 middle row, left: Sean Ellis; 143 bottom row, left: David McLain/Aurora; 145 middle: Photodisc/Getty Images RF; 145 right: Newsweek Magazine/NASA/National Science Data Center, U. S. Geological Survey. Newsweek research by Peter Burkholder. Copyright September 23, 1996, Newsweek Inc. All rights reserved. Reprinted by permission. 170 Lebrecht Music & Arts Photo Library; 184 Image Bank/Getty Images; 185 top, Library of Congress. Prints and Photographs Division; 185 center, Library of Congress. Prints and Photographs Division; 185 bottom, *Passing/Posing/Female Prophet Ann, Who Observes the Presentation of Jesus on the Temple*, oil on canvas, 2003 © Kehinde Wiley; 188 photo of Caracas, Venezuela by Rob Crandall; 190 David Young-Wolff/PhotoEdit Inc.;

Part 5: Opener: Dorling Kindersley Media Library; 194 Lisette Le Bon/Superstock, Inc.; 200 Getty Images/Taxi; 214 Bill Aron/PhotoEdit, Inc.; 216 David Fischer/Digital Vision/Getty Images.

Part 6: Opener: Photonica Amana America, Inc./Getty Images; 224 Jamie Marshall/Dorling Kindersley Media; 226 Lonely Planet Images/Photo 20/20; 230 National Geographic Image Collection; 252 AP/Wide World Photos; 260 PhotoDisc/Getty Images; 264 AP/Wide World Photos.

Part 7: Opener: Dorling Kindersley Media Library; 268 PhotoEdit, Inc.; 272 Corbis/Reuters; 274 Creative Eye/Mira.com; 276 Allstock/Getty Images.

Part 8: 290 Alan Oddie/PhotoEdit, Inc.; 292 Stockbyte/Getty Images; 297 Photodisc/Getty Images RF; 298 Kayte Deioma/PhotoEdit, Inc.; 311 Photodisc/Getty Images RF; 321 Klaus Tiedge/Corbis; 356 RF Bloomimage/Corbis; 366 top left, Dorling Kindersley Media Library; 366 bottom left, Lake Country Museum/Corbis; 366 top right, Dorling Kindersley Media Library; 366 center, ©Ed Young/Corbis; 366 bottom center right, Dorling Kindersley Media Library; 366 bottom right, ©Kristy-Anne Glubish/Design Pics/RF Corbis; 367 top left, Terry Sirrell/ RF@images.com /Corbis; 367 left top center, Dorling Kindersley Media Library; 367 left center, ©Bettmann/Corbis; 367 left center bottom, Pablo Corral/Corbis; 367 left bottom, ©Gideon Mendel/Corbis; 367 top right, Free Agents Limited/Corbis; 367 right center, RF Corbis; 367 bottom right, Dorling Kindersley Media Library.

Part 9: Opener: The Stock Connection; 476 The Granger Collection; 480 top center, Frank Siteman/

Omni Photo Communications, Inc.; 480 bottom center, Photo Researchers, Inc.; 481 top right center, Dorling Kindersley Media Library; 481 top right, David Young-Wolff/PhotoEdit, Inc.; 481 bottom center right, The Image Works; 481 bottom right, Superstock RF; 489 top left, Frank Siteman/Omni Photo Communications, Inc.; 489 top right: David Young-Wolff/PhotoEdit, Inc.; 489 middle left: Photo Researchers, Inc.; 489 middle right: Superstock RF; 489 bottom left, Corbis - Comstock Images RF; 489 bottom center, The Image Works; 489 bottom right: David Young-Wolff/PhotoEdit, Inc.; 492 top, George Eastman House; 492 middle, Oscar Burrill/Photo Researchers, Inc.; 492 bottom: Richard Hutchings/ Photo Researchers, Inc.; 498 top left, Getty Images, Inc./Taxi; 498 top left center, Tom Stillo/Omni Photo Communications, Inc.; 498 top right center, David Parket/Omni Photo Communications, Inc.; 498 top right, David Parket/Omni Photo Communications, Inc.; 498 middle left, William Mullins/Photo Researchers, Inc.; 498 middle left center, Frederick Ayer III/Photo Researchers, Inc.; 498 middle right center, David Parket/Omni Photo Communications, Inc.; 498 middle right, Terry Wittaker/Photo Researchers, Inc.; 498 bottom left, Phil Mislinski/ Omni Photo Communications, Inc.; 498 bottom left center, Ardea, London, Ltd.; 498 bottom right center, Jeanne White/Photo Researchers, Inc.; 498 bottom right, Richard Hutchings/Photo Researchers, Inc.; 526 Stone/Allstock/Getty Images; 584 Stockbyte/Getty Images.

Exercises section: 595 ©Fancy/Alamy RF

TEXT

Part 2

47 Cover, *African Journal on Conflict Resolution*, © The African Centre for the Constructive Resolution of Disputes (1991-2008).

47 Cover, *Peabody Journal of Education*, Routledge, Taylor & Francis Group.

47 Cover, *Social Neuroscience*, 1.1, March 2006, Routledge, Taylor & Francis Group.

49 See Jane Compute screenshot, seejanecomoute.blogspot.com Used with permission

49 Screen shot, Neil Gaiman blog/website. http://www.neilgaiman.com. Photo by Sopia Quach. Used with permission

50 *Crooked Timber* screen shot, crookedtimber.org. Used with permission.

50 Google™ screenshot. GOOGLE is a trademark of Google, Inc. By permission.

51 Pew Internet & American Life Project, accessed September 2007, www.pewinternet.org. Used with permission.

52 Reprinted with the permission of Kairos: A Journal of Rhetoric, Technology, and Pedagogy <http://kairos.technorhetoric.net>

53 Reprinted with permission from Encyclopaedia Britannica Online, ©2009 by Encyclopsedia Britannica, Inc.

53 GMU Free Doc

57 University of Louisiana Library, Advanced Search screenshot. Powered by SirsiDynix. Used by permission of SirsiDynix.

60 Michigan Tech, Van Pelt Library Database search screen shot. Used by permission.

61 Michigan Tech, Van Pelt Library Database search results screen shot. Used by permission.

62 Copyright 2007 LexisNexis, a division of Reed Elsevier Inc. All Rights Reserved. LexisNexis and the Knowledge Burst logo are registered trademarks of Reed Elsevier Properties Inc. and are used with the permission of LexisNexis.

63 Image published with permission of ProQuest LLC. Further reproduction is prohibited without permission.

64 From Gale. Screen shot from *Power Search Database*. © Gale, a part of Cengage Learning, Inc. Reproduced by permission. www.cengage.com/permissions.

65 From OCLC's WorldCat® database, used with OCLC permission. WorldCat® is a registered trademark of OCLC Online Computer Library Center, Inc.

Part 3

84, 120 Used by permission of Hachette Book Group, Inc. USA

87, 91 Used by permission of Hachette Book Group, Inc. USA

87, 89, 91 Cover, *The Little Friend* by Donna Tartt. New York: Knopf, 2002.

89 Used by permission of Hachette Book Group, Inc. USA

95 "Food ad blitz," *The San Francisco Chronicle*, Editorial, March 29, 2007, B8. Copyright 2007 by San Francisco Chronicle. Reproduced by permission of San Francisco Chronicle in the format print and other book via Copyright Clearance Center.

106 Screenshot "Bacteria Salad" from Persuasive Games. Used by permission of Persuasive Games.

111 Copyright © 2006 Conde Nast Publications. All rights reserved. Originally published in *The New Yorker*. Reprinted by permission.

129 Screenshot from *Wired News*, July 14, 2005. Copyright © 2005 Condé Net, a dision of Condé Nast Publications.

133 Title page, "The Avian Flu: How Scared Should We Be," *Time*, October 17, 2005.

137 GMU Free Doc

Part 4

158 Memo to STC Arts Projects Teams written by Jason Dryja, 2006. Used by permission of Jason Dryja.

165 "Letter to the editor" written by Daniel Moshenberg, George Washington University. *The New York Times*, Oct. 2006. By permission of the author.

167 Copyright 2007 by Ben Carmichael. First published in *OnEarth* (www.onearth.org) Fall 2007. Reprinted by permission.

168 Home page from Steve Berlin Johnson's blog page, www.stevenberlinjohnson.com. Used by permission.

169 Courtesy A. Reindeer.

173 Laurence Gonzales, *Deep Survival; Who Lives, Who Dies, and Why*. New York: W. W. Norton & Company, 2003.

177 Richard Rhodes, *Deadly Feasts: The "Prion" Controversy and the Public's Health*. New York: Simon & Schuster, 1997.

177 Christian Hoard, "The Boys Are Back in Town," *Rolling Stone*, October 5, 2006

178 Michael Pollan, *The Omnivore's Dilemma*. New York: Penguin Press, 2006.

179 ©2007, Washington.Newsweek Interactive Company, LLC. All Rights Reserved.

180 Charles Siebert, "An Elephant Crack Up?" *New York Times Magazine*, October 8, 2006.

181 Paul Bloom, "Is God an Accident?" *The Atlantic Monthly*, December 2005.

183 Mike Rose "Extol Brains As Well As Brawn of the Blue Collar," *Los Angeles Times*, September 6, 2004.

Part 6

229 Bühner, M. et al. (2006). "Working memory dimensions as differential predictors of the speed and error aspect of multitasking performance," *Human Performance*, 19, 253-275.

229 J. Balzar, J., "One Thing at a Time, Please," *Los Angeles Times*, April 27, 2003.

240 John Edgar Wideman, "Who's War," *Harper's Magazine*, March 1, 2002.

Part 7

270 Quote from student Jun Liu, *Reflections on Multiliterate Live*, ed. Diane Dewhurst Belcher and Ulla Connor. Multilingual Matters Limited 2001. Used by permission of Multilingual Matters, Ltd.

275 Quote from student Miyuki Sasaki, *Reflections on Multiliterate Live*, ed. Diane Dewhurst Belcher and Ulla Connor. Multilingual Matters Limited 2001. Used by permission of Multilingual Matters, Ltd.

276-277 From *My Year of Meats* by Ruth L. Ozeki, copyright © 1998 by Ruth Ozeki Lounsbury. Used by permission of Viking Penguin, a division of Penguin Group (USA) Inc.

284 American Psychological Association, APA Online, http://apastyle.apa.org/disabilities.html.

288 *Longman Dictionary of American English*. London: Pearson Education, 2008.

Part 8

299 Ravi Purushotma, "You're not studying, you're just…" *Language Learning & Technology*, Jan 2005. Used by permission of Ravi Purushotma. See updated version at http://www.lingualgamers.com/thesis

313 Cover and title page, *Gorls Make Media* by Mary Celeste Kearney, published by Routledge. Copyright 2006 by Taylor & Francis Group LLC-Books. Reproduced with permission of Taylor & Francis GroupLLC – Books in the format Textbookand Other book via Copyright Clearance Center.

314 Title page, *Sorting Things Out* by Geoffrey C Bowker and Susan Leigh Star, Published 1999, MIT Press. Used by permission of MIT Press.

315 Title page, *Images of an Era: The American Poster*, 1945-1975, MIT Press. Used by permission of MIT Press.

315 Title page, *Aesthetic Computing* by Paul Fishwick, MIT Press 2006. Used by permission of MIT Press.

315 *The Elements of Style* by William Strunk, Jr, Longman Publishers. Used by permission. of Pearson Education, Inc.

317 Oxford University Press

317 "Contesting the Objectivist Paradigm" by Lee Brasseur, *IEEE Transactions on Professional Communication* 36.3 (1003):114-123. Used by permission of IEEE and author.

319 Screenshot, Brittany Huntley, "My Global Study Experience in Dubai," *The Black Collegian*, First September Super Issue, 2006. By permission of *The Black Collegian*.

319 Screenshot, "Inside This Issue" *The Black Collegian*, First September Super Issue, 2006. By permission of *The Black Collegian*.

320 *Milwaukee Journal Sentinel*, September 23, 2007.

321 Science News

323 Velo News screenshot. VeloNews.com. Used by permission of Velo News. Inside Communications, Inc.

324 Screenshot jill/txt. Used by permission of Jill Walker Rettberg.

325 Used by permission of The Union of Concerned Scientists.

325 Screen shot from http://www.salon.com, featuring excerpt from Laura Miller, "Panic in the Pages," Salon.com, March 24, 2008. Reprinted by permission.

Part 9

527 Pico Iyer, "In Praise of the Humble Comma," *Time*, June 13, 1988.

INDEX

A

Assignment *(continued)*
    summary for, 11, 15
    terms for, 11
    understanding of, 5, 10, 11, 17
Assumption
    about audience, 108, 281, 287
    about author, 86
    about religious beliefs, 287
    through analogy, 100
    as appropriate, 112, 279
    through experience, 279, 281
    of heterosexuality, 286
    for shared values, 98, 105
Attitude, of audience, 3, 198. *See also* Audience; Experience, personal
Audience
    as academic, 145–51, 218, 228, 242–43
    analysis of, 14, 338–39
    anecdote for, 191
    assumptions about, 108, 281, 287
    attitude of, 3, 198
    background of, 5, 13
    beliefs of, 5, 13
    for blog, 50, 52
    characteristics of, 195, 196–97
    choices for, 7, 9, 44, 45
    classroom as, 3
    coherence for, 172–75
    communication with, 1, 3, 14, 15, 88, 106, 108, 109, 127, 221, 227, 234, 254–57
    for composer, 3, 20, 86, 109, 157, 193, 199, 200
    composition for, 1, 2, 3, 5, 7, 20, 44, 86, 88, 92, 106, 108, 109, 127, 157, 193, 199, 200, 221, 225–27, 234, 254–57, 275
    connection with, 3, 218, 277
    consideration of, 5, 18, 194–97, 206–7
    context for, 3, 7, 9, 10, 14, 44, 45, 84, 109, 110–15, 122–23
    culture of, 5, 13
    emotions of, 9, 88, 99
    emphasis for, 227
    engagement of, 1, 2, 3, 5, 7, 20, 44, 86, 88, 92, 106, 108, 109, 127, 157, 193, 199, 200, 221, 225–27, 234, 254–57, 275
    ethos by, 86, 109, 121, 201
    evidence for, 96–98, 109, 110–15, 122–23, 131, 135, 197
    examples for, 109, 110–15, 201, 227, 234, 254–57
    expectation of, 9, 11, 241
    experience of, 198
    focus of, 5, 9, 13, 108, 198
    genre and, 144–47
    as global, 273
    identification of, 21
    as immediate, 13
    for journal/magazine, 46
    language for, 45
    medium for, 11, 46
    for nonprofit, 51
    observations of, 195
    oral presentation for, 1, 190, 191, 264–65
    orientation of, 190
    passive voice for, 238–39, 402–3, 465
    pathos and, 109, 110–15, 121, 122–23, 201
    for periodical, 46, 52, 196
    for popular writing, 40, 42, 44, 46, 49, 145, 164–69, 229
    prior knowledge by, 120
    questions by, 34
    relationship with, 3, 9, 13, 240, 252
    relevance to, 125, 126, 128–29
    repetition for, 190
    research strategies for, 124, 195
    respect for, 278–79
    response by, 5, 88, 105–6, 109, 110–15, 121, 122–23, 138, 184, 197
    salutation for, 283
    as secondary, 13
    sentence length and, 225, 228–29, 239, 271
    shared values of, 13, 105–7
    as specialized, 45
    strategies for, 3, 10, 11, 195
    style for, 225–27, 240–41
    teachers as, 3, 5, 10
    for topic, 5, 30, 196, 198
    visuals for, 120–23
    vocabulary for, 225
    for website, 50
    in workplace, 145, 156–63, 229
Author
    as anonymous, 423
    APA citation for, 420–23
    approval by, of book, 87
    assumptions about, 86
    book cover approval by, 87
    CMS citation for, 447
    as corporate, 48, 315, 423
    credentials of, 39, 131, 135
    CSE citation for, 442
    as journalist/reporter, 39
    MLA citation for, 368–70
    pseudonym for, 371
    of revision, 315, 442
Authority
    of database, 52
    for ethos, 116–17, 201, 210–11
    from experts, 178
    through in-text citations, 342–51, 410–13, 438, 439, 444–45
    MLA citation for, 332–33
    through quotation, 298, 300–301, 303
    source of, 103, 116–17, 210–11, 300–301

B

Background, of audience, 5, 13, 107
BARTLEBY.COM, 68
Behavior, shared values for, 5, 13, 107
Beliefs, of audience, 5, 13
The Best Essays of 2003, 241
Bibliography, of source, 39, 45, 48, 205, 295, 296–97. *See also* also Citation

O

Observations
for analysis, 92
of audience, 195
by composer, 199
evaluation of, 104
as field research, 25, 39, 41,
73, 104
protocol for, 73
Onelook, 68
Online Archives, 68
Onlinenewspapers.com, 68
Online synchronous discussion,
citation for, 394. *See also*
Citation; Internet
Opinion, popular
blog for, 40, 42, 49, 50, 126,
168, 385, 435, 443, 448
facts v., 103
genre for, 145, 164–69
magazine for, 40, 42
on topic, 40, 42
Organization
of analytic papers, 148
of composition, 142–43, 184,
192, 271
through genre, 144
through heading, 271, 406
of ideas, 192
for oral presentation, 190
of paragraph, 184, 221
of photographs, 185
through statement of thesis,
152–55, 193, 200–201,
336–39
of text, 142–43, 184
of visual, 184, 186, 190
Outline, after draft, 192
Overhead, as visual, 190
Ozeki, Ruth L., 276

P

Painting/drawing
as abstract, 185
arrangement in, 185
citation for, 296, 367, 393
MLA citation for, 367, 393
text with, 185

title for, 185
Pamphlet, MLS citation for, 371
Paper, scientific/technical. *See
also* Composition
abstract for, 11, 396–97, 429
arrangement of, 7, 11, 150
citation for, 395
composing for, 7, 11, 150, 228,
239, 395, 585
quotation marks in, 228, 239,
302, 571, 574
words/phrases for, 228, 239,
571, 574, 585
Paragraphs
for academics, 231
analogy in, 176, 181
categories of, 171
categorization/division through,
182
for cause/effect, 176, 183
claim in, 235
clarity of, 208–9
for classification/division, 176,
183
coherence of, 172–75
for comparison/contrast, 176,
182
complexity of, 183
in composition, 170–83
as concluding, 92–93, 109,
114–15, 118–19, 149, 153,
192, 212–13, 221,
232–33, 266, 338–39
content of, 225
context of, 225
coordination/subordination in,
246–47
definition through, 176, 178
as descriptive, 176–77
development of, 176
emphasis of, 231
as engaging, 230
examples in, 180
expectations for, 170
focus of, 336–37
as introductory, 234–35, 266
length of, 231
linking words/phrases in,
174–76, 236
as narrative, 176, 179

for online reading, 231
organization of, 184, 221
pathos in, 176
process development in, 183
purpose of, 171, 176, 221
qualities of, 171–83
questions in, 235
quotation in, 233, 235, 266
revision of, 232–33, 266
rhythm in, 230, 231
sentence length in, 230
strategy for, 172–74, 233, 235,
266
style for, 225–27
summary of, 212–13, 233, 266
as syllogistic, 176
topic for, 234–35
transition between, 192, 206–7,
221, 223, 236–37
as unified/coherent, 172–75
unity through, 182
vocabulary for, 225
Parallelism
coherence and, 175
for composition, 175, 248–49
as faulty, 249
in ideas, 248–49
in oral presentation, 265
patterns and, 249
through words/phrases, 248
Paraphrasing
by academics, 298
citation for, 309
length of, 308–9
plagiarism and, 295, 309
of quotations, 206–7, 210–11,
294
as summary, 296, 309
for technical modification, 298
Parentheses, 556–57
Passive voice. *See* Voice
Pathos
analogy for, 101
assumptions through, 100
audience response for, 109,
110–15, 121, 122–23, 201
in book cover, 89
as comparison, 100
evaluation of, 101
example as, 110–15, 201

REVISION CHECKLIST

STYLE

ORGANIZATION

ACADEMIC INTEGRITY; ATTENTION TO THE VALUES OF CRITICAL THINKING

COMMON ERRORS

NOT PROOFREADING CAREFULLY

GRAMMAR

PUNCTUATION

SENTENCE-LEVEL CONCERNS

BEING UNFAMILIAR WITH THE CONVENTIONS

NOT WRITING WITH THE EXPECTED LEVEL OF FORMALITY

REVISION SYMBOLS

Boldface numbers refer to pages in the handbook

ab	abbreviation	590	*sp*	spelling error	586
agr	agreement	456	*shift*	shift in voice or number	464
awk	awkward diction or construction	244	*sub*	sentence subordination	246
cap	capitalization	588	*t*	verb tense error	462, 494
coh	coherence	172	*trans*	transition needed	236
coord	coordination	246	*var*	sentence variety	240
cs	comma splice	470	*vb*	verb form error	593
d	diction, word choice	252	*w*	wordy	259
dev	development needed	36, 176	*ww/wc*	wrong word; word choice	253
dm	dangling modifier	474	//	faulty parallelism	248
doc	check documentation	292	. ? !	end punctuation	580, 582, 583
frag	sentence fragment	466	:	colon	550
fs	fused sentence	470	'	appostrophe	568
hyph	hyphen	562	—	dash	558
ital	italics	585	( )	parentheses	556
lc	lowercase letter	588	[ ]	brackets	560
log	logic	90, 94	...	ellipses	566
mm	misplaced modifier	474	/	slash	564
no ¶	no paragraph needed	170	;	semicolon	549
num	number	592	" "	quotation marks	570
¶	paragraph	170	,	comma	528
¶ dev	paragraph development needed	176	⌒	close up	
ref	unclear pronoun reference	472	∧	insert a missing element	
search	check research or citation	20, 292	⌿	delete	
			∼	transpose order	

QUESTIONS ABOUT RESEARCH